Introducing Autodesk® Revit® Architecture 2012

Introducing Autodesk® Revit® Architecture 2012

AUTODESK® OFFICIAL TRAINING GUIDE

PATRICK DAVIS

WITH STEPHEN STAFFORD | MARTIN TAURER | CHARLIE BUSA | ANGELA MCDONNELL

Wiley Publishing, Inc.

Senior Acquisitions Editor: Willem Knibbe

Development Editor: Tom Cirtin

Technical Editor: Jon McFarland

Production Editor: Rachel Gunn

Copy Editors: Liz Welch, Linda Recktenwald

Editorial Manager: Pete Gaughan

Production Manager: Tim Tate

Vice President and Executive Group Publisher: Richard Swadley

Vice President and Publisher: Neil Edde

Book Designer: Caryl Gorska

Compositor: Kate Kaminski, Happenstance Type-O-Rama

Proofreader: Sheilah Ledwidge, Word One

Indexer: Jack Lewis

Project Coordinator, Cover: Katherine Crocker

Cover Designer: Ryan Sneed

Main Image: © Dwayne D. Ellis

Left Image: © Dwayne D. Ellis

Middle Image: © Maria Vishnevskaya / iStockPhoto

Right Image: © Andrey Prokhorov / iStockPhoto

Library of Congress Cataloging-in-Publication Data.

Davis, Pat, 1968–

 Introducing Autodesk Revit Architecture 2012 / Patrick Davis. — 1st ed.

    p. cm.

  ISBN: 978-1-118-02996-1 (pbk.)

  ISBN: 978-1-118-14156-4 (ebk)

  ISBN: 978-1-118-14159-5 (ebk)

  ISBN: 978-1-118-14157-1 (ebk)

  1. Autodesk Revit. 2. Architectural drawing—Computer-aided design. 3. Architectural design—Data processing. I. Title.

NA2728.D383 2011

720.28'40285536—dc23

                        2011018497

Dear Reader,

Thank you for choosing *Introducing Autodesk Revit Architecture 2012*. This book is part of a family of premium-quality Sybex books, all of which are written by outstanding authors who combine practical experience with a gift for teaching.

Sybex was founded in 1976. More than 30 years later, we're still committed to producing consistently exceptional books. With each of our titles, we're working hard to set a new standard for the industry. From the paper we print on, to the authors we work with, our goal is to bring you the best books available.

I hope you see all that reflected in these pages. I'd be very interested to hear your comments and get your feedback on how we're doing. Feel free to let me know what you think about this or any other Sybex book by sending me an email at nedde@wiley.com. If you think you've found a technical error in this book, please visit http://sybex.custhelp.com. Customer feedback is critical to our efforts at Sybex.

Best regards,

Neil Edde
Vice President and Publisher
Sybex, an Imprint of Wiley

To my future wife Debbie, thanks for the support and patience.

—Patrick Davis

Acknowledgments

Writing *Introducing Autodesk Revit Architecture 2012* in the allotted time-frame required a lot of support. A special thank-you to Jon McFarland for stepping into the role of technical editor. Your contribution made this a better book. We also want to thank the editors—Willem Knibbe, Tom Cirtin, Pete Gaughan, Rachel Gunn, Liz Welch, and Linda Recktenwald—for all their support and patience: We really do appreciate it. Thanks to Dwayne Ellis (www.dwayne-ellis.com) for creating a awesome rendering of our project file. Thanks also to the firms and individuals who provided images for the color insert. There are just way too many people at the "Factory" to thank each of them for their support and hard work. We do need to single out Anthony Hauck for answering the many emails. We want to thank our families, friends, and employers. Even though the timeline was short, it required a lot of effort, and your patience is appreciated. Finally, I want to thank Steve, Charlie, Martin, and Angela for all the hard work and effort that went into this. The writing of the *Introducing Autodesk Revit Architecture* books has been challenging, and I enjoyed being a part of the authoring team.

—*Patrick Davis*

About the Authors

Patrick Davis is the manager of virtual design and construction for Atkins. He has used Autodesk Revit Architecture since 2004 to complete projects of all scopes and sizes. He is one of the founders of the Kansas City and Tampa Bay Revit User Groups. He has also been involved in the development of national BIM standards and has served as the communication task chairman for the National Building Information Model Standard (NBIMS). In his spare time, he enjoys riding his Harley to visit new parts of the country.

Steve Stafford started using Autodesk Revit Architecture at work in 2002, though he used it informally from its inception in 2000. In May 2005 he started working as a consultant to provide training and implementation support to firms that are using or intend to use Autodesk Revit Architecture. Steve has been very active in the Autodesk Revit Architecture community. In 2003 he joined the Autodesk Revit Architecture community forum at Zoogdesign, and he currently serves as the forum manager for the Autodesk User Group International (AUGI) Revit community. He also served as a member of AUGI's board of directors from 2006 to 2008. He has presented classes at Autodesk University since 2004 and at the Revit Technology Conference in Australia since 2006. He created, writes, and manages three Autodesk Revit Architecture blogs: www.revitoped.com, www.revitinside.com, and www.revitjobs.com. He lives in Southern California with his wife and two children.

Martin Taurer joined Revit Technology Corporation in 2001 after a decade as architect and CAD consultant in Austria and Germany, researching product requirements and design and construction industry workflows and methodologies internationally in Australia, Japan, and China. His main interest lies in integrating

architecture, structure, and MEP. In 2008 Martin joined Livingroomcraftz, a Dutch company specializing in BIM consulting and implementation services mainly serving the Dutch and German region. He is a frequent presenter at Revit Technology Conference since 2008 and blogs on `www.livingroomcraftz.com/blog`. Outside of work, Martin follows his passion for music and Italian cuisine.

Charlie Busa joined Autodesk in 2007 after more than a decade and a half of experience in the AEC field, working primarily with architects, engineers, and corporate management staff to help them determine and plan optimal methods for implementing Revit BIM solutions that meld with their current, and future, processes. His product focus is on Autodesk Revit Architecture and Autodesk Revit Structure. He spent the majority of time prior to joining Autodesk operating his own firm, providing consulting and design services, as well as training and implementation offerings. Charlie is also a frequent presenter at Autodesk University on multiple Autodesk products and multiple topics ranging from BIM to visualization. When not involved with BIM, Autodesk Revit Architecture, and computers, Charlie enjoys good food, both cooking and eating it, as well as spending time in the garage performing motorcycle maintenance on his road-racing bikes.

Angela McDonnell has been an interior designer in the built environment for 12 years. She has extensive experience overseeing the design and construction of projects for the commercial building industry and has been a mentor on the instruction and implementation of Autodesk Revit Architecture. Angela is currently a consultant to the AEC field and is LEED CI certified.

CONTENTS AT A GLANCE

Contents

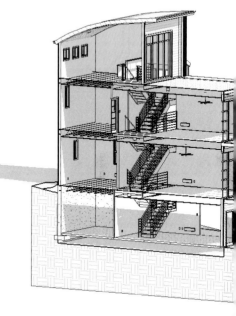

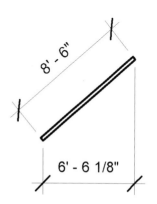

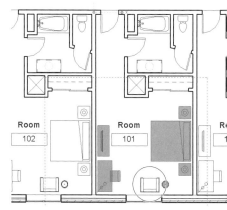

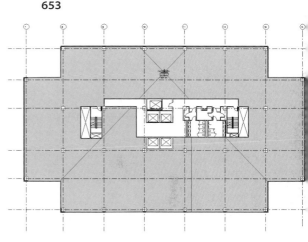

Introduction

Welcome to *Introducing Autodesk Revit Architecture 2012*, the fourth edition of the Introducing Autodesk Revit Architecture series. This book covers the fundamentals of using the key features of Autodesk Revit Architecture, including many features that are new additions to the 2012 version. Moreover, this book offers numerous Revit tips and tricks, with ample expert-recommended advice and techniques. The goal is for you to be able to identify and readily adapt these best practices to your daily Revit Architecture usage.

Revit Architecture allows you—an architect, designer, or technician—to design and document a virtual representation of your project. Revit Architecture is an integrated architectural design and documentation environment. You create a virtual building model of your design with intelligent building elements. These smart, parametric building elements automatically adjust and interact with the design environment, and at the same time you are creating views such as floor plans, sections, elevations, and schedules.

With the maturity of Revit Architecture in recent years, more and more firms and users are switching from AutoCAD or MicroStation. General contractors and owners are realizing the potential of BIM and Revit Architecture and requiring it as a deliverable. Although easy to learn, Revit Architecture is nonetheless a complicated product, and most advanced users would agree that they learn something new every day. This book is for the new user who is looking to understand the fundamentals of Revit Architecture and how 3D can be more efficient than just drawing lines, arcs, circles, and so on.

Whether you are new to BIM or Revit Architecture or you are an existing Revit Architecture user who simply wants to make your job or upgrade to Revit Architecture 2012 easier, this book is an invaluable resource for learning Revit Architecture.

Who Should Read This Book

This book was written to help today's owners, builders, contractors, architects, engineers and technicians. Hopefully it will do that in a variety of ways. For one thing, it can be used purely as a reference. It covers a wide range of the Revit platform. Most of these will be used in everyday work, but there are a few new features and some lesser-known tools to keep things interesting.

The book is much more than a reference, though. It is a tutorial; as such, it steps you through important topics with information that includes everything from guidance to tips and tricks.

This book assumes that you know little or nothing about Revit Architecture. It starts out slowly, covering important basics, and then progresses to more intermediate topics. The concepts in this book are laid out in order of importance, beginning with four basic requirements for working in Revit: user interface, views, geometry creation, and documentation.

Although it is intended for beginning Revit users through intermediate users, it covers some advanced topics as well. In truth, Revit Architecture has so many features and offers so many benefits that no one book could realistically hope to fully cover them all. Thus, each chapter provides an overview of the tools and workflow for that particular process or task-related area, covering it with illustrations, tips, and techniques from authors who use, teach, and support the application every day.

What Is Covered in This Book

Here is a glance at what is in each chapter of *Introducing Autodesk Revit Architecture 2012*:

Chapter 1: The Autodesk Revit Architecture User Interface The opening chapter introduces you to the Revit Architecture 2012 user interface and jump-starts you into your first project.

Chapter 2: Views This chapter demonstrates working with view controls such as zoom and pan and creating views of your building model such as plans, sections, elevations, and 3D views.

Chapter 3: Constraints and Dimensions Here we demonstrate the constraint and dimensions functions. We explore temporary and permanent dimensions, constraints, and best practices to ensure that your modeling project is properly constrained.

Chapter 4: Modeling This chapter demonstrates fundamental tools you need for creating geometry or modeling elements. We start by using the basic wall tools and move into stacked walls and adding doors and windows. Along the way, we also introduce the basic editing commands such as copy, move, rotate, trim, and so on.

Chapter 5: Advanced Modeling In this chapter we demonstrate advanced tools you need for creating stairs, railings, ramps, and curtain walls.

Chapter 6: Visibility Controls In this chapter we show you how to use the visibility controls. We start by creating and using filters, using graphic overrides, using and creating custom line styles and line patterns, and using fill patterns, and we wrap up with using scope boxes.

Chapter 7: Introduction to Families   This chapter discusses the fundamental building blocks used in Revit families. We explain how to load them into the project, the basic editing tools, and the different types of families that you will utilize in your project.

Chapter 8: Creating Families   Creating families is very powerful because the Revit parametric change engine drives them. In this chapter, we cover using templates and other modeling tools to create families.

Chapter 9: Massing   Here we explore the fundamentals of using the massing tools. Topics include dealing with visibility issues, creating basic forms, and constraining masses.

Chapter 10: Groups   This chapter discusses using 2D and 3D groups in your project. We start with creating and placing a group and then go into editing, saving, and linking groups.

Chapter 11: Rendering   We examine the fundamentals of rendering in this chapter. This includes working with basic still images, adding and managing lights, and applying materials.

Chapter 12: Working with Other Files   This chapter discusses working with files from other applications. It may not always be feasible to create your entire building project in Revit. In these cases, it will be necessary to import or export to other file formats. We discuss the tools and procedures you need to work successfully with other file formats being imported or exported from Revit.

Chapter 13: Rooms and Areas   This chapter focuses on working with rooms and areas. Topics covered include placing rooms; creating room schedules, rooms, and phases; area plans; and the issues associated with rooms and linked Revit files.

Chapter 14: Tags, Schedules, and Keynotes   We explore creating schedules, drawing lists, and creating material takeoffs.

Chapter 15: Detailing   This chapter discusses creating the 2D embellishments, such as text, dimensions, and fill patterns, to your views for documenting your design.

Chapter 16: Sheets   We examine creating the printed documentation required for your building projects. We talk about creating sheets and title blocks, printing, and managing revisions.

Chapter 17: Design Options   This chapter is all about design options. Sometimes it is necessary to explore different scenarios. Design options provide you with the flexibility to explore and retain different options in your building project.

Chapter 18: Phases   Phases are distinct, separate milestones within the life of the project. They can represent either the time periods themselves or the status of the project at specified points in time. In this chapter, we discuss the techniques used to create, edit, and manage phases.

Chapter 19: Autodesk Revit Architecture for Interiors   Here we explore the basics of using Revit for interior design. There are a number of tools in Revit that can be used by the interior designer to streamline and improve the production process. We discuss using Revit for the creation of your programming documents to verify that your proposed spaces meet the project programming requirements. We also cover how to use Revit to efficiently create finish schedules using key schedules, which help automate the process of populating repetitive data. When a finish schedule is not adequate to properly detail all the finish, then we demonstrate how to use elevations and plans to show this information.

Chapter 20: Worksharing   The final chapter discusses the basic concepts that allow multiple users to access and edit one Revit project file. These principles allow multiple team members to concurrently work on the same Revit project and keep changes synchronized.

Appendix A: Decoding Autodesk Revit Architecture Warnings   This appendix discusses a unique feature in Revit that tracks potential problems in the project model. Warning messages occur when Revit detects a problem while you are working in your model, such as multiple rooms located in the same enclosed region and walls and room separation lines that overlap. Warning messages are sometimes confused with error messages. Warning messages inform you of a potential problems that could impact the integrity of the model, the design intent, and the reliability of your documentation. When a warning is presented, Revit allows you to ignore the issue and continue working. Error messages, on the other hand, require that you take immediate action to correct the problem in order to continue.

Appendix B: Autodesk Revit Architecture Tips and Tricks   This appendix discusses some tips and tricks. You will find information on drafting and groups, working with CAD files, file size issues, annotations, and the user interface.

All the demo and tutorial files that are mentioned in the book are available for download from the book's online catalog page: www.sybex.com/go/introducingrevit2012.

How to Contact the Authors

We welcome feedback from you about this book or about books you'd like to see from us in the future. You can reach the authors by writing to authors@IntroRevitArchitetcure.com. For more information about our work, please visit our website at IntroRevitArchitecture.com.

Sybex strives to keep you supplied with the latest tools and information you need for your work. Please check their website at www.sybex.com/go/introducingrevit2012, where we'll post additional content and updates that supplement this book if the need arises.

CHAPTER 1

The Autodesk Revit Architecture User Interface

If you have never used Autodesk Revit Architecture before, then you will quickly notice that its look and feel doesn't even come close to resembling AutoCAD or MicroStation. There is no command prompt, there are no crosshairs, and the background is white, not black (though you can adjust that). Revit Architecture is similar to other Windows-based applications that utilize the Microsoft Office ribbon interface. Users familiar with the ribbon should find learning Revit Architecture's user interface (UI) relatively straightforward once they grasp the underlying concepts.

This chapter covers the following topics:

- ▪ **Getting to know the home screen**

- ▪ **Navigating the main screen**

- ▪ **Application menu and Quick Access toolbar**

- ▪ **The ribbon**

- ▪ **Options bar**

- ▪ **Properties palette**

- ▪ **Project Browser**

- ▪ **Drawing area**

Getting to Know the Home Screen

After you start Revit, you are taken to the Recent Files screen (see Figure 1.1). This window provides you with quick access to a list of the most recently opened projects or families. The main area of the screen is divided into three areas:

Projects The top section, Projects, provides options for opening and creating new projects as well as icons to the right listing any recent projects that you have been working on.

Families The middle section, Families, provides options for opening and creating new families as well as icons to the right listing any recent families that you have been working on.

Resources The bottom section, Resources, provides access to additional resources on learning Revit.

Figure 1.1

Recent Files screen when starting Revit for the first time

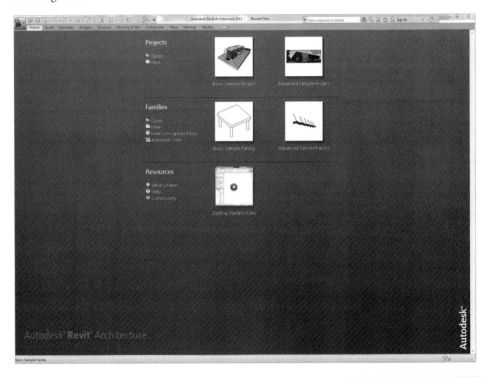

If you have started Revit for the first time, you will only be given the option to open or create new projects or families. The recent files icons will display two sample projects and two sample families.

So you can further explore the user interface, we will explain how to create a new project. Revit provides two methods to accomplish this. The first is to click the New button in the Projects area. When you do so, Revit will create a new project using the default settings found in the default template called default.rte (DefaultMetric.rte). This method allows you to start working immediately but is normally not the best approach.

Navigating the Main Screen

Now that you have started a project using the template file by clicking New, the window shown in Figure 1.2, which is the main screen, appears. The UI is divided into several areas; we will discuss each of them in the following sections.

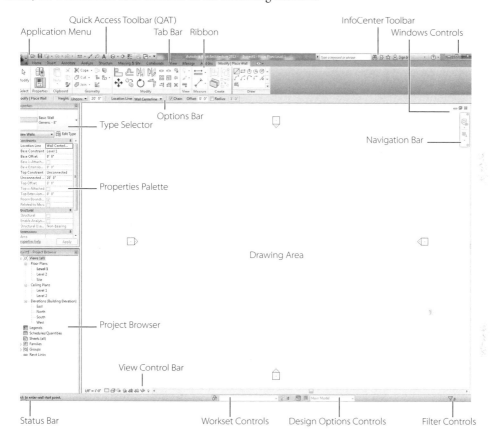

Figure 1.2

Main screen

Application Menu and Quick Access Toolbar

Located at the top left of the screen (see Figure 1.3), the Application menu gives you access to most of your file management tasks such as New, Open, Save, and so on, as well as access to export tools, printing features, recent documents, and the Options dialog box (which allows you to tailor custom settings in Revit that we will discuss later in the book). The right side of the Application menu contains a list of recently opened files. You can use the pushpin icon located to the right of the filename to "pin" that file to the list, making it easier to find that file each time you start Revit. In addition to providing quick access to project operations in one place, the Application menu allows you to sort and access recent documents.

The Quick Access toolbar (QAT) is filled with some of the most popular commands and is user customizable (Figure 1.4). There are two ways to customize the QAT:

- To add a tool to the QAT, right-click the tool on the ribbon, and then choose Add To Quick Access Toolbar.

  You can also right-click the QAT to remove icons, add a QAT separator line, and customize the QAT.

- Use the Customize button (Figure 1.5) at the end of the QAT to add, remove, and rearrange the buttons on the QAT.

The QAT can appear above or below the ribbon. To change its location, follow these steps:

1. Click the Customize Quick Access Toolbar drop-down.

2. Scroll to the bottom of the list, and select one of the following:

   - Show Below The Ribbon.

   - Show Above The Ribbon.

Figure 1.3

Application menu

Figure 1.4

Quick Access toolbar

1. Click the Add/Remove button.

Figure 1.5

Customizing the QAT

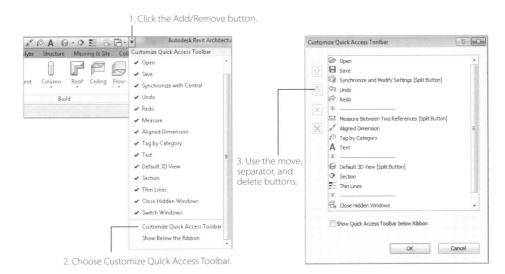

3. Use the move, separator, and delete buttons.

2. Choose Customize Quick Access Toolbar.

To the right of the QAT is the InfoCenter toolbar (Figure 1.6). You use the InfoCenter to search for information using keywords or phrases, to access subscription services, and to search for topics in the help files.

Figure 1.6
InfoCenter toolbar

When you want to choose a template for creating your project, use the following steps after you've started Revit:

1. Click the Application menu, and select New → Project.

   Doing so opens the New Project dialog box (Figure 1.7). Here, you have the ability to choose which template you want to utilize to start your project. You can also start your project without using a template file or create a new template file.

2. In the New Project dialog box, click Browse under Template File.

3. Navigate to your local project template location, select the template file (.rte file extension), and click Open.

4. In the Create New area, make sure that the Project radio button is selected.

5. Click OK.

Figure 1.7
New Project dialog box

The Ribbon

Below the Application menu and QAT is the ribbon (Figure 1.8). The ribbon is the most common method for initiating commands in Revit to help you define your building project. The Revit user interface is based on Microsoft Office 2007's ribbon interface. The interface is a set of dynamic or contextual toolbars that are placed in tabs in a tab bar. What we mean by that is if you are placing a wall, a new Modify | Place Wall tab is displayed with specific functionality for placing or modifying walls. These new contextual tabs are visible only when that tool is active.

Figure 1.8
The ribbon

The ribbon is broken up into two main parts. The top is the tab bar. Ten main tabs hold all the tools. Clicking a tab makes it active. Table 1.1 provides an overview of the tools in each tab.

Table 1.1

Ribbon tabs

TAB NAME	TOOLS
Home	The tools provided are commonly used tools for creating and placing building elements.
Insert	The tools provided are for linking, importing, and loading families, as well as for searching for family content online.
Annotate	The tools provided are for dimensioning, detailing, adding text, tagging, keynoting, and adding symbols.
Analyze	The tools provided are for basic energy analysis.
Structure	The tools provided are for adding structural members, foundations, and datum elements.
Massing & Site	The tools provided are for creating conceptual masses and creating and editing site elements.
Collaborate	The tools provided are for collaborating with both internal and external team members.
View	The tools provided are for controlling graphic settings of objects, creating views, adding sheets, and managing views.
Manage	The tools provided are for managing the project settings and environment, which include project settings, the project location, design options, phasing, and macros.
Modify	This a contextual tab that will change based on the operation being performed. The tools provided are for modifying and tagging elements.

The second part of the ribbon consists of the panels, with each panel holding tools or options pertaining to a specific activity or function. If you find yourself using a particular panel over and over again, it can be "torn off" the ribbon and placed where you want it on the screen (Figure 1.9). When you do this, you are making a floating toolbar on your screen. So if you are using multiple monitors, you can place some of your favorite and most often used ones on one screen, while your model is on another. When you do this, Revit will remember the user-defined locations of the panels the next time you open Revit. You can move a panel by clicking and dragging the panel label to the new location either within the toolbar or into the drawing area or other location on your desktop.

Figure 1.9

Panels can be "torn off" the ribbon and repositioned.

Drag to move panel

Click icon to reset panel to original location

Figure 1.10

Panel positioning controls

If you have "torn off" a panel and want to restore it, do the following:

1. Move your mouse cursor over the panel you want to restore.

   Gray bars will appear on both sides of the floating panel (Figure 1.10).

2. Use the gray bar on the left side to drag the panel to the new location.

3. On the right side of the gray bar, you will see a small icon; click that icon to restore the panel to the original location.

You can customize the ribbon further by changing the view state to one of the four settings. You can adjust the view state by clicking the arrow control to the far right of the tab bar to cycle through the options (Figure 1.11), as described here:

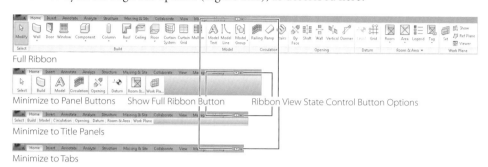

Full Ribbon

Minimize to Panel Buttons   Show Full Ribbon Button   Ribbon View State Control Button Options

Minimize to Title Panels

Minimize to Tabs

Figure 1.11

The four ribbon view states

Show The Full Ribbon This is the default state and shows the tab labels, panel labels, and tool icons.

Show The Tab and Panel Labels When you move your cursor over the panel label, the tools for those panels will be displayed.

Show Tab Labels When you click the tab label, the tools for those panels will be displayed.

Ribbon Tool Controls

The final elements of the ribbon are the tool controls, of which there are three types:

Buttons Initiate a command, function, or option.

Expanded Panel Arrow Allows you to expand the panel to display additional related tools and controls.

Dialog Launcher Buttons Allow you to open another dialog box to define additional options or settings to complete a task. The dialog launcher buttons are the small icons to the far right of a panel on the same line as the panel name (Figure 1.12).

Figure 1.12

Dialog launcher button

Buttons come in three different types: button, drop-down, and split buttons. If you look on the Home tab, you can see the Door and Window tools on that Build panel; they are examples of buttons. When you click this type of button, the tool is invoked, and you are provided with options to place a door or window. In the Model panel, the Model Group tool is an example of a drop-down button (Figure 1.13). When you click that type of button, a list appears showing the various options for the tool. You can then pick a tool option.

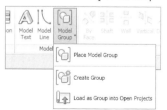

Figure 1.13

Example of a drop-down button

The split button serves two functions; when you move your cursor over a split button, you will see either a horizontal or a vertical divider line on the icon:

- The portion of the button that contains the small block triangle (Figure 1.14) functions like a drop-down button.

- The other half of the button functions like a regular button.

Figure 1.14

Example of a split button

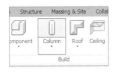

The Wall and Column buttons are examples of split buttons.

Some ribbon panels have a drop-down arrow next to the panel title (Figure 1.15) that indicates that the panel can be expanded to display additional related tools and controls (Figure 1.16). These are known as *expanded panels*.

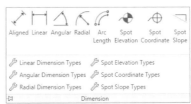

Figure 1.15

Dimension panel with expanded panel arrow

Figure 1.16

Dimension expanded panel

Understanding Ribbon Clues

Figure 1.17

Examples of two grayed-out buttons

You might have noticed that some buttons on different toolbars are grayed out (Figure 1.17). If a particular tool is not available, then it will be grayed out because the tool will not function. An example of this is the Level tool in the Datum panel of the Home tab or the View Reference and Area Tag buttons shown in Figure 1.17. If you are in a plan view, Revit does not permit you to create a new level in a plan view, so the Level tool is grayed out. Title blocks can be added in plan views, rendering needs to be done in a 3D view, and walls can't be drawn in elevation views—these are just some of the examples of the restrictions. If a tool is grayed out, switch to a different view type.

Figure 1.18

Expanded tooltip for the Trim/Extend To Corner tool

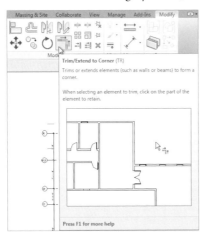

Another feature of the ribbon are tooltips (Figure 1.18). Tooltips provide a brief description of the tool's function. When you move your cursor over a tool on the ribbon, by default Revit will display a tooltip. If you leave your cursor over the tool a little longer, additional information in the form of an expanded tooltip will be displayed. While the tooltip is visible, you can press F1 for context-sensitive help to provide additional information about the tool. (Elements that are traditionally called *tooltips* are typically a word or phrase, but as you can see in Figure 1.18, some of Revit's tooltips are much larger, even a whole panel and illustration.)

Options Bar

The Options bar (Figure 1.19) is located just under the ribbon and displays options that are specific to the active tool or selected elements. For example, if you are placing a wall, you are presented with options that include Height, Location Line, Chain, Offset, and Radius. When you place a window, you are presented with options for Window Tag Orientation, Tag Type, Leader Usage, and Leader Offset.

Figure 1.19

Options bar examples for different tools

The Options bar is also active when you select an existing element to edit. If you select a door and want to copy that multiple times, simply select the window, click the Copy button on the Modify tab, and then select the Multiple check box on the Options bar (Figure 1.20).

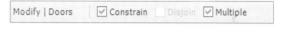

Figure 1.20

Options bar example with the Multiple copy option

It is very important to pay attention to the Options bar as you work, no matter your experience level. The Options bar will provide you with options to help you create elements in your project.

Properties Palette

The Properties palette (Figure 1.21) is where you can view and modify the various parameters that define the properties of elements in Revit. By default the Properties palette is located under the Options bar and to the far left; it is broken up into two main areas:

- Type Selector
- Instance properties

The top portion is the Type Selector and lists all the various types available for given elements that are currently loaded into the project file. In Revit, *families* are components you use to build your model, such as walls, windows, doors, columns, and so on. A door family can

Figure 1.21

Properties palette

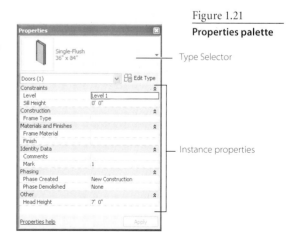

Type Selector

Instance properties

have multiple variations or, in Revit terms, *types*. Types are different sizes, materials, and so on. For example, a Single-Flush window might have several standard-size configurations. If you make a change to a type that is already used in the project, then it is updated in every instance throughout the project. If you have a window type called 24″× 80″ and you change the size to 30″× 75″, then all the 24″× 80″ windows will be updated so that they are now 30″× 75″, regardless of their name.

UNITS

This book references both imperial and metric units (imperial first, followed by metric equivalent in parentheses). We make an exception for instances like this, where we're talking only about the element in general rather than the actual dimensions of something.

When you create new elements, you use the Type Selector to select the family and type that you want to insert into your project. If you select an element that is already in the model, you can use the Type Selector to change it to a different type.

Families are broken up into different element categories. Some examples of categories are doors, walls, windows, floors, and so on. When you use the Door tool to place a door, only door categories will be shown in the Type Selector. So, the Type Selector is only going to display the appropriate category, families, and types for the one in use. We will discuss more about families in later chapters.

The bottom portion of the Properties palette contains the instance properties. *Instance properties* control only the instances (in other words, the elements) you have selected.

Instance properties are sometimes referred to as *element properties*. For example, when you change the door's finish material, then only the door you selected will have that finish description. When you change the door mark, then only that particular door is changed.

If you have selected multiple elements, the Type Selector will display the common type if possible. For example, if you selected five windows but they are not the same type (Single-Flush and Double-Flush) or if you have elements of different categories such as a door and window, Revit will display a message in the Type Selector: Multiple Categories Selected. The instance properties will display only those properties that are common to the selected elements (Figure 1.22).

While we are on the subject of properties, we should also discuss *type properties*. You can access them from the Properties palette by clicking the Edit Type button under and to the right of the Type Selector (Figure 1.23). Type properties control every instance (or all elements) of a specific type in the project, regardless of whether they are selected. Like

Figure 1.22

Properties palette with door and window selected

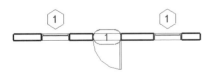

instance properties, if multiple elements are selected, the Type Properties dialog box includes only those properties that all the selected elements have in common. Figure 1.24 shows an example of the type properties for a door.

The Properties palette displays properties that are both user-editable and read-only. To edit a user-editable property value, click in the field to the right of the property name, and enter a new value, select one from a drop-down list, or select/deselect a check box. For some properties, the value box contains a button to the far right that opens a dialog box or browser window in which you define the desired value.

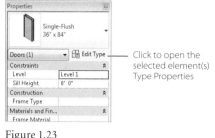

Click to open the selected element(s) Type Properties

Figure 1.23

Click the Edit Type button on the Properties palette to access the element's type properties.

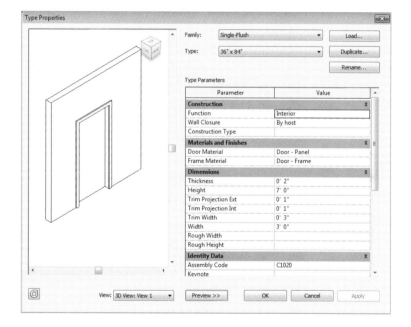

Figure 1.24

Type properties for a Single-Flush 36″×84″ door

Project Browser

As you work with Revit, you are going to find you are working on a fully integrated model. This means that all your views, details, sheets, schedules, and so on are generally in a single workspace. Other applications, such as AutoCAD Architecture or Bentley Architecture, use a federated model approach where you might have tens if not hundreds of drawing files in multiple folders for a project. Rather than using Windows Explorer or some other tool to manage files, in Revit you can use the Project Browser to manage and navigate your projects.

You can find the Project Browser under the Properties palette (Figure 1.25). The Project Browser is organized by category in a Windows Explorer–like tree. All the different

Figure 1.25

Project Browser

view categories such as Floor Plans, Ceiling Plans, 3D Views, Legends, Schedules, Details, Sections, Elevations, Sheets, Families, Groups, and Revit Links are displayed. These views in the Project Browser can be sorted, grouped, and filtered to help you organize your project. The Project Browser, like other dialog boxes in Revit, can be docked, or you can drag it to a new location such as a second monitor.

Using the Project Browser is very straightforward. We will cover a few of the basics here and get into more detail throughout the text. When you double-click a view name, that view is opened in the drawing area. When a view is active, the view name in the Project Browser is now bold.

Drawing Area

The drawing area is the large workspace under the Options bar; it's to the right of the Project Browser and Properties palette. The drawing area displays the current view that you are working on, and a new window will open for each view. If you have multiple views open and the views are maximized, the other views will be under the current view.

View Control Bar

The View Control bar is located in the lower-left corner of each drawing area window. Figure 1.26 (top) shows the View Control bar for 2D views such as plans, sections, and elevations. Figure 1.26 (bottom) shows the View Control bar for 3D views. The View Control bar serves a couple of purposes to control the graphical view for each window. Working from left to right are the following functions for the View Control bar:

Figure 1.26

View Control bar

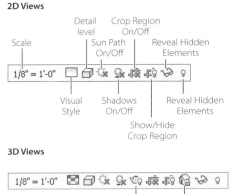

Scale This function allows you to change the scale of a view. When you click the scale text, a pop-up menu will display, allowing you to change the scale of your view (Figure 1.27). One of the great things about Revit is that when you change the scale of a view, annotations and symbols will automatically adjust. You don't have to worry about the scale factor or making adjustments to text sizes or dimension scales.

Detail Level This function allows you to select from three detail levels: Coarse, Medium, and Fine. If you want to see more graphical information, set your detail level from Coarse to Fine.

Visual Style This function allows you to you to specify visual style options, which are one of the following:

> **Wireframe** Displays the image of the model with all the edges and lines drawn but without surfaces
>
> **Hidden Line** Displays the image of the model with all edges and lines drawn except those obstructed by surfaces
>
> **Shaded** Displays the image of the model with all surfaces shaded according to their material color settings and project light locations
>
> **Consistent Colors** Displays an image of the model similar to Shading With Edges with more consistent colors
>
> **Realistic** Displays the image of the model with materials in the active view

Sun Path On/Off This function allows you to specify Sun Settings and to turn Sun Path on or off.

Shadows On/Off This function allows you to specify to turn shadows on or off. There are additional graphic display options consisting of Shadows and Silhouette Edges.

Show/Hide Rendering Dialog This function allows you to either display or hide the Rendering dialog box.

Crop Region On/Off This function allows you to turn a crop region on or off.

Show/Hide Crop Region This function allows you to show or hide a crop region.

Temporary Hide/Isolate This function allows you to temporarily hide or isolate elements or categories.

Reveal Hidden Elements This function allows you to reveal hidden elements in the view.

Figure 1.27

Scale listings from View Control bar

Status Bar

The Status bar (Figure 1.28) is located at the very bottom of the UI. It provides you with the following information:

Figure 1.28

Status bar prompting for additional information

- Displays the name and family type of the element your cursor is over
- Prompts you for additional information regarding the active tool such as hints or what to do next

KEYBOARD ACCELERATORS

If you are a seasoned AutoCAD user, then you probably initiated most of your commands by pressing a one- or two-key shortcut on the keyboard rather than clicking a button or selecting a tool from a menu. Revit provides the same functionality for using and editing shortcuts. Many of Revit's tools have predefined keyboard shortcuts. You can find them in several ways. In the example shown here, the first line of the Place A Component tooltip lists the name of the tool followed by the two-key shortcut.

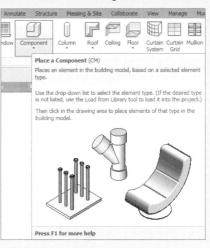

You can also display and edit keyboard shortcuts using the Keyboard Shortcut dialog box. You can access the dialog by clicking the View tab, clicking the User Interface drop-down in the Windows panel, and then selecting Keyboard Shortcuts.

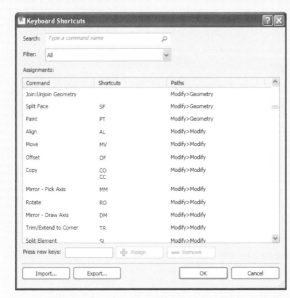

In addition to providing feedback and information, the Status bar contains the following controls:

Worksets Provides access to the Worksharing dialog box and displays the active workset when worksharing has been enabled

Design Options Provides access to the Design Options dialog box and displays the active design option

Exclude Options (not shown) Provides the ability to filter components that are part of a design option

Editable Only (not shown) Allows you to filter your selections to only select editable work-shared components

Press & Drag Allows you to drag an element without selecting it first

Filter Allows you to refine your selection set using element categories

CHAPTER 2

Views

Views are an essential part of your building project. Autodesk Revit Architecture is basically a large database, and many of your projects will consist of a single model or file (unlike AutoCAD projects, which can consist of hundreds of drawing views). For this single model to work effectively, you need a system to create different views of your building project. With Revit's view tools, you can create views of your model—such as floor plans, ceiling plans, detail views, section views, and schedules—to graphically display that information.

The views that you create display specific information related to your building project, and Revit provides you with view property controls to specify what information is represented and how it is represented.

In this chapter, we will discuss the various view types, their relationship to the model, and how they are organized in the Project Browser. You will learn how to create views and how to use view controls to edit and manage the display of elements in the views. We will discuss view properties, view templates, and best practices for working with views.

This chapter covers the following topics:

- **Zoom and Pan tools**
- **View properties**
- **Other view controls**
- **Adding new views**

Zoom and Pan Tools

You can use the Zoom and Pan tools to assist in navigating and editing elements in the building model and to change the viewable area in a drawing window. The Zoom tool provides the means for changing the magnification of the view, either increasing or decreasing. The Pan tool in a 3D view moves the camera left or right. In a 2D view, Pan scrolls the view in the direction you move the cursor. Revit provides the following zoom options:

- Zoom In Region
- Zoom Out (2X)
- Zoom To Fit
- Zoom All To Fit
- Zoom Sheet Size
- Previous Pan/Zoom
- Next Pan Zoom

Figure 2.1

The Zoom and Pan tools on the navigation bar

Revit provides several methods for accessing these tools, one of which is the navigation bar (Figure 2.1), displayed in the upper-right corner of the drawing window. You can also access the ViewCube and SteeringWheels, described in a moment, from this navigation bar. If the navigation bar is not active, do the following:

1. Click the View tab.
2. In the Windows panel, click the User Interface drop-down list.
3. Select the Navigation Bar check box to activate the navigation bar.

   Deselecting the check box will hide the navigation bar.

Zoom In Region

You use the Zoom In Region tool when you need to zoom into a certain area or window. To zoom into a region, you must specify a rectangular window by identifying diagonal opposite corners. Here are the general steps:

1. Start the Zoom In Region tool.
2. Move your mouse pointer, and click at the start point of your rectangle.
3. Move the mouse pointer to define the opposite diagonal corner of the Zoom In Region window, and click.

   Notice that as you define the window, a dynamic window is created (Figure 2.2).

   The region within your Zoom In Region area is enlarged in the current view (Figure 2.3).

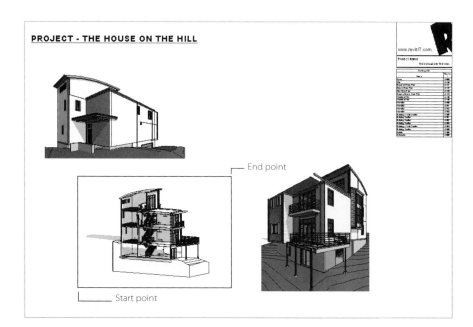

Figure 2.2

Defining the start and end points for Zoom In Region

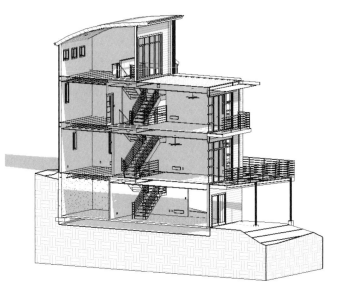

Figure 2.3

Results after using Zoom In Region

One-Click Zooms

One-click zooms are quick actions you can take to change the magnification or range of your view with a single mouse click:

Zoom Out (2X) Use this tool when you need to zoom out of an existing view by twice the size of the current view. In other words, when you use this tool the new view is going to show twice the length and width of the original view.

Zoom To Fit Use this tool when you want to display the entire extents of the model and annotation elements in the available view space on the screen.

 Zoom All To Fit This tool works the same way as Zoom To Fit but in all the views that are open.

Zoom Sheet Size Use this tool when you want the drawing window to match the print size based on the scale of the view. This tool is useful when you want to make sure that you are showing the correct level of detail based on the scale of the drawing.

Previous Pan/Zoom Use this tool when you need to revert to the last view displayed using the Zoom and Pan tools. You can think of this tool as an undo function for zooming and panning.

Next Pan/Zoom Use this tool when you want to undo the previous pan/zoom operation.

ViewCube

The ViewCube is a *persistent* tool that can be used to switch between standard and isometric views. When the ViewCube is displayed, it is shown with one of the edges, faces, or corners highlighted. This represents the current orientation of the view. Clicking one of the faces, edges, or corners will switch to that view.

The ViewCube has two display states:

- When *inactive*, it appears in halftone so that it does not interfere with the view of your model.
- When *active*, it is opaque and may obscure the view of the model.

The ViewCube also acts as a compass and indicates which direction is north for the model. When you click the cardinal direction letter on the compass, the view will rotate. You can also click the compass ring and interactively rotate the view around the pivot point.

The real power of the ViewCube, though, is revealed when you right-click it. When you do, you can quickly create 3D sections, plans, elevations, and so on. The ViewCube context menu has the following options (Figure 2.4):

Go Home Restores the home view saved with the model

Save View Allows you to save the current view

Lock To Selection Uses the selected objects to define the center of the view when a view orientation change occurs with the ViewCube

Set Current View As Home Defines the home view of the model based on the current view

Figure 2.4

The ViewCube context menu

Set Front To View Allows you to define a new front view from a predefined list

Reset Front Resets the front view of the model to its default orientation

Show Compass Toggles on and off the ViewCube Compass

Orient To View Lets you select from a set of preset views to reorient the model's current view

Orient To A Direction Lets you select from a set of preset view directions to reorient the model's current view

Orient To A Plane Lets you specify a new orientation plane to reorient the model's current view

Help Launches the online help system and displays the topic for the ViewCube

Options Opens the Options dialog box where you access options for adjusting the appearance and behavior of the ViewCube

SteeringWheels

SteeringWheels are special tracking menus that follow your mouse pointer as you move it across the drawing area. In theory, these wheels can save you time since they combine multiple navigation tools into a single menu. Typically these wheels allow you to zoom, rewind, orbit, and so on. Because different types of operations have different view requirements, there are seven SteeringWheels (Figure 2.5) for navigating and orienting models in different views.

In the next example, we will walk you through the process of utilizing the Zoom and Rewind functions from the SteeringWheels:

Figure 2.5

The seven different SteeringWheels

Full Navigation Wheel · Tour Building Wheel · View Object Wheel · 2D Steering Wheel

Mini Full Navigation Wheel · Mini Tour Building Wheel · Mini View Object Wheel

1. Click the SteeringWheels icon on the navigation bar (Figure 2.6).

2. Move the SteeringWheels to an area in the drawing area you want to zoom in and out of.

3. Place your mouse pointer over the Zoom tool. Notice that as you move your mouse pointer over a function, it will highlight.

4. Click and hold the Zoom tool. Moving your mouse forward zooms in, and moving the mouse backward zooms out. Notice that varying the mouse speed varies the speed of the zoom.

5. Release the mouse button to stop the Zoom command and return to the Steering-Wheels.

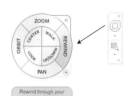

Figure 2.6

Activating the Steering-Wheels from the navigation bar

Now that you have used the Zoom tool, you will use the Rewind tool to return to your previous zoom state. As you perform zooms and pans, Revit keeps track of these actions. When you use the Rewind tool, Revit displays a strip of previous zooms and pans.

1. In the SteeringWheels, move your mouse over the Rewind tool.

2. Click the Rewind tool.

3. Move your mouse pointer over the rewind strips (Figure 2.7). Revit will change the zoom or pan location.

4. When you find the view that you desire, click, and you are returned to the Steering-Wheels.

Figure 2.7

Using the Rewind tool allows you to select a previous zoom or pan.

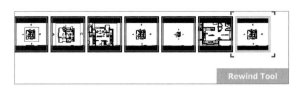

The SteeringWheels also offers a wheel menu (Figure 2.8). You can use this menu to switch between the big and mini wheels that are available. The behavior and options available in the wheel menu are dependent on the current wheel and program. Table 2.1 lists the complete wheel menu options.

Figure 2.8

Full Navigation wheel with menu for 3D and Camera views

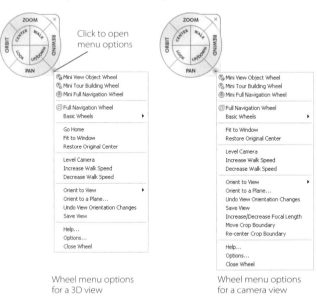

MENU ITEM	DESCRIPTION/FUNCTION
Mini View Object Wheel	Displays the Mini View Object wheel.
Mini Tour Building Wheel	Displays the Mini Tour Building wheel.
Mini Full Navigation Wheel	Displays the Mini Full Navigation wheel.
Full Navigation Wheel	Displays the big Full Navigation wheel.
Basic Wheels	Displays the big View Object or Tour Building wheel.
Go Home	Switches to the home view saved with the model.
Fit to Window	Resizes and centers the current view to display all objects.
Restore Original Center	Restores the center point of the view to the extents of the model.
Orient to View	Orients the camera to match the view angle of the selected view. This function is also available in the ViewCube menu.
Orient to A Plane	Adapts a view according to the user specified or selected plane. This function is also available in the ViewCube menu.
Save View	Saves the current view orientation with a unique name. Save View allows you to save a 3D view only when working in the default 3D view. If you are working in a previously saved 3D or perspective 3D view, the view is simply saved with the new orientation and you are not prompted to supply a unique name.
Increase/Decrease Focal Length	Changes the focal length (zoom lens).
Move Crop Boundary	Moves the position of the crop boundary around the perspective view.
Re-center Crop Boundary	Repositions the crop boundary to the center of the perspective view.
Help	Opens the help system to the wheel topics.
Options	Displays the dialog box where you can adjust the options for the wheels.
Close Wheel	Closes the wheel.

Table 2.1

Wheel menu options

View Properties

You use view properties (Figure 2.9) to set the various settings for the active view. These settings consist of the scale, detail level, underlay, phase, and so on. Table 2.2 lists some common view properties and a brief description of how they function.

INSTANCE PARAMETER	FUNCTION/DESCRIPTION
View Scale	Changes the scale of the view.
Scale Value	Defines the custom view scale. This option is available only when View Scale is set to Custom.
Display Model	Normal: Displays all elements in the view normally.
	Do Not Display: Hides the model elements and displays only detail/annotation view-specific elements such as lines, text, dimensions, and symbols.
	Halftone: Displays all detail/annotation view-specific elements normally, and model elements appear dimmed.
Detail Level	Sets the detail level for newly created views based on a view scale. View scales are organized under the detail level headings Coarse, Medium, and Fine. When you create a new view in your project and set its view scale, its detail level is automatically set according to the arrangement in the table.

Table 2.2

View Instance Properties

continues

continued

INSTANCE PARAMETER	FUNCTION/DESCRIPTION
Visibility/Graphic Overrides	Allows you to control the display and appearance of element categories on a view-by-view basis.
Graphic Display Options	Offers settings to enhance the visual display of your model view.
Underlay	Displays another plan view under the current plan view. The underlay can be set to any level above, below, or at the same level as the current view. Underlays are used for coordinating levels and other building content. Underlays will print.
Underlay Orientation	Sets the underlay's view orientation. If the value is set to Plan, then the underlay displays as if you are viewing from above, like a plan view. If the underlay is set to Reflected Ceiling Plan, then the underlay displays as if you are viewing it from below. Setting this property to Reflected Ceiling Plan is useful when you want to see the furniture layout and how it coordinates with the lighting.
Orientation	Switches the orientation of the project between Project North and True North. Our projects are generally set to Project North to make it easier to model and draft. True North enables you to set up your project with the true orientation.
Wall Join Display	Sets the behavior of wall joins.
Discipline	Sets the discipline for the view to Architecture, Structural, Mechanical, Electrical, or Coordination.
Color Scheme Location	Sets the color scheme location to either the front of the model (foreground) or the back of the model (background).
Color Scheme	Opens the Edit Color Scheme dialog box to create new or edit existing schemes.
View Name	Specifies the name of the active view and is what will be displayed in the Project Browser (as well as the name of the viewport on the sheet unless you rename it using the Title On Sheet parameter).
Title on Sheet	Specifies the name of the view as it will appear on the sheet.
Referencing Sheet	Comes from the referencing view that is placed on a sheet (read-only).
Referencing Detail	Comes from the referencing view that is placed on a sheet (read-only).
Default View Template	Sets the default view template for the active view.
Crop View	Activates the crop region for the view, which can limit the extents of the visible area of the view.
Crop Region Visible	Makes the crop region visible or invisible.
Annotation Crop	Shows or hides the annotation crop region when crop regions are visible in the view.
View Range	Also known as *visible range*, View Range is a set of horizontal planes that control object visibility and appearance in the view.
Associated Level	Lists a view that may be associated with this view (read-only).
Scope Box	Similar to Crop Region, limits the extents of levels and grids.
Phase Filter	Allows you to control which of the defined phases are displayed in the view.
Phase	Allows you to control the phase visibility properties for the view.

Overriding Visibility/Graphics

As you work on your building project, there will come a time when you find that you have too much going on in the view and you want to turn on or off certain element categories, such as all furniture or all columns. You may also want to change the way that different element categories display in the view. Most of the time you will use the Visibility/Graphic Overrides dialog box (Figure 2.10), usually just called Visibility/Graphics or VG, to control the visibility per view. Therefore, you want to be very familiar and comfortable using this dialog box. There are a few other methods of controlling the visibility of objects in a view, and we will cover those in this section as well.

When you start a new project, the Visibility/Graphic Overrides dialog box is broken up into five tabs. Additional tabs will be displayed if you enable phasing, link files, or worksharing. The first tab in Visibility/Graphic Overrides is Model Categories. On this tab, you have the ability to turn on and off model categories in the view and to override the cut, projection and surface, halftoning, transparency, and detail level of an element category. Generally speaking, model elements are the geometry or 3D objects that make up your building project, such as doors, walls, windows, and floors.

The Visibility column contains a list of all the Revit element categories available. You can display subcategories for each element category by clicking the expand button. For example, Doors is a category, and when you expand Doors, you are provided with several door subcategories, including Elevation Swing, Frame/Mullion, and Glass.

Figure 2.9

The Properties palette

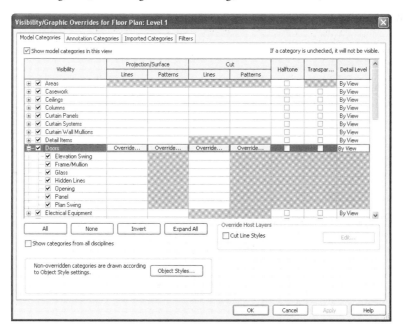

Figure 2.10

Visibility/Graphic Overrides dialog box with Model Categories tab active

Next to the category or subcategory name is a check box. When you select the check box, the category or subcategory will be displayed in the view. Deselecting will turn the visibility off in the current view. Turning the visibility of the category off will also turn off the visibility of the subcategory items.

In the exercise that follows, you are going to override the first floor Visibility Graphic Overrides settings to hide the furniture and plumbing fixtures. This will allow you to explore the Visibility Graphic Overrides settings.

1. Open the source file `Dataset_02_01.rvt` from the book's web page (`www.sybex.com/go/ introducingrevit2012`).

2. Save the file elsewhere, naming it **02_01_VG.rvt**.

3. Switch to the First Floor, Floor Plan.

4. Zoom into the southwest corner of the building where the bedroom and bathroom are located.

5. On the View tab's Graphics panel, click Visibility/Graphics.

6. In the Visibility/Graphic Overrides dialog box, deselect the check box next to the Furniture and Plumbing Fixtures categories.

7. Click Apply and then OK to close the dialog box.

> Throughout this book we will often suggest that you click Apply and then OK to close a dialog box. Clicking the Apply button applies any changes you make to the model or view immediately. Doing so allows you to verify that the desired changes occurred or make further changes as needed while in the dialog box. Clicking OK makes the changes to the model or view and then closes the dialog box. It is good practice to verify the changes you made are the desired results before leaving the dialog box.

After deselecting the Furniture and Plumbing Fixtures categories, the bedroom furniture and bathroom plumbing fixtures are turned off. Remember that when you deselect a category in the Visibility/Graphic Overrides dialog box, that category is turned off in the current view only.

Another shortcut for controlling the visibility of elements in a view is to use the Hide In View tool. To use this tool, select an element in the view in which you want to turn off the visibility, such as a door. Right-click and choose Hide In View (Figure 2.11).

You are then presented with three options:

Elements Only the element or elements selected will be turned off. For example, if a single chair is selected, only that chair will be turned off.

Category This will turn off the entire category for the element selected. For this example, if you select a single chair, all the furniture elements will have their visibility turned off in this view because a chair is part of the Furniture category. This is the same as going to the Visibility/Graphic Overrides dialog box and turning the category off.

By Filter This will turn off the group of elements that you defined in your filter. We will discuss filters in more detail later in this chapter.

Click Category. All of the doors in the view now have visibility turned off.

In our previous exercise, we turned off all the furniture and plumbing fixtures in the view. You may want to turn them back on. If you turned off the entire category, you could simply go back to the Visibility/Graphic Overrides dialog box and turn the category back on. But if individual elements have been hidden, how do you find them? Revit provides a tool called Reveal Hidden Elements. This tool displays any elements that are currently hidden in the view. To reveal hidden elements, continue using the file from the previous exercise and follow these steps:

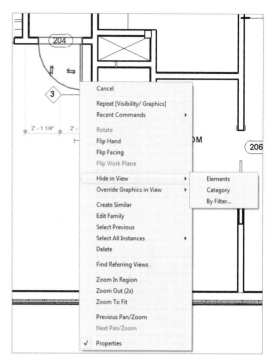

Figure 2.11

Options for Hide In View

1. On the View Control bar, click the Reveal Hidden Elements icon.

   When this icon is active, the lightbulb on the View Control bar will have a red border and the lightbulb will be on. The border of the drawing window will be in red, indicating that you are in Reveal Hidden Elements mode. All the hidden elements will be displayed in red, and the visible elements will be in halftone (Figure 2.12).

2. Select the elements you want to unhide.

3. On the ribbon in the Reveal Hidden Elements panel (Figure 2.13), click Unhide Element or Unhide Category.

The Unhide Category button in the Reveal Hidden Elements panel is enabled when the item selected has the entire category hidden (turned off). If individual elements are hidden and not the entire category, then the Unhide Element button in the Reveal Hidden Elements panel is enabled.

Colored border and label
indicates we are in Reveal
Hidden Elements mode

Visible elements are gray

Figure 2.12

The thick border (red in Revit but dark gray here) indicates that you are in Reveal Hidden Elements mode.

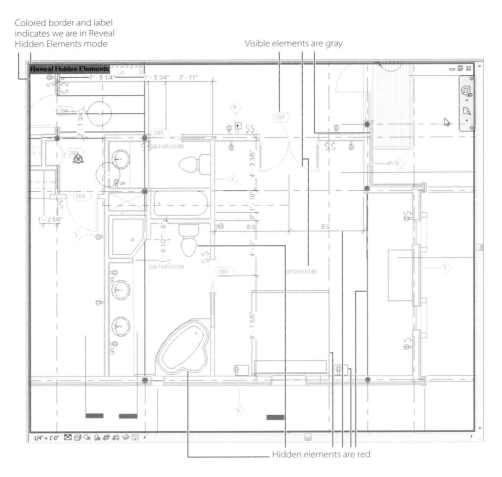

Hidden elements are red

Figure 2.13

Ribbon options for revealing hidden elements

4. When you have unhidden all the elements, click the Toggle Reveal Hidden Elements Mode button on the ribbon to turn off Reveal Hidden Elements mode. You can also click the lightbulb on the View Control bar to exit Reveal Hidden Elements mode.

5. Save and close the file 02_01_VG.rvt.

Another method of restoring the visibility of elements while in Reveal Hidden Elements mode is to select an element, right-click, and choose Unhide In View.

In addition to being able to control the visibility of element categories, Visibility/Graphics also enables you to override the visibility and graphic display of model elements, annotation elements, imported elements, linked Revit model elements, and workset elements for each view in a project. These settings that you are overriding are those specified at the project level. If you want to change the settings for all views in the project, you should modify them in the Object Styles dialog box.

Using Visibility/Graphic Overrides to Poche Walls

In this example, you are going to override the visibility and graphic display of walls in the view. You will first duplicate a view and then apply a transparency to faces on model elements, and then you will poche the exterior walls.

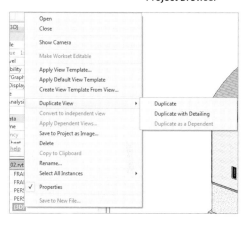

Figure 2.14

Duplicate View options on the context menu in the Project Browser

1. Open the source file `Dataset_02_02.rvt` from the book's web page (`www.sybex.com/go/introducingrevit2012`).

2. Save the file elsewhere, naming it `Views_Poche.rvt`.

3. In the Project Browser, make the {3D} view active.

   You are going to duplicate this view and then apply your transparency.

4. Right-click the view name (Figure 2.14).

   Right-clicking any view name in the Project Browser and highlighting Duplicate View provides you with three duplication options:

   Duplicate This option makes a copy of the view without any annotation objects with the exception of levels, grids, and reference planes. Model changes made in the original view will appear in the duplicated view. Annotation changes (with the exception of levels, grids, and reference planes) made in the original view will not appear in the duplicated view (Figure 2.15).

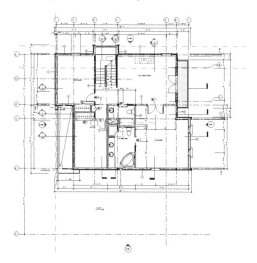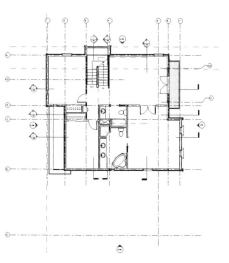

Figure 2.15

The view on the right was created by duplicating the view on the left. Because we used Duplicate here, annotation objects were not copied.

Duplicate with Detailing   This option makes a copy of the view with the annotation objects. Model changes made in the original view will appear in the duplicated view. Annotation changes (with the exception of levels, grids, and reference planes) will not appear in the duplicated view.

Duplicate as a Dependent   This option makes a complete or exact copy of the view, including all annotations. The copy of this view is also dependent on the original view. Any changes in the model or annotation made in either of the two views will appear in the other view.

HOW TO CHOOSE A DUPLICATE OPTION

Use Duplicate when you need a copy of that view for various reasons but the annotations are not important.

Use Duplicate With Detailing when the annotations are important but you need to develop the new plan differently. For example, you may want to duplicate many of the annotations on your Level 1 plan and your Level 1 Furniture plan.

Use Duplicate As A Dependent when you have a large plan that needs to be broken up into several plans to drop on sheets or you need to place the same view on multiple sheets.

---

5. Choose Duplicate View → Duplicate.

    In the Project Browser, a new view named Copy of {3D} was created. Let's rename this view to something more meaningful.

6. Right-click the view called Copy of {3D}, and select Rename.

7. Name the view **Transparent Walls and Floors**.

    You will now begin the process of applying transparency to model face categories.

8. Open the Visibility/Graphic Overrides dialog box by choosing one of these actions:

    •   On the View tab's Graphics panel, click Visibility/Graphics.

    •   Right-click a wall in the drawing area, and choose Override Graphics In View → By Category.

    •   Press VG or VV on the keyboard without hitting the Enter key.

9. In the Visibility/Graphic Overrides dialog box, make sure that the Model Categories tab is active.

10. Click the Walls cell under Visibility to highlight the entire row.

11. In the Transparent column, select the check box.

12. Repeat steps 9 and 10 for Floors.

13. Click Apply and OK to view your changes (Figure 2.16).

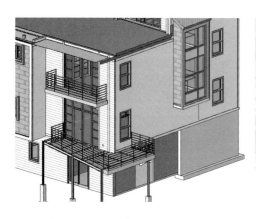
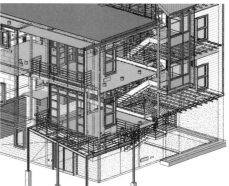

Figure 2.16

View with transparency off (left); model with transparency on (right)

In the next example, you are going to use the Visibility/Graphic Overrides dialog box to poche walls in a view. Let's continue using the Views_Poche.rvt file.

1. Switch to First Floor, floor plan view.

2. Open the Visibility/Graphic Overrides dialog box.

3. Select the Walls row, and click the Override button for Cut Patterns. This will open the Fill Pattern Graphics dialog box (Figure 2.17).

4. Set Color to Blue.

5. Set Pattern to Solid Fill.

6. Click OK to close the Fill Pattern Graphics dialog box.

7. Click Apply and OK to view your changes (Figure 2.18).

Figure 2.17

Fill Pattern Graphics dialog box for our poche walls

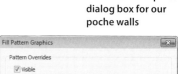

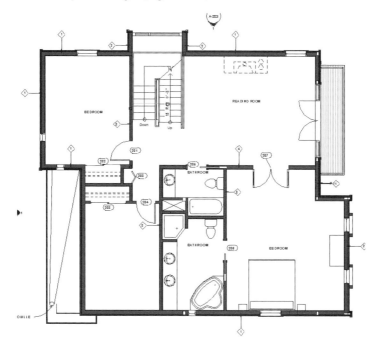

Figure 2.18

Example of poched walls using Visibility/Graphic Overrides

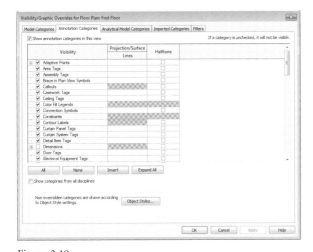

Figure 2.19
Visibility/Graphic Overrides dialog box's Annotation Categories tab

The second tab in the Visibility/Graphic Overrides dialog box is Annotation Categories (Figure 2.19). This includes objects such as text, tags, legends, dimensions, and so on. The third tab (and new in Revit 2012) is the Analytical Model Categories tab. This tab is used to control the display of categories from Revit Structure and Revit MEP models and includes boundary conditions, structural loads, analytical beams, and so forth found in categories (Figure 2.20). The fourth tab is Imported Categories (Figure 2.21). If you have linked in any CAD files, you will be able to control the visibility and graphic display of layers. The fifth tab, Filters, is discussed in the next section.

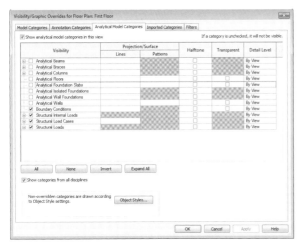

Figure 2.20
Visibility/Graphic Overrides dialog box's Analytical Model Categories tab

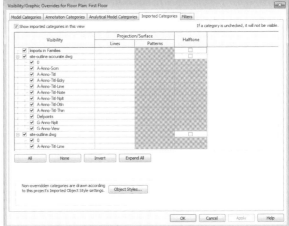

Figure 2.21
Visibility/Graphic Overrides dialog box's Imported Categories tab

Using Filters

Filters are a very powerful tool and give you the ability to control the visibility of a group of elements that you define. In this section, we will discuss using the Filter tool to sort and control elements. In this example, you are going to use the Filter tool as a method to check your models for accuracy. You will create a filter that looks at the walls in the view and changes the poche of walls that have an assembly description of "exterior walls" to a solid black poche.

1. On the View tab's Graphics panel, click the Filters button [Filters].

2. In the Filters dialog box, click the New button (Figure 2.21).

   Using Figure 2.22 as a reference, complete the following steps to create a filter for walls that have a Type parameter Function of Exterior.

3. Name the new filter **Exterior Walls**.

4. Under Categories, select Walls.

> Categories allow you to determine the parameters that are available in the Filter By lists. You can select more than one category. For example, if you wanted to create a filter that shows two-hour rated walls and doors, then you would select both the Doors and Walls categories.

5. Under Filter Rules, change Filter By to Function.

6. For the filter operator, select equals.

7. For the filter value, enter **Exterior**.

8. Click Apply and OK to save and close the Filters dialog box.

   Because you used the equals filter operator, when you type in the filter value you must use the exact spelling and capitalization. You have now created a new filter that will find any walls in a view that have a Function of Exterior.

9. Open the Visibility/Graphic Overrides dialog box.

10. Switch to the Filters tab.

    Using Figure 2.22 as a reference, complete the following steps to poche walls that have a Type parameter Function of Exterior.

11. Click the Add button to add a new filter.

12. In the Add Filters dialog box, select the Exterior Walls filter.

13. Click OK to close the Add Filters dialog box.

    Back in the Visibility/Graphic Overrides dialog box on the Filters tab, notice that the Exterior Walls filter is now added, and you

Figure 2.22

Visibility/Graphic Overrides dialog box's Filter tab

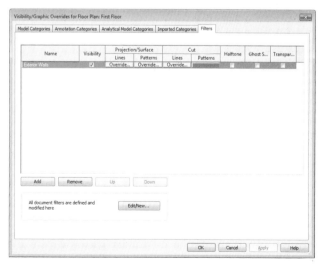

have options similar to the Model Categories tab. You have the following options that you can adjust:

Visibility Determines whether your filter overrides will be visible in the view.

Projection/Surface Used in Elevation views or anything in the distance that is not being cut or sliced by the view. The Lines and Patterns overrides provide you with the ability to change the line color and thickness, as well as a fill pattern color and thickness.

Cut Used in views where the objects are displayed as cut. This could be plans, sections, or details. The Lines and Patterns overrides provide you with the ability to change the line color and thickness, as well as a fill pattern color and thickness.

Halftone Allows you to halftone the filtered element category.

Ghost Surface Displays surfaces with a 30% transparency.

Transparent Allows you to make the filtered element category transparent.

In this particular view, you want all walls with a Type parameter Function of Exterior to display with a solid red poche.

14. Click the Cut Patterns Override button.

15. In the Fill Pattern Graphics dialog box, set Color to Red.

16. Set Pattern to Solid Fill.

17. Click OK to close the Fill Pattern Graphics dialog box.

18. Click Apply and OK to close the Visibility/Graphic Overrides dialog box.

Figure 2.23 shows the results of the filter you applied to the First Floor view. Note that the interior walls still have a blue poche that we applied to all walls in the previous section, "Using Visibility/Graphic Overrides to Poche Walls." Using this filter method, you could poche walls based on fire rating, function, structural usage, and so forth to help validate your model.

Figure 2.23

**Filter applied to the current view with walls with a function of 'exterior'
being poched solid red**

Other View Controls

In this section we are going to discuss some of the other view controls. These include changing the level of detail, using crop regions, and using temporary hide/isolate features.

Changing the Level of Detail by View Scale

In Chapter 1, "The Revit User Interface," we briefly touched on using the View Control bar to change the level of detail in a view. You can also make these changes using the Properties palette. Detail level and view scales go hand in hand. In Figure 2.24, you can see an example of a wall at Coarse and Fine/Medium detail levels.

The level of detail is important when you need to print your drawings. For example, if you have a drawing at $\frac{1}{16}'' = 1'-0''$ (1:200) and your detail level is set to Fine, then your printed drawing is more likely to lose detail because of all the lines that are being printed. So, using the proper level of detail is important to ensure a consistent look for your drawings.

Revit provides a mechanism to control how Revit should automatically set the level of detail for a specific scale. This is done through the View Scale-To-Detail Level Correspondence dialog box (Figure 2.25). To adjust the detail level scale values, follow these steps:

1. On the Manage tab's Settings panel, click the Additional Settings drop-down, and click Detail Level.

2. Click the left and right move arrows to move scale values from one detail level to another.

3. If you want to return to the original settings, click Default.

4. Click OK to close the View Scale-To-Detail Level Correspondence dialog box.

Later in this chapter, you will create a schedule to help you manage your detail levels in Revit.

Using Crop Regions

The crop region defines the boundaries of the project view. A crop region consists of two parts:

Model Crop Crops model elements, detail elements, section boxes, and scope boxes at the model crop boundary.

Annotation Crop Crops annotation elements when it touches any portion of the annotation element so that no partial annotations are drawn. Annotations that reference cropped or hidden model elements are not

Figure 2.24

Wall example at Coarse (top) and Fine/Medium (bottom) detail levels

Figure 2.25

Setting the detail level scale values

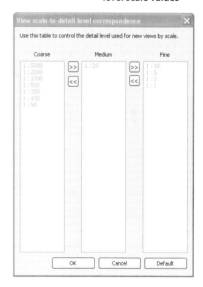

displayed in the view, even if they are inside the annotation crop region. In other words, if any portion of an annotation is touching the annotation crop, the entire annotation is not displayed. By default, the annotation crop is not displayed.

There are three check boxes (Figure 2.26) in the view's Properties palette to show and adjust the crop region:

Crop View Enables or disables the crop region

Crop Region Visible Shows or hides the crop region

Annotation Crop Shows or hides the annotation crop

Crop regions can be adjusted either graphically or explicitly. Figure 2.27 shows the model and annotation crop turned on. To adjust the model and annotation crop regions graphically, drag the blue drag controls. The View break controls can be used to remove a portion of the crop region to break the view into separate regions. To explicitly set the height and width of a crop region, follow these general steps:

1. Select a crop region.

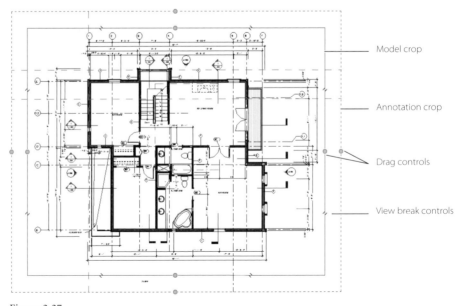

Figure 2.27

Model and annotation crop turned on

2. Click the Modify | *viewtype* tab, select the Crop panel, and click the Size Crop button. This opens the Crop Region Size dialog box (Figure 2.28).

3. Modify the value for Width, Height, and Annotation Crop Offsets.

4. Click OK to close the Crop Region Size dialog box.

Figure 2.28

Using the Crop Region Size dialog box to explicitly size a crop region

Using Temporary Hide/Isolate

Temporarily hiding or isolating elements or element categories can be handy when you want to see or edit only a few elements of a certain category in a view. The Hide tool hides the selected elements in the view. The Isolate tool shows the selected elements and hides all other elements in the view. Temporary Hide/Isolate is useful since the changes are temporary. Any changes you make using Temporary Hide/Isolate will revert to the original state when you close the project and will not impact printing.

To temporarily hide or isolate an element or element category, select one or more elements in the drawing area; then on the View Control bar, click the Temporary Hide/Isolate button that looks like a pair of glasses, and select one of the following operations:

Isolate Category Of the elements selected, only those element categories will be displayed. All other element categories will be hidden.

Hide Category Of the elements selected, only those element categories will be hidden.

Isolate Element Only the selected elements will be displayed.

Hide Element The selected elements will be hidden.

When Temporary Hide/Isolate is active, the border of the drawing area will be cyan and a label in the upper-left corner will read Temporary Hide/Isolate.

To exit Temporary Hide/Isolate mode, choose one of these approaches:

- To exit without saving the changes:

  1. Click the Temporary Hide/Isolate button on the View Control bar.

  2. Click Reset Temporary Hide/Isolate. All temporary hidden elements are then restored.

- To exit and make the changes permanent:

  1. Click the Temporary Hide/Isolate ibutton on the View Control bar.

  2. Click Apply Hide/Isolate To View.

If you make temporarily hidden elements permanent, you can reveal them later using the Reveal Hidden Elements tool.

Adding New Views

When working on your building project, you will need to create different views such as floor plans, ceiling plans, details, section, schedules, and so on, to develop and document the building project. Revit provides a number of methods for creating new views. The most common method is to duplicate an existing view. Duplicating views allows you to use different view settings that display the same portion of your building project.

When duplicating an existing view, you have three options:

Duplicate Creates a copy of the selected view. Note that on the model, elements will be duplicated, but annotation or detailing elements will not be duplicated.

Duplicate With Detailing Creates a copy of the selected view and contains both the model and annotation elements from the original view.

Duplicate As A Dependent Creates a copy of the selected view, contains both the model and annotation elements, and inherits the view properties of the primary view. Any changes made to either the original or dependent views will be synchronized. You use this option when you need to create views that show portions of a plan when the entire plan is too large to fit on a drawing sheet.

Creating Floor and Ceiling Plans

As you work on your building project, you will find that you have to create new levels and plans in order to build and document your project. In this section, you are going to create new floor and ceiling plans based on existing levels. Floor plans (Figure 2.29) are the default plan for your building project; a floor plan is a horizontal slice of your building project. Reflected ceiling plans (Figure 2.30) are also a horizontal slice of your building. In Chapter 4, "Modeling Basics," we will go into detail about creating new levels. To create a new floor plan, follow these steps:

1. Open the source file `Dataset_02_03.rvt` (`mDataset_02_03.rvt`) from the book's web page (`www.sybex.com/go/introducingrevit2012`).

2. Save the file elsewhere, naming it `Create_Plans.rvt`.

3. In the Project Browser, do the following:

    a. Expand Views (By Type).

    b. Expand Elevations (Building Elevation).

    c. Double-click the West Elevation.

4. Zoom into the lower three level datums, as shown in Figure 2.31.

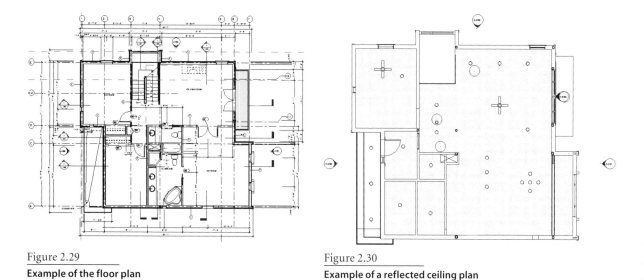

Figure 2.29

Example of the floor plan

Figure 2.30

Example of a reflected ceiling plan

Notice that some of the elevation datums symbols are blue and some are black. The blue elevation datums have a floor or ceiling plan associated with them. Black elevation datums are not associated with either a floor or an elevation plan. In the next steps, you are going to create floor and ceiling plans for the levels with the black datums.

5. From the View tab's Create panel, click the Plan Views drop-down, and choose Floor Plan. Doing so opens the New Plan dialog box (Figure 2.32).

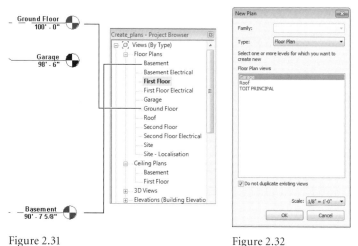

Figure 2.31

Elevation datums from default template

Figure 2.32

New Plan dialog box

6. In the Floor Plan Views section, select the Garage and Roof levels to create new plan views.

   If you want to create an additional plan view for a level that has an existing plan view, deselect Do Not Duplicate Existing Views.

7. Set the scale to ¼″ = 1′-0″ (1:50).

8. Click OK.

To create a new ceiling plan, follow these steps:

1. From the View tab's Create panel, click the Plan Views drop-down, and choose Reflected Ceiling Plan. Doing so opens the New Reflected Ceiling Plan dialog box.

2. In the Reflected Ceiling Plan Views section, select the Garage and Roof levels to create new RCP views.

3. If you want to create an additional reflected ceiling plan view for a level that has an existing RCP view, deselect Do Not Duplicate Existing Views.

4. Set the scale to ¼″ = 1′-0″ (1:50).

5. Click OK.

The Project Browser in Figure 2.33 shows the new floor and ceiling plans you've added.

Figure 2.33

The Project Browser with updated views

Creating Elevation Views

Elevations provide a view of your model projected onto a vertical plane. Elevation views can be used to evaluate and document building exterior and interior wall elevations. When you start a new project using one of the Revit template files, Revit will automatically create exterior elevation views for north, south, east, and west (Figure 2.34). With Revit, you can create both exterior and interior elevations.

Elevations are created by placing the elevation tags in your model. To create an elevation view, from the View tab's Create panel, open the Elevation drop-down. Click Elevation, and in the drawing area, move the mouse pointer near the exterior walls.

Notice that as you move the mouse pointer near the wall, the elevation symbol (Figure 2.35) appears. As you continue to move the mouse pointer around the walls in the project, the arrowhead of the elevation symbol will automatically align perpendicular to the wall. When you are creating interior elevations, Revit displays the extent of the elevation of the room to where the bounding walls, floors, and ceilings are located.

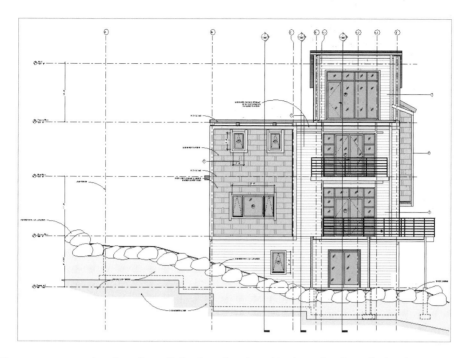

Figure 2.34

Sample elevation view

To create an exterior elevation, click when the elevation arrowhead symbol points toward the desired direction.

To create an interior elevation:

1. Move your mouse pointer inside the walls.

2. Click when the elevation arrowhead symbol points toward the desired direction.

Notice that in the Project Browser the new views have been added.

The elevation symbol consists of several components. When you click the square or round part of an elevation tag (Figure 2.36), you have the ability to create four different elevation views by selecting or deselecting the check boxes.

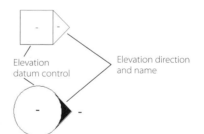

Imperial Exterior Elevation symbol

Elevation datum control

Elevation direction and name

Metric Exterior Elevation symbol

Figure 2.35

Exterior elevation symbol

When you click the elevation arrow, you get an additional option to change the width and depth on an elevation. In Figure 2.37, the solid bar represents the width of the elevation. The dashed line represents the depth of the elevation and can be adjusted by moving the arrows. Double-clicking the elevation direction arrow will open that elevation view.

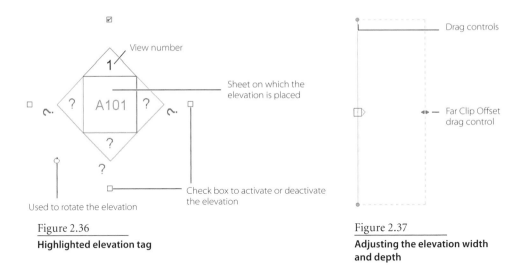

Figure 2.36

Highlighted elevation tag

Figure 2.37

Adjusting the elevation width and depth

Creating Section Views

Section views are a vertical slice through your building project (Figure 2.38). You can create section views in plan, section, elevation, and detail views.

Figure 2.38

Section view example

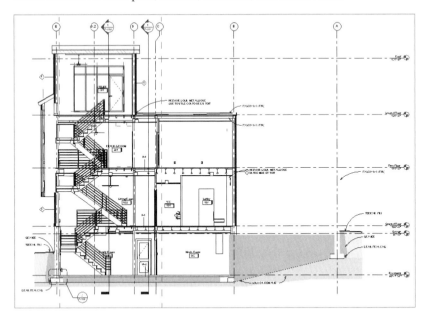

To create a section view, follow these steps:

1. Open a plan, section, elevation, or detail view.

2. Click the View tab's Create panel, and click the Section button.

3. In the Properties palette, click the Type Selector and select one of the following:

   - Detail

   - Building Section

   - Wall Section

4. On the Options bar, select the view scale.

5. In the drawing area, place the mouse pointer at the starting point of the section and drag through the model or family.

6. Click when you reach the end point of the section.

7. If applicable, resize the crop region by dragging the blue controls.

8. Click Modify or press Esc to exit the Section tool.

To open a section, you can double-click the section head or select the section view from the Sections or Detail Views groups of the Project Browser.

When you click the section, you get an additional option to change the width and depth on an elevation. In Figure 2.39, the solid bar represents the width of the section. The dashed lines represent the width and depth of the section and can be adjusted by moving the blue arrows. Double-clicking the arrowhead will open that section view. The view and sheet number of the section are added when the section has been dropped on a sheet. This topic is discussed in greater detail in Chapter 16, "Sheets."

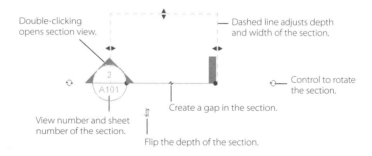

Figure 2.39

Section view controls

Sections in Revit can also be split or jogged. You do so when you need to show elements that are not necessarily in line with one another. To jog a section, use the following steps:

1. Select a section that you have already created.

2. On the Modify | View tab, and in the > Section panel, click the Split Segment button.

   In the drawing area, notice that your mouse pointer has now turned into an X-Acto knife blade .

3. Pick a point along the section line where you want to create the split.

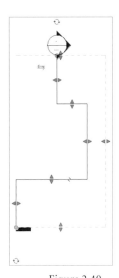

Figure 2.40

Example of a jogged section

4. Move your cursor to the left or right to create your jog (Figure 2.40).

5. Hit the Esc key on the keyboard twice to exit the Split Segment function.

Creating Callout Views

Callout views are typically enlarged or detail views of a *parent view* from your building project. For example, in Figure 2.41 the left image shows a floor plan view with a callout. The image on the right is the callout view. The callout view is a *child view* of the plan view. You can create callout views from plan, section, elevation, and detail views, and they are dependent on the parent view in which they were created.

To create a callout view, follow these steps:

1. Open a plan, section, elevation, or detail view.

2. Click the View tab's Create panel, and click the Callout button.

3. In the Properties palette, click the Type Selector and choose either Detail or Floor Plan.

4. On the Options bar, select the view scale.

5. In the drawing area, define the callout area by picking one point and then dragging the cursor from that to another point to create a rectangular shape to define the callout boundary.

6. If applicable, resize the callout area by selecting the callout and dragging the blue controls.

7. Click Modify or press Esc to exit the Callout tool.

Figure 2.41

Callout view example

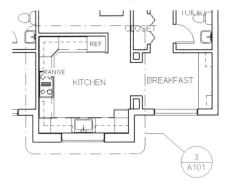
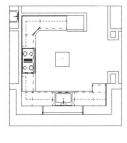

Creating Drafting Views

When we think of *building information modeling* (BIM), most of us probably think about 3D. In reality, though, it is just not possible to completely model every component of a project in 3D. The effort and computer hardware required to model every component is impractical even on small projects. Most projects utilize a hybrid approach to fully documenting a project. This approach consists of the following:

- 3D modeling
- Embellishing 2D views (sections, elevations, detail views) of the model
- Stand-alone 2D views

Drafting views are 2D views used to generate geometry or information that would not normally be visible in the model. These drafted details are not directly based on model geometry. You can use drafting views for just about anything because they have no relationship to any portion of the model unless you specifically reference it to the model.

To create a drafting view, click Drafting View in the View tab's Create panel. In the New Drafting View dialog box, provide a name for the drafting view and change the scale of the view as desired. You can now use any of Revit's drafting tools to create your 2D details.

Drafting views can be used to bring in existing CAD geometry to make it part of your Revit documentation. You or your organization probably has a collection of typical details that are used on many of your projects. Manufacturers also offer available details of their products as AutoCAD details. With Revit, you can leverage those existing CAD details by importing or linking them into a drafting view.

Revit allows you to import or link DWG, DXF, or DGN file formats. When these files are brought into Revit, they become a special Revit element called an *import symbol*.

The key to success when using CAD details is determining whether to link or import the file. There are pros and cons to each method, which we will discuss next.

Linked CAD Files

When you link a CAD file in Revit, a link is maintained to that file. If the DWG file changes, Revit will automatically update the link the next time you open the Revit project or manually refresh the link. This is an important consideration if the CAD file might change during the course of the design. Linked files cannot be exploded into Revit elements. The more linked CAD files you have in the project, the longer it can take for the project to open, since the links must be refreshed.

In the next example, you will create a new drafting view and link in an AutoCAD jamb detail:

1. Start a new project using the default Revit template. Click Application → New.
2. On the View tab, click the Create panel and select Drafting View.
3. In the New Drafting View dialog box, name the file **Jamb Detail**.
4. Set Scale to 3″ = 1′-0″ (1:5), and then click OK to close the New Drafting View dialog box.
5. On the Insert tab, select the Link panel, and click the Link CAD button.

6. Browse to open the CAD file `Dataset_02_DWG.dwg`, (`mDataset_02_DWG.dwg`) but do not click the Open button yet. The file can be downloaded from the book's web page (`www.sybex.com/go/introducingrevit2012`).

7. At the bottom of the Link CAD Formats dialog box, set Colors to Black And White. Doing so will convert the colors of the CAD file to black and white.

8. Set Layers to All.

9. Set Import Units to Auto-Detect. Revit will try to detect the units of the CAD file.

10. Set Positioning to Auto – Center To Center.

11. Click the Open button to link the CAD file.

12. Type **ZA** to perform a Zoom All in the drafting view.

13. Select the detail.

14. On the Modify | Dataset_02_DWG01.dwg tab, select the Import Instance panel and click the Query button.

15. Select any CAD geometry element in the view.

    Revit now provides some basic information about the selected element in the view. You also have the ability to hide the selected element in the view.

16. Click Esc twice to exit the Query tool.

Imported CAD Files

When you import a CAD file into Revit, there is no link to the original file and any changes made to that CAD file will not be reflected in the Revit project. You can explode an imported CAD file into Revit elements, but that is not necessarily a good thing. When you explode a CAD file, Revit will create a new text style and line style for each unique line and text style in the CAD file. Explode CAD files with caution.

To import a CAD file into Revit:

1. If you are continuing from the previous section, use that file, or you can start a new project using the default Revit template (click Application → New).

2. On the View tab, select the Create panel and click Drafting View.

3. In the New Drafting View dialog box, name the file **Soffit Detail**.

4. Set Scale to 12″ = 1′-0″ (1:1), and then click OK to close the New Drafting View dialog box.

5. On the Insert tab, select the Import panel and click the Import CAD button.

6. Browse to open the CAD file `Dataset_02_DWG02.dwg`, (`mDataset_02_DWG02.dwg`) but do not click the Open button yet. The file can be downloaded from the book's web page.

7. At the bottom of the Link CAD Formats dialog box, set Colors to Black And White. Doing so will convert the colors of the CAD file to black and white.

8. Set Layers to All.

9. Set Import Units to Auto-Detect. Revit will try to detect the units of the CAD file.

10. Set Positioning to Auto – Center To Center.

11. Click the Open button to link the CAD file.

12. Type **ZA** to perform a Zoom All in the drafting view.

13. Select the detail.

14. On the Modify | `Dataset_02_DWG02.dwg` (`mDataset_02_DWG02.dwg`) tab, select the Import Instance panel and click the lower portion of the Explode Split button; then click the Partial Explode button.

The CAD file has now been exploded into Revit elements. You can edit the text, modify the 2D geometry, and so forth.

> **FULL EXPLODE VS. PARTIAL EXPLODE**
>
> Full Explode explodes all blocks and Xrefs into their most basic elements, such as lines and arcs.
>
> Partial Explode explodes the instance into its nested blocks and references. For example, if you have a block within a block, the first partial explode explodes the file and leaves the nested block. The second partial explode explodes the nested block, leaving a single block. The third partial explode explodes the block into the most basic elements, such as lines and arcs.

Creating Camera Views

An orthographic 3D view (Figure 2.42) is a 3D view that shows the building model where all the components are the same size regardless of the camera's distance. Revit can also create 3D perspective views (Figure 2.43) that show the model in 3D where the building components that are farther away appear smaller and components that are closer appear larger. We cover creating 3D perspective views in Chapter 11, "Rendering."

To create a 3D orthographic view, follow these steps:

1. Open a plan, section, or elevation view.

2. On the View tab's Create panel, click the 3D View drop-down and choose Camera.

3. On the Options bar, deselect the Perspective option.

4. Click once in the drawing area to place the camera, and click again to place the target point. Revit then creates the view and opens it.

To create a 3D perspective view, follow the previous steps but skip step 3.

Figure 2.42

Sample orthographic view

Figure 2.43

Sample perspective view

Adjusting the Camera

Once you have created your camera view, there are several options to tweak the view. You can use the ViewCube; be sure to hold down the middle mouse button (MMB)+Shift key to create more desirable results. You can also adjust the camera by following these steps:

1. Make the plan view where the camera view was originally created.

2. In the Project Browser, right-click on your 3D camera view.

3. Click the Show Camera option.

The camera will now appear in the plan view. You can select the camera and make adjustments by either moving the camera or modifying the camera's properties in the Properties palette.

Adding Legends

Legends are another type of view that allows you to place graphical representations of elements in the model to explain the symbols used in the project. When working in a legend view, you can add legend components, which are symbolic versions of all families and types in your project. To create a legend, follow these steps:

1. On the View tab's Create panel, select the Legends drop-down and click Legend.

2. In the New Legend View dialog box, type the legend name, such as **Doors**.

3. Choose the scale, and click OK.

   A new blank drawing window will open. In the view, you will use the Legend Component tool to place a symbolic representation of the families and types used in your project.

4. On the Annotate tab's Detail panel, click the Component drop-down and click Legend Component.

   The Options bar (Figure 2.44) provides the means to select the family and view to use.

Figure 2.44

Options bar for the Legend Component tool

5. From the Family list on the Options bar, select the family name.

6. From the View list on the Options bar, choose the view type.

7. Click to place the symbolic view of the family on the sheet.

8. Repeat the process for as many family and types as you need to document in your legend.

9. Add labels, notes, and dimensions as appropriate.

CHAPTER 3

Constraints and Dimensions

Autodesk Revit Architecture provides a unique method of embedding your design intent in the form of locks and constraints with dimensions. In this chapter, you will become acquainted with dimensions, the use of constraints on objects within your design, and the flexible relationship that these offer for changes that will take place in your project.

This chapter covers the following topics:

- **Understanding dimensions**
- **Equality constraint and lock**
- **Spot dimensions**
- **Units**

Understanding Dimensions

Dimensions are annotation elements within the project that convey the distance or angle between elements or parts of elements in the model. The dimensions are bidirectional annotations that behave like a tag for the distance and size of project elements. Calling it *bidirectional* means that you can edit the dimension value shown, which will move your element to match the value entered. Or if you move the element, it will update the dimension value to display the true value.

Dimensions are view-specific elements within your project, meaning that when placed, they will show up only in the view in which they are placed and will not be automatically added to other views. To help you understand them a bit better, we will look at the types and options available, starting with *temporary dimensions*.

Temporary Dimensions

Temporary dimensions are displayed as you create or select geometry. As the name implies, they are temporary and are there for the purpose of placing elements in the model more accurately. Temporary dimensions do not print.

When you create or select an element, Revit displays temporary dimensions around the component. The temporary dimensions display values as they relate to the nearest

Figure 3.1

Temporary dimensions are displayed while you place a wall.

perpendicular component. These dimensions are unique in that they exist and are displayed while you are placing a component (see Figure 3.1).

Once you place a new component, any temporary dimensions that were displayed while you placed a previous component will no longer be visible. When you select a component, the temporary dimensions will again be displayed, as shown in Figure 3.2.

When multiple components are selected, the temporary dimension will not be displayed, as shown in Figure 3.3.

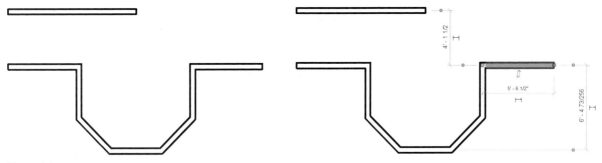

Figure 3.2

Left: Unselected walls with no temporary dimensions displayed. Right: Selecting a single wall will display temporary dimensions relative to the nearest perpendicular components.

To enable temporary dimensions, you can click the Activate Dimensions button on the Options bar, as shown in Figure 3.4, which will then show the temporary dimensions.

With a component selected and the temporary dimensions displayed, you can adjust the location or size of the component by editing the dimension value. To do so, click the dimension value and it becomes an editable text field. Enter the desired numerical value; if there are no constraints, Revit will move the selected component to the specified location.

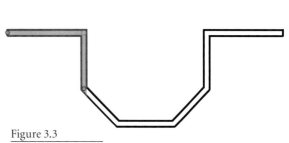

Figure 3.3

Selecting multiple components will not display temporary dimensions.

Temporary Dimension Settings

You can control the display and reference placement used with temporary dimensions for walls, doors, and windows by using the following settings:

- Selecting one of the following Measure From Walls options:
  - Centerlines
  - Center Of Core
  - Faces
  - Faces Of Core

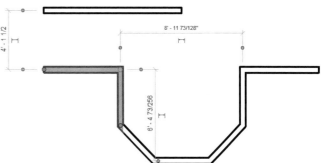

- Selecting one of the following Measure Doors And Windows options:
  - Centerlines
  - Openings

Figure 3.4

With multiple components selected, the Activate Dimensions button will be available in the Options bar.

You access these settings by selecting the Manage tab and on the Additional Settings panel, clicking Temporary Dimensions, as shown in Figure 3.5. Doing so opens the Temporary Dimension Properties dialog box, as shown in Figure 3.6.

Figure 3.7 shows an example of placing a window within a wall using the default options, with Doors And Windows set to Centerlines.

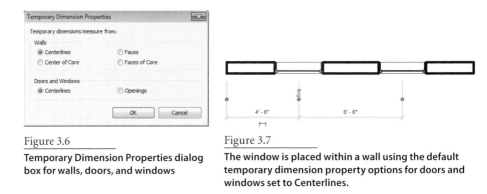

Figure 3.6

Temporary Dimension Properties dialog box for walls, doors, and windows

Figure 3.7

The window is placed within a wall using the default temporary dimension property options for doors and windows set to Centerlines.

Figure 3.8 shows the same window being placed within a wall with Doors And Windows set to Openings. Here the nearest perpendicular element is the wall and existing window, which displays the dimensions to the outside of the window being placed.

Figure 3.5

Click Temporary Dimensions on the Additional Settings panel.

Figure 3.8

The window is placed within a wall using the additional settings for doors and windows set to Openings.

Snap Increments

When sketching a wall or other component and moving the cursor from left to right in the drawing area, the temporary dimensions that are displayed for the wall increase or decrease. This distance is based on the value provided for the *snap increment*. You can access the snap increment values from the Manage tab; just click Snaps in the Settings group (see Figure 3.9).

Figure 3.9

The Snaps option allows you to set the snap increment that is used by the temporary dimensions when you're placing components.

The Snaps dialog box has a Length Dimension Snap Increments setting (see Figure 3.10). Here, you can enter new or edit existing values, or add new increments. Although there is no limit to the number of increments you can have when adding or removing increments, be sure each value you enter has a semicolon after it. Revit uses these increments when the zoom level changes, and the closer you are zoomed in, the smaller the increment that is used.

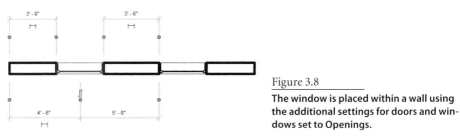

> When adding values to the Length Dimension Snap Increments or Angular Dimension Snap Increments setting, Revit will automatically change the displayed order of the entries—sorting them from larger to smaller—after you click OK.

When adjusting the Angular Dimension Snap Increments setting, as shown in Figure 3.10, you enter the angle value, and Revit will automatically place the degree symbol after you click OK in the dialog box.

Figure 3.10

Snaps dialog box: the temporary dimensions that are displayed will increment based on the values in this dialog.

Converting Temporary Dimensions

With an object selected and the temporary dimensions displayed, you can turn them into permanent dimensions (described in the following section) by selecting the dimension symbol ⊟ that appears near the temporary dimension.

In Figure 3.11, you can see a selected wall with a temporary dimension displayed and the dimension symbol available. After selecting the symbol, the dimension is converted to a permanent dimension, as shown in Figure 3.12. The dimension will now be visible after the object is no longer selected, as shown in Figure 3.13.

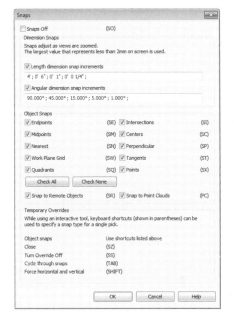

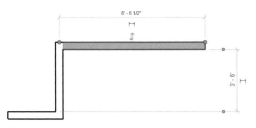

Figure 3.11

Wall selected with the temporary dimension shown and the blue dimension symbol available to convert this to a permanent dimension

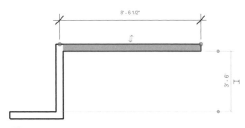

Figure 3.12

The temporary wall dimension is now converted to a permanent dimension while selected.

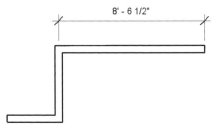

Figure 3.13

The permanent dimension for the wall is now displayed in the view.

Permanent Dimensions

A *permanent* dimension is one that is placed specifically for the purpose of conveying the distance or angle between elements or parts of elements in the model and is visible only within the view in which it is created. Dimensions are annotation elements, and like other annotations, if the scale of the view is changed, the dimensions will automatically resize (scale up or down).

You can create permanent dimensions either by converting a temporary dimension (as shown earlier in the "Converting Temporary Dimensions" section) or by selecting a dimension option on the Annotate tab and selecting the desired dimension type (see Figure 3.14).

Figure 3.14

Choosing a dimension type on the Annotate tab

When you select a dimension type, the Options bar will display available dimension options to aid you in placing your dimensions correctly. Figure 3.15 shows the options available when you use the Aligned dimension tool.

Figure 3.15

These options are available when you use the Aligned dimension tool: (top) Modify | Place Dimensions options, (middle) snap to option, and (bottom) Pick drop-down options.

Place Dimension Options

The Place Dimension options help you choose what Revit will snap to when dimensioning. The first option lets you specify references in walls you would like to dimension to and from during placement. These options include the following:

- Wall Centerlines
- Wall Faces
- Center Of Core
- Faces Of Core

> When placing dimensions, you can change the Place Dimension option by pressing the Tab key while placing the dimension to cycle through nearby references (see Figure 3.15, middle image).

Pick Options

The Pick drop-down (Figure 3.15, lower image) lets you do one of the following:

- Use individual references to select your dimension reference one entity at a time.

- Use the Entire Walls option to pick a wall and let Revit automatically find the ends of the wall and place a dimension at the desired location.

Additionally, when you are using the Entire Walls option, clicking the Options button (displayed in Figure 3.15, the upper image) opens the Auto Dimension Options dialog box. This dialog box provides options that can be used to automate the dimensioning of openings, intersecting walls, and grids when you are using the Entire Walls option (see Figure 3.16).

In Figure 3.17, the top dimension is using individual references. The bottom dimension string is using the Entire Walls pick option with Openings set to Widths in the Auto Dimension Options dialog box.

Figure 3.16

The Auto Dimension Options dialog box is available when you use the Entire Walls option.

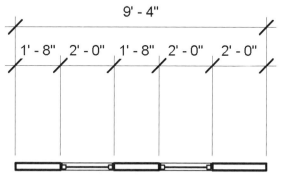

Figure 3.17

Using two different pick methods for placing dimensions

Dimension Styles

You can select from the following dimension styles; each is described in more detail for your reference in the following section:

Aligned Aligned dimensions are the most common dimension type used. When you choose this option, Revit places dimensions between two or more parallel elements or two or more points (such as wall ends). With an angled wall, the dimension reads parallel to the direction of the angled wall (see Figure 3.18).

Linear Linear dimensions are placed between selected points, and when placed they are in alignment with the horizontal or vertical axis of the view (see Figure 3.18 and Figure 3.19).

Angular Angular dimensions show the angles between two selected elements that share a common intersection (see Figure 3.20). To create an angular dimension, follow these steps:

1. Select the Annotate tab, and in the Dimension panel, click the Angular button.

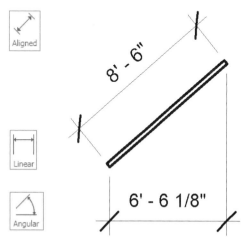

Figure 3.18

This wall is dimensioned with the Aligned (angle) and Linear (horizontal) dimensioning tools.

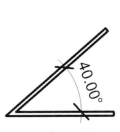

Figure 3.19

This irregular wall layout is dimensioned with the Linear dimension style.

1' - 7 5/8" 8' - 0 3/32" 21' - 2 17/32" 3' - 10 7/8" 1' - 2 7/32"

3' - 10 3/4"

15' - 10 31/32"

6' - 4 1/16"

4' - 2 1/8"

3' - 7"

6' - 9 3/16"

8' - 5 5/16"

5' - 8 3/16"

5' - 3 1/8"

26' - 1 25/32"

35' - 11 11/32"

40.00°

Figure 3.20

Here, angled walls with a common intersection are dimensioned using the Angular dimension style.

Radial

Arc
Length

2. Place the cursor on a component and click to create the starting location for the dimension.

3. Place the cursor on a component not parallel to the first and click.

4. Drag the cursor to the size of the angular dimension and click to place the dimension.

Radial Radial dimensions show the radius of an arc or circle (see Figure 3.21). To create a radial dimension, follow these steps:

1. Select the Annotate tab, and in the Dimension panel, click the Radial button.

2. Place the cursor on the arc and then click.

3. Drag the cursor to the desired location and click to place the dimension.

Arc Length Arc length dimensions show the length of an arc (see Figure 3.22). To create an arc length dimension, follow these steps:

1. Select the Annotate tab, and in the Dimension panel, click the Arc Length button.

2. On the Options bar, select the Snap option.

3. Place the cursor on the arc and click to select the radial point.

4. Select the end points of the arc and then move the cursor up and away from the arc wall.

5. Drag the cursor to the desired location and click to place the dimension.

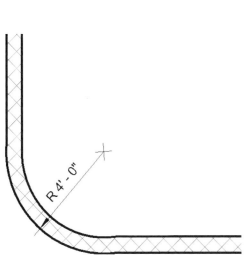

Figure 3.21

In this arc wall, the radius is dimensioned using the Radial dimension style.

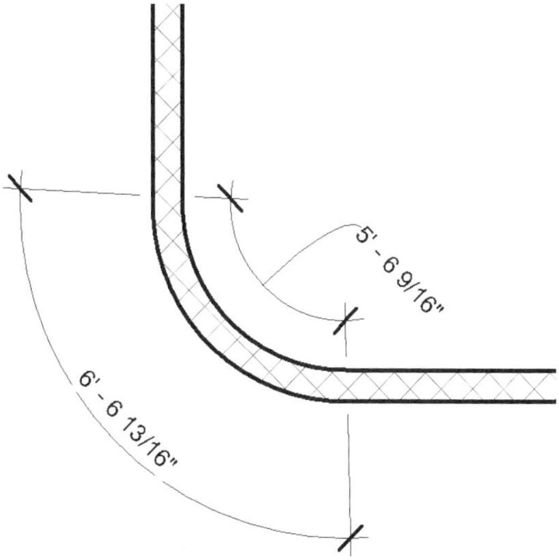

Figure 3.22

An arc wall with the arc length (inside and outside) dimensioned using the Arc Length dimension style

Baseline and Ordinate Dimensions

Baseline dimensions are multiple dimensions measured from the same baseline point, as shown in Figure 3.23. Ordinate dimensions measure the perpendicular distance from a picked origin point called the *datum*, as shown in Figure 3.24.

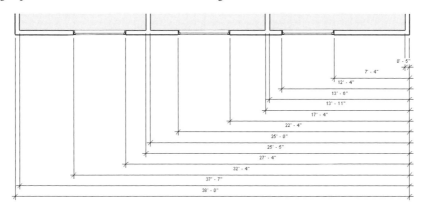

Figure 3.23

Floor plan layout dimensioned using baseline dimensioning

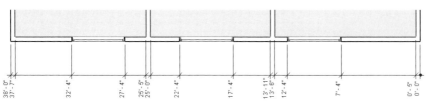

Figure 3.24

Floor plan layout dimensioned using ordinate dimensioning

Figure 3.25

**The Properties pal-
ette shows the cur-
rent dimension type
being used; choose
Edit Type to create a
new type.**

You can use the Aligned or Linear dimension style to display baseline or ordinate dimensions. But first you will need to edit the dimension type settings and create a new type with the proper settings. Start by selecting the Aligned dimension and choosing the Edit Type option in the Properties palette (see Figure 3.25).

Figure 3.26 shows the Properties palette with the Type Selector displaying the current dimension style. If you do not already have a type created for the baseline or ordinate type, you can duplicate an existing type by clicking the Duplicate button. You will be prompted to enter a name for this new type, as shown in Figure 3.27. It is a good idea to keep a standard naming format. For variations, add text that will help you and others know why the type was created.

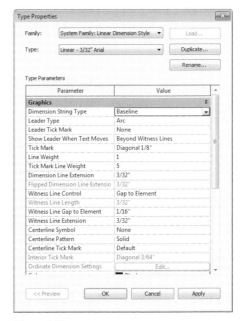

Under Graphics in the Type Properties dialog box, do the following:

1. From the Dimension String Type drop-down, choose Continuous, Baseline, or Ordinate. In Figure 3.28, we chose the Baseline value.

2. Click OK in the dialog box to create this new type.

3. Select the elements for dimensioning.

Figure 3.27

**Duplicate a dimen-
sion type and enter
a new name.**

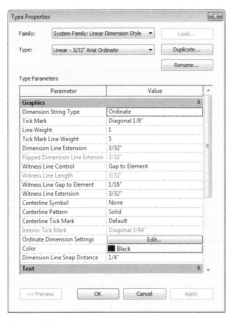

Figure 3.26

**Use the Type Properties dialog box to create a
new dimension type.**

Figure 3.28

Choosing a dimension string type

A sample file (Dataset_03_01.rvt) that shows these two dimension styles is available at the book's web page at www.sybex.com/go/introducingrevit2012.

An additional set of options becomes available when you set Dimension String Type to Ordinate. As shown in Figure 3.29, an Edit button appears next to Ordinate Dimension Settings under Graphics. Clicking Edit opens the Ordinate Dimension Settings dialog box, shown in Figure 3.30, with additional options for the graphical display of the ordinate dimension style. You can repeat this process as needed to create additional dimension styles to meet your project needs.

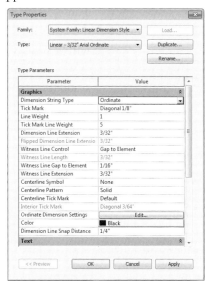

Dimension Text Overrides

Dimensions in Revit always report their exact value and do not allow the use of fake or inaccurate dimensions. For example, if the width of a room is modeled 8¢-0², Revit will not allow you to add a dimension and override the width dimension to 12¢-0², or some other value, as you can do in AutoCAD. There will be times while working with dimensions where you will need to add supplemental text such as a suffix or prefix. Supplemental text can be added on any side (above, below, left, or right) of the permanent dimension value and in some cases replace the actual dimension value with text, as shown in Figure 3.31.

Figure 3.30

Ordinate Dimension Settings dialog box

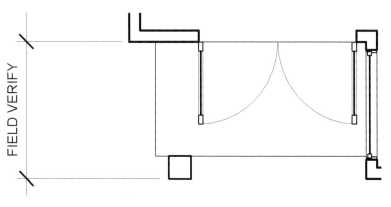

Figure 3.31

Text has been added in place of the dimension value.

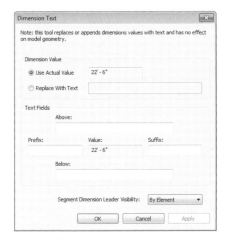

To add a dimension text override to your dimension, follow these steps:

1. Select your dimension.

2. Click the dimension value to display the Dimension Text dialog box, shown in Figure 3.32.

3. Specify how you want to display the dimension value (Use Actual Value or Replace With Text). If you choose text, you must specify how you want to display that text above or below the dimension value, or with a prefix or a suffix.

When using overrides, you do not have to enter text in all the available fields.

Figure 3.32

Dimension Text dialog box

Equality Constraint and Lock

Dimension constraints allow elements to be locked or tied together to create a relationship based on dimension constraint types. Constraining elements helps maintain design intent if changes occur in the model. The equality constraint is used to maintain an equal distance between multiple elements. For example, you might place three windows in a wall and want the spacing between each window to be equal. The equality constraint makes this simple. The lock constraint is used when you want to lock the relationship between elements. For example, you might place a window next to a door and want to maintain a 2′-0″ (600mm), spacing between the two elements, regardless of where the door is placed. Locking the dimension for the door and window spacing will accomplish that.

The Equality option is available for objects that have a multisegment dimension and is indicated by the EQ symbol EQ within the dimension string. Figure 3.33 shows a permanent dimension string that has been placed for the walls and windows in the project. With the dimension string selected, you can use the EQ option (which by default has a red diagonal line through it indicating that the values are not equally constrained) by picking the symbol to make the actual dimension distance between each window equal, as shown in Figure 3.34. If the dimensions were not created as a dimension string but one dimension at a time, the equality constraint will not be available.

Figure 3.33

Floor plan with dimensions and Equality option visible

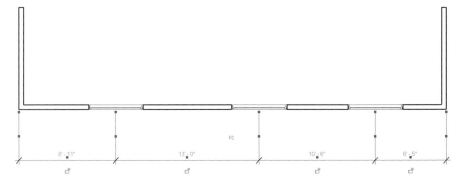

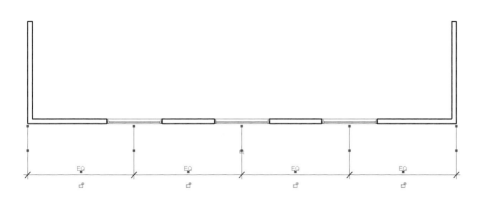

Figure 3.34

**Floor plan with
dimensions and
Equality option
selected**

When you use an equality constraint, the default value
(Equality Text) changes from displaying the numeric value
to showing the letters *EQ* at each dimension location
(Figure 3.34). You can instead display the actual value. To
do so, select your dimension string, and in the Properties
palette (see Figure 3.35), under Other, select Value from
the Equality Display drop-down and click Apply. Doing so
changes the dimension display, as shown in Figure 3.36.

Figure 3.35

**Dimension equality
display options**

Figure 3.36

**Floor plan with
dimensions and
equality constraint
display set to Value**

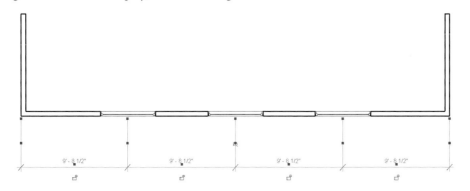

With the equality constraint applied, the walls or other references used will remain at
equal distances from one another as long as the constraint remains active. To remove the
constraint, select the dimension string and then click the blue EQ option. The dimensions will remain the same, but the actual constraint will be removed. Now you can independently move any of the objects, and the dimension will change only for that reference
and not for other related elements along the dimension string.

Locking Dimensions

When using permanent dimensions, you can also *lock* the dimensions, which will create a
relationship between the referenced objects that cannot be changed unless the constraint
is purposefully removed. Figure 3.37 shows an example floor plan that has walls and a

door with dimensions. The door needs to maintain the 1′-4″ (450mm) distance from the inside face of the bottom wall.

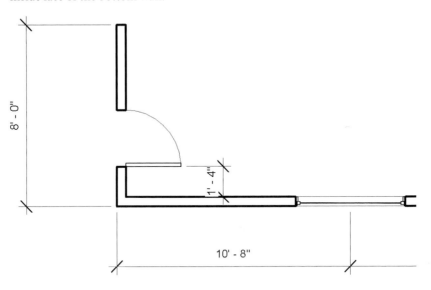

As the floor plan develops, the exterior is shifting, and the use of a lock constraint will help you maintain that relationship. In Figure 3.38, we have selected the dimension, and in Figure 3.39 we are going to click the small lock icon. Doing so will change the icon from an unlocked to locked. Later when the bottom wall is moved down, we can see the distance for the door will be maintained, and the door will stay 1′-4″ (450mm) from the inside face of the bottom wall, as shown in Figure 3.40.

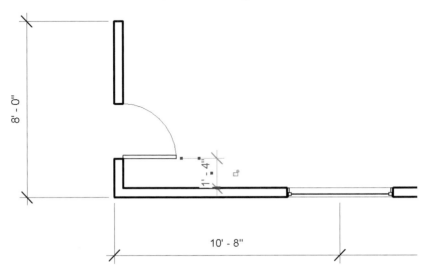

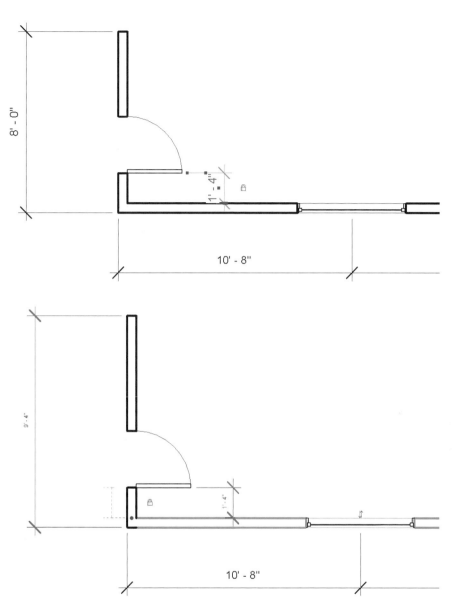

Figure 3.39

Floor plan with dimension and lock constraint picked

Figure 3.40

Floor plan with dimensions and lock constraint applied. Compare with Figure 3.39; the bottom wall has moved, but the distance from the inside face of the wall to the door is maintained.

If you delete the dimension, Revit gives you a warning (Figure 3.41) letting you know that a lock relationship exists and that you can delete the dimension and keep the relationship or delete the dimension and remove the constraint.

If the dimension is removed and the lock constraint remains, when you select an element that has been constrained you will see the lock icon selected on the temporary dimension displayed when the element is selected, as shown in Figure 3.42.

Figure 3.41

You'll see this warning when removing a dimension that has a lock constraint applied.

Figure 3.42

Door selected and showing the lock constraint in the temporary dimension

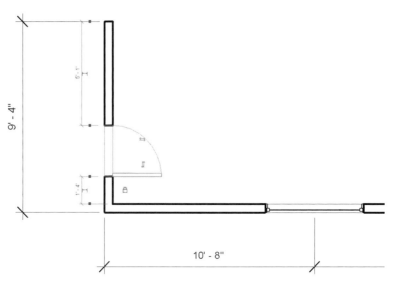

Figure 3.42

Door selected and showing the lock constraint in the temporary dimension

Spot Dimensions

Spot dimensions offer the ability to report information about a single point or slope in relation to a chosen set of points. Spot dimensions can be used to display the heights of reference points or the north/south and east/west coordinates of a reference point. In the Revit environment, these coordinates can be placed as Spot Elevation, Spot Coordinate, or Spot Slope using the Annotate tab on the Dimension panel (see Figure 3.43):

Figure 3.43

Spot dimension options on the Dimension panel

Spot Elevation Displays the actual elevation (height) of a selected point and can display the top and bottom elevations of an element with a thickness (see Figure 3.44).

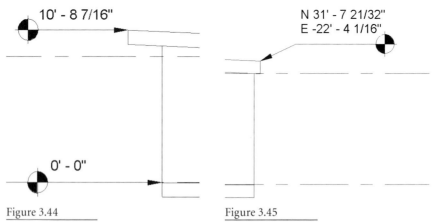

Figure 3.44

Choosing Spot Elevation displays a roof's top and bottom elevations.

Figure 3.45

Spot Coordinate showing roof coordinates

Spot Coordinate Displays the north/south and east/west coordinates of a selected point and can display the elevation (height) of the selected point (see Figure 3.45). You can add the elevation to the spot coordinate by checking the Include Elevation check box in the Type Properties dialog box for Spot Coordinates (Figure 3.46).

Spot Slope Displays the slope at a specific point on a face or an edge of an element (see Figure 3.47).

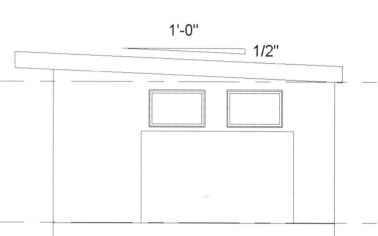

Figure 3.46

Click Include Elevation in the spot coordinate's Type Properties dialog box to display the elevation.

Figure 3.47

Spot Slope showing the roof pitch

Units

The dimension types provided in the out-of-the-box Revit templates take advantage of the units and accuracy assigned to the project (on the Manage tab, click Project Units). At some point you will need to adjust the units and/or level of accuracy to achieve the results you desire. For example, in a project that is using imperial units, you may have to show metric units or use different rounding options. To do any of these things, you must override the dimension type.

   To create a dimension with an override, follow these steps:

1. On the Annotate tab, select the Dimension panel and from the drop-down, choose the dimension style you want to override. You can also select a dimension in the

drawing area that you want to override and select Edit Type from the Properties palette.

Doing so opens the Type Properties dialog box, as shown in Figure 3.48.

2. Click the Duplicate button to create a copy.

3. Provide a name for the new type.

4. Under Type Parameters in the Text group, you will see Units Format. Click the button under the Value column for Units Format to open a Format dialog box for the dimension units. By default, the Use Project Settings check box is selected.

5. To make your override, deselect this check box, as shown in Figure 3.49. Doing so makes the entries available for editing.

6. Make the changes that you need.

7. Click OK in the Format dialog box, and then click OK in the Type Properties dialog box.

Your changes are now part of the style; from here you can place new permanent dimensions using the modified type or select existing dimensions and change the type used from the Properties palette. Figure 3.50 shows a partial floor plan that was created using an imperial template, and Figure 3.51 shows the same floor plan with the dimension type units formatted to display meters.

Figure 3.48

Dimension type properties

Figure 3.49

Format options for dimension units

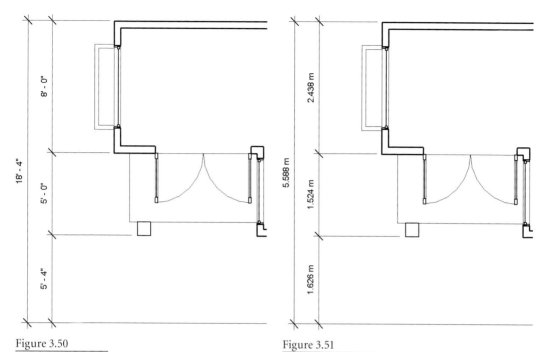

Figure 3.50

Partial floor plan based on the imperial template and dimension type using imperial project units

Figure 3.51

Partial floor plan based on the imperial template and dimension type with an override set to meters

CHAPTER 4

Modeling

In this chapter, we cover the basics of modeling in Autodesk Revit Architecture. We begin with a discussion of object selection and how to filter a group of objects that you have selected. We then move into a discussion on walls and wall properties.

This includes selecting objects; creating and editing walls, doors, and windows; using levels and grids; grouping; and adding columns. We will start by showing you how to select, move, copy, trim, extend, cut, delete, rotate, mirror, array, align, and match.

This chapter covers the following topics:

- Levels

- Basic editing tools

- Creating and modifying column grids

- Working with walls

- Introducing parts

- Creating doors and windows

- Creating floors

- Creating ceilings

- Creating roofs

- Assemblies

Levels

Levels are horizontal planes that go on indefinitely. These planes act as references in your building project to host certain elements such as walls, floors, roofs, and ceilings. Levels allow you to define floor elevation and key vertical elevation elements. What's a key vertical elevation element? The top of a parapet is one example. The nice thing about levels is that you can choose whether you want them associated with a floor and reflected ceiling plans. In the case of the top of the parapet, you would not necessarily need to create a floor plan or reflected ceiling plan of that view. Levels are key to modeling because you use them to help you define the vertical extents of certain elements and for the vertical placement of other elements such as furniture.

In any given project, you should be creating levels for all the key heights and datums. You do this so that you can constrain your elements to those levels, and if for some reason you make a change to the floor-to-floor heights, your elements will adjust in height accordingly. If you didn't do this, then it would be necessary to create your elements and assign absolute values to the height of the walls. But if you needed to change the height of the parapet or floor-to-floor heights, then you would have to select all the objects and change their heights manually, which is very time-consuming.

It is not as simple as saying, "I have a five-story building that consists of five levels." That is not really the case; you will definitely have many more than five levels in that project. Nor should you have 115 levels in a typical four-story project, which we have actually seen.

WHAT ARE DATUMS?

Datums are nonphysical items such as levels, grids, and reference planes that are used to establish project context. Grid lines, for example, are used for placing columns and other building elements. The grid lines are nonphysical elements that are not part of the building but are used to help define and constrain the building model.

Datums can host elements. If you assign a wall's base to a specific level, then when the elevation of that level changes, the wall will move with the level. Grids are similar to levels. If an element is constrained to a grid line, then when the grid moves, that element moves.

Another important feature of levels is that you can associate views with your levels. Levels can be associated with floor plan views and reflected ceiling plan views. Views and the level should both have the same name. If you change the name of the level, you will be asked whether you want to change the names of the floor plan and reflected ceiling plan views.

Let's look at levels in a project. Start a new project using the default template. In the Project Browser, the Revit tree shows the different view categories. Under Views (All), look at the views under Floor Plans. Notice that there are three views: Level 1, Level 2, and Site. Under Elevations (Building Elevation), four views have been defined: East, North, South, and West (Figure 4.1). If you double-click one of the elevation view names, that view will open in the drawing area. In the drawing area, below the level name is the vertical height of the level (Figure 4.2).

Before you add or modify the levels, let's look at the various controls for adjusting the appearance of a level. To follow along, zoom in on the Level 2 datum. Select either the level reference line or the level name or elevation (Figure 4.3).

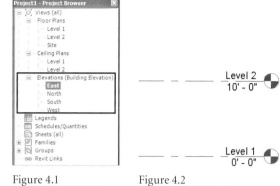

Figure 4.1

Elevations in the Project Browser

Figure 4.2

Level examples

Figure 4.3

Selected level

When you select an element and a blue object or object controls appear, this indicates you can perform some kind of action to that object or object controls.

To change the name of the level, perform the following steps:

1. Double-click the level name, and type a new name (Figure 4.4). Or you can select the level and change the name in the Properties palette.

2. Type **Roof** for the new name, and press Enter.

   Revit will open a dialog box asking whether you really want to rename any corresponding views. Because levels are typically tied to floor plan and ceiling plan views, Revit can automatically keep the level and corresponding view's name the same.

3. Choose Yes, and note in the Project Browser that the Level 2 floor and ceiling plan views have also been renamed to Roof (Figure 4.5).

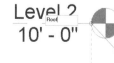

Figure 4.4

Renaming a level to Roof

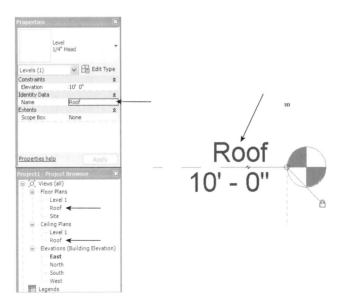

Any time a view is renamed, whether it is a floor plan, ceiling plan, or level name, if there is a corresponding view, Revit will always ask whether you want to rename the corresponding view. If you allow Revit to perform this task, which is recommended, then your Project Browser's corresponding view names will be renamed. If you do not allow Revit to rename corresponding views, then you could have a floor plan with a different name than its corresponding ceiling plan and level.

To change the elevation of the level, you can follow similar steps as you did with changing the level name. You can double-click the elevation value and type in a new value (Figure 4.6). You can also change the Elevation value in the Project Browser.

Another method involves changing the temporary dimension constraint of the level. Zoom out in your view so that you can see two levels. When you select the Roof level, a temporary dimension will be displayed between the two levels (Figure 4.7). Notice that the dimension value is blue, indicating that you can edit it. If you click the dimension text and change it to **14 6**, the roof-level elevation will adjust accordingly.

When you type in units, the default Revit templates will automatically assume that you are typing in feet and inches or millimeters. If you are working with Imperial units, typing **10 6** in a dialog box is the same as typing **10′ 6″**. Revit sees the space between the 10 and the 6 as a feet/inch separator. If you only want to type in six inches, you could type either **6″** or **0 6**.

You can move levels by selecting the level or levels and dragging them up or down to the new location. The temporary dimension and snap settings increment will assist in positioning the levels.

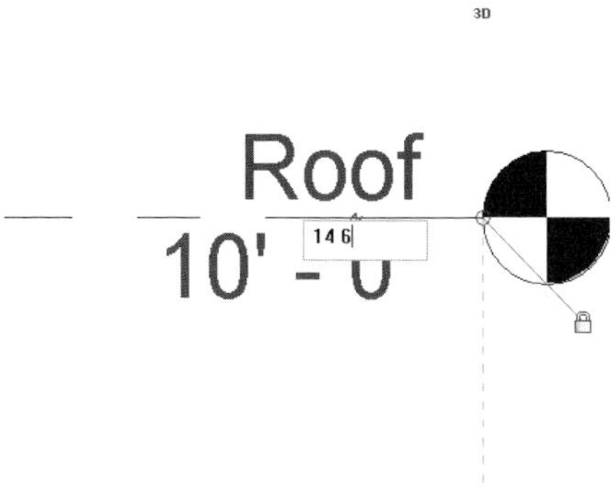

Roof
10' - 0
14 6

Roof
14' - 6"

Level 1
0' - 0"

Figure 4.6

Changing the elevation of level

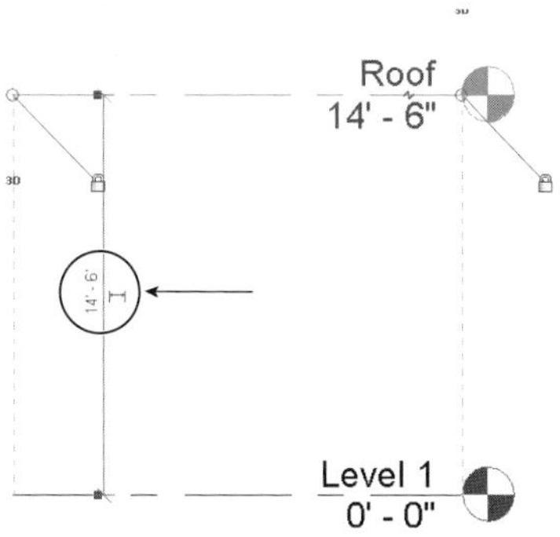

Figure 4.7

Selected level showing temporary dimensions

SNAP SETTING INCREMENTS

When you place or move an element in a view, it will snap at user-defined dimension increments. For example, when you are moving the elevation of a level, as you move the mouse pointer up or down in the drawing area, you see the dimensions for the level increase or decrease according to the defined length dimension snap increments. The same applies to rotating an element; angle snap dimensions increase or decrease according to the defined angle dimension snap increments.

Unlike in AutoCAD, in Revit you can define multiple length and angle snap increments to account for changes as you change your zoom level (the closer you zoom in, the smaller the increment; the farther you zoom out, the larger the increment).

To set or review snap increments, follow these steps:

1. Click the Manage tab, go to the Settings panel, and click Snaps.

2. Select Length Dimension Snap Increments and Angular Dimension Snap Increments to turn on the snaps. Deselect to turn off the snaps.

3. Edit or add the snapping increment values, separating each increment with semicolons. There is no limit to the number of increments you can specify.

4. Click OK to apply the changes.

Creating a Level

Two methods are available to create a level: the Pick Lines tool and the Sketch tool. To add new levels to a project with the first method, use the following steps:

1. Change the active view to a section or elevation view.

2. Click the Home tab, select the Datum panel, and click Level.

Notice that the ribbon switches to the Modify | Place Level tab.

You have two options to draw the level:

- The first allows you to draw a line segment (by default).
- The second option allows you to pick lines.

3. Select the Pick Lines tool in the Draw panel.

4. On the Options bar, make sure that Make Plan View is checked, and specify an Offset value of **10′ 0″ (3050mm)**.

5. Move the mouse pointer over one of the existing level lines that you want to use as an offset to create the new level (Figure 4.8).

Notice the new level line that appears above the previous level line, based on the location of your cursor.

Figure 4.8

Creating a new level using the Pick and Offset method and getting a preview of the location

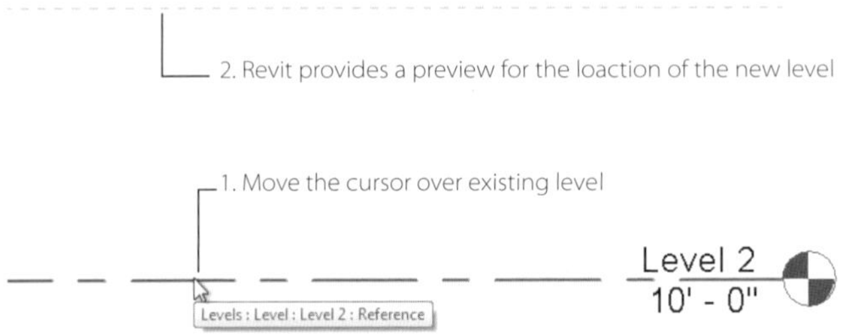

2. Revit provides a preview for the loaction of the new level

1. Move the cursor over existing level

Level 2
10' - 0"

Levels : Level : Level 2 : Reference

6. Click the left mouse button to create the new level.

The Options bar for the Level tool has several options (Figure 4.9):

Figure 4.9

Placing a level, Options bar

Modify | Place Level   ☑ Make Plan View   Plan View Types...   Offset: 10′ 0

Make Plan View When this option is selected, after you draw your level line, the floor plan and reflected ceiling plan views will be automatically created. If this option is not selected, then the level is considered a reference or nonstory level, and no associated floor or ceiling plan view is created.

Plan View Types This opens a dialog box that allows you to choose the view types (floor plan and ceiling plan) that will be created when Make Plan View is selected.

Offset Specifying an Offset value will create a new level parallel to the level selected by the amount that is specified.

Lock Lock is enabled only when Offset is set to 0. This locks the level to the reference picked. If you try to move the reference, say a floor, for example, after you have locked the level, you will get an error. If you move the level, the floor will follow.

7. Right-click and select Cancel to exit the Level command.

Now, let's create another level using the Sketch tool:

1. Click the Level tool on the Home tab's Datum panel, and click the Line option.

2. In the drawing area, move your mouse pointer in the general area where you want to place your level.

   Notice that a temporary dimension is displayed, showing the offset from the nearest level.

   As you move the mouse pointer near one end of an existing level line, a dashed cyan alignment line appears, indicating its alignment with an existing level.

3. Click to specify the first point of the level reference line, and move the mouse pointer to the left or right.

   Notice that level name, level line, datum, and elevation appear.

4. When the alignment line appears, click to place the level head.

   The level line is created, and the temporary dimension is displayed, indicating the level offset.

   When you finish drawing the new level, the Level tool is still running.

5. To stop a tool in progress, either select the Modify tool from the ribbon or hit the Esc key twice.

If you want to place multiple levels, using the Level tool is one method, but it's not very efficient. You can use some of the basic editing tools to help with this task.

Clicking a level line displays the graphic controls shown in Figure 4.10. The blue squares on each end of the grid are check boxes used to control the visibility of the level heads. The blue circles on the end of the grid lines are the drag controls. These enable to you to extend or reduce the length of the grid line. The Add Elbow drag control allows you to move the grid bubble away from the grid line. When you use the Add Elbow drag control, the change will appear in the current view only.

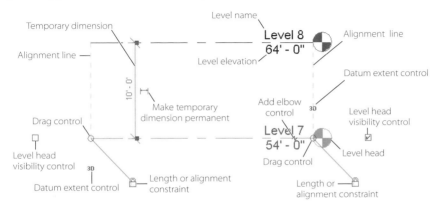

Figure 4.10

Level graphic controls

The final control you want to look at is the Datum Extent control. When the grid line shows the 3D designation, the grid line is in Model Extent mode. This means that if you drag and change the length of the grid line, the change will appear in all other parallel views, provided these grid lines also are set to the 3D Model Extent control. If the Datum Extent control is set to 2D, then the resizing of the grid line will take place only in that view.

With the intelligence of *building information modeling* (BIM) and the ability to share this intelligence with other applications, it is important to be able to display your levels at the correct elevation above sea level. Revit provides you with the ability to use project and shared elevations. The project elevations are what we use and typically show in our document sets. Shared elevations allow you to display the true elevation of the project without moving the project.

Basic Editing Tools

Before you get too far into learning basic modeling techniques, you need to learn how to use the various editing tools so you can modify the elements that you have created. You can find these tools on the Modify tab (Figure 4.11).

Figure 4.11

Modify tab

Selecting Objects

To edit an element, you need to be able to select it. Revit provides a number of ways to do this, some of which are similar to AutoCAD. The basic method for selecting objects is to use the mouse.

You can select a single element simply by clicking it. The element will turn light blue, indicating that it has been selected.

To select multiple elements, several methods are available:

- Ctrl+clicking
- Creating a "window" or "crossing window" marquee
- Chain selecting (walls and lines)
- Using the Select All Instances command

Ctrl+clicking each element individually adds it to a selection set. The elements turn light blue, indicating that they have been added to the selection set.

You can create a window selection by using a click-and-drag operation in the drawing area: pressing the left mouse button and dragging the mouse pointer diagonally from left to right to create a selection box around the elements to be selected. Only the elements that are completely within the window will be selected (Figure 4.12). The window selection rectangle will be a solid light gray line. Items added to the selection set will turn light blue.

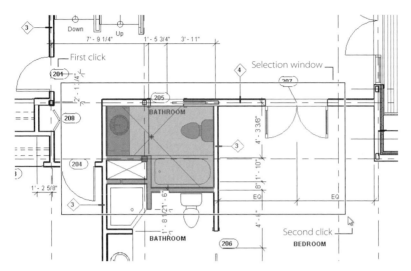

Figure 4.12

Window selection—blue elements (here, gray) selected

You can create a crossing window selection by pressing the left mouse button and dragging the mouse pointer diagonally *from right to left* to create a selection box around the elements to be selected. All elements that either are in the window boundary *or are touched by it* are added to the selection set (Figure 4.13). The crossing window rectangle will be a gray dashed line. Items added to the selection set will turn light blue.

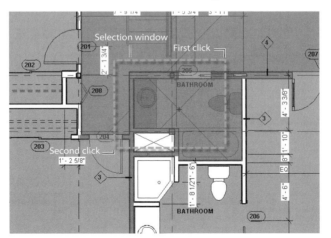

Figure 4.13

Window crossing selection—blue elements (here, gray) selected

You can use the Chain option to select objects such as walls and/or lines that are joined in a continuous chain. To create a chain selection, first select one element by clicking it or hovering the mouse pointer over it (Figure 4.14). Press the Tab key once, and

Revit highlights all the elements in the chain (Figure 4.15). You may have to press the Tab key more than once for more complex chains. Left-click to create the selection.

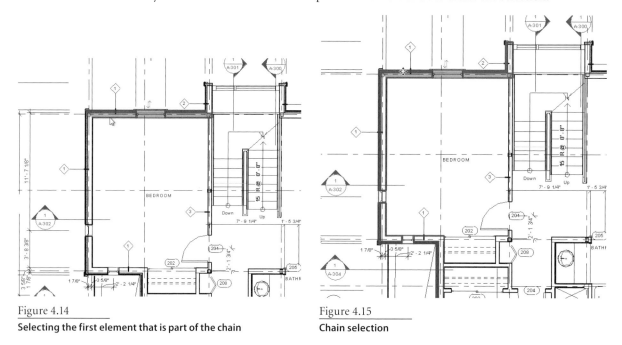

Figure 4.14

Selecting the first element that is part of the chain

Figure 4.15

Chain selection

You can also use the Select All Instances options to select all instances of an element type that is used in the project. You might want to do this to globally change element properties, such as manufacturer or finish information. You might want to change the element type to switch from a single-flush to a double-flush door. You might also need to delete or modify a specific element type.

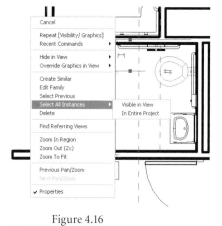

Figure 4.16

Select All Instances context menu

To use Select All Instances, first select a single instance of the element type that you want to add to the selection set. You can do this in any view. In Figure 4.16, we have selected a toilet, right-clicked to open a context menu, and selected the Select All Instances item. You have two options:

Visible In View This option will select only instances of the elements that are visible in the current view. By *view*, Revit means the view that you have open, such as the Level 1 floor plan, and not just the area that is visible in the drawing area window.

In Entire Project This option will select every instance of the element in the entire project.

Filtering and Element Selection Count

When you select multiple elements, you often end up selecting unintended elements. Hold down the Shift button and click the unwanted elements to remove them from the selection set.

For more complicated changes to the selection set, you can use the Filter tool (the item that looks like a funnel on the status bar) to eliminate elements by category from your selection set. When you have elements selected, the selection count will display the total number of elements selected on the status bar. Figure 4.17 shows that 44 elements are selected.

To remove element categories from a selection set, follow these steps:

1. Click the Filter tool on the status bar.

   This will open the Filter dialog box (Figure 4.18). The Filter dialog box lists the selected elements categories. It also displays the number of selected elements in each category and the total number of selected elements.

2. Clear the check boxes to deselect categories of elements.

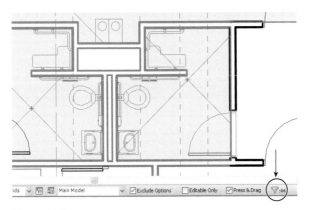

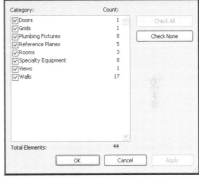

Figure 4.17
Selection count tool and filter listing on status bar

Figure 4.18
Filter dialog box

Moving Objects

Revit provides numerous methods for moving and copying elements in the drawing area: ribbon options, keyboard actions, and onscreen controls. The first option for moving an element is to utilize the temporary dimensions.

As you create or place elements in Revit, temporary dimensions will be displayed around the element. This helps you accurately define and place an element relative to the surrounding elements in your building project. There are two different types of temporary dimensions: *listening* and *viewing*.

LISTENING DIMENSIONS

When you are sketching, rotating, moving, and so on, Revit will provide temporary reference dimensions. These are known as *listening dimensions*. At any time during the editing, you can enter a new value for length or rotation.

If you do not like the size of the listening dimension, you can change the size. Click the Application button and choose Options. In the Options dialog box, switch to the Graphics tab. Near the bottom of the dialog box in the Temporary Dimension Text Appearance, there is an option to adjust the text size.

Listening dimensions are present when you are creating or placing elements, and you can specify values during placement. Listening dimensions appear bold and blue, and they update when you move your mouse pointer, such as dragging the length of a wall.

Viewing dimensions become active when you select an element. They display a dimension in reference to the nearest element. You can move the witness lines (dimension extension lines) of a temporary dimension to a new location to reference specific elements.

Figure 4.19 displays a wall selected that shows temporary dimensions. Clicking the witness line grip (the blue square grip on the temporary dimension witness line) allows you to toggle between the center of the wall, finish face, core face, and so on, depending on the type of wall. Changes you make to the witness line are saved for the current Revit session.

Figure 4.19

Selected wall temporary dimensions

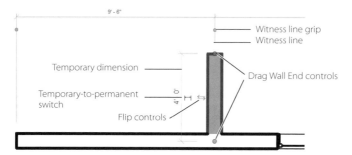

The blue circles are the Drag Wall End controls. The position of the blue circles indicates the wall location line and the ability to change the length of a wall by dragging. The two opposite-facing arrows are flip controls. Flip controls on elements are always on the exterior side of the object. Clicking a flip control changes the orientation of an element. For example, when you flip a compound wall, you reverse the order of its component layers. Walls use their location line as the axis line of the flip. Doors with a swing will often have two flip controls:

- Flip The Instance Facing controls whether the door swings in or out.
- Flip The Instance Hand controls whether the door swings right or left.

Temporary dimensions also have a switch to convert a temporary dimension to a permanent dimension.

FAKING DIMENSIONS IN REVIT

In Revit you are not able to fake a dimension. A dimension's value is the actual distance, and if you change a dimension value, the model will change to reflect the new dimension.

Another method for moving as well as copying an object involves using the dragging option. To move or copy an object using the dragging option, follow these steps:

1. Select an object in the drawing window.

2. On the status bar, make sure that the Press & Drag check box is selected.

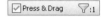

3. Move the mouse pointer over the element, and click and hold the left mouse button.

4. Move the mouse pointer to the desired location.

   As you drag the mouse pointer, Revit will display the original element and an image of the element moving with the drag, as shown in Figure 4.20.

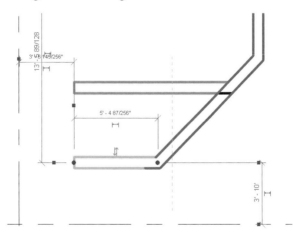

Figure 4.20

Moving a wall with preview image

5. When the element reaches the desired location, release the left mouse button.

As you move, copy, or perform editing tasks on elements, Revit will provide you with visual cues regarding the result of what you are trying to accomplish.

Another method for moving elements is to use the Move tool. The Move tool is very similar to Press & Drag, except that you will not get the same preview of the elements. The Move tool will also provide more precision, allowing you to take advantage of the temporary dimensions.

To use the Move tool ✥, follow these steps:

1. Select the element(s) to be moved.

2. On the Modify tab's Modify panel, click the Move tool. The Options bar for this tool has a couple options:

   Constrain Selecting this restricts the movement of the selected elements along vectors that run perpendicular or collinear to the element.

   Disjoin Selecting this breaks the association of an element with its associated elements and moves it to a new location. An example use would be when you want to move a wall that is joined to another wall.

3. Click in the drawing area to pick the start point for moving.

4. Move the mouse pointer to the desired move location, and click to specify the end point.

   You can also move the mouse pointer and edit the temporary dimension to specify the new location.

   The elements are moved to the new location.

Copying Objects

Using the Copy tool 📋 is very similar to using the Move tool:

1. Select the elements to be moved.

2. On the Modify tab's Modify panel, click the Copy tool.

   The Options bar for the Copy command shares several of the same options as the Move tool. In addition, Copy also utilizes the Multiple option. Select this check box to create multiple copies of the elements, and then click where you want to place them.

3. Click in the drawing area to pick the start point for copying.

4. Move the mouse pointer to the desired copy location, and click to specify the end point.

   You can also move the mouse pointer and edit the temporary dimension to specify the new location.

   The element(s) are moved to the new location.

   The following list is a general set of rules regarding moving and copying:

- Walls that are moved or copied using the click-and-drag method will have the wall joins adjusted automatically.

- Some elements can be moved only in a particular direction. Pressing Shift removes this constraint.

- Some elements can be moved in all directions. Pressing the Shift key restricts the direction of movement.

- When moving and copying elements, specify a distance with the listening dimension (Figure 4.21) to move in the direction you move the mouse pointer. Specifying a negative dimension value will move the element in the opposite direction of the mouse pointer.

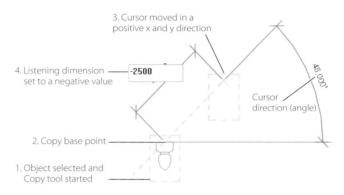

Figure 4.21

Using listening dimensions to move or copy an element along the direction of the mouse pointer

Rotating Objects

The Rotate tool ⟳ allows you to rotate elements around a specified axis or point. In floor plans, ceiling plans, elevation views, and section views, elements will be rotated around an axis perpendicular to the view. In 3D views, elements will be rotated about an axis perpendicular to the current work plane of the view.

The trick to using the Rotate tool is understanding the rotate controls shown in Figure 4.22. The center of rotation symbol is used to change the center of rotation. By default, Revit will position the center of rotation symbol by finding the center of the objects selected. This may not be the location that you need for the origin of your rotation. By left-clicking and dragging the center of the rotation symbol, you can relocate it. The symbol automatically snaps to points and lines such as walls and intersections of walls and lines.

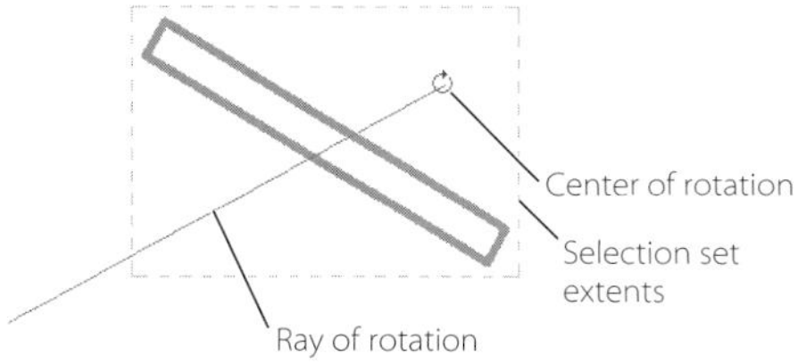

Figure 4.22

Rotate controls

To rotate an element, follow these steps:

1. Select an object to rotate.

2. On the Modify tab's Modify panel, click the Rotate tool.

3. On the Options bar, select any of the following options if applicable:

   Disjoin Selecting this option breaks any connection between the selection and other elements before the rotation.

   Copy Selecting this option creates a copy of the selection, and the original remains in place.

Angle With this option, you can specify the angle of rotation. After you press Enter, the rotation is performed, and no further steps are necessary.

Center Of Rotation The Place option allows you to relocate the origin of the rotation. This is similar to selecting the origin point and dragging to a new location. The Default option allows you to restore the center of rotation origin to the original location.

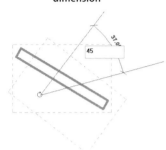

Figure 4.23

Rotating by editing the listening dimension

4. In the drawing area, click to specify the first ray of rotation.

   A line will be displayed to indicate the first ray.

5. Move the mouse pointer to place the second ray of rotation, or specify an angular dimension (Figure 4.23).

6. Click to place the second ray, and finish rotating the selection.

   If you are trying to rotate and the rotation symbol does not appear, this means that the active workset is turned off in the view. Change the active workset to one that's visible or turn on its display in the view, and the rotation symbol will reappear.

Arraying Objects

When you need to create multiple copies of selected elements in a rectangular or radial fashion, use the Array tool ⊞. The Array tool has two options:

Linear (Default) Allows you to copy items along a straight line.

Radial Allows you to copy items around a circle or arc and is very similar to the Rotate tool.

To create multiple copies along a straight line, use the Linear Array option. In the next example, you will array a series of doors along a wall:

1. From the book's web page (available at www.sybex.com/go/introducingrevit2012), open Dataset_04_01.rvt (M_Dataset_04_01.rvt)

2. Open the South Elevation view.

3. Select the door.

4. On the Modify tab's Modify panel, click the Array tool.

   The Options bar (Figure 4.24) for the Array tool provides these settings:

Figure 4.24

Options bar for the Array tool

Linear/Radial The first two buttons indicate whether you will be creating a linear or radial array.

Group And Associate This check box enables you to create a group of the selected elements, which are then copied as a group rather than as individual elements. If deselected, once placed, each copy acts independently of the others.

Number Specifies the total number of copies (of the selected elements) in the array.

Move To Indicates how Revit should space the objects in the array:

- The option named 2nd specifies the distance from the original selected member to each member of the array. Additional array members will appear after the second member.

- The option Last specifies the entire span of the array from the first to the last; the array members are evenly spaced between the first and last members of the array.

Constrain This check box will restrict the movement of array members along vectors that run perpendicular or collinear to the selected elements.

Activate Dimensions When you select multiple elements in Revit, temporary dimensions and constraints may not display. Temporary dimensions also may not appear; as more and more elements fill up the screen, Revit decides not to show temporary dimensions to improve performance. The Activate Dimensions button will force the showing of these temporary dimensions. Be aware that system performance can significantly decrease when the temporary dimensions and constraints are displayed.

5. In the Options bar, set the number of items to **4**, and set the Move To radio button to Last.

6. Click in the drawing window to pick the start point of the array.

7. Move your mouse pointer along the wall until the length is 50′ 0″ (15240mm) (Figure 4.25).

8. Click to accept the length.

9. Hit the Esc key twice to exit the Array tool and selection set.

Figure 4.25

Specifying a linear dimension for array

The array is then completed, and you are provided with an option to change the number of elements in the array (Figure 4.26).

Figure 4.26

Final array with the number of items in array displayed for editing

Creating a radial array is similar to creating a linear array. The Options bar for creating a radial array provides a new Angle edit box to specify the angle at which the array is to be created.

Resizing Objects

You can use the Scale 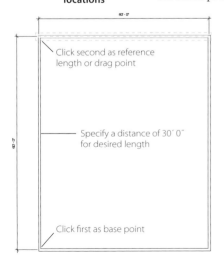 tool to modify the scale of a single element or a selection of elements. This tool is limited to walls, lines, images, DWG and DXF imports, reference planes, and the positions of dimensions. Items such as doors, windows, and furniture cannot be scaled. In the following example, you have a rectangle of four walls and are going to change the length of the vertical walls to 20′ 0″ (6070mm) from 10′ 0″ (3035mm).

1. Continue using the file from the previous section or from the book's web page (available at www.sybex.com/go/introducingrevit2012), open Dataset_04_01.rvt (M_Dataset_04_01.rvt).

2. Open Level 1.

3. Select the wall.

4. On the Modify tab's Modify panel, click the Scale tool. The Options bar provides two options:

    Graphical When this option is enabled, you will scale your elements graphically in the drawing area. To use this option:

    a. Specify three points, the first to specify the origin of scaling and the other two to define the scale vectors.

    b. Once you have defined the origin, move the mouse pointer and click to specify the length of the first vector.

Revit will then calculate the proportion of the two vectors and resize the element in the same proportion using the specified origin.

Figure 4.27

Scale reference locations

Click second as reference length or drag point

Specify a distance of 30′ 0″ for desired length

Click first as base point

Numerical When this option is used, you specify a numeric value for the scale.

5. Select the lower end point of the wall for the first input, the origin point, or the base point (Figure 4.27).

6. Select the upper end point of the wall for the second input, the reference length, or the drag point.

7. Select the midpoint of the wall for the third input or the desired length.

    The walls then immediately adjust.

    The following list is a general set of rules regarding resizing:

• All elements must lie in parallel planes.

- All walls in the selection must have the same base level.

- Resizing changes the position of dimensions but not their values. If you resize an element that a dimension references, the dimension value does not change.

- When you resize a wall, inserts remain at a fixed distance from the wall's midpoint.

- Resizing moves the position of the location line of the walls, but it does not change either the height or the thickness.

Mirroring Objects

The Mirror tool is used to create a mirror image of the selected elements around an axis defined by a line passing through two points. To create this reference axis line, you can either draw an axis line or pick geometry to be used as the axis for the mirroring. When you start the Mirror tool, the Options bar will present you with the Copy option. By default this option is selected and will create a mirrored copy of the elements. If this option is not selected, then the selected elements are mirrored to the new location. To mirror an element, follow these steps:

Figure 4.28

Using the Mirror Draw Axis option to define a mirror axis

1. Select the elements that you want to mirror (Figure 4.28).

2. Click the Modify tab's Modify panel, and click Mirror Pick Axis or Mirror Draw Axis.

   - If you select Mirror Pick Axis, select a line or element to use as the axis line.

   - If you choose Mirror Draw Axis, then you will need to sketch a temporary mirror axis line.

3. Select or draw the line or element you want to use as a mirror axis.

   After you select or draw a reference line, a new element will be created.

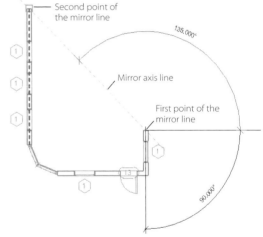

> You can only pick a line or a reference place that the mouse pointer can snap to. You cannot mirror a component around empty space.

Revit then either moves or copies the selected elements and reverses its position opposite the selected axis (Figure 4.29).

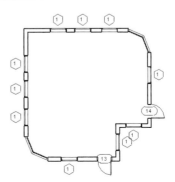

Figure 4.29

Results of the mirroring

Aligning Objects

As you work on your building project, you will find a situation when you need to align 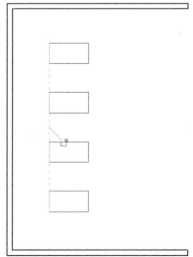 two or more objects with one another. You can choose an element that acts as a reference line or a place along which the other elements can be aligned.

When you align them, a padlock is displayed, which represents the alignment constraint. With the padlock, you can lock or unlock the alignment of the elements. Once elements are alignment locked, when one is moved, they will all move together.

In the following example, you have a group of desks that need to be aligned with one another, as shown in Figure 4.30. The topmost desk is properly positioned, and you will use the leftmost edge of the desk as your reference point.

1. On the Modify tab's Modify panel, click the Align tool. The Options bar provides you with two options:

   Multiple Alignment Selecting this option allows you to align multiple elements with a selected element.

   Prefer This drop-down indicates the method of how the selected wall will be aligned. The options are Wall Faces, Wall Centerlines, Face Of Core, and Center Of Core.

2. Select the Multiple Alignment option on the Options bar.

3. Select the top desk's left edge for the reference element.

4. Select the left edges of the bottom three desks to align to the top desk.

   After you make this selection, the desks will align (Figure 4.31).

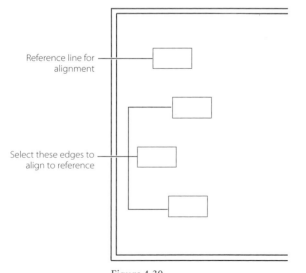

Reference line for alignment

Select these edges to align to reference

Figure 4.30
Selecting desk edges for alignment

Figure 4.31
Selecting desk edges for alignment with alignment lock unlocked

Trimming and Extending Objects

Unlike some CAD applications, the trim and extend actions are integrated into a single tool. You can trim or extend an element to meet other elements at a boundary, which is defined by selecting an element. You can use this tool with walls, lines, beams, and braces.

If you want to trim or extend two selected elements to form a corner, follow these steps:

1. On the Modify tab's Modify panel, click the Trim/Extend To Corner tool.

2. Click the first line or wall to define the trim/extend boundary. When trimming, make sure that you click the part of the element you want to keep.

3. Move your mouse pointer over a second line or wall to trim/extend.

   Notice the dashed blue line. This provides a preview of what the result of the operation will be.

4. Click the part of the element you want to keep, and that element will automatically be trimmed or extended (Figure 4.32).

You can also trim or extend multiple elements using a common boundary or edge. Figure 4.33 shows the walls you want to trim and extend.

1. On the Modify tab's Modify panel, click the Trim/Extend Multiple Elements tool.

2. Click the first line or wall to define the trim/extend boundary. Make sure that you pick the part of the element you want to keep.

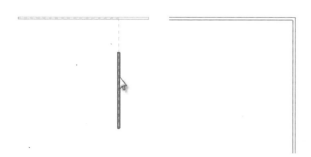

Figure 4.32

Selecting the wall to trim/extend, and the walls after trim/ extend is complete

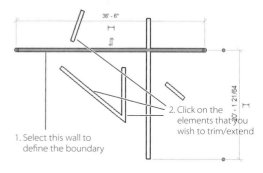

Figure 4.33

Selecting the wall to trim or extend to

3. Move your mouse pointer over a second line or wall to trim/extend.

   Notice the dashed blue line. This provides a preview of what the result of the operation will be. Make sure that you click the part of the element you want to keep.

Figure 4.34

Walls after trimming and extending

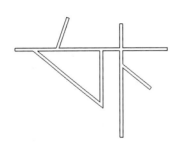

4. Click additional elements that you want to trim/extend, making sure that you click the part of the element you want to keep.

5. Click the Modify tool on the ribbon, or hit the Esc key to end the command.

The walls should now look like Figure 4.34.

Creating and Modifying Column Grids

Grids in Revit are finite vertical planes that are represented as lines in plan, section, and elevation views (Figure 4.35). In plan views, you can create grid lines as either straight lines or arcs. In a section or elevation view, you can create only straight grid lines. If you create an arc grid line in plan view, it will not be displayed in section and elevation views.

Figure 4.35

Column grid example

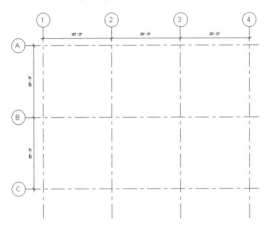

You can use grids for spacing, aligning, and placing elements such as columns in your building project. You can also use grids to be references to the position of building elements in plan, section, and elevation views.

Grids will not be displayed in 3D views. If you need to show your grids in a 3D view, then the grid lines in Revit need to be exported to a DWG file and then imported back into your 3D view.

You have two methods for creating grid lines:

• Draw them and use the various sketch options to draw either a line or an arc.

• Use the Pick tool to create grid lines from existing geometry. This can be from other Revit geometry or geometry from an imported or linked CAD file.

In the following example, you are going to create a sample column grid, add dimensions to place and constrain the grid, and add structural columns to that grid.

Revit provides three options for drawing grid lines:

Line Used to create straight-line grid segments

Arc Tools Used to create curved grid lines

Pick Lines Used to select an element

To create a straight grid line, follow these steps:

1. Start a new project using the default template.

2. On the Home tab's Datum panel, click Grid.

3. In the drawing window, click a start point, and move the mouse pointer to the right.

   As you start to sketch the grid line, notice that the start point of the grid line remains fixed. As you move the mouse pointer, a temporary dimension indicating the angle of the line with the horizontal axis is displayed if the grid line is being drawn off the horizontal axis, as shown in Figure 4.36.

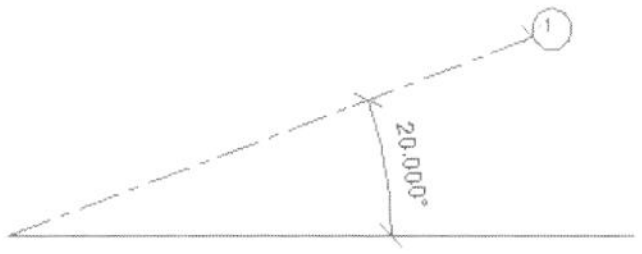

4. Click to specify the end point of the grid line.

Figure 4.36

Sketching a straight grid line

> When drawing orthogonal grids, hold down the Shift key to force the movement of the mouse pointer to be on either the horizontal or vertical axis.

As you create grids, Revit will automatically number each grid line. Each grid line must have a unique identifier. No two grids can have the same number. To change a grid number, you can click the grid and then the number; or click the grid and edit the grid number in the Properties Palette; or without a grid selected, double-click the grid number, enter the new value, and press Enter. Numbers and letters can be used for grid values.

Clicking a grid line displays the graphic controls, as shown in Figure 4.37. The blue squares on each end of the grid are check boxes used to control the visibility of the grid bubbles. The blue circles on the end of the grid lines are the drag controls. These enable to you to extend or reduce the length of the grid line. The Add Elbow control allows you to move the grid bubble away from the grid line. When you use the Add Elbow drag control, the change will appear in the current view only.

Figure 4.37

Grid line graphic controls

The final controls we'll cover are the Datum Extent controls. When the grid line shows the 3D designation, the grid line is in Model Extent mode. This means that if you drag and change the length of the grid line, the change will appear in all other parallel views, provided these grid lines are also set to the 3D Model Extent control. If the Datum Extent control is set to 2D, then the resizing of the grid line will take place only in that view.

A quick way to create a structural grid is to draw the first grid line and then use the Copy command for the other grid lines. The number or letters will automatically increment as you copy. If your grid lines are going to be evenly spaced, then use the Array tool.

Keep the following issues in mind when working with column grids:

- If you have multiple grids to place in a row, you can select one of the grids and use the Copy tool with the Multiple option or use the Array tool.

- Revit does not permit grid lines to have the same name.

- Grid lines can be a single-line or arc segment only.

- You can pin grid lines after they have been created to prevent the lines from being inadvertently moved. To pin the location of the grid:

    a. Select the grid lines.

    b. Use the Pin tool on the Modify tab's Modify panel.

- It is recommended that when you draw your grid lines, you keep the end points aligned with each other.

Adding Columns

Revit provides two tools for adding columns to a project: Architectural and Structural. Architectural columns can and should be viewed as placeholders or decorative elements. Architectural columns also inherit the material of other elements to which they are joined, such as walls. Compound layers in walls also wrap at architectural columns.

Structural columns are used to model vertical load-bearing elements in your building project. Structural columns share many of the same properties as architectural columns. Other structural elements such as beams, braces, and isolated foundations join to structural columns; this is not the case with architectural columns.

To place columns in this example, you are going to use the column grid from Figure 4.35:

1. To place a column, on the Home tab's Build panel, click the Column drop-down, and select the Architectural Column tool.

2. In the Type Selector of the Properties palette, select the column type `Rectangular Column 24˝×24˝` (`M_Rectangular Column 610×610mm`).

    On the Options bar (Figure 4.38), Height and Room Bounding are self-explanatory. The Rotate After Placement check box allows you to rotate the column after it has been placed. An alternate option for rotating the column is by hitting the spacebar as you are placing the column.

3. Place columns by clicking a grid line intersection in the drawing area.

Options bar for Structural columns

Options bar for Architectural columns

Figure 4.38

**Options bar for plac-
ing structural (top)
and architectural
(bottom) columns**

When placing architectural columns, the columns will snap to the column grid and grid line intersections. You can also place a column in the drawing area independent of a grid line or grid line intersection. You can use the temporary or listening dimensions to aid in the placement of the columns. After you've placed the columns, you can use the basic editing tools such as Move, Copy, and Array to aid in the placement of columns.

To place structural columns, you have several more options to speed up the process. You can find these options on the Modify | Place Structural Column tab on the ribbon (Figure 4.39) after selecting Structural Column from the Column drop-down:

Placement → Vertical Column

Placement → Slanted Column

Multiple → At Grids

Multiple → At Columns

Tag → Tag on Placement

Structural columns and architectural columns share some of the same Options bar options.

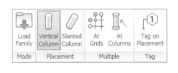

Figure 4.39

**Structural column
placement options**

In this example, you are going to place multiple columns by grid using the column grid from Figure 4.35:

1. To place a column, on the Home tab's Build panel, click the Column drop-down, and select Structural Column.

2. From the Type Selector of the Properties palette, select the column type W-Wide Flange-Column W10X49 (M_W-Wide Flange-Column W250X49.1).

3. On the Options bar, set the height of the columns.

4. On the Modify | Place Structural Column tab's Multiple panel, click the At Grids button.

5. Select all grid lines.

6. On the Modify | Place Structural Column tab and then on the At Grid Intersection tab's Multiple panel, click Finish.

The columns are automatically placed at every intersection of the selected grid lines (Figure 4.40).

Figure 4.40

Columns placed at grid intersections

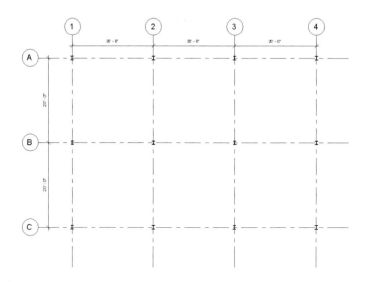

Working with Walls

Walls are one of the fundamental building blocks of building projects. Walls are 3D para-metric elements that can host elements such as door and windows. They can also host other wall-based elements such lights, light switches, and electrical outlets. Wall sweeps and reveals can also be applied to walls. Walls also define rooms. In this section, we will cover the basic concepts of creating walls, modifying wall properties, and understanding the different basic wall types.

Revit provides several predefined wall types that are divided into families based on usage:

Basic Basic walls can be either

- Monolithic and have a simple structure with varying wall thickness.
- Composed of multiple layers that represent the material types that define the wall. Some examples of layers are gyp board, studs, insulations, bricks, and so on.

Curtain Curtain walls consist of panels divided by grid lines.

Stacked Stacked walls consist of basic walls stacked on top of one another.

Walls are part of a special group of families called *system families*. This means they reside and are defined in either a project or project template files. There are not wall family templates that allow you to create new wall types outside your project environ-ment. The good news is that you can still define new wall types and share them between projects.

For more information on families, see Chapters 7, "Introduction to Families," and 8, "Creating Families."

There are several different methods for accessing these different wall styles in Revit. One method is to access the wall styles through the Project Browser (Figure 4.41).

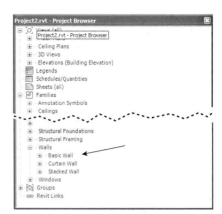

Creating a Basic Wall

The Wall tool button is a split button (Figure 4.42), allowing you to choose between creating a wall, structural wall, wall by face, wall sweep, and reveal. A structural wall is the same as a normal wall with the usage set to structural for creating load-bearing or shear walls. The Wall By Face tool allows you to create a wall from the face of a mass or generic model. Wall sweeps and reveals are applied to existing walls, which is why those options are grayed out here.

Figure 4.41

Accessing a wall style through the Project Browser

Whenever you are creating or editing an element, the Modify tab will be displayed, and the ribbon is broken up into two parts. The leftmost part has the basic editing and element-creation tools such as the Move, Copy, Element Properties, and Clipboard tools. These will be available for every tool. The rightmost part of the ribbon has the tools specific to the element category you are editing. These panel names have a light green background and will vary depending on the element being edited or created.

The Modify | Place Wall ribbon has the following options (from left to right):

Select Panel When active, this is used to select elements.

Properties Panel These buttons provide access to instance properties for an individual wall or the type properties for the wall type you are working with.

Clipboard Panel This provides tools for copying and pasting elements to the Windows clipboard.

Geometry Panel This provides tools used to modify 3D elements, such as Cut and Join, and apply materials.

Modify Panel This provides tools used to modify the elements, such as Move, Copy, and Extend.

View Panel This provides tools for changing the display options for the view.

Measure Panel This provides tools for dimensioning or measuring a distance.

Create Panel This provides tools to either duplicate the element or create groups.

Draw Panel There are a variety of tools that can be used to define walls. Some of these tools allow you to sketch the location for the walls, and the Pick Lines option allows you to pick existing lines to define your walls. The Pick Faces option allows you to pick faces from masses or other 3D geometry.

Figure 4.42

Wall tool split button options

From left to right are the following options for a wall's Options bar:

Height This option allows you to specify the wall's top constraint (level) or enter a fixed top constraint. There are two options for setting the height of a wall:

- You can specify a fixed unconnected height of a wall to a fixed distance. If any changes are made to the level heights, then walls set to an unconnected height would not be impacted by the level change.

- You can specify a level to constrain the top of the wall to.

Figure 4.43 shows two walls. The wall on the left has the height set to an unconnected height of 15′ 0″. The wall on the right has the height constrained to the Roof level.

Location Line This option determines where the wall sits in relation to the line that you sketch to define the wall location. A wall's Location Line property sets which vertical plane is used to position the wall in relation to the sketch you are creating to define the wall. The six different wall vertical planes are Wall Centerline, Core Centerline, Finish Face: Exterior, Finish Face: Interior, Core Face: Exterior, and Core Face: Interior (Figure 4.44).

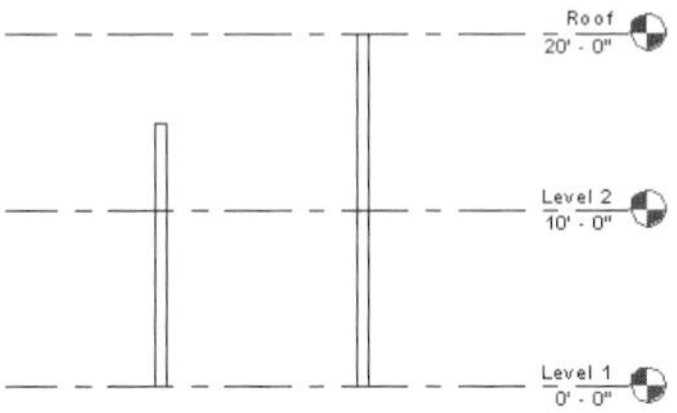

Figure 4.43

Walls with unconnected and connected heights

Chain When this option is selected and you are drawing a series of walls, the different wall segment end points will be connected.

Offset Use this field to specify how far from the mouse pointer position the wall's location line will be and how much the wall will be offset.

Radius Use this option when you need to create rounded corner joins, such as during the wall-creation process.

Figure 4.44

Wall location line examples

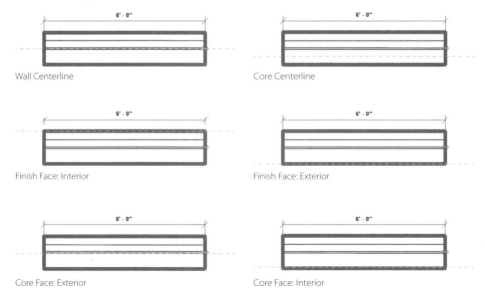

Wall Centerline   Core Centerline

Finish Face: Interior   Finish Face: Exterior

Core Face: Exterior   Core Face: Interior

In the Revit world, the "core" of a wall is the main structural layer or layers. In a typical stud wall, the core is the metal or wood studs.

The following steps describe the basic procedure for creating walls by sketching:

1. In the Home tab's Build panel, click the Wall drop-down, and select Wall. The Modify | Place Wall tab is displayed (Figure 4.45).

Figure 4.45

Modify | Place Wall ribbon and Options bar

2. In the Properties palette's Type Selector, select the Interior - 4 7/8″ Partition (1-hr) wall type (Figure 4.46).

As you start to draw, Revit will display a temporary listening dimension. As you drag your mouse, you can use this as a reference, or you can directly enter a distance value. To do this, after you pick a start point, just type in the value for the length of the wall and press Enter. The light-blue dashed line indicates the location line.

Figure 4.46

Type Selector for walls

3. On the Modify | Place Wall tab's Draw panel, click the Line tool.

4. Anywhere in the drawing window, click a point, and then move your mouse pointer to either the left or the right (Figure 4.47).

Prior to clicking to define the wall's end point, you can hit the space-bar to flip the interior/exterior orientation of the wall. This features works on other elements as well.

5. Pick a second point to finish the wall.

6. Hit the Esc key twice to exit the Wall tool.

Now that you have the basics of creating a wall by sketching, let's look at some of the other options, starting with creating walls by using the Pick Lines tool and Offset option.

1. From the book's web page, open Dataset_04_02.rvt (M_Dataset_04_ 02.rvt).

2. In the Project Browser, verify that the Level 2 floor plan is active. (The text will be bold if it is the active view.) If it is not active, then either double-click the view name or right-click it and choose Open (Figure 4.48).

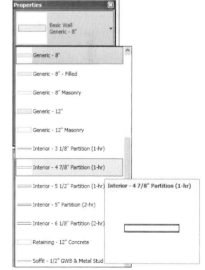

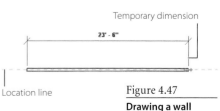

Temporary dimension

23′ - 6″

Location line

Figure 4.47

Drawing a wall

Figure 4.48

Context menu
options

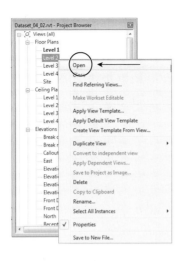

In the next steps, we are going to split the VP HR office into two offices.

3. Zoom into the offices on the south end of the building between grid lines 8 and 10.

4. Click the Home tab's Build panel, click the Wall drop-down, and select Wall.

5. On the Draw panel, click the Pick Lines option (Figure 4.49).

6. On the Options bar, set the Height constraint to Level 3; then for Offset, type **15 0** (**4572mm**), and press Enter to set the offset to 15′ 0″ (4572mm) (Figure 4.50).

7. Move your mouse pointer over the wall to the right of grid line 9 between grid lines E and F until you see the dashed blue alignment line appear to the left of grid line 3, as shown in Figure 4.51.

8. Click, and the new wall is offset 15′ 0″ (4572mm).

Figure 4.49

**The Pick Lines tool
from the Draw panel
will allow you to use
existing geometry.**

Figure 4.50

**Options bar settings
for creating a wall
by offset**

| Modify | Place Wall | Height: Level 3 ▾ | 12′ 0″ | Location Line: Wall Centerline ▾ | Offset: 15′ 0 |

Figure 4.51

**Creating a wall
using the offset
function**

Modifying Wall Parameters

Now that we have covered the basics of creating walls, let's look at the different element properties that control the definitions of walls and other elements in Revit.

Every element in Revit is an instance of a family type. A family could be a single-flush door, and that single-flush door could consist of a half-dozen different sizes, each size being a different type. Each element in Revit—such as a Single-Flush 36″×84″ (M_Single-Flush 0915×2134mm) door—has two sets of element properties, called *type properties* and *instance properties*.

Instance Properties

Whenever you click an element in Revit, the Properties palette (Figure 4.52) displays the properties for that element, and you can immediately edit the instance parameters. If you select multiple elements, the Properties palette will display the common instance properties for all the selected elements. Instance parameters are those parameters that change only the individual object being added or modified.

The instance parameters will vary for each different element type. Figure 4.52 shows an example of the various parameters for walls. These parameters are broken up into several different categories, including Constraints, Structural, Dimensions, Identity Data, and Phasing. The twin arrows to the right of the category name either expand or collapse the parameters for each category. Table 4.1 describes the various instance parameters for walls.

Figure 4.52

Properties palette for a wall

INSTANCE PARAMETER	DESCRIPTION
Location Line	Reference plane for sketching a wall.
Base Constraint	Level or reference plane of the wall.
Base Offset	Distance of the height of the wall from the base constraint.
Base Is Attached	Check box showing whether the wall is attached to another model component such as a floor (read-only).
Base Extension Distance	Distance that the base of the layers in the wall has been moved.
Top Constraint	Whether the wall height is defined by a specific level or a specific unconnected height.
Unconnected Height	Specific height of the wall.
Top Offset	Distance of the top of the wall from the top constraint.
Top Is Attached	Check box showing whether the wall is attached to another model component such as a roof (read-only).
Top Extension Distance	Distance that the top of the layers in the wall has been moved.
Room Bounding	Check box showing whether the wall constitutes the boundary of a room.
Related To Mass	Check box indicating whether the wall was created from a mass (read-only).
Structural	Check box to enable structural property settings. When unchecked, the wall will have a Structural Usage of Non-bearing.

Table 4.1

Instance parameters for walls

continues

continued

INSTANCE PARAMETER	DESCRIPTION
Enable Analytical Model	Check box to enable the structural analytical model.
Structural Usage	Sets the structural usage for the wall.
Length	Length of the wall (read-only).
Area	Area of the wall (read-only).
Volume	Volume of the wall (read-only).
Comments	Text field to add comments to describe the wall.
Mark	Unique label or value; must be unique to every wall.
Phase Created	The phase when the wall was created.
Phase Demolished	The phase when the wall was demolished.

ROOM BOUNDING

It might seem out of place to discuss rooms during a topic of walls, but walls are the key elements to creating rooms. By default, whenever you create a wall, it is a boundary element for the room elements. There are times, though, when you may not want this to happen. Figure 4.53 shows an example where you have a large office. Notice the room in the upper-left corner. By default, the walls are room bounding. When the Room Bounding check box in the wall instance Properties palette is deselected, you are left with one large room.

Figure 4.53

Room Bounding selected (left); deselected (right)

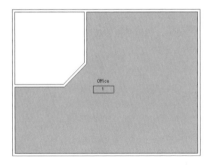 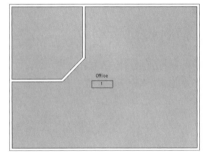

STRUCTURAL USAGE

Structural Usage can be set to define whether an element can "support" structural elements. Figure 4.54 shows the different options. Setting the Structural Usage option correctly is important when coordinating with the structural engineer. Figure 4.55 shows

Figure 4.54

Structural Usage drop-down

the different display options and how the walls will appear in Revit Architecture and Revit Structure. A wall created in Revit Architecture with its usage set to Non-bearing will not display in Revit Structure (Figure 4.55).

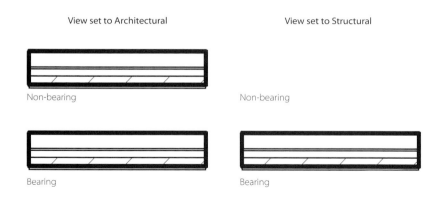

View set to Architectural   View set to Structural

Non-bearing   Non-bearing

Bearing   Bearing

Figure 4.55
Visibility with View set to Architectural (left); visibility with View set to Structural (right)

Type Properties

Type parameters will alter every item in that type in the model. To access type parameters, select an element and click the Edit Type button below and to the right of the Type Selector in the Properties palette to open a separate Type Properties dialog box (Figure 4.56). These parameters are also broken up into several different categories, including Construction, Graphics, and Identity Data. When you make a change to a type parameter, that change will impact *every instance* of that wall type. Table 4.2 describes some of the type parameters for walls.

Figure 4.56
Click the Edit Type button to access type properties for a wall.

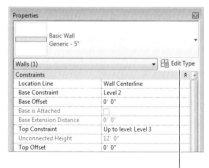

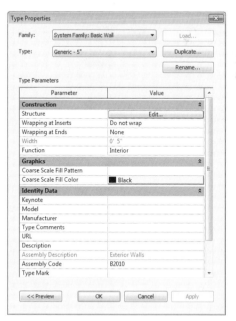

Clicking the Edit Type button brings up the Type Properties button

TYPE PARAMETER	DESCRIPTION
Structure	Allows you to define the composition for the wall type
Wrapping At Inserts	Sets the wrapping around complex inserts such as doors, windows, and nonrectangular shapes
Wrapping At Ends	Defines layer wrapping of wall end caps
Width	Defines the width of the wall (read-only)
Function	Used to define whether a wall is Exterior, Interior, Retaining, Foundation, Soffit, or Core-shaft
Coarse Scale Fill Pattern	Sets the fill pattern for the wall in a coarse view
Coarse Scale Fill Color	Sets a user-defined color to the fill pattern for a wall in a coarse view
Keynote	Keynote for the wall
Model	Model information (generally not used for walls)
Manufacturer	Manufacturer information (generally not used for walls)
Type Comments	General comments about the wall type
URL	Hyperlink to a web page or file
Description	Description of the wall
Assembly Description	Description of the wall assembly, which is based on the Assembly Code selection (read-only)
Assembly Code	Uniform at assembly classification code
Type Mark	Mark number for wall; must be unique for each wall in the project
Fire Rating	Fire rating of the wall
Cost	Cost of the wall

Defining Wall Structure

As you start creating walls in Revit, you will notice that it is a relatively simple task working with walls. But when you need to use a wall type that does not ship with Revit, creating that new wall type can be tricky and time consuming. The tools to accomplish this could be better, but with plenty of practice and patience, you can create new wall types. The real trick to doing this is understanding how Revit defines the structure of walls. This can be confusing, and it is not surprising that issues related to walls are some of the top issues that Autodesk's Revit support team has to address. In this section, you are going to dive into the structure of walls and create and edit wall types.

In Revit, walls are composed of different layers. Figure 4.57 shows a cutaway of the different components (layers) that make up a wall, in this case a wall in Revit. Each layer is a different component of the actual wall composition, such as gyp board, metal studs, insulation, and so on. Each layer can be a different thickness, can serve a different purpose, and of course can be made up of different materials.

> The term *layer* in Revit has a completely different meaning than in AutoCAD. AutoCAD uses layers to help you categorize your drawings so that you can add or remove drawing elements all at once. They provide a means for managing and controlling the individual layout of the drawing. In Revit, *layer* refers to a building material that is part of a wall assembly such as a metal stud, insulation, gyp board, and so on.

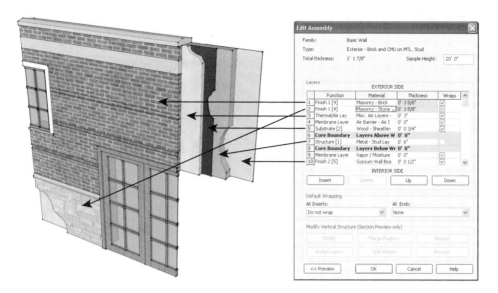

Figure 4.57

Anatomy of a wall

Figure 4.58 is the Edit Assembly dialog box. This dialog box contains the tools necessary for defining or editing your wall types. In the following example, you are going to take a generic 8″ (200mm) wall and modify it to create an 8″ (200mm), two-hour STC 60-rated interior partition.

1. Start a new project from the default template.

2. Open the Level 1 floor plan.

3. On the Home tab's Build panel, click Wall.

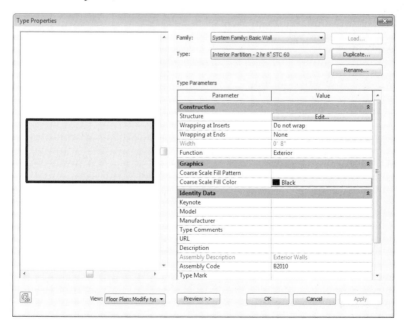

Figure 4.58

Edit Assembly dialog box with the preview pane opened

4. In the Properties palette, click the Type Selector, and change the wall type to `Basic Wall Generic - 8"` (`Basic Wall Generic - 200mm`).

5. On the Options bar, set Height to Level 2.

6. Draw a wall in the drawing window.

7. After you have drawn a wall segment, cancel the Wall tool by hitting the Esc key twice or clicking the Modify button on the ribbon.

8. Select the wall you just created.

9. In the Properties palette click the Edit Type button.

   This will bring you to the type properties for the wall.

10. Because you are going to be modifying this wall to create a new wall type, click the Duplicate button.

11. Call the new wall `Interior Partition - 2 hr 8" STC 60` (`Interior Partition - 2hr 200mm STC`).

12. Under Type Parameters in the Type Properties dialog box, click the Edit button in the Structure row under the Construction category.

    Figure 4.58 shows the wall Edit Assembly dialog box for our completed wall type. In this dialog box you can edit or create new wall types. The top-right portion of the dialog box contains basic information about the wall you are editing. Below that is a section marked Layers. This is where you define the different layers of your wall assembly.

13. At the bottom of the Edit Assembly dialog box, click the Preview button.

14. With the preview window open, to the left of the Preview button, change the View list to Floor Plan: Modify Type Attributes (Figure 4.59).

    Figure 4.60 shows the Layers fields of the Edit Assembly dialog box. This area allows you to modify or define new layers or the components that define the compound wall structure. When you define the wall, the exterior side of the wall is always defined toward the top of the dialog box and the interior side toward the bottom. In the example in Figure 4.60, you see three layers; two of them are core boundaries. These two layers define the boundary for the structure of the wall. Any layers that are within the core boundaries will be part of the wall structure.

    This is very important. When you create a new wall and use a location line such as

Figure 4.59

View drop-down

Figure 4.60

Layers of a wall, from the Edit Assembly dialog box

Core Centerline, the location line will be set in the middle of those two boundaries regardless of the number of components and thickness of the compound wall structure. In the following steps, you are going to change the structure of the wall by adding a stud layer and metal furring layers.

15. In the Layers field, click in the Material field in row 2.

16. Click the browse button ⌈ ... ⌋ to open the Materials dialog box.

17. Select the material Metal – Stud Layer (Figure 4.61), and click OK.

18. In the Layers field, click in the Thickness field in row 2, and change the thickness to **6″** (**150mm**).

19. In the Layers field, click the number 3 that marks the bottom, Core Boundary, row.

20. Click the Insert button to add an additional layer. This new layer should now be item 3.

21. Verify that the new layer is selected, and then use the Up button to change the location to item 2.

22. Click the Material cell, and click the Browse button to open the Materials dialog box.

23. In the Materials tab change the material/finish to Metal – Steel, and click OK.

24. Change the thickness to ½″ (12mm), and press Enter.

Figure 4.61

Materials dialog box

You will now add two layers of gyp board to the exterior side of the wall definition.

25. Click row 1 to highlight the entire row that reads Core Boundary Layers Above Wrap 0′ 0″.

26. Click the Insert button. A new layer will appear as the new row 1.

27. Change Function to Finish 1 [4].

When you define a new wall layer, you must also define a function associated with it. Table 4.3 describes the six layer functions.

Table 4.3

Wall layer function and wall cleanup priority list

PRIORITY	LAYER FUNCTION	DESCRIPTION
1	Structure	Structural core of the wall
2	Substrate	Secondary structural member that acts as a foundation for another material
3	Thermal/Air Layer	Insulation layer
4	Finish 1	Exterior finish layer
5	Finish 2	Interior finish layer
n.a.	Membrane Layer	Vapor barrier with zero thickness

28. Change the material to Gypsum Wall Board, and click OK.

29. Change the thickness to ½″ (12mm).

The first layer is complete. You will follow similar steps to complete the second layer:

30. Click row 1 to highlight the entire row that reads Finish 1 [4] Gypsum Wall Board ½″ (12mm).

31. Click the Insert button. A new layer will appear as the new row 1.

32. Change the function to Finish 2 [5].

33. Change the material to Gypsum Wall Board, and click OK.

34. Change the thickness to ½″ (12mm), and press Enter.

The second layer is complete.

You now need to add one final layer, the gyp board on the interior side of the wall definition.

35. Click 6 to highlight the entire row that reads Core Boundary Layers Below Wrap 0′ 0″.

36. Click the Insert button.

A new layer will appear as the new row 6 and is inside the core boundary. This layer needs to be moved outside the core boundary.

37. Click 6 (new layer) to highlight the entire row.

38. Use the Down button to move the row so that it becomes 7.

39. Change the function to Finish 1 [4].

40. Change the material to Gypsum Wall Board, and click OK.

41. Change the thickness to ½″ (12mm), and press Enter.

42. Click OK twice to finish editing the wall type.

Figure 4.62 shows the completed compound wall layer definition.

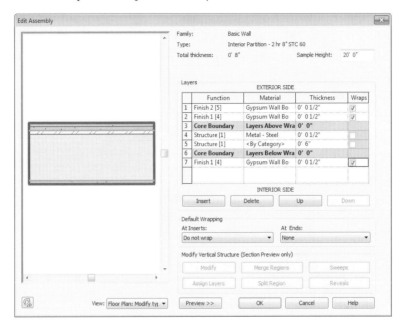

Figure 4.62

Wall assembly for Interior Partition – 2 hr 8″ STC 60

Wall Joins

One of the great features of Revit is the almost-always automatic wall join cleanups. These joins represent the display of intersection wall layers in plan view and are displayed in either a medium or fine view detail level. When two or more walls join, Revit will look at the walls' layers and prioritize how they should be joined. Wall layers have different functions and are represented by a hierarchy of numbers. This is used to determine how one layer should clean up with a layer from an adjoining compound wall. Table 4.3, shown earlier, described the priority and function for the six different types of wall layers.

The rules for how layers join is fairly simple: 1s will clean up with 1s, 2s with 2s, 3s with 3s, and so on. Also, the lower the number, the higher the priority when a cleanup is required. For example, when two walls join, the structure layer (Priority 1) will clean up before finish layers. This means that higher-priority layers will pass through lower-priority layers. Revit does this by prioritizing how the various layers of the wall will join together. This system generally works very well and requires little to no user interaction unless you want to change how the walls are joined or prevent walls from automatically joining.

Figure 4.63 shows the three different wall join classifications: Butt, Miter, and Square Off. By default, Revit creates butt joins. If a join has an angle that is less than 20 degrees, then a miter join is created. If there is an end wall join condition with the angle being 90 degrees, then a square-off join is created.

Figure 4.63

Wall join example

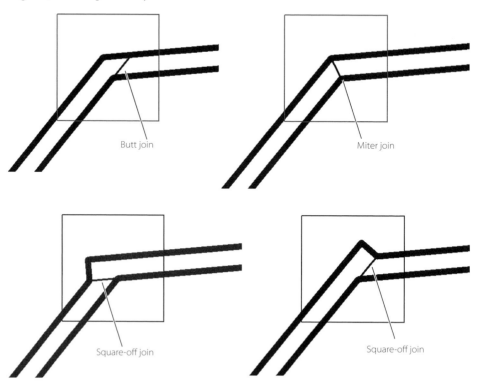

The last type of join is a radius join. A radius join is created when you have a rounded corner wall intersection. The radius join is created by drawing a wall using the Fillet Arc draw option and then selecting the two walls to create a fillet between them. You then specify the radius or drag a radius to create the wall join.

To edit a wall join, use the following steps:

1. Start a new project using the default template.

2. Switch to a plan view. Make sure that your View Detail level is set to either Medium or Fine.

3. Create two walls using Figure 4.64 as a reference using Exterior – CMU on Mtl. Stud.

4. On the Modify tab's Geometry panel, click Wall Joins.

5. Move your mouse pointer over the wall join that you want to edit.

   A large square will be displayed around the wall join (Figure 4.64).

6. Click to select that wall join.

7. On the Options bar, select Clean Join from the Display drop-down to clean up the join by forcing the internal wall layers to join.

8. From the Configuration Options bar, select either Butt, Miter, or Square Off. (The Square Off option is grayed out for 90-degree joins.)

9. Click the Previous or Next button to cycle through the various join options.

10. Press Esc to end the command and to set your wall join.

There might be times when you do not want walls to automatically join, such as when creating expansion joints. In those cases:

1. Select one of the walls.

2. Right-click the blue circle at the intersection.

3. Select Disallow Join in the context menu.

If you want to re-enable automatic joining,

1. Select the wall again.

2. Right-click the blue dot.

3. Select the Allow Join option.

The following are some rules regarding layer joining:

• Higher-priority layers are connected before lower-priority layers.

• Higher-priority layers will pass through lower-priority layers.

• Layers need the same material applied to them in order for them to join properly.

• Walls can have multiple core layers. An example is a plumbing chase wall.

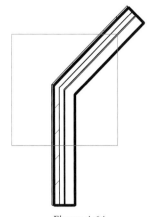

Figure 4.64

Selecting a wall join for editing

Modifying Wall Profiles and Adding an Opening to a Wall

At some point when working with walls, it will be necessary to create an opening in the wall. Revit provides numerous options for creating openings in walls. Each method has its own pros and cons. We will discuss two methods, the Wall Opening tool and Wall Edit Profile tool.

The first method is to use the Wall Opening tool, which will allow you to create a rectangular opening in a wall:

1. Open a section or elevation view where you can see the wall you need to create an opening in.

2. On the Home tab's Opening panel, click Wall button.

3. Select the wall to which the opening will be applied.

4. Sketch the rectangle of the opening. Once the sketch is complete, the opening is created.

You can modify the opening by either using the drag controls to modify the size and location, or editing the temporary dimensions (Figure 4.65).

Figure 4.65

**Using the Wall
Opening tool to cre-
ate an opening in
the wall**

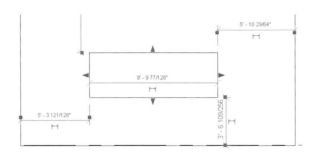

The following are issues to keep in mind when using the Wall Opening tool:

- It will create only a rectangular opening.

- It will cut only one wall at a time.

- It will create an opening in a curtain wall.

- The opening will be perpendicular to the wall.

- The opening is level based. If the level moves, so does the opening.

- It is not room bounding.

The second method is modifying the profile of the wall (Figure 4.66). This allows you to create an opening and to also change the shape of the wall.

1. Open a section or elevation view where you can see the wall you need to create an opening in.

2. Select the wall you want to add an opening into.

3. On the Modify | Walls tab's Mode panel, click Edit Profile.

   The original outline of the wall will turn magenta, and Revit will switch your view into Sketch mode.

4. Using the basic 2D editing tools in the Draw panel on the ribbon, create new openings or change the shape of the wall.

5. When finished editing your sketch, on the Modify | Walls tab's Mode panel, click Edit Profile and click the green check ✓ to finish the sketch.

Figure 4.66

**Edit profile exam-
ple. Left to right: the
original wall, while
the profile is being
edited, and the
edited wall.**

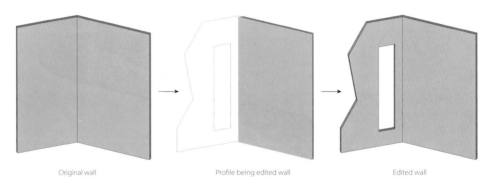

Original wall   Profile being edited wall   Edited wall

You can edit the opening or profile change as follows:

1. Select the wall.

2. On the Modify | Walls tab's Mode panel, click Edit Profile.

If you want to reset the wall to the original shape, on the Modify | Walls tab's Mode panel, click Reset Profile.

The following are issues to keep in mind when modifying the profile of a wall:

- It will create just about any shape.

- It will cut only one wall at a time.

- The opening will be perpendicular to the wall.

- The opening is wall base offset based. Move the wall base, and the opening will move.

> When you place components like doors and windows, Revit will automatically create the opening when the component is placed.

Embedding Walls

Embedding walls means to place one wall within a wall of another type. A common use for embedding walls is to place a curtain wall inside walls of another type to represent glazing. Another use is to add a masonry panel into a brick wall.

> A curtain wall is not a window. So if you embed a curtain wall into another wall to represent a window, be aware that it will not schedule as a window.

> Automatically Embed allows curtain walls to be embedded into another wall. The curtain wall is then associated with the host wall. If you move or rotate the host wall, the embedded curtain wall moves with it. The embedded curtain wall will act in a similar fashion to that of a door or window in a wall.

In this example, you are going to embed a Curtain Wall Exterior Glazing wall in a brick wall, but this could also easily be a masonry panel:

1. Start a new project using the default template.

2. Draw a wall using the `Basic Wall Exterior - Brick on Mtl. Stud` type.

   a. Set the Height to Level 2.

   b. Make the Length **20′ 0″** (**6070mm**).

3. Create a new wall using the Curtain Wall Exterior Glazing wall type.

4. Draw the new curtain wall shorter and directly over the existing wall.

    a. Set the Height to **8′ 0″** (**2440mm**).

    b. Make the Length **10′ 0″** (**3045mm**).

As soon as you finish placing the second wall, Revit will beep and display the Warning dialog box (Figure 4.67). What this message is indicating is that two walls are overlapping, and they may not work properly with rooms. You will use the Cut Geometry tool to correct the issue.

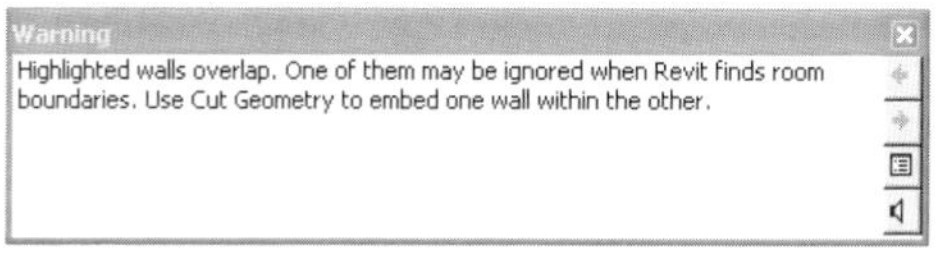

Figure 4.67

Warning dialog box about walls overlapping

Warning

Highlighted walls overlap. One of them may be ignored when Revit finds room boundaries. Use Cut Geometry to embed one wall within the other.

5. On the Modify | Place Wall tab's Geometry panel, click the Cut tool.

6. Pick the host or main wall.

7. Pick the curtain wall.

By adjusting the height and adding both horizontal and vertical grids and mullions, you quickly added a glazed viewing window into the wall (Figure 4.68).

Figure 4.68

3D view of the completed curtain wall embedded in the wall

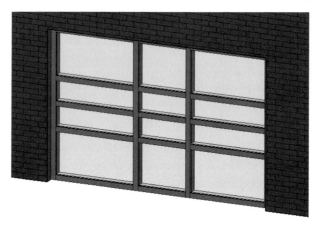

The following are the issues to keep in mind when working with embedded walls:

•   When using the Cut Geometry tool, pick the host wall (main wall) first and then the wall to be embedded.

•   By default, a curtain wall will embed into a host wall.

•   Profiles of embedded walls can be edited.

•   Embedded walls can be edited (length, width, and height).

Stacked Walls

Sometimes on your building project you will need to create a compound wall by vertically stacking two or more walls. A stacked wall uses a main wall for the base and one or more subwalls that are stacked on top of each other. The stacked walls are attached and have their geometry joined to each other.

In the next example, you are going to create a stacked wall that uses a standard interior partition, and you will stack a metal stud wall that goes up to the ceiling. The first step to accomplish this is to create your two different wall types. Revit ships with a wall type that you can use for your base. You will also use this as the basis to create the metal stud wall with no gyp board.

1. Start the Wall tool, and change the type to `Basic Wall Interior - 4 7/8″ Partition (1-hr)` (`Basic Wall Interior - 123mm Partition (1-hr)`).

2. Click the Edit Type button.

3. In the Type Properties dialog box, click Duplicate, name the new wall type **`Interior - 3 5/8″ Stud Wall`** (**`Interior - 80mm Stud Wall`**), and click OK.

4. Click the Edit button in the Structure row under Type Parameters to edit the wall structure.

5. Delete both the Finish 2 [5] Gypsum Wall Board layers.

   Your wall definition should now look like Figure 4.69.

6. Click OK to close the Edit Assembly dialog box.

7. Click Apply to save your changes and then OK to close the Type Properties dialog box.

Figure 4.69

Interior – 3 ⅝″ Stud Wall layer definition

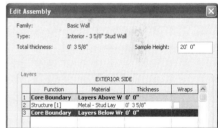

The next step in the process is to define your new stacked wall type. To do this, you are going edit the existing stacked wall type in the project.

1. Start the Wall tool, and change the type to `Stacked Wall Exterior - Brick Over CMU w Metal Stud`.

2. Click the Edit Type button.

3. In the Type Properties dialog box, click Duplicate, name the new wall type **`Interior - 4 7/8″ Partition - Unfinished Above Ceiling`** (**`Interior - 123mm Partition - Unfinished Above Ceiling`**), and click OK.

4. Click the Edit button in the Structure row under Type Parameters to edit the wall structure.

   Notice that the middle section of the Edit Assembly dialog box displays types rather than layers. The items listed in the Types list are displayed from the top of the stacked wall to the base. You are going to change the wall types listed to meet your needs.

5. Click Type 1, `Exterior - Brick on Mtl. Stud.`

6. Click in the Name field, and then click the down arrow to enable the drop-down.

7. Select `Interior - 3 1/8″ Partition (1-hr)` (`Interior - 79mm Partition (1-hr)`) for the top wall type. Leave Height set to Variable because you want this top wall to grow or shrink in height as needed.

8. Click Type 2, `Exterior - CMU on Mtl. Stud.`

9. Click in the Name field and then on the down arrow to enable the drop-down list.

10. Select `Interior - 4 7/8″ Partition (1-hr)` (`Interior - 123mm Partition (1-hr)`) for your base wall type.

11. Change Height to **9′ 0″ (2750mm)**. This will set the base wall to always be 9′ 0″ (2750mm) tall and will be the starting point for your top wall.

12. Click the Preview button. Figure 4.70 shows the newly defined stacked wall.

13. Click OK to close the Edit Assembly dialog box.

14. Click Apply and OK to save the Type Properties changes.

Keep the following issues in mind when working with stacked walls:

- They are made from predefined basic wall types and are stacked vertically.

- Curtain walls can't be stacked.

- One of the subwalls must be of a variable height.

- Subwalls are scheduled and tagged individually.

- To edit the structure of a stacked wall, you edit each subwall individually.

- You can't edit the profile of either the stacked wall or the individual subwalls.

- You can separate a stacked wall into the individual wall types by right-clicking the wall and selecting Break Up.

Figure 4.70

Finished Interior partition stacked wall

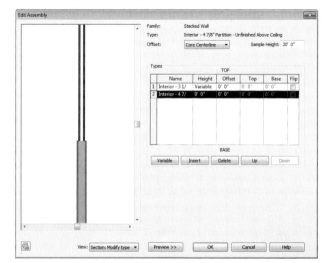

You can separate a stacked wall into the individual wall types by right-clicking the wall and clicking Break Up. The subwalls will have a Base Constraint value assigned based upon their relevant offset. The Top Constraint value will be assigned as Unconstrained with a correct Unconnected Height. Once you break up a stacked wall, it cannot be rejoined, unless you use the Undo command.

Introducing Parts

Parts are a new feature in Revit 2012 that allows disassembling multilayer components into their individual subcomponents. For example, using parts you can access the individual layers in a multicomponent wall, geometrically modify them individually, as well as tag and schedule them with their detail quantities.

A typical use for parts would be in an advanced design stage where you need to provide detailed quantity take-offs as well as construction documentation that requires individual layers of multilayer components to be modified to exactly represent the built result.

While parts need to be enabled individually for each multilayer component, visibility of parts is handled on a per-view basis. That means enabling parts for specific multilayer components will not change existing views in your project; only if you select specific views to actually display parts will they become visible.

The behavior of a multilayer component with parts enabled will also remain consistent with other multilayer components where parts have not been enabled. That means a multilayer wall with parts enabled will still join the same way as it did before without parts being enabled.

Using Parts

In order to use parts you need to enable them individually for each multilayer component. Multi-selecting components is possible, which means that in a view you can select multiple multilayer walls or floors and enable parts for them all at once.

To enable parts, with the relevant components selected, click the Parts button located in the Create group of the Modify | Multi-Select panel of the ribbon.

1. From the book's web page, open Dataset_04_03.rvt (M_Dataset_04_03.rvt).

2. Switch to view Sections (Building Section): Section 1.

3. Select the floor displayed in the section.

4. On the Create group of the Modify | Multi-Select panel, click the Create Parts button (Figure 4.71).

When you now hover with your mouse pointer over either the wall or the floor, you will notice that Revit will not highlight the entire component anymore but instead will highlight the individual layers within the component.

Figure 4.71
Create Parts button

When you click one of the layers, the Parts feature will appear in the Properties window (Figure 4.72).

Figure 4.72

Parts properties

To enable manipulation of individual parts, you need to set Show Shape Handles to Enabled by clicking the check box in the part's properties. Now shape handles will appear for the part selected, and you can drag the extents of the individual layer.

Instead of using the shape handles to drag the layers extents, you can also use the Align tool to align layer extents to other references in your view.

In the following example, we illustrate how the feature can be used to clean up a wall floor join using parts. The initial display for the floor join after we modeled it is shown in Figure 4.73.

1. Select the left wall and enable the Parts feature by clicking the Parts button on the Create group of the Modify | Walls panel of the ribbon.

2. Select one layer of the wall.

3. In the Properties palette, click the Show Shape Handles check box for that part.

   Shape handles will now appear at the end of the wall layer, enabling you to drag its extents individually.

4. Repeat this procedure for the individual layers in both the wall and the floor.

You can use shape handles as well as the Align tool to individually align layers within the components. By doing so, you can achieve the appropriate result for a construction documentation level (Figure 4.74).

Figure 4.73

Wall - floor join

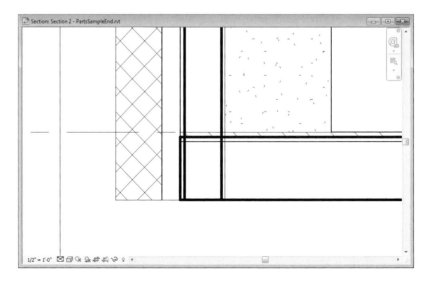

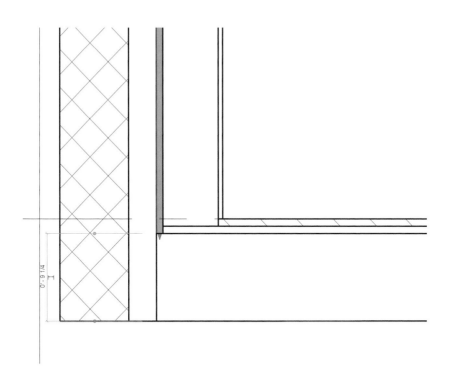

Figure 4.74

Parts used to edit the join

Editing Parts

When parts are enabled for a multilayer component, subdividing them also can modify them. That means, for example, within the Finish layer of a wall you can now sketch an area that represents a different finish material. To do so, follow these steps:

1. Select a part and then click Divide Parts on the Modify | Parts panel of the ribbon (see Figure 4.75).

   Divide Parts puts you into sketch mode, and you can sketch an area on the part (Figure 4.76).

2. To divide a floor layer in the previous example, switch to the default 3D view, 3D Views {3D}.

3. In the Properties palette for 3D Views {3D}, select Show Parts For Parts Visibility.

4. Select the floor layer on top of the floor.

5. Click the Divide Parts button in the Part group on the Modify | Parts panel of the ribbon.

   You can now sketch an area on the part.

6. End sketching by clicking Finish Edit Mode.

   You have now created a subcomponent within the part.

Figure 4.75

Modify | Parts panel

This procedure has now created a separate object within the part. You can now see its individual Area and Volume dimensions in the Parts Properties palette as well as assign a different material to it (Figure 4.77).

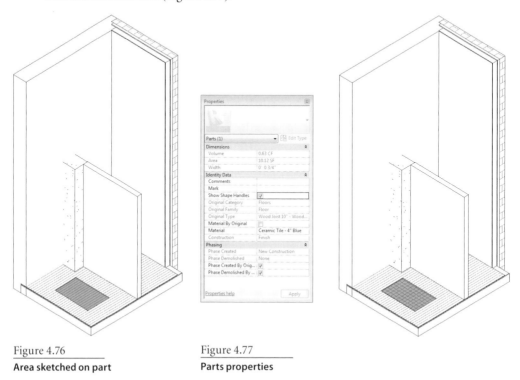

Figure 4.76
Area sketched on part

Figure 4.77
Parts properties

To remove all subdivisions in a part:

1. Select any subdivision previously created.

2. Click Delete.

   Revit will delete all associated subdivisions, and the original element will be made visible.

To edit a subdivision within a part:

1. Select any subdivided part.

2. Click Edit Division in the Part group on the Modify | Parts panel of the ribbon.

   This will return you to sketch mode, and you will be able to change the sketch that determines the division of the part.

You can also add another subdivision to an existing subdivision by using Divide Parts. Revit allows two levels of subdivision; that means you can add another subdivision to an existing subdivision, but you then cannot subdivide this second-level subdivision any further (Figure 4.78).

Parts Properties

Three significant parameters for parts determine their appearance and behavior in the model:

Material By Original When this check box is activated, the part will inherit the original material as defined in the layer of the multilayer host. This means that if you want to assign a different material to the part or any subdivision of this part, you need to have this check box cleared.

Material This parameter becomes available as soon as Material By Original is not activated anymore. This enables you to set a different material than defined in the multilayer component itself for that specific layer.

Show Shape Handles When turned on, shape handles appear for parts and allow dragging the extents of the individual part in all views (Figure 4.79).

Further properties for parts include the following:

Volume The actual volume of the part that will reflect any geometric changes applied to the part

Original Category The category to which the multilayer component that was used for creating a specific part belongs

Original Family and Type The Family and Type of the multilayer component that was used for creating a specific part

Layer Function The Layer Function of the layer within the multilayer component the part was derived from, such as Structure, Substructure, or Finish

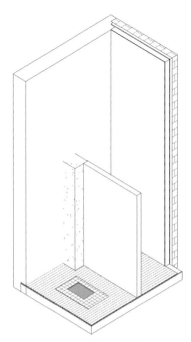

Figure 4.78

Subdivided parts

Figure 4.79

Shape handles for parts

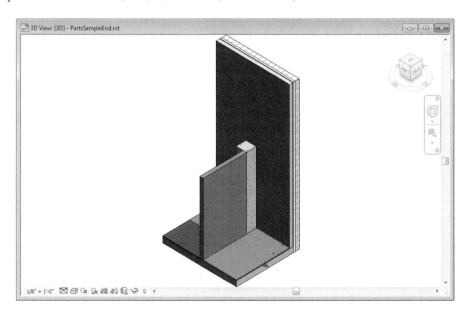

Scheduling Parts

One of the most powerful features of parts is that they can be individually scheduled. This enables you to create detailed schedules of materials in multilayer components according to their actual quantities as they are derived from the individual parts.

The following steps will take you through the workflow of creating a schedule for parts:

1. From the book's web page, open Dataset_04_04.rvt (M_Dataset_04_04.rvt).

2. Click Schedules and choose Schedule/Quantities on the Create Panel of the View tab on the ribbon.

3. In the New Schedule dialog box, scroll down to Parts and click OK.

4. Add the following fields by selecting them in the Available Fields list using the Ctrl key:

     Original Category

     Original Family

     Original Type

     Material

     Volume

5. Click Add to add those fields to the Scheduled Fields (In Order) list.

6. Click OK.

The resulting schedule (Figure 4.80) will now display Volume quantities for each individual layer of the part.

Figure 4.80

Part Schedule

Material	Original Category	Original Family	Original Type	Volume
Wood - Sheathing - plywood	Floors	Floor	Wood Joist 10" - Wood Finish	5.24 CF
Structure - Wood Joist/Rafter Layer	Floors	Floor	Wood Joist 10" - Wood Finish	69.57 CF
Gypsum Wall Board	Walls	Basic Wall	Exterior - CMU on Mtl. Stud	8.54 CF
Metal - Stud Layer	Walls	Basic Wall	Exterior - CMU on Mtl. Stud	107.54 CF
Wood - Sheathing - plywood	Walls	Basic Wall	Exterior - CMU on Mtl. Stud	13.44 CF
Misc. Air Layers - Air Space	Walls	Basic Wall	Exterior - CMU on Mtl. Stud	57.46 CF
Masonry - Concrete Masonry Units	Walls	Basic Wall	Exterior - CMU on Mtl. Stud	154.49 CF
Gypsum Wall Board	Walls	Basic Wall	Exterior - CMU on Mtl. Stud	5.52 CF
Metal - Stud Layer	Walls	Basic Wall	Exterior - CMU on Mtl. Stud	66.71 CF
Wood - Sheathing - plywood	Walls	Basic Wall	Exterior - CMU on Mtl. Stud	8.99 CF
Misc. Air Layers - Air Space	Walls	Basic Wall	Exterior - CMU on Mtl. Stud	36.30 CF
Masonry - Concrete Masonry Units	Walls	Basic Wall	Exterior - CMU on Mtl. Stud	95.57 CF
Gypsum Wall Board	Walls	Basic Wall	Interior - 6 1/8" Partition (2-hr)	3.30 CF
Gypsum Wall Board	Walls	Basic Wall	Interior - 6 1/8" Partition (2-hr)	3.30 CF
Metal - Stud Layer	Walls	Basic Wall	Interior - 6 1/8" Partition (2-hr)	19.13 CF
Gypsum Wall Board	Walls	Basic Wall	Interior - 6 1/8" Partition (2-hr)	3.30 CF
Gypsum Wall Board	Walls	Basic Wall	Interior - 6 1/8" Partition (2-hr)	4.06 CF
Wood - Flooring	Floors	Floor	Wood Joist 10" - Wood Finish	4.26 CF
Ceramic Tile - 4" Blue	Floors	Floor	Wood Joist 10" - Wood Finish	0.98 CF

Tagging Parts

Parts can be individually labeled using part tags, once parts have been enabled in a multilayer component. To tag parts, you need to select Tag By Category from the Tag section on the Annotate panel of the ribbon.

After selecting Tag By Category, a part tag will show when you hover above a part with your mouse pointer. Clicking will now place the part tag (Figure 4.81).

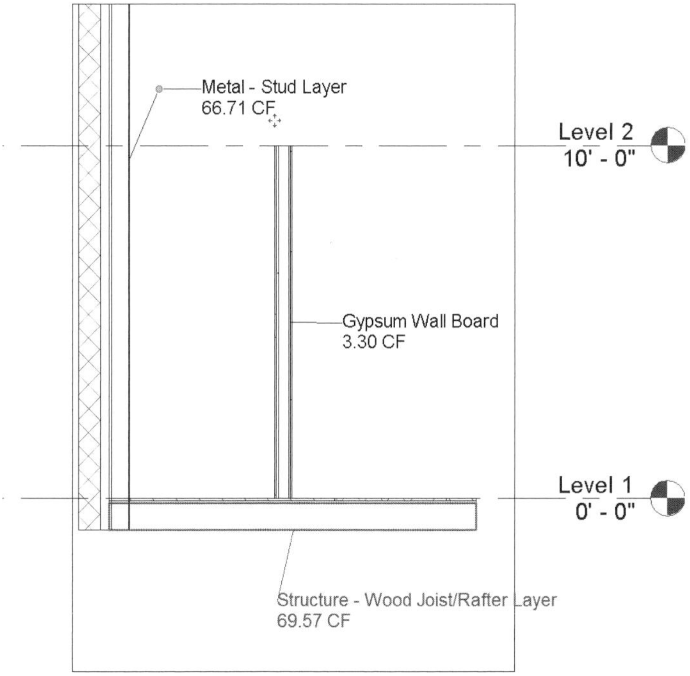

Figure 4.81

Parts tagged

Tags will display only if Parts Visibility in the view is set to Show Parts or Show Both. If it is set to Show Original, parts tags will not display.

Creating Doors and Windows

In this section, we will cover adding and modifying doors and windows to the building project. Doors and windows are wall-hosted elements. If you try to place a door or window into your project, it must be within a wall, or Revit will not permit the insertion. Generally speaking, doors and windows can be placed into any type of wall, with the exception of curtain walls. Curtain walls require you to swap a panel with a special door panel. Doors and windows can be placed in a plan, elevation, or 3D view.

Doors and windows are component elements in Revit. Components are defined in separate Revit family (RFA) files. You can edit existing files and create new door and window families to develop your own library.

To add a new door and window to a project, follow these steps:

1. Start a new project using the default template.

2. Switch to the Level 1.

3. Draw a wall using the `Basic Wall Exterior - Brick on Mtl. Stud` type.

   a. Set the Height to Level 2.

   b. Make the Length **20′ 0″** (**6070mm**).

4. On the Home tab's Build panel, click the Door tool.

5. Select `Single-Flush 36″×84″` (`M_Fixed 0406×0610mm`) from the Type Selector.

   The Options bar for doors has one option related to the placement of the door and three related to the placement of the door tags:

   Orientation This drop-down allows you to choose either Horizontal or Vertical orientation.

   Tags This button allows you to load new tags.

   Leader This option allows you to create a leader line between the tag and the door.

   Dimension This field allows you to change the default length of the leader.

6. In the drawing area, position the mouse pointer along the wall.

   The precise location is not important. As you move your mouse pointer to one side of the wall or the other, this will flip the orientation of the door. Pressing the spacebar will allow you to change the swing orientation of the door prior to placing it.

7. Once you have located the door correctly, click the left mouse button to add the door.

Figure 4.82

**Door controls
and listening
dimensions**

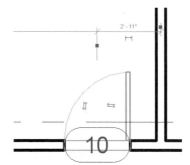

After the door is placed, the Door tool is still active. The temporary or listening dimensions are still active, displaying the distance between the door and either wall.

Figure 4.82 shows the different door controls. Clicking the double arrows that are perpendicular to the wall will flip the face of the door so that it opens outward and back again. Clicking the double arrows that are parallel to the wall will flip the hand of the door from right to left and back again.

In the next step, you will add a window to the left of the door you just placed.

1. On the Home tab's Build panel, click the Window tool.

2. Select `Fixed 36″×48″` (`M_Fixed 0406×0610mm`) from the Type Selector.

   The Options bar is the same as it was in the preceding procedure.

3. In the drawing area, position the mouse pointer along the wall.

   The precise location is not important. As you move your mouse pointer along the wall, the position of the window will change.

4. Click to add the window.

After the window is placed, the Window tool is still active. The temporary or listening dimensions are still active, displaying the distance between the window and either door or wall.

Figure 4.83 shows the different window controls. The location of the double arrows indicates which side of the window is the outside face. Clicking the double arrows will flip the window.

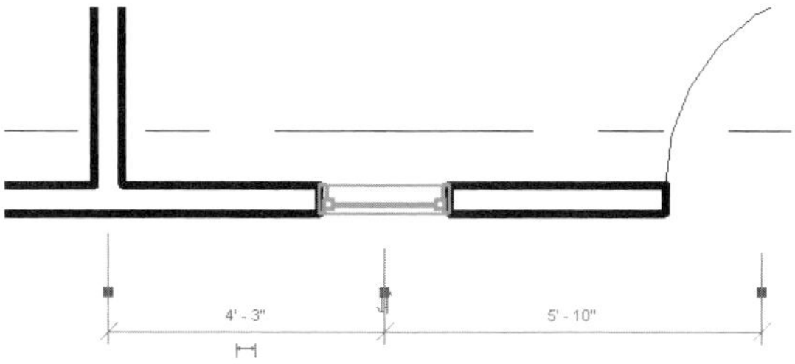

Figure 4.83

Window controls and listening dimensions

As you work on your building project, you will need to load additional door and window families. To load additional content, on the Insert tab's Load From Library panel, click the Load Family tool. This will open the Load Family dialog box, which will allow you to select additional content to be loaded into your project file.

Editing Door and Window Properties

After you create a door or window, you can modify both the type and instance parameters. Type parameters include dimensions and materials. Instance parameters include swing direction and side, materials, and level. Keep in mind that any changes you make to the type parameters apply to all instances of that type in the project. Changes to instance parameters apply only to the selected instances of that particular door or window.

Keep the following issues in mind when working with doors and windows:

- Deselect the Tag On Placement check box on the Options bar if you do not want to place tags automatically when a door or window is placed.

- Select the tag with the door or window if you want the tag to move with the door and window.

- Use the spacebar to change the door swing while positioning the door for placement.

- Place doors and windows quickly in their general location, and use the temporary or listening dimensions for precise placement.

- If door and windows are identical on multiple floors, use the Copy tool in an elevation or section view or copy to the clipboard to speed the process.

- Sometimes it is much easier and faster to place doors and windows without tags.

Creating Floors

A floor is a horizontal surface supported by the structure of the building. Floors are level based, and you can create either flat or sloped or tapered floors (Figure 4.84). To create a floor, you need to define a boundary of the floor. The boundary must be a closed loop, and boundary loops cannot overlap or cross any other floor boundary. When a floor is created, you specify its vertical position by creating it on a level. The top of the floor is placed on the level where it is created, with the thickness of the floor projecting downward. Floors are like walls and use one or more layers of materials to define the floor type. To create floors, you need to sketch their perimeters.

Figure 4.84

Horizontal, sloped, and tapered floor examples

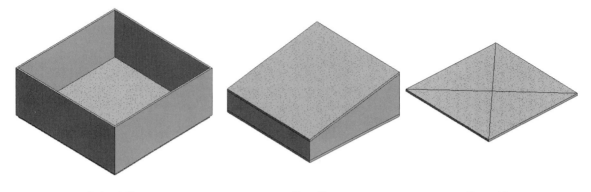

Horizontal floor   Sloped floor   Tapered floor

1. From the book's web page, open `Dataset_04_05.rvt` (`M_Dataset_04_05.rvt`).

2. Verify that the Level 1 floor plan is active. You will create a floor on this level.

3. On the Home tab's Build panel, click the Floor tool.

4. On the Modify | Create Floor Boundary tab's Draw panel, click the Pick Walls button.

    On the Options bar, leave the Offset set to 0′ 0″, and ensure that Extend Into Wall (To Core) is selected.

5. Click each of the exterior walls.

    Revit will automatically define the boundary to the core of the wall and form a closed boundary.

6. On the Modify | Create Floor Boundary tab's Mode panel, click the Finish Edit Mode button (the check mark) to create the floor.

7. Switch to the Level 2 floor plan. Repeat steps 2 through 5.

8. On the Modify | Create Floor Boundary tab's Mode panel, click the Finish Edit Mode button (the check mark) to create the floor.

   Revit will display a dialog box and ask, "Would you like the walls that go up to this floor's level to attach to its bottom?"

9. Click Yes to have the wall attach to the bottom of the floor.

10. Click Yes to join geometry and cut the overlapping volume out of the wall(s).

11. Open the 3D Cutaway 3D View (Figure 4.85).

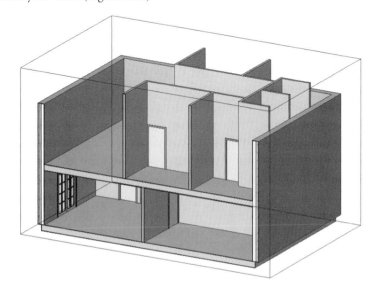

Figure 4.85

3D section view showing the floors added to the model

Creating a Sloped Floor

As you work on your building project, it may be necessary to create a sloped floor. This is a very straightforward process. To do this, follow these steps:

1. Select an existing floor.

2. From the Modify | Floors tab's Mode panel, click the Edit Boundary button.

3. Click the Slope Arrow button, and then choose either Line or Pick Lines.

4. Place a slope arrow in the floor sketch so that it is parallel to the direction of the desired slope. In the Properties palette, you can define the height offset for both the head and the tail.

5. In the Mode panel, click the Finish Edit Mode button to create the sloped floor (Figure 4.86).

6. Click Yes to join geometry and cut the overlapping volume out of the wall(s).

Figure 4.86

A sloped floor

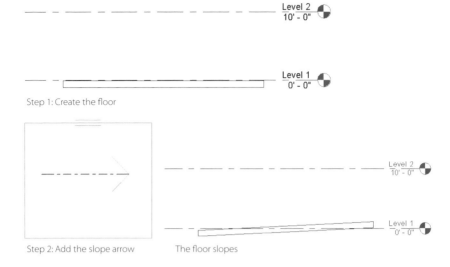

Creating a Tapered Floor

Creating a tapered floor is useful when you want to create a floor of a variable thickness. To do this, follow these steps:

1. From the book's web page, open `Dataset_04_06.rvt` (`M_Dataset_04_06.rvt`).

2. Select the existing floor.

3. On the Modify | Floors tab's Shape Editing panel, click the Add Point button.

4. On the Options bar, set Elevation to **–6″** (**–150mm**).

5. In the drawing window, move the mouse pointer to the center of the floor, and click to place the point.

   The Add Point tool does not provide you with temporary dimensions for precision. If you need to define a precise point, draw some reference lines to define the precise insertion point.

6. Click the Esc key twice to exit the Modify | Floors mode.

7. Open the Section 1 section (Building Section).

   Figure 4.87 shows that the point that was added tapered the floor and the floor maintains a consistent thickness. You need to make one further adjustment so that your floor has a variable thickness.

8. From the section view, select the floor, and click the Edit Type button in the Properties palette.

Figure 4.87

Tapered floor with a consistent thickness

Level 1
0' - 0"

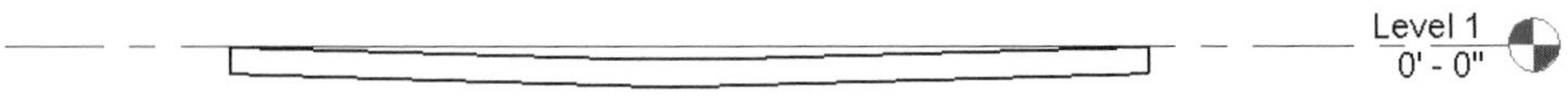

9. In the Type Properties dialog box, click the Duplicate button.

10. Name the new type `Generic - 12″ Variable`, (`Generic - 300mm Variable`) and click OK.

11. Click the Edit button to the right of Structure. This opens the Edit Assembly dialog box.

12. In the Edit Assembly dialog box, select the Variable check box for row 2. This allows this layer of the floor assembly to have a variable thickness.

13. Click OK twice to finish the variable thickness floor (Figure 4.88).

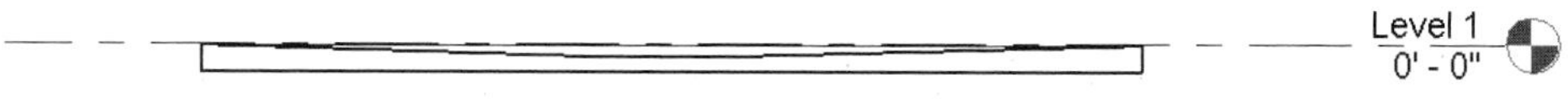

Figure 4.88

Tapered floor with a variable thickness

Creating Ceilings

A ceiling is a building element in Revit that can host ceiling components such as lights, electrical equipment, smoke detectors, fire sprinklers, and ventilation elements. Ceilings can be sloped and contain complex structures. Ceilings are level-based elements and are automatically offset from a level. You view and add elements to ceilings in ceiling plan views.

Automatic Ceiling Creation

In this section, you will use the Automatic Ceiling tool to create your ceiling on the first level of your sample project:

1. From the book's web page, open `Dataset_04_07.rvt`.

2. Open the Level 1 ceiling plan.

3. On the Home tab's Build panel, click the Ceiling button. This opens the Modify | Place Ceiling tab.

4. On the Ceiling panel, ensure that the Automatic Ceiling button is enabled.

   When you click inside walls that form a closed loop, the Automatic Ceiling tool places a ceiling within those boundaries. It ignores room separator lines.

5. In the Properties palette, make sure Compound Ceiling 2′×4′ ACT System (Compound Ceiling 600×1200 ACT System) is selected.

6. In the Properties palette, under Height Offset From Level, set the value to **8′ 6″ (2032mm)**.

7. In the drawing window, move your mouse pointer into the southwest corner room (Figure 4.89).

8. Click to add the ceiling.

9. Using Figure 4.90 as a reference, add ceilings to the rest of the enclosed spaces.

10. Hit the Esc key to exit the Automatic Ceiling tool.

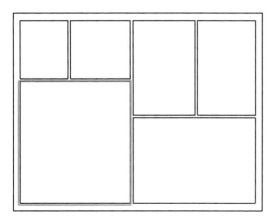

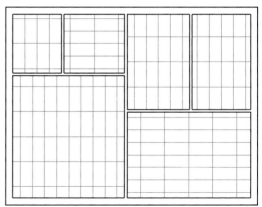

Figure 4.89

When you click inside a wall that forms a closed loop, Revit automatically generates a ceiling boundary.

Figure 4.90

Ceilings added to Level 1

With your ceilings in place, you can demonstrate several techniques for editing the ceiling grid. When you place a ceiling, Revit will center the grid in the room. In the next steps, you will change the placement of the grid by shifting the grid to the right.

1. Zoom into the southeast corner room (Figure 4.91).

2. Place your mouse pointer over one of the ceiling grid lines, and click to select it.

   The Modify | Ceilings tab is now displayed on the ribbon. You can use any of the Modify tools to edit the ceiling grid.

3. From the Modify panel, click the Move button.

4. For the move start point, click anywhere on the line you selected in step 2.

5. For the move end point, drag the mouse pointer right, and click the interior wall face. The grid then shifts to the right.

Figure 4.91

Using the Move tool to shift the grid

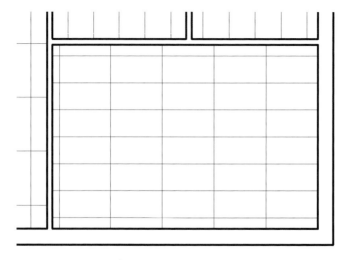

Manual Ceiling Creation

In this section, you will create a ceiling by manually defining the ceiling boundary on the second level of your sample project. You will also walk through the steps to create a new ceiling type.

1. Open to the Level 2 ceiling plan.

2. On the Home tab's Build panel, click the Ceiling button. This opens the Modify | Place Ceiling tab.

3. On the Ceiling panel, click the Sketch Ceiling button.

4. In the Properties palette, click the Edit Type button.

5. In the Type Properties dialog box, click the Duplicate button.

6. Name the new type `2´×2´ ACT System` (`600×600mm ACT System`).

7. Click OK to close the Name dialog box.

8. Click the Edit button.

9. In the Edit Assembly dialog box in the Layers section, click the Browse button 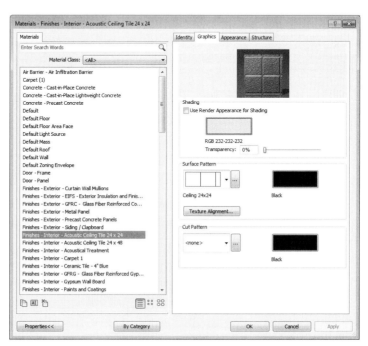 of row 4 in the Material column.

10. In the Materials dialog box, select `Finishes - Interior - Acoustic Ceiling Tile 24×24` (600×600) (Figure 4.92).

11. Click OK three times to exit the Materials, Edit Assembly, and Type Properties dialog boxes.

Figure 4.92

Assigning a material definition to the ceiling tile

12. In the Properties palette, under Height Offset From Level, set the value to **8′ 6″** (**2032mm**).

13. On the Modify | Create Ceiling Boundary tab's Draw panel, click the Pick Walls button .

14. Using Figure 4.93 as a reference, select the indicated walls.

    When using the Pick Walls tool, make sure that after you have picked the wall, the magenta lines drawn are on the inside of the wall for which you are creating a ceiling. Use the flip arrows as necessary to select the interior edges of the walls.

Figure 4.93

Using the Pick Walls tool, select the indicated walls.

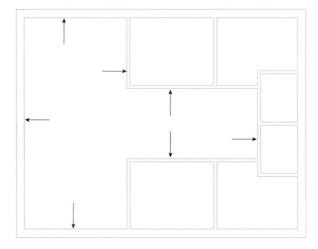

15. When defining a ceiling boundary, the boundary must form a closed loop. Trim the boundary using the Trim tool found in the Modify panel.

16. Click Finish Edit Mode ✓ on the Mode panel to create the ceiling.

    If you want to discard the operation to define the ceiling boundary, click the Cancel Edit Mode ✕ button on the Mode panel.

17. Create ceilings using the manual method for the remainder of the enclosed spaces on the Level 2 ceiling plan (Figure 4.94).

Figure 4.94

Ceilings on the second floor

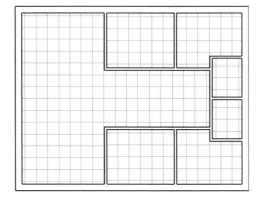

Placing Components in a Ceiling

With your ceilings created, you can begin the process of adding ceiling-hosted elements such as lights, electrical equipment, smoke detectors, fire sprinklers, and ventilation elements. In this section, you will add a light fixture, align it, and lock it to your ceiling grid. Should you move the grid, the light fixture will move with it.

1. From the book's web page, open `Dataset_04_08.rvt` (`M_Dataset_04_08.rvt`).

2. Open the Level 1 ceiling plan.

3. On the Home tab's Build panel, click the Component button.

4. In the Properties palette's Type Selector, select `Troffer Light - 2x4Parabolic 2´ × 4´` `(2 Lamp) - 120V` (`Troffer Light - 50x100mm Parabolic 50x100mm (2 Lamp) - 120V`).

5. In the drawing window, click somewhere in the middle of southwest corner ceiling to place the light (Figure 4.95). The exact placement and rotation are not important.

6. Click Esc twice to exit the Component tool.

    You now need to align the light fixture with your ceiling grid.

7. Move the mouse pointer over the light, and click to select it.

8. Press the spacebar once to rotate the light fixture 90 degrees.

    You now need to align the light fixture with the vertical gridline.

9. From the Modify | Lighting Fixtures tab's Modify panel, click the Align button .

10. Pick a vertical gridline for the reference point of alignment, and then select the left edge of the light fixture to align it with the gridline (Figure 4.96). The light fixture is then aligned with the vertical gridline.

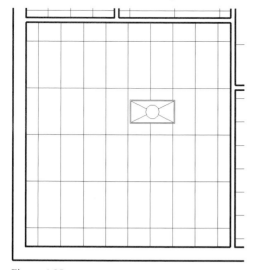

Figure 4.95

Light fixture placed in the ceiling

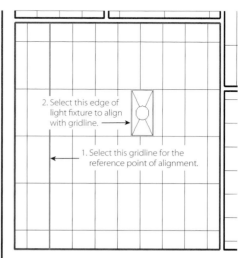

Figure 4.96

Using the Align tool to align the edge of the light fixture with the gridline

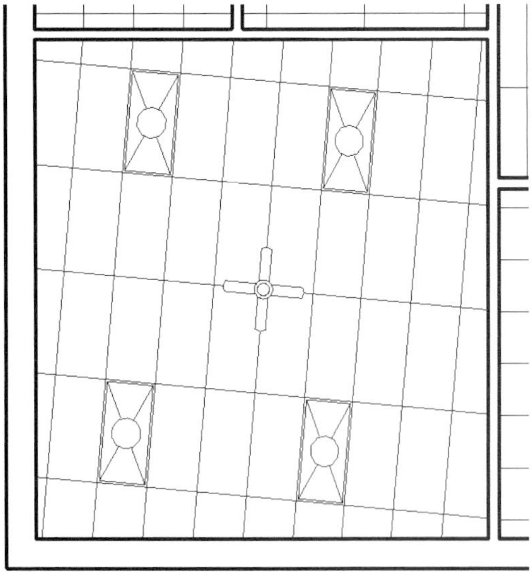

Figure 4.97

Example of a rotated ceiling grid with lights, ceiling fan

11. After the light fixture has been aligned, click the padlock to lock the left side of the light fixture to the vertical gridline.

12. While still in the Align tool, pick a horizontal gridline for the reference point of alignment, and then select the top edge of the light fixture to align it with the gridline. The light fixture is then aligned with the horizontal gridline.

13. After the fixture is then aligned with the horizontal gridline, click the padlock to lock the top edge of the light fixture to the horizontal gridline. This locks the alignment of the fixture to the gridline.

Since you locked the alignment of the light fixture to the grid, if the grid moves, so will the light fixtures or any other element locked to a gridline. You can now add additional light fixtures and other additional ceiling-based items such as the ceiling fan shown in Figure 4.97.

Creating Roofs

Revit provides multiple options for creating roofs. Like walls and floors, roofs are system components and are defined in the project file, not as separate family components. There are three basic roof types in Revit: Roof By Footprint, Roof By Extrusion, and Roof By Face (sometimes referred to as Roof From Mass), as shown in Figure 4.98.

Figure 4.98

Examples of Roof By Footprint, Extrusion, and Face

By footprint   By extrusion   By face

Roof By Footprint

To create a Roof By Footprint, you are going to sketch the perimeter of the roof. This sketch must form a closed boundary. You'll create a gable roof.

1. From the book's web page, open Dataset_04_09.rvt (M_Dataset_04_09.rvt).

2. Open the Level 3 floor plan.

3. On the Home tab's Build panel, click the Roof button.

4. On the Modify | Create Roof Footprint tab's Draw panel, click the Pick Walls button 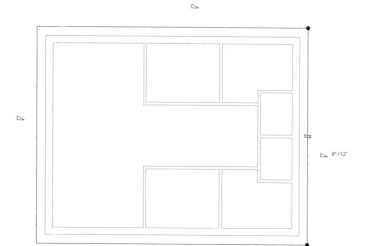 .

5. On the Options bar, set the following:

   - Defines Slope = selected

   - Overhang = **2′ 6″** (**750mm**)

   - Extend To Wall Core = selected

   The last option allows you to measure the overhang from the core of the wall.

   > If you try to add a roof at the lowest level of your project, a dialog box will prompt you to move it to a higher level. If you do not move the roof to a higher level, Revit will then notify you that the roof is too low.

6. Pick the walls to form a closed loop.

   When picking the walls where you have specified an overhang, make sure you use the dashed line on the side of the wall where you want the overhang to be displayed. This dashed line provides a preview of where the boundary line will be placed. Moving the cursor to one side of the wall or the other will change the location of the overhang in some circumstances.

   Figure 4.99 shows the sketch of the roof by footprint. If you were to create the roof now, the result would be a hip roof because you are sloping all four sides of the roof. You want to create a gable roof, sloping only the north and south sides of the building. When a roof boundary line has the slope symbol ▱ adjacent to it, this defines a slope for that roof line. You need to remove the slope symbol from the east and west roof boundary lines.

Figure 4.99

Sketch of roof footprint

7. On the Mode panel, click the Finish Edit Mode button.

8. Click Yes when asked if you would like to attach the highlighted walls to the roof.

9. Open a 3D view (Figure 4.100).

In the following steps, you are going to modify your hip roof to create a gable roof.

1. Open the Level 3 Floor Plan view.

2. Select the roof, and in the Modify | Roofs tab, click the Edit Footprint button on the Mode panel.

3. Select the west roof boundary line, and on the Options bar, deselect the Defines Slope check box.

4. Repeat step 3 for the east roof boundary line.

5. On the Mode panel, click the Finish Edit Mode button.

6. Open a 3D view (Figure 4.101).

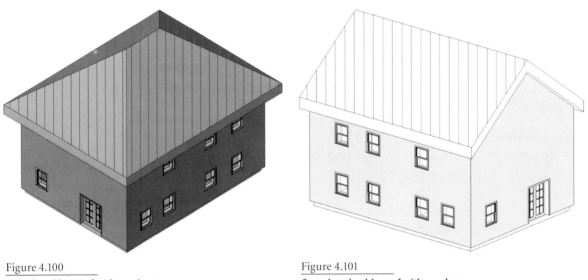

Figure 4.100

Completed hip roof with overhang

Figure 4.101

Completed gable roof with overhang

Roof by Extrusion

To create a roof by extrusion, you sketch a profile of the roof. This determines the height of the roof. You can do this in section or elevation view, and then you extrude that profile. The Roof By Extrusion sketch must be a series of connected lines and/or arcs that do not form a closed loop.

1. From the book's web page, open Dataset_04_10.rvt (M_Dataset_04_10.rvt).

2. Open the West elevation (Building Elevation).

3. On the Home tab's Build panel, click the bottom portion of the Roof split button, and select Roof By Extrusion.

   When the Roof By Extrusion command is started, Revit will display the Work Plane dialog box so that you can specify which workplace you will sketch on. In an elevation or section view, you need to set the work plane. In this particular case, you are going to use the Pick A Plane option and then select an element in the elevation to use as a reference for your work plane.

   The Work Plane dialog box has three options for specifying a new work plane:

   Name This allows you to select an existing named work plane in the project.

   Pick A Plane This option creates a plane that is coincident to the selected plane. You can select any plane that can be dimensioned. Some examples are wall faces, faces in linked models, extrusion faces, levels, and grids.

   Pick A Line And Use The Work Plane It Was Sketched In This option creates a work plane that is coplanar with the work plane of the selected line.

4. In the Work Plane dialog box, click the Pick A Plane radio button, and click OK to close the dialog box.

5. Move your mouse pointer over the west wall, and click.

   The Roof Reference Level And Offset dialog box will be displayed, asking you to specify the Roof Reference Level and Offset. You can use this to raise or lower the roof from the reference level. When you click OK in this dialog box, Revit will create a reference plane that can be used to control the position of the roof in relation to the level.

6. In the Roof Reference Level And Offset dialog box, specify an offset value of **4′ 0″** (**100mm**),and click OK.

   Using Figure 4.102 as a loose reference, sketch a profile for the roof, making sure that it is not a closed loop.

7. On the Modify | Create Extrusion Roof Profile tab's Draw panel, click the Sketch tools.

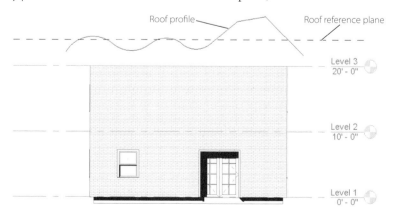

Figure 4.102

Sketch of roof by extrusion profile

8. On the Mode panel, click the Finish Edit Mode button.

9. Switch to 3D view and select the roof.

10. In the Properties palette, change the roof type to Basic Roof Generic - 9″ [Generic - 125mm]; the result is shown in Figure 4.103.

Figure 4.103

A roof by extrusion

Attaching Walls to Roofs

In the previous section, you created a roof by extrusion, but the walls are not attached to the roof. This can lead to some serious drafts for the residents on the third floor. Revit provides an option that allows you to set or override the initial top and base constraints by attaching a wall's top or base to another element in the same vertical plane. A wall can attach to a floor, a roof, a ceiling, a reference plane, or another wall that is directly above or below. The height of the wall automatically increases or decreases as necessary to conform to the boundary represented by the attached element. When you attach a wall to another element, you can avoid having to manually edit the wall's profile when your design changes.

1. From the book's web page, open Dataset_04_11.rvt (M_Dataset_04_11.rvt).

2. Open the {3D} 3D view.

3. Select one of the exterior walls that you want to attach to the roof.

4. On the Modify | Walls tab's Modify Wall panel, click the Attach Top/Base button.

5. On the Options bar, for Attach Wall select Top, because you want to adjust the top attachment of the wall.

6. Select the roof to attach the top of the wall to the roof.

7. Repeat steps 3 through 6 for the remaining exterior walls that need to be attached to the roof (Figure 4.104).

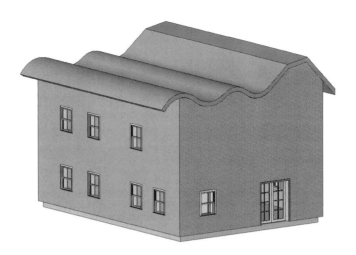

Figure 4.104

Completed roof by extrusion with walls attached

Adding Roof Soffits

Revit allows you to add other roof elements including soffits, fascias, and gutters. In this section, you are going to walk through the process of creating a soffit. Because design intent for soffits can widely vary, the method for creating soffits in Revit varies.

1. From the book's web page, open `Dataset_04_12.rvt` (`M_Dataset_04_12.rvt`). Open the file `AddSoffit.rvt`.

2. Open the Roof floor plan.

3. On the Home tab's Build panel, click the lower portion of the Roof split button, and select Roof Soffit.

4. On the Modify | Create Roof Soffit Boundary tab's Draw panel, click the Pick Lines button.

5. Click the north and south roof edges, as shown in Figure 4.105.

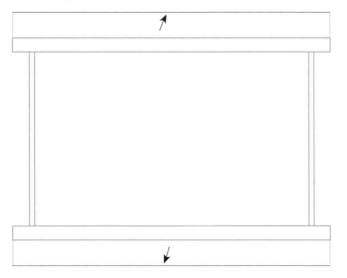

Figure 4.105

Roof edges selected

6. On the Draw panel, click the Pick Walls button 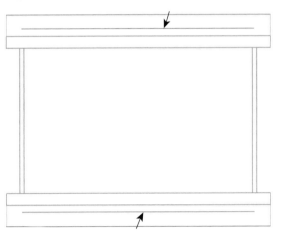.

7. Highlight the outside face of the north wall beneath the roof, and click to select.

8. Repeat steps 6 and 7 for the south wall (Figure 4.106).

Figure 4.106

Sketch lines for walls for the soffit

9. Using the Sketch tools and Trim tools, complete the sketch of the soffit as a closed loop (Figure 4.107).

Figure 4.107

Complete soffit sketch

10. On the Mode panel, click the Finish Edit Mode button. The soffit is created.

To complete the operation, you need to join the soffit to the roof, join the soffit to the wall, and join the wall to the roof:

1. Open the Section 1 section (Building Section) view.

2. On the Modify | Roof Soffits tab's Geometry panel, click the Join button.

3. Click the soffit and then the roof.

4. Select the soffit and wall. Press Esc to exit the Join command.

5. Select the wall.

6. On the Modify | Walls tab's Modify Wall panel, click the Attach Top/Base button.

7. On the Options bar, for Attach Wall select Top, because you want to adjust the top attachment of the wall.

8. Select the roof to attach the top of the wall to the roof (Figure 4.108).

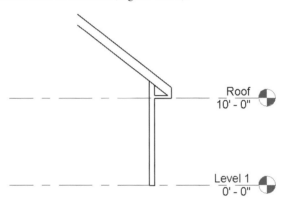

Figure 4.108

Complete roof soffit

Assemblies

Assemblies are a new feature in Revit 2012. Assemblies allow you to create a logical unit consisting of multiple components in your building model. Unlike with groups, components within assemblies can still be accessed and edited without the need to enter a dedicated edit mode for the assembly.

Assemblies can be scheduled as a category of their own. Assemblies also allow automated creation of views, including plan, section, and 3D views, as well as parts lists and material takeoffs and assembly sheets.

Creating Assemblies

The following process illustrates how to create an assembly:

1. From the book's web page, open `Dataset_04_13.rvt` (`M_Dataset_04_13.rvt`).

2. Open 3D Views: {3D}.

3. Making a crossing selection, and select all the elements visible in the 3D view.

4. Click the Filter button located on the Modify | Multi-Select panel of the ribbon.

5. In the Filter dialog box, uncheck Walls (because they cannot be included in an assembly) and leave all the other categories checked.

6. Click OK to exit the dialog box.

7. In the Create panel of the Modify | Multi-Select tab, click the Create Assembly button (Figure 4.109).

Figure 4.109

Modify | Assemblies Create panel

In the New Assembly dialog box. you can now name the assembly as well as select a category for it.

8. Type **Elevator** as a Type Name and select Specialty Equipment as its Naming Category.

9. Click OK to exit the dialog box.

You have now created an assembly. We will now look at the assembly parameters.

Assembly Parameters

Available Instance parameters for assemblies are Naming Category, Comments, and Mark, as well as the Phasing parameters Phase Created and Phase Demolished common in all Revit model objects (Figure 4.110).

Figure 4.110

Assembly Instance parameters

Naming Category

The most significant parameter for an assembly is Naming Category. Here you can select any category of component the assembly encompasses. In our example `Dataset_04_13 .rvt`, the components we selected were Roofs, Structural Columns, Structural Framing, Curtain Panels, and Specialty Equipment. These categories are subsequently available as Naming Category for the assembly.

Available Type parameters are common with all other Revit components and include Keynote, Model, Manufacturer, Type Comments, URL, Description, Assembly Description (derived from Assembly Code), Assembly Code, Type Mark, and Cost.

Creating an Assembly Schedule

To create as Assembly Schedule, continue in `AssemblySample.rvt`.

1. Click Schedules and choose Schedules/Quantities located in the Create group of the View tab of the ribbon.

2. In the New Schedule dialog box, select Assemblies as a Category.

3. In the list of available fields, select Family And Type, Naming Category, and Count and click the Add button to add them to the scheduled fields. Click OK.

Revit will create the Assembly Schedule and list the assembly you previously created (Figure 4.111).

Figure 4.111

Assembly Schedule

Assembly Schedule		
Count	Family and Type	Naming Category
1	Specialty Equipment Assembly: Specialty Equipment 001	Specialty Equipment

Creating Assembly Views

The following will explain how to create assembly views and add them to a sheet:

Continue in `AssemblySample.rvt`.

1. In the 3D View: {3D}, select the assembly you previously created.

2. On the Modify | Assemblies tab of the ribbon, click the Create Views icon  .

3. In the Create Assembly Views dialog box, check all available check boxes under Views To Create, select ¾″ = 1′-0″ (1:100) as Scale, and use the B 11 × 17 (A2 metric) Horizontal entry as Titleblock.

4. Click OK to exit the dialog box.

   Revit will now open one of the views created.

5. On the Project Browser, scroll down to Assemblies. Expand the node and expand the Specialty Equipment 001 assembly. Here all views created will be accessible (Figure 4.112).

Revit will have created plan, section, and detail views, as well as a Part List (not to be confused with the Part feature), listing all the individual components in the assembly, and a Material Takeoff of all the components in the assembly.

You can now use the Sheet created with the assembly to place all the views (Figure 4.113).

Figure 4.112

Assembly views

Figure 4.113

Sheet showing assembly views

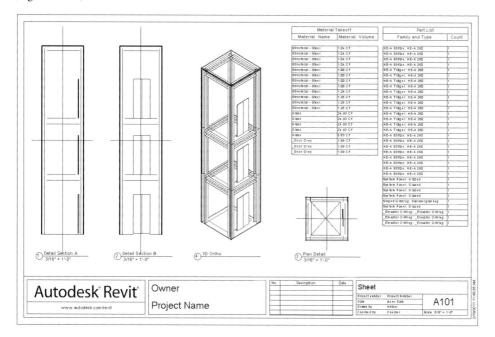

Editing Assemblies

To edit an assembly, select an assembly and click the Edit Assembly button located on the Modify | Assemblies tab of the ribbon (Figure 4.114).

The assembly editor will open and, similar to Edit Groups, will allow you to add or remove components to or from the assembly.

Disassembling Assemblies

To disassemble an assembly, select the assembly you want to disassemble and click the Disassemble button located on the Modify | Assemblies tab of the ribbon (also shown in Figure 4.114).

When disassembling an assembly, all dependent schedule entries as well as all views and sheets created from the assembly will be removed from the project.

Figure 4.114

**Edit Assembly
button**

CHAPTER 5

Advanced Modeling

In this chapter, we will elaborate further on modeling techniques for core complex building elements. We will begin by creating stairs, followed by a discussion about stair parameters. From there, we will move on to ramps and railings.

Another topic this chapter will explore is curtain walls. We will explore curtain wall properties and the methods used to create them.

This chapter covers the following topics:

- **Creating stairs**
- **Creating railings**
- **Creating ramps**
- **Creating curtain walls**

Creating Stairs

Stairs and railings can be very simple to extremely complex, and you could fill a book on just this one topic. In this section, we'll explore how to create a basic stair with railings. Stairs are created by defining the run of the stairs or by sketching riser and boundary lines. Revit allows you to create several styles of stairs, including straight runs, L-shaped runs with a platform, U-shaped stairs, and spiral stairs. When stairs are created in Revit, the railings are automatically created for the stairs. In multistory buildings, you can design one set of stairs, and Revit creates identical sets up to the highest level defined in the stair properties.

To create stairs, you need to be in a plan or 3D view. You click the start point of the stairs, and Revit will automatically calculate the number of treads, based on the distance between the floors and the maximum riser height defined in the stair properties. Revit will generate a rectangle representing a preview footprint of the run of the stairs. As the mouse pointer is moved, the rectangle adjusts accordingly. If you move the mouse pointer outside of the end preview footprint and click, Revit will create the stairs.

When creating stairs, you begin by creating a sketch of the start and end points of the stair. Stairs have two Sketch modes:

Run Sketching a run is the easiest method. As you sketch the run, the boundaries and risers are generated automatically. After you finish sketching and create the stair, the railing is automatically added. With the Run tool, you are limited to following types of stairs:

- Straight runs
- Straight runs with landings
- Spiral staircases

Boundary and Run When you create a stair using the Boundary and Run mode, two separate tools are used to define the stair. To create a stair, you define the boundary and riser. You use this method when you want more control when sketching the footprint of your stair.

In the following sections, you will create the three types of stairs available with the Run tool and learn to use Revit's Stair tool.

Straight Run Stair

In this section, you are going to create a straight run stair from Level 1 to Level 2:

1. From the book's companion download files (available at www.sybex.com/go/introducingrevit2012), open the file Dataset_05_01.rvt [Dataset_05_01_metric.rvt].

2. Open the Level 1 floor plan.

3. On the Home tab's Circulation panel, click the Stairs button.

4. On the Modify | Create Stairs Sketch tab's Draw panel, click the Run button.

5. In the Draw panel, click the Line tool.

6. Using Figure 5.1 as a reference, use the intersection of the two reference planes as the start point of the run of the straight stair.

7. Drag the mouse pointer to the right to define the run. You will need to create 18 risers. Click to define the end of the run (Figure 5.2).

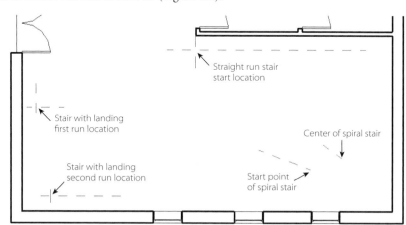

Figure 5.1

Stair creation reference

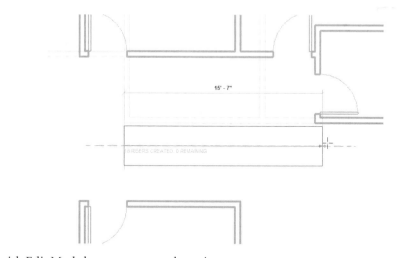

Figure 5.2

Defining the run of the straight stair

8. Click the Finish Edit Mode button to create the stair.

The stair has been created correctly; however, there is no opening in the Level 2 floor for the stair. You need to create an opening in that floor.

9. Open the Level 2 floor plan. Notice that parts of the stair's railings are visible on the second floor (Figure 5.3).

10. Select the floor on Level 2.

Figure 5.3

Railings extending through the second floor

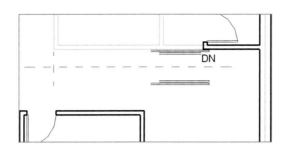

11. On the Modify | Floors tab's Mode panel, click the Edit Boundary button.

    The boundary of the floor will turn magenta. To create an opening in the floor, you will use the sketch tools.

12. In the Draw panel, click either the Rectangle or the Line tool to sketch an opening, as shown in Figure 5.4.

Figure 5.4

Sketching an opening in the Level 2 floor

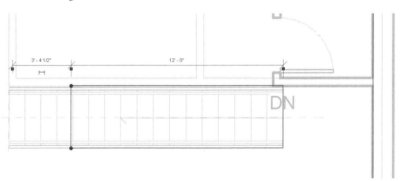

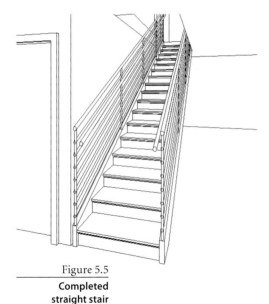

13. Click the Finish Edit Mode button to finish the editing of the floor boundary sketch.

14. Click Yes to accept having the walls attach to the bottom of the floor level.

15. Open the 3D view 3D – Straight Stair (Figure 5.5) to view your completed stair.

16. Save the file to your local computer.

Stair with Landing

In this section, you will create a stair with a landing. Unlike the previous section, where you created a single run from Level 1 to Level 2, you will now create a short run of stairs, followed by a landing, then another run of stairs to Level 2.

Figure 5.5

Completed straight stair

To create a straight stair with a landing, do the following:

1. If you are continuing from the previous lesson, use that file; otherwise, from the book's companion download files (available at www.sybex.com/go/introducingrevit2012), open the file Dataset_05_01[Dataset_05_01_metric.rvt].

2. Open the Level 1 floor plan.

3. On the Home tab's Circulation panel, click the Stairs button.

4. On the Modify | Create Stairs Sketch tab's Draw panel, click the Run button.

5. In the Draw panel, click the Line tool.

6. Using Figure 5.1 as a reference, locate "Stair with landing first run location." Use the intersection of the two reference planes as the start point for the run of the stair with landing.

7. Click and drag the mouse pointer until the dynamic feedback on the risers reads "9 RISERS CREATED, 9 REMAINING," and click (Figure 5.6).

8. Using Figure 5.1 as a reference, locate "Stair with landing second run location." Use the intersection of the two reference planes as the start point for the run of the stair with landing.

9. Click and drag the mouse pointer until the dynamic feedback on the risers reads "18 RISERS CREATED, 0 REMAINING," and click to complete the stair sketch (Figure 5.7).

10. Click the Finish Edit Mode button to create the stair.

11. Open the 3D view 3D – Stair With Landing (Figure 5.8) to view your completed stair.

12. Save the file to your local computer and then close it.

The stair is created correctly; however, you still need to create an opening on the second floor, as outlined in the previous example and shown in Figure 5.8.

Spiral Staircase

In this section, you will learn how to create a spiral staircase.

To create a spiral stair, follow these steps:

1. If you are continuing from the previous lesson, use that file; otherwise, from the book's companion download files (available at www.sybex.com/go/introducingrevit2012), open Dataset_05_01.rvt[Dataset_05_01_metric.rvt].

2. Open the Level 1 floor plan.

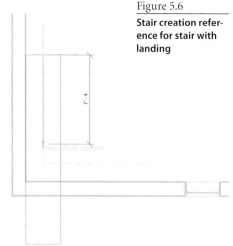

Figure 5.6

Stair creation reference for stair with landing

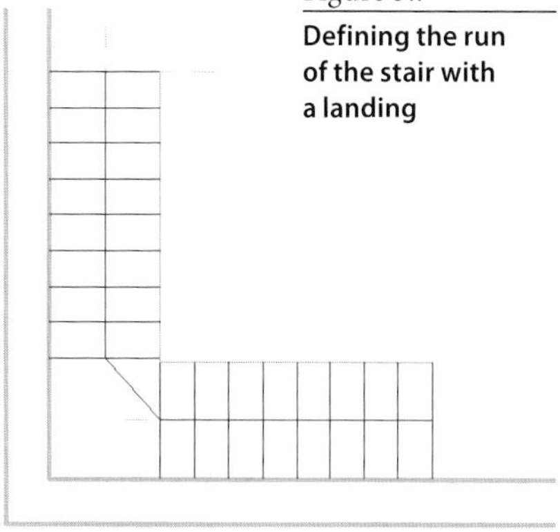

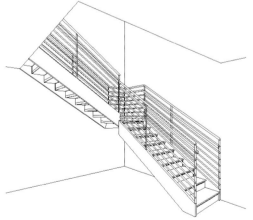

Figure 5.7

Defining the run of the stair with a landing

Figure 5.8

Completed stair with a landing with an opening on the second floor

3. On the Home tab's Circulation panel, click the Stairs button.

4. On the Modify | Create Stairs Sketch tab's Draw panel, click the Run button.

5. On the Draw panel, click Center-ends Arc.

6. Using Figure 5.1 as a reference, click the center of the spiral stair as the center point of the spiral stair.

7. Using Figure 5.1 as a reference, drag the mouse pointer to the start point of the spiral stair to define the arc run radius. Then drag the mouse pointer until the dynamic feedback on the risers reads "18 RISERS CREATED, 0 REMAINING," and click to complete the arc boundary radius (Figure 5.9).

8. Click the Finish Edit Mode button to create the stair.

9. Open the 3D view 3D – Spiral Staircase (Figure 5.10) to view your completed stair.

10. Save the file to your local computer.

The stair is created correctly; however, you still need to create an opening on the second floor, as outlined in the previous examples and shown in Figure 5.10.

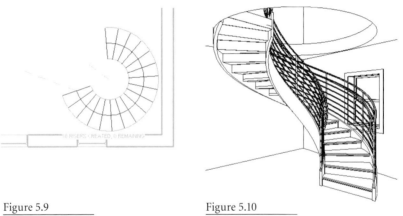

Figure 5.9
Completed sketch of the spiral staircase

Figure 5.10
Completed spiral staircase

Stair Parameters Explained: Using the Stairs Tool

In construction reality, stairs are complex assemblies of parts ranging from simple monolithic straight run concrete stairs to highly complex multimaterial curved assemblies.

The Stairs tool in Revit offers a high degree of flexibility that allows you to cater to those differing requirements; however, this also means that some aspects of this tool can be challenging to grasp intuitively. The following will outline some of the feature's advanced possibilities.

Stair Instance Parameters

Let's start by creating a stair using the default values and explore its instance parameters and settings:

INSTANCE PARAMETERS VS. TYPE PARAMETERS

To understand the difference between instance and type parameters, you need to consider that Revit structures the building model hierarchically. The hierarchy follows the principle of components, types, and instances.

One particular window in a building model is an instance of a specific type of the component window in the building model.

So, for example, if you change a setting for a type parameter in a door, the change will affect all occurrences (instances) of that particular type of door throughout your entire model.

On the other hand, when you change an instance parameter, the change will only affect the particular door you have selected.

In the Revit user interface, the difference between instance and type parameters is clearly visible. When you select any object in Revit, its instance parameters will be immediately visible in the Properties palette.

To access the type parameters of an object you selected, you have to click the Edit Type button in the Properties palette.

1. From the book's companion download files (available at www.sybex.com/go/introducingrevit2012), open the file Dataset_05_02.rvt [Dataset_05_02_metric.rvt].

2. Select the stair and expand the Properties palette to get a complete overview of the stair's instance parameters (Figure 5.11).

   The constraints section of the stair's instance parameters determines on which level the stair originates and to which level it will lead. While settings for level and offset are quite obvious, the setting for Multistory Top Level is quite powerful.

3. Open Section 1 view.

4. If not still selected from the previous exercise, select the stair again; be sure to select the stair and not the railing hosted by the stair.

5. In Stair Properties, select Level 3 as value for Multistory Top Level.

Figure 5.11

Stair's instance parameters

The result of changing this setting is that you will have created a second stair, connecting Level 2 to Level 3. This feature is especially handy when you are creating staircases spanning multiple floors.

Multistory stairs require all levels they are connecting to to be equidistant. That means that you cannot use a multistory stair to connect multiple levels with different story heights. The main purpose of this feature is to provide a quick way of vertically connecting repetitive levels, such as in high-rise constructions.

The Graphics section of the stair's Properties palette provides options for automatically created graphic annotations of stairs in plan views. Depending on your locale and office graphic standards, this set of parameters allows you to control the way a stair will display annotation in plan views.

The Dimensions section of the stair's Properties palette lets you control aspects of the stair's dimension after its initial creation.

6. Go to Floor Plan Level 1.

7. Select the stair.

8. In stair's Properties palette, change the value for width from 4′ 0″ [1200 mm] to 5′ 0″ [1500 mm] by typing **5′ [1500]** in the Width field.

The stair will widen accordingly to the new setting.

Stair Type Properties

Stair type properties control the appearance and construction of stairs in Revit. The following will give you an overview of the possibilities and settings for parameters that determine the stair geometry.

Parameters in the Construction section of the stair's Type Properties dialog box control the overall geometry of the stair, as follows:

Calculation Rules The Calculation rules defined in the Stair Calculator allow you to set a rule based on x * riser height + y * tread depth = z. During stair creation, Revit will attempt to calculate riser height and tread depth based on the formula defined. It will honor the values set for Maximum Riser Height as well as Minimum Tread Depth (Figure 5.12).

Figure 5.12

Stair Calculator

Extend Below Base A negative value will extend the stair below the base level, and a positive one will extend the stair above the base level (Figure 5.13).

Monolithic Stairs The Monolithic Stairs parameter will create a monolithic (also commonly known as concrete) stair (Figure 5.14).

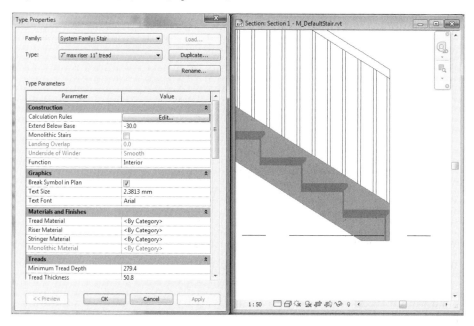

Figure 5.13
Extend Below Base

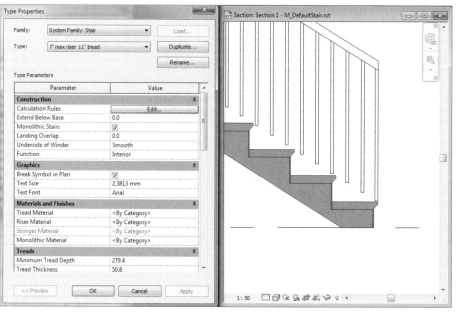

Figure 5.14
Monolithic Stairs

Landing Overlap This parameter is only available with monolithic stairs. This value determines the horizontal overlap of the landing under the following riser when Underside Of Winder is set to Stepped (Figure 5.15).

Underside Of Winder Possible settings are Stepped or Smooth. This parameter will change the underside of a curved monolithic stair accordingly. It will not affect straight sections of a monolithic stair (Figure 5.16).

Figure 5.15

Landing Overlap

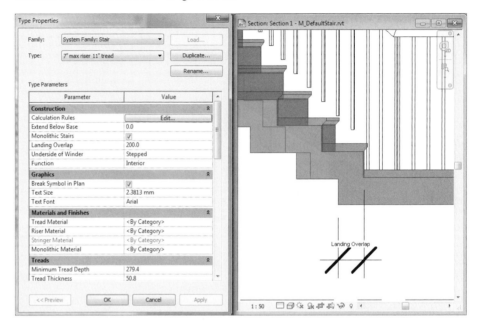

Figure 5.16

Using the Underside Of Winder parameter, the left stair shows a smooth underside and the right stair shows a stepped underside.

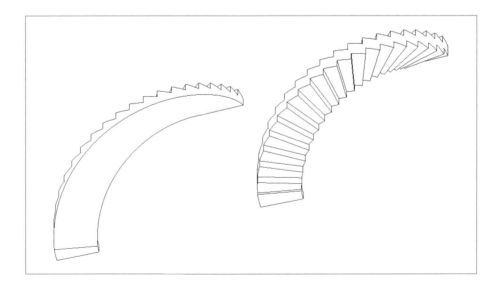

Function This parameter defines the functional use of the stair; the value can be either Exterior or Interior. The parameter has no impact on the stair geometry itself, but it's helpful for scheduling purposes.

- Parameters in the Graphics section determine the graphic appearance of the stair in plan views.

- Parameters in the Materials And Finishes section allow you to select materials for treads, risers, and stringers individually. In the case of a monolithic stair, the monolithic material can also be set here.

- Parameters in the Treads section allow various settings for adjusting treads.

Minimum Tread Depth This value is used by Revit to calculate the stair layout while sketching the stair.

Tread Thickness This value defines the thickness of the tread.

Nosing Length This value defines the length of the nosing.

Nosing Profile This parameter allows you to select any loaded stair nosing profile family loaded in the project.

Apply Nosing Profile This parameter allows you to use a combination of left, right, and front for applying the stair nosing profile (Figure 5.17).

Parameters in the Risers group will affect how risers are created. Revit offers different settings for the riser geometry as well as placement of risers.

Figure 5.17

Stair treads

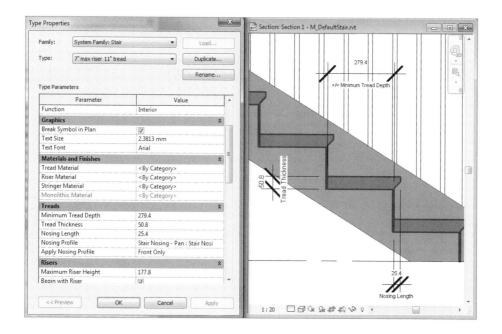

Maximum Riser Height The value for Maximum Riser Height will be used when Revit calculates the overall geometry of the stair during sketching. The actual riser height will be smaller or equal to the Maximum Riser Height value.

Riser Thickness This value determines the thickness of the riser (Figure 5.18).

Riser Type The value for Riser Type can be None, Straight, or Slanted. Setting the value to None will produce an open stair without any risers; setting it to Slanted will produce slanted risers. A slated riser goes from the back of the nosing profile to the back of the tread below at whatever angle is required to fill the gap (Figure 5.19).

Figure 5.18

Riser height and thickness

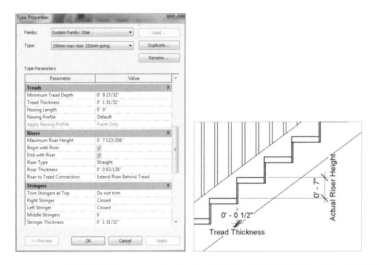

Figure 5.19

Slanted risers with the default nosing profile

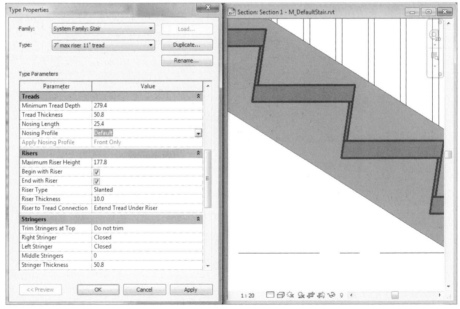

Begin With Riser and End With Riser These two settings affect the overall geometry of the stair. When both values are set, the stair will start with a riser first and then end with a riser on the stair top (Figure 5.20).

When both settings are unchecked, the stair will actually become one riser short. A warning message will appear and you may need to add another riser to make the stair meet its desired target (Figure 5.21).

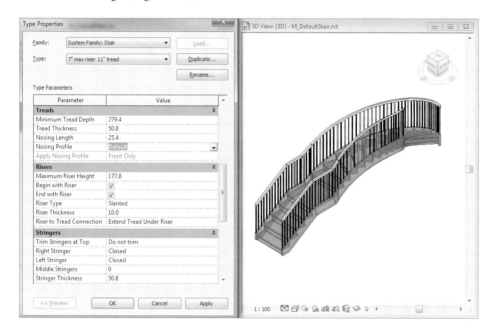

Figure 5.20

Begin With Riser and End With Riser check boxes selected

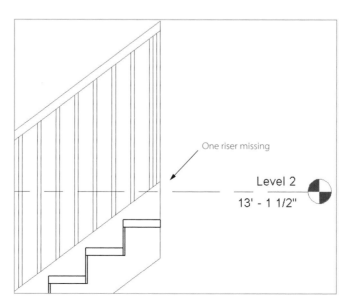

Figure 5.21

The Begin With Riser and End With Riser check boxes are deselected, and the stair is short one riser/tread.

Riser To Tread Connection This parameter affects the way the riser and treads connect. Possible values are Extend Riser Behind Tread or Extend Tread Under Riser. The settings in the Stringers section of the stair's type properties allow you to determine the number and shape of stingers created with the stair. In order to change values for properties in the Stringer section, you must deselect the Monolithic check box.

Right Stringer, Left Stringer Possible values for those two parameters are Open, Closed, and None.

Stringer Height This parameter is the actual height of the stringer, measured at a closed stringer from the top to the bottom of the stringer.

Stringer Thickness This parameter specifies the thickness of the stringer.

Landing Carriage Height This parameter specifies the height measured from the bottom of the stringer to the bottom of the tread at a stair landing.

Stringer Carriage Height This parameter specifies the height measured from the bottom of the stringer to the bottom edge of the tread (Figure 5.22).

Open Stringer Offset When one or both stringers are set to Open, this value allows you to push the open stringers toward the center of the stair (Figure 5.23).

Figure 5.22

Stringer dimension parameters

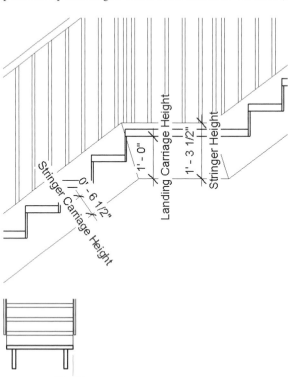

Figure 5.23

Open Stringer Offset

Open Stringer Offset

Trim Stringer At Top This parameter can be set to three different values:

Do not Trim Will not perform any trim of the stringer at the top of the stair.

Match Level Cuts off the stringer at the top level set for the stair.

Match Landing Stringer Results in a cutoff performed at the theoretical height of the landing stringer. (The actual value will be Stringer Height – Landing Carriage Height – Tread Thickness.)

Middle Stringers This parameter can be set to any number (Figure 5.24). Note that middle stringers will be spaced equidistant along their centerlines from the outside edge of the treads.

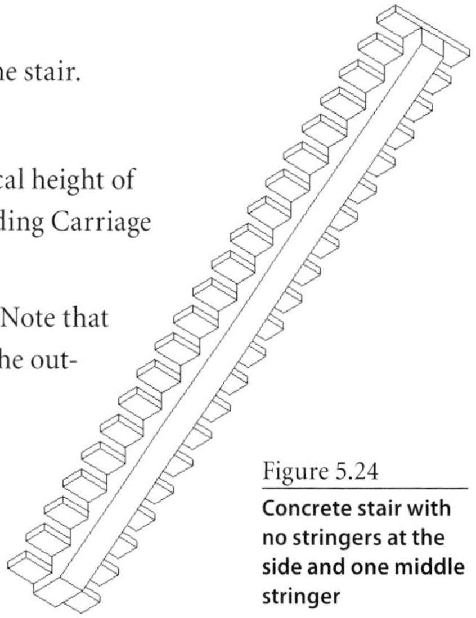

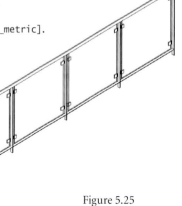

Creating Railings

Railings in Revit can be added to the model either as elements that are attached to, or hosted by, other elements such as floors, ramps, and stairs or as freestanding elements on levels.

Figure 5.24

Concrete stair with no stringers at the side and one middle stringer

Railings are *sketch-based elements*, which means that when creating a railing you will start by sketching its path.

To create a simple railing, do the following:

1. From the book's companion download files (available at www.sybex.com/go/ introducingrevit2012), open the file Dataset_05_03.rvt [Dataset_05_03.rvt_metric].

2. On the Home tab of the ribbon, click Railing in the Circulation group.

3. Start sketching the railing at the indicated point and end your sketch at the point indicated in the project.

4. Close the Sketch Editor by clicking the green check mark in the ribbon.

5. Switch to a default 3D view to inspect the result.

Your project will now look like Figure 5.25, and you will have created the railing.

Figure 5.25

Railing created

Railing: Basic Parameters

Railings in Revit consist of three major parts: rails, posts, and balusters. The geometric appearance of each can be changed using its properties. These settings determine the structure and appearance of the railing.

Figure 5.26 illustrates samples of different railings that can be built with Revit. Their visual appearance as well as construction is primarily determined by their properties and the families that are used to construct a particular railing type.

Figure 5.26

Railing samples

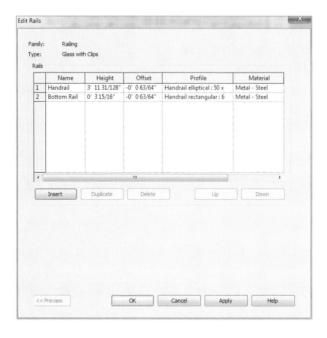

Creating Rails

Rails follow the length of the railing. Depending on the particular railing, they can be horizontal, such as the guardrails along a balcony, or slanted, such as the rails in a stair railing. They consist of profiles that sweep along the sketched path.

To change the horizontal components of a railing you need to:

1. Select the railing previously created.

2. On the Properties palette, click Edit Type.

3. In the Type Properties dialog box, for Rail Structure, click on Edit. The Edit Rails dialog box will open.

4. In the Edit Rails dialog box, change the Height value for Rail 1 (Handrail) from 3′-11 31/128″ [1200 mm] to 4′-0" [1300 mm].

5. Click OK to exit the Edit Rails dialog box and then click OK to close the Railing Type Properties dialog box.

The railing will change its height according to the new value.

Adding Posts and Balusters

Posts and balusters compose the vertical elements of the railing. The concept behind balusters and posts in Revit railings is that together they form the Main pattern of the railing.

Depending on the railings type properties, Revit will attempt to spread the Main pattern equally within the individual segments of the railings sketch. Posts can then be used at any break in the sketch, such as start, corner, or end.

To familiarize yourself with the basic concept behind posts and balusters, try this short exercise:

1. Select the railing previously created.

2. Make sure that you have a 3D view of the file open and position it in a way that you can see the railing while changing its type properties.

3. Zoom into the railing; you will notice that there is a gap between the glass panels and the posts of the railing.

4. On the Properties palette, click Edit Type.

5. In the Type Properties dialog box, for Baluster Placement, click Edit.

   The Edit Baluster Placement dialog box will open.

6. In the Main Pattern section of the dialog box, click on the Justify drop-down and select Center from the list of options.

7. Click Apply and then click OK.

   This will bring you back to the Railing Type Properties dialog box.

8. In the dialog box, click Apply again.

You will notice that the adjustment of the glass panels in the railing has changed. Now there is no gap between panels and posts left; however, when you zoom into the railing you will notice that there is now a gap at the beginning and the end of the railing.

If you want to use different posts to start or end the railing, you can do the following:

1. Select the railing previously created.

2. On the Properties palette, click Edit Type.

3. In the Type Properties dialog box, for Baluster Placement, click Edit. The Edit Baluster Placement dialog box will open.

4. In the Posts section of the dialog box (at the bottom part), change the baluster Family for Start Post and End Post to Baluster – Rectangular: 1″ × 1″ (35 × 35mm).

5. Click Apply and then click OK to exit the Edit Baluster Placement dialog box.

6. Click Apply in the Railing Type Properties dialog box.

You will notice that the shape of the Start and End posts will now have changed to the selected family type.

Hosted Railings

Railings can be hosted by other building components such as stairs, ramps, and floors. This means that whenever the geometry of the host changes, the railing will adapt to the new situation. An example for this would be a railing that is hosted by a stair. In a case where the stair changes due to changes in the floor height, the railing will follow the stair.

The following is an exercise that will illustrate the concept of hosted railings:

1. From the book's companion download files (available at `www.sybex.com/go/ introducingrevit2012`), open the file `Dataset_05_04.rvt` [`Dataset_05_04_metric.rvt`].

2. Open Floor Plans: Level 1 and Sections (Building Section): Section 1 and tile them side by side.

3. In Section 1, change the height of Level 2 from 13′-1″ [4000 mm] to 13′-0″ [3800 mm].

Notice that not only the stair will change its height to meet Level 2 at the new height, but also the railing will have changed its slope to accommodate the new setting. In this case the railing did not change because the height of Level 2 changed, but because the geometry of its host, the stair, has changed. To validate this, try the following:

1. Open Floor Plan: Level 1 and Sections (Building Section): Section 1 and tile them side by side.

2. In Section 1, select the stair.

3. In the stair Properties panel, specify 0′- 2″ [100 mm] as Top Offset.

4. Click Apply.

As in the previous exercise, the stair will now end at a top offset of 2″ [100 mm] above the level. The railing will have adjusted to the new geometry of the stair.

Switching Hosts

The concept of a hosted railing also allows switching hosts for a railing. In that scenario, the railing sketch line has to be within the projected geometry of the host in a plan view. To examine this behavior, try the following exercise:

1. Open Floor Plans: Level 1 and 3D Views: {3D} and tile both windows.

2. In Floor Plan: Level 1, select one of the stairs railings and click Edit Path on the Mode panel of the Modify | Railings tab.

3. In the Tools panel of the ribbon, click Pick New Host and then click on the ramp visible in the 3D view.

4. Click the green check mark to exit edit mode.

   You will notice that the railing is now completely flat: It follows neither the slope of the stair nor the slope of the ramp.

5. If not still selected, select the railing again and click Edit Path on the Modify | Railings tab.

6. In Floor Plan: Level 1, align the railing path sketch to the edge of the ramp using the Align tool.

7. Click the green check mark to exit edit mode.

8. Check the result in Section: Section 1: Now the railing will follow the slope of the ramp.

Understanding Railing Joins

The way in which railings join—for example, at a stair landing—is determined by settings in the Baluster Placement section of the Railing Type Properties.

Parameters controlling the way in which railings join in different conditions are explained in the following sections.

Angled Joins

The Angled Joins type parameter allows you to either use no connector or add vertical/ horizontal segments to the railing. It controls the join of railing segments that are angled—in other words, that do not follow a continuing tangent. A typical example of this type of rail join can be found where stair runs meet landings: Inclined rails following the stair run will meet horizontal stretches of rail and then meet with inclined rails that follow the next stair run.

Tangent Joins

The Tangent Joins type parameter lets you specify the connections of different segments of a railing that are on a continuing tangent (line-to-line or line-to-tangent arc). Here are the available settings:

No Connector Setting this value to No Connector will result in Revit not creating a rail element between the individual railings of each stair run.

Extend Rails To Meet When the Tangent Joins property is set to Extend to Meet, Revit will try to create railing elements that connect the individual rail elements of each stair run.

Add Vertical/Horizontal Segments When this property is set to Add Vertical/Horizontal Segments, Revit will try to create railing elements that connect the individual rail elements of each stair run using horizontal and vertical elements only.

Figure 5.27 shows a railing condition at a landing. Angled Joins is set to Add Vertical/ Horizontal Segments; Tangent Joins is set to No Connector. Notice the gap on the outer side of the railing—this is due to the fact that No Connector is specified for this particular join condition.

Figure 5.27

Railing at stair landing

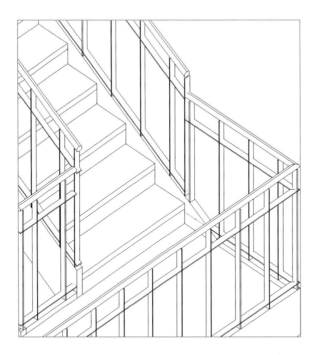

Changing the value for Tangent Joins to Extend Rails To Meet will now create a smooth connection at this particular point (Figure 5.28).

Figure 5.28

Tangent join condition changed

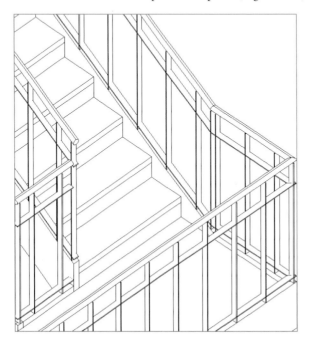

Rail Connections

The Rail Connections setting controls how Revit will join rails that meet. When it's set to Weld, Revit will miter all rail connections. In most cases, Weld will only be successful when mitering rails along one axis and will not produce a meaningful result in a situation where rails need to miter in two directions, such as the inner rail joins on a stair landing (Figure 5.29). When it's set to Trim, Revit will cut back any rail connection that it cannot miter in one axis.

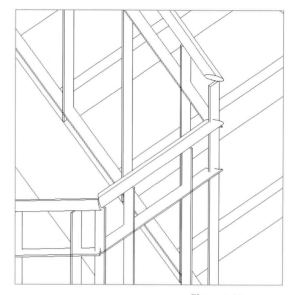

Use Landing Height Adjustment

This parameter lets you specify the height of the railing at a landing independently from the properties of the rail structure. Using this parameter, you can raise or lower the railing at landings. You can specify a positive or negative value. This setting is helpful for cleaning up complex join conditions such as at the inner turns of U-shaped stairs.

Note that when in Sketch mode you will have control over individual rail joins. The Edit Rail Joins tool found in the Options bar while editing the railing path allows you to select any join in the sketch.

Figure 5.29

Rail connection set to Weld

When a rail join is selected, the tool allows you to specify the join with the following options (Figure 5.30):

ByType When the Rail Join property is set to Type, any of the three following options defined as a type property can apply.

Figure 5.30

Options for individual rail joins

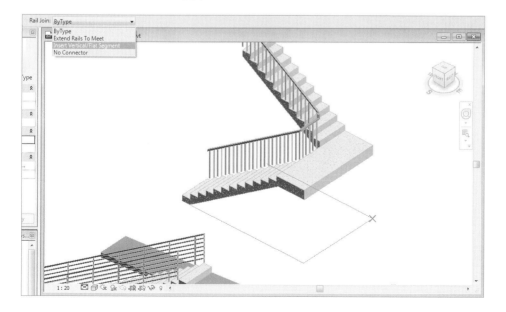

Extend Rails To Meet When the Rail Join property is enabled, Revit will try to create railing elements that connect the individual rail elements of each stair run.

Insert Vertical/Flat Segment When the Rail Join property is set to Extend Rails To Meet, Revit will try to create railing elements that connect the individual rail elements of each stair run using horizontal and flat (vertical) elements only.

No Connector Setting the Rail Join property to No Connector will result in Revit not creating a rail element between the individual railings of each stair run.

Advanced Settings for Railings

Railings are the single most complex building component in Revit. So far we have covered the most important properties of railings that you must set correctly to achieve the results you want in situations where railings are commonly used.

We will provide an in-depth description of all railing properties in order to help you grasp how these properties affect the composition and behavior of railings in Revit.

Balusters: Main Pattern

In the Railing Type Properties, Edit Baluster Placement offers control over all aspects of the railings baluster pattern. The number of options can easily be overwhelming. In this section we will explain the basic concepts of baluster placement and examine some of the advanced features.

Figure 5.31 shows a railing that uses two different baluster families—one for the vertical posts and another one for the cross wire section of the railing

The Main Pattern section of the Edit Baluster Placement dialog box is the primary editor for placement of balusters (Figure 5.32).

Delete, Duplicate, Up, and Down let you control individual balusters used in a particular railing type.

Figure 5.31

Railing sample

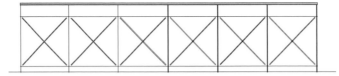

Figure 5.32

Main Pattern section

The individual columns of the Main Pattern grid control offer the following settings:

Name The name of the baluster, useful for identifying individual balusters in complex railing types.

Baluster Family The family used for a specific baluster; the drop-down list will list all loaded baluster families in a project.

Base Allows you to select a base reference for the baluster. This setting will show all the rails available in the railing type as well as the host of the railing.

Base Offset This value determines the offset of the baluster to the base specified in Base.

Top Allows you to select a top reference for the baluster. This setting will show all the rails available in the railing type as well as the host of the railing.

Top Offset This value determines the offset of the baluster to the top of the railing specified in Top.

Distance From Previous Allows you to place balusters at a defined distance from one another. You need to know the dimensions of the balusters involved before setting this value. These values are required to properly define the space between the balusters. The sum of all values in the Distance From Previous column must add up to the value defined in Pattern Length (Figure 5.33).

Offset This value defines the lateral offset of a given baluster to the centerline of the railing (Figure 5.34).

Figure 5.33

Distance From Previous

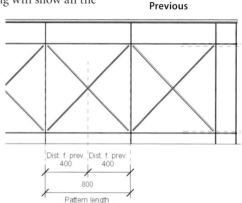

Figure 5.34

Offset value set to 2″ (50mm)

Justify

The way in which the values in the Distance From Previous column work also depends on the Justify setting. Revit offers the choice of four ways to justify the balusters: Beginning, End, Center, and Spread Pattern To Fit.

In the example in Figure 5.35, the pattern length is 4′ (600mm), the entire railing is 10′ (3000mm) long, and Justification is set to Beginning. The result is a remaining field of 2′ equals 10′ (3000mm) minus 2 times 4′ (2400mm).

Figure 5.35

Justification set to Beginning

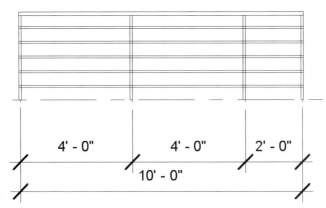

The options for Center and End will work accordingly. The option for Spread Pattern To Fit, though, works differently; here Revit will try to find the closest match of number of balusters per given railing length and then attempt to spread the pattern. In the sample in Figure 5.36, we extended the railing length to 11′ (3300mm) and set the Option To Spread pattern to Fit.

Figure 5.36

Justification set to Spread Pattern To Fit

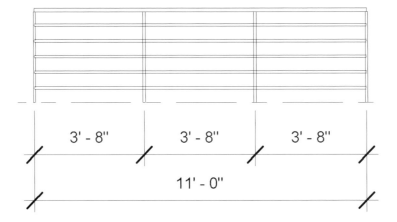

Revit has now adjusted the pattern length to 3′-8″ (1100mm). In cases where a railing is set up to use a baluster family with a fixed baluster length (such as in Figure 5.36), the railing segment length needs to be exactly a multiple of the pattern length to avoid gaps at the beginning or end of the railing. In cases where it is impossible to create the railing with segment lengths that are an exact multiple of the baluster length, Revit offers a solution: Excess Length Fill.

For Excess Length Fill you can choose None, Truncate Pattern, or any loaded baluster families. In the sample in Figure 5.37, we set the value to Baluster: Rectangular 1/4″×1″ (25×100mm)and the spacing to 4″ (100mm). You can set the spacing using the Spacing input field next to the Excess Length Fill drop-down list.

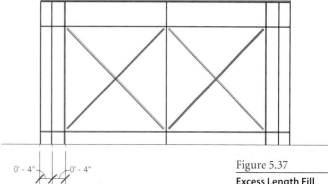

Figure 5.37
Excess Length Fill

The truncate pattern option can only be applied if the axis distance between the last post and the baluster is bigger than the baluster pattern length.

Break Pattern At

There are also options for how the Main pattern should start. The three options offered are:

Each Segment End Revit will create a Main pattern for each segment of the sketch of the railing.

Angle Greater Than Revit will only start a new Main pattern at segments that start at an angle greater than the one specified. You can specify the angle using the Angle input field next to the Break Angle At drop-down list.

Never Revit will attempt to create the entire length of the railing with one Main pattern. This option will not create meaningful results if the segment length differs too far from multiples of the Main pattern length. Figure 5.38 shows such a situation: Revit cannot create a valid solution for the corner when Break Pattern At is set to Never.

Figure 5.38
Break Pattern At set to Never

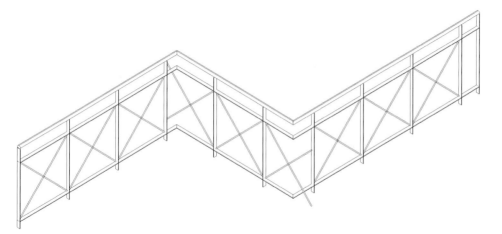

Use Balusters Per Tread On Stairs

Figure 5.39

Use Baluster Per Tread On Stairs

With Use Balusters Per Tread On Stairs, you can specify the number of balusters per tread on stairs as well as specify the baluster family. Figure 5.39 shows the same railing family used flat and hosted by a stair. The Use Baluster Per Tread On Stairs parameter is set to 1 and Baluster: Rectangular 6′ (45mm) is used.

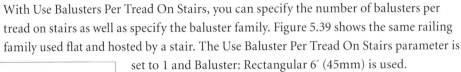

The following section will explain the properties found in the lower Posts section of the Edit Baluster Placement dialog box.

Posts

The Posts section of the Edit Baluster Placement dialog box allows you to define start posts, end posts, and corner posts for the railing. The options for the individual columns offer settings similar to the Main Pattern section:

Name The name of the post. The value is defined by Revit as Start Post, Corner Post, or End Post.

Baluster Family The baluster family used for a specific post; it will list all loaded baluster families in a project.

Base Allows you to select a base reference for the post. This option will show all the rails available in the railing type as well as the host of the railing.

Base Offset This value determines the offset of the post to the base specified in Base.

Top Allows you to select a top reference for the post. This option will show all the rails available in the railing type as well as the host of the railing.

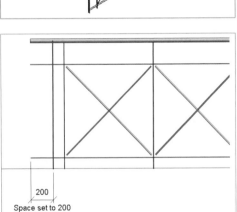

Figure 5.40

Space setting in Posts properties

Top offset This value determines the offset of the post to the top of the railing specified in Top.

Space The value in the Space column defines the distance of the post centerline to the railing viewed in a longitudinal direction (Figure 5.40).

Offset The value chosen for Offset defines the lateral offset of the post to the rail position (Figure 5.41).

Railing Sketch: Advanced Options

When you're sketching the railing, Revit offers tools for slope and height correction, as shown in Figure 5.42. You can find these settings in Revit's Options bar when creating a railing sketch. To see these settings, you must have a railing sketch line selected.

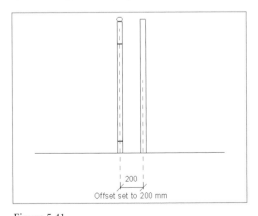

Figure 5.41

Offset setting in Posts properties

Slope Allows you to define whether the segment is horizontal or sloped in respect to the host. These settings can be found in the left drop-down list in Revit's Options bar when you're creating a railing sketch:

> **By Host** The host defines the slope of the railing.
>
> **Flat** The slope defaults to horizontal.
>
> **Sloped** The slope is set to a defined slope.

Height Correction Height Correction allows you to override the railing height set in the Railing Type Properties. These settings can be found in the right drop-down list in Revit's Options bar when you're creating a railing sketch:

> **By Type** The railing height for the selected segment will derive from the height set in the type properties of the railing.
>
> **Custom** Allows you to change the height to a different value and thus override the railing height.

Slope and Height Correction allow you to emulate railings following the top of a wall. In Figure 5.43 we used Slope and Height Correction to allow the railing to follow the top of the wall.

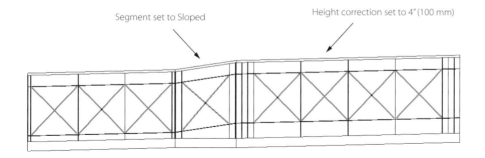

Segment set to Sloped

Height correction set to 4" (100 mm)

Figure 5.42

Slope and Height Correction settings

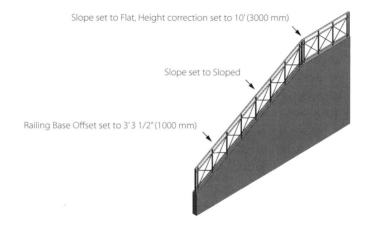

Figure 5.43

Railing on top of a wall

Slope set to Flat, Height correction set to 10' (3000 mm)

Slope set to Sloped

Railing Base Offset set to 3'3 1/2" (1000 mm)

Creating Ramps

Revit allows you to create different styles of ramps, including straight ramps, ramps with landings, and spiral ramps. As with stairs, when ramps are created in Revit, the railings are automatically created for the ramps. The overall workflow for creating ramps is similar to that for creating stairs.

To create ramps, you need to be in a plan or 3D view. You click the start point of the ramp, and Revit will automatically calculate the required length of the ramp, based on the distance between the levels and the maximum length between landings as well as the maximum incline defined in the type properties. Revit will generate a rectangle representing a preview footprint of the ramp. As you move the mouse pointer, the rectangle adjusts accordingly. If you move the mouse pointer outside of the end preview footprint and click, Revit will create the ramp.

When creating ramps, you begin by creating a sketch of the start and end points of the ramp. As with stairs, ramps have two Sketch modes: Run and Boundary And Riser. Sketching a run is the easiest method. As you sketch the run, the boundaries are generated automatically. After you finish sketching and create the ramp, the railing is automatically added. With the Run tool, you are limited to straight runs, straight runs with landings, and spiral ramps. When you create a stair using the Boundary And Riser mode, there are only two methods: Run and Boundary And Riser. Two separate tools are used to define the ramp. To create a ramp, you define the boundary start and end. You use this method when you want more control when sketching the footprint of your ramp.

Although both methods bear a great number of similarities to the workflow used to create a stair, there are a few fundamental differences. To help you understand those differences, we will take a look at the most important type properties of ramps.

Parameters for Ramps

There are four type properties that will significantly determine the shape of a ramp in Revit:

Shape This property can be found in the Other section of the Type Properties dialog box.

Possible values for Shape are either Thick or Solid:

- Thick will create a ramp with constant thickness as defined in the Thickness parameter setting.
- Solid will ignore the value set for thickness and create a wedge-shaped ramp with a flat surface at the bottom level (Figure 5.44).

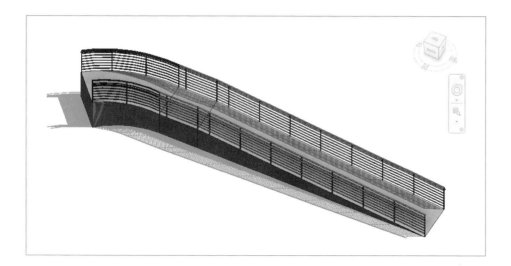

Figure 5.44
Solid ramp

Ramp Max Slope (1/x) This property can be found in the Other section of the Type Properties dialog box. The setting for this parameter will define the maximum possible slope the ramp can have. The value needs to be set as a fraction. For example, an input value of 12 will result in setting Slope to 1/12 and will create a ramp that will rise 1″ (25mm) for every 1′ (2500mm) horizontal running length. That means the smaller the number, the steeper the ramp will be. Revit will use this value together with the value for Maximum Incline Length to determine the length of each run of the ramp while sketching.

Maximum Incline Length This property can be found in the Dimensions section of the Type Properties dialog box. This setting determines the maximum length for each run of a ramp before a flat (horizontal) section needs to be inserted.

Thickness This property can be found in the Construction section of the Type Properties dialog box. It determines the thickness of the ramp when Shape is set to Thick (Figure 5.45).

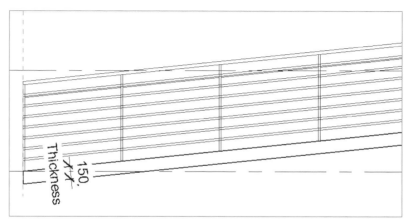

Figure 5.45
Ramp thickness

Creating a Straight Ramp

The process of creating a straight ramp is very similar to creating a stair. We will introduce you to sketching a ramp consisting of two inclined parts and a horizontal part connecting them as well as show how to change its construction using instance and type properties.

1. From the book's companion download files (available at www.sybex.com/go/introducingrevit2012), open the file Dataset_05_05.rvt [Dataset_05_05.rvt_metric].

2. Open the Level 1 floor plan.

3. On the Home tab's Circulation panel, click the Ramp button.

4. On the Modify | Create Ramp Sketch tab's Draw panel, click the Run button.

5. In the Draw panel, click the Line tool.

6. Click on the intersection of the reference planes where the annotation indicates the start of the first part of the ramp.

7. Move the mouse pointer to where the annotation indicates the start of the landing and click again (Figure 5.46).

8. Click where the annotation indicates the start of the second part of the ramp (Figure 5.47).

9. Drag the mouse pointer to where the annotation indicates the end of the second part of the ramp and click again.

10. Click the Finish Edit Mode button to create the ramp. Revit creates the ramp, as shown in Figure 5.48.

Figure 5.46

Defining the first part of a straight ramp

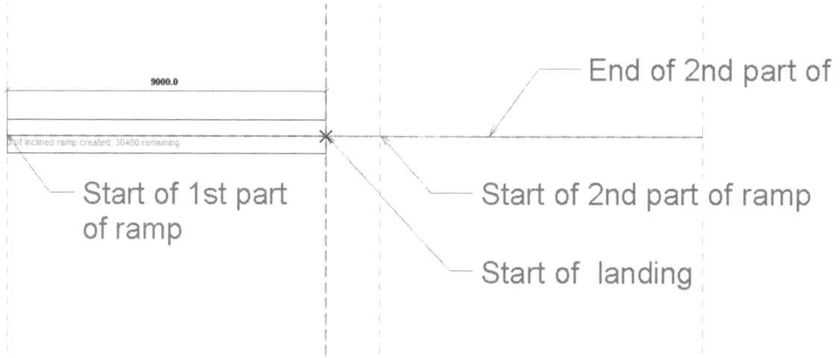

Figure 5.47

Defining the second part of a straight ramp

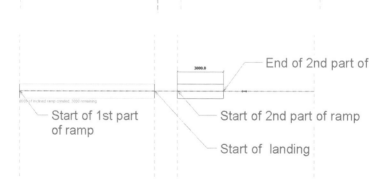

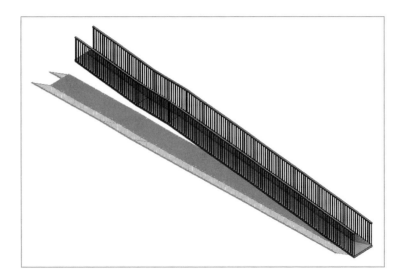

Figure 5.48

Finished ramp

Advanced Techniques for Sketching a Ramp

The following will illustrate how to create a vehicle ramp with a 180-degree turn. We will first start to construct a ramp that consists of two inclined parts and a horizontal part connecting them that will represent the turn:

1. Prepare a ramp type that will allow you to create a ramp long enough to connect two levels 9′ 10 ⅛″ [3,000 mm] apart with one single run. To do so:

   Set the Maximum Incline length to 150′ [46,000 mm].

   Set the Ramp Max Slope (1/x) to 10 (see Figure 5.49).

2. Sketch the first run of the ramp, and draw a 49′ 2 ½″ [15,000 mm] long run (Figure 5.50).

3. Draw the second run in opposite direction.

   Revit assumes that you want to place a flat segment whenever you create ramps out of multiple runs. For now, don't worry about the curve you want to place but continue with the straight second segment. In the example shown, the center lines of the inclined parts of the ramp are 24′-7½″ [7,350 mm] apart (Figure 5.51).

Figure 5.49

Type Properties for vehicle ramp

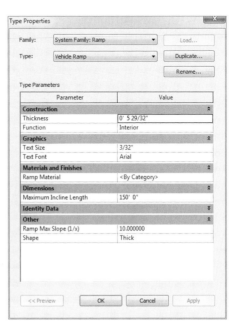

After you place the second run, Revit will automatically provide a solution for the flat segment of the ramp, as shown in Figure 5.52.

4. Since you want a curve between the two segments, erase the boundary lines of the flat segment so that you can sketch a curve (Figure 5.53).

5. Sketch the curve by using Start-End-Radius Arcs to create the inner and outer curves (Figure 5.54).

The result is a ramp with two inclined segments and a flat curve (Figure 5.55).

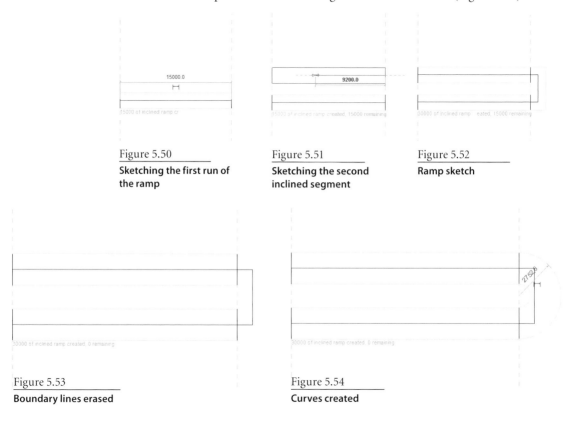

Figure 5.50

Sketching the first run of the ramp

Figure 5.51

Sketching the second inclined segment

Figure 5.52

Ramp sketch

Figure 5.53

Boundary lines erased

Figure 5.54

Curves created

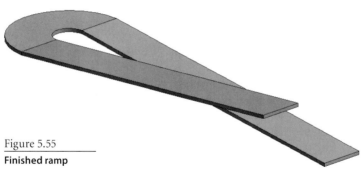

Figure 5.55

Finished ramp

If you now want the ramp to be continuously inclined along the entire length, you need to do the sketch again. Since Revit assumes a flat segment between any inclined segments of the ramp, follow these steps:

1. First sketch a ramp that consists of a straight incline, a short straight flat segment, an inclined curve, and again, a short flat straight segment and the final inclined segment, as shown in Figure 5.56.

   The intention is to have the inclined curve created by Revit and to remove the horizontal flat straight segments afterward to create a ramp continuously inclined along its entire length.

Figure 5.56

Initial sketch

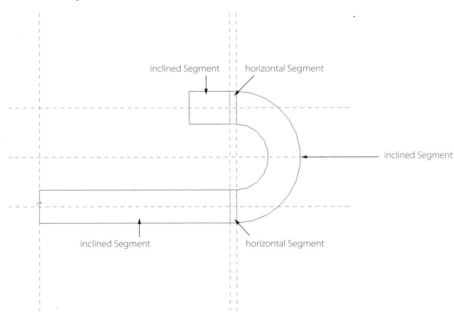

inclined Segment   horizontal Segment

inclined Segment

inclined Segment   horizontal Segment

While still in Sketch mode, you will now reduce the length of the flat segments to zero.

2. For each flat straight segment, select the riser lines of the straight segments at the left side of the straight segment, and drag them toward the end of the curved segment.

3. Revit will warn you that the boundary lines are now too short. Dismiss the warning by clicking Delete Element(s) (Figure 5.57).

   The result is a ramp with a continuous incline along its path, as shown in Figure 5.58.

Figure 5.57

Removing the flat ramp segments

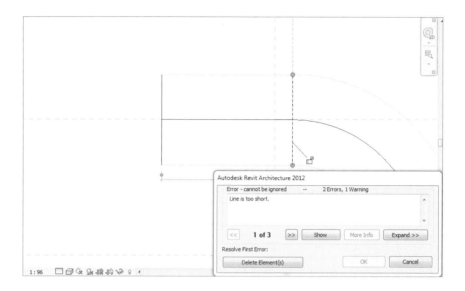

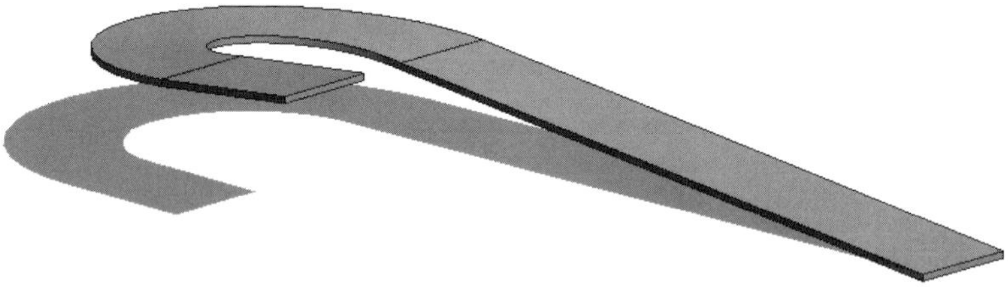

Figure 5.58

Resulting ramp

Figure 5.59

Example of a curtain wall

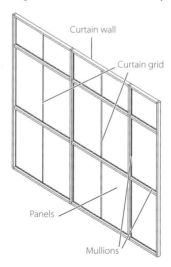

Creating Curtain Walls

Curtain walls in Revit are vertical panelized wall systems that are attached to the building structure but do not carry any floor or roof loads of the building. A typical curtain wall consists of panels, curtain grids, and mullions, as shown in Figure 5.59. Each of these curtain wall elements can be edited individually. Curtain walls come in two different varieties: curtain wall and curtain systems.

Curtain walls are drawn in a similar manner to walls. Curtain walls consist of panels that are divided by grid lines. These panels can consist of different materials, and mullions of specific shapes, sizes, and materials can be placed on grid lines to represent actual mullions. When you draw a curtain wall, Revit will create either a single panel that is extended the length of the wall or a panel that is subdivided into several panels based on the curtain wall type.

A curtain system is a component that consists of panels, grids, and mullions and is not normally rectangular in shape. Curtain systems are created by using faces from other geometry, such as masses. This approach allows for more complex forms such as sloped and curved.

Revit provides three curtain wall types:

Curtain Wall This is a single panel with no grids or mullions. This type of curtain wall has no rules associated with it and provides the most flexibility.

Exterior Glazing This type has predefined grids that can be adjusted.

Storefront This type has predefined grids and mullions that can be adjusted.

The curtain wall types are shown in Figure 5.60. You can access these types from the Type Selector when you are using the Wall tool.

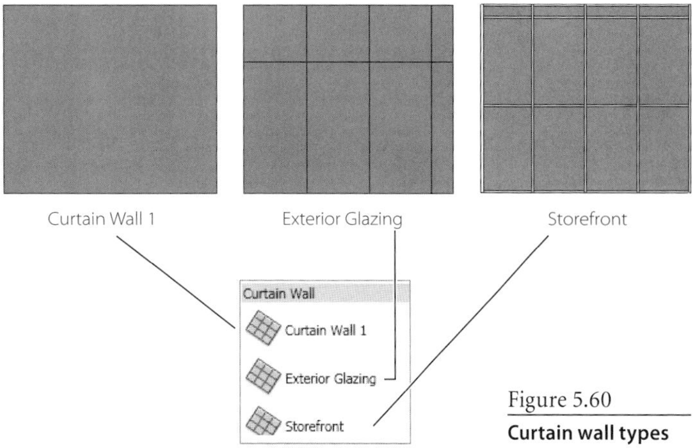

When you create a curtain wall using the Wall tool and select the Curtain Wall 1 type, the curtain wall is created as a single panel. You then use the Curtain Grid tool (go to the Home tab's Build panel and click Curtain Grid) to define the curtain grid system. You will create your first curtain wall using the Wall tool:

Curtain Wall 1   Exterior Glazing   Storefront

Curtain Wall

Curtain Wall 1

Exterior Glazing

Storefront

Figure 5.60
Curtain wall types

1. Start a new project using the default template, and make sure you are on the Level 1 floor plan.

2. On the Home tab's Build panel, click the Wall tool.

3. In the Properties palette's Type Selector, click Curtain Wall: Curtain Wall 1.

4. On the Options bar, set the height to Unconnected with a height value of 17′-0″ [5,200 mm] and deselect the Chain check box.

5. In the drawing window, click the start point and drag the end point to create a wall 30′-0″ [9,150 mm] long.

6. Switch to a 3D view by clicking the Default 3D View button on the Quick Access toolbar.

7. On the View Control bar, set the visual style to Shaded With Edges.

Figure 5.61
Curtain wall panel

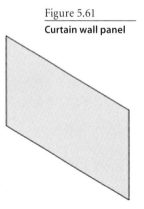

When you create a curtain wall using the Curtain Wall 1 type, Revit creates a single panel, as shown in Figure 5.61. To make this single panel look and behave like a curtain wall, you need to add curtain grids and then apply mullions to those grid lines. You can manually or automatically place the grid lines.

You will now add your horizontal grid lines by adjusting the type properties of the wall. Table 5.1 describes some of the curtain wall type properties that you will be working with.

1. Select the curtain wall panel you just created.

2. In the Properties palette, click Edit Type.

3. In the Type Properties dialog box, click the Duplicate button.

4. Name the new type **My First Curtain Wall**, and click OK.

Table 5.1	NAME	DESCRIPTION
Curtain Wall 1 Type Properties	Function	Purpose of the wall: Interior, Exterior, Retaining, Foundation, Soffit, or Core-Shaft
	Automatically Embed	Determines whether the curtain wall automatically embeds into the wall
	Curtain Panel	Sets the curtain panel family type for the curtain element
	Join Condition	Controls how the mullions join at an intersection
	Layout	Sets the automatic horizontal and vertical layout for the curtain grid lines
	Spacing	Specifies the grid line spacing
	Adjust for Mullion Size	When enabled, automatically ensures panels are of equal size
	Interior Type	Specifies mullion family for interior mullions
	Border 1 Type	Specifies mullion family for vertical mullions on the left border
	Border 2 Type	Specifies mullion family for vertical mullions on the right border

Remember, when you make a change to a type property, it impacts all instances of that type. So, it is a good idea to create new types rather than editing the default types that ship with Revit.

5. Make the following change to the type properties:

   Curtain Panel: System Panel : Glazed

   Horizontal Grid Pattern: Layout: Fixed Distance

   Horizontal Grid Pattern: Spacing: 5′ 0″ [1500 mm]

   Adjust For Mullion Size: Checked

6. Click OK to close the Type Properties dialog box.

Your curtain wall is now divided into four panels, as shown in Figure 5.62.

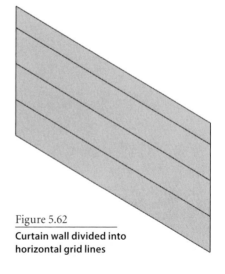

Figure 5.62

Curtain wall divided into horizontal grid lines

To create the vertical grid lines, you will use the Curtain Grid tool:

1. On the Home tab's Build panel, click Curtain Grid.

   The Modify | Place Curtain Grid tab will be displayed, and the last panel, Placement (Figure 5.63), will provide you with three options for defining your curtain grids:

   All Segments Places a grid segment on all panels. A preview is provided to aid in placement.

   One Segment Places one grid segment on one panel. A preview is provided to aid in placement.

   All Except Picked Places a grid segment on all panels except those you choose to exclude.

2. From the Placement panel, select a placement type.

3. Move the mouse pointer along the edge of the curtain panel.

4. A temporary grid line with dimensions will be displayed, allowing you to preview the placement. Click to place the grid line.

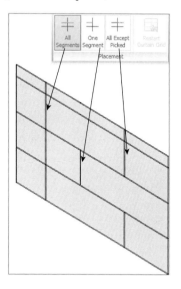

Figure 5.63

Curtain grid placement options

Modifying Curtain Wall Grids

Curtain wall grids are created in one of two methods: automatic and manual. When you edit the type properties of a curtain wall, this will create an automatic curtain grid. Curtain walls created in this manner are known as an *automatic curtain grid*. The vertical and horizontal grid pattern parameters are used to divide the curtain wall with the user-defined number of grid lines. The position of the curtain grids in an automatic curtain grid remain fixed if the length or height of the wall is modified. The wall types Curtain Wall Exterior Glazing and Curtain Wall Storefront are examples of curtain walls that use the automatic curtain grid.

If the Curtain Grid tool was used to manually create curtain grid lines in your curtain wall manually, then that curtain wall uses the manual curtain grids.

Modifying Automatic Curtain Grids

Modifying the curtain wall grid is a straightforward process once you unpin the grid lines.

When you create a curtain wall in Revit, the grid lines automatically have their position pinned or locked in place so that you do not accidentally adjust them during the editing process.

In Figure 5.64, we have clicked a grid line, and in addition to the temporary dimensions, there is a small icon that resembles the head of a pushpin.

Figure 5.64

Curtain grid with pushpin locking the grid line

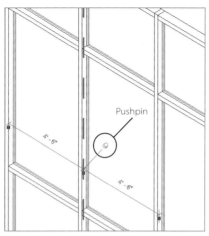

The pushpin is a control that provides a quick way to either allow or prevent changes to an element's location. You use the Pin Position to lock a modeling component in place. When you pin a modeling component, it cannot be moved. If you try to delete a pinned component, Revit warns you that the component is pinned. A pushpin control appears near the element to indicate that it is locked.

If you pin a component, it can still move if the component is set to move with nearby elements or if the level where it is placed moves up or down.

1. From the book's companion download files (available at www.sybex.com/go/introducingrevit2012), open the file Dataset_05_06.rvt [Dataset_05_06_metric.rvt].

2. Switch to the {3D} 3D view, and select one of the curtain grid lines that you want to modify.

    You are modifying a storefront curtain wall, which contains grids, panels, and mullions. If you are having trouble selecting a grid, move your mouse pointer over a grid line, and press the Tab key to cycle through available selection options. The status bar at the bottom-left corner of the Revit window displays which element is ready for selection.

3. Click the pushpin to unlock the curtain grid line.

4. Move the grid as desired. This can be done either by dragging the grid to a new location or by editing the temporary dimension (Figure 5.65).

Figure 5.65

Automatic curtain grid unlocked and grid relocated

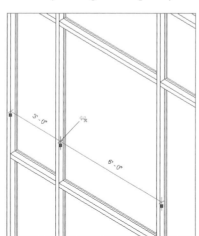

At any time, you can return a modified automatic curtain grid line to its original location by clicking the pushpin with the red X (Figure 5.66).

Figure 5.66

Clicking the pushpin with the red X (gray in this image) will return the automatic curtain grid line to the original location.

Modifying Manual Curtain Grids

Modifying a manual curtain grid is a straightforward process:

1. From the book's companion download files (available at www.sybex.com/go/ introducingrevit2012), open the file Dataset_05_07.rvt [Dataset_05_07_metric.rvt].

2. Switch to the {3D} 3D view, and select one of the curtain grid lines that you want to modify.

3. Click the pushpin to unlock the curtain grid line.

4. Move the grid as desired. You can do so either by dragging the grid to a new location or by editing the temporary dimension.

At any time, you can return a modified automatic curtain grid line to its original location by clicking the pushpin with the red X.

Adding Mullions

Once you have created a curtain wall grid, you can then add mullions to the grid. The nice thing about mullions in Revit is that they will automatically resize to fit your grid. When placing mullions, if you add a mullion to an inside grid, then the mullion is centered on the grid. If you add a mullion to the perimeter grid, the mullion will align itself so its border is flush with the outside of the wall.

1. From the book's companion download files (available at www.sybex.com/go/ introducingrevit2012), open the file Dataset_05_08.rvt [Dataset_05_08_metric.rvt].

2. Switch to the {3D} 3D view.

3. On the Home tab's Build panel, click the Mullion button.

4. In the Properties palette, select the Rectangular Mullion 1.5″ × 2.5″ rectangular [30 x 60 mm – rectangular] in the Type Selector.

5. On the Modify | Place Mullion tab's Placement panel, click the Grid Line button.

6. In the drawing window, move the mouse pointer over one of the vertical grid lines, and click to place the mullion.

7. Continue to add mullions to the six remaining vertical mullions (Figure 5.67).

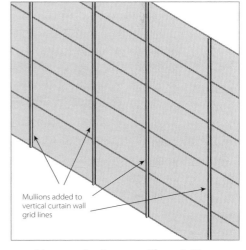

Mullions added to vertical curtain wall grid lines

Figure 5.67

Mullions added to vertical grid lines

In the next few steps, you will create a new mullion type for the top and bottom horizontal curtain wall grid lines:

1. With the Place Mullion tools active, click the Edit Type button in the Properties palette.

2. In the Type Properties dialog box, click the Duplicate button.

3. In the Name dialog box, enter **6″ × 6″ rectangular** [150 x 150 mm – rectangular] for the new Type name, and click OK.

4. In the Type Properties dialog box, enter the following under Dimensions:
   - Width On Side 2: **3″** [75 mm]
   - Width On Side 1: **3″** [75 mm]

5. Click OK to close the Type Properties dialog box.

6. On the Modify | Place Mullion tab's Placement panel, click the Grid Line button.

7. Ensure that the 6″ × 6″ rectangular [150 x 150 mm rectangular] mullion is active in the Type Selector.

8. In the drawing window, move the mouse pointer over the bottom horizontal curtain wall grid line, and click to place the mullion. Repeat for the top horizontal curtain wall grid line.

You now need to add a 1.5″ × 1.5″ mullion to the remaining horizontal mullions:

1. With the Place Mullion tools active, click the Edit Type button in the Properties palette.

2. In the Type Properties dialog box, click the Duplicate button.

3. In the name dialog box, enter **1.5″×1.5″ rectangular [40×40 mm – rectangular]**, and click OK.

4. In the Type Properties dialog box, enter the following under Dimensions:
   - Width On Side 2: **3/4″ [20 mm]**
   - Width On Side 1: **3/4″ [20 mm]**

5. Click OK to close the Type Properties dialog box.

6. On the Modify | Place Mullion tab's Placement panel, click the Grid Line button.

7. Ensure that the 1.5″×1.5″ rectangular [40 x 40 mm rectangular] mullion is active in the Type Selector.

8. In the drawing window, move the mouse pointer over one of the remaining horizontal curtain wall grid lines, and click to place the mullion.

9. Repeat for the remaining horizontal curtain wall grid lines (Figure 5.68).

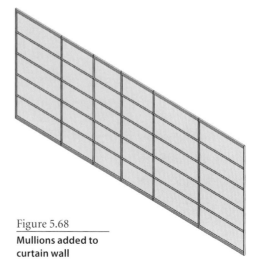

Figure 5.68

Mullions added to curtain wall

Adding a Door to a Curtain Wall

As you work with your curtain wall, you will need to place a door or change a panel from glazed to solid. A curtain wall, however, does not allow you to use the Door tool like you would if you were working with a basic wall type. With a curtain wall, you need to swap out a wall panel for a door panel. The first thing you need to do is load a door panel from the Revit library. Then you will need to remove a mullion and grid line to accommodate your door. Finally, you will modify a row of panels.

To load a door panel, follow these steps:

1. From the book's companion download files (available at www.sybex.com/go/introducingrevit2012), open the file Dataset_05_09.rvt [Dataset_05_09_metric.rvt].

2. On the Insert tab, click Load Family.

3. In the Doors folder of the default Revit library, select Curtain Wall Dbl Glass.rfa [M_Curtain Wall Dbl Glass.rfa] (which is also included as part of the companion files), and then click Open.

   The family will then be loaded into your project.

4. Switch to the {3D} 3D view.

   You need to remove the two mullions and one grid line, as indicated in Figure 5.69.

5. Select the two mullions, and delete them. You can do this individually or both at the same time.

   You can now delete the curtain wall grid line.

6. Select the curtain wall grid line. This will be the second grid line from the bottom.

7. On the Modify | Curtain Walls Grids tab's Curtain Grid panel, click the Add/Remove Segments button.

8. Click the curtain wall grid line, and the grid line will be deleted (Figure 5.70).

   You can now replace the panel with your curtain wall door.

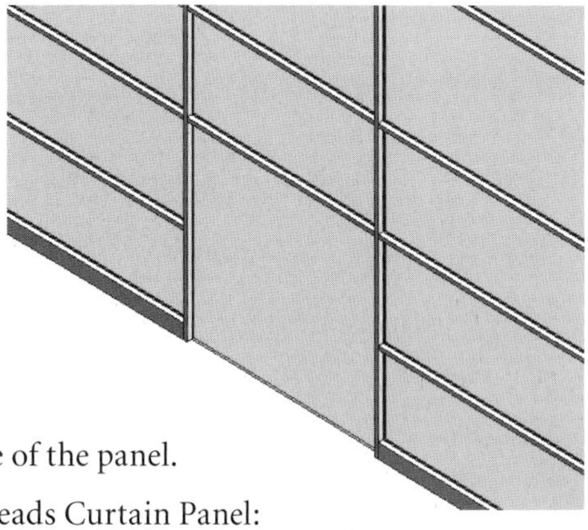

9. Select the glazed panel by placing the mouse pointer over an edge of the panel.

10. Press the Tab key repeatedly, and monitor the status bar until it reads Curtain Panel: System Panel: Glazed and the panel is highlighted; then click.

11. In the Properties palette, click the Type Selector drop-down, and select the Curtain Wall Dbl Glass element.

    The Glazed panel has now been replaced with the Double Doors. In the next step, you will swap out the entire row of glazed panels above the door with a solid panel.

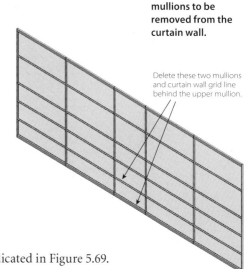

Figure 5.69

Select the indicated mullions to be removed from the curtain wall.

Delete these two mullions and curtain wall grid line behind the upper mullion.

Figure 5.70

Curtain wall with mullions and grid line removed

12. Select the glazed panel above the double doors.

13. In the Properties palette, click the Type Selector drop-down, and select the System Panel Solid element.

14. Repeat step 12 for all the glazed panels in the row above the door (Figure 5.71).

Figure 5.71

Completed curtain wall

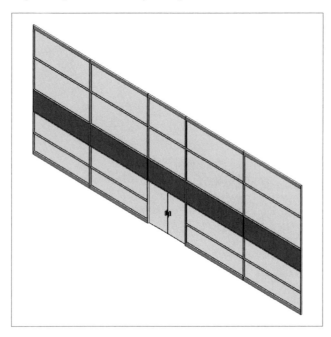

TAB KEY

You can press the Tab key for a wide variety of time-saving techniques. One of the uses is for object selection. You can use the Tab key to cycle through objects that either overlap or are close enough together to cause selection difficulties. When trying to select an object, move your mouse pointer over one of the objects. Revit will highlight the object and provide information about the object in the status bar. Hitting the Tab key will allow you to cycle through other nearby objects.

Exterior Glazing and Storefront

In the next example, you will embed a storefront curtain wall into the sample project:

1. From the book's companion download files (available at www.sybex.com/go/introducingrevit2012), open the file Dataset_05_10.rvt [Dataset_05_10_metric.rvt].

   In the next step, you will use the Split Element tool to divide the wall into three segments.

2. On the Modify tab, click the Split Element tool (Figure 5.72).

3. Click on the wall in two places to divide a wall into three segments.

The middle wall segment should be longer than the two other segments. You will then switch the middle wall segment to a Storefront wall type.

Figure 5.72

Locating the Split Element tool on the Modify tab to split a wall

4. Press the Esc key to exit the Split Element tool.

5. Switch to a 3D view.

6. Select the middle wall segment.

7. In the Properties palette's Type Selector, change the wall type to Walls: Curtain Wall: Storefront (Figure 5.73).

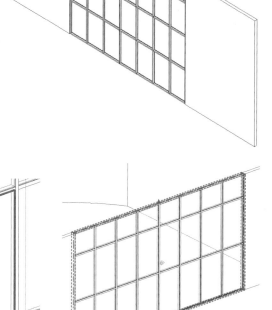

Figure 5.73

Wall with storefront

Now that you have created a couple of basic curtain walls, let's explore modifying the grid and placing mullions. Select the Storefront curtain wall. When selecting a curtain wall, you have four object selection options (Figure 5.74):

• Mullions

• Curtain Wall Grids

• Curtain Wall Panels

• Entire Curtain Wall

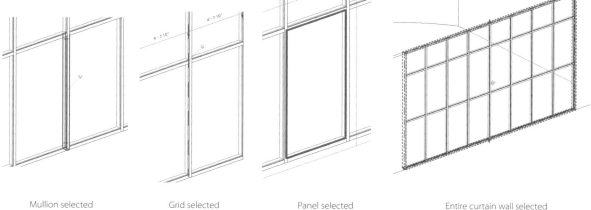

Mullion selected   Grid selected   Panel selected   Entire curtain wall selected

Figure 5.74

Curtain wall selection examples

Make sure that you select the entire curtain wall. Use the Tab key to cycle between objects until you find the entire curtain. Use the status bar to help identify what object is selected.

Figure 5.75

**Type properties
for the Storefront
curtain wall**

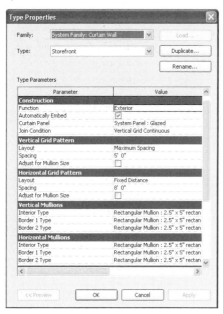

With the Storefront selected, open the Storefront type properties (Figure 5.75). Through the Type Properties dialog box, you can modify the grid pattern and mullions.

CHAPTER 6

Visibility Controls

We all want control. A design document has a purpose, and how it is prepared either enables or hinders that purpose. Autodesk Revit Architecture has a collection of features and tools that are intended to provide the control you want in order to ensure that your documents fit their purpose. Some tools are exceedingly simple, and others are a bit complicated. Often, the more complicated a tool or feature is, the more granular the control you have becomes. This control not only helps define how well your documents tell their story, but unfortunately it also can create the need to be a very good detective when the plot of the story goes astray.

Chapter 2, "Views," focused on how views work and what you can do with them. This chapter focuses on the appearance of your model within the views of the project, the management of information that you add to views, and the various tools you can use to accomplish these tasks.

This chapter covers the following topics:

- **Essential concepts of visibility**
- **Object styles**
- **Properties palette for views**
- **Visibility/graphics overrides**
- **View range**
- **Filters**
- **View templates**
- **Linked files**
- **Worksets**

Essential Concepts of Visibility

With all the Revit tools at your disposal, four concepts help define just how much control you have. At the highest level, a single change will have far-reaching implications, usually affecting the entire project. Although efficient and fast, this kind of control is usually a bit too general and will leave you wanting for exceptions. At the lowest level you will find it possible to affect individual items so that you have a great deal of control.

The following are the four important visibility control concepts:

Global vs. Local When you need to change something, you have to choose whether you want that change to happen in all views or in an individual view instead. You must keep this in mind as you work. Revit's tools are intended to let you balance your desire to do something fast and globally against your need to deal with very specific exceptions locally. You use the Object Styles feature to manage the appearance of elements globally. You use the Visibility/Graphics Overrides dialog box to manage this locally.

Category vs. Element Once you begin to focus on the local level, you find that the global/local concept repeats itself, in a way, but with regard to element categories and the elements themselves. The changes you make in individual views (locally) can be applied to an entire category of elements (global) or to an individual element (local). It is simpler to manage elements as a category since it changes many at once. It's more work to deal with elements individually, but it's much more flexible.

It is important to have this kind of flexibility, and most people wouldn't trade it away despite it taking more effort. Ultimately, it is up to you to find the right balance. You manage the visibility and appearance of categories using the Visibility/Graphics Overrides feature. Individual control of elements is accessed either through the ribbon or via context (right-click) menu options. Either route assumes you are selecting an element or elements first and then choosing the action to take.

Hiding vs. Overriding Many times you just want to hide an element simply because you don't want people to see it in a given view. Other times you just need to change (*override*) the appearance of an element, such as to make it lighter or darker or use a dashed line instead of solid. The tools address both naturally. You can hide or override elements by category (which is faster because it affects many at once) or by element (individually, which is slower because you have to select elements first).

When elements are hidden, you may need to find them later or see what someone else has hidden. The Reveal Hidden Elements tool makes it easy to see which elements are affected (Figure 6.1). Elements that have had their appearance overridden are more difficult to assess. You'll have to examine a view carefully to find these and evaluate them.

Figure 6.1

The Reveal Hidden Elements tool

Temporary vs. Permanent By *permanent*, we don't mean that you can't ever alter or restore something later. *Permanent* in this context means that your changes will be persistent and that they will print and export this way until you change them again. When collaborating with other users in the same project, *permanent* also means what they see will be affected by your changes. The use of the word *temporary* in this case means that the changes you make will not affect printing or exporting information. Technically speaking, changing a value and then restoring it shortly thereafter qualifies as a temporary action too, just not what we have in mind here.

Truly temporary changes are limited to the Temporary Hide/Isolate tool on the View Control bar (the "sunglasses" icon, as shown in Figure 6.2). This tool affects only what you see onscreen; it doesn't affect anyone else working on the project and will be reset when you close the project, assuming you haven't already done so.

1/8" = 1'-0"

Figure 6.2

The Temporary Hide/Isolate tool on the View Control bar

If you refer to Figure 6.3, you'll see that you have these four options: Hide Element, Hide Category, Isolate Element, and Isolate Category. You can remove all the temporary changes you've made using Reset Temporary Hide/Isolate. You can choose to make a temporary change permanent using Apply Hide/Isolate To View. It isn't possible to reset just one or a few of the elements that have been temporarily hidden/isolated. Everything affected by the tool will be restored.

Figure 6.3

The other Temporary Hide/Isolate options

Apply Hide/Isolate to View
Isolate Category
Hide Category
Isolate Element
Hide Element
Reset Temporary Hide/Isolate

Object Styles

Returning to the notion of global settings or behavior, object styles are defined in a project template and determine how all elements will appear in all views initially. This is an essential part of implementing Revit well in your practice. You can open the Object Styles dialog box from the Settings panel of the Manage tab of the ribbon. This dialog box contains four tabs: Model Objects, Annotation Objects, Analytical Model Objects, and Imported Objects (see Figure 6.4). All the categories that are defined by Revit are listed in the Category column, and the settings you control for each are Line Weight for Projection and Cut, Line Color, Line Pattern, and Material. The available settings vary slightly for each tab, but the purpose for each is the same, which is

Figure 6.4

The Object Styles dialog box

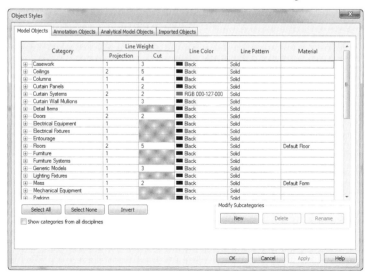

to give you a way to decide how your model, annotation, and imported elements should look as a rule.

Quite often, you can resolve any dissatisfaction you might have about how your documents look initially by making relatively minor adjustments in the Object Styles dialog box. Each category has subcategories, and you can adjust these too. For example, the way a door panel appears in a plan is configured in the Panel subcategory, as shown in Figure 6.5. Just remember, these are global settings that affect the entire project.

Figure 6.5

A door's Panel subcategory

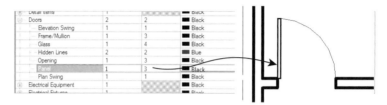

As a practical example, let's assume you are dissatisfied with the way door panels look in a plan view. To increase or decrease the line weight that Revit uses to draw a door's panel, you follow these steps:

1. Open any project file and open a view so you can see at least one door in a floor plan view.

   Alternatively, sketch a couple walls and add some doors in a new project file.

2. Click the Manage tab on the ribbon.

3. On the Settings panel, click the Object Styles button.

4. Scroll the list of categories, and select the Doors category.

5. Click the + symbol next to Doors to expand the list of subcategories.

6. Select the subcategory Panel.

   Notice that you can click in either of the columns for Line Weight—Projection or Cut—and a button appears to let you choose a new line weight.

7. Increase the line weight for Cut: Change it to a higher number (the default is usually 3; try 4 instead).

8. Click Apply.

   If you move the dialog box so you can see the door family, you should see the panel's rectangular lines become thicker.

Remember that earlier we wrote that object styles are for global changes, so this change will affect all the views that show doors in the project, assuming some manner of overrides is not being used.

Properties Palette for Views

The Properties palette provides quick access to a great many view controls. This palette is docked above the Project Browser as its default location. You can move it to other locations and even outside the Revit workspace onto another monitor if one is available to you.

THE VIEW CONTROL BAR AND THE PALETTE

The View Control bar isn't part of the Properties palette, but it complements it, so we'll mention it briefly here. Located at the bottom-left corner of most of the view types, the View Control bar provides fast access to a select few features. It offers access to different features according to the kind of view you are working in (3D versus 2D, which doesn't show up in schedules). It was added to Revit originally to help you avoid the need to open the Properties dialog box. The View Control bar was covered in depth in Chapter 1.

The Properties palette is a relatively recent addition to provide access to element properties; think "information," if that helps (see Figure 6.6). If you keep it open all the time, as the product's designers anticipated you will, you get quick access to a view's properties at either location (View Control bar or Properties palette). Within the Properties palette are buttons that provide access to deeper parts of Revit, which often provide access to still other features; see the Edit buttons in Figure 6.6. It can be a bit labyrinthine. These additional routes to features are provided primarily to save you the hassle of retracing your steps to alter related settings only to have to return to your original agenda afterward.

> Keep in mind that the Properties palette does not always show you buttons that provide access to more information or features until you click in the field. Don't be afraid to click in a field to see if Revit will offer you more options/information.

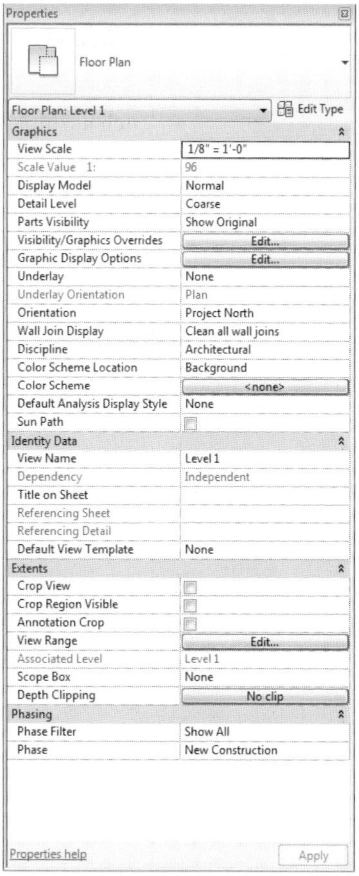

Figure 6.6

The Properties palette for a floor plan view

Graphics Group

Let's examine the first group of features found in the Properties palette for the floor plan view called Floor Plan: Level 1 (as found in a default template), as shown in Figure 6.7. The Graphics group includes the following properties:

View Scale	Underlay Orientation
Scale Value	Orientation
Display Model	Wall Join Display
Detail Level	Discipline
Parts Visibility	Color Scheme Location
Visibility/Graphics Overrides	Color Scheme
Graphic Display Options	Default Analysis Display Style
Underlay	Sun Path

When you examine the properties of other views such as elevations or sections, you'll find another setting, Hide At Scales Coarser Than. When design options are being used, you'll also find the Visible In Option setting. You'll learn more about these in more detail a little later in this section.

Figure 6.7
**Properties palette's
Graphics group**

View Scale and Scale Value

The first two are pretty obvious because of their names, but it may not be obvious that each view defines its own scale (first two rows in Figure 6.7). This means that the model you build in Revit is full size at all times, but you are consistently conscious of an intended drawing scale, or at least Revit is. This helps you determine how well a design will fit on paper.

The field under View Scale, called Scale Value, is the expression of a scale's numeric ratio as opposed to the traditional feet and inches or metric values displayed above it in View Scale. It serves little purpose other than to inform the curious since you can't alter the value here.

Display Model

The Display Model setting has three choices: Normal, Halftone, and Do Not Display (see Figure 6.8):

Normal The first and most common setting is Normal, and this displays the model without bias according to the settings that have been defined in your project's template and the Object Styles dialog box.

Halftone Using Halftone will cause Revit to apply a halftone to the model elements in the view so that you can draft details over the model and let your drafting work take precedence.

Figure 6.8

Display Model property

Do Not Display The last choice, Do Not Display, is intended to hide the model when the drafting exercise produces everything required by the view and the model will only serve as a distraction.

The second two choices allow you to blur the distinction between 2D and the Revit 3D model, where the abstract can take priority over the virtual reality of the building model. The Display Model setting is most commonly used in conjunction with details rather than in conventional floor plans, elevations, or building sections. As with anything, we're sure there are reasonable exceptions to be found that counter this claim.

If you choose to use the Halftone setting, Revit provides some control over the intensity of the effect. It is a global setting, so it will affect halftone used in all views. To adjust it, take the following steps:

1. Click the Manage tab on the ribbon, and on the Settings panel click the Additional Settings button.

2. Click Halftone / Underlay.

   The Halftone frame provides a slider and a numerical option to input a specific value.

3. Adjust this as you see fit, remembering that it affects all views that are using this feature.

   We suggest making a small change and printing to evaluate the result.

4. If you change the setting, you can click the Reset button to restore the default value of 50 percent that Revit uses.

Detail Level

Detail Level is a clever method that allows you to transition between simple and complex or, put another way, between preliminary/schematic design and later design phases (see Figure 6.9). There are three settings: Coarse, Medium, and Fine.

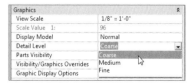

Figure 6.9

Detail Level choices: Coarse, Medium or Fine

Coarse Elements appear at their simplest with a Coarse setting. Walls are shown as just two lines. The same is true for floors, ceilings, and roofs (see Figure 6.10).

Medium A simple switch to Medium will show the additional subtle construction layers of walls, floors, ceilings, and roofs (see Figure 6.10).

Fine The Fine setting has no bearing on walls, floors, roofs, or ceilings, but for other content like doors, windows, or casework, it can have dramatic impact.

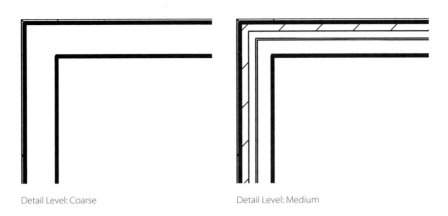

Detail Level: Coarse   Detail Level: Medium

Casework, for example, could show drawer pulls and locking hardware at Fine while showing only door or drawer forms when the view is set to Medium. At Coarse these same cabinets could be simple rectangular forms with little definition.

This feature is also available as part of the Visibility/Graphics Overrides dialog box that can be used to adjust the appearance of individual views. (We'll cover Visibility/Graphics Overrides in more detail in the later section by the same name.) This allows Detail Level to be altered category by category. For example, you may want walls to be represented with only two lines (Coarse) but want to show more detail for structural columns (Medium or Fine).

The ultimate goal is to provide a sophisticated level of display control with a modest amount of effort while working in the project environment. To truly make the most of this feature, you must build the content you use and make yourself with it in mind. This feature is also available for view-specific (local) changes to customize how elements are displayed. We'll revisit this concept in the Family Editor chapters (Chapters 7 and 8) in this book.

Parts Visibility

The Parts feature, which is covered in Chapter 4, "Modeling," allows us to create actual elements of the graphical representation of the layers that are defined in walls, roofs, ceilings, and floors. Before this feature is used, a view is assigned to Show Original, meaning the normal wall, roof, ceiling, or floor is displayed. When you invoke the feature on

Figure 6.11

Parts Visibility choices

one of these kinds of families, Revit will change the Parts Visibility setting (for the view you are working in) to Show Parts instead (see Figure 6.11). One other setting, Show Both, is intended to let both be visible so it is easier to see how they relate to one another and/or how they have been altered. Each view can be assigned its own value to help display the information you need to show.

Visibility/Graphics Overrides

The Visibility/Graphics Overrides feature (and the slender Edit button that appears next to it, see Figure 6.12) is a much deeper topic and deserving of more than a simple paragraph. We will devote more time to this a bit later in this chapter in its own section. VG (its keyboard shortcut too), as you'll probably come to refer to this feature, lets you tailor an individual view to your needs while leaving all others alone.

Figure 6.12

Visibility/Graphics Overrides Edit button

Graphic Display Options

These are probably familiar concepts to you, consisting of Wireframe, Hidden Line, and Shaded (see Figure 6.13). Veteran users may remember these being called Model Graphics Style and then Visual Style. They've been combined into this new larger dialog box in an attempt to simplify where we find things to set up how our views should look.

Recent additions (beginning with release 2011) are Consistent Colors and Realistic:

Consistent Colors The Consistent Colors setting turns off the light source used in the Shaded setting so that the colors are not altered by the shadows that are cast on the model.

Realistic Realistic is the first step toward real-time material representation in views; enabling Show Edges enhances the view by overlaying lines that represent the edges where elements intersect one another.

Refer to Figure 6.14 for examples of each graphic style.

Overall, the Graphic Display Options dialog box provides access and control for Surfaces, Silhouettes, Shadows, Lighting, and Sun and Shadow Intensity. With it you can choose to display shadows and even define how the shadows should be cast. They can respond to time/day/date or a specific orientation. It is also possible to create a single-day or multiple-day shadow study. Silhouettes allows you to override the appearance of the model so that outer boundaries such as walls and roofs, as well as the boundary edges of openings in walls, "pop" by assigning a heavier line weight to them. The intention is to take an

Figure 6.13

Graphic Display Options button in the Properties palette and the View Control bar access location

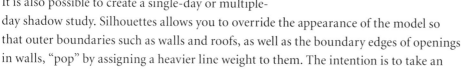

otherwise drab exterior elevation view and make it more dramatic. This release introduces a new feature called Ghost Surfaces, which makes the surfaces of elements transparent (see Figure 6.15 for a couple of examples).

Figure 6.14

Graphic Display Options examples

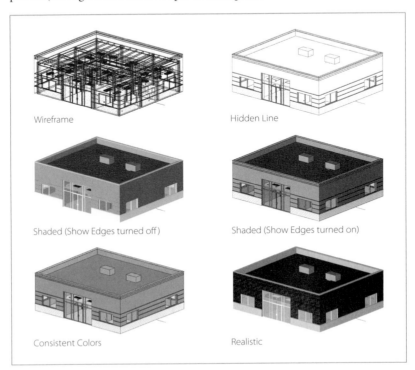

Wireframe

Hidden Line

Shaded (Show Edges turned off)

Shaded (Show Edges turned on)

Consistent Colors

Realistic

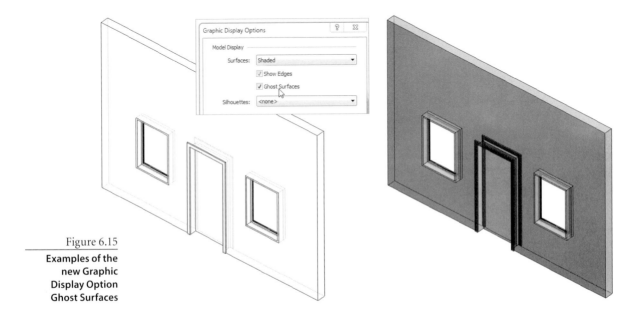

Figure 6.15

Examples of the new Graphic Display Option Ghost Surfaces

Underlay and Underlay Orientation

It can be handy to display a portion of the model that is above or below the current plan elevation. For instance, lining up shaft walls is not as easy unless you can "see" them. The Underlay and Underlay Orientation settings control whether Revit shows another level and which way the information should be displayed—either according to plan or according to reflected ceiling plan view (see Figure 6.16).

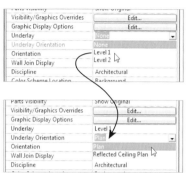

Most of the default templates that come with Revit have an underlay assigned to the floor plan views that use the plan orientation. When it comes time to print a view, you may want to adjust the Halftone / Underlay settings so that your underlay will print dark enough (see Figure 6.17). There is also a setting in the Print Setup dialog box called Replace Halftone With Thin Lines, as shown in Figure 6.18.

First selection leads to second option becoming available

Figure 6.16

Underlay Settings: setting Underlay to something other than None activates the Underlay Orientation option.

Figure 6.17

Halftone / Underlay settings

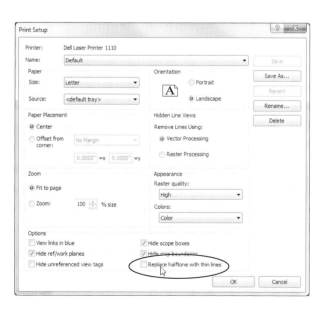

Figure 6.18

Replace Halftone With Thin Lines setting

Earlier we provided steps to access and alter the settings for Halftone, which happens to share the Underlay settings. Like Halftone, changing the Underlay Weight and Pattern is a global change, so it will affect all views that display an underlay. To adjust the Underlay settings, take the following steps:

1. Click the Manage tab of the ribbon, and on the Settings panel click the Additional Settings button.

2. Click Halftone / Underlay.

   The Underlay frame provides selection options for Weight and Pattern (Lines) as well as an Apply Halftone check box. You can also open the Line Patterns dialog box by clicking the browse button next to the Pattern drop-down list.

3. Adjust these as you see fit, remembering that your change affects all views that are using this feature.

   We suggest making a small change and printing to evaluate the outcome.

4. If you change the setting, you can click the Reset button to restore the default value of 50 percent that Revit uses.

> Be careful not to use the Apply Halftone option *and* Underlay overrides without verifying that the results print satisfactorily. Combining them may result in printed documents that are not dark enough to be practical.

Orientation

A project is usually drawn so that it is easy to describe on a printed page. The actual north bearing of a project is important but is not often conducive to creating drawings. Therefore, a common practice is to create drawings that use a project north orientation (the easy-to-draw orientation) while providing a north arrow symbol that tells the reader which direction is true north.

The templates that come with Revit have their plan-oriented views assigned to Project North (see Figure 6.19). This means that you should start by being just a little ambivalent about which direction north really is, making it easy to sketch the design and get it on paper first. It is easy to let Revit know which direction true north is later via the Rotate True North tool (Manage tab of the ribbon → Project Location panel → Position button). Once you create the design, then any plan view can be assigned to either True North or Project North as needed.

Figure 6.19
**Orientation
property**

Wall Join Display

Wall Join Display is a bit arcane and available only in views that use a Detail Level setting of Coarse. There are just two choices, Clean All Wall Joins and Clean Same Type Wall Joins (see Figure 6.20):

Clean All Wall Joins As you can imagine, the first choice will cause Revit to clean up all the intersections between walls that occur in the view.

Clean Same Type Wall Joins The second choice is intended to be a bit more selective by having Revit focus on cleaning up the intersection of walls that are the same type of wall.

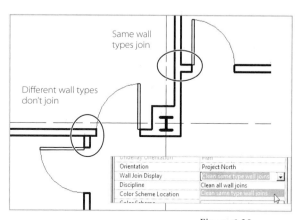

Figure 6.20

Wall Join Display choices

The first setting is used the most, by far. The second can be useful if you don't want dissimilar walls to appear as though they blend together.

Imagine shaft walls or rated walls that have a nonrated wall that comes into contact with them. It is fairly common practice to show a line where these walls touch instead of having the software show them blending together. This can be useful in overall plan views until you use enlarged plans that will likely use a Detail Level of Medium to make this difference more obvious and relevant to the reader because differences in material assignment are displayed.

> In elevation or section views, this setting isn't present because it is irrelevant. Revit only automatically considers how walls join in plan-oriented views.

Discipline

Revit uses the Discipline setting to alter the appearance of the model according to how each discipline tends to display information. These disciplines include Architectural, Structural, Mechanical, Electrical, and Coordination (see Figure 6.21). In Revit Architecture, this setting may not get as much use compared with Revit Structure or Revit MEP.

Figure 6.21

Available disciplines in Revit views

Architectural All views in Revit Architecture's stock templates are assigned this as the default choice of discipline. Architecture elements take precedence over other disciplines. In reality you'll see differences only when you switch from Architectural to one of the others.

Structural The Structural discipline setting alters the view to display structural items only. Walls that are not assigned as bearing (structural purpose) are hidden from view, for example.

Mechanical and Electrical The Mechanical and Electrical disciplines alter the view so the architectural and structural elements are transparent and halftone. Each discipline takes precedence in the view over the others.

Coordination The Coordination discipline displays everything as equal without overrides.

> It isn't possible to add/remove or change the disciplines offered in the list. You may encounter a subdiscipline parameter in some project files/templates. This has been added to allow for further view organization in the Project Browser. You'll be able to enter whatever value you need for that parameter.

Color Scheme Location and Color Scheme

Two items in this group of properties are dedicated to views that will have color schemes applied: Color Scheme Location and Color Scheme (see Figure 6.22):

Color Scheme Location This property offers you a choice between Background or Foreground. The Background setting keeps the color scheme beneath (behind) walls and

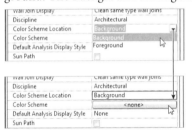

Figure 6.22

Color Scheme settings: defining the color scheme location and choosing a color scheme

other elements in the view. The Foreground setting moves it above (in front of) other elements. This works nicely when you are interested in large blocks of color, uninterrupted by walls, to define a portion of the plan. The Background setting works better for views that need to focus more on individual rooms but still indicate their relationship with other rooms through color.

Color Scheme Color schemes can be applied to rooms and areas in Revit Architecture. If you are collaborating with an engineering firm using Revit MEP, then you might find it useful to know that this feature works for their spaces and ducts too.

Hide At Scales Coarser Than

When you examine this group for other kinds of view, such as elevations or sections, you'll find another setting called Hide At Scales Coarser Than (see Figure 6.23). This

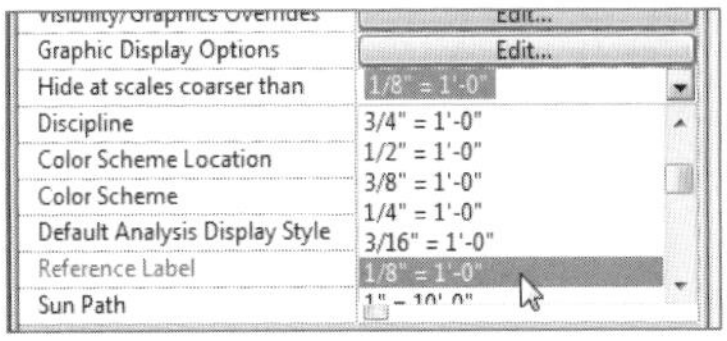

Figure 6.23

Hide At Scales Coarser Than setting

allows you to choose a plateau below which the annotation for these view types will not display. This makes it easier to prevent finer-scale wall sections or detail sections from having their annotation appear in your overall plan views or elevations.

Just choose the last scale value you want them to show up in, and they won't appear in any below that value.

Default Analysis Display Style

This is a new feature intended to support third-party applications for analysis. Clicking the small browse button that appears when you place your cursor in the field next to the label (see Figure 6.24) will open a dialog box that offers two reporting styles that are supported at this time: Colors (coloring of surfaces) and Legends (text information).

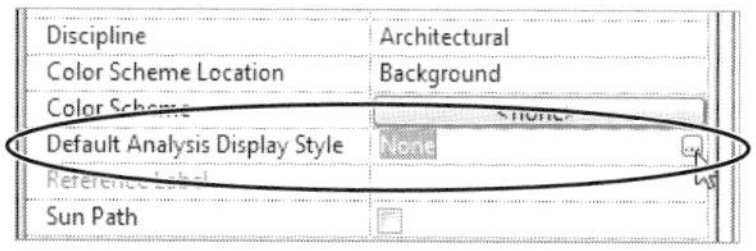

Figure 6.24

Default Analysis Display Style setting

Discipline	Architectural
Color Scheme Location	Background
Color Scheme	
Default Analysis Display Style	None
Reference Label	
Sun Path	

> The dialog box isn't much use yet because, as of this writing, it isn't apparent which applications will take advantage of it. However, some relevant examples of a third-party application that could use this are reports for lighting levels, thermal radiation levels, and structural analysis.

Visible In Option

You find this property only when your project has a design option (refer to Figure 6.25). This setting determines whether the annotation for this view should be visible in all views or only when a specific design option is assigned to a view. For example, a section view has an associated annotation, and when you create a new section view while editing the main model, it will be assigned to All. If you are editing a specific option when you create the section view, it will be assigned to that option instead. This makes it easier for you to change it back to All or assign it to appear in a specific option only.

Figure 6.25

Visible In Option setting

Color Scheme	<none>
Default Analysis Display Style	None
Visible In Option	All
Sun Path	
Identity Data	Option Set 1 : Option 1 (primary)
View Name	Option Set 1 : Option 2
Dependency	Option Set 1 : Option 3

Sun Path

This feature will display a representation of the sun and its path around and over your project (see Figure 6.26). It provides a tactile and interesting (and more useful and fun, too) way to manipulate the sun-positioning information for the project instead of using the established Location and Position dialog boxes. You can turn this on by selecting the Sun Path setting, by checking a check box in the Properties palette, or by clicking the View Control bar button (the small sun icon).

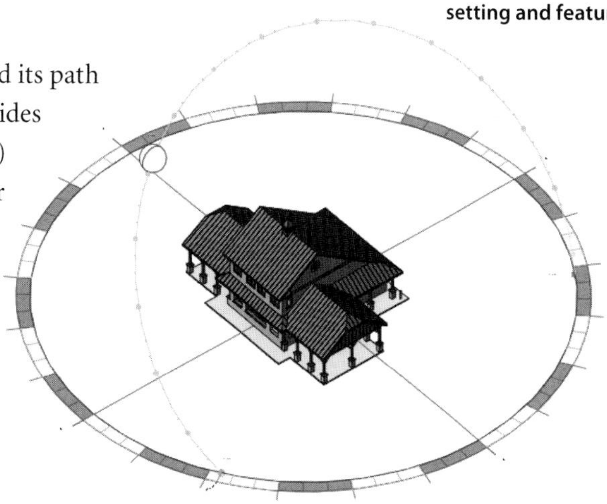

Figure 6.26

The new Sun Path setting and feature

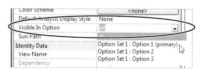

Identity Data Group

The next group listed in View Properties is Identity Data (see Figure 6.27). This is intended to manage information related to the view, such as its name and the Title On Sheet parameter. There is one important visibility control item here, though, called

Default View Template. This setting is a critical part of managing your project and its views. If you spend a significant amount of time adjusting the way a view looks, you won't be thrilled to repeat the entire exercise many times. You will be thrilled, however, to learn that a view template can be assigned to a view to make short work of that repetitive task. Revit assigns a view template to the view when you apply one. Later, you can apply the default view template to several views at one time, and Revit will use the template that is assigned to the view. You will see more about this later in the chapter in the sections "View Range," "Filters," and "View Templates."

You can apply a view template quickly by following these steps:

1. Place your cursor over the view you'd like to change in the Project Browser.

2. Right-click the view to bring up the context menu.

3. Choose Apply View Template.

4. Choose a view template from the Apply View Template dialog box.

   You can filter the list with the Show Type drop-down list.

5. Click OK.

   Alternatively, you can apply a view template via the ribbon by taking these steps:

1. Open the view you want to change.

2. Click the View tab on the ribbon → View Templates → Apply Template To Current View.

3. Choose the appropriate template from the Apply View Template dialog box (more about view templates later).

4. Click OK.

Extents Group

The Extents group in View Properties provides control over the following features: Crop View, Crop Region Visible, Annotation Crop, View Range, Associated Level, Scope Box,

and Depth Clipping (see Figure 6.28). In other view types, there are some additional settings: Far Clipping, Far Clip Offset, and Parent View.

Cropping

It is possible to crop a view, such as a floor plan, elevation, or section, to either increase or decrease how much of the model is visible. Some views do not allow it, such as drafting, legend, and schedule views. Cropping is typically applied to a view to create partial plans or enlarged scale views of the building model. You can choose to display the crop region (boundary) with the Crop Region Visible setting. Some don't mind seeing it, while others are distracted by the extra rectangle in the view—it's your call (see Figure 6.29).

The Annotation Crop is a secondary boundary that defines when the annotation in the view should show up. For example, room tags identifying rooms that are partially displayed in the view because of the crop boundary will appear only if they are within the Annotation Crop boundary (see Figure 6.30). Naturally, you can adjust the extents of the crop region and the annotation crop separately.

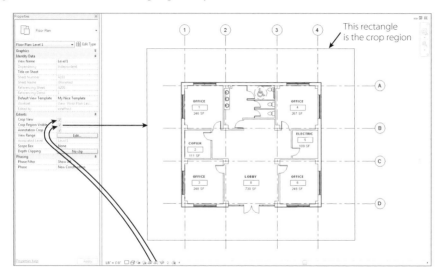

Figure 6.29

Cropping a view

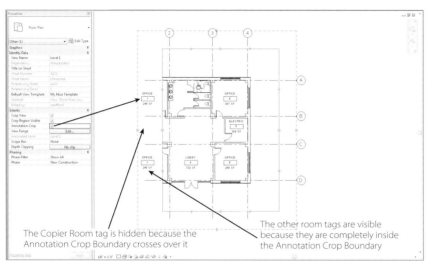

Figure 6.30

Annotation Crop boundary

View Range

View Range determines how elements are drawn (displayed) in the view. It defines where Revit cuts a plan or ceiling plan and whether elements use a thick, thin, or thinner pen. This little paragraph won't do it justice, so we'll discuss it in greater detail later in this chapter in the sections "View Range," "Filters," and "View Templates" (see Figure 6.31).

Figure 6.31

View Range property, Edit button, and View Range dialog box

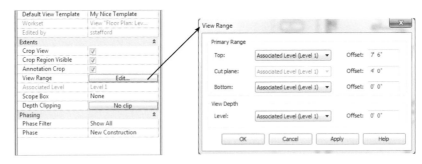

Associated Level

Associated Level is a read-only setting (you can't change it—sorry!), as shown in Figure 6.32. Each plan-oriented view type is forever associated with a specific level. We occasionally see a user trying to create a new level by duplicating a floor plan view and

Figure 6.32

Associated Level (read-only) setting

just renaming it. Unfortunately for them and their team, they end up with a view with a nice name that is still associated with a different level, and confusion ensues. Just keep in mind that you can quickly check this setting for any view to confirm it is being used as intended.

Scope Box

Imagine a project that has several floors and is large enough that an overall plan doesn't fit on a single sheet. This is where scope boxes and this setting come in handy (see Figure 6.33). When you need a consistent portion of the building to appear in each floor's plan view, you'll want a scope box.

You sketch a rectangular boundary to define the scope for each partial plan. Each view can be assigned to a specific scope box, and as a result the crop region adheres to this new boundary. All the partial plan views for a given part of the project can be assigned to the same scope box. This provides control that is easy to manage as well as effective. You can also apply this feature to other views and datum (levels, grids, and reference planes) to help manage their visibility. Scope boxes are a very useful, often-overlooked portion of Revit's arsenal of features.

Let's take a little closer look at a scope box:

1. From the book's companion download files (available at www.sybex.com/go/
introducingrevit2012), open the dataset file IARA CH06 Visibility A.rvt.

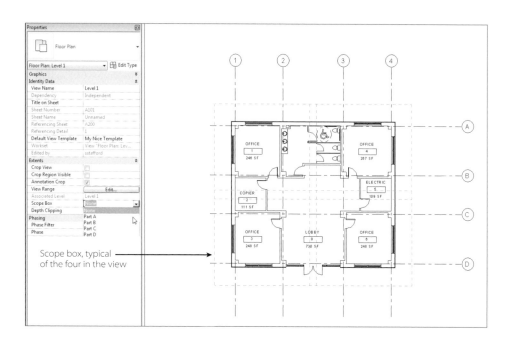

Figure 6.33

Scope box setting

2. Open the 3D View: {3D}.

   You can see the scope box in the view surrounding the building, the box with the green dashed lines.

3. Select the scope box, and examine its properties. Its name is Scope Box 1.

4. Click the Views Visible Edit button (Properties palette).

   The Scope Box Views Visible dialog box that opens controls when scope boxes are visible in views and whether or not levels and/or grids that are associated with a scope box are visible.

5. Click OK to close the dialog box.

6. Open the Floor Plan view: Level 0.

   Surrounding the building is a rectangle; it is the crop region.

7. Look at the Properties palette for the floor plan view, and look for the Scope Box parameter.

   Note that it is assigned to Scope Box 1.

8. Click the View tab on the ribbon → Windows panel → Close Hidden.

   This will close all views other than the floor plan Level 0.

9. Open the floor plan view: Site.

10. Click the View tab on the ribbon → Windows panel → Tile.

    This will place the two floor plan views next to each other.

11. On the Navigation bar → Zoom tools → click Zoom All To Fit.

    This will zoom both views at the same time so you can see the entire plan.

12. Select the scope box, visible in the Site floor plan view (rectangle with green dashed lines).

13. Use the triangular drag grips on the right side to decrease the size of the box so that it is closer to the building.

    Watch the result in the other floor plan.

14. Try the other sides.

Plan, section, and elevation views can all be assigned to a scope box. Once they're assigned, the scope box assumes control over the crop region that governs how much of the model we see in a view. Changing the scope box from one view can alter a great many views very quickly as well as ensure that the same portion of the model is offered to people who see the resulting documents printed from the project.

Depth Clipping

This feature is related to a view's View Range settings, which, as we mentioned earlier, are covered a bit later in the chapter in the sections "View Range, "Filters," and "View

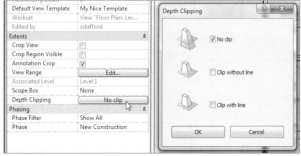

Templates." When you click the slender gray button labeled No Clip (the button wording changes according to the setting chosen), you'll see the Depth Clipping dialog box shown in Figure 6.34. The graphics in the dialog box explain what it is intended to do pretty effectively.

The most likely reason to use this is for a slanted wall that extends beyond the current level's view range. If you want Revit to stop displaying the wall as if it were not continuing below, then you should choose Clip With Line. The Help documentation has nice graphic images that help explain the concept well.

Figure 6.34

Depth Clipping options

Far Clipping and Far Clip Offset

There are two other settings in section, elevation, and camera views called Far Clipping and Far Clip Offset (see Figure 6.35). These govern the depth of these views and how far forward Revit will look and therefore display information. These are especially important

Figure 6.35

Far Clip settings

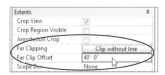

when rendering views to limit how much of the model Revit will attempt to render to just the part that is actually necessary or actually visible. There's little to gain by rendering the portion of the model hidden by walls and other elements.

Phasing and Camera Groups

We'll now wrap up the contents of the View Properties palette. For most of the view types you'll see a small group with just two Phasing tool settings: Phase Filter and Phase. The phasing features in Revit are intended to graphically aid the documentation of Existing, Demolished, Temporary, and New Construction conditions. Phasing is primarily a graphical tool to change the appearance of elements according to their phase conditions. It can also be manipulated to create a series of construction sequence views, but often this use contradicts the primary purpose of the tool.

The Camera Properties group appears when you start using the Default 3D View, Camera, and Walkthrough view tools (see Figure 6.36). These settings allow you to adjust the orientation of the camera position with numerical input. Most users find it is more natural and intuitive to use the other navigation tools that Revit provides to orient a camera.

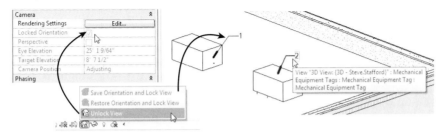

Figure 6.36

Properties palette group: Camera and the new 3D features: tagging and lock 3D orientation

3D views (except the Default 3D view) and camera views can now be locked to allow you to tag elements (refer to Figure 6.36). Tagging in 3D views has been a longstanding wish list item. If you unlock a 3D or camera view that has tags, they will disappear. If you choose Restore Orientation And Lock View, the tags will return. If you reorient the view and then choose Save Orientation And Lock View, you'll get a message asking if you want to lock the orientation (which deletes the tags permanently) or continue without locking (which returns you to the view but without the tags). Just make sure you are satisfied with the orientation of your 3D views before you do any tagging. Otherwise, you'll end up redoing some work.

As you can see, we weren't kidding when we said that there are a lot of features and tools tucked away in this palette.

Visibility/Graphics Overrides

This section will tackle how you can selectively redefine how an individual view will look. For example, a plan view dedicated to showing the scope of work for furniture, fixtures, and equipment (FF&E) needs to look a bit different than a construction plan intended to explain how to build all the partitions for the offices on a given floor. The Visibility/Graphics Overrides dialog box gives you this sort of control as well as provides access to other related features.

Let's start by taking a look at the dialog box; it is one of the biggest that Revit has (see Figure 6.37). You open it either by using the standard keyboard shortcut VG or clicking the View tab of the ribbon → Graphics panel → Visibility/Graphics button. It features tabs (five at a minimum) across the top. How many tabs are displayed depends on the other features that you use for your project. For example, if you are using a linked Revit model, worksets, or design options, you'll find that new tabs join the five default ones. These default tabs correspond to the nature of information presented in a view: Model Categories, Annotation Categories, Analytical Model Categories, Imported Categories, and one tab dedicated to a special view control tool called Filters. We've written more about Filters later in this chapter, in the section by the same name.

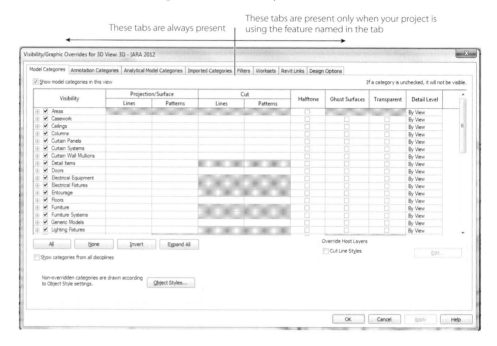

These tabs are always present   These tabs are present only when your project is using the feature named in the tab

Figure 6.37
Visibility/Graphics Overrides dialog box

The first column of the Model Categories tab, Visibility, lists each category used in Revit. Above the column is a check box that can be used to turn off or on the visibility of everything listed on the tab. This can be useful, as an administrative technique, to see only annotation elements like text or symbols in the view, for example. Doing so will also hide annotation elements that are tied to model elements like a wall tag or a dimension between two walls. For each category in the Visibility column, the accompanying check box is a switch that will turn off or on the category or its subcategories. The little plus sign next to a category indicates that it has at least one subcategory, if not many (see Figure 6.38).

Figure 6.38
Turning on/off a category/subcategory

Once you've decided which categories should be visible, you can deal with the individual appearance of each according to the Projection/Surface Lines, Projection/Surface Patterns, Cut Lines, and Cut Patterns settings. Remember, all views initially adhere to the settings defined in Object Styles (global settings), while Visibility/Graphics Overrides allows for unique situations (local settings). Ideally, your Object Styles settings will cover the majority of the conditions you have. Revit has a button in this dialog box to access the Object Styles settings just in case you decide that changing something there is the best course of action instead (see Figure 6.39).

Several other settings such as Halftone, Ghost Surfaces, Transparent, and Detail Level can be quite useful to adjust the intensity or priority of various categories so that your view tells the correct story. For example, your architectural floor plan may want to use a Detail Level setting of Coarse to show information as simply as possible. Structural steel elements only show as "stick" symbols when you choose Detail Level: Coarse. They become more obvious steel shapes only when you choose a setting of Medium or Fine instead. It is an easy change, one setting, to show steel beams (Structural Framing) in a more meaningful way (see Figure 6.40).

Figure 6.39

Object Styles button

Figure 6.40

Example of Detail Level overrides

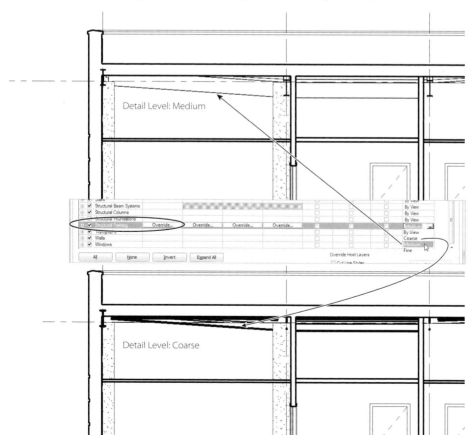

If you assigned the view property Discipline to anything other than Architectural or Coordination, be careful with the Halftone setting. The Structural, Mechanical, and Electrical disciplines apply halftone to the view automatically. Using the Visibility/Graphic Overrides tool to assign a category to halftone doubles the halftone, making it even lighter. It is reasonable to expect that this will cause some printing/plotting problems!

View Range

As we mentioned earlier, the View Range feature requires a bit more explanation for you to appreciate how it affects what you see in your views. It is applied individually to views, and it allows Revit to choose which line weight settings to apply to elements in plan-oriented views.

You can use view templates to apply changes to the view range more efficiently—and to lots of other settings too!

Imagine you are standing on the second floor of a building. Revit uses a metaphorical knife to cut and present a plan view to you. This knife's height above the floor is Revit's *cut plane*. Any element that is cut by this plane will use Revit's Cut line weight setting, if it has one, found in Object Styles or overridden with Visibility/Graphics Overrides. Elements in the view that are not specifically cut by Revit will display using the Projection line weight found next to the Cut line weight in either location. Revit uses two more planes to establish how far above the cut plane you want it to "look" and how far below the cut plane it should "look." As long as an element exists between the Bottom and Top planes, Revit will see it and use the Projection line weight to show it. Before you go further, refer to the View Range dialog box to see these settings (see Figure 6.41).

Figure 6.41

View Range dialog box for a floor plan

To help resolve situations where there is more information below the floor, like standing on a mezzanine level looking down to the floor below, Revit has one additional plane called View Depth. If the elements in the view are not found between the Bottom and Top planes but are located between the Bottom and View Depth planes, Revit will use another line style called Beyond to show them. Therefore, Revit is capable of using a combination of three different line weights to show elements in a plan-oriented view, all according to their vertical relationship to the floor they are related to.

It is important to think of each plane (Primary Range: Top, Cut Plane, and Bottom; and View Depth: Level) as physical entities (plates of glass stacked one above another, for example) that cannot travel past each other. You cannot enter a value that would push the Bottom plane beneath the View Depth plane. They can share a value, but they can't travel past one another. You can avoid getting error messages if you remember this fundamental rule.

All plan views in a template start with basic, viable settings. You may have to adjust them from time to time, and it is important to understand the role templates play in controlling the visibility of elements.

To tackle a practical example, let's consider the stock template default.rte and the ceiling plan View Range settings.

1. Start a new project using the template default.rte.

2. Open the Ceiling Plan view: Level 1.

3. Click the View Range Edit button in the Properties palette.

    The View Range settings in this template are adjusted to prevent allowing the cut plane to pass through doors, at least doors that are less than 7′-6″ (2280mm) tall.

4. Click OK to close the View Range dialog box.

5. Open the Floor Plan view: Level 1.

6. Sketch a wall about 10′-0 ″ (3m) long.

7. Place a door in the wall.

8. Open the Ceiling Plan view: Level 1 again.

    The resulting ceiling plan view doesn't give you any indication where door penetrations are. Some users don't like this because they are in the habit of showing where openings are in walls.

Let's compare two ceiling plan views using a simple model to focus on the settings, not the design. The first ceiling plan uses the stock settings captured on top of the plan (see Figure 6.42).

Figure 6.42

Ceiling plan, stock settings

The next image to consider is the revised ceiling plan using different settings, also captured in place (see Figure 6.43). Now you see the doors, but you also see the panel and the arc of the door swing. Many firms don't show these this way at all. A short visit to the Visibility/Graphics Overrides dialog box to turn off the categories for them will resolve that (see Figure 6.44). If you expand on what you just learned about Visibility/Graphics Overrides and combine it with this View Range adjustment, you can fix the problem with the doors (see Figure 6.45).

Figure 6.43

Ceiling plan, modified settings

Figure 6.44

Visibility/Graphic Overrides applied

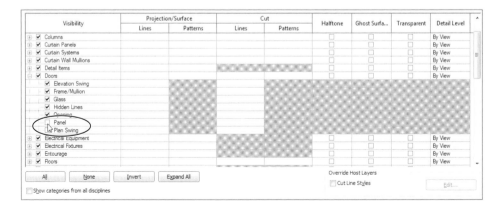

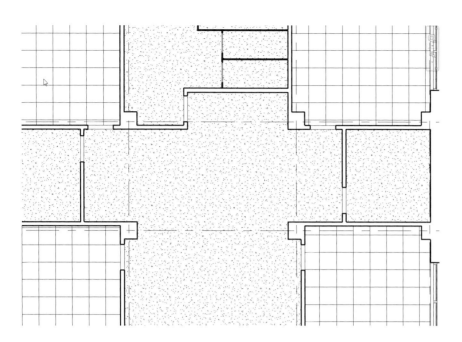

Figure 6.45

Ceiling plan after Visibility/Graphic Overrides

Another approach is when you have a slightly unusual ceiling plan that shows you the panel and swing of the doors so it is easier to determine where light switches should go (see Figure 6.46).

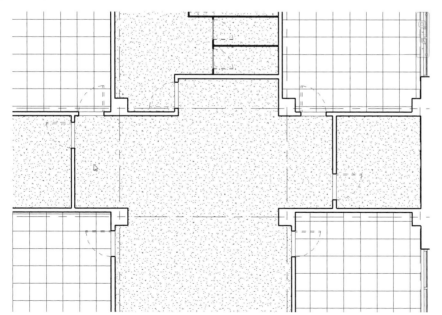

Figure 6.46

Ceiling plan, modified View Range and Visibility/Graphic Overrides

These are the settings used to adjust the appearance of the door Panel and Plan Swing subcategories. Pay close attention to the fact that the Panel subcategory is adjusted under the Cut Lines column (see Figure 6.47), and the Plan Swing subcategory (see Figure 6.48) is adjusted under the Projection/Surface Lines column. These are created using separate Object Styles subcategories in the family to provide individual control over them.

On this subject, we want to encourage you to review the Help documentation that comes with Revit. Its technical documentation team has put quite a bit of effort into making this quirky subject more accessible.

Figure 6.47
Visibility/Graphic Overrides of Panel settings

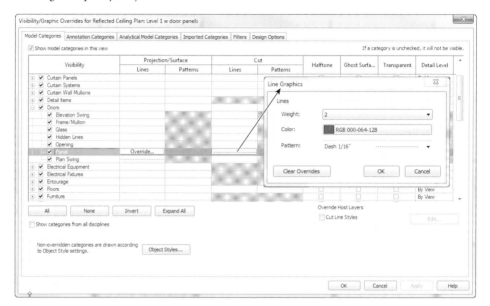

Figure 6.48
Visibility/Graphic Overrides of Plan Swing settings

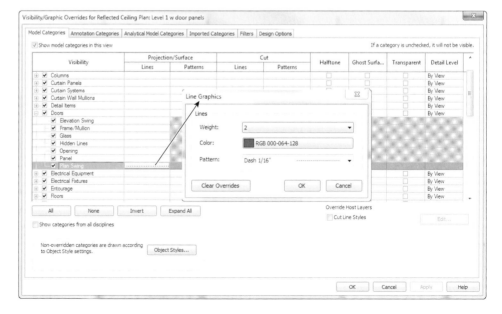

Filters

You can use filters to hide elements or to alter their appearance. How they affect elements depends on the criteria being used to apply them and how many elements share the criteria that you use to create the filter. There are two roads you can take to create a filter: managerial and user.

The managerial road starts at the View tab of the ribbon, and the Filters tool is found on the Graphics panel (see Figure 6.49). You can create and edit filters using this route, but you can't apply them. As the manager, you are planning for their eventual application by users.

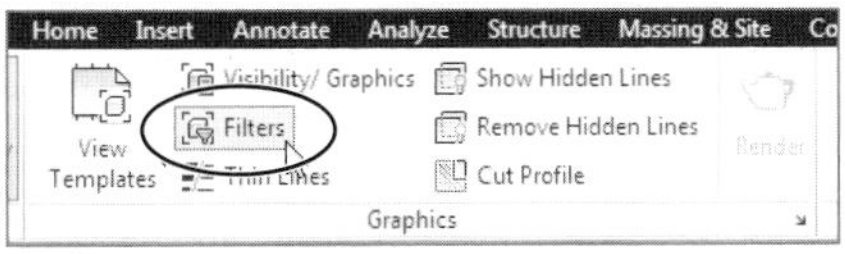

The user road is found by working from within the Visibility/Graphics Overrides dialog box (see Figure 6.50). It is also possible to apply them by selecting an individual element or elements and using the context menu option Hide Element Or Override Graphics In View and choosing By Filter. The result, however, is that Revit just opens the Visibility/Graphics Overrides dialog box to let you choose and apply a filter. It is also possible to create/edit a filter from within the Visibility/Graphics Overrides dialog box.

When you create a filter, you usually have a problem to solve—something doesn't look the way you want it to. Architects tend to use filters to solve documentation subtleties. Engineers using Revit MEP tend to use filters as much to help them see different systems of equipment as they work, such as supply air versus return air ducts or hot/cold and sanitary piping, as they do for documentation.

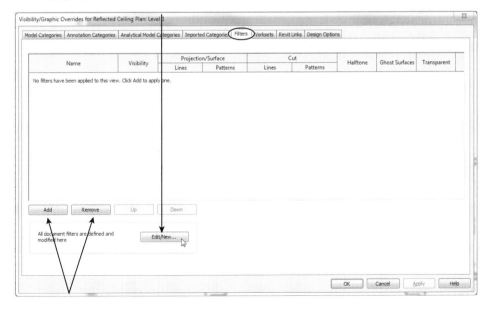

Figure 6.49

Filters tool on the ribbon

Figure 6.50

The Filters tab in the Visibility/Graphic Overrides dialog box: click Add or Remove to apply or remove existing filters, and click Edit/New to open the Filters dialog box.

You can take a closer look at a practical example based on sketching a quick bathroom partition layout with walls instead of using component families. It isn't an obvious approach for some, but those who want a faster way to get an idea on paper might find it useful.

The ingredients for this are a filter, a wall type, and a door type. Mix them together, and you can get the kind of result shown in Figure 6.51. We called the wall type Toilet Partitions, and it is just 1″ (25mm) thick, like a real toilet partition. The trouble with this thickness is that it will print poorly, as a single, really heavy line, because the two wall faces are so close together. The door type will also be altered to be thinner than a regular door for the same reason as the wall. The Type Comment parameter for both the wall and door types can be used to store values that the filter can use. We used TP for our special criteria. The filter will fix these graphical issues quickly. The result is a quick toilet room layout, which doesn't force you to make very specific equipment selections too soon. Being successful in early design phases with Revit comes from being able to differentiate between what you need now and what you'll need later.

Figure 6.51

Toilet Partition walls before and after filter

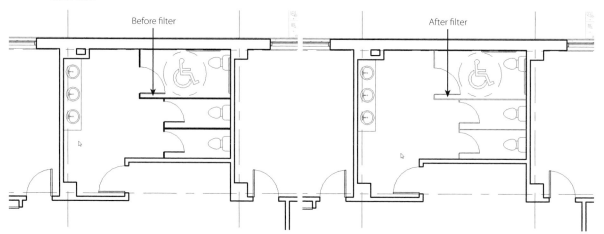

Creating the filter is easy; just take these steps:

1. From the book's companion download files (available at www.sybex.com/go/introducingrevit2012), open the file we've provided called IARA CH06 Visibility.rvt.

2. Open the Filters dialog box (go to the View tab's Graphic panel).

3. Create a new filter by clicking the New button.

4. Name the filter **Toilet Partitions**.

5. In the center section of the dialog box, choose the categories your filter applies to (Doors and Walls). Note the check box for Hide Un-checked Categories; this will reduce the number of categories displayed to just those you have selected. Don't check it at first.

6. In the right section of the dialog box, choose the criteria your filter will use to find your elements (see Figure 6.52).

   In this example we've entered the letters *TP* into the Type Comments parameter for the wall family type used for the partitions.

7. Click OK to save the filter.

   Applying the filter to your view is easy too:

1. Open the sample file IARA CH06 Visibility.rvt or continue using the file from the previous steps.

2. Open the Floor Plan view: Level 1, and zoom in on the toilet room.

Figure 6.52

Creating a new filter called Toilet Partitions

3. Open the Visibility/Graphics Overrides dialog box (keyboard shortcut VG).

4. Click the Filters tab, and then click the Add button. This opens the Add Filters dialog box.

5. Choose your new filter from the list (Toilet Partitions), and then click OK to return to the Visibility/Graphics Overrides dialog box.

6. To test the filter, deselect Visibility, and then click Apply. Did it turn off the toilet partitions and doors?

   If it did, select the Visibility option again, and override the settings (see Figure 6.53).

Figure 6.53

Overriding the settings

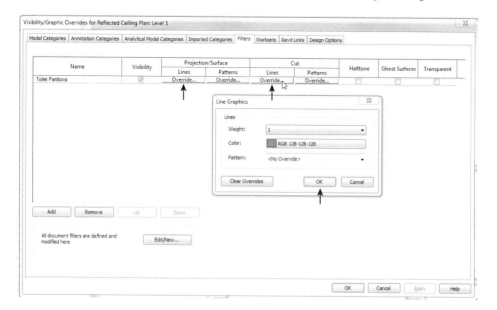

If it didn't, your criteria are incorrectly defined (case-sensitive and logic issues).

7. Override the settings for Projection/Surface: Lines and Cut: Lines. Assign both to use Weight: 1.

Following these steps should help you create and apply any filter you need. Eventually you will need to become comfortable with defining your own custom parameters to provide criteria that aren't available out of the box. For more information refer to Chapter 7, "Introduction to Families," and the section "Shared Parameters."

View Templates

Templates allow you to apply consistent changes to multiple views quickly. View templates are not aggressive, however. They don't automatically apply changes to views that have been assigned to them. The product designers stopped short of doing this because they have just as much potential to harm as to help. In the wrong hands, a view template can create some serious problems. For example, view templates can get changed and applied incorrectly on the day of a big deadline. Reapplying the correct view template(s) will often undo the damage pretty easily. Just remember that they are powerful, and it is necessary to be careful with powerful things.

As we mentioned with filters, View templates can be created from two points of view, user and manager:

User As a user, you are likely to create a template using a view that you spent some time adjusting carefully with View Properties and/or Visibility/Graphics Overrides. It just makes sense to use something you've fine-tuned well as the template for the template.

Manager If you are the manager, then you'll probably be comfortable with just creating or editing a raw template without seeing the results immediately in the view itself.

First, let's consider this from the user's perspective:

1. Open the sample file IARA CH06 Visibility.rvt.

2. Open the Ceiling Plan: Level 1 w door panels.

3. Assuming that this view is correct, use the context menu in the Project Browser, by right-clicking this view's name.

4. Choose Create View Template From View (see Figure 6.54).

    Choosing this will prompt you to provide a name for the template.

5. Enter the name **RCP with door panels**.

    Once you satisfy that request, Revit will open the View Templates dialog box. This gives you a chance to review the settings before saving the template to the project.

6. Examine the listed properties and choices available to you.

7. Click OK when you have finished.

The View Templates dialog box is loaded with things to adjust. It is a combination of the View Properties and Visibility/Graphics Overrides features. You can also reduce the number of view templates displayed in the list of names by choosing from the Show Type selector to filter by view types. In the area dedicated to adjusting View Properties, Revit provides a row for each kind of visibility control, that a View Template provides, such as Display Model, V/G Overrides Model, or Shadows. The "Include" column check boxes provide a way to tell Revit that you don't want it to apply a particular view property when you apply the view template to a view or views.

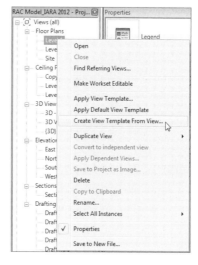

Figure 6.54

Right-click and choose Create View Template From View.

As a manager you can open this dialog box at any time by clicking the View Templates button on the Graphics panel on the View tab of the ribbon. You can create/delete or edit a template by choosing View Template Settings. Once you've finished making changes or adding a new template, you close the dialog box and then either apply the view template(s) or let your project team know that you've updated their view template(s).

Each view can be assigned to a template, and later you can apply a template to many views quickly by right-clicking and choosing Apply Default View Template. Regardless of the views you have selected, Revit will only apply the view template that is assigned to each view, ignoring the view if none is assigned yet (refer to Figure 6.55).

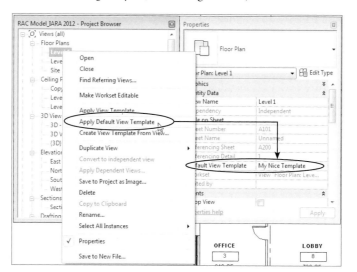

Figure 6.55

Apply the Default View Template option via the context menu.

Linked Files

Chapter 12, "Working with Other Files," delves into working with linked files, so this section will only touch on the control you have over the visibility of them. It is often necessary to link other data into your project, whether it is from other CAD applications or other Revit models. The features discussed in this chapter extend to managing the information in these linked files too. For links based on DWG file data, you can manage the layers of the link with the Visibility/Graphics Overrides settings. This means it is necessary for these external files to be well made so that you have as much control over the information stored on their layers as possible.

Revit files that are linked together enjoy a bit deeper level of control than you have for external CAD file data. You can choose to let the host file "drive" the link, or you can use the link's own appearance and settings. At the most granular level, you can access categories and elements individually even though they are part of a link. This control isn't exactly equal to being part of the host file, but it gives you much greater control than just letting the host control the link.

Imported DWG files have their layers added to the Revit database, and this gives you control over the elements on those layers similar to what AutoCAD users have over their DWG files. The file and its layers are listed on the Imported Categories tab in the Visibility/Graphics Overrides dialog box. As long as the elements in the file are defined By Layer, you can override their color, line type, and line weight (see Figure 6.56).

Figure 6.56

Imported Categories tab in the Visibility/Graphic Overrides dialog box

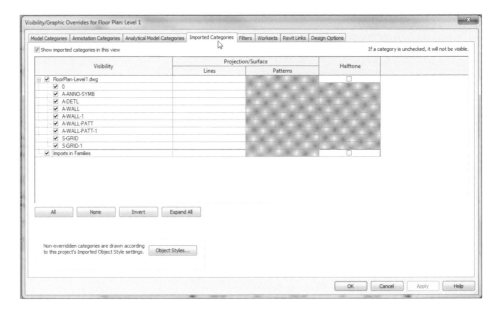

When you link a Revit project file, a new tab called Revit Links is added to the Visibility/Graphics Overrides dialog box for it just as for DWG files (and other formats), as shown in Figure 6.57. Initially the linked file is controlled by the host project. It is through this tab that you can dig deeper into the link to have more control over its elements. The next level of control is to display information by linked view (see Figure 6.58). This will expose the views of the linked project and let you choose which one to display instead. This means you also see notes and other annotations that otherwise are not visible at all in the host project (see Figure 6.59).

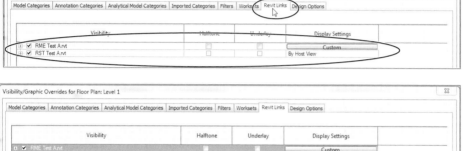

Figure 6.57

Revit Links tab in Visibility/Graphic Overrides

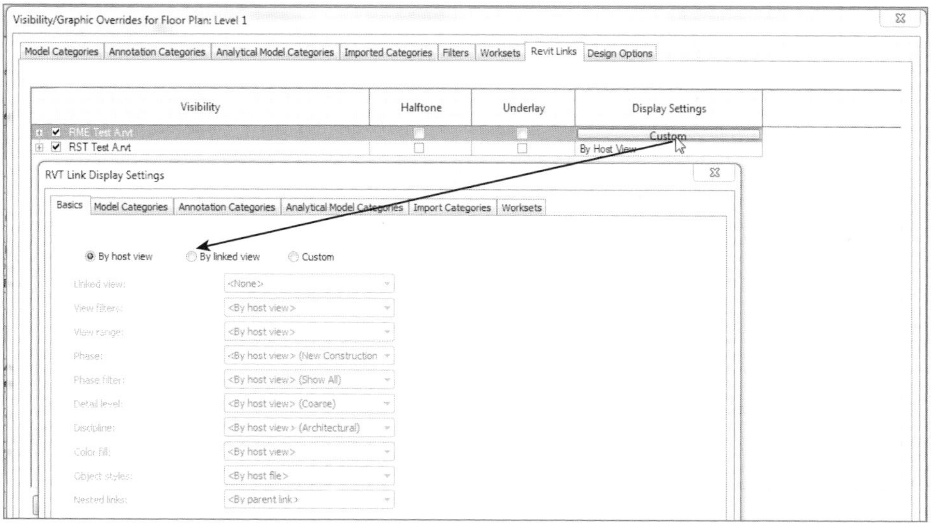

Figure 6.58

Changing to By Linked View

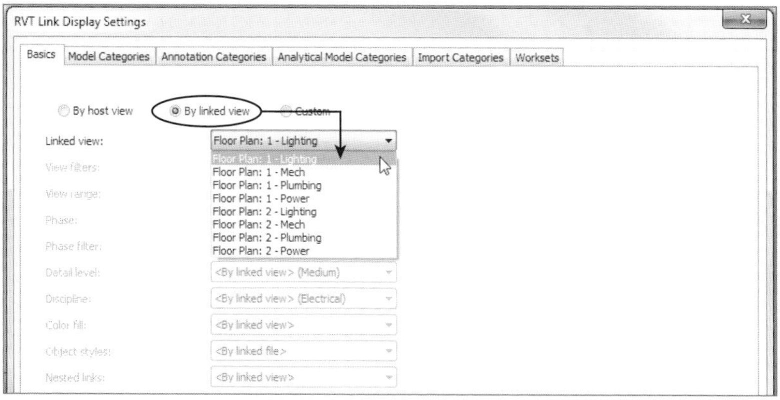

Figure 6.59

Choosing a linked view to show

Linked files ordinarily do not show any annotations (text, symbols, tags, dimensions, and so on) that are in their views; only the model is visible. You can ask the team that is providing the other Revit model to create specific views for you so that you can use these overrides to include annotations that otherwise would not be available. The new tagging features may limit the necessity for this to some degree but not completely.

The next level you can descend to offers quite a bit more control but also represents much more effort to get what you want. When you click the Custom option, you'll see all the settings exposed for your consideration (see Figure 6.60). If you examine the other tabs, such as Model Categories, Annotation Categories, and Import Categories, you'll find that the Custom option changes each of them too. This is the deepest level of control that you have now. When you choose Custom on each tab, you have access to each category in the linked project file as if you were working within the file itself, at least as far as the Visibility/Graphics Overrides settings are concerned (see Figure 6.61).

Ideally you will get what you need to see of an external file just by going to the trouble of linking it. If you need more control, Revit has it. It is there waiting for you to take advantage of it.

Figure 6.60

Choosing custom overrides for the Basics tab

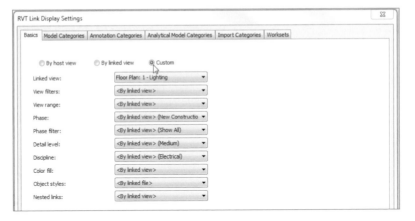

Figure 6.61

Choosing custom overrides for the Model Categories tab

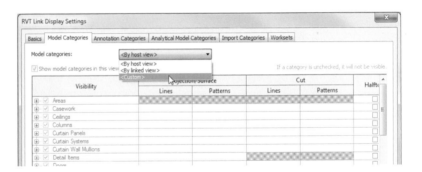

Worksets

We lied. We told you just a moment ago that you had reached the deepest level of control for linked files. Worksets are a feature that we will cover in Chapter 20, "Worksharing." Suffice it to say for now that worksets are necessary when you want to work on the same project at the same time, sharing the same model data with other users. You may prefer to skip this section for now and come back later.

Linked Revit projects that are using worksets provide yet another option for taking control over their visibility. The Worksets tab (see Figure 6.62) in the Visibility/Graphics Overrides dialog box isn't new, but it provides different options with this release. When a workset is created, Revit offers a Visible In All Views option in the New Workset dialog box. This is a time-saver when the elements you want to assign to this workset don't need to be visible in many views but just in a few.

Figure 6.62

Visible In All Views setting

It is less work to turn the workset on in a few views than to turn it off in many.

In the past, this feature negatively affected other projects that imported this project. The worksets that you chose not to make visible in all views caused them to be invisible in the host project as well. The only recourse then was to reassign the elements to a new workset that was set to be visible in all views.

When you examine the dialog box, you'll see that Revit provides three (new) options: Use Global Setting (Visible), Show, and Hide (see Figure 6.63):

- Use Global Setting (Visible) means that it will work the way it did in the past: the Workset property for Visible In All Views takes precedence.

- Show and Hide override this setting in this view and do what they suggest, that is, show or hide the workset.

Thus far we are only discussing what affects the worksets of the host project. It is now possible to turn on and off worksets in a linked file on a view-by-view basis. When you reexamine the Visibility/Graphics Overrides dialog box, look at the Revit Links tab, as shown in Figure 6.64, and click the button that appears in the Display Settings column to open the RVT Link Display Settings dialog box. You should see the Worksets tab (assuming the link uses worksets). When you have selected the Custom option on the Basics tab, you get the right to override the setting for worksets, which you can change to Custom too. Now you can turn on or off each workset listed.

Figure 6.63

New visibility options for worksets

Figure 6.64

The Revit Links tab of the Visibility/ Graphic Overrides dialog box

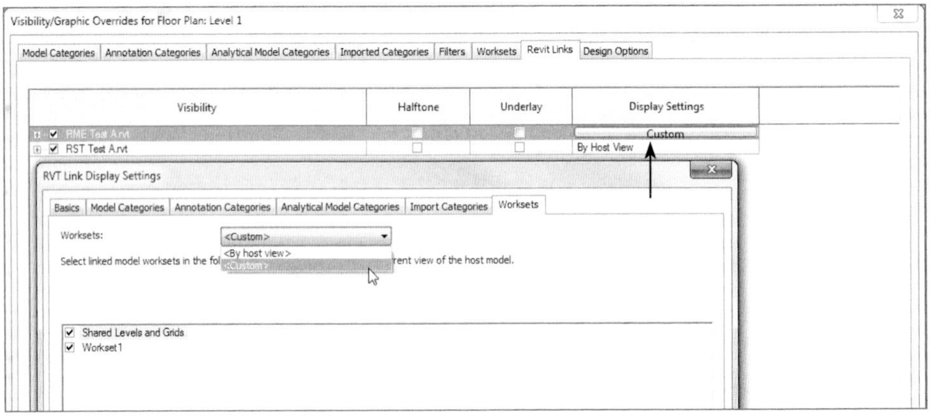

CHAPTER 7

Introduction to Families

You have already encountered families such as walls, doors, and windows in the previous chapters. In fact, every element in Autodesk Revit Architecture can also be referred to as a family. The founders chose the word family to describe the elements you use in Revit because it aptly applies to the relationships that each has in a building project as well as to each other. For example, a cabinet manufacturer offers various kinds of cabinets, and each has a range of sizes. You just need to exchange "kind of cabinets" with "family of cabinets" to see how well it works. Each size that is available is a child of the parent cabinet family. The family parent-child relationship is present in many of Revit's features.

This chapter covers the following topics:

- **Understanding family organization**

- **Working with families**

Understanding Family Organization

Everything you use in Revit is referred to as a family, so it is important to explain how Revit manages families and then makes them available to you. Fundamentally, families are divided into three functions: model, annotation, and datum. Beneath these functions, families are all expressed in a family tree structure consisting of category, family, type, and instance. Finally, you interact with families according to three concepts: system family, loadable family, and in-place family.

Functions of Families

The following functions make up the grand scheme underlying Revit and its families. All projects are composed of tasks that use each of them. What sets Revit apart from other applications is the way that it integrates the families among their unique functions: model, annotation, and datum (see Figure 7.1).

Figure 7.1

Examples of each function in a view

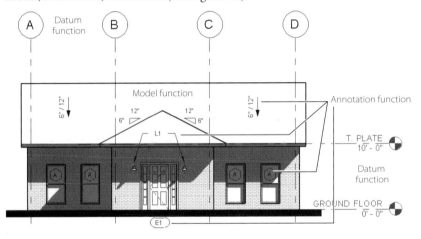

Model These families are usually three-dimensional and represent real objects in or on a building. They will appear in all model views of your project as well as being listed in schedules. Some easy examples are walls, floors, doors, windows, furniture, and roofs.

Annotation These are families that do not have a three-dimensional purpose, though it is possible to use tags in 3D views in 2012. They also do not appear in multiple views. They are intentionally limited to be visible only in a single view so you can add specific information to your documentation. Some examples for these are text, dimensions, symbols, tags, detail lines, and detail components.

Datum This function is reserved for three items: levels, grids, and reference planes. These families straddle model and annotation functions because they have some capabilities of both. Datums appear in multiple views without extra intervention on your part. They also provide view-specific features that make it possible to format your documents well.

For example, there are model-to-model relationships such as a wall and door. There are model-to-annotation relationships such as a door or wall and a related door or wall tag. Datum elements such as a level can revise an entire building's floor elevation, moving everything associated with it at the same time as well as updating every view and sheet for the project. Dimensions can both display important information and allow you to change a family's position in the model.

The Family Tree

Families are organized on four branches: category, family, type, and instance.

Category Every family, at the uppermost branch, is assigned a category. The Doors category, for example, deals with all the doors of a project (see Figure 7.2).

Family The next branch addresses the definition of specific families in your project. The Single-Flush door (in Figure 7.2), for example, represents something you can actually use.

Type The third branch, type, transitions to inside the family and provides the list of its children (sizes or kinds; see the list of sizes in Figure 7.2).

Instance The top three branches represent the idea or notion of a door (the door and its sizes are available), but the lowest branch—instance—represents the actual occurrence of a door when you place one in your project.

For many of the categories of families, you can see the top three branches expressed in the Project Browser and the lowest in the project's views when you interact with the individual families you use (refer to Figure 7.2). The top three are also displayed for you in a tool tip (when your cursor is over a family and it is highlighted) and on the status bar. The family your cursor is over represents the lowest branch, the instance. This organization is present for every family in your project whether it is a door, a wall, a view, a dimension, text, or a wall tag.

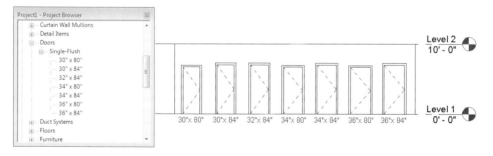

Figure 7.2

Category (Doors), family (Single-Flush), types, and instances in the Project Browser and a view

Classifying Families

Families are divided into three classes (refer to Figure 7.3):

- System families (sometimes also called *host families*)
- Loadable families (also known as *components*)
- In-place families

Each presents families to you differently, and each is different in how much work is required to create and use them.

Figure 7.3

**Examples of
each class**

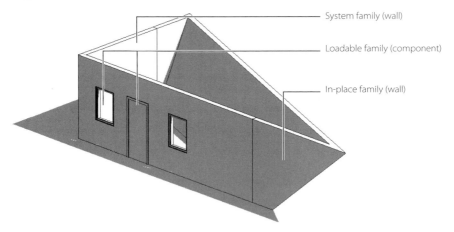

- System family (wall)
- Loadable family (component)
- In-place family (wall)

It might be helpful if you think of system families as internal and loadable families as external with respect to the project environment. In-place families are a combination of system and loadable family capabilities.

System Families

System families are entirely defined by the Revit product developers. You have only the features and options that they designed into them. For example, walls can be a system family, and you can alter only the properties that Autodesk has provided. You cannot introduce new behavior to a wall, for example, or introduce a lean or angle property. The system family is not designed to lean; therefore, you can't cause walls to lean with the available properties.

When you start a project, your template contains a collection of walls, as well as other system families. If you don't find a wall family that you need, then you have to duplicate an existing wall to create a new version, as shown in Figure 7.4. You do this right in your project, which is why we suggested you think of them as having an internal relationship with your project. The more you anticipate what is needed and establish these system families in your office's template, the quicker you can start your design.

Figure 7.4

**Creating a new wall
type by duplicating
an existing one**

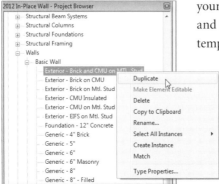

Some system families are also called *host families*. The words *system* and *host* are often used interchangeably, which can be a bit confusing. The use of the term *host* is meant to explain that some families—such as walls, floors, ceilings, and roofs—can hold other families, such as doors, windows, and light fixtures (Figure 7.5). A *hosted* family cannot be placed in a project without its host. (A hosted family is always a loadable family, by the way.)

Stairs, railings, and ramps are also system families. Stairs and ramps can act as hosts for railings (see Figure 7.6), but they don't host other families, such as doors or windows, because they don't do so in actual buildings either. Hosting is meant to mimic real building element-to-element relationships. Not all system families are host families, such as railings. They are managed internally, in the project, but don't provide hosting for other families.

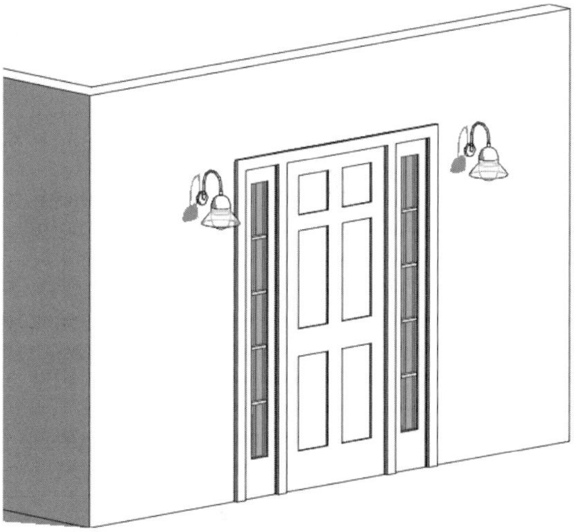

In addition to the three classifications used for families (system, loadable, and in-place), a fourth concept applies to them but is really a hybrid of system and loadable classes. There is no official terminology used to describe them other than to call them system families too. In some families, a loadable family such as a profile defines their shape or appearance, but system family behavior is designed into the software. You can control the shape or appearance but not what Revit lets you do with the family when you use it in your project. The level, grid, wall sweep, floor slab edge, repeating detail, and roof gutter are examples of this hybrid (see Figure 7.7).

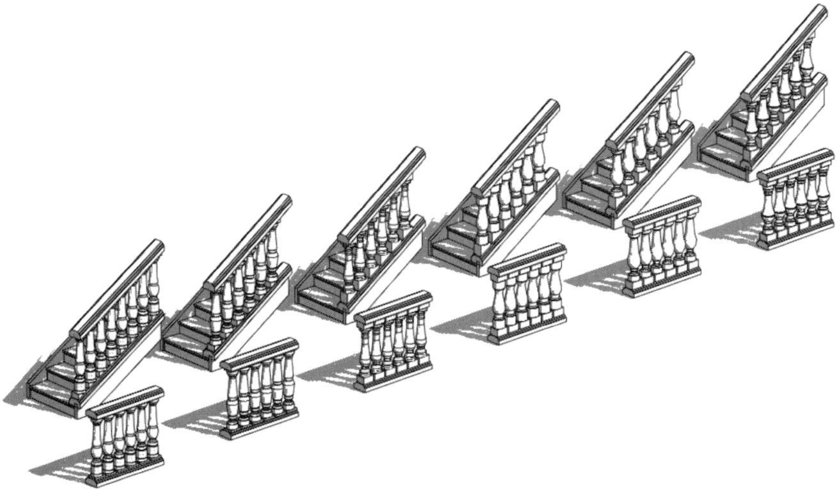

Figure 7.5

Wall hosting a door and two lights

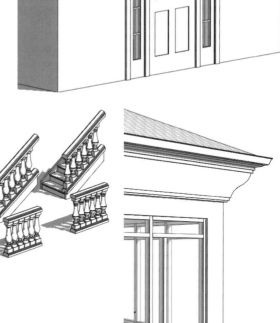

Figure 7.6

Sample railings hosted by stairs

Figure 7.7

Wall sweep and roof gutter families

Loadable Families

As mentioned earlier, *loadable families* (also called *component families*) can be thought of as external items; in other words, families that are added to your project from an external source. Doors, windows, casework, and furniture are all loadable families (see Figure 7.8). In a perfect world, all the families you need would be already made; you'd just need to find them, add them to the project, and use them. The reality is that no matter how many families are provided by Autodesk or created by others, you will eventually need something that isn't there.

Figure 7.8

Examples of loadable door and window families

Doors

Windows

Loadable families are built outside the project environment from templates (.rft) and saved using their own file format (.rfa) in a special mode of the Revit user interface called the Family Editor. Revit doesn't display this title or inform you of this subtle change; it only offers the tools that are relevant for creating a family. As soon as you open a family file, you are using the Family Editor.

> Remember that these families play into the model and annotation functional roles described earlier. Therefore, a door is a model family, while a door tag is an annotation family. Both are loadable families and are created in the Family Editor mode, but they play different roles. It is important to know that these families are restricted from using the same categories as system families.

In-Place Families

In-place families are built using all the same tools as loadable families except that you create them within the context of your project (internal versus external). As we mentioned earlier, a wall (system) family cannot be induced to lean. We also just explained that loadable families are not allowed to use categories reserved for system families. This means you can't build a leaning, loadable wall family, thus the in-place or "in-between" family. The in-place family doesn't share this restriction, so you can build an in-place wall family that leans. It takes a bit more work than just sketching a wall with the Wall tool, but you have much more control over the outcome. The penalty for this flexibility is the singular, unique nature of the final result.

The in-place family is not intended to be used extensively or for many of the same items; it's not for repetition. Using them too much or inappropriately is less efficient and takes more effort. Regardless, there are design features that cannot be created in any other way, so they exist to provide the flexibility you need to convey your ideas. Figure 7.9 shows an example of a Sprung roof structure (`http://sprung.rtrk.com/`). The system family roof tools don't lend themselves to modeling this kind of structure. In fact, this type of structure is not just a roof or just a wall, but acts as both by stretching a membrane over a skeleton frame. Judicious use of loadable families and in-place families provides a way to do a project that might, at first glance, be deemed not possible for Revit.

Figure 7.9

In-place Sprung roof design

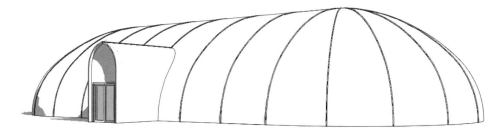

Working with Families

This section is dedicated to the routine interaction you will have with loadable families. Working with system families such as walls, floors, and roofs is covered in other chapters. It is possible to be quite productive with the concepts covered here long before you ever need to make or design a loadable family yourself. In fact, some people never need to create a family from scratch because someone at their firm handles family creation and editing for everyone else. We will delve into designing and creating families in Chapter 8, "Creating Families."

This section is devoted to finding, loading, placing, and replacing families (hosted and nonhosted); creating new types; and using type catalogs. We will also introduce you to nested families, shared families, and shared parameters. These are more advanced concepts, but you should be aware of them as you start using families.

Finding and Loading a Family

Some "stock" families are provided with Revit. A growing number of websites are dedicated to peers sharing families as well as product manufacturers providing families for their products. Some companies create families for you as a (paid) service. You just need to make sure that a team has access to content and knows where to find it and, if necessary, how to acquire it. Your project template can simplify this process by having the content the team needs already loaded. When that's impractical, then the process to load a family is easy enough to learn and remember.

Loading a family is easy; take these steps from within any project file:

1. Choose the Insert tab on the ribbon.

2. Select the Load From Library panel, and click the Load Family button.

3. Browse to the US Imperial or Metric library folder (or your own company library folder), and then choose the category you need, such as Doors.

4. Choose the family or families you need from those in the folder (press Ctrl to add individual files or Shift to select a group).

5. Click Open to add them to your project.

> There are a few other ways to load a family. You can click Load Family when using the Component tool, you can click the Load button when viewing the type properties of a family, or you can drag and drop a family from a folder view using Windows Explorer.

Placing a Loadable Family

Placing content varies according to the kind of family you are dealing with, but again, it is easy to learn and remember.

Placing a family is easy:

1. Click the Place A Component button, which is the upper portion of the Component split button (on the Home tab's Build panel), or click the specific buttons for Door, Window, or Column.

2. Choose the type from the Properties palette's Type Selector.

3. Review the instance parameters in the Properties palette, and make any necessary changes.

4. Click in the drawing area (on a host family if required) to place the family.

There are other techniques to place a loadable family. You can drag and drop a family type from the Project Browser; you can right-click a family and choose Create Similar from the context menu; with a family selected, you can click Create Similar on the ribbon (on the Modify | "selected category" tab's Create panel); or you can just use the Copy tool after selecting an existing family nearby.

Replacing a Loadable Family

It is quite common to use a family as a placeholder during the conceptual and schematic design phases. A generic door or window is probably sufficient to convey your intentions during that time. Later you may need to replace these generic placeholder families with more accurate representations of products that have been selected. Fortunately, this is pretty easy too.

To replace one door family or type for another, take these steps:

1. Select the current family.

2. Choose a different family or type from the Type Selector (on the Properties palette).

3. Click Apply in the Properties palette.

You can do the same thing to replace many doors at once—just select multiple families in the same category in step 1.

You can replace every single occurrence of one type of family by using the Select All Instances → Visible In View, or Select All Instances → In Entire Project option on the context menu when you right-click a family. Once you've selected one of those options, you can use the same steps listed earlier. You can also use the Match Type Properties tool on the Modify tab's Clipboard panel.

Adding More Information to a Family

Sometimes you just need to add some missing information in an existing family. For example, you could decide that you want to include the manufacturer and model information for the windows in your project. Revit has standard parameters for both of those. You might also choose to use a different identifying window type value in your window tags. A specific window might need a unique comment to warn the contractor that it has to meet emergency exit requirements. The first few changes affect a family's type properties, while a single unique comment should apply to a specific window, not all, which means that it should be applied as an instance property.

To add manufacturer and model information to a window family, follow these steps:

1. Select the family.

2. In the Properties palette, click the Edit Type button.

3. Enter values for Manufacturer and Model.

4. Click OK.

To add a unique comment to a window family, follow these steps:

1. Select the family.

2. Enter the information in the Comments parameter found in the Properties palette.

3. Click Apply.

> The most likely place to show the information for either of these examples is in a schedule. Part of Revit's charm is that you can enter this information as described earlier in the schedule or in a tag if one is available in the view. Revit makes it easy to enter and keep these things coordinated. You'll get a reminder warning that changes you make (for Type properties) will affect all the occurrences of that family and type that are present in the model.

Working with Hosted and Nonhosted Families

All model families are related to the levels of your project (think of the floors or stories of the building). When you place a family (a door, for example) in a plan view of the second floor of your project, it is associated with the level family that defines the second floor. You can see this parameter in the Properties palette when you select a family, such as a door.

In addition to this notion of being related to or associated with a level, a family can be hosted by a system family, such as a wall. When you click the Door or Window button on the Home tab, you are using a hosted family, and hosted families are intended to be hosted by wall families. They can't exist without a host wall. These families are created in a template that contains a placeholder host wall. (We'll cover creating families in Chapter 8.) When you click the Place A Component button and place a chair family, you are using a family that isn't hosted. A chair family is assigned to the furniture category, and they are usually not hosted. They are associated with a level in the project, though. Like with the door mentioned previously, Revit will display the level the chair is associated with in the Properties palette.

Hosted families naturally need a host to exist first in order to be placed. Families can also be hosted by the face or surface of various parts of the building model. This kind of family is referred to as *face-based*, and it is less particular about the kind of host you want to place the family on. It can be a wall, floor, top of a table, ceiling, underside of a steel beam, and more. You get three options for placing a face-based family: Place On Vertical Face, Place On Face, and Place On Work Plane.

Figure 7.10
Work Plane-Based option

Family Parameters	
Parameter	Value
Work Plane-Based	☐
Always vertical	☑
Cut with Voids When Loaded	☐
Can Host Rebar	☐
Part Type	Normal

Just to keep things interesting, each family category that isn't a face-based family already can elect to be work plane-based as an option (see Figure 7.10). As shown in Figure 7.11, when you see only two options on the ribbon's Placement panel—Place On Face and Place On Work Plane—you are attempting to place a family that has the Work Plane-Based option selected. Just remember to examine the ribbon placement options that appear for each kind of family you use.

Figure 7.11

Placement cue on the ribbon: left, face-based; right, work plane-based

Face-Based Family Placement Options

Work Plane-Based Placement Options

You do not have to choose to have your family hosted unless your family needs to cut or alter the host, like the slab depression family shown in Figure 7.12. If the family has no actual relationship with a building other than with a specific host, then it makes some sense to make the family hosted by that host, like a wall.

Many objects in a building, such as a light switch, power receptacle, or thermostat, might normally be part of a wall, but even these items can be found on other surfaces than walls. For example, cabinetry might have receptacles or switches mounted on them. Therefore, choosing to make a light switch family wall-based might actually be a hindrance at some point in a project. A similar classic example is a ceiling fan. These are often mounted to ceilings, but you'll also at times find them attached to the underside of the floor structure above, to beams, and to other structural elements. Therefore, a ceiling-based ceiling fan will eventually be rather inconvenient (see Figure 7.13).

This is where the face-based template becomes useful. This family has a host element, but it isn't a wall, floor, ceiling, or roof. It is a "host" that can pretend to be whatever surface you want to believe it is. Revit is equally willing to believe that your family is as at home attached to the underside of a beam as it is to the top of a table.

> You can create nonhosted families, and if you really need them to be hosted later, you can just nest them into a hosted template. It is much easier to do this than rebuild the family to not require a host.

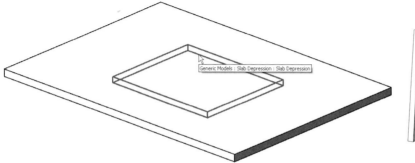

Figure 7.12

Floor-based slab depression family

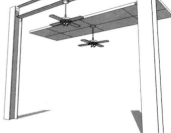

Figure 7.13

Face-based and ceiling-based ceiling fans

Creating a New Family Type

Quite often a family is nearly sufficient, but you just need a new type. For example, a stock Single-Flush door family has a 36″ × 84″ (900 × 2100 mm) door as its largest type (size).

These are the steps required to add a 42″ wide (1050 mm) door type:

1. Select the family that you want to be the larger size in the drawing area.

2. Click the Edit Type button on the Properties palette.

3. Click the Duplicate button, and provide a new name, such as **42″ × 84″ (1050 × 2100 mm)**.

4. Change the Width parameter to **42″ (1050 mm)**; change the Height parameter if necessary.

5. Click OK to close the Type Properties dialog box. The selected family is now using the new size.

When you select the family type listed (right-click and then select Duplicate) in the Project Browser, you aren't dealing with a specific occurrence of the family, so only the new type will be added without changing any families. This is a better way to create a new type when you don't want to alter an existing family.

> This is the same process you use to create a new wall family, so it applies equally well to system families. In fact, this process is used for nearly every kind of family in Revit. It should become second nature pretty quickly.

Updating the Family in Your Library

In the previous exercise, you created a new type in the family that is part of your project. The original family in the Revit library or your own office's library has not been altered. This is both good and bad. It is good if the new type is a unique situation and not commonly used. In this case, it doesn't need to be in the library version. It is bad when the opposite is true—that everyone else who encounters this family in their own projects will end up repeating the same steps to add a very common type. The responsible thing to do instead is to make the change to the library version of the family and load this updated version into your project. This gives you what you need for the short term but accommodates the longer-term needs of your co-workers and the firm.

To update the family and load the new version, follow these steps:

1. Select the family, and click the Edit Family button (on the Modify tab's Mode panel).

2. Click the Family Types button (on the Home tab's Properties panel).

3. Click the New button, and provide a new name for the type.

4. Edit the parameters to reflect the new type size or information needed, and then click OK.

NAMING CONVENTIONS

Be judicious when naming families and their types. Erratic naming habits will affect their usefulness in schedules. Other people who use the families where you've added new types will also find any naming inconsistency frustrating.

The naming we see ranges from subtle to complex. For example, we've seen names that refer to Door 1 and then Door2 (space and no space). Then we see doors that are named Flush Panel with Kick Plate and EOH. We also see names created with abbreviations like SPKPEOH that require a secret decoder ring. Depending on how organized your firm is (and the number of users you have), you'll find that naming like this helps: DR-Single-Flush or DR-Double-Flush. The prefix *DR* allows for sorting in the Type Selector, which makes it a little easier to find doors, and more so for other family categories. The short description that follows the prefix means that it will (hopefully) fit in the various places that Revit displays the family name.

We won't presume to tell you exactly how to name your families, but we do encourage you to consider your process and create consistent habits that make everyone's interaction with your family library as good an experience as possible.

5. Click the Save button on the Quick Access toolbar.

If this is the stock content or in a protected folder, Revit will prompt you for a new filename. This means you need special permission to modify the library of families available to you. Save the new version elsewhere if necessary, and have someone with the necessary permission put the new file in the folder for you later.

6. Click Load Into Project (on the Home tab's Family Editor panel).

7. Place or replace the family as required.

You can also edit a family by using the context menu (right-click) and choosing Edit Family. Remember, it is better to open the file separately from the project, make the changes, and save the file. Later when you are back in the project, you can load the family.

Placing Loadable Families That Use Type Catalogs

A type catalog is used to create a list of all the parameters for each family type, and the information is saved in a separate text file (.txt). It is intended to provide an easier way to deal with families that have many types. Most families have a modest number of types, such as the Single Flush.rfa door family that has seven types (sizes). When a family can represent many more different types (think sizes or configurations), it often makes more sense to use a *type catalog*. Many of the structural detail component families, such as

`Nominal Cut Lumber-Section.rfa`, use a type catalog to make it more practical to load just the types your project actually needs.

When you load a family that uses a type catalog, Revit will open the Specify Types dialog box (refer to Figure 7.14). Take these steps to select types and load the family:

Figure 7.14

Type catalog sample with multiple families selected

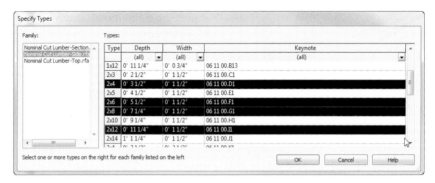

1. Select the type(s) you need.

   When you choose more than one family that has a type catalog, you will see a list of each selected family on the left side of the dialog box.

   - Press Shift+click to select a group.
   - Press Ctrl+click to select various individual types.

2. It is possible to filter the listed types by clicking the small drop-down arrow in the heading of a column.

3. Click OK after all the types are selected.

   Take these steps to place the family:

1. Choose the Place A Component tool or one of the specific component tools like Door or Window.

2. Select the type you need.

   Notice that only the types (sizes) you chose previously are listed, not all the types that were visible in the Specify Type dialog box.

3. Click in the drawing area to place the family.

Encountering Advanced Features

You will run into a few features as you work with families that are worth explaining. We'll explain how you create a family that uses them in Chapter 8. For now, we'll limit the discussion to just what you need to know about them or should expect from them as you find, load, place, edit, and replace families.

Nested Families

Most of us are familiar with nested drawings in CAD (called *external references or Xref's*) but in Revit they are referred to as *Linked Files* and you *insert* them via the Insert ribbon. Nested families are similar but you use Load Family (Insert ribbon → Load from Library panel → Load Family) to add them to a *host* family. Using this technique you can create very useful families as a "kit of parts" so you can minimize or eliminate redundant tasks and reuse these parts effectively (see Figure 7.15).

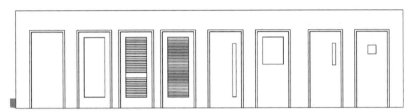

Figure 7.15

Door panel "kit of parts"

A well-made family that uses a nested family or families will not be all that noticeable unless you attempt to create a new type or take a closer look at the family by opening it. The doors pictured in Figure 7.15 consist of panel families that you can exchange for one another by changing one parameter. If you examine the properties of a family closely and you see a parameter that has what looks like another family name listed, then you are seeing a nested family in use.

Several stock families use a nested family or families, such as DLH-Series Bar Joist.rfa (structural framing folder), Alternating Tread Device.rfa (specialty equipment folder), and Outlet Duplex.rfa (electrical fixtures folder). The first two use them to allow for variable-length/height families by creating an array of a nested family. The outlet family uses a nested annotation family to represent the symbol graphics you see in a plan view.

To take a closer look at the DLH-Series Bar Joist family, follow these steps:

1. Click the Application menu, select Open → Family, and navigate to US Imperial/Structural/Framing/Steel.

2. Choose the file DLH-Series Bar Joist.rfa.

3. Expand the Families branch of the Project Browser, expand the Structural Framing branch, and expand the Angled Web branch.

4. Select the type Angled-Web, right-click, and choose Select All Instances → Visible In View.

   The elements that are highlighted in the drawing area are the nested families.

5. If desired, repeat steps 3 and 4 for each of the other two Structural Framing families listed in the Project Browser.

6. Close the file without saving changes when you are finished.

If you take the steps listed earlier in this section to create a new type in a family and you get errors that you don't understand, it is possible that you have encountered a family that uses a nested family, and it isn't prepared sufficiently to provide the change you need. The concepts covered in Chapter 8 should help prepare you for such a situation.

Shared Families

When a family is nested and its host is loaded into a project, Revit loads only enough of the nested family to be able to display it—a symbol of it, not the real family. As a result, it does not appear in the Project Browser under the Families branch. It doesn't really exist in the project even though you can see it.

When the nested family is shared, then Revit loads it into the project in addition to its host family. As a result, this family is listed in the Project Browser under the Families branch. This means you can place the nested family alone as well as have it appear whenever its host family is placed. More important, since the actual family is loaded, it becomes possible to schedule the nested family as if it were an individual apart from its host. Numerous interesting possibilities are available to you as a result.

For example, a schedule can report how many cabinets you have in a project. Using shared families Revit can now also provide a schedule of cabinet doors and hardware. This might be an extreme example, but it could be quite effective for a firm that could use this level of detail.

There are not many examples of these in the stock library, but you can examine one more closely. To see an example of a shared family, take these steps:

1. Click the Application menu, select Open → Family, and navigate to US Imperial/ Casework/Domestic Kitchen.

2. Choose the family `Counter Top-L Shaped w Sink.rfa`, and click Open.

3. Select the sink that is visible in the drawing area.

   Notice that it is a family and its type (Sink Kitchen-Double 42″ × 21″) is displayed in the Type Selector of the Properties palette.

4. With the sink selected, click the Edit Family button on the Modify | Plumbing Fixtures tab's Mode panel.

   Revit opens the sink family (you are now two family files deep into the Family Editor mode).

5. Click the Family Category And Parameters button on the Home tab's Properties panel.

   You should find that the shared parameter in the Family Parameters frame is selected. Also notice that the assigned family category is Plumbing Fixtures.

6. Close each family file without saving any changes.

This setting means that the sink can be scheduled separately as a plumbing fixture even though it is part of the countertop family. The counter can be scheduled too, but because the sink belongs to a different category, it won't be part of the casework schedule.

Shared Parameters

Parameters exist for every family in Revit. Some are created by the software developers and designed to work without any extra effort on your part. Others are created by you as you develop or modify content. Parameters are part of projects and families. You can create project parameters that are assigned to specific categories. These project parameters can be included in schedules and are an elegant way to include important information that applies to many families of one or more categories but that doesn't actually alter the physical family itself (think "information only").

When you create families, you can define more parameters than what you find in each template. Many of these are just family parameters that only have the role inside the family to determine how big or small it should be and what should be visible. These parameters are available to you in the project, but you can't schedule them or display their values in tags. When you need to do either, you need to plan for shared parameters (Figure 7.16).

Figure 7.16

Shared Parameters button on the Manage tab

Think of a shared parameter file as a dictionary (see Figure 7.17). It contains definitions that you can make available to projects and families as you work in either environment. When you want a parameter to both change the physical nature of a family *and* schedule it or tag it, you just need to create the shared parameter and assign it in the family. When you get back to your project, you add the same shared parameter to the project. This common definition helps Revit understand that the information we enter in a family and in projects is really the same information.

If you are going to be the go-to person for Revit families, then you'll want to become familiar with shared parameters. You'll also want to read Chapter 8 as well as get hold of the Revit Family Style Guide mentioned in that chapter.

Figure 7.17

Selecting a shared parameter

CHAPTER 8

Creating Families

In Chapter 7, "Introduction to Families," we discussed the broader role that families play in Autodesk Revit Architecture. A single chapter cannot do this subject true justice. This entire book—even perhaps several books—could be consumed with the vagaries of creating families, if you consider the full scope of the work you do.

This chapter serves, as the book's title suggests, as your introduction to creating Revit families. It will delve into the concepts and features that you need to appreciate in order to modify existing families as well as create your own.

This chapter covers the following topics:

- **Preparing to create a family**

- **Examining the tool chest**

- **The bigger picture**

- **Dissecting some practical examples**

Preparing to Create a Family

You can consider a family to be a smaller representation of the complexities of a project. Like a project, a family has unique requirements, and the choices you make during early design discussions can have considerable impact later when the family is being used in the project. It is often easier to create a family for yourself because you have all the answers (in an ideal world). When you are responsible for making families for other users, it can be just as tricky to find out what they really want as it is for you to figure out what your client really wants for their project.

When you create a family, you need to consider how it will be used and what it should look like. You are trying to both create a meaningful representation of a real object as well as improve the way a project is designed, documented, and ultimately built. The process will likely challenge your understanding of the components you include in the buildings you design. It is also very easy to be lulled into thinking that every family you create must be highly parametric. However, it is reasonable to create a simple version or a placeholder initially and then refine it as the project matures. You might just replace it entirely with a specific manufacturer's family when one is available.

The process to create a family can be reduced to the simple relationship that exists with our own bodies. In the Family Editor environment, certain terms can be compared with Revit elements:

Bones Reference planes and reference lines

Muscle Dimensions, constraints, and parameters

Skin The visible part of your family—solid and void forms as well as lines and regions

You and Revit are the "brains" of the operation. You tell Revit what you want the family to do, and Revit delivers the information to the muscle. The bones follow the instructions of the muscle. Skin has no choice but to follow the bones it is attached to, as long as the family isn't involved in a skiing accident.

You need to consider several things before you start creating a family from scratch. Since Revit is organized according to categories, you will need to start there. Then it is necessary to decide whether your family needs to be hosted by system families. A family can be placed by a single "pick" (a door) or by two "picks" (a plywood detail component). You need to choose which makes the most sense for your family. Once you've made these decisions, you can start working inside the family.

Modify an Existing Family or Start from Scratch?

Initially, the most common way a Revit user gets acquainted with families is by editing something in the stock library. They might need a door or window in another size, so they just create a new type, change a few parameters, and go back to what they were doing. It is very easy and quick—that is, until they can't find what they need. Even when a perfect version isn't available, they might be able to make some minor changes to something that is reasonably close. In this case, it makes sense to edit an existing family as well but save it as a different filename. There is a point, however, where editing an existing family is a complete waste of time. If you think it will take 20 minutes just to understand how a family was put together, then you should probably consider starting with a fresh template. This is where the learning curve gets a bit steeper.

Apart from editing something you already have, starting from scratch offers you nearly complete freedom. You don't have to contend with existing decisions or habits. You are the boss (at least to some extent). You start to design your family with a template, and choosing a template is the first of several decisions you must make.

Choosing a Category

All elements in Revit are organized into specific categories according to their role; you have model elements such as doors, walls, and windows and you have annotation elements such as tags, detail components, symbols, grids, and levels, to name just a few.

When you start creating a family, your first decision is to figure out which category you need. That shouldn't be too hard. When what you want to make doesn't fit neatly into a category, you can choose the catchall category Generic Models, as shown in Figure 8.1.

There is another catchall called Specialty Equipment, but this category does not provide a Cut representation, whereas Generic Models does, as shown in Figure 8.2. If you need a Cut representation for your family, be careful to choose Generic Models.

To choose your family template, there are two ways to access the template: the Recent Files window and the Application menu. The Recent Files window offers you the following choices:

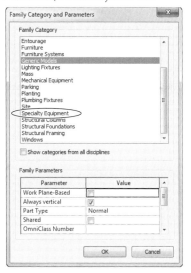

Figure 8.1

Family Category And Parameters dialog box

- Open
- New
- Conceptual Mass
- Web Library

Figure 8.2

**Object Styles' Cut
Line Weight**

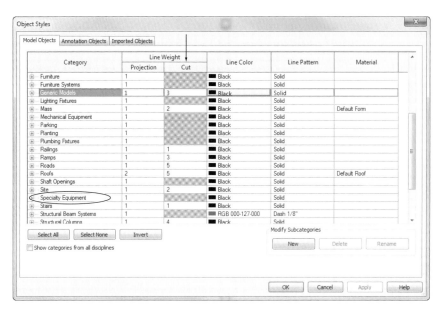

When you use the Application menu and choose New, the following options are offered:

- Project
- Family
- Conceptual Mass
- Title Block
- Annotation Symbol

Each of these (except for Project) is a family as far as Revit is concerned, but their templates are segregated into separate folders. Clicking one of the listed options will open the corresponding folder and offer you templates to choose from. There are many templates, and a little separation can help. Since Revit is organized around categories, you have to make the correct choice to get started properly. If you make a mistake, you can still change it later, but it is best to start well.

To create a new room tag, do the following:

1. Click the Application menu and select New ⇒ Annotation Symbol.

2. Choose the room tag.rft family template.

3. Click Open.

To create a new furniture family, do this:

1. Click the Application menu and select New ⇒ Family.

2. Choose the `furniture.rft` family template.

3. Click Open.

> You probably noticed that Revit offers two templates with *furniture* in the name: `furniture`
> `.rft` and `furniture systems.rft`. They exist because it is quite common to provide sum-
> maries of discreet furniture items such as chairs and tables apart from *system* furniture such
> as those made by Haworth or Steelcase, for example. This intentional separation makes it
> very easy to provide schedules that have a bias for one or the other.

If you decide that you need to change the category of the family after you've made your
selection, it isn't the end of the road; just take these steps:

1. Open the family and click the Home tab.

2. Go to the Properties panel, and click the Family Category And Parameters button.

3. Choose the new category you need, and click OK.

Catchall Sometimes it is not easy to choose. Are you making an awning family for a
front entrance? If you are making the brackets for this awning as a family that will support a roof, you may struggle with the category choices. Should it be Structural Framing,
Specialty Equipment, or just Generic Models? Structural families bring with them analysis implications. There may be no implications if you don't include analytical lines (or
aren't using Revit Structure), but then you aren't creating anything that helps an engineer
using Revit Structure. But that might be OK if you really don't have any training in structural design. Your family can be an excellent placeholder until something gets properly
sized or designed.

Generic Models This is a catchall category that has both a Cut and a Projection line
weight representation in views. If you need your component to provide both a Cut and
a Projection line weight, then Generic Models is your choice. If that isn't desirable, then
Specialty Equipment is a better choice because it does not have a Cut line weight.

Specialty Equipment This too is a catchall category that has only a Projection line weight
representation in views. If you need your component to provide both a Cut and a Projection
line weight, then Generic Models is your choice. If that isn't desirable, then Specialty
Equipment is a better choice because it doesn't have a Cut line weight.

Level Behavior Does your family need to be constrained from a level to one above? Does
it matter if your family just sits on a level? There are some families that provide two levels in the template (columns and structural columns, for example), while most others
provide just one. In some cases, you must start with one of these and change to a more
appropriate category just to get the extra level to manage your family's behavior. This can
also be considered as part of the next topic.

Are Hosted Families/Face-Based Families Required?

To host or not to host, paraphrasing the Bard, that is the question. This choice can be a bit murky, but the only time a family must absolutely be hosted is when you expect the family to alter the host in some way. If your family needs to cut a hole in a wall, roof, floor, or ceiling, then it either must be hosted by a host family or must use the face-based family template, as shown in Figure 8.3.

Figure 8.3

Floor-based Slab Depression family

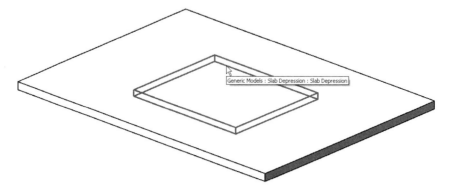

The language is a bit confusing too. We are referring to *host* or *hosted*, but the templates don't mention the word *host*, just *based*: wall based, floor based, ceiling based, and so on. The terms *host* and *based* are interchangeable. People are more likely to understand the term *host* than *based*. We wouldn't disagree if you suggested that the templates ought to be named with the term *hosted* instead of *based*.

Except when you need to alter a host, you do not have to choose to have your family hosted. If the family has no actual relationship with a building other than with a specific host, then it makes some sense to make the family hosted by that host, like a wall. Many objects in a building might normally be part of a wall, like a light switch, power receptacle, or thermostat, but even these items have been found on other surfaces than

Figure 8.4

Face-based and ceiling-based ceiling fans

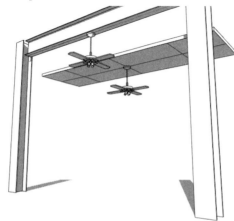

walls. For example, cabinetry might have receptacles or switches mounted on it. Therefore, choosing to make a light switch family wall based might actually be a hindrance at some point in a project. A similar classic example is a ceiling fan. These are often mounted to ceilings, but at times you'll find them attached to the underside of floor structure or from the bottom of beams and other structural elements. Therefore, a ceiling-based ceiling fan will eventually be rather inconvenient, as shown in Figure 8.4.

This is where the face-based template becomes useful. This family has a host element, but it isn't a wall, floor, ceiling, or roof. It is a "host" that can pretend to be whatever surface you want it to be. Revit is equally willing to believe that your family is as at home attached to the underside of a beam as to the top of a table. You can create non-hosted families, and if you really need them to be hosted later, you can just nest them into a hosted template. That is much easier to do than remaking the family to not require a host.

Choosing a Placement Technique

If you examine the templates that exist in the folders provided with Revit, you will find a couple templates that include the description "line based," as shown in Figure 8.5. These are different from hosted or based families. This description applies to how you use them in the project, specifically, how you place them. Most families are single-pick families, meaning that you click once to place them, whether on a face or just on the level like a desk or a chair.

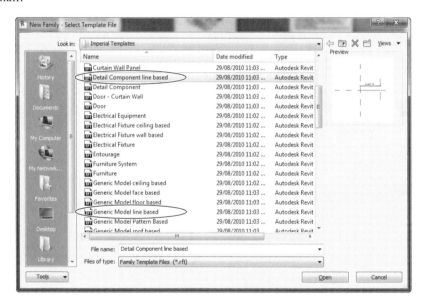

Figure 8.5

The available line-based templates

The line-based template allows you to create a family that is placed with two picks, very much like clicking a wall or sketching a line. For example, you could create a family that represents decorative rafter tails on the exterior facade of your building, as shown in Figure 8.6. Another example might be a sunscreen louver system. To place either of these, the user would only need to click the start and end points. These families are not the easiest to make if you are just getting started. If you are patient, you will gain some experience with some project-inspired ideas, which can be quite useful.

Figure 8.6

Rafter tails created using a line-based family template

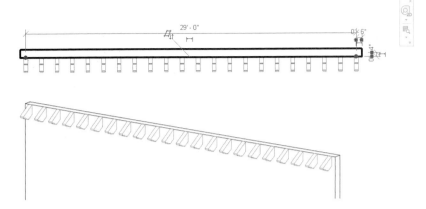

Level of Detail

The phrase *level of detail* (LOD) is emerging in the broader context of design and building information modeling (BIM). Organizations attempting to specify BIM are wrestling with defining LOD. How much detail is required, and when is it required? Also important is to decide when there is too much or inappropriate detail. In the context of a building project, it is certainly an important topic. It is equally relevant for each family you create and use. It isn't hard to imagine that families that are too detailed or complex will ultimately have an impact in the project context too.

As you have already learned, Revit uses the Detail Level feature to allow you to display three different LODs in your views. These are simply referred to as coarse, medium, and fine. Each family you use and create can take advantage of each setting by choosing to display only the relevant information at the corresponding detail level. As you add features to a family, you can decide which view orientation is relevant.

A detailed column does not need to show all the detail at the base in a plan view, usually preferring to show only the overall extent of the base, as shown in Figure 8.7. An elevation view might benefit from the more elaborate appearance of the column, but even that might be excessive if the scale used in the view is fairly coarse like $\frac{1}{8}'' = 1'\text{-}0''$ or $\frac{1}{16}'' = 1'\text{-}0''$ (1:100 or 1:200). It might be better to use a combination of view orientation selection and detail level.

Subcategories

Each model family has at least one subcategory called Hidden Lines that is used in conjunction with the Show Hidden Lines and Remove Hidden Lines tools. Many families have several subcategories; doors, for example, have the following subcategories: Elevation Swing, Frame/Mullion, Glass, Hidden Lines, Opening, Panel, and Plan Swing. These are intended to provide additional control over how doors are presented to you in various views. The Doors subcategories (refer to Figure 8.8) are what come with Revit, but you can choose to create additional subcategories for your own content if you need similar control over them too.

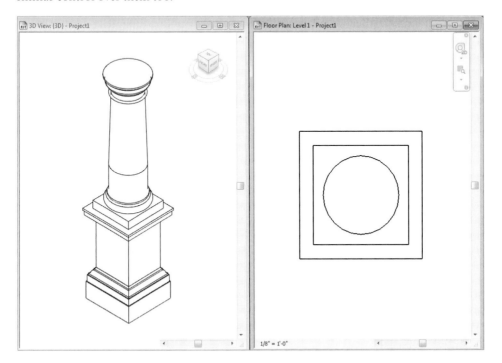

Figure 8.7

Plan view of column showing less detail than the actual column base has in a 3D view

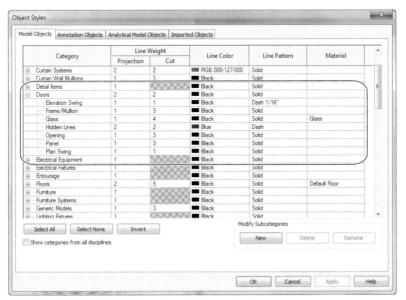

Figure 8.8

Doors subcategories

TYPING MATTERS

You need to be careful when adding subcategories. If too many different people do this, you can end up with chaos such as different spelling and words attempting to describe the same thing.

Category	Line Weight		Line Color	Line Pattern	Material
	Projection	Cut			
⊟ Generic Models	1	1	■ Black		
Hidden Lines	1	1	■ Black	Dash	
My Subcategory	1	1	■ Black	Solid	
My-sub-category	1	1	■ Black	Solid	
MY-SUBCATEGORY	1	1	■ Black	Solid	
my_sub_category	1	1	■ Black	Solid	
MySubCategory	1	1	■ Black	Solid	

Parametric vs. Nonparametric

There is a natural tendency when people begin using Revit to gravitate toward creating fewer but highly parametric and flexible families that represent what would have been many more components in their earlier product libraries. We find it interesting that after several years of using Revit, the same people who took this approach are now gravitating toward more individual and simpler families. So-called *super families* can be harder for novices to use and understand. They see many possible settings and are easily confused about what they can or should change. We've seen families that require an hour "lunch-and-learn" session to explain how to use them. Although the feature is cool, the very practical problem of helping regular users be efficient is important, probably more important than having super families. The average user might just be more productive returning to the library to get another kind of family than trying to figure out how to make some changes in the single super family instead. It is a balancing act, and each firm and team will have to assess their strengths and weaknesses to find that elusive equilibrium.

Believe it or not, there are perfectly good reasons to make families that are not parametric at all. One size, one configuration, and that's all you want. In early design, the rush to get your ideas on paper and in front of your client can demand that you model just the individual family you need without taking more time to make it flexible. You can always return to the family later if it survives the various design meetings you have with your client. There are also products that have only a couple configurations, and it is just as easy to make two families as one. In particular are items that are oriented in one way but not offered in a mirrored configuration. You are probably better off with separate families so these special configurations aren't misrepresented. Again, you are seeking a balance between parametric, flexible, and reusable families and the fast, efficient use of your time.

Examining the Tool Chest

The Family Editor features fewer tools than the regular project environment, but they are no less useful or powerful. This section will describe how these features factor into the families you make. Before we get into them, we'll look at several parts of the interface that get a bit more attention in Revit than others. Some of these are no different in either the project or the family. Two are not used outside the Family Editor. It won't be hard to remember them after you make a couple families.

Family Category And Parameters This dialog box allows you to change the category assignment for your family. This way, you can start with a family template and change your mind to some degree. You cannot change to the mass category or change from the mass category. You will find that not all categories are offered to you either. If a category is missing, you can't change your family to that category.

Family Types This dialog box is the primary interface between you and the parameters you define to control your family. Once you associate a parameter/label with a dimension, it is a good habit to change the parameter with this dialog box. When the parameter value is locked (as shown in Figure 8.9), you cannot simply select the constrained geometry and alter the dimension value as you can in a project. You will very likely open this dialog box as often as you use the Properties palette in a project.

> Make a keyboard shortcut! You can define a keyboard shortcut to open this dialog box.

Options Bar This location is no less important in the Family Editor than in a project. If you have trouble remembering where the Options bar is, you are probably still struggling with Revit in general. This spot is dynamic, and you have to remember to look there when you work.

Figure 8.9

The lock feature to prevent changing parameters directly "in canvas"

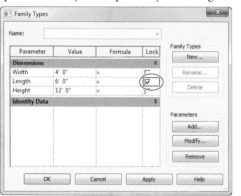

Type Selector With version 2012, the Type Selector is now part of the Properties palette. If you're familiar with previous versions of Revit, that will take a little getting used to. It is in the same place in the project environment. Just remember, it is a frequent place for your cursor to visit.

Properties Palette Also new to 2012, you'll visit this as much in the Family Editor as in a project, except now you don't have to open it all the time because it is normally open already. Revit is built around this dialog box, and the Family Editor is no different.

Visibility/Graphic Overrides This is used in both the family and project environments. It is less intrusive in the Family Editor, but you will need to use it from time to time to manage what you see—or don't see, for that matter. The keyboard shortcut for this (VG) is probably one you'll remember the easiest.

Reference Planes and Lines: The "Bones"

These provide the structure a family needs to provide consistent flexible behavior.

Reference Planes

A reference plane (as shown in Figure 8.10) defines a work surface, so to speak. Imagine a sheet of glass under your feet. Now imagine a sheet of glass in front of you extending from the sheet beneath you up toward the sky. Each of these sheets of glass can be thought of as a work plane. All objects in Revit are based on a work plane that either you deliberately choose or Revit chooses in the absence of a decision by you.

Figure 8.10

Reference plane in use in an elevation and 3D view

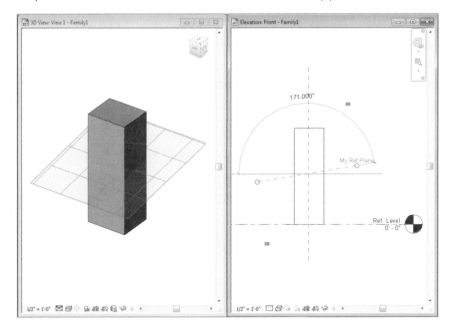

You need consider how your family should adjust. Do you want it to flex (increase or decrease in size) from the middle? Would it be better to increase in size from the left side instead? You need to place the reference planes, name them, and constrain them to allow the family to grow the way you intend. Like any element in Revit, reference planes have properties. We'll take a few minutes to explain how these properties affect the role that reference planes play in your families. Each of the properties listed here is found by selecting a reference plane and then looking in the Properties palette.

WALL CLOSURE

The Wall Closure setting is used along with settings in your walls to define how far the finish layers of a wall should turn and enter the opening created by doors and windows. If your design involves a detail that wraps the opening with the finish, such as brick, for example, then this feature will be helpful. Revit allows for two planes to use this setting, one for the exterior finish and the other for the interior finish.

NAME

It is a good habit to provide a unique name. It must be unique! You cannot use the same name twice in a project or family. The name appears at the "head" of the reference plane. It must be named if you want to select it to define a work plane at another time. The positive direction of a solid is determined by the location of the "head" of a reference plane (as shown in Figure 8.11). The positive direction is to the right of the head for reference planes created by Autodesk in the Revit templates, and any that are copies of them. For those that you sketch yourself, the positive direction is to the left of the head.

SCOPE BOX

The Scope Box setting is irrelevant in the Family Editor and families. It is a project-only feature and plays no role in families.

IS REFERENCE

The Is Reference value sets the priority that Revit will use in the project when you use the Dimension or Align tool with your family. Let's say you have a door in a wall (as shown in Figure 8.12), and you've decided to make sure the door is 4′- 0″ (1200mm) from the nearest wall. You need to add a dimension and lock it.

When you decide to use a different door, Revit seems to know how to switch the doors yet maintain the same position, as shown in Figure 8.13. If you don't add a specific locked dimension defining how this door should be positioned, Revit will assume the Center (Left/Right) reference plane will take precedence. The doors will be swapped and aligned with their common centerline.

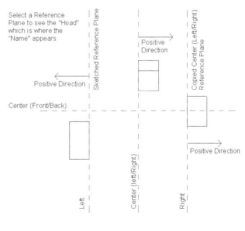

Figure 8.11

Depicting the orientation of reference planes and positive/negative values for geometry depth

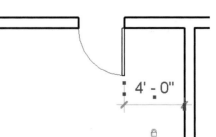

Figure 8.12

You can manage a door's location with a dimension and the Is Reference setting.

Most stock content uses the Is Reference setting. The default setting for a new reference plane is the Weak Reference option. Figure 8.14 shows the properties for the reference plane named Right in the imperial door family template. Providing a name for

Figure 8.13

Exchanging a single door for a double, but the side position is maintained.

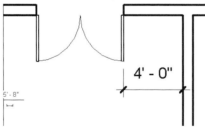

each reference plane will help you and others remember why it was created. Adding a name will also let you choose the reference plane from a list when you need to assign a different work plane to a view when you are creating solids or voids. This is true for the project environment too.

In Figure 8.14, notice there is no Name value assigned. Each reference plane can be Strong or Weak. You can choose Strong, Weak, Not A Reference, and specific names such as Right, Top, or Bottom. A strong reference has the highest priority for dimensioning or snapping. A weak reference means you may need to use the Tab key feature in order to use it for your dimension. Zooming in and out also affects how Revit will see reference

Figure 8.14

Door family reference plane properties

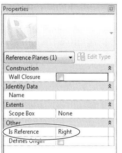

planes. Just remember that a strong reference gets Revit's attention first when other lesser reference planes are present.

By choosing one of the predefined names, you are establishing two things: a strong reference and a common reference plane for Revit to use when you want to switch families. If you don't want a reference plane to take on such a role, choose the Not A Reference option instead. If you want your reference plane to be unnamed and play a lesser role than other strong reference planes, choose Weak Reference.

Revit can display grips (blue triangles) for parts of your family so you can stretch them manually within a project. This is true for parameters that are defined as instance parameters. When you make a reference plane and assign a strong or weak reference or other predefined named option (see the following list), Revit will display these grips (as shown in Figure 8.15). If you don't see them, you just need to make sure that the reference plane is strong or weak and the dimension is associated with an instance parameter. When you assign a reference plane to Not A Reference, the grips will not be available.

Here's a list of the predefined names you can use (no, you can't add your own, sorry!):

- Not A Reference
- Strong Reference
- Weak Reference
- Left
- Center (Left/Right)
- Right
- Front
- Center (Front/Back)
- Back
- Bottom
- Center (Elevation)
- Top

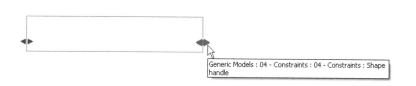

Generic Models : 04 - Constraints : 04 - Constraints : Shape handle

Figure 8.15

Grips appear in families using instance parameters and strong or weak Is Reference settings.

DEFINES ORIGIN

Two reference planes that are not parallel in plan views can be used to define the origin of a family. One reference plane at an elevation can define a vertical (Z) origin.

> There is a coordinate origin in a family as well. Be careful to avoid moving your origin, as defined by reference planes, from the actual coordinate origin in the family. Although Revit will let you see the project origin, it isn't possible to see the coordinate origin of a family yet. You can find it if you import a DWG file that contains a line that starts at the origin. Just import the file using the positioning option Auto – Origin To Origin. You can use this technique to ensure that content is at the real origin. Remember to remove the imported file when you are finished with it.

Reference Lines

These were created specifically to resolve the angular constraints you may need in your families. Reference planes do not respect the spring point (intersection) of an angular relationship between them. This is because they don't really have an endpoint; they have just a graphical control that lets you manage how much of the reference plane you see. Reference lines have actual endpoints and have four work planes. You can see them in Figure 8.16. There is one vertical plane parallel to the line, one plane perpendicular to the line, and one plane perpendicular to each endpoint.

This makes it possible to create dependant relationships between the work planes of several reference lines. When these were first introduced, one of Revit's original designers, David Conant, demonstrated (at Autodesk University 2004) the concept using an articulated task lamp as inspiration, as shown in Figure 8.17. There are few examples of families using them in the stock library for Revit Architecture. In contrast, however, practically all the pipe and duct fitting content for Revit MEP uses them extensively. They are also increasingly important in the new conceptual design environment (massing).

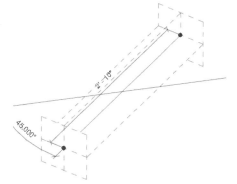

Figure 8.16

A reference line has four work planes you can use.

Figure 8.17

Reference lines
applied to an articu-
lated task lamp

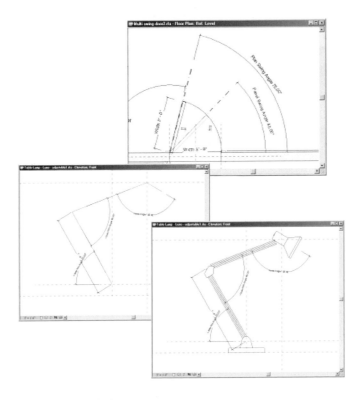

Defining Rules: The "Muscle"

You add dimensions in a project to provide important information to the person using your documents. When you create a family, the dimensions you add are there only to explain what your requirements are to Revit. The only time anyone will ever see them is when they choose to edit the family itself. Providing a properly dimensioned drawing isn't the intention. Rather, it is necessary to define how the family should behave and what you want Revit to do.

Dimensions can be constrained by using a lock (padlock icon), by using equality (EQ icon), and by assigning a parameter using a label. It is also possible to use the lock constraint when you use the Align tool. The lock and equality constraints work the same way they do in the project environment.

Locks

Using the padlocks that appear next to the dimension values when a dimension string is selected can lock the dimension value so that Revit will maintain that value while others are permitted to change, as shown in Figure 8.18.

The padlock (as shown in Figure 8.19) also appears when using the Align command.

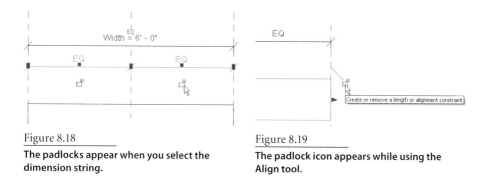

Figure 8.18

The padlocks appear when you select the dimension string.

Figure 8.19

The padlock icon appears while using the Align tool.

Judicious use of locking will ensure that you don't overconstrain your project so you can avoid causing poor computer performance. In families, however, it is very important to avoid ambiguity, and therefore it is important to use constraints like these to explicitly tell Revit what to do.

Equality

This concept is a feature of dimensions that permit you to ensure referenced elements stay equally spaced relative to each other. There is a difference between equality as a constraint and the existence of equality as "EQ" on a dimension string. The icon shown in Figure 8.20 is the constraint.

Figure 8.21 shows the context menu option to display the text *EQ* instead of a dimension value. If you'd rather see the dimension value, just use the context menu option to turn off EQ Display. Just don't use the visible icon to do it. If you do, you will remove the constraint you want to be equal.

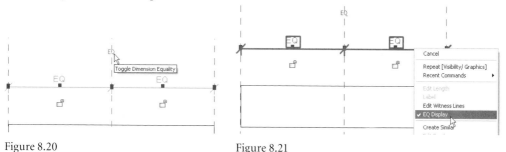

Figure 8.20

The equality constraint icon appears when you select a dimension string that references three or more elements.

Figure 8.21

You can display *EQ* or the actual dimension value.

You should pay special attention to the anchor symbol (as shown in Figure 8.22) that will appear when a member of equality constrained elements is selected. This anchor will determine how the constraint is applied and therefore how the elements will stretch or flex.

Figure 8.22

The anchor symbol appears to help define how the equality constraint should flex the reference planes.

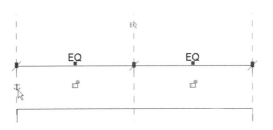

This anchor can be dragged to the middle element so the three elements will flex equally from the middle. As pictured in Figure 8.22, these three reference planes will flex from the left side toward the right.

Parameters

Parameters (also called *labels* when they are applied to dimensions) are the underlying information of all objects. They are how you communicate with Revit. Parameters include the height of a wall, the width of a door, the thickness of a counter, the material of a floor, the elevation of a level, and the scale of a view. Every piece of information you might want to supply, change, schedule, calculate, or study is a parameter.

These are the rules that you define and permit your users to alter once they are loaded into their projects. The other constraints we've described are locked behaviors that users cannot alter when they use them in the project. The only way to change them is to edit the family and reload it. Labels and parameters provide your users with the flexibility they are used to with Revit.

TYPE AND INSTANCE PARAMETERS

This should be a familiar concept by now, but just to be thorough, let's discuss this concept again briefly. All parameters in Revit apply to either the kind or type of object you are working with or the individual instance of the object. A wall style whose type is 8″ (200mm) Masonry has *type parameters* that affect every individual instance of the wall, while its *instance parameters* affect only a single wall instance. The thickness of the wall is a type parameter. Every instance of the wall will be the same thickness. The height of the wall is an instance parameter, so each wall can have a different height if necessary.

PARAMETER ROLES

Parameters are broken down into three roles: project, family, and shared. Either they are created in advance for you (system) by Autodesk or you create them yourself (user) as needed.

PROJECT (ENCOUNTERED IN A PROJECT ENVIRONMENT)

- System (type or instance)
- User-defined (type or instance)

FAMILY (ENCOUNTERED IN A PROJECT OR FAMILY EDITOR ENVIRONMENT)

- System (type or instance)
- User-defined (type or instance)

SHARED (ENCOUNTERED IN A PROJECT OR FAMILY EDITOR ENVIRONMENT)

- Project (type or instance)
- Family (type or instance)

Shared parameters combine the natures of system and user-defined parameters. Shared parameters exist to allow you to tell Revit you are talking about the same information whether it originates in a family or a project. They can be used to create a parameter in both a family and/or a project to allow the information assigned to them to be displayed in a schedule and/or tags.

Keep in mind that when you create a parameter from a shared parameter, there is no active link to the file it comes from. Think of the shared parameter file as a dictionary that Revit uses to look up definitions of parameters. This definition is stored in your project and families afterward. When Revit encounters a parameter in a family within a project that also uses the parameter, it automatically knows they are using the same definition. This allows you to schedule and tag objects.

Parameters exist either because Revit made them for you (system) to use in advance or because you chose to make them yourself (user). You can't change or alter a system parameter's character or how it will work except to provide a different value for it. Every element in Revit has some system parameters. Here are some system parameter examples (with parameter names in quotes):

- Wall "Top And Bottom Constraint"
- Wall "Location Line"
- Floor Object Layer "Thickness"
- Casework "Manufacturer"
- Window "Width"
- Project "Name"
- Project "Client Name"
- View "View Scale"

You can create parameters yourself to control a family and to store information. It is important to appreciate that user-defined parameters that are created in a project can appear in that project's schedules but not in tags. Those user-defined parameters created in a family cannot be used in schedules or tags unless they are created using a shared parameter definition. These are some user parameter examples (again with parameter names in quotes):

- Room "Occupancy Classification"
- Project "Issued Date"
- Project "Issued Description"
- Door "Undercut"
- Door "Jamb Detail Type"
- Window "Glazing Area"

CONSISTENCY

Parameters in Revit's system and component families as well as project parameters all use Title Case, meaning every word gets a capitalized first letter. Some users prefer to use all uppercase for their parameters because that makes them look different and therefore makes it more obvious which parameters belong to them. Still others prefer to use all lowercase for much the same reason and perhaps because they have some aversion to the Shift key. Whatever you decide, please be consistent!

To create a parameter called Width, follow these steps:

1. Create a new family using the `Generic Model.rft` family template.

2. Click Family Types on the Home tab of the ribbon.

3. Click Add in the Parameters frame.

4. Supply the following information:

   Name: Width

   Discipline: Common (Architecture uses Common)

   Type of Parameter: Length (default setting)

   Group Parameter Under: Dimensions (default setting)

   Type/Instance: Type

5. Click OK when you're finished.

You now have a parameter listed under the Dimensions category.

The Reporting Parameter feature is available when you choose Instance instead of Type. This feature arrived with the 2011 release, and it provides access to information that wasn't available to you in the past. For example, with a door family, you can use this feature to determine how thick the hosting wall is. With this knowledge, the family can then respond to alter the size of the frame accordingly as the hosting wall thickness changes or the door is placed in a variety of wall types. You wouldn't put this feature in beginner territory, but seasoned "family editors" are quite happy with this development.

Dimensions

Every dimension (using the dimension tools) you add to a family is effectively a rule. If the rule isn't necessary, then the dimension isn't needed. Adding another dimension just because it is good drafting practice will, more often than not, end up generating an error message telling you that doing so will overconstrain the family.

It is important to realize that Revit is focused on the orthogonal relationship between elements when you attempt to constrain them with dimensions. When you want to define angular relationships, you need to make sure that those dimensions are really referencing the elements you intend them to reference. This means paying close attention to the information provided in tool tips and on the status bar to ensure the correct elements are referenced. If you aren't careful, you will get strange results as you flex and test a family.

AUTOMATIC SKETCH DIMENSIONS

In addition to temporary and permanent dimensions, Revit has automatic sketch dimensions. It creates them behind the scenes to locate everything you make in Revit. These are the glue or magic of the Revit Family Editor. If you don't realize they exist or don't understand them, you'll have a little harder time getting comfortable.

They won't be called into action until your family has at least one parameter label assigned to a dimension or the family uses an equality constraint. If those are present, when you add a line, solid, or void, they will start to appear. For solids and voids, they appear during Sketch mode. Revit starts using them, but you still won't see them because the family templates all have them turned off. If you are diligent, they don't need to be visible, and they can clutter a view unnecessarily. It's just important to understand that they exist and that you can verify they are helping you make your family.

To see sketch dimensions come to life, take the following steps:

1. Start a new family using the `Generic Model.rft` family template.

2. Add a new reference plane parallel to the right of the existing Center (Left/Right) reference plane.

3. Add a dimension between the vertical reference planes.

4. Create a parameter called Width (this was outlined in the previous section).

5. Select the dimension string.

6. Click the Label: <None> field on the Options bar.

7. Choose the Width parameter from the list.

   This assigns it to the dimension.

8. Using Visibility/Graphic Overrides, turn on Automatic Sketch Dimensions.

   This is on the Annotation Categories tab.

9. Sketch a model line somewhere between the reference planes.

   The dimensions that appear are the automatic sketch dimensions.

What do automatic sketch dimensions do? Revit uses them to infer your intent once you start using parameters and labeled dimensions or the equality constraint. If Revit does well, you get automatic obedience from your family with a minimum of effort.

When it doesn't, you get less-predictable behavior. It is important to tell Revit what you want when this happens. Reviewing these automatic sketch dimensions can help you decide what other constraints or parameters you really need to add to eliminate any confusion.

> If you want to create an angular relationship between elements, consider using reference lines. You should also avoid drawing your lines directly on a reference plane. The automatic sketch dimensions may assume a relationship with the reference plane incorrectly. It is more reliable or predictable to sketch lines, those that are intended to be changed with labeled angular dimensions, away from reference planes entirely. Sketch them at an angle first, and then constrain them at the angle.

Creating What You See: The "Skin"

Assuming you've created "bones" (reference planes) and added some "muscle" (dimensions and parameters) to your family, you are now ready to deal with adding what everyone will see, the "skin" of your family. It isn't absolutely required to build a family in this order (bones, then muscle, then skin). If you do it consistently, though, you should find that your families work correctly the first time more often than if you don't.

Geometry

The basic building blocks of a Revit family are solids and voids. They can be created using five distinct processes: extrusion, blend, revolve, sweep, and swept blend. There are also a few different kinds of lines that can be used to convey the proper amount of information in each view.

Extrusion A solid or void extrusion is a three-dimensional object that is described by first sketching a profile with lines forming a closed boundary and then providing a depth. A familiar example of an extrusion is a mullion for a curtain wall. Mullions are extrusions made of aluminum, typically. They have a profile and are "extruded" to a depth/length. A solid extrusion is used to represent columns, the seat of a chair, or a door panel—virtually anything you need to make can be described with a solid extrusion in some fashion.

A void extrusion is created exactly the same way except that a void is permitted to cut a solid. A void can also explicitly cut one solid while not cutting another, according to your demands.

Blend A blend solid or void is exactly the same concept as an extrusion except that you have two profiles: base and top. These profiles can be different shapes and sizes. They can be placed in different positions relative to each other. In this way, a leaning column or tapering table leg can be fashioned. Stacking tapering or twisting blends can create forms that you are beginning to see in more and more building forms.

Revolve A solid or void revolve is also created using a profile, but instead of providing a depth, you provide a value for rotation around an axis that you must also sketch or pick. The combination of a profile and axis defines the shape and where that shape should "spin" around the axis. Imagine a wine glass or a corner molding detail. A revolve also requires a work plane for the axis, which should be created first.

Sweep A solid or void sweep uses a profile, but instead of using an axis like a revolve, it needs a path to follow. Crown molding is a nice example of a sweep in action. You can sketch a path or pick the edges of other elements to describe a path and then either sketch a profile or use a separate profile family created at another time.

Swept Blend As the name suggests, this form combines the features of the sweep with the blend. It uses a single segment path with a profile at each end. The resulting form changes from each profile as it is created along the path.

Lines

Several kinds of lines are available in the Family Editor. They each play an important role when creating your family.

Symbolic These are similar in purpose and behavior to detail lines in a project. In the Family Editor, however, they are called *symbolic* because they are intended to provide a simpler graphical (symbolic) representation of a family that might be too complex to justify displaying the three-dimensional geometry at various scales. A highly detailed column base might print as muddy line work at coarse scales. If symbolic lines (found on the Annotate tab of the ribbon) are used for this base instead, they can provide a simpler profile or plan representation and save the fullness of the 3D form for finer scales.

Symbolic lines appear only in views that are parallel to the view they are created in. A symbolic line sketched in a Left elevation will also appear in the Right elevation. The same is true for Front and Back elevations. Carefully using the detail levels Coarse, Medium, and Fine and assigning these symbolic lines to them appropriately are key parts of making quality families. Symbolic line styles are provided for each object style that exists in the family template and for any that are added to the family. If a family is "cuttable" in the project environment, there are both Projection and Cut line styles to choose from.

Model Model lines are equivalent to model lines in the project environment. A model line exists for each category and subcategory of the family you are using as well as a cut and projection version, assuming the family can be cut.

Lines When you are creating a detail component, a profile, a tag, a title block, or any 2D-only element, there is only one Line tool. This is because these are 2D elements, and there is no need to differentiate between Model and Symbolic, so they are just called lines. It's confusing a bit perhaps, but actually it makes sense.

Analytical (RS) These are a special feature reserved for structural component families. These are used to describe the path that loads take through a structural component. It is important to properly place these in order for third-party analysis tools to correctly evaluate them.

 You can use the Convert Lines tool if you decide that you should have used symbolic lines instead of model lines, or vice versa.

Family Visibility Controls

Just as important as creating the things you see is having some control over how or when they are displayed. Chapter 6 dealt with the wide range of control that Revit offers you while you're working on a project. These items apply to families and set the stage for them to be used later in the project. Lines, solids, text (in annotation families), and labels all offer visibility control features.

Visible Parameter This parameter (as shown in Figure 8.23) has a check box and can also be connected to a Yes/No parameter (more about this later). If you deselect the parameter, that element will not be visible in the project environment no matter what your user does to the family, short of editing and changing the family itself. This allows you to create line work or other geometry that might drive design intent but should not be visible itself. For example, this can be useful to define a clearance or conflict solid element that can be detected with Revit's Interference Detection tool—detected but not seen.

Figure 8.23

The Visible parameter

Visibility Each element has Visibility/Graphic Overrides options as well. You can find them within the Properties palette or simply by clicking the Visibility Settings button on the ribbon when the element is selected. Figure 8.24 shows the options you have within this dialog box.

Figure 8.24

The Family Element Visibility Settings dialog box

Simply deselecting an option will prevent the element from being visible according to each condition. When combined with the model and symbolic lines, you have a great deal of control over the graphic display of your content.

Creating Forms (Solids/Voids)

As mentioned earlier, solids and voids are the visible part of your family; they're the "skin" that everyone will see. These solid form tools—Extrusion, Blend, Revolve, Sweep, and Swept Blend—as well as the void versions of them are found on the Home tab's Forms panel, as shown in Figure 8.25. While editing, you use a variety of tools on the ribbon. To finish, you click the large green check mark, formally called Finish Edit Mode.

Figure 8.25

The Forms and Mode panels are critical for creating forms.

Solid Extrusion

A solid extrusion uses a single sketched profile and a depth. To create a solid extrusion, follow these steps:

1. Select the Home tab on the ribbon → Forms panel → Extrusion button.

2. Sketch a rectangle (or other shape) to define your sketch.

3. Click the green check mark to complete the extrusion.

> Notice the Depth parameter on the Options bar prior to sketching; it is not active from when you start sketching until you stop sketching. You can assign the depth via the Properties palette. You can disregard these options and simply associate the extrusion with a reference plane in an elevation view instead, dragging the visible grip of the solid until the reference plane is highlighted, releasing the grip, and then using the padlock icon that appears.

4. Open the view Elevations: Front to assign the top of the extrusion to a reference plane.

   The result should look like Figure 8.26.

Blend

A solid blend consists of two sketches: a base sketch and a top sketch. This is easy when you think in terms of plan orientation, but it's less obvious when you are sketching in an elevation orientation. Regardless, just consider that *a blend needs two sketches whether you think of them as base/top or front/back.* Once the two sketches are defined, you need only define the depth of the blend or, in other words, the offset between each sketched profile. To create a solid blend, follow these steps:

1. Select the Home tab on the ribbon → Forms panel → Blend button.

Figure 8.26

The finished solid extrusion

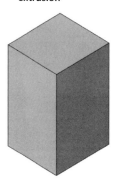

Figure 8.27

The finished solid blend

You are sketching the base profile at this time. The presence of the Edit Top button on the ribbon indicates this. You can't draw the top first because you can't switch to this mode until there is a valid sketch for the base.

2. Sketch a profile for the base.

3. Click Edit Top on the Mode panel.

4. Sketch a profile for the top.

5. Click the green check mark to complete the blend.

6. Open the view Elevations: Front to assign the top of the blend to a reference plane that should be created for it in advance.

The finished result should look something like Figure 8.27.

Figure 8.28

A profile to consider for your sketch

Revolve

A revolve, which is a shape (profile) that "spins" around an axis (imagine turning a wooden spindle on a lathe), requires three things: a work plane, an axis line, and a boundary line (profile):

Work Plane The work plane is needed to define the orientation of the form.

Axis Line The axis line defines where the profile will "spin," or revolve.

Boundary Line The boundary line defines the shape you want to "spin" or revolve.

To create a solid revolve, follow these steps:

1. Select the Home tab on the ribbon → Forms panel → Revolve button.

2. Open the Elevations: Front view, and choose Set Work Plane from the Work Plane panel to confirm the work plane is Center (Front/Back).

Figure 8.29

The finished solid revolve

3. Use the AXIS Line tool from the Draw panel to sketch the axis on top of the Reference Plane Center (Left/Right).

4. Click the Boundary Line tool to sketch half of the profile (as shown in Figure 8.28).

5. Click the green check mark when you are finished.

6. Select the revolve.

7. Change the Start and End Angle parameters (in the Properties palette). Notice the effect they have on the revolve form.

The result should resemble Figure 8.29.

Your sketch must not cross beyond the axis; the sketch must be completely on one side of the axis. A sketch will produce a hollow revolve if it represents the "skin" of your shape. It will produce a solid if it just represents the outside profile or shape.

Sweep

A sweep (imagine crown molding along a wall at or near a ceiling) comprises a path and a profile. You start with a path that you define by sketching lines or by picking the edges of other elements present in the family. You must finish the path and then start to create the profile. It can be defined by sketching with lines too, or you can choose to use an external profile family. The advantage of using an external family is that you can reuse it easily. It is more efficient since you can make the profile once and use it many times. To create a solid sweep, follow these steps:

1. Select the Home tab on the ribbon → Forms panel → Sweep button.

2. Click Sketch Path on the Sweep panel.

3. Open the Floor Plans: Ref. Level view, and sketch a rectangle.

   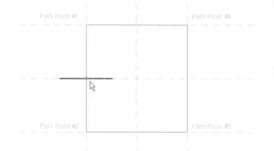

   Notice the origin of your path. This can be relocated to another segment or the beginning/end of any segment. It is a good idea to place the origin on a straight segment that is perpendicular to a view to make it easier to sketch a profile. You cannot change the origin after a profile is sketched, so make sure to set it correctly now.

4. Click the green check mark.

5. Click Edit Profile.

6. When prompted to do so, select one of the elevation views offered to you.

   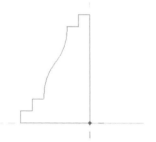

   The views that are offered are parallel to the origin of your path, which is the small blue line with a red dot perpendicular to one segment of your path. If you sketch something like this profile, you'll end up with what is shown here.

7. Click the green check mark when you are satisfied with your sketch path.

8. Open the Elevations: Front view.

9. Click Select Profile on the Sweep panel, and then click Edit Profile.

10. Sketch something like the profile shown in step 5.

11. Click Finish Edit Mode when you are satisfied with your profile sketch.

12. Click the green check mark to finish the sweep completely, as shown in Figure 8.30.

Swept Blend

This form requires a path just like the sweep, and it uses two profiles just like the blend; that's why it's called a *swept blend*. It is limited to one segment for the path, but it does allow the use of the Spline tool. The spline isn't the best thing for documenting a design, but it does permit creating interesting forms. If you need a swept blend that has more than one path segment, you'll need to piece them together with multiple swept blend forms.

Figure 8.30

The finished solid sweep

Follow these steps to create a modest swept blend:

1. Select the Home tab on the ribbon → Forms panel → Swept Blend button.

2. Open the Floor Plans: Ref. Level view, and click Sketch Path from the Swept Blend panel.

3. Sketch an arc using the Start-End-Radius Arc tool.

4. Click the green check mark; this completes the path.

5. Click Select Profile 1 (the first pick point of your path).

6. Click Edit Profile – Select 3D View: View 1 from the list; orient the view so you can see the work plane well.

7. Sketch a small rectangular shape at the origin.

8. Click the green check mark.

   This completes the first profile.

9. Click Select Profile 2 (the second pick point of your path).

10. Click Edit Profile; orient the view so you can see the work plane well.

11. Sketch a larger rectangular shape at the origin.

12. Click the green check mark.

This completes the second profile.

13. Click the green check mark again.

This completes the swept blend.

Your result should look something like Figure 8.31.

Figure 8.31

The finished swept blend form

Voids

The process for creating voids is exactly the same as for solids. The difference is that voids can cut solid geometry. They will cut solids automatically if the solid(s) they intersect is already present. If a void is created first, it will not cut a solid created afterward. If a void does not intersect a solid when its sketch is finished, it will not cut a solid when its shape or position is altered to cause it to intersect with a solid later. To resolve the relationships between solids and voids, Revit has the Cut Geometry and Uncut Geometry tools.

To experiment with a void extrusion, follow these steps:

1. Select Home tab on the ribbon → Forms panel → Extrusion button (create the solid form first so you have something to cut).

2. Open the Floor Plans: Ref. Level view, and sketch a simple rectangular profile.

3. Click the green check mark.

4. Select the Home tab → Forms panel → Void Forms button → Void Extrusion option.

5. Sketch a smaller rectangular profile that overlaps the solid form at one corner.

6. Click the green check mark and select Open 3D View: View 1.

Notice that this void cuts the solid immediately. If you place your mouse pointer near the edge where the void cuts the solid, you should see that the void is still there.

7. Select the void.

8. Click Edit Extrusion on the Mode panel.

9. Change the sketch a little (you can also drag the grips that appear at the edges of the void).

10. Click the green check mark to see the result.

To experiment with a void that does not cut immediately, follow these steps:

1. Select the Home tab → Forms panel → Extrusion button (create the solid form first so you have something to cut).

2. Open the Floor Plans: Ref. Level view, and sketch a simple rectangular profile.

SKETCHING VOIDS—CAREFULLY

When sketching voids, be careful not to place your sketch directly on the edge of a solid that is getting cut. If the finished sketch will result in a tiny sliver of geometry being left on the solid, Revit may generate an error. It is better to extend a void beyond the edges of the solid it will cut. The portion of the sketch that passes through the solid is the "knife" edge. The other edges are extraneous.

It might help to imagine a void as the cutting blades of a router bit that is cutting the edge of a wooden plank. One side of the bit cuts the plank, while the other side spins harmlessly in space away from the edge of the wood.

3. Click the green check mark.

4. Click the Home tab's Forms panel.

5. Select Void Forms → Void Extrusion.

6. Sketch a smaller rectangular profile above the solid extrusion so that it won't intersect its volume.

7. Click the green check mark when you're finished.

8. Select the void, and click and drag a grip control far enough to intersect the existing solid.

Notice that this void does not cut the solids. Let's pause to discuss the concept of joining and cutting geometry.

A solid can be changed into a void, and a void can be changed into a solid via the Solid/Void parameter for the solid/void. When Join Geometry is used between solids, you can no longer change a solid to a void unless you use the Unjoin Geometry tool. A void cannot be changed into a solid if it is cutting a solid. Within the conceptual massing Family Editor environment, Revit now also allows one solid to cut another solid.

Joining and Cutting Geometry

Similar to their role in projects for walls and other elements, in the Family Editor the Join Geometry, Unjoin Geometry, Cut Geometry, and Uncut Geometry tools permit you to define the relationship between intersecting solids and voids. With solids, Revit does not automatically create a line representing an intersection between them. You must use Join Geometry to tell Revit which solids should have this condition. Unjoin Geometry removes this relationship between solids.

Revit doesn't join geometry automatically in an attempt to reduce the computational effort required when solids intersect. By using the tool, you are explicitly telling Revit which relationships matter more to you. Revit will then generate line(s) to show how the elements intersect. If it isn't possible to see that two solids don't join cleanly (a line at their joint or intersection) in most (or any) of the views of a project, it may not be important to join solids at all.

The Cut Geometry and Uncut Geometry tools are similar to the Join tools except they apply to the way that solids and voids interact. A void can cut one solid and not another intentionally. It isn't obvious, but a void will remember that it is supposed to cut a solid that it doesn't actually come into contact with. This means that you can use dimensions and parameters to push and pull a void to cut or not cut a solid. Imagine a conference table that has a data port that can be lifted above the surface for access. You could model this in such a way that the void that cuts the tabletop intersects the table only when the data port is above the table. When the data port is beneath the surface, there is no hole indicated because the void no longer cuts the table top. There are many clever possibilities.

Continuing from the previous exercise, you can follow these steps to formally cut the geometry of the solid:

1. Choose the Modify tab of the ribbon → Geometry panel → Cut button → Cut Geometry option.

2. Select the void.

3. Select the solid.

    Notice that the void now cuts the solid.

4. Select the void, and drag it away from the solid so that it no longer intersects the solid.

    Notice that the solid is no longer cut.

5. Select the void, and drag it back into place.

    Notice that the solid is cut once again, as shown in Figure 8.32.

Figure 8.32

Void cutting, not cutting, and then cutting again as the location of the void's edge is changed

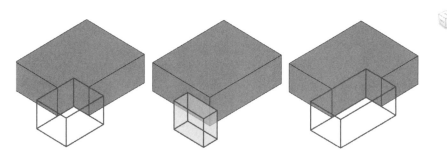

Voids can be hard to select once they are cutting solids. Just select one of the solids, and the voids will appear. Now you can see the voids more easily. Select the void you want to work with.

Assigning Materials to Families

There are two approaches to material assignment you can take when designing a family:

- Defined internally (family)
- Defined in projects

It comes down to whether you want to define specific materials now or let the user decide later in the context of a project. For manufacturer-specific content, it may be important to preset materials to just those that are actually available. For all others, it is more efficient to allow users to define the material in the project. It's more efficient because you don't waste time creating materials in the family that might not be used. Multiply this by the number of similar families you might need, and this can get quite time-consuming to keep all your content materially in sync.

By Categories If you assign forms to categories, you can avoid assigning a material in your family at all. The project you use the family in will determine how your family looks and will render automatically according to its category settings in Object Styles or Visibility/Graphic Overrides.

By Subcategories The same is true for subcategories. If you take the time to map out a strategy for subcategories, you can avoid assigning or creating material libraries for your families. This way, a project determines what your family looks like and how it renders as soon as you assign materials to the categories and subcategories you've defined. If your templates are already set up for this, it is even easier for your users to get to work.

By Parameters Using parameters and assigning them to each solid element that needs a material assignment is probably the most versatile approach. You create a parameter and simply connect it to the solid. The family is loaded into a project, and its materials are defined in the project by editing the properties of the family. No time is required of you to create specific materials in the family itself, and it is completely flexible for the end user.

When using material parameters, you need to create parameters and assign them to each solid in the family that needs a material assignment. There are two ways to define these parameters:

- Via the Family Types dialog box (in advance)
- While editing the properties of a solid (on the fly)

Solids that have had Join Geometry applied to them can share only one material assignment.

To create a Material parameter in advance, follow these steps:

1. Click Family Types on the Properties panel.

2. Click Add from the Parameters frame, and add this parameter data:

   Name: Table Leg Material

   Discipline: Common (Architecture uses Common)

   Type of Parameter: Material

   Group Parameter Under: Materials And Finishes

   Instance/Type: Type

3. Click OK to finish the parameter.

4. Select the solid to which you want to assign a material.

5. On the Properties palette, click the small square button on the far right of Material parameter row.

6. Choose the parameter you just created from the list.

7. Click OK to finish assigning the parameter to the solid.

To create a Material parameter on the fly, follow these steps:

1. Select the solid you want to assign a material to.

2. On the Properties palette, click the small square button on the far right of Material parameter row.

3. Click Add Parameter and add this parameter data:

   Name: Your Material Name

   Discipline: Common (Architecture uses Common)

   Type of Parameter: Material

   Group Parameter Under: Materials And Finishes

   Instance/Type: Type

4. Click OK to finish the parameter.

5. Choose your new parameter from the list.

6. Click OK to finish assigning the material to the solid.

Visibility and Yes/No Parameters

This is another equally effective way to manage what is visible in your family. Solids and lines can be assigned to parameters (a Yes/No check box), which will let you turn them on and off when you add the family to your project. A nice example you can open and examine is the stock Revit Room Tag family. It uses this concept to show either a room area or volume or neither. As mentioned earlier, each element has a Visible parameter. If you use the little "sneaky" square button at the far right, you can connect its Visible parameter to a parameter.

Follow these steps to associate a Yes/No parameter with your solid:

1. Create your parameter in advance as described earlier.

2. Select the solid that you'd like to assign to your new parameter.

3. On the Properties palette, click the small square button on the far right of the Visible parameter's row.

4. Choose the parameter name, or create one now as described earlier.

5. Click OK to finish assigning the parameter.

You can control the application of Material and Yes/No parameters in advance by assigning them in the family, or you can leave it up to the project team to decide what is needed. The beauty of using parameters to do these tasks is that it puts control in the hands of the project team. Your library of families will be a bit easier to manage because the project team is adjusting the things that make the families unique where it matters, in the project.

The Bigger Picture

There are several features—type catalogs, shared families, and shared parameters—that improve the user experience, allows for scheduling more information as well as make the process of creating families more efficient. These features play an important role in the ever-present need for reasonable standards to help improve your workflow as well as to get an upper hand on your family's libraries.

Types and Type Catalogs

Each family has one type initially, and it just uses the name of the family as its type name. When your family can represent several different types (think sizes or configurations), you can add more types. When you have many types, it can become a bit of a chore to check each size for accuracy. Revit provides the ability to create a catalog of types.

Type catalogs are simple text files that just require carefully defining each parameter that the catalog needs to set when the family is loaded into your project. When you choose to load one of these families, Revit will first open a dialog box that lists all the available types. When you choose more than one family that has a type catalog, you see a list of each family on the left, as shown in Figure 8.33. You make your selections for each, and then click OK.

STANDARDS: NAMING YOUR FAMILY AND TYPES

First, it is a good practice to create one type for each family so that it will be easier to update as you test and flex your family. As we just finished saying about types, "anything goes" should not be your motto, as tempting as it might be. Schedules might rely on the family name to help identify them meaningfully. Erratic naming habits will really start to show up in these schedules. People who use your families will also find inconsistency frustrating, and that can lead to all sorts of other undesirable issues. We won't presume to tell you exactly how to name your families, but we do encourage you to consider your process and create consistent habits that make everyone's interaction with your family library as good an experience as possible.

THE REVIT FAMILY STYLE GUIDE

The Revit Family Style Guide was created by Autodesk to help define standards for creating and managing content that will be posted at Autodesk's Seek website: `http://seek .autodesk.com/`. It also attempts to define the many parameters that other disciplines need to have for Revit MEP and Structure. If you are going to get serious about Revit families, you'll want to get this collection of documents and files.

The following list comes partially from the Revit Family Style Guide and offers some advice to consider for naming your family:

- Create unique names for each family.
- Use natural language to name the family.
- If possible, do not include the family category in the family name, unless the functional type is the same as the category.
- Capitalize the leading letters in each portion of the family name (Title Case).
- Keep filenames as short as possible.

The following list also partially comes from the Revit Family Style Guide and offers some advice for naming family types:

- Do not include the family name or category in the type name.
- Type names should mirror actual usage.
- Type names should indicate the key difference between types and standard sizes.
- When types are named by size, use dimensions only.
- Type names should include units unless they represent nominal sizes.
- Metric types should reflect local standards; use "soft" metric unless nominal sizes.
- Keep type names as short as possible.

Figure 8.33

Type catalog sample with multiple families selected

Nested Families

This should be a familiar concept; you nest drawings in CAD all the time, except there it's called *referencing* or *external references* (Xrefs). In Revit, you can create families as a "kit of parts" so you can minimize or eliminate redundant tasks and reuse these parts effectively, as shown in Figure 8.34. For example, you'll soon tire of making door panels in every door family for your firm's library, especially if you put the same panel in a half-dozen other doors just because the frame is different.

Figure 8.34

Door panel "kit of parts"

You could also tire of making frames for the same reason. Windows offer many reasons, as do casework families. There are examples of required nested behavior too, such as electrical families for switches and receptacles. These use a nested symbol family for the plan graphics and a 3D solid to create the outlet box and cover plate for elevation and 3D views.

It is also important to be careful how far you take nesting, because you can find yourself making that "super family" we mentioned earlier as well as making a family that is quite large (file size) and sluggish for users to deal with. Most families can be quite effective with a single level of nesting. Complex families can require a few levels of nesting, but these will also perform poorly when loading and making changes. Experimentation and testing should always be done prior to turning them over to the team to start using on the project.

Shared Families

This is a single check box in each family with a fairly significant impact; just click the Family Category And Parameters button to see it (Figure 8.35). The Shared option also applies only to the family when it is nested in another family. When a family is nested and its host is loaded into a project, Revit loads only enough of the nested family to be able to display it or a symbol of it, not the real family. As a result, it does not appear in the Project Browser under the Families branch. When the nested family has its Shared option selected, then Revit loads it into the project in addition to its host family. As a result, this family is listed in the Project Browser under the Families branch. This means you can place the nested family alone as well as have it appear whenever its host family is placed. More important, since the actual family is loaded, it becomes possible to schedule the nested family as if it were an individual apart from its host. There are numerous interesting possibilities available to you because of this.

Figure 8.35

Click the Family Category And Parameters button to make a family shared.

For example, a schedule can report how many cabinets you have in a project. Using shared families, Revit can now also provide a schedule of cabinet doors and hardware. This might be an extreme example, but it could be quite effective for a firm that could use this level of detail. Hospitals have various types of suites that are repeated considerably throughout a design. It is also possible to build a composite hospital room equipment family that nests each of the equipment families used.

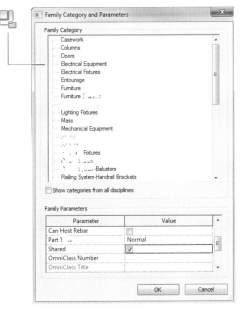

It might not be as useful to schedule the composite room, but it might be very useful to place them quickly and then schedule the individual pieces of equipment as if they had been put in each room individually. With some clever use of parameters, many of the nested families that are most likely to shift around can be repositioned as needed. This is definitely on the verge of qualifying for "super family" status, but in some cases the effort is justified by the result.

Shared Parameters

Parameters exist for every family in Revit. Some are created by the software developers and designed to work without any extra effort on your part. Others are created by you as you develop or modify content. Parameters are part of projects and families. You can create project parameters that are assigned to specific categories. These can be included in schedules. These are an elegant way to include important information that applies to many families of one or more categories but don't actually alter the physical family itself (think "information only").

When you create families, you can define more parameters than what you find in each template. Many of these are just family parameters that have a role inside the family only to determine how big or small it should be and what should be visible. These parameters are available to you in the project, but you can't schedule them or display their values in tags. When you need to do either, you need to plan for shared parameters (Figure 8.36).

Figure 8.36

Shared Parameters button on the Manage tab

Think of a shared parameter file as a dictionary, as shown in Figure 8.37. It contains definitions that you can make available to projects and families as you work in either environment. When you want a parameter to both change the physical nature of a fam-

Figure 8.37

Selecting a shared parameter

ily and schedule it or tag it, you just need to create the shared parameter and assign it in the family. When you get back to your project, you add the same shared parameter to the project. This common definition helps Revit understand that the value it finds in the family and project are really the same information.

If you are going to be the go-to person for Revit families, then you'll want to become familiar with shared parameters. You'll also want to get hold of the Revit Family Style Guide we mentioned earlier.

Practical Matters

We should mention a couple items that are beyond just becoming familiar with clicking and picking tools: file size and complexity. It takes time to become really competent when making families. It is easy to make complex families, so to speak. Complexity isn't a worthy goal, though. Creating really effective families that are not a burden on your projects or your co-workers is worthy, and it is the result of careful craftsmanship. You also have to evaluate your results, test/flex them often as you create them, and once you are finished, test again.

File Size Smaller is better. Most of the stock content varies from between 100 and 300 KB (as shown in Figure 8.38). Structural steel families are a bit bigger, but most of them also include a bit more complexity. The LH-Series Bar Joist family is a little more than 550 KB, but it has a nested family and uses an array to create the cross braces (as shown in Figure 8.39).

Figure 8.38

The files sizes of some stock structural families

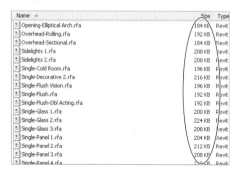

It is perfectly reasonable to expect that some content may be a bit larger when the complexity it has offers significant benefits. But you should keep an eye on your file sizes primarily to make sure that none are arbitrarily large without justification. For example, a nested family might be part of a door family that doesn't actually use it anymore. We have seen instances where a

Family Editor has tried a few different ideas, eventually settled on a different approach, and never cleaned out the earlier nested components. This can cause a file's size to be two or three times larger than necessary. One or two families like this won't hurt your project, but hundreds of them with similar inconsistency will affect performance.

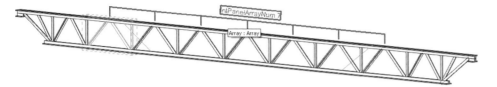

Figure 8.39

The Bar Joist family uses an array to create the bracing you see (the "skin").

Complexity As mentioned earlier, it is an asset that Revit can provide a high level of parametric capability. It is also a curse because you can abuse this power. You need to be mindful of complexity because users may be stymied by it, and projects may suffer for it. What are examples you might choose to avoid?

- Avoid using the Array feature with the Group And Associate option selected.
- You might also prefer to avoid using a great many parameters that are derived through sophisticated calculations. Each calculation will require a bit more work than a simpler family version will.

There is no hard-and-fast rule. This is where the artist and technician blend together and where family editing is as much art as science (refer to Figure 8.40).

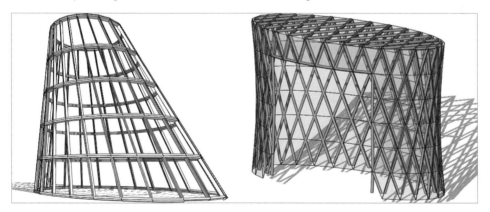

Figure 8.40

A couple complex forms created with families

Evaluation Test! You must test your family both in the Family Editor and in a project. A family can work perfectly in the Family Editor, but a user can find one circumstance in a project that doesn't support your assumptions and you have to fix it. The project also provides you with what the regular Revit user will experience when they try to use your family. Just as it is good advice not to proof your own writing, it is good advice to not proof (test) your own families. A couple other people will usually find things that you didn't expect and save you the trouble of rushing around after users have started to put it in their project.

Dissecting Some Practical Examples

We have assembled a collection of exercises that provide some practical tasks. These build on what we've discussed in this chapter as well as broader concepts we discussed in Chapter 7, "Introduction to Families." It is our hope that, once you've tried these, you'll see opportunities to apply what you learn to other content you need in the future. You may even find yourself inclined to revisit some content you've already made. The following are the exercises:

- Creating a door with variable swing
- Nesting a variable swing (in a door family too)
- Modifying a room tag and shared parameter
- Modifying an existing column's visibility and material settings

The first two exercises deal with providing an adjustable door swing for a door family. The first one just alters an individual family, while the second introduces the concept of nesting a family in another. It is a bit more complex, but it has the benefit of reusing one family to provide consistent results in many other families. The third example shows you how to create a room name abbreviation and apply it to your room tag family. The last example deals with a column family and shows you how to simplify what you see in a plan view versus a 3D view.

Creating a Door with Variable Swing Angle

A fair number of Revit users wonder whether a door can change the angle of the door panel. The stock content is fixed at 90 degrees, or perpendicular to the wall. Some plan views need the doors to be able to decrease or increase this angle because either they interfere with another graphically or it is desirable to show how far the door will swing into an area. This exercise will take you through the necessary steps to modify the existing Single Flush.rfa door family found in the Imperial Library. The metric version is called m_Single Flush.rfa.

Begin with the preparation:

1. Open Single Flush.rfa.

2. Save the file. Provide a unique name to preserve the existing file.

3. In the Floor Plan view: Ground Floor, delete the symbolic line work (five lines, one arc, and four lines).

4. Add a new reference plane along the exterior face of the host wall.

5. Lock the padlock that appears when you sketch the plane.

6. Name the reference plane (Exterior Face) so it is easier to understand what it is for later.

7. Create three types for the host wall using three different values for thickness.

This makes it easier to test for different wall thickness inside the Family Editor.

8. Temporarily hide the host wall, opening cut, flip controls, trim, and door panel solids.

This makes it easier to sketch new symbolic lines and make sure constraints are correct.

Create the symbolic panel:

1. Sketch a rectangle (representing the panel) using the symbolic line subcategory Panel [cut]:

   a. Start at the intersection of reference planes Right and Exterior Face (the new one you added), and sketch at a 45-degree angle to the left.

   b. Make the rectangle 3′-0″ (900mm) long and 2″ (50mm) thick.

2. Add Aligned dimensions between each parallel side of the rectangle:

   a. Assign the Thickness parameter to the narrow dimension.

   b. Assign the Width parameter to the long dimension.

3. Add Angular dimensions between each long line segment and the upper short perpendicular segment.

4. Lock their angle at 90 degrees.

5. Repeat steps 3 and 4 for the lower short segment, but only one (Angular dimension) of them is necessary, between the outer long line and the lower short segment.

Attempting to add both dimensions and locking them will generate an error message concerning overconstraining the sketch.

6. Add an Angular dimension between the exterior side of the panel and the reference plane Exterior Face.

7. Select this Angular dimension, and create a parameter for it.

8. Name it **2D Swing**, and assign it to the Graphics group.

9. Select the Instance box.

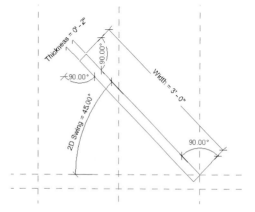

This will allow you to change the swing angle for doors individually. This is what your work should look like so far.

10. Flex your door:

   a. Open Family Types, and change the 2D Swing parameter from 45 to 90 degrees.

   b. Change the door type to a different size. Make sure that it does not break.

If the panel does not change correctly or generates any error messages, return to the previous steps and repeat until there are no errors.

Create the symbolic arc:

1. Hide the Panel symbolic lines to make it easier to sketch the arc.

2. Sketch the arc for the door swing using the symbolic line subcategory Plan Swing [projection]:

    a. Choose the Center-Ends Arc tool, and place the arc center point at the intersection of the reference planes Right and Exterior Face (the new one you added).

    b. Place the first arc endpoint at the intersection of the reference planes Left and Exterior Face.

    c. Place the second endpoint of the arc randomly above the first, between 0 and 45 degrees.

3. Select the arc, and drag the bottom endpoint down until it meets the other reference plane (unnamed).

    Doing this prevents the arc from becoming zero length if the door swing is set to zero degrees. The wall's line weight will hide the arc for this door so it won't be visible.

4. Add a Radial dimension to the arc, and assign it to the Width parameter.

5. Reset the temporarily hidden elements.

6. Select the arc and drag the upper endpoint up to meet the upper-inside corner of the symbolic lines for the panel.

    Your work should look like this now.

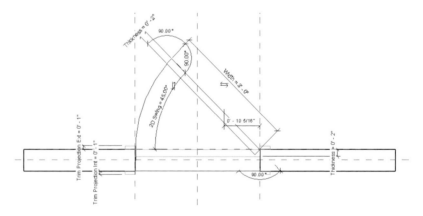

7. Flex/test the family again by changing the parameter setting for 2D Swing as well as choosing different door types to change the Width and Thickness parameters.

8. If there are no errors to contend with, load the family into a project to test it in that environment.

If you run into errors, you'll need to work through each of them so your users won't have to. Pay close attention to the error message descriptions; hopefully they'll help you figure out what you did wrong.

Remember, the value you assign to the new 2D Swing parameter is the default value that Revit will use when you place the family; assign it accordingly. It is still possible for a user to break this swing if they place the door in a very thin wall, because the arc may become too short for Revit to show or create. It isn't all that common for a door to be "closed," however, which means it isn't likely to be a real issue. Here's what the door should look like in a project after you finish it.

Nesting a Variable 2D Swing

Repeatedly taking the steps in the previous section for every door in your family library might feel a bit repetitive. Another strategy you can consider is to create a separate family that represents the 2D swing graphics. This separate family is then nested into your door families. It is only necessary to position the family and associate the parameters that allow for width, thickness, and swing angle to the host family. This section will provide the outline for taking this approach.

Begin with the preparation:

1. Start a new family using the `Generic Model.rft` template file.

2. Save the file; name it **2D Swing.rfa** (just a suggestion).

3. Change the category from Generic Models to Doors.

   Doing this eliminates the host wall that exists in the door template and provides the subcategories that are part of the door template.

4. Open the Object Styles dialog box from the Manage tab.

5. Click the New button in the Modify Subcategories frame.

6. Type the name **Plan Swing**, and click OK.

   It is important to type it the same way you typed it here in the instructions so that it will be the same as all the other door families that use this object style. Just compare yours against the other door families in the Revit library.

Add the bones (reference planes):

1. Add a vertical reference plane parallel and to the left of the existing vertical reference plane.

2. Set it at 3′-0″ (900mm) from the existing vertical reference plane.

3. Name it **Left**, assign the Is Reference parameter to Left, and click Apply.

4. Select the existing vertical reference plane. It is named Center (Left/Right).

5. Change its name to **Right**, and reassign the Is Reference parameter to Right.

   Notice that the check box is selected for Defines Origin, which is correct. The reference plane is also pinned. If you want to change the extent of the reference plane, you'll have to unpin it first.

6. Select the horizontal reference plane, rename it to **Front**, and reassign the Is Reference parameter to Front.

   You'll have to unpin it too if you want to change how long the reference plane is. It too defines the origin of the family.

Add some muscle (dimensions and parameters):

1. Place an Aligned dimension between the Left and Right reference planes.

2. If necessary, adjust the Left reference plane to ensure they are 3′-0″ (900mm) apart.

3. Assign the parameter Width to the dimension.

   The Width parameter is already available because Revit added it when you switched from the generic model category to the door category.

> We should point out that the following steps are nearly the same as those we described in the previous steps for the panel in the earlier exercise.

Create the door panel (adding some skin and some more muscle):

1. Sketch a rectangle (representing the panel) using the symbolic line subcategory Panel [cut]:

   a. Start at the intersection of reference planes Right and Front, and sketch at a 45-degree angle to the left.

   b. Make the rectangle 3′-0″ (900mm) long and 2″ (50mm) thick.

2. Add Aligned dimensions between each parallel side of the rectangle:

   a. Assign the Thickness parameter to the narrow dimension.

   b. Assign the Width parameter to the long dimension.

   These are also already available because you changed from the generic model category to the door category.

3. Add Angular dimensions between each long line segment and the upper short perpendicular segment.

4. Lock their angle at 90 degrees.

5. Repeat for the other end, but only one of them (Angular dimension) is necessary.

   Attempting to add both dimensions and locking them will generate an error message that you are overconstraining the sketch.

6. Add an Angular dimension between the exterior side of the panel and the reference plane Exterior Face.

7. Select this Angular dimension, and create a parameter for it.

8. Name it **2D Swing**, and assign it to the Graphics group. Select the Instance box.

   This will allow you to change the swing angle for doors individually. This family should look like this now:

9. Flex your panel; in Family Types, change the 2D Swing parameter from 45 to 90 degrees.

10. Try some other angles greater and less than 90. Make sure that it does not break.

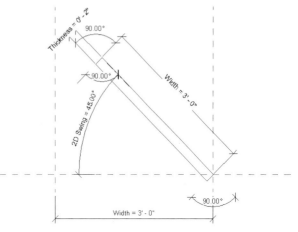

   If the panel does not change correctly or generates any error messages, repeat the previous steps until there are no errors.

   Add more skin and muscle (the arc):

1. Hide the Panel symbolic lines to make it easier to sketch the arc.

2. Sketch the arc for the door swing using the Symbolic line subcategory Plan Swing [projection]:

   a. Choose the Center-Ends Arc tool, and place the arc center point at the intersection of the reference planes Right and Front.

   b. Place the first arc endpoint at the intersection of the reference planes Left and Front.

   c. Place the second endpoint of the arc randomly above the first, a value between 0 and 45 degrees.

3. Sketch a symbolic line using the subcategory <Invisible Lines> from the intersection of reference planes Right and Front to the left just below the Front reference plane at a slight angle of 0.5 degrees.

4. Select the invisible line, and deselect the Visible property.

   This means it will not be visible in the project at all; if it's selected, it will be visible when you hover your mouse pointer over the family but not visible otherwise.

5. Place an angular dimension between the reference plane Front and the new symbolic invisible line.

6. Lock the dimension (angle should be 0.5 degrees).

7. Select the arc, and drag the bottom endpoint down until it meets the invisible line you just sketched.

Doing this prevents the arc from becoming zero length if the door swing is set to 0 degrees. The wall's line weight will hide this tiny extension of the arc, so it won't be visible.

8. Reset the temporarily hidden elements.

9. Select the arc and drag the upper endpoint up to meet the upper-exterior corner of the symbolic lines for the panel.

   The family should look like this now:

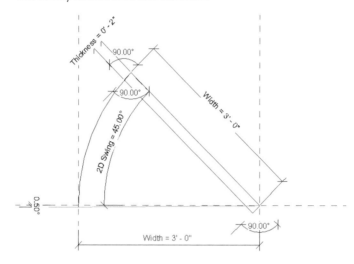

10. Flex/test the family again by changing the parameter setting for 2D Swing as well as choosing different door types to change the Width and Thickness parameters.

11. If there are no errors to contend with, load the family into a project to test it in that environment.

    As mentioned before, if you do encounter error messages, read the warnings text carefully for clues about what Revit objects to.

Be careful not to test the angle by trying 0 degrees or 90 degrees. When you nest the family into the host door, it will tolerate these values. The arc tends to distort the constraints if you use those values in the swing family itself. You could fuss with the family trying to resolve this only to find out later that once it is nested, it doesn't matter.

Nest the 2D swing (preparation):

1. Open Single Flush.rfa.

2. Save the file with a different name to preserve the original.

3. In the view Floor Plan: Ground Floor, delete the symbolic line work (five lines, one arc, and four lines).

4. Add a new reference plane along the Exterior face of the host wall.

5. Lock the padlock that appears when you sketch the plane.

6. Name the reference plane **Exterior Face** so it is easier to understand what it is for later.

7. Create three types for the host wall using three different values for thickness.

   This makes it easier to test for different wall thickness inside the Family Editor.

8. Temporarily hide the host wall, opening cut, flip controls, trim, and door panel solids.

   This makes it easier to constrain the nested 2D Swing family.

   Load the family and place it (nesting):

1. Load your 2D Swing family from the Insert tab's Load From Library panel.

2. Select Load Family, and place it near the opening of the door.

3. Using the Align tool, align and lock the right side of the 2D Swing to the Right reference plane, and do the same for the base of the swing to the Exterior Face reference plane.

4. Select the 2D Swing family, and click the small gray button next to the Instance parameter 2D Swing on the Properties palette.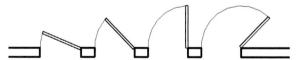

5. Click the Add Parameter button to create a new parameter called 2D Swing in the host family.

6. Assign the parameter to the Graphics group, and select the Instance option.

   This allows you to change the swing of individual doors as required in the project.

7. Click the Edit Type button to do the same task for the Width and Thickness parameters.

   These parameters are already present in the host family, so you only need to select the matching parameter name.

8. Reset the temporarily hidden elements, and test the family to make sure everything flexes properly.

9. Save the file and load it into a project to test it there.

Modifying a Room Tag and Shared Parameter

This task is minor editing for a family, but it gives you a chance to create a parameter to store a room name's abbreviation. This is useful when a room is pretty small in a plan view and the tag and its full name tend to hide the room itself. This exercise will modify the existing room tag and show you how to create the necessary shared parameter as well as add it to your project to make everything work together.

To create the shared parameter, follow these steps:

1. On the Manage tab, click Shared Parameters.

2. If you have a shared parameter file you can do testing with, click Browse, or click Create to make a new one for this exercise only. The following steps assume you'll create one.

3. Choose a folder location and provide a name, such as **RAC Intro SP**. It will be a .txt-formatted file.

4. Click New in the Groups frame.

5. Provide a new group name such as **Room and Area Data**.

6. Click New in the Parameters frame.

7. Provide a new name such as **Abbreviation**; use the Discipline: Common, and assign the Type Of Parameter: Text.

   If you make a mistake, it will be here; make sure you select Text!

8. Click OK.

   Your parameter awaits you for use in the room tag family.

9. Click OK in the Edit Shared Parameters dialog box.

Create the new room tag family and add the parameter:

1. Open the stock family Room Tag.rfa(M_Room Tag.rfa "metric") from the US Imperial (or US Metric, varies by geographic location) /Annotations folder.

2. Save the file in another folder location as Room Tag Custom.rfa (just a suggestion).

3. Select the label for Room Name.

4. Create a copy of it, and place it above the existing one.

5. Click Edit Label, and then click the small Add Parameter button (bottom-left corner of the Edit Label dialog box).

6. Click Select (Shared Parameter is the only option offered).

7. Select the Abbreviation parameter.

   If you aren't using a new shared parameter file, you may have to select a different group to see your Abbreviation parameter.

8. Click OK twice (first to select and second to apply).

9. Select Abbreviation from the list of available Category Parameters.

10. Click the Add Parameters(s) To Label button (green arrow pointing to the right).

11. Select row 1 (Name parameter), and click the Remove Parameter From Label button.

12. Supply a sample abbreviation value: **Abbr**.

13. Click OK.

Create a Yes/No parameter to control the visibility of the Abbreviation label:

1. Select the Abbreviation label.

2. Click the Associate Family Parameter button for the Visible parameter (the little square gray button on the Properties palette).

3. Click Add Parameter.

4. Provide the following:

   Name: Show Abbreviation

   Group Parameter Under: Graphics

   Select: Type

5. Click OK.

Create a Yes/No parameter to control the visibility of Room Name label:

1. Select the Room Name label.

2. Click the Associate Parameter button for the Visible parameter (the little square gray button on the Properties palette).

3. Click Add Parameter.

4. Provide the following:

   Name: Show Full Name

   Group Parameter Under: Graphics

   Select: Type

5. Click OK.

Adjust the family types, and save the file:

1. Click the Properties palette, and select Family Types (there are three types already).

2. Rename the existing types:

   Rename Room Tag to **Full Name-Number**.

   Rename Room Tag with Area to **Full Name-Number-Area**.

   Rename Room Tag with Volume to **Full Name-Number-Volume**.

3. Create three new types:

   Short Name-Number

   Short Name-Number-Area

   Short Name-Number-Volume

4. Create a formula for Show Full Name; enter the following in the Formula column next to the parameter Show Full Name: **not(Show Abbreviation)**.

5. For each type, change the values of each parameter so the result matches each type's name.

See the example here for Short Name-Number-Area.

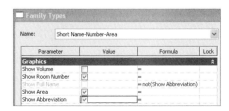

6. Click OK.

7. Move the Abbreviation label so that it sits directly on top of the Room Name label.

The parameters assigned to their visible parameters will govern when they are supposed to show up so they don't compete with each other.

8. Save your work.

9. Click Load Into Project.

If you don't have a project open already, you'll need to do that first.

10. Apply the tag to rooms and experiment with various versions of the tag.

You should notice that you can't supply a value for the abbreviation yet, though. That's next!

Add the shared parameter Abbreviation to your project:

1. On the Manage tab, click Project Parameters.

2. Click Add.

3. Click to select Shared Parameter, and click Select.

4. Choose Abbreviation from the list, and click OK.

5. Provide the following:

Group Parameter Under: Identity Data

Select: Instance

Assign Category: Rooms

6. Click OK, select Abbreviation, and click OK.

7. Select a room tag (using the Short Name tag versions, naturally).

You can now provide a value for Abbreviation.

8. Select the Room element directly, and find the parameter listed among the other parameters in the Identity Data group in the Properties palette.

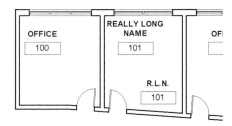

You should see something like this when you apply the tags to your rooms:

Modifying the Existing Column Visibility and Material Settings

The column family called `Doric Column.rfa` is provided with the content that is installed with Revit. When you load, place, and then examine how it looks in various views, you may find that it needs a little adjustment to make it look better in plan views. Left alone, it appears a bit too heavy because many of the columns' forms are visible in the plan. This exercise will change the settings to simplify its plan representation. We will also take this opportunity to revisit how the materials are assigned to the column.

Open the family, examine it, and get it ready:

1. Open the stock family `Doric Column.rfa` from the Imperial library.

2. Save the file in another folder location under a new name, something like **Our Doric Column.rfa** (which is just a suggestion).

3. Open a new project template.

4. Load the column, and place it to take a close look at it in a plan view.

The cylindrical portion of the column has too many lines showing, which cause it to appear too bold. You need to adjust this:

1. Select the column, and click Edit Family.

2. Open the view Floor Plan: Lower Ref. Level.

3. Zoom in, and select the Revolve form (circles that you see).

4. Click Visibility Settings on the Mode panel.

5. Deselect Plan/RCP and When Cut In Plan/RCP, and click OK.

> In the Family Editor you will find that elements are not hidden when these settings are changed. They become muted (halftone) in order to show they are affected by a visibility setting.

6. Save the family file, and click Load Into Project.

7. Choose Overwrite The Existing Version, and review the result.

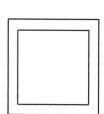

   You should see just the rectangular base form now.

   Add symbolic lines for the circular form:

1. Back in the column family, sketch a symbolic circle using the Columns [Projection] subcategory.

2. Save the family file, and click Load Into Project.

3. Overwrite the existing version, and review the result.

   Manage the material assignment for the column:

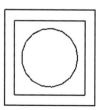

1. Select the column, and click Edit Family.

2. Open the 3D View: View 1.

3. Select the Revolve form (the upper portion of the column).

4. Click the Associate Family Parameter button for the Materials parameter (the small gray button).

   This form is assigned to a material already; the equal sign symbol on the button indicates this subtlety. Change nothing yet.

5. Repeat step 4 for the forms that make up the base; all are assigned to the same material.

6. Select the Revolve form again, and click the Associate Family Parameter button.

7. Click Add Parameter, and supply the following:

   a. Set Name to Column Upper.

   b. Leave Discipline set to Common.

   c. Leave Type Of Parameter set to Material.

   d. Group the parameter under Materials And Finishes.

   e. Choose Type, click OK, and click OK again.

8. Click Family Types.

9. Select the Material parameter, and click Modify.

10. Replace the name Material with **Column Base**.

11. Click OK, and save the family.

12. Choose Load Into Project, overwrite the existing version, and open a 3D view.

13. Select the column, and click Edit Type.

14. Change the Material parameters to assign two new materials from the available materials in the project.

CHAPTER 9

Massing

Three-dimensional modeling tools have many uses within a building project. Two types of modeling tools are available in Autodesk Revit Architecture. The solid modeling tools are covered in Chapter 7, "Introduction to Families," and this chapter concentrates on the tools used to create conceptual building models for design analysis and spatial planning. The specific need and family type chosen will determine which set of tools is available for use.

This chapter covers the following topics:

- **Understanding Mass Objects**
- **Understanding references and work planes**
- **Creating mass forms**
- **Editing forms**
- **Employing loadable mass families**
- **Using face-based modeling**
- **Creating mass families from imported geometry**

Understanding Mass Objects

The Mass Object category within Revit has unique capabilities that differ from other categories and types of three-dimensional elements. Mass objects are used to define the shape and geometric design of the building. Once a building shape is modeled using a mass object, area and volumetric calculations can be automatically calculated and reported. If desired, walls, floors, roofs, and curtain systems can also be created directly from the faces of the mass object for conceptual design exploration. These models help you quickly visualize the building shape, compare floor areas, and add exterior finishes generated directly from the faces of the mass.

You can take two approaches when creating mass objects:

In-Place Family Create the mass object as an in-place family within a project. This type of mass is used for creating elements that are unique within a project, that access other project geometry directly, and that occur only once in the project.

External Mass Family Create a loadable, or external, mass family that is then loaded into a project and placed as needed, once or multiple times. Any edits to the mass family will then be applied to all instances of that mass family when the family is reloaded.

Table 9.1 defines some key terms you'll need to know to learn about massing.

Table 9.1

Massing glossary

TERM	DEFINITION
Massing	The process of visualizing, studying, and resolving building forms using mass instances. The shapes created may be as simple as basic block shapes that are used to visualize the building and report spatial information about the structure.
Mass family	A family of shapes, belonging to the Mass category. An in-place mass is saved with the project; it is not a separate file.
Mass instance or mass	An instance of a loaded mass family or an in-place mass.
Conceptual design environment	A type of Family Editor that creates conceptual designs using in-place and loadable family mass elements.
Mass form	The overall form of each mass family or in-place mass.
Massing study	A study of one or more building forms made from one or more mass instances.
Mass face	A surface on a mass instance that can be used to create a building element, such as a wall or roof.
Mass floor	A horizontal slice through a mass at a defined level. Mass floors provide geometric information about the dimensions of the mass above the slice, up to the next slice or the top of the mass.
Building elements	Walls, roofs, floors, and curtain systems that can be created from mass faces.
Cross section shapes	Cross section shapes represent slices through the objects that are being modeled and are used to create forms. Shapes can be open or closed. A closed shape consists of a continuous series of lines, arcs, and so on that returns to the original starting point. A closed shape cannot overlap, cross, or intersect itself. An open shape is a series of continuous lines, arcs, and so on that does not return to the original starting point. An open shape may intersect or cross over itself and will still be a valid shape to create a form. Cross section shapes are also referred to as profiles, curves, and shapes.

Visibility and Display

The Conceptual Mass panel (Figure 9.1) displays the Show Mass By View Settings button as well as the In-Place Mass and Place Mass buttons. Mass elements are not set to display by default in the project environment. The Show Mass button is a flyout that has four display options:

Figure 9.1

Conceptual Mass panel

Show Mass by View Settings Mass elements are displayed using the setting selected in the Visibility/Graphic Overrides window, including any elements set to a specific subcategory. This setting is a view setting and only applies to the current view.

Show Mass Forms And Floors This is a project setting that applies to all views in the project. This setting displays only elements set to the following subcategories:

- Forms
- Gridlines
- Hidden Lines
- Mass Floor
- Nodes
- Pattern Fill
- Pattern Lines
- None

Show Mass Surface Types Available only after using the Analyze Mass Model tool. The model displays surfaces using construction types specified in the Energy Settings window.

Figure 9.2

Edit Visibility/ Graphic Overrides

Show Mass Zones And Shades Available only after using the Analyze Mass Model tool. Mass zones are displayed so that properties can be changed or viewed.

To enable the visibility of mass objects per view and also allow them to print, use the Visibility/Graphic Overrides window to modify the visibility and graphic settings of the view:

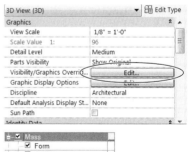

1. Open the Visibility/Graphic Overrides dialog by selecting the Edit button, as shown in Figure 9.2.

   This setting makes the mass objects visible in a single view and overrides the Show Mass tool.

2. Select the check box beside the Mass category to turn on the visibility of mass elements and their associated subcategory elements, as shown in Figure 9.2.

The default material for mass objects is named Default Form, as shown in Figure 9.3. This is the material assigned to the Mass Object category in the Object Styles setting on the Manage tab; this material will automatically be assigned using the <By Category> setting. Other materials can be assigned to the mass object in the Properties palette while creating, or later while editing, the mass object.

Figure 9.3

Materials dialog box

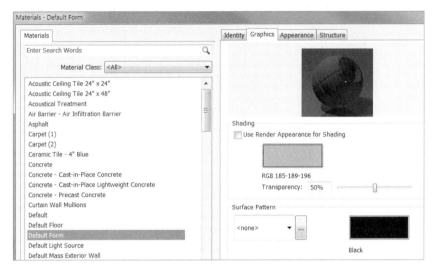

To change the material assigned to a mass object:

1. Select the mass object.

2. Click the <By Category> material parameter setting in the Properties palette, as shown in Figure 9.4.

Figure 9.4

Material instance parameter

3. Click the ellipsis button that appears at the right end of the slot.

4. Select a different material from the material window.

5. Click OK to complete the material change.

Creating In-Place Mass Families

In-place mass families are used when creating objects that are unique to the project and will be used only once. Examples include an overall building mass model or unique building element. If a mass family is to be repeated multiple times in a project—for example, a tower feature or silo—then creating a mass family outside of the project and loading the family into the project is the preferred method. This approach will help reduce file size and simplify the updating of the families.

To explore the menu and tools available for creating solid and void forms, follow these steps:

1. Start the In-Place Mass tool from the Conceptual Mass panel on the Massing & Site tab.

   Once the tool is activated, you will be prompted to provide a name for the mass object.

2. Type a name.

3. Click OK.

Note that if Show Mass mode has not been enabled prior to starting the In-Place Mass tool, an alert message will be displayed informing you that Show Mass mode has been enabled. Select Close to dismiss the alert; if you want, select Do Not Show Me This Message Again before selecting Close to permanently disable the alert.

> Assigning a logical name for mass objects will enable easier selection later in the project. With a logical name, you will be able to easily locate the mass in the Project Browser families section listing by name.

Once you click OK in the Name dialog box, you are working in the mass Family Editor environment. The Home tab and associated panels are shown in Figure 9.5.

Figure 9.5

In-Place Editor Home tab

Mass objects are created by drawing cross section shapes using model lines and/or reference lines and then creating forms from those objects. Additional tools used for creating and controlling forms are reference planes and reference points. The Draw panel contains the tools used for creating the base elements of forms.

The forms can be categorized into five basic types, listed here and demonstrated in Figure 9.6:

- Surface forms
- Extrusions
- Lofts
- Revolves
- Sweeps

Figure 9.6

Five types of mass object forms

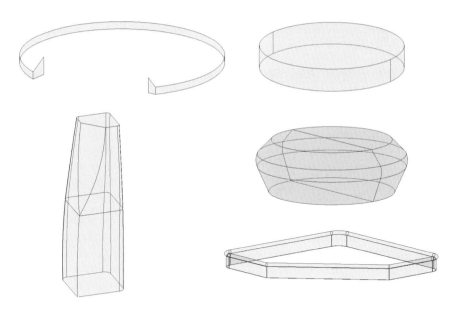

These forms can be modeled as *solids* or *voids*:

Solids Additive; used to create or add to the model.

Voids Subtractive; used to remove portions from the solids.

Mass models can be assembled with multiple form types using combinations of solid forms and void forms. The in-place mass objects created later in this chapter are separate in-place families, but they could have all been combined into one. Creating the mass objects as separate in-place families may allow for a simplified creation process but limits interaction between the objects and requires the maintenance of multiple families.

To close the In-Place Editor, select Cancel Mass from the In-Place Editor panel. Note that if you try creating cross section shapes or forms, you will receive a warning alerting you that you may be discarding elements; click Yes to cancel (Figure 9.7).

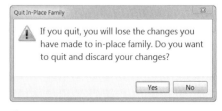

Figure 9.7

Warning message. Click Yes to cancel your mass.

Understanding References and Work Planes

References and work planes are the planes that model elements and objects are created on. Objects in Revit are sketched or modeled on work planes, which control their placement and location. Understanding how to create references and how they can be used to control the model elements is critical to using Revit efficiently.

Reference Planes

Reference planes are infinite flat planes created by selecting two pick points. They are used to align and locate separate elements of a model or to control the location of model elements using parameter-driven dimensions. Reference planes have the following characteristics:

- Can be created in the project file and used to control numerous separate objects in the project.

- Can be created within families for controlling or aligning objects modeled within the family.

- Can be used for dimensioning within the family or outside of the family directly in the project. This is true whether the reference plane was created inside the family or directly in the project.

- Can be named in the Properties palette once the reference plane is selected. This provides easier management and allows them to be selected from a name list and used for alignment when creating elevations.

To create a reference plane:

1. Select Reference Plane from the Draw panel.

2. Select the Line tool, as shown in Figure 9.8.

3. Pick a start point and an end point to create the reference plane.

Reference planes cannot be created in a 3D view in the project environment. You have two options when creating reference planes, which allow you to draw the lines or pick lines. This in turn allows you to select the edges of existing model objects and linework.

Figure 9.8

Draw panel's Line tool

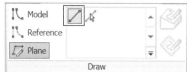

Reference Lines

Reference lines are used to control geometry or sketch elements in multiple types of families, including loadable mass families and in-place mass families. For mass forms, they can also be used as cross section shapes, curves, or paths for sweeps. The use of reference lines as paths and shapes is particularly valuable because they create their own perpendicular reference planes on which curves and shapes can be sketched. Reference lines have the following characteristics:

- Have a start point that can be used as their center of rotation when being controlled by an angular parameter.

- Are visible in 3D views.

- Can be linear shapes, such as lines, rectangles, and polygons. These create four work planes per segment on which you can draw elements and perform modeling.

- Can be curved, including splines. These create work planes perpendicular to the start and end of the shape (as shown in Figure 9.9).

Figure 9.9

Reference lines showing work planes

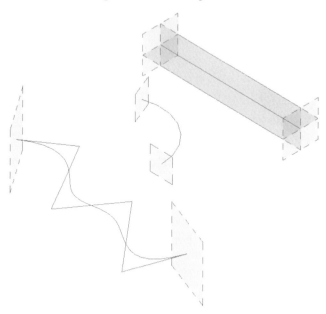

- Can be used as cross section shapes directly to create forms or can be used as a path for swept forms.
- May be created in any family.

To create a reference line:

1. Click the Reference Line button on the Draw panel (Figure 9.10).

2. Select a shape to draw.

Any shape in the Draw panel may be used to create a reference line or multiple reference lines at one time.

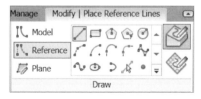

Figure 9.10

Draw panel's Reference Line tool

Reference Points

Reference points are used to define coordinates in three-dimensional work spaces, to define specific points along a shape, and to control geometry. There are three types of reference points: free, hosted, and driving.

FREE POINTS

- Created based on a work plane and maintain an association with the work plane. Free points can be moved in three axes: x, y, and z. If the work plane is moved, the points will maintain their offset from the work plane.

- Are visible in 3D views.
- Available for use for mass families, both in-place and loadable.

HOSTED POINTS

- Can be placed on existing lines, arcs, ellipses, splines, or surfaces.
- Appear visually smaller than free or driving points.
- Are added to an existing object.
- Will move with their host surface.
- Will move along a spline or line.
- Create three planes for drawing or modeling. The planes define a local XYZ system with one of the planes perpendicular to the line or spline host or in the case of a surface, parallel to that surface.

DRIVING POINTS

- Used to create surfaces or linework by picking on the preexisting points.
- Become part of the form they are used to create.
- Can be edited to manipulate the form after creation or the spline created using the Spline Through Points tool.
- Can be created and selected prior to starting the Spline Through Points tool to automate the creation of the spline.

To create a reference point, select the Point Element tool on the Draw panel (Figure 9.11); a reference point will be created by default based on the conditions outlined previously.

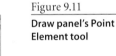

Figure 9.11

Draw panel's Point Element tool

Setting and Showing the Active Work Plane

Once references have been created, a work plane of the reference needs to be set active in order to sketch or model on that work plane. The Set Work Plane tool in the Work Plane panel on the Home tab will allow you to set a work plane as active by one of three methods:

- By name from a drop-down list
- By picking a work plane
- By selecting an existing model line and setting the work plane it was created on active

Choose a Plane by Name The Name drop-down list contains the following:

- All project levels (both story and nonstory levels)
- Grid lines
- Named reference planes

If you select a work plane that is perpendicular to your current view, Revit will open the Go To View dialog box, which will show a list of views parallel to the selected work plane in the upper portion and a list of 3D views in the lower portion. This will happen immediately when you are using either the "pick a plane" or "pick a line" method; when the Name list is used to select a work plane, the dialog box opens after you click OK.

Pick a Plane The user selects a reference plane, reference line, reference point, or face of existing model element to set that work plane active. When selecting elements with multiple work planes, such as reference lines or reference points, hovering over the element and pressing the Tab key will cycle through the available work planes. Once the desired work plane is highlighted, left-click to make that work plane active. See Figure 9.12.

Figure 9.12

Reference line planes

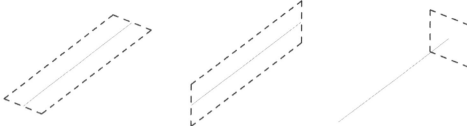

Pick a Line and Choose the Work Plane It Was Sketched In Model lines record the work plane that was active when the line was created. This option allows the user to pick a model line and set that work plane active.

Work planes can also be set using the Placement Plane drop-down list on the Options bar when you are sketching cross section profiles.

In the Work Plane panel, the Show tool will toggle the visibility of the active work plane in the current view.

Creating Mass Forms

Here we will create a new project and add levels and reference planes to the project. This new project will be used to create mass forms using the Extrusion, Loft, Revolve, Sweep, Surface, and Void form tools. The steps outlined for creating the forms will allow you to create mass form models for building design and analysis.

Save your changes to any open files prior to starting the new project.

Preparing to Create Mass Forms

The following steps show you how to create a new project using the default template. The template will then be prepared to model the remaining mass elements.

1. From the Application menu, select New to begin a new project.

The default template and template location for Revit Architecture is as follows:

C:\ProgramData\Templates\US Imperial\default.rte

2. If this is the template listed in the template file list, click OK. If the default template is not listed, select Browse and navigate to the folder shown in step 1.

    This opens a new project with the Level 1 view active.

3. Open an elevation view of the project.

    There are two levels already created.

4. Change the height of Level 2 to 16′.

5. Add five additional levels above the existing two. The heights and names of the levels will be as follows:

    Level 7: 266′

    Level 6: 214′

    Level 5: 162′

    Level 4: 110′

    Level 3: 58′

    You will use these levels later in this chapter.

    The mass model you are building in this exercise will be composed of multiple separate in-place family elements, and you will use reference planes to maintain the coordinated center point of the model.

6. Double-click the Level 1 view in the Project Browser to make it the active view.

7. Choose the Ref Plane tool from the Home tab.

8. Using the Line tool from the Draw panel (Figure 9.13), draw two reference planes, one horizontal and one vertical, as shown in Figure 9.14.

9. Once you have completed the two reference planes, click Modify at the left end of the ribbon, or press the Escape key twice to return to Modify mode.

10. Select the vertical reference plane, and in the Properties palette, fill in a name for the reference plane using **Building Center Left/Right** for the Name property.

11. Select the horizontal reference plane, and repeat the step, naming this reference plane **Building Center Top/Bottom**.

Figure 9.13

Reference Plane tool

Figure 9.14

Creating reference planes

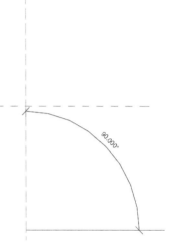

Note the names will appear on the screen only when the reference plane is selected or highlighted, as shown in Figure 9.15.

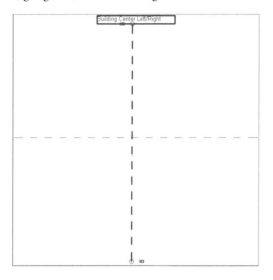

The intersection of these planes will be used as the center point of the building mass object.

Building an Extrusion Form

Extrusion forms are created by defining a closed cross section profile using model lines or reference lines and then creating a form from those closed shapes. There are numerous common instances of objects most easily modeled using the extrude form. Glazing panels, circular pedestals, and water heaters are just a few examples.

1. Start the In-Place Mass tool from the Conceptual Mass panel on the Massing & Site tab.

   Once the tool is activated, you will be prompted to provide a name for the mass object.

2. Name it **Main Building Form**, and then click OK.

3. Double-click the Floor Plan Level 1 view in the Project Browser to make it the active view if you have changed to a different view.

4. Select Model Line from the Draw panel, and then select the Circle tool.

   Leave the Make Surface From Closed Loops check box on the Options bar empty (Figure 9.16).

5. Create a circle centered at the intersection of the crosshairs with a radius of 52′.

6. Once the circle profile is created, click Modify on the ribbon to exit the Model Line tool.

7. Change to the default 3D view by clicking the Default 3D View button on the Quick Access toolbar. If a default 3D view already exists, it will switch to that view; if it doesn't, a default 3D view will be created.

8. Use Zoom Extents (ZE) if you do not see the circle, and then select the circle (Figure 9.17).

9. From the Form panel in the ribbon, click the Create Form tool.

   At the bottom center of the screen, you will see two buttons (Figure 9.18). The button on the left will create a cylindrical form from the circle profile, and the button on the right will create a spherical form from the circle.

10. Click the cylindrical form button.

11. Double-click the South elevation view to make that the active view.

12. Use the Align tool from the Modify panel to align and lock the top of the extrusion form to Level 2 (Figure 9.19).

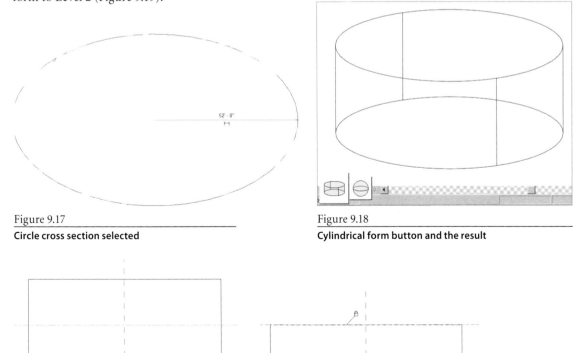

Figure 9.17

Circle cross section selected

Figure 9.18

Cylindrical form button and the result

Figure 9.19

The original form and the form aligned and locked

By locking the top of the form to Level 2, the height of the form will automatically change to match any height changes made to the level. The bottom of the form will automatically be locked to Level 1 because that was the active work plane on which the profile was created.

13. Choose Finish Mass from the In-Place Editor panel.

   This finishes this editing session for this mass object.

14. To save the project file, you must exit in-place editing by selecting either:

   • Finish Mass, which will save changes to the mass

   • Cancel Mass, which will discard any changes made to the mass object during that editing session

15. Choose Finish Mass to exit in-place editing.

   This completes the extrusion form. The steps that follow will build on this extrusion exercise.

16. Save the file as `Extrusion Form.rvt` for use in the following exercise.

Building a Loft Form

Similar to the extrusion form, a loft form begins by drawing a closed cross section profile on the desired level or reference plane. Examples of common loft objects are tapering furniture legs, twisting building forms, and numerous columns.

Unlike the extrusion form, a loft form can use multiple cross section profiles and will interpolate the loft form surfaces between the different shape profiles. The shape profiles are created at the desired distances along the loft form. Shape profiles can be any closed shapes, but more than one profile cannot exist at the same distance along the length or height of the loft.

The loft shown in Figure 9.20 is formed using three circles all created at different levels. The cross section shape profile shown in Figure 9.21 has two circles drawn at the midlevel and cannot be used to form a loft.

Figure 9.20

Good loft cross section shapes and loft

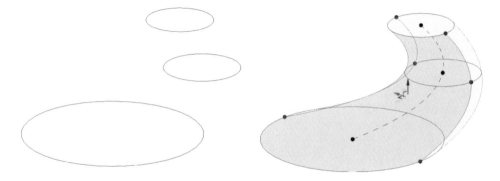
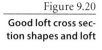

Cross section profiles can be created on project levels, on reference planes, or on reference lines. The loft created will be perpendicular to the reference selected or on the face of existing model geometry, such as walls, where the loft will also be perpendicular to the face selected.

We will use the levels created in the previous exercise to place the cross section shapes for a loft form. Continue working in the `Extrusion Form.rvt` file saved previously, or reopen the file to continue.

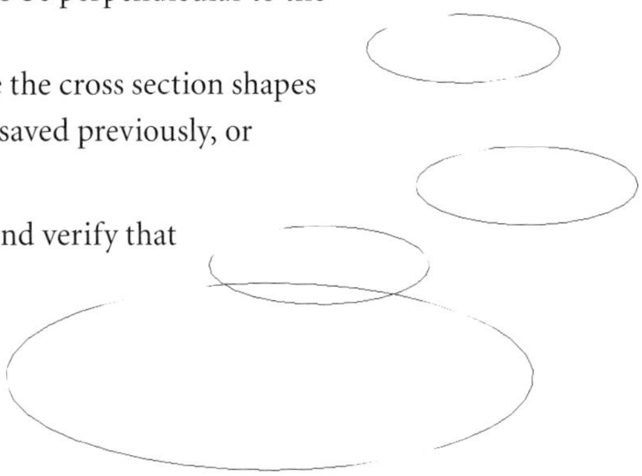

1. Double-click Floor Plan Level 3 to make it the active view, and verify that Show Mass Form and Floors is set on the Conceptual Mass panel.

2. From the Massing & Site tab, select In-Place Mass on the Conceptual Mass panel.

3. Name the mass **Loft Tower**.

   The reference planes that were placed in the project earlier are visible and can be used to ensure alignment with other objects.

4. To view the extrusion created previously, ensure that the current view name, Floor Plan: Level 3, is listed in the Properties palette. (Alternately you can set the underlay before clicking In-Place Mass.)

5. Click in the Edit column beside Underlay, and select Level 1 (Figure 9.22).

6. From the Draw panel, select Model Line, and then select the Rectangle tool.

   You may select the rectangle, or any other shape, first, which will also create a model line.

7. Open the Placement Plane drop-down list that shows Level 3 and select Level 3 to ensure the shape is drawn on that level (Figure 9.23).

8. Create a rectangular cross section profile that is 36′ square, as shown in Figure 9.24.

   The lower-right corner of the rectangle will be at the intersection of the reference planes.

Figure 9.21

Bad loft cross section shapes

Figure 9.22

Floor Plan Properties palette

Figure 9.23

Options bar's Placement Plane drop-down list

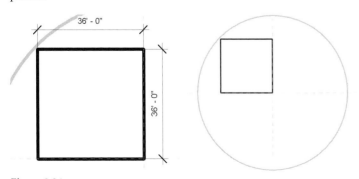

Figure 9.24

A rectangle size and location

9. Create the following cross section shapes on the level listed (Figure 9.25).

The *upper-left* corner of the square shape will remain a consistent point for all cross section shapes. This is the corner shown highlighted in Figure 9.25. Dimensions are shown for reference, but there is no need to dimension the shapes; their sizes are as follows:

Figure 9.25

Cross section shapes

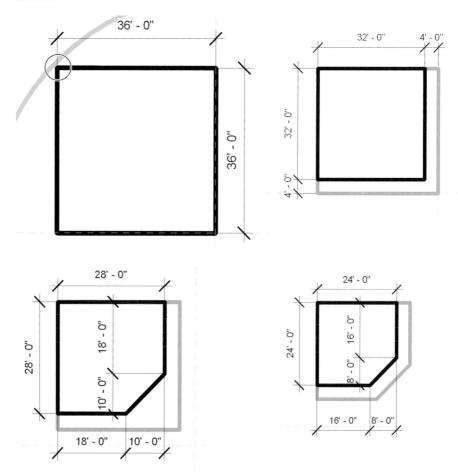

Level 4: 36′ × 36′

Level 5: 32′ × 32′

Level 6: 28′ × 28′, with angled corner

Level 7: 24′ × 24′, with angled corner

10. Once you have sketched all the cross section shapes, click the Default 3D View tool on the Quick Access toolbar to activate the default 3D view.

11. Select the five shapes (Figure 9.26), and verify that you've selected all segments of the shapes.

12. Choose Create Form from the Form panel.

> You can Ctrl-click or use a window or crossing window to select the shapes.

13. Choose Finish Mass from the In-Place Editor panel to complete the loft form (Figure 9.27).

14. From the Application menu, use the Save As command to save a copy of the file named Loft Form.rvt.

Building a Revolve Form

Revolve forms are created by turning a cross section shape around a single centerline element. Examples include turned handrail balusters, vases, and donut shapes. Both the shape and the centerline element must be drawn on the same work plane. The cross section shapes can be closed or open shapes (if the shape is open, a surface form will be created), and the line element can be a model line or a reference line. When using a reference line, the line will remain in the mass family for future use. If a model line is used as the center point, it will be discarded once revolve form is created.

The centerline element will not be part of the revolve form regardless of which type of line is created. If two line elements are selected, the first line element created will be the default centerline. There will be up to three options available using the onscreen buttons: Default Centerline, Switch Centerline, and Create Surface. The number of

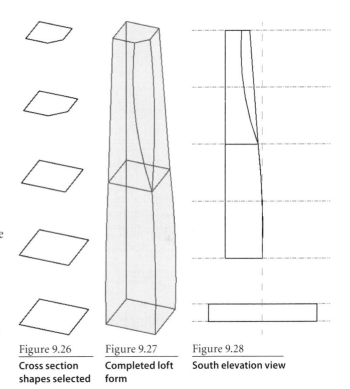

Figure 9.26
Cross section shapes selected

Figure 9.27
Completed loft form

Figure 9.28
South elevation view

options available will vary depending on the shapes selected. Selecting two open shapes will provide more options than a line and a closed shape. When option buttons are displayed onscreen, select the desired option or cycle through the options by pressing the spacebar.

Let's create a revolve form that fills the open space between the previously modeled extrusion and loft forms. Continue working in the Loft Form.rvt file saved previously, or reopen the file to continue.

1. Double-click the South elevation view in the Project Browser to make it the current view, as shown in Figure 9.28.

2. Select the In-Place Mass tool to begin a new mass object.

3. Name the mass **Meeting Facility**.

4. Click Set Work Plane from the Work Plane panel, and select Reference Plane : Building Center Top/Bottom from the Name drop-down (Figure 9.29). Click OK.

5. Using Model Line from the Draw panel, sketch a closed cross section shape similar to what is shown in Figure 9.30.

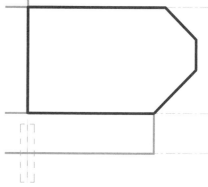

Figure 9.29

Work Plane dialog box

Figure 9.30

Cross section shape and reference line

6. Select Reference Line and then Line to draw a vertical reference line.

7. Select both the closed cross section shape and the reference line, and then click Create Form.

8. Click the Default 3D View tool on the Quick Access toolbar (QAT).

   The closed shape is turned around the reference line to build a 360-degree shape.

9. Select Finish Mass from the In-Place Editor panel to complete the revolve form (Figure 9.31).

10. From the Application menu, use the Save As command to save a copy of the file and name it `Revolve Form.rvt`.

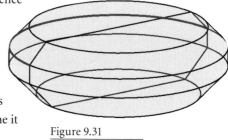

Figure 9.31

Finished revolve form

Building a Sweep Form

Sweep forms, like the one in Figure 9.32, are created when a cross section shape, or multiple shapes, is extruded along a path. Building-related examples commonly modeled include most moldings applied in a building, handrails, and hoses. The sketching method used for both the cross section shape and the path affect whether the sweep form will be created.

Here are the options when modeling a sweep form:

- Cross section shapes can be either open or closed.

- Cross section shapes must be created perpendicular to the segment of the path that they are sketched on.

- Paths can be single segments or multisegmented.

- Paths may be closed when sweeping a closed cross section shape.

- Open shapes can be swept only along single segment paths.

- Multiple cross section shapes can be swept along single-segment paths.

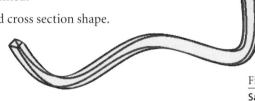

Figure 9.32

Sample sweep form

A sweep form will be used to create an equipment screen element on the roof of the loft form previously modeled. Continue working in the `Revolve Form.rvt` file saved previously, or reopen the file to continue.

1. Double-click Floor Plans Level 7 in the Project Browser to make it the current view (the lineweights in the figure have been adjusted so they are easier to see).

2. Click the In-Place Mass tool, and name the new mass **Screen**.

3. Click Reference Line and then Line from the Draw panel.

4. Sketch a chain of reference lines, offset from the edge of the Loft Tower, as shown in Figure 9.33.

   The reference planes shown are offset from the edge of the Loft Tower mass by a distance of 1′-0″; the exact distance does not matter.

5. Using the Point Element tool from the Draw panel, place a point at the midpoint of the left-side vertical reference line segment, as shown in Figure 9.34.

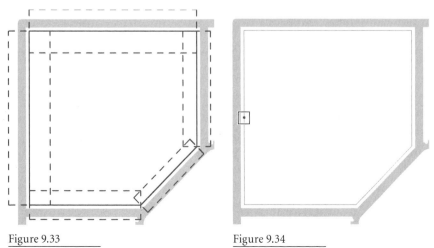

Figure 9.33

Chain of reference lines

Figure 9.34

Reference point added to sketch

6. Click Default 3D View on the QAT, and adjust your point of view close to what is shown in Figure 9.35.

7. Select Set Work Plane from the Work Plane panel, and hover over the reference point.

8. Press Tab, if necessary, until the reference plane that is perpendicular to the reference line highlights, and then left-click.

9. Use the Model Line tool to create a cross section shape similar to the shape shown in Figure 9.36. The shape is roughly 3′-0″ tall.

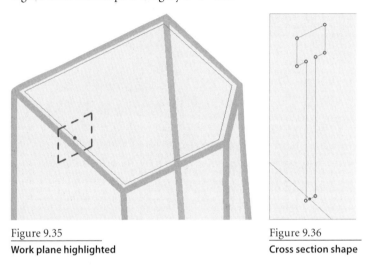

Figure 9.35
Work plane highlighted

Figure 9.36
Cross section shape

10. Select the closed cross section shape and the path of reference line segments, and then click Create Form.

11. Click Finish Mass to complete the sweep form.

12. From the Application menu, use the Save As command to save a copy of the file named Sweep Form.rvt.

Building a Surface Form

Surface forms are created from closed or open shapes and have no thickness. Unlike other forms, the shapes used to create the form can be on the same level or work plane or on different work planes. When sketching a shape for a surface form, selecting the Make Surface From Closed Loops check box on the Options bar will automatically create a surface form when you finish sketching a closed shape. Common examples of surface forms would be hanging fabrics, screen walls, and free-form curving panels.

A surface form will be used to create a privacy screen element on Level 3. This surface form will appear on the top surface of the revolve form created in the earlier exercise.

Continue working in the Sweep Form.rvt file saved previously, or reopen the file to continue.

1. Double-click the Floor Plans Level 3 view to make it the current view.

2. Select the In-Place Mass tool once again, and assign the name **Privacy Screen**.

3. Prior to creating the sketch, open the Placement Plane drop-down list and select Level 3 regardless of the current plane displayed.

4. Sketch a Model Line arc similar to what is shown in Figure 9.37, with a radius of 48′-0″ and linear segments returning to the loft form.

   Use the Center – Ends Arc tool to initially draw the arc only to an angle of 180 degrees.

5. Click Modify to activate Modify mode.

6. Select the arc and lines, and then choose Create Form.

7. Double-click the South elevation view to make it the current view, and select Finish Mass from the In-Place Editor panel to finish the surface form (Figure 9.38).

   The message window that appears is informational; it alerts you that the mass has no volume. You can dismiss it.

8. From the Application menu, choose Save As to save a copy of the file and name it Tower Mass.rvt.

Figure 9.37

Surface model line curve

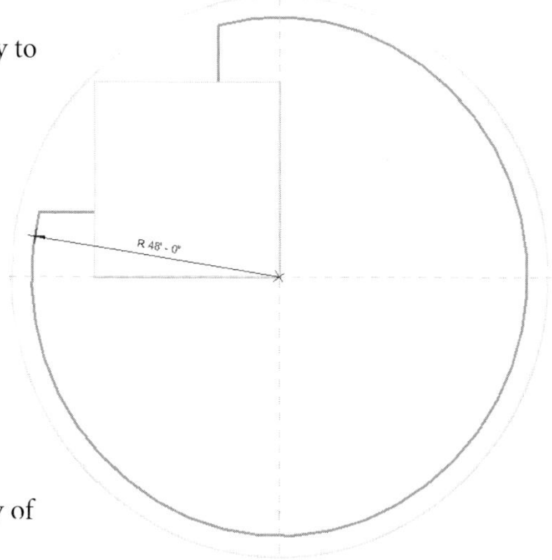

Building Void Forms

Void forms can be created using any of the five types of forms shown earlier in this chapter. Voids are negative forms that make openings or subtract their shape and volume from solid forms. Void forms can be modeled within the solid form mass at the same time the mass is created or after the mass has been finished by editing the mass solid. While editing the mass solid, void forms may be added or deleted. You will add mass void forms to your previously created mass tower.

Figure 9.38

Finished surface form

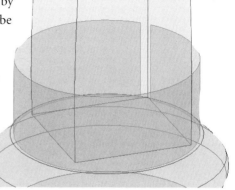

1. Continue working in the Tower Mass.rvt file saved previously, or reopen the file from the book's website to continue.

2. Make sure the default 3D view is the current view, and orbit the view to approximately the SW view direction.

   You can observe the compass on the ViewCube while orbiting to verify view direction. This view direction will enable easy selection of both corners of the loft that will be used as the center points of the cylindrical forms.

3. Select the Loft Tower element previously created.

4. From the View Control bar, choose Temporary Hide/Isolate, and then choose Isolate Element (Figure 9.39).

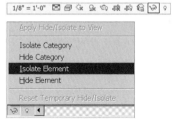

This will turn off the display of all other elements in the model and provide a clear view in which to model the voids. The Drawing Area is now surrounded by a cyan colored border and the upper-left corner of the drawing area is labeled Temporary Hide/Isolate.

Figure 9.39

View Control bar, Temporary Hide/Isolate control

5. Once the tower mass is isolated, select the Edit In-Place tool from the Model panel.

6. Click Set Work Plane from the Work Plane panel, and select Level 3 from the Placement Plane drop-down list on the Options bar; this will set the work plane at the base of the loft.

7. Sketch two circles with a radius of approximately 12′, as shown in Figure 9.40. You will create void forms using each circle.

8. Select the right circle, expand the Create Form tool on the Form panel, and choose Void Form, as shown in Figure 9.41 (Click the lower half of the Create Form tool to expand the drop-down.)

9. Choose the leftmost icon that displays on the screen similar to the cylindrical extrusion created earlier in order to create a cylindrical extrusion.

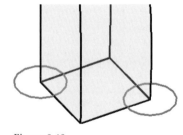

Figure 9.40

Circle sketches

The void is created and automatically subtracts itself from the solid form. The void extrusions will be created at a height of 10′-0″ by default. In the following steps, the height of the extrusions will be changed to better fit the model.

Figure 9.41

Choosing Create Form → Void Form

10. Without deselecting the void element, pick the 10′-0″ dimension text, as shown in Figure 9.42; change the dimension to 48′; and press Enter.

The void element extends to a height of 48′ and subtracts that volume from the mass solid.

11. Clear the selection by clicking in an empty area of the graphics screen to see the result (Figure 9.43).

Void forms are invisible unless selected and therefore disappear once the selection is cleared.

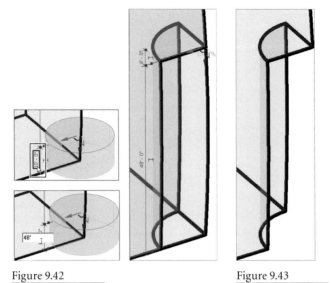

Figure 9.42

Temporary dimensions and void updates

Figure 9.43

Deselect to see final results.

12. For the next void form, select the sketch circle on the left, and create a void form.

13. Use the same methods as before to change the default 10′-0″ height of the void to 24′-0″ tall.

SELECTING A VOID

If a void form becomes deselected after being created, do the following:

1. Hover over an edge that is coincident with the solid form.

2. Press the Tab key until you see the void highlight.

3. Left-click to select the void.

Note both voids will highlight, but only one will be selected.

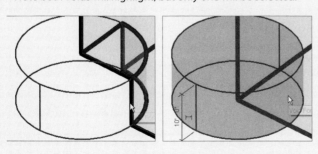

Converting Solid Forms to Void Forms

Converting solid forms to void forms can be done in the Properties palette (Figure 9.44). Creating the form as a solid first provides more visual feedback and simplified selection when creating, editing, and placing the form. Once the desired design has been achieved, the solid form can be converted to a void.

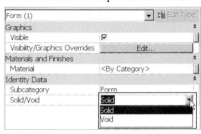

The procedure to convert solid forms to void forms (Figure 9.45) is as follows:

1. Select any part of the form, or the entire form.

2. In the Properties palette, open the Solid/Void list, and select Void.

Figure 9.44

Converting a solid form to a void in the Properties palette

If you are having difficulty determining what form you are selecting hover over the form to be converted, press Tab repeatedly until the entire form highlights, and then left-click to select the form.

Forms can be converted from solids to voids but not from voids to solids. Although voids cannot be converted back to solids, they can still be edited using the same methods as solids.

Figure 9.45

Two solid forms converting to a void

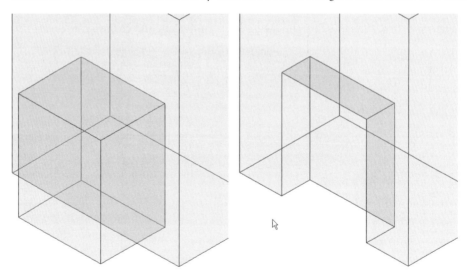

Using the Cut and Join Geometry Tools

Void forms will only automatically cut, or subtract, their mass from solid forms that exist in the mass family prior to the creation of the void form. If a solid form is added after the void form, the Cut Geometry tool will need to be used to cut the void from the solid.

1. Using the Cut Geometry tool from the Geometry panel, select the new solid form (Figure 9.46).

2. Select the void form by clicking the Tab key until it is highlighted.

3. Left pick to finalize the selection.

4. Close the current file, and save changes if desired.

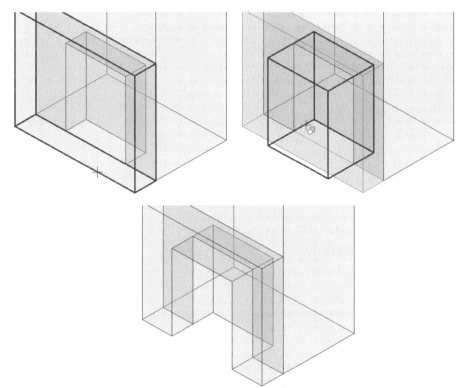

Figure 9.46
Solid form selected

Join Geometry will merge the two solid forms into one object and remove the lines where they meet (Figure 9.47). Use Join Geometry whenever you need to join multiple forms together whether they are in the same mass family or separate mass families. The Join Geometry tool will clean up the model, remove any overlapping volumes, and create edges at form and mass intersections. Individual elements, both forms and masses, will remain editable independently after joining. Start the Join Geometry tool, and select one form and then the other.

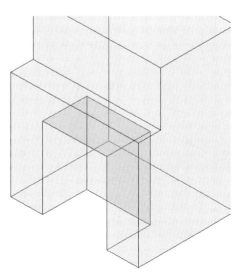

Figure 9.47
Joined solid forms

Editing Forms

Through the conceptual and schematic design stages of a building project, massing models evolve and change, and mass forms will require editing in order to still match the design intent. Form-editing tools, shown in Figure 9.48, provide a method to manipulate and adjust the model in order to modify existing forms or to finalize forms that are difficult to model directly by means of cross section curves and shapes. In addition, the form can be broken down to the component parts used when originally creating the form, which can be a fast method of quickly making major changes.

Figure 9.48

Editing tools

The void forms and the Cut and Join tools introduced in the previous section are a type of editing operation that is performed using the same tools that were used to create the solid forms initially. In addition, editing tools are available for mass forms that provide the ability to stretch and manipulate the form by pulling and pushing surfaces, edges, and vertex points. These editing tools allow rapid changes to size and shape and also provide a more intuitive process for creating organic mass elements. These tools can be used in conjunction with the solid and void form creation tools.

Editable subcomponents are as follows:

- Surfaces

- Edges

- Vertexes

Placing the cursor over the edge, vertex, or surface will highlight the subelement to be edited (Figure 9.49). Pressing the Tab key will cycle through available subelements and also allow selection of the entire form for editing. Selections and edits can be made in any view where the form is visible, including orthographic 3D views. In camera views, selection is possible, but editing is limited to deleting subelements or deleting the entire form.

Figure 9.49

Highlighting subelements

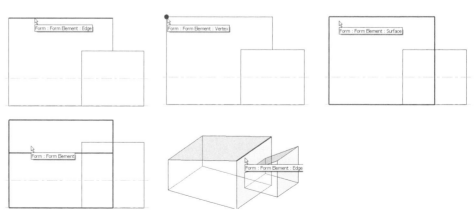

Push/Pull Editing

Once the selection is made by left-clicking, the subelement 3D Control object will display. The 3D Control object allows manipulation of the subelement by clicking and dragging. By hovering over the x-, y-, or z-axis and clicking and holding, the stretch move will be constrained to that axis. To constrain stretches to a double axis:

1. Hover over the small planes between the 3D Control axes.

2. Pick and hold to constrain the movement to either XY, YZ, or XZ.

In Figure 9.50, the highlighted axis, or plane, will appear bolder than the other axes and planes. On your computer screen, the highlighted axis or plane will be much clearer.

The orientation of the 3D Control object will be aligned to the local coordinates of the subelement selected by default, and the three axes will be aligned to the edge or face being manipulated. Pressing the spacebar will toggle the 3D Control orientation from local coordinates back to global coordinates (Figure 9.51).

Figure 9.50

3D Control object and axis constraints

Curved cross section solid form edges will display additional editing options not available for linear edge segments. Closed cross section shapes will allow editing of the circle radius by dragging the 3D control (Figure 9.52), and the center of the form will remain fixed. Open cross section edges on surface forms will allow either editing the radius as above or editing the radius and having the endpoints remain fixed. This option will not function when you are editing a closed circular shape.

Figure 9.53 shows examples of the radius-editing options on a curved surface form.

Figure 9.51

Changing alignment of the 3D Control object

Figure 9.52

3D Control radius editing fixed center and fixed end points

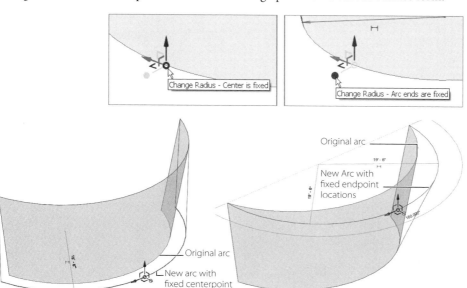

Figure 9.53

Arc editing with fixed center and arc editing with fixed end points

Dimensional Editing

As is standard with all Revit object editing, you can use temporary dimensions to exactly control dimensional changes to the form during editing operations. Temporary dimensions for editing forms will be available for vertex, edge, or surface editing.

1. Select the subelement to be edited.

2. Click the temporary dimension to edit and type a new dimension (Figure 9.54).

3. Press Enter; the form will resize to reflect the dimensional change.

Figure 9.54

Dimensional radius editing

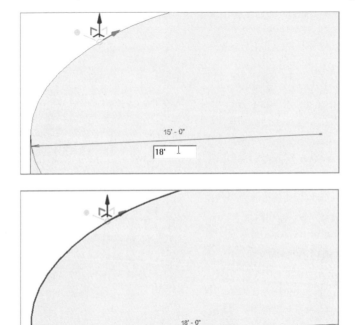

The direction of the view, plan, elevation, section, or 3D will affect which temporary dimensions are displayed. If the desired temporary dimensions are not readily available, permanent dimensions can be added to the form, or form subelements, to allow accurate manipulation and modification. The temporary dimensions can also be used to control and adjust the two-dimensional cross section shapes and curves prior to creating forms from them.

Permanent dimensions can be added manually using the tools on the Dimension panel located on the Annotate tab or by making the temporary dimensions permanent by clicking the Make This Temporary Dimension Permanent icon displayed at the midpoint of the dimension (Figure 9.55).

Permanent dimensions can be added manually in plan, section, elevation, and orthographic 3D views. Once the permanent dimension is added to the mass model, it will be visible and editable in all appropriate views, including 3D (Figure 9.56), regardless of which view it was created in. Dimensions, either permanent or temporary, are not available in a camera view.

Permanent dimensions added in the mass family will behave and display the same whether they were created on the two-dimensional cross sections or on the three-dimensional form element. These dimensions will be visible and accessible for editing while in the In-Place Editor only and will not display once the mass has been finished.

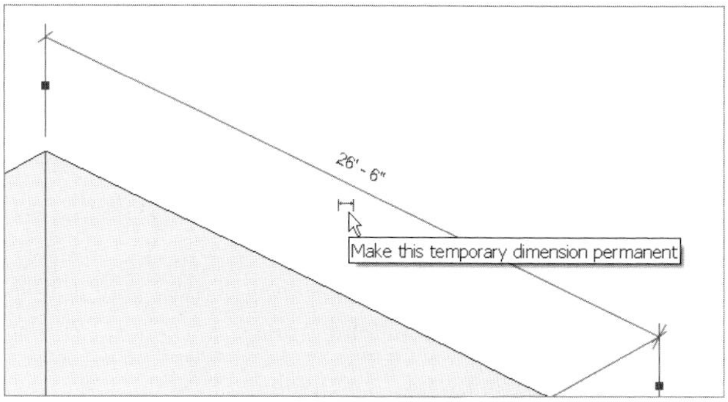

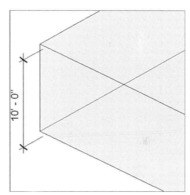

Figure 9.55

Click to make a temporary dimension permanent.

Figure 9.56

Vertical aligned dimension created in elevation and the same dimension displayed in 3D view

When you are creating permanent dimensions in 3D orthographic views (Figure 9.57), the dimension will be created on the active work plane. Using the Set Work Plane tool to pick the dimension plane will allow dimensions to be created on any plane needed.

Figure 9.57

Dimensions created in 3D view

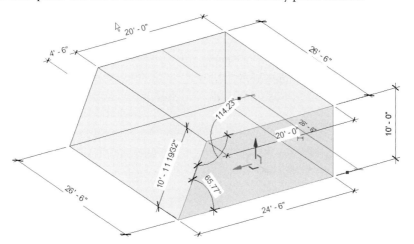

To place the dimension parallel to the angled face:

1. Choose Set from the Work Plane panel.

2. Hover over the angled face.

3. Pick the face to make it the active work plane (Figure 9.58).

4. Start the Aligned Dimension tool on the Home tab.

5. Pick two edges of the plane.

6. Pick away from any edge, or pick back on the dimension segment already created to place and finish the dimension (Figure 9.59).

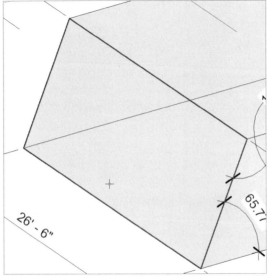

Figure 9.58
Setting the face as the active work plane

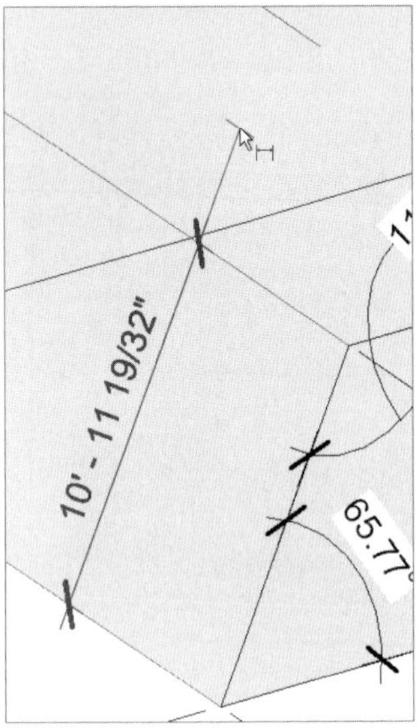

Figure 9.59
Creating the aligned dimension

Parametric Controls: Dimensional Parameters

By using dimensional parameters, you will gain the capability to adjust the dimensions of a mass element from outside of the In-Place Editor and also provide the capability to edit multiple dimensions at one time by changing a single parameter value. Once the parameter value is changed, the mass will update to reflect the dimension changes. These changes can be performed within the mass family or in the project itself.

Dimensional parameters are created using one of two methods. The easiest method of adding parameters to dimensions is as follows:

1. Create the dimension.

2. After the dimension is created, select it.

3. Open the Label list on the Options bar, and choose Add Parameter (Figure 9.60).

You can select multiple dimensions at one time when adding a parameter, and that parameter will be applied to all the selected dimensions.

Figure 9.60

Choosing Add Parameter

> When you are adding dimensional parameters to already existing dimensions, the dimension values should be the same when selecting multiple dimensions, or the values will be changed to a common value when the parameter is created and attached and could cause unexpected changes to the form or shape. The dimension value of the first dimension created in the Selection Set will be the value used for multiple dimensions.

The parameters can also be created using an alternate method before you attach them to a dimension by opening the Family Types dialog box on the Properties panel on the Home tab (Figure 9.61). This opens the Family Types dialog box, where you can add parameters to the family, modify or remove parameters, or change parameter values (Figure 9.61). Once the parameter has been added to the family, it is attached to the dimension by selecting the dimension (or multiple dimensions), opening the label list on the Options bar, and choosing the previously created parameter to attach. When using this method, verify that the type of parameter is set to Length in the Parameter Properties dialog box. This is the default type of parameter and is the only type that can be attached to a dimension.

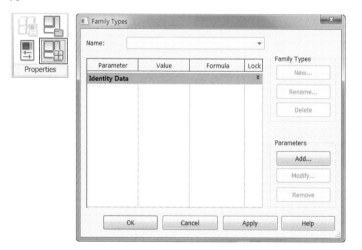

Figure 9.61

Click the Family Types tool to open the dialog box.

We will not use the check box in the Lock column for these parameters. Leaving a parameter unlocked allows you to edit the elements controlled by the dimensional parameter using push/pull techniques.

When a dimensional parameter is locked, the form and that parameter can be changed only in the Family Types dialog box or by changing the dimension value on the screen. The ability to lock parameters applies only to dimensional parameters and includes Length and Angle parameters.

Creating Dimensional Parameters

The next steps will walk through both methods of creating parameters and attaching them to two separate dimensions:

1. Begin a new project using the default template as used previously.

   This creates a new project and opens with the Level 1 view active.

2. Create a new in-place mass family, working in the Level 1 Floor Plan view for simplicity.

3. Create a rectangular cross section shape of approximately 30′ × 20′ (10m × 7m).

4. Add two aligned dimensions for width and depth, as shown in Figure 9.62.

Figure 9.62

Rectangular shape

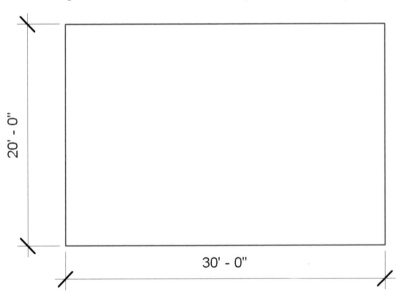

5. Select the 30′ (10m) dimension, open the Label drop-down list on the Options bar, and then choose Add Parameter.

   This opens the Parameter Properties dialog box where the parameter will be created, as shown in Figure 9.63.

Using this method of parameter creation automatically forces the Type Of Parameter setting to Length and groups the parameter in the Dimensions group. This parameter will be both a family parameter and created as an instance parameter.

6. In the Name text box, type **Width**.

7. Select the Instance radio button, and then click OK at the bottom of the dialog box. Keep your file open for now.

> The name of the parameter or group it is assigned to has no effect on the function of the parameter; that name is used only to identify the parameter in the Family Types dialog box or Properties palette.

Figure 9.63

Parameter Properties dialog box

Instance parameters (Figure 9.64) allow the objects to vary from one another. Type parameters control all elements of that family type—whenever the parameter setting is modified, all elements of that family type are modified. For in-place mass families, the selection of parameter type will not have any effect on the function but will control only whether the parameter appears in the instance or type properties of the mass.

When the dialog box closes, you will see the parameter name has been added to the dimension value (Figure 9.65). This always alerts you that a family dimension is controlled by a parameter. This type of dimension is called a *labeled dimension*.

Still in the same file where you just created the Width parameter, let's continue. Let's use an alternate method to create the Depth parameter:

1. From the Properties panel on the Modify tab, select the Family Types tool to open the Family Types dialog box.

   The already created Width parameter appears in the dialog box. All family parameters will appear in this dialog box regardless of which method is used to create them or which type of parameter they have been created as.

2. Click Add in the Parameters area at the right side of the dialog box (Figure 9.66), which will open the Parameter Properties dialog box. (This is the same dialog box you just used to create the Width parameter.)

3. Type the name **Depth**, and verify that Type Of Parameter is set to Length.

Figure 9.64

Name and instance settings

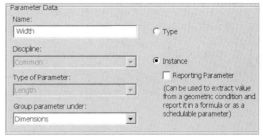

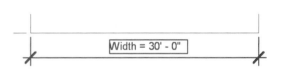

Figure 9.65

Parameter attached to dimension

The parameter is not forced to be Length using this method!

Figure 9.66

Adding a parameter

4. Verify that the parameter will be grouped in the Dimensions group.

5. Select the Instance radio button, and leave Parameter Type set to Family Parameter.

6. Click OK to close the Parameter Properties dialog box. The new Depth parameter appears in the Family Types dialog box along with the previously created Width parameter. Click OK again to close the dialog box.

7. To attach the Depth parameter to the dimension, select the vertical dimension (currently 20′ or 7m), and open the Label list on the Options bar.

8. Select the Depth parameter.

> All Length parameters will be available in this drop-down list regardless of which method was used to create them. Only Length parameters will be listed because they are the only type of parameter that can be attached to a linear dimension.

The Depth parameter is now attached to the vertical dimension and appears as part of the dimension text.

Testing Dimensional Parameters

Testing dimensional parameters in Revit is a very important step when you are building families. To test the dimensional parameters, the Family Types dialog box will be used to "flex" the model. *Flexing* the model in Revit means assigning new parameter values and observing that the changes to the model are as expected. It is easier to confirm that the behavior is correct before proceeding any further. If the behavior is not as expected, it will be easier to make changes and fix the error before moving on.

1. Click the Family Types tool to open the Family Types dialog box.

2. Arrange the screen similar to what is shown in Figure 9.67 so that you can see both the dialog box and the shape and dimensions. If this is not possible, do the following:

   a. Close the dialog box.

   b. Pan the shape to allow a clear view.

   c. Reopen the Family Types dialog box.

Figure 9.67

**Screen layout for
flexing parameters**

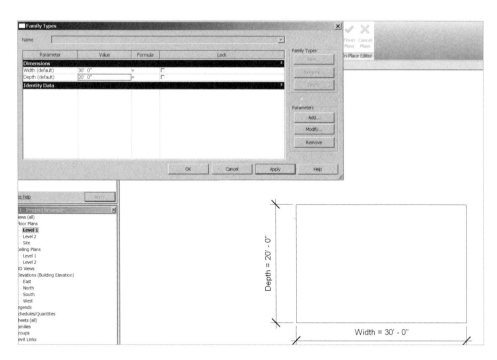

3. In the Value column beside the Width parameter in the Family Types dialog box, highlight the Width value (currently 30′ or 10m), and change it; then click Apply at the bottom of the dialog box.

   The shape should update to reflect the new dimension value.

4. Perform the same type of change to the Depth parameter, and verify that the model updates to reflect the change.

5. Set both parameters back to their original values (optional), and click OK.

   If the shape did not update as expected, verify that the dimension is associated with the desired edge of the shape. If necessary, the dimension could be deleted and a new dimension created to replace it. The parameter will still be available to be attached to the dimension and will not need to be re-created.

6. Select the rectangular shape only, and choose Create Form from the ribbon.

   If the dimensions are included in the selection set, the Create Form button will not be available. If this happens, either reselect only the shape or hold down the Shift key and select the dimensions to remove them from the selection set.

7. Choose Finish Mass from the ribbon, and open the default 3D view from the QAT.

   If the mass does not display, use the Zoom Extents (ZE) command to bring the mass into view. Remember the display settings, from earlier in the chapter, that control mass elements if you still are unable to view the mass.

8. Select the mass, and in the Properties palette, you will see the Width and Depth parameters.

9. Change the value of the parameters in the Properties palette (Figure 9.68), and the mass should update to reflect the new dimensions.

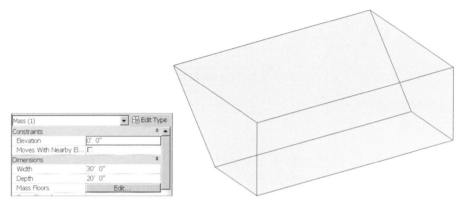

Figure 9.68

Width and Depth parameters in the Properties palette and the modified mass

The mass should have updated but may not have responded as expected. The parameter-controlled dimensions were created using the 2D cross section shape, or profile, of the mass form. The mass form extrusion, as with all mass forms, now also has a bottom and top cross section shape, and each can be manipulated independently of the other. To force the mass to retain its original box shape, do the following:

1. Select the mass family in the graphics area.

2. Choose Edit In-Place from the ribbon.

3. Once in the Form editor, hover over the form.

4. Press Tab until the entire form highlights.

5. Select the form.

6. In the ribbon on the Form Element panel, as shown in Figure 9.69, choose Lock Profiles to lock the shape of the form cross sections together so that the form maintains a rectangular shape.

Figure 9.69

Lock Profiles tool

7. Select Finish Mass from the ribbon, and retest the parameters in the Properties palette.

To unlock the profiles:

1. Use Edit In-Place.

2. Select the form.

3. Click the closed padlock icon that appears above the form (Figure 9.70).

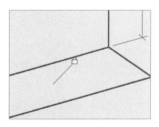

Figure 9.70

Modified mass with an icon showing that it's locked

When you are creating dimensions that will have their values controlled by parameters, the subelement selection—whether vertex, edge, or surface—will control the dimensional changes. When placing the dimensions on the three-dimensional form, ensure that the desired subelement is being dimensioned. The subelement selected when the dimension is created will be the subelement that moves when the dimension value is modified.

Vertex, edge, and surface dimensions will each generate different changes to the mass. By changing the dimensional parameter values, you are stretching, pushing, and pulling the form in the same way as you would be by using the 3D Control object. The subelement selection when stretching determined the results of the stretch, and the same is true using parameters. When adding dimensions to the form, ensure that you are dimensioning to the appropriate vertex, edge, or surface (Figure 9.71) in order to get the desired result.

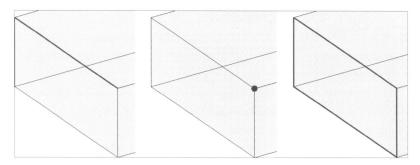

Figure 9.71

Subelements selected when dimensioning: left, edge; center, vertex; right, surface

A Height parameter with a default setting of 10′ (3.3m) has been added to a dimension in the same mass family used earlier. The profiles have been unlocked. Figure 9.72 shows the results when changing the height from 10′ (3.3m) to 15′ (5m) using dimensions that were added to an edge, a surface, and a vertex.

This finishes our use of this file; save the changes if desired or discard the changes and close the file.

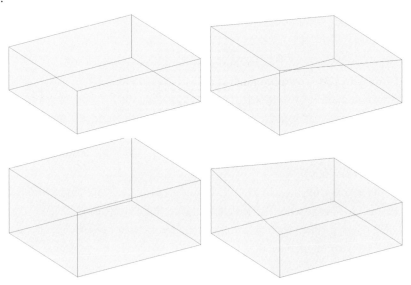

Figure 9.72

A box mass with dimension parameter changes, in order of Edge, Surface, and Vertex

Employing Loadable Mass Families

Loadable, or external, mass families are created outside the project environment and loaded into a project for use. This is the preferred method of creating mass families that are either going to be duplicated within a single project or are going to be used in multiple projects. Creating the family outside the project environment also allows you to update the mass model outside the project where the file performance may be faster. Once the loadable family has been modified, it can be reloaded into the project, or projects, and all instances of that family will update to reflect the updated model. This will not be the behavior when you are copying an in-place mass family that you created using the techniques earlier in this chapter. If there is a chance that the mass may be duplicated, creating the mass as a loadable family is strongly encouraged.

All of the techniques introduced during the in-place family portion of this chapter will apply to loadable families. The only changes are the user interface and the conceptual mass environment, which has additional display capabilities not available in a project environment.

The default Revit installation creates two conceptual mass templates. One is provided (`Mass.rft`) for creating loadable mass families, and one template (`Adaptive Component.rft`) is provided for creating loadable mass or generic model families. The adaptive component template creates families primarily to be inserted into other loadable mass families or into in-place mass families.

Creating a Loadable Family

To create a loadable mass family, open the Application menu and choose New → Conceptual Mass. Doing so opens a list of templates used for creating loadable mass families.

You can also create a loadable mass family from the Recent Files window by selecting New Conceptual Mass from the Families area and then choosing the desired template. The default Imperial Windows 7 template location is as follows:

`C:\ProgramData\Autodesk\RAC 2012\Family Templates\English\Conceptual Mass`

You can create customized mass family templates by starting with one of the provided templates, making any needed changes, and saving the file using the `.rfa` file extension. This is the only extension available for saving a family in Revit. Once the file has been saved, the file extension can be changed to `.rft`, and the file can be placed in the family templates folder. The file will then be available for selection when you are creating a new loadable mass family.

The new family file opens in the default 3D view. One level and two reference planes are included in the template and are visible in three-dimensional views (Figure 9.73). These references will be visible only in the Family Editor environment and not in the project environment once the family has been loaded into a project.

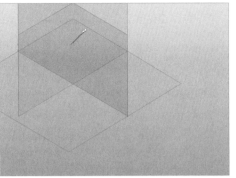

Figure 9.73

Conceptual mass design environment and the same environment with Level and Reference planes highlighted

You can use levels in conceptual mass families as work planes and also for adjusting the height of the conceptual mass while in the Family Editor. The levels created in the mass will not interact with or be available for use in a project file. If the family is being created to match levels in a project, the levels will have to be created in the family file with the matching height settings.

1. From the Application menu, select New → Conceptual Mass.

2. Select `Mass.rft` from the list.

3. Using the South elevation view, start the Level tool from the Home tab, and add two levels in the mass family file.

   The level lines will automatically align with the existing lower level when you hover near the ends. The two new levels will be placed at 60′ (20m) and 120′ (40m). The default level, Level 1, will remain at its current location.

   These levels will be used to sketch the cross section shapes for our mass family and also to control the height of the cross section shapes once the form is created.

4. In the Level 1 Floor Plan view, sketch the elliptical shape shown in Figure 9.74 using model lines and the Ellipse tool from the Draw panel on the Home tab.

   The horizontal, major axis will have a radius of 120′ (40m), and the vertical, minor axis will be 60′ (20m).

5. In the Level 2 Floor Plan view, sketch a circle with a radius of 60′ (20m); this circle will be centered on the ellipse below.

6. Then, on the Level 3 Floor Plan view, sketch another ellipse with a horizontal radius of 60′ (20m) and a vertical axis of 30′ (10m).

   This ellipse will be centered on the two sketch shapes already created.

7. After creating the three cross section shapes, open the default 3D view (Figure 9.75).

   You will see the two new levels and the three shapes created in the previous steps.

8. Select the three shapes, and then choose Create Form from the Form panel.

Figure 9.74

The Ellipse tool and the ellipse on Level 1

Figure 9.75

The default 3D view and the newly created form

 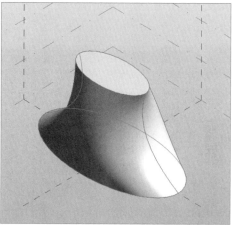

9. To better see what the form is composed of, select the form or any part of the form, and enable X-Ray mode by picking the X-Ray tool from the Form Element panel, as shown in Figure 9.76.

   X-Ray mode displays the form and the underlying elements that the form is composed of. This mode allows for easier editing of the form and also gives you a means of aligning and locking shapes to levels using their automatically created reference points.

   If there is a 3D Control visible, select a blank area of the screen to clear the face previously selected. This mode is also available for in-place mass families.

10. Using the Align tool (Figure 9.77), from the Modify panel, align and lock the cross section shapes on Levels 2 and 3 to their respective levels.

    The cross section shape on Level 1 will automatically be locked to the Level 1 plane, but the other two levels will not automatically lock to the levels they were created on.

Figure 9.76

The form viewed using the X-Ray tool

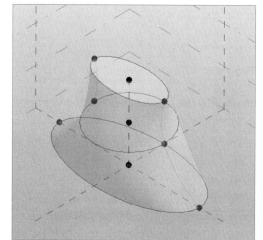

After starting the Align tool, pick Level 2 as the first pick point, and then select the reference point at the center of the circular cross section shape sketched on Level 2 (Figure 9.78).

11. Click the open padlock icon to lock the shape to Level 2.

12. Perform the same steps to align and lock the elliptical shape created on Level 3 to the Level 3 plane.

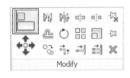

Figure 9.77

Align tool

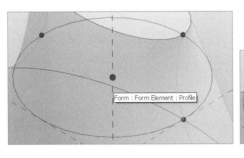

Figure 9.78

Reference point, before and after locking the shape to the level

13. After both shapes are locked to their planes, cancel the Align tool by clicking Modify at the left end of the ribbon.

14. Flex the model to make sure that the shapes move with the levels as expected: Pick one of the levels, and in the Properties palette, change the Elevation setting, and then click Apply.

As the elevation of the levels is changed, the shapes should move up and down (remaining locked to the levels), and the form should adjust as well. If the shapes do not remain locked to the levels, repeat the Align tool again, and ensure that the shape is locked to the level.

15. Click the Undo tool from the QAT to restore the Elevation setting.

When a form requires significant changes, you can select the form and choose Dissolve from the Modify tab's Form Element panel, as shown in Figure 9.79. This will deconstruct the form back to the current component cross section shapes. There will be one reference point left on each cross section that can be deleted. The form could then be easily reconstructed using the shapes.

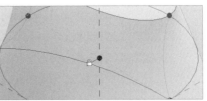

Figure 9.79

Dissolve tool

If you tested the Dissolve tool, use the Undo tool to bring the form back.

16. The family is complete: save the family file, naming the file `Core Building Shape.rfa`, and keep it open.

The family name that you use will appear in the Project Browser once you have loaded the mass family into a project. As with in-place mass families, logical names will be easier to work with later when selection and editing is necessary.

Using a Loadable Family in a Project

Now that the family is complete, let's load it into a new project file:

1. From the Application menu, choose New → Project. Click OK to use the default template.

   The new project will open in the Level 1 Floor Plan view by default. This is the view you will use to place the mass family.

2. Save the project with the name **Building A**. Switch the active view to the conceptual mass family that was previously saved. This can be done on the View tab by using the Switch Windows tool in the Windows panel:

   a. Locate the view name in the list.

   b. Select a view of the conceptual mass family

   The specific view will not matter. Alternately, you could cycle through open views and files by pressing Ctrl+Tab.

Load into Project

Family Editor

3. Once the mass family is in the active view, choose Load Into Project from the Family Editor panel.

   If the family and the newly created project are the only Revit files open, even if there are multiple views of the same file, the family will be automatically loaded into the open project, and the active view will be changed to that project. If there are multiple other files open, you will see a selection window where you can select the project, multiple projects, or other families into which to load the family. If a pop-up window opens, select the project named Building A. You can also load families into a project directly from the project by selecting Load Family and then navigating to the family file. You may also see the message alerting you that Show Mass has been enabled.

4. Click Close to proceed.

   The Place Mass command is automatically activated when Load Into Project is initiated from the family file.

> If the Load Family command is used from the project to load the family, the Place Mass command will need to be activated manually, and the correct family will need to be chosen from the Type Selector.

5. To place the mass family on a work plane, and not on a face, select Place On Work Plane on the Placement panel in the ribbon.

6. Click a point roughly centered in the view to place an instance of the conceptual mass family, and then click Modify to finish the Place Mass command. Activate the default 3D view to view the mass family.

Editing a Loadable Family

When mass families are created as loadable families, and not as in-place families, editing of the family can be done only in the family file and not in the project. To edit the loadable mass family, open the family file and modify it, and then reload the family into the project where any changes you made will update all instances of the conceptual mass family.

1. To quickly open the file for editing, select the family, and choose Edit Family from the Mode panel in the ribbon.

   This opens the family in the Conceptual Mass Family Editor, and you can now manipulate the form.

2. Activate the default 3D view, and select Level 3.

3. In the Properties palette, change Elevation to 300′ (100m), as shown in Figure 9.80.

   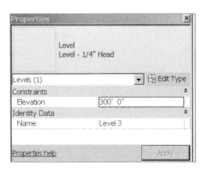

   Figure 9.80

   Changing Level 3 Elevation in the Properties palette

4. Click Apply in the Properties palette to update the form, as shown in Figure 9.81.

5. Save the family file.

   The family could be loaded into the project at this point, and the conceptual mass family would be updated in the project file, but the changes would not be saved in the family file.

6. Select Load Into Project on the ribbon.

   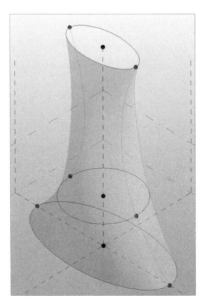

   Figure 9.81

   Updated form

7. If there is only one project open, the view will change to the open project. If there are more than one project or family file open, a selection window will open; choose the Building A project file and click OK.

   The dialog box shown in Figure 9.82 alerts you that the family already exists in this project file. If the family is reloaded, it will be updated in the project file, and all instances of the family will be updated. This dialog box offers three choices:

   Overwrite The Existing Version This option will replace the current version of the family in the project that it is being loaded into.

Overwrite The Existing Version And Its Parameter Values If you select the override option, the parameter values of the existing family are overridden by the parameter values of the family you are loading. If you do not select this option, then any family types in the family file not currently in the project file will be loaded. Any family types that already exist in the project file will be ignored.

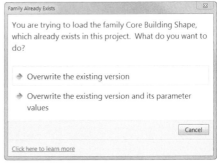

Figure 9.82

Warning message

Cancel Clicking Cancel will not reload the family into the project file, and no changes will be made to the family in the project.

8. Choose Overwrite The Existing Version.

   The conceptual mass family already placed in the project file updates to reflect the dimensional change made in the Family Editor (Figure 9.83).

9. Save the file, and continue working through the next exercises.

Figure 9.83

The updated family

Using Face-Based Modeling

Mass families can be used to quickly build conceptual design models by selecting the faces of the mass and then creating model objects directly from the geometry of the face. Here are the Model By Face objects:

Curtain Systems Curtain systems are similar to curtain walls but can be created only by face. Curtain system family types can be created, modified, and saved. Curtain systems are controlled by the face object that was used to create it and cannot be edited independently of the face.

Walls Typical project wall family types can be created by using faces to model complex geometry not possible with the Wall command. Vertical walls can be edited independently of the face once created.

Floors Typical project floor families are available to be placed on mass floors. Floors can be edited independently of the face once created.

Roofs Typical project roof families are available to be modeled on mass faces. Roof sketches cannot be edited independently of the face.

Mass Floors A mass floor is created directly from the shape of the mass by selecting the mass and then selecting which floors are to be created. Mass floors are used for scheduling, for area calculations, and as the host objects when creating floors by face.

All of these objects can be updated so that they still follow the shape of the face after the conceptual mass object has been changed. The update is not automatic but is accomplished by the Update To Face tool. Certain changes will be discarded when updating the model object to the face; for example, wall profile edits will be discarded.

You will add some levels to your project file. Mass floors are created on levels in the project file. To create mass floors, you must have levels present in the project.

1. Continue working in the Building A file that you used in the preceding section on loadable families, or reopen it if it has been closed, and activate the South elevation view. Select the existing Level 2, and change its elevation to 15′ (5m).

2. You can use the Array tool here: Select Level 2 again if needed, and start the Array tool (Figure 9.84).

Figure 9.84

Array tool, on the ribbon and on the Options bar

3. In the Options bar, choose Linear, and deselect the Group And Associate option to make the levels easier to work with once they are arrayed.

Figure 9.85

Finished array

4. Set Move To as 2nd and Number to 20.

5. In the drawing window, pick the selected Level 2, move the pointer straight up, and then type **15′ (5m)** and press Enter.

6. Save the file.

    The resulting array should appear as shown in Figure 9.85.

Leave the file open because you'll continue with it in the next section. Creating the levels using the Array command did not create story levels, but the levels will still be available to the Mass Floors tool.

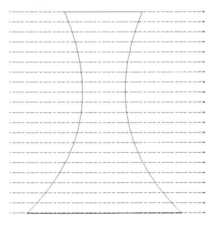

Adding Mass Floors

The next step is to create the mass floors. The mass floors are created using the existing levels of the project. A selection window allows the selection of all or only certain levels when adding mass floors to the conceptual mass. Mass floor elements are planar and do not display a thickness. For final building modeling, they will be used as the faces from which to create Model By Face floors.

Still in your Building A file, follow these steps:

1. Select the conceptual mass.

2. Pick Mass Floors from the Model panel of the Modify | Mass tab on the ribbon.

3. In the Mass Floors selection dialog box (Figure 9.86), select Level 1.

4. Scroll down, and while holding the Shift key down, select Level 20 (Level 21 will be the roof level, so a mass floor is not needed).

5. Select any check box next to one of the highlighted levels, and the check will appear in all 20 selected levels.

6. Click OK at the bottom of the dialog box to create mass floors at each of the levels selected in the dialog box.

7. Open the default 3D view to see the mass floors, as shown in Figure 9.87.

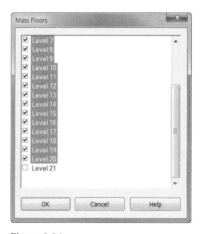

Figure 9.86
Selecting mass floors

Figure 9.87
Mass floors in default 3D view shown using the Shaded Visual style

At each selected level, a mass floor has been created that follows the shape of the mass family; because of the shape of the family, the mass floors may appear to be twisted or sloped. Adjust the 3D view to better visualize the mass floors using the Nav Cube or by holding down the Shift key, holding down the middle mouse button, and moving the mouse.

8. Save the file, and continue working through the next exercises.

Modeling Tools

The Model By Face tools are located on the Massing & Site tab in the Model By Face panel (Figure 9.88). Unlike the mass floors created earlier, using the tools available on the Model By Face panel creates Revit model elements. The model elements will be linked to the faces from which they were created and can be updated to reflect any future changes made to the mass family. During preliminary design, this is a very fast method of putting together a presentation model for design analysis and review. Once the model elements have been added to the mass, Show Mass is disabled, leaving only the actual model elements visible.

Figure 9.88

Model By Face panel

Creating Floors

The Floor By Face tool requires mass floors in order to create the floor objects.

Continue working in the file from the end of the "Adding Mass Floors" section:

1. Start the Floor By Face tool.

2. On the Options bar, set Offset to **12″** (**300mm**).

   A positive offset will offset the sketch edge of the floor inward, whereas a negative offset will offset the floor sketch edge outward. The inside offset would allow room for exterior curtain systems or walls. You can edit the floor sketch manually as well by using the standard Edit Boundary tool.

3. Verify that Select Multiple is activated in the Multiple Selection panel on the ribbon.

4. Use a window or crossing window to select all of the mass floors.

5. Finish the floors by selecting Create Floors from the same Multiple Selection panel.

   You can select the type of floor before creating the floors by face or you can change the type after. The Floor Family type can be left set to Floor Generic 12″ (Floor Generic 300mm) in the Properties palette.

Figure 9.89

Completed Floors By Face

6. Zoom in, if necessary, on the mass model.

7. Verify that the floor objects are now created.

8. Display the 12″ (300mm) thickness, as shown in Figure 9.89.

9. Save the file, and continue working through the next exercises.

The floors will be more clearly visible if you select Show Mass By View Settings on the Conceptual Mass panel.

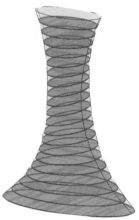

Adding Walls

The Wall By Face tool will use the actual faces of the conceptual mass as the basis for the wall. There is no need to create an intermediate object as was needed by the Floor By Face tool.

Figure 9.90

Pick Faces button

1. Select the Wall By Face tool from the Model By Face panel.

2. Verify that the Pick Faces button is active in the Draw panel (Figure 9.90).

   This is the default setting. This tool can also be activated directly from the Wall tool on the Home tab.

3. On the Options bar, set Location Line to Wall Centerline.

4. Verify that Basic Wall Generic – 8″ (200mm) is the current wall type in the Properties palette.

5. Select the near-side vertical curving face, as shown in Figure 9.91.

   The wall will be created automatically once the face is selected. The tool remains active, and you could select additional faces if desired.

6. Select Modify at the left end of the ribbon to cancel the Wall By Face tool.

Figure 9.91
Face selection and a finished wall

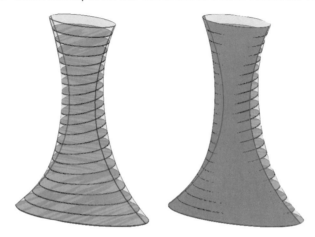

7. Save the file, and continue working through the next exercises.

Creating a Curtain System

The Curtain System By Face tool will use the actual faces of the conceptual mass as the basis for the curtain system. There is no need to create an intermediate object as was needed using the Floor By Face tool.

1. Orbit the 3D view so that you can see the far side of the conceptual mass.

2. Select the Curtain System By Face tool from the Model By Face panel.

3. Select the near vertical face of the conceptual mass (Figure 9.92).

   The Select Multiple option will be active by default but you can deselect it if you want. The Curtain System By Face tool allows you to create a selection of faces before creating the curtain system. Faces can be selected one by one, without the need to hold the Ctrl key, or they can be selected using window or crossing window selection methods. If you select a face inadvertently, you can remove it from the selection set by Shift-clicking it once again. There is also a tool in the panel that lets you clear the entire selection set (Clear Selection) and begin selecting faces again.

Curtain System 5´ × 10´ (1500 × 3000mm) is the default curtain system family type and is listed in the Type Selector at the top of the Properties palette. Curtain System family types can be created and edited as needed similar to Curtain Wall family types.

4. Choose Create System from the Multiple Selection panel.

5. Save the file, and continue working through the next exercises.

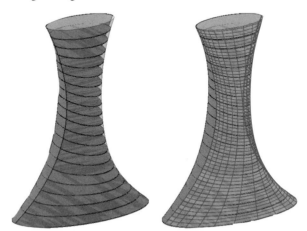

Figure 9.92

Left: face selection; right, finished curtain system

Adding a Roof

The Roof By Face tool has the same selection options noted for Curtain Systems. The Roof By Face tool makes use of typical roof family types available through the standard roof command.

1. Select the Roof By Face tool from the Model By Face panel.

   Select Multiple will be the active selection option in the Multiple Selection panel.

2. On the Options bar (Figure 9.93), set Offset to **8″** (**200mm**) by using a positive offset.

   The sketch edge of the roof will be offset 8″ inward.

3. Select the top face of the conceptual mass.

Figure 9.93

Options bar

Modify | Place Roof by Face   Level: Level 21   Offset: 0´ 8″

4. Choose Create Roof from the Multiple Selection panel to create the roof object, as shown in Figure 9.94.

Figure 9.94

Face selection and finished roof

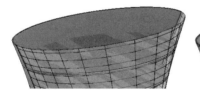
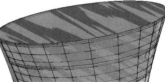

5. On the Massing & Site tab's Conceptual Mass panel, click the Show Mass tool and choose Show Mass By View Settings option.

   Doing so turns off the display of the conceptual mass and shows only the model elements (Figure 9.95).

6. Save the file, and continue working through the next exercises.

Updating Model Elements

Model elements that have been created based on the faces of a conceptual mass family can be updated as necessary. When edits are made to the mass family and the family is loaded back into the project, the model elements can be updated to represent any changes.

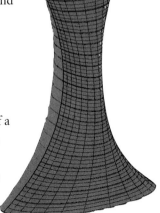

Figure 9.95

Finished model (using Show Mass By View Settings)

1. To make changes to the mass family, select Show Mass Form And Floors from the Conceptual Mass panel.

   Doing so makes the conceptual mass family visible on the screen and selectable.

2. Select the mass family. Using the Tab key will allow you to cycle through the elements available on the screen.

   a. Hover over an edge of the mass family.

   b. Press Tab until the family is highlighted.

   c. Left-click.

   You can check the status bar at the bottom-left corner of the Revit screen to ensure that the mass family Core Building Shape is highlighted.

3. Once the mass family is selected, choose Edit Family from the ribbon.

4. Open the default 3D view in the Family Editor, select Level 2, and change its elevation to 150′ (50m).

5. When the change is complete, choose Load Into Project from the ribbon.

   Remember, the save is needed only if you want to save the changes to the original family file in addition to the project file.

6. Select Overwrite Existing Version; then you will see the updated mass on screen (see Figure 9.96).

7. Use a crossing window—right to left dragging—to select the conceptual mass family and all of the model elements.

8. Use the Filter tool from the ribbon or from the lower-right corner of the Revit window to filter the selection.

9. In the Filter dialog box (Figure 9.97), deselect all check boxes except for the model geometry.

   This will leave Curtain Systems, Floors, Roofs, and Walls selected.

10. Click OK.

11. From the ribbon, choose Update To Face, which will update all the selected model elements created using the Model By Face commands.

There is quite a bit of remodeling taking place, so the final result will take a few seconds to complete (Figure 9.98).

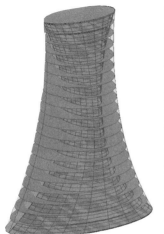

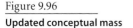

Figure 9.96

Updated conceptual mass

Figure 9.97

Filter dialog box

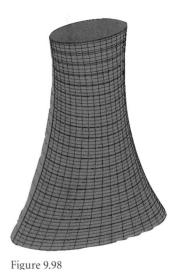

Figure 9.98

Updated model

Creating Mass Families from Imported Geometry

Using previously created three-dimensional models from other applications can be a very fast method of creating mass building studies. Imported geometry can be used to create face-based models, mass floors, and schedules. This is the same capability as masses that were created originally within Revit. The imported geometry mass models can also be created as in-place families or as loadable, or external, families.

To use the imported geometry as a conceptual mass object in Revit, you must import the model object into a conceptual mass family. If the file is not imported directly into a family, either loadable or in-place, then the expected tools will not be available.

1. To start, create a new mass family.

2. Once the new family is created, import the external model.

The tools to create a new loadable family are available on the Application menu by selecting New → Conceptual Mass Family. The Mass.rft template will be one of the two listed by default.

3. On the Insert tab's Import panel, select Import CAD (Figure 9.99).

Figure 9.99

Import CAD tool

The imported file cannot be linked into a conceptual mass family; even though the Link CAD tool is active, the external file will be imported.

4. Navigate to the location in which the file has been saved.

5. Set the color, positioning, and level as desired for the model.

6. Click Open.

The external file is then loaded into the conceptual mass family file.

> For additional information on importing and linking CAD files, see Chapter 12, "Working with Other Files."

7. Save the conceptual mass family.

8. Load the family into a project.

Once loaded into the project, the model can be used to generate mass floors, floors, walls, curtain systems, and roofs.

Note that the imported CAD file is imported into the mass family and not linked. If updates are made to the original CAD file and the file is reimported into the family file and reloaded into the project, the Update To Face command will not function because the mass faces of the model will have changed. These are the file formats supported for import:

- DWG
- DXY
- DGN
- SAT
- SKP

CHAPTER 10

Groups

A group is a collection of individual elements like walls, doors, and windows that are added together to form a new, single entity (the group). Most Autodesk Revit Architecture projects have design elements that are repeated or reused; for example, a hotel has guest rooms, medical facilities have exam rooms, and so on. It isn't practical to model each element over and over for every one of these repeated aspects of a design. Not only is it inefficient to do so, but doing so increases the likelihood for errors and omissions. Groups provide yet another way to manage repetition within your building models.

This chapter covers the following topics:

- Understanding groups

- Creating and editing a group

- Placing a group

- Making special changes to a group

- Saving, loading, and reloading groups

- Practical considerations

Understanding Groups

Groups provide you with a way to combine component and system families into a coherent, repeatable named entity. Easily identifiable examples include a hotel room, apartment unit, or hospital patient room. Groups are also useful to help create consistent annotation and documentation, such as common notes, phrases, or comments that various drawings require.

A Revit component family provides a reliable and efficient way to manage repetition as long as the elements you need to manage are not system families (hosts), such as walls, floors, or ceilings. System families are excluded from the scope of component families (as discussed in Chapter 7, "Introduction to Families"). A component (loadable) family will provide better results when considering pure file performance. Groups excel when using a component family isn't possible.

There is a bit of a paradox, however, because Revit treats *model elements* differently than it does *annotation elements*. Model elements appear in nearly all views automatically. Annotation elements, on the other hand, do not appear in all views by design; they appear only in the views they are deliberately placed within. Each view has a purpose, and the annotation that is included helps serve this purpose. This segregation and behavior means that a group cannot include both model and annotation elements. For this reason, there are three kinds of groups: Model, Detail, and Attached Detail.

Model Groups These are reserved for model elements only, such as walls, doors, windows, floors, model lines, rooms, and other 3D elements that are visible in all views.

Detail Groups These contain only the annotation elements that are view specific, such as tags, symbols, dimensions, text, filled regions, detail components, and detail lines.

Attached Detail Groups These are Detail groups that have an inherent relationship with a Model group. They are created when you use the Create Group tool with both model and annotation elements selected.

Figure 10.1

Groups listed in the Project Browser

Groups have their own branch at the bottom of the listed nodes in the Project Browser (see Figure 10.1). Detail groups appear first in the list, followed by Model groups. Each Attached Detail group, if any exist, is listed and nested beneath its own related Model group.

Creating and Editing a Group

Creating a group is as easy as going to the Home tab, finding the Model panel, clicking the Model Group button, and selecting the Create Group tool from the drop-down menu (see Figure 10.2). You can start with nothing selected in advance, or you can carefully select everything you want to include in the group first. Regardless of the approach you take, Revit will ask you to name your group. Choosing a descriptive name is helpful later when you are working with other people and they have only the names listed in the Project Browser to help them decide which to use. We suggest that you avoid names like Group 1 or Group 2 because they aren't very effective, even if you are working alone.

When you start without a selection set (by clicking the Create Group button), Revit will prompt you for a name and ask you to choose which kind of group you'd like to make (see Figure 10.3). Starting with a selection set (selecting more than one element first and then clicking Create Group) will change the ribbon to a contextual tab (Modify | Multi-Select) and will display a new Create Group button (see Figure 10.4). Once you click Create Group in the Create panel, Revit will offer you one of two different dialog boxes, depending on whether your selection set includes model elements, annotation elements, or a combination of both.

Figure 10.2

Model Group button's Create Group command

Figure 10.3

The Create Group dialog box when no selection is previously set

Figure 10.4

Click the Create Group button. The Create Model Group dialog box then differs based on what you had previously selected.

Since you can select a variety of elements, first Revit needs to evaluate your selection set in order to figure out how to create a group for you. You can choose to create a new Model group, Annotation group, or a Model group with its Attached Detail group. You also have an option to open the Group Editor as soon as the group is defined. Doing so is most useful when you start without a selection first, such as when you realize that you've neglected to include something or need to remove something that is part of your selection set.

If you elect to use the Group Editor immediately, then you'll find that the interface changes a little. A slight color change, reminiscent of the beige tracing paper many of us have used for sketching, is applied to the view. Revit also provides an Edit Group panel, which appears within the drawing area just below the Options bar (see Figure 10.5). It

Figure 10.5

**Group Editor
panel tools**

has the following tools: Add, Remove, Attach, Finish, and Cancel. The panel can be returned to the ribbon if you prefer. Just click the small button in the upper-right corner.

Add Click this tool to add new elements that are already present in the model to your group. You can also create new elements while in the Group Editor, and these new elements are added to the group. You don't have to add them with this tool. While you are editing a group, if the elements are bold, when compared with other elements, then that means they are part of your group.

Remove Click this tool to remove elements from your group. Doing so does not delete them from the project; the removed element is left in place but is no longer part of the group. If you want to remove the element from the project as well as from the group, you need to delete the element instead while in the Group Editor.

Attach Click this tool to attach a Detail group to your Model group. This feature doesn't apply when you're editing a Detail group, so you'll find it is disabled. If you select this tool when there are no Detail groups to attach, you'll be prompted to create one and then to add, remove, or create new elements to include in the group.

Finish and Cancel Click these tools when you are either done editing the group or decide to abandon your work during the Group Editor session.

When you finish creating or editing a group, it remains selected, and an origin icon appears (see Figure 10.6). This icon is located at the center of the overall extent of the group initially, but you can move it to another location as well as rotate it if necessary. You just click the icon control grips to reposition it. Click the X or Y grip to rotate, and where the X and Y lines meet, click to move the origin location. This serves to define a common point and rotation for this group and any other that might be exchanged for it later. Imagine a king-bed hotel room design that might be swapped out for a queen-bed configuration. If these two rooms did not share the same origin location, you wouldn't be able to swap one for the other without having them move out of position.

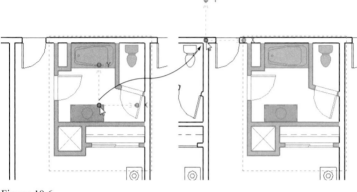

Figure 10.6

The group origin icon appears on your new group but can be moved to a new location.

PRACTICING WITH GROUPS

We have provided a sample project file—2012 IARA Ch 10 Groups.rvt—so you can experiment with the concepts explained in this chapter. It is our hope that, once you have a good grasp of these concepts, you'll see opportunities to apply what you've learned to other content you need in the future.

A little preparation is required. The file that we've provided was a Central File (Workset/Worksharing) originally. The process of copying it from place to place results in Revit regarding it as a Local File that is looking for the original Central File name and location.

To use the sample file, follow these steps:

1. Copy it from the source location (website/folder) to a folder for practice purposes.

2. When you open the file in Revit, check the Detach From Central option (found in the File Open dialog box).

3. When the Detach Model From Central dialog box appears, click the Detach And Preserve Worksets button.

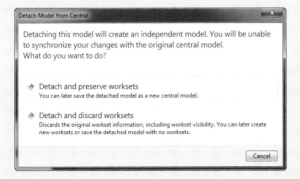

4. If a message about upgrading the file appears, you can disregard it.

   These steps will create a temporary file that will become a new Central File if you choose to save it. If you do decide to save the file, just provide a new name and you can work without becoming too preoccupied with the Central File/Local File concepts.

   The reason this file uses worksets is to permit you to experiment with Revit's worksharing concepts and groups later if you choose to.

Using the dataset file we just mentioned, let's create a group. Room 105 in the sample project file has some furniture that could serve as a Double Bed version of a unit. Let's take a closer look at creating a group with these elements. To get started, refer to the steps provided in the section "Practicing with Groups" first, and then take the following steps. The view you see initially is just our "Opening View," added as a convenience to list things to do or consider doing.

1. Open the Floor Plan view: Chapter 10 Tasks (Level 1).

2. Zoom in to see Room 105.

3. Click the Home ribbon tab, click the Model Group button on the Model panel, and click Create Group (this approach assumes that you will use the Add tool to place existing furniture in your new group).

4. When the Create Group dialog box appears, provide a name for the group: **Unit Double Bed Furniture.**

5. Leave the Model option selected because you are adding Model elements; click OK.

6. Click Add in the Edit Group "floating" panel (the button should have a blue background when active).

7. Select the furniture in Room 105 (there are nine elements).

   There is a Multiple check box on the Options bar (refer to Figure 10.7) that you can use to allow window selection or crossing window selection. You have to click Finish or Cancel to complete or stop the Multiple selection mode.

8. Click Finish in the Edit Group floating panel after you have everything selected.

   You now have a new group; check the Project Browser to see it.

9. Select your new group; then reposition (drag) the origin of the group to the intersection of the horizontal corridor wall and the vertical shared wall between Room 106 and Room 105 (refer back to Figure 10.6 for a similar result).

Swapping or switching one group for another is very much the same as swapping one family for another using the Type Selector. You must take into account which group is compatible or intended to be exchanged for another. For example, you can't swap a Model group for an Annotation group. Let's see how this works firsthand now.

If you are not continuing to use the file we just used to create the Unit Double Bed Furniture group, then repeat the steps in the section "Practicing with Groups" first.

1. Open the Floor Plan view: Chapter 10 Tasks (Level 1).

2. Select the group called Unit King Bed Furniture in Room 101.

3. Use the Type Selector, from the list of Model groups choose Group: Unit Queen Bed Furniture.

You should see the bed, side table, and lamp arrangement adjust slightly. Look closely and you'll see that the Unit Queen Bed Furniture group is missing the chair that is visible in Room 100. If you examine this more closely, by selecting the group or the chair you'll see that the angled chair in the corner isn't part of the Unit King Bed Furniture group. However, the chair you see in Room 102 is part of the group. Let's add the chair to the Unit Queen Bed Furniture group and remove the lamp:

1. If necessary, open the Floor Plan view: Chapter 10 Tasks (Level 1).

2. Select the Unit Queen Bed Furniture Group.

3. Click Edit Group in the Group panel of the Modify | Model Groups contextual ribbon tab.

4. On the Home ribbon tab, in the Build panel click the bottom half of the Component button and then select Place A Component.

5. Choose the Chair-Corbu family from the Type Selector.

6. Place the chair family near the nightstand by the bed; rotate and adjust as desired.

   Putting it here will interfere with the current position of the lamp.

   If you placed the chair before editing the group, you could click the Add button on the Edit Group floating panel. Since you added it after using Edit Group, it is already part of your group.

7. Click Remove, and select the lamp family (the circle near the bottom exterior wall). The lamp should turn gray.

8. Click Finish.

   Your group now has the chair but the lamp is still there—still a part of the project but now separate from the group. You could delete the lamp to remove it, or move it and then add it to the group, or move it next to the chair and just leave it separate from the group. It's up to you!

9. Switch the Queen Bed Furniture Group for another King Bed Group and you'll find the chair and lamp arrangement changes accordingly.

   If you don't delete the lamp from the Queen Bed group, it will be sitting uncomfortably on top of the King Bed group because it isn't part of the Queen Bed group anymore. New groups that you place after making the changes to the group won't have the lamp, but the older groups will have a "loose" lamp, which you can either delete or reposition.

10. Extra Credit: Put the lamp back in the group so it works better with the new chair.

Placing a Group

Once you've created a group, you'll want to use it and place it where it belongs in your project. Remember that a group is much like a component family, such as a desk or chair, except that it can include many such elements.

There are three ways to place a group:

- On the Home tab's Model panel, click the Model Group drop-down (see Figure 10.8) and choose Place Model Group.

- You can right-click on a group listed in the Project Browser and select Create Instance from the context menu (see Figure 10.9).

- You can drag and drop the group from the Project Browser.

Figure 10.8

Model Group tools

Regardless of the method you choose, you place a group the same way you place a component family—by clicking the appropriate location in the drawing area. The group's origin is at your mouse pointer's tip to help you place it accurately. If you see a group in the view and want to place another just like it, you can also take advantage of the Create Similar tool via the context menu or by clicking the Create Similar button on the Modify tab that appears when you select the existing group.

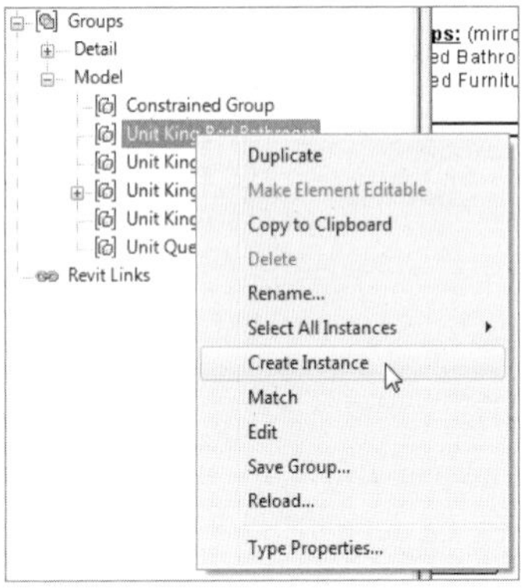

Figure 10.9

Context menu's Create Instance option

As we mentioned earlier, placing a group isn't much different from placing a family like a door, window, desk, or a chair. You just start from a different tool or location, or from the Project Browser as you can with a family. When you have a group at your cursor, its origin will be at the tip of your cursor. Let's see how it works now.

To get started, refer to the steps provided in the section "Practicing with Groups" first. Then move on to the following exercises.

To place a group from the Project Browser, perform these steps:

1. Open the Floor Plan view: Chapter 10 Tasks (Level 1).

2. Zoom in to see Room 104 more closely.

3. Expand the Groups node of the Project Browser.

4. Expand the Model node under Groups.

5. Select/drag Unit King Bed Bathroom to the empty room; once your cursor is within the drawing area you can release the left mouse button (a dashed rectangle appears and the origin of the group is at your cursor tip).

WHAT ABOUT THE LOAD AS GROUP INTO OPEN PROJECTS OPTION?

You may have noticed the third option listed under the Model group tool—Load As Group Into Open Projects. This tool is intended to provide a way to create repetitive design elements outside the project in a separate project file, each in its own "sandbox," so to speak.

Let's say you created a design for a typical hotel room in a separate project file. You can use this option to load your new design (the current file you are working in) into the hotel building project file (another open file), but instead of individual elements, it is created as a group that can be placed repeatedly. The group can be edited externally and reloaded, and it can be edited locally—which means you can choose to abandon the external original. The group can also be altered internally and then saved to a separate file. Once you've used this feature to load the file into your project, you can use one of the three ways we've mentioned to place it in the project wherever you need it.

6. Click at the intersection of the vertical (shared between 104 and 105) and horizontal wall (corridor). The group should appear in the room.

   Note that the Edit Pasted ribbon panel is displayed. This operation is using Window's Cut/Copy/Paste technology.

7. Click the Finish button on the ribbon.

8. Repeat the steps to add another group or groups until you are comfortable. The rooms on other floors in the model have no groups yet.

   To place a group from the ribbon, perform these steps:

1. Zoom in to see one of the "empty" rooms closer.

2. Click the Home ribbon tab → Model panel → Model Group button → Place Model Group.

3. From the Type Selector, select Unit King Bed Bathroom.

   As when you drag a group, a dashed rectangle appears as you move your cursor toward the room.

4. Choose the same intersection of vertical and horizontal walls (corridor). The group should appear in the room.

5. Click the Finish button to complete the task.

Making Special Changes to a Group

Earlier we described the simple add and remove functions for editing a group. Two additional features, called Exclude and Move To Project, provide a different kind of control over the elements of a group. There may be an occasion when you will want to remove an element from a group or possibly from the group *and* the project. We'll explain the difference between these two situations and how to accomplish each.

The Exclude feature allows you to create a complete group that represents the worst-or best-case scenario of a design. Take a classroom, for example. You can create a desk and chair arrangement that satisfies all but a few room conditions. For the few rooms where a desk or chair won't work, you can use Exclude to remove them from individual groups. These excluded elements won't appear in the model or be included in schedules.

As you work with groups and the project's design evolves, it wouldn't be surprising to us if you decide that something doesn't belong in a particular group instance. That's where Move To Project comes into play.

These features are explained in the following sections.

Using the Exclude Tool

To exclude elements, you first need to select the element (or elements) you want to exclude. To do this, place your mouse pointer over it and press the Tab key to cause Revit to highlight it apart from the rest of the group. Click the element when it highlights and you'll see an icon appear to let you quickly exclude elements. You can also use the context (right-click) menu, as shown in Figure 10.10.

When your project is using worksets and you select a group or single element, Revit displays the Make Element Editable icon instead. You need to click that to borrow the element so you can see and then click the Exclude icon. It is a little faster to just make

Figure 10.10

Context menu's Exclude option

your selection and use the context menu instead; just choose Exclude. It's faster because Revit will also make the elements editable for you. This is particularly useful when you have multiple elements selected.

Once an element is excluded, it is easy to restore it. Just hover over the location where an element used to be, and you'll see that it highlights as if it were still there (it is still there technically). You need to use the Tab key to highlight the element; then click to select it and click the icon that appears. Alternatively, you can use the same context (right-click) menu technique to access Restore Excluded Member. The icon and the context menu are both visible in Figure 10.11.

When you select a group and use the context menu, you should also see the Restore All Excluded command (as shown in Figure 10.12). This command restores all the ele-

Figure 10.11

Context menu's Restore Excluded Member command

Figure 10.12

Context menu's Restore All Excluded command

ments you've excluded earlier for the group(s) that are currently selected. Other instances of the same group that are not selected won't be affected. If you've used the Exclude tool on several items in a single group, this command provides a quick way to restore them all.

The secret to using the Exclude and Restore Excluded features is the Tab key. You place your cursor over the family you want to change and then press the

Tab key. Doing so causes Revit to highlight the individual element instead of the entire group so that you can click to select it separately. Let's try using the Exclude features now.

If you are not continuing from the previous exercise, repeat the first steps in the procedure in the section "Practicing with Groups" to open the file to get started again.

To exclude the table and lamp, perform these steps:

1. Open the Floor Plan view: Chapter 10 Tasks (Level 1).

2. Zoom in to see Room 101 closer.

3. Place your cursor over the nightstand nearest the chair and lamp, and press the Tab key.

   The table should highlight by itself; don't move your mouse when you use the Tab key because you might lose the highlighting.

4. Click to select the table when it is highlighted by itself.

5. With your cursor over the table still, right-click and choose Exclude.

   You can also click the Exclude icon instead to achieve the same result.

6. Click in empty space away from the table to see that it is no longer visible.

7. Repeat steps 2–6 for the lamp.

   To restore the excluded table and lamp, follow these steps:

1. Zoom in to see Room 101 closer if you aren't already.

2. Place your cursor where the table used to be; it should highlight even though you can't see it otherwise.

3. Press the Tab key to highlight the table, separate from the rest of the group.

4. Right-click and choose Restore Excluded Member.

   You could also select the group and then choose Restore All Excluded to bring back the table and the lamp at the same time.

5. Repeat for the lamp location except click the Restore Excluded icon that appears near the lamp.

Using Move To Project

Move To Project is available only from the context menu (Figure 10.13). To move elements out of a group instance and into the project:

1. Hover over the element and use the Tab key to highlight it.

2. Right-click and select Move To Project.

The selected element(s) are still part of the group instance but are excluded (not visible or counted in schedules). Revit adds a new entity in the same place that is not part of the

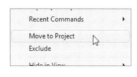

Figure 10.13

Context menu's Move To Project command

group; it has been moved to the project. Another way of looking at this is that Revit has copied the element from the group and hidden the original one so you can alter the copy separately. This allows you to deal with some variation by changing this new element to a larger size or even a different element entirely. If you choose to abandon the change later, the group still has the original member, and you can use the Restore Excluded Member tool. Other copies of the group are unaffected by the action.

Removing Elements

As you work on your project and remove elements from groups, there are two more questions to consider. Do you want to remove the element from just the group, or do you want to remove the element from the group and the project as well?

Removing an Element from the Group Only

At times you may decide that you don't want an element or elements in a group, but you want to keep it in the project and maybe even in its current location. To accomplish this, you need to:

1. Select the group.
2. Click Edit Group button on the Group panel of the Modify | Model Groups contextual ribbon.
3. Click Remove on the floating Edit Group panel.
4. Select the element(s) you want to remove.
5. Click Finish to wrap up your change(s).

The element will remain in place, but it is no longer part of the group's definition (refer to Figure 10.14). Keep in mind that this applies to all the groups you've placed so far. For example, if you remove a chair from a classroom group that has been placed in 20 locations, the removal will affect each of the 20 locations. You'll find 20 individual elements that are no longer part of the group definition, in the same location they were in when they were still in the group.

Removing an Element from the Group and the Project

You remove an element from the group *and* the project when you don't want the element at all—not in the group and not in its current location as part of the project outside of the group. This process has nothing to do with removing it from other locations in the project that are not using groups, but only in the context of a group and the elements it contains. To take this approach, follow these steps:

1. Select the group.
2. Click the Edit Group button on the Group panel of the Modify | Model Groups contextual ribbon.

3. Select the element you want to remove.

4. Press the Delete key or click the Delete button on the ribbon.

5. Click Finish when you are done.

Following these steps will remove the element from the group as well as in any other copies of the group. The element is also no longer present in the model (refer to Figure 10.15).

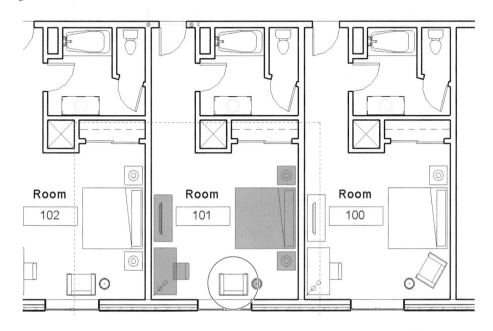

Figure 10.14

The chair is removed from the group but is still part of the project.

Figure 10.15

The chair is removed from all groups and not present in the project; independent chairs are still part of the project.

Saving, Loading, and Reloading Groups

Groups are defined inside a project file, and most are created within the context of your *active* project. As mentioned earlier, it is possible to create a group in a separate project file and then load it into a project to use as needed. You can choose to save a group to an external file so that it can be altered by someone else or shared with another project. If you work on a group outside the project in its own file (it also uses the .RVT file format), you can load and, if necessary, reload it into your project. These three concepts are called saving, loading as a group, and reloading.

Save Group

The Save Group feature will save a group as a Revit project file (with the extension .rvt). This will allow you to share it with other projects and to edit the group in its own file. The file will not be a group or require you to edit a group as you would in the project it came from. The primary method for saving a group is found on the Application menu; select Save As → Library → Group. If you prefer the context menu, right-click the group name in the Project Browser and choose Save Group (refer to Figure 10.16).

Figure 10.16

Choose Save Group from the context menu.

Revit will choose to use the group's name as the name for the new RVT file. In fact, the value you'll see for File Name in the Save Group dialog box is Same As Group Name. If you want to use a different name just provide one. You can browse through the groups listed in the Group To Save drop-down. If you have attached details associated with your group, choose the Include Attached Detail Groups As Views check box to generate a view that can show those details when the new project file is created. This is subtle but necessary since attached details are visible only in the views you intentionally add them to.

When you click Save you will briefly see the group open in a view but close quickly as Revit creates the new file from the group, opens it, and then finishes the process with a save and close operation. If you want to work on the group or let someone else know it is ready, you just need to open the file like any other project file.

Saving a group to a file allows you to create an isolated copy of your group outside your project. This creates interesting opportunities to share and/or isolate certain work with the best people to deal with it. Let's see how easy it is to do it.

If you are not continuing from the previous exercise repeat the steps in the section "Practicing with Groups" to create a new file and get started, then follow these steps:

1. Expand the Project Browser so you can see the groups listed beneath the Group node.

2. Expand the Model node.

3. Right-click on the Unit King Bed Bathroom Group and choose Save Group.

4. Browse to find an appropriate folder to store your new group as a Revit project file (note that it uses the extension `.rvt`).

5. Accept the File Name entry, which is `Same As Group Name`.

6. Deselect the option Include Attached Detail Groups As Views.

7. Click Save.

   You'll see Revit display the group briefly in the separate file before finalizing the work and closing the file.

   At your leisure you can open this new file and experiment with redesigning it.

Load As Group

The Load As Group feature starts with the Load From Library panel on the Insert tab on the ribbon. If you are not continuing from the previous exercise, repeat the steps in the section "Practicing with Groups" to get started. Then follow these steps:

1. Click the Insert ribbon tab, and click Load As Group on the Load From Library panel.

2. Browse to the file you previously saved called `Unit King Bed Bathroom.rvt`.

3. Deselect the option Include attached detail.

   The other two options, Include levels and Include grids, should already be unchecked.

4. Click Open.

5. Accept the message regarding duplicate types, and click OK.

6. Click Yes when asked about replacing the existing group using the same name.

   If you use this feature to load a file that is already in your project file, you'll get a dialog box asking if you'd like to replace the existing group (see Figure 10.17). Revit is just trying to protect your existing work. As mentioned in step 5, you may also see a message about duplicate types. This means that you have content in the external file that is using the same family name and type names. Revit will just reuse the ones that are already in the current project in order to protect them from any differences that may exist in the external file. If Revit finds differences in families in your group and the project it will create renamed versions for those families (those in the group), renamed by adding a "1" to the name.

Figure 10.17

Duplicate Group Names dialog box

Ultimately, you are just overwriting the one you saved earlier. A warning may appear about pasting duplicate types. You can disregard this message. You aren't actually placing the group at all; you're just updating the existing versions. You can place one after the command completes if you'd like to. Experiment with this process by making some minor changes to the external version of the group and then use Load as Group again.

Reloading

Maybe it is obvious, but you can reload a file using Load As Group if you select a file that you previously saved as a group. There is also a method available when you right-click the group name in the Project Browser. Keep in mind that reloading a group will generate similar warning messages, as mentioned in the previous section.

Linking

You use the Link tool when you decide that an external linked file will serve your needs better than a group. Groups provide a higher level of interaction than linked files between walls that are and are not part of the group. With groups, walls clean up with other walls and look better (the way one wall appears to "flow" into another). This means that performance can suffer. If this kind of issue isn't as important to you, then a linked file might be a better choice. Even if it isn't ideal, it might be a decent solution for the short term while the design shifts back and forth.

For example, in a hospital project, you might have a series of meetings with the nursing staff to work through patient treatment room design proposals. The patient treatment rooms could be linked into the overall building model to demonstrate how well they are distributed. The design team and nurses involved in the meeting can review the separate linked smaller files for each patient room design as well as seeing them in the context of the building overall. Using links for this stage of design development can yield better performance in the building model while the designs for the patient rooms are changing frequently.

To convert a group to a link, follow these steps:

1. Select a group.

   You'll see the Link button appear on the contextual tab Modify | Model Groups on the ribbon. It is on the Group panel.

2. Click Link, and Revit will display the Convert To Link dialog box, as shown in Figure 10.18. You have three choices:

   - Replace With A New Project File
   - Replace With An Existing Project File
   - Cancel

The first choice is similar to Save As Group because you have to create a file to use as your link. If you already saved a group as a file, you can use the second choice. You can also change your mind and click Cancel.

3. Choose one of the options in the Convert To Link dialog box.

After Revit completes the command, you'll find that the group you selected to create the link has been replaced with a linked file. The Project Browser will show a linked file, as shown in Figure 10.19. It is important to understand that only the selected group(s) will be replaced with the linked file. You'll have to remove and replace the other groups or use the Link tool on them as well; then you repeat the command but use the second choice to replace with an existing project file (the one you already used/created).

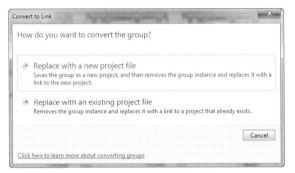

Figure 10.18

The Convert To Link dialog box

Figure 10.19

Project Browser lists a linked file now.

Binding

The Bind Link tool allows you to reverse a decision to create a link from a group, by letting you turn the link back into a group instead. It also allows you to choose to convert a linked file into a group even if you didn't use the Link tool before. If you consider the patient room example mentioned earlier, you may decide to bind the links once the designs have been approved. Doing so will allow the walls in the bound links (which became groups) to clean up nicely with the rest of the walls in the building model, which provides for better-looking drawings and documents.

Bind Link

The process starts with the selection of a linked file. When you have at least one linked file selected, you'll find the Bind Link button on the ribbon's Link panel. If you click the Bind Link button, Revit displays the Bind Link Options dialog box (see Figure 10.20) to let you define how the link should be reassembled into a group.

Figure 10.20

Bind Link Options dialog box

Figure 10.21

The Duplicate Group Names dialog box appears to let you decide how to deal with duplicate group names.

Figure 10.22

Warning that all instances of the linked file have been removed

If you happen to choose a link that shares its name with a group already, then you'll see the Duplicate Group Names dialog box, as shown in Figure 10.21. If you bind all the linked files, you'll get another message asking whether you want to remove the link completely or keep it around, just in case you need it again later (see Figure 10.22).

Practical Considerations

In past years and versions, seasoned users habitually avoided the Group feature because it was often either unreliable or too quirky. This was unfortunate. In recent releases, the Revit product team has devoted quite a bit of research and effort to rectify this situation. Groups are still a bit quirky, and this section delves into some slightly arcane things you should know.

Getting Rid of a Group

If you use groups, it is pretty likely that eventually you'll decide that you don't need one anymore. At the very least, you'll decide that you don't need one in a specific location. You can ungroup and delete a group. In each case, you affect only the selected group or groups. If you want to completely eliminate a group:

1. Select it in the Project Browser.

2. From the context menu, choose Select All Instances → In Entire Project.

3. Either press the Delete key or click the Delete button in the Modify panel on the Modify | Model Groups ribbon tab.

When there are no more groups of that type present in the model, you find that selecting the group in the Project Browser and using the context menu again will provide the option to delete the group. Choosing this option will eliminate the group from the project completely. Any unused groups should be removed to reduce their impact on the project file size and performance.

Keep in mind that you can use the Purge Unused tool to remove unused groups quickly. Just make sure you click the Check None button before you cavalierly use Purge Unused. If a group isn't used now, it doesn't mean that you won't want to use it later. Too often users purge things they don't realize they'll need sooner rather than later.

Avoiding Complexity

As with anything, the more complicated you choose to make something, the more difficult it becomes for all concerned, including Revit. A group that includes everything on an entire floor of your building is much more likely to become a problem for you and the project team than more discrete groups used to compile the same entire floor's design. Seek to build smaller reusable groups that focus on the aspect of the design that differentiates one solution from another. Since a group must be exactly the same for each instance, a group that contains a great many elements is much more likely to encounter design issues that might require subtle differences between groups.

For example, a multifamily apartment project might have a pretty consistent unit design, while the kitchen and bathroom configurations are where variety becomes apparent. The units might be best described using groups that don't include the bathroom and kitchen elements. Use additional groups for the bathroom and kitchen concepts. This means a bit more analysis and planning, but the groups will be much more likely to work well for you.

Nesting

You might consider rereading the previous section about complexity; nevertheless, the fact remains that you can nest one group inside another. This approach to using groups provides yet another way to manage repetition despite the obvious complexity it implies. A hotel room unit plan can include a nested group for the bathroom configuration. One designer can adjust the bathroom group design while another is focused on some other aspect of the room or project. The nested group is still altered by editing the original either within the host or where it is placed elsewhere on its own.

Mirroring

Creating a "mirror" image of a design feature is a common requirement. For example, hotel room configurations are frequently mirrored; it's the same layout but appears exactly opposite of the other, as if seen in a mirror, on either side of a shared wall. It is a natural inclination to want to use Revit's Mirror tool to create mirrored versions of groups, but we don't recommend mirroring groups. Despite this caution, Model groups are fairly tolerant when you mirror them. Attached Detail groups, however, aren't very stable when applied to a mirrored group. In particular, dimensions may not reference the same part of an element or generate error messages.

Mirroring some model elements in the group may not be appropriate; for example, furniture, equipment, or plumbing fixtures may have specific right or left versions. In addition, in-place families that are included in groups have been a problem for groups that are mirrored. With these examples in mind, you will find it more reliable (or safer) to create a mirrored version for each group facing this requirement. Doing so will help ensure that groups are as effective as possible.

Worksharing

When you create a group that has elements assigned to more than one workset, Revit will reassign them to the active workset. For this reason, it is a good habit to establish a group workset or worksets so you can manage them apart from other workset items. If you choose to use Ungroup later, the elements will remain assigned to the workset to which the group was assigned.

Wall Top Level Setting

Groups and the walls that are part of them don't tolerate different floor-to-floor elevation changes well. It isn't a good idea to constrain walls to a Top Level setting other than Unconnected (this is true only for walls that are to be part of groups). If you choose to do so, Revit won't object until a level elevation changes, and you'll be presented with a fairly scary dialog box, shown in Figure 10.23. Your choices at this point are Fix Groups and Cancel. Choosing Fix Groups will present you with another dialog box (Figure 10.24). You can choose to ungroup the inconsistent groups, create new group types, or cancel.

The Ungroup choice defeats the purpose of using the group in the first place. The second choice, creating a new group based on the variance Revit is concerned with, at least provides a solution that lets you continue to use groups. The last choice, canceling, means you've let Revit scare you away for now.

This next procedure is intended to demonstrate the potential problem that could occur when you constrain the top of a wall to a specific level "above." It won't be a problem until you change the level-to-level relationship between levels that hosts such a group.

Figure 10.23

Error dialog box: Fix Groups or Cancel?

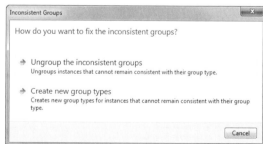

Figure 10.24

Inconsistent Groups dialog box

Keep in mind that this issue primarily exists for walls and columns that are included in groups. It is, however, possible to create an issue with any family that can be constrained to a level. When the height of an element causes Revit to regard it as "different," it will generate the warnings we describe here.

If you are not continuing from the previous exercise, repeat the steps in the section "Placing a Group" to get started, then follow these steps:

1. Open the Floor Plan view: Level 3.

2. Click the Home ribbon tab, click Model Group in the Model panel, and select Place Model Group.

3. Choose the Model Group: Constrained Group from the Type Selector.

4. Place one above the building that is visible in the view (it doesn't matter how many you place).

5. Open the Elevation view (Building Elevation): West.

6. You should see the group sitting on Level 3.

7. Select Level 4.

8. Change the elevation value to 34′-0″ (increase it by 24″ or 600mm).

    As soon as you apply the new elevation, you should get the error dialog box shown earlier in Figure 10.23.

9. Choose Cancel to abandon the attempt.

The best way to prevent this situation is to assign the Top Constraint of walls in a group to Unconnected. For floors that have different floor-to-floor elevations, you'll need "identical groups" that have taller walls. Revit sees the different height as a "difference," even though we see the floor plan and concept as the "same." This is the difference between a computer interpreting "facts" and our ability to deal with abstract ideas.

File Size

File size is a bit of a distraction. People tend to get overly concerned about Revit files when compared with other CAD files because by comparison they seem much bigger. In a simple experiment, we created two separate files that had just four walls in each, and we eliminated everything else Revit would let us remove by using the Purge Unused tool. The first file with four walls came in at 696 KB. We created a total of 10 sets of four walls for a total of 40 walls, and this file came in at 744 KB, an increase of 48 KB.

For groups we used another set of four walls that we used to create a group. This file came in at 720 KB. This resulted in a difference of 24 KB to create and have one instance of a group. We created nine more instances of the group to replicate the same 40 walls we used in the file without groups. The resulting file with 10 instances of one group to reach the same total of 40 walls came in at 748 KB, just 4 KB larger than the file with the same number of walls but no groups.

Even placing 90 more copies of the group for a total of 400 walls increased the file size only by 356 KB (file size 1104 KB). This translates to a little less than 1 KB for each wall. Our conclusion is that file size isn't as serious a concern with groups as is the way that Revit ponders the existence of a group when elements are changed.

Revit must evaluate all the instances of a group whenever an element that touches a single instance of the group is altered. Changing a single wall that touches a member of a group will likely take longer to process than for relationships that don't involve a group. This isn't an argument to cast groups aside. It is something to consider as you choose to take advantage of groups.

CHAPTER 11

Rendering

There are several points in your project when you will want to represent your building model with real-world materials, texture, and lighting. To achieve this in Autodesk Revit Architecture, you are going to create renderings from your 3D views. The Revit platform uses the mental ray render engine as a renderer, which in turn allows you to create realistic renderings from within the software. This chapter will show you how to generate images directly within Revit. This approach lets you keep working on the design while you create presentation images for your clients.

Rendering can be a complicated and time-consuming process because you want to develop an image that is visually accurate and appealing. It is not uncommon for firms to employ visualization experts who utilize a variety of tools to produce photorealistic renderings. In this chapter, the objective is to provide an overview of the tools to enable you to produce appealing images.

This chapter covers the following topics:

- ■ **The basics of rendering**
- ■ **Adding lighting to your rendering**
- ■ **Setting the background**
- ■ **Adding and adjusting materials**
- ■ **Real-time rendering**
- ■ **Exporting a model for rendering in an external application**

The Basics of Rendering

Revit offers a variety of possibilities to create rendered images for presentation purposes. They range from real-time shaded model representations, to renderings using the Revit render tool, to renderings produced outside of Revit still using a seamless workflow for lighting and materials.

Your choice of technique depends on various factors, such as current design stage and downstream use of the rendered output.

In the following sections we will introduce you to the basic steps required to produce high-quality rendered output from your model. After those basic steps, we will discuss the individual aspects that contribute to the quality of your rendering in greater depth.

Understanding Rendering Workflow

Rendering can be a complicated and time-consuming task. How you approach this process can either reduce or increase your rendering tasks and efforts. When creating renderings, the general workflow is as follows:

1. Create and position cameras.

2. Add and adjust lights.

3. Add and adjust materials.

4. Add entourage, such as people, cars, and decorative items.

During this process, you should follow some general guidelines to facilitate rendering:

Lights Turn off lights you are not using. This will speed up the rendering process.

Geometry To create a rendering, you need to be in a 3D view:

- Crop the 3D view to show only what you need to see. The more elements that are displayed, the more elements that have to be processed.

- Adding entourage such as people, trees, and so on, can improve the appearance of a rendering.

Materials Materials need to be applied to all surfaces.

Rendering To initiate the rendering process, you need to take the following steps:

- To test lighting, materials, exposure, and so on, use the Region option. This renders a small area rather than your entire view.

- Use the Draft render option to quickly create test renderings.

- Consider the resolution of your output. If you are printing to a 300 dots per inch (dpi) printer, rendering to a file at 600 dpi requires more time with no improvements in print quality.

Adding planting and entourage is a straightforward process just like adding doors, walls, and so on. As a result, this book will only cover the basic workflow required to add individual planting and entourage elements.

Choosing Your Rendering Method

Revit offers real-time rendering, which means the rendering is updated when changes are made in real time. Revit provides an internal rendering tool that you can use to create photorealistic images of your design along with related entourage. You can also export your model to other applications such as 3ds Max to create high-quality rendered images.

When you are deciding whether to use real-time rendering, use the Revit rendering tool, and/or export to an external application, it is important to take the purpose of the rendering into consideration. The pros and cons of each methodology are as follows:

Real-Time Rendering Real-time rendering will update simultaneously with any model change (Figure 11.1). This method is most suitable for early design stages where frequent design changes are expected. A real-time rendered view placed on a sheet will consistently be up-to-date with the model, which means no dedicated action needs to be taken when printing a new sheet set after finishing a design change. The limitation of real-time rendering, though, is that the actual quality of the image is lower than the quality of a rendered view using the Revit rendering tool.

Figure 11.1

Real-time renderings update any time the model is changed.

Revit Rendering Tool When you use the Revit rendering tool, any model change (Figure 11.2) updates the view to be rendered; previous settings such as lighting, materials, and view settings are preserved during a design change. However, as a result of the rendering, the rendered image itself will need to be re-created after the design change. Any rendered images placed on sheets will have to be replaced with the newly rendered images.

The benefit of the Revit rendering tool is that the overall quality of the rendered image, depending on the quality settings of the rendering process, will generally surpass the quality of a real-time rendered view. The Revit rendering tool is therefore most appropriate in scenarios where fewer design changes affecting the rendering are expected.

Figure 11.2

Here's the same scene using Revit's rendering tool.

Exporting to an External Application Exporting to an external dedicated application such as 3ds Max offers the best possible quality of a rendered image. It further enables a CG artist to add realism to a scene beyond the realms of what is achievable in Revit itself. The disadvantage of this workflow, though, is that with any design change done in the model, a significant amount of the effort that resulted in the rendered image utilizing external software will need to be redone. Therefore, this approach is most suitable in cases where a high-quality still image is required in a phase of the project where *no* further design changes are expected.

Preparing the Scene for Rendering

Before rendering in Revit, you need to prepare the scene. This preparation involves creating a new view, assigning materials to your model elements, and setting and adjusting lights. While these are three distinctly different functionalities to create a rendered image, they share a similar workflow in preparing the model for rendering:

1. Create a new view.

   Regardless of rendering technique used, Revit will render the content of the actual 3D view from which the rendering feature has been launched. It will support view visibility overrides to enable you to turn categories and/or objects on and off for rendering. It will also support section boxes so you can create partial model renderings or cutaway images.

2. Assign materials to your model elements.

   Materials are shared across the various rendering methodologies in Revit. The same material setting that will be used to create a real-time rendered image in Revit utilizing the Realistic visual style will also be used by the rendering tool to create a photo-realistic rendering. Material settings will also be exported via the FBX interface when utilizing an external application such as 3ds Max and can be used in that application as a basis for extended material adjustments.

3. Set and adjust the lighting.

   Lighting of 3D View used for both real-time rendering as well as by the rendering tool is determined by the settings made in the Graphic Display options for the specific view. Again, as with materials, these settings will be exported when you export the model to an external application via the FBX interface and can be used there as a starting point for advanced lighting settings.

Those three steps do not necessarily have to be taken in any specific order. Furthermore, although setting up the view itself (size and camera position) as well as setting up lighting are view-specific—which means they can be different for any 3D view to be rendered—defining materials will impact the entire model. In other words, once material definitions are made for the model in one particular 3D view, they are not required to be repeated for a subsequent rendering of any other 3D view, as they affect the model globally.

Exterior Rendering: Day

In this section, you will create an exterior rendering. You will do this by:

- Creating and positioning a camera
- Cropping a view
- Adjusting the rendering settings

Exterior renderings are generally easier and faster to create, so that's a good starting place. Exterior renderings are generally simpler because you are working with only one light. The following exercise will walk you through a simplified process for rendering:

1. Open the source file rac_basic_sample_project.rvt.

   This file is installed by default with your standard Revit Architecture installation.

   You are using this model because it has materials assigned and will give you an opportunity to explore the rendering settings rather than focusing on the model geometry.

2. Switch to the Site floor plan view.

3. Save the file as **Rendering11.rvt**.

   The Site floor plan has Crop View enabled, which will make placing the camera more difficult. You need to turn it off for camera placement.

4. In the Properties palette, scroll down to the Extents section, and deselect the Crop View check box.

   The next step is to create a 3D view for your rendering. You can use a default 3D view or create a perspective (camera) view.

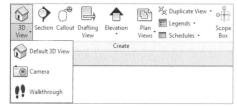

5. On the View tab's Create panel, click the 3D View drop-down and select Camera (Figure 11.3).

Figure 11.3

3D View drop-down

6. Using Figure 11.4 as a reference, click to place the camera location or where you would be standing, and then click to place the target location or where you would be looking.

Figure 11.4

Marking the camera and target locations

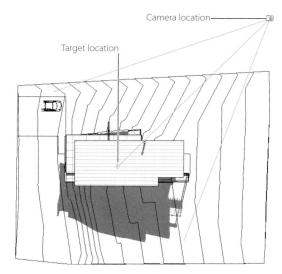

With your camera placed, a new 3D view is created. To minimize render time, you want to minimize as much of the view as possible because the image size and/or resolution of a rendered image has a predictable effect on rendering time.

7. In your view, click on the crop region.

8. Use the blue dots on the crop region to display only the model geometry, similar to what's shown in Figure 11.5.

Figure 11.5

Camera view of the sample project

Clicking on the crop region also enables the view's instance properties. Here you can make further adjustments, such as changing Eye Elevation and Target Elevation.

9. On the View tab's Graphics panel, click Render.

    Doing so opens the Rendering dialog box (Figure 11.6). The Rendering dialog box in Revit contains settings that determine the results of the rendering. Another way you can start the render process is by clicking the rendering icon (the teapot) on the View Control bar.

10. Make sure the Lighting Scheme drop-down is set to Exterior: Sun Only.

11. To the right of the Sun Setting field, click the Choose A Sun Location button right underneath the Lighting Scheme drop-down. Doing so opens the Sun Settings dialog box.

12. In the Solar Study panel, select the Single Day radio button, as shown in Figure 11.7.

Figure 11.6

The Rendering dialog box

13. For Presets, click <In-session, Single Day>.

14. Click the Browse button to the right of the location.

    This will take you to the Location Weather And Site dialog box.

15. Set the Define Location By option to Default City List, and then select **Orlando, FL** from the drop down list (Figure 11.8).

16. Click OK to close this dialog box.

17. Back in the Sun Settings dialog box, set Date to 6/1/2011 and set the Time fields to 10:00 AM and 4:00 PM.

18. Select the Ground Plane At Level check box, and set the level to Level 1.

19. Click the Save Settings button, and name the settings **Orlando, FL 6.01.10, 10am**.

20. Click OK to close the Sun Settings dialog box.

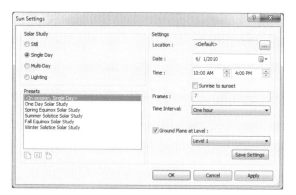

Figure 11.7

Sun Settings dialog box

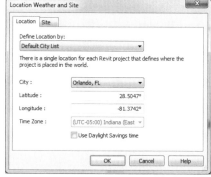

Figure 11.8

Location Weather And Site dialog box

Render Quality Settings

The Quality drop-down is where you will determine the quality of your rendering. The quality setting controls the overall quality of the rendering based on predefined settings. You can create custom settings and assign them to a specific 3D view. Note that rendering times will increase when you switch to higher-quality presets. The lower you set the quality, the faster the rendering is produced. Revit provides seven preset options for quality, as described in Table 11.1. These preset options dictate how good the quality of your rendering will be and how long it will take to render.

A number of factors determine the quality of your renderings, including lighting, materials, and the render quality settings you choose. Generally speaking, images that will be presented to clients will be rendered at a medium level or higher. Draft and low settings are more ideally suited to provide a quick check of the lighting, materials, and overall composition of the scene before rendering at a higher setting. The Region check box above the Quality drop-down is used to specifically render a user-defined section of the scene. Choose this option when you want to check an area of the scene with a Best or higher quality setting to accurately check the scene lighting or a material without having to render the entire scene.

QUALITY	RELATIVE RENDERING SPEED	DESCRIPTION
Draft	Fastest	Poorest quality, fastest rendering. Many artifacts. Used for testing settings and to get a general idea of what the image will look like.
Low	Fast	Better quality than Draft with fewer artifacts.
Medium	Medium	Normally provides an image that can be used in presentations. Image quality can still be improved upon.
High	Slow	Render quality can be used for presentation. Very few artifacts. Slow.
Best	Slowest	High-quality images with minimal artifacts. Slowest rendering times.
Custom (view specific)	Varies	Uses settings specified by the user in the Render Quality Settings dialog box. Render times will vary depending on the custom settings.
Edit	Varies	Allows you to define a new view-specific custom rendering setting.

Table 11.1

Render quality settings

Changing the rendering quality settings to a higher level does not necessarily mean a higher-quality image. As you are trying to refine your render settings, utilize lower render quality settings, or create a region when using a higher quality setting. Each time you increase the render quality one level, you increase the rendering time two, three, or even four times. We recommend that you use a combination of the Draft setting and Region check box until you are ready for your final renderings.

Setting the Image Output Size

One of the nice features of rendering in Revit is that you do not need to perform a great deal of customization in order to get good-quality renderings. When setting the render quality settings, you also need to think about the image output and resolution (Figure 11.9). As we previously discussed, you can save an image to the project and render it to a specific resolution.

Keep in mind that the image size or resolution setting has a predictable effect on the rendering time. Generally speaking, if you double the image resolution from 150 dpi to 300 dpi without changing any other setting, the average render time increases 2.7 times. Double the resolution again, from 300 dpi to 600 dpi, and the average render time is increased by 2.7 × 2.7 times, or about 7.3 times. When defining the view area to render, be sure to check the image size. Usually, the larger the image area you choose, the longer the rendering will take.

Figure 11.9

Rendered image output settings

Output Settings determine the actual size of the rendering. Smaller sizes will render faster; larger sizes will render more slowly. Under Output Settings, for Resolution you have two options:

Screen When this option is selected, Revit will calculate the screen resolution based on the defined view area to render. It will include the width and height in pixels as well as in an uncompressed image file size.

Printer When this option is selected, the user is required to specify the dpi to use when printing the image. The lower the dpi value, the grainier the picture will look like, whereas a higher dpi value will produce a smooth image. For printing purposes, we recommend a minimum dpi value of 300. The values shown on the Rendering dialog will include the image width and height as well as the uncompressed image file size.

Adjusting Exposure

In the next few steps, you will adjust the exposure control settings. As you would do in photography, you will have to control your exposure in your renderings. Elements such as exposure value and saturation can be specified. Table 11.2 describes the exposure control settings.

Table 11.2

Exposure control settings

SETTING	DESCRIPTION
Exposure Value	Overall brightness of the image. Values can be set between –6 (brighter) and 16 (darker).
Highlights	Controls the level of the highlights (brightest area) in the image.
Mid Tones	Controls the level of the midtone (between highlights and shadows) in the image.
Shadows	Controls the level of the shadows (darkest area) in the image.
White Point	Controls the temperature of the image. You can make the image look warmer (more orange) or colder (bluer).
Saturation	Allows you to increase or decrease the intensity of the colors.

Now let's further refine the rendering:

1. In the Rendering dialog box, click the Adjust Exposure button.

2. In the resulting Exposure Control dialog box, use these settings:

   Exposure Value: **14**

   White Point: **7000**

   Saturation: **1.25**

   Shadows: **0.4**

3. Click OK to close the Exposure Control dialog box.

4. Back in the Rendering dialog box, deselect Region, and change the Setting option under Quality to High.

5. Click Render to see your final image (Figure 11.10).

Figure 11.10

Finished rendering

Exposure settings are very touchy. A small change can result in major changes in your rendering.

Now that you have a nice rendering, Revit provides you with two options for saving your image. You'll find these settings in the Image section of the Rendering dialog box:

Save To Project Saves the image in a project view. Rendered images will be displayed in the Project Browser under Views (All) → Renderings.

Export Saves the image to a file. Revit can save the file to the following formats: BMP, JPEG, JPG, PNG, and TIFF.

To save a rendered image as a project view:

1. In the Rendering dialog box, click Save To Project in the Image section.

2. In the Save To Project dialog box, enter a name for the rendered view.

3. Click OK. The rendered imaged can now be dropped onto a sheet.

To save a rendered image to a file, follow these steps:

1. In the Rendering dialog box, click Export in the Image section.

2. In the Save Image dialog box, for the Save In location, navigate to the desired location where you want to store the save rendered image.

3. For Filename, enter the name of the image file.

4. Click Save.

Adding Lighting to Your Rendering

Lighting allows the choice of natural and/or artificial lights to illuminate the particular 3D view to be rendered. Natural light renders fastest; the more light sources set up in a view, the longer the rendering time will be. Lighting is an important factor in bringing your design to life. Revit allows you to create lights that mimic natural light, artificial light, or both, to illuminate the project.

PRACTICAL CONSIDERATIONS

Before setting up materials for the model and lighting for the specific 3D view to be rendered, do a draft rendering of the view using the preset values, Draft quality, and a relatively small size for the actual resolution of the rendered image, as shown here.

This approach will help you determine the extent of the next steps you'll take. It will help you see which materials require adjustments as well as whether the default lighting setting will suffice for a desirable result.

The rendering dialog box gives you a choice between exterior and interior lighting schemes, which are based on exterior and interior lighting setups of the model. Revit provides three main light types that you can draw upon:

Sun System Lights Natural light. Sun System lights allow you to specify the direction of the sunlight, or the location, date, and time of day to generate a realistic representation of sunlight on the building. You can use this for your sun paths, solar studies, walk-throughs, and rendered images.

Standard Lights Artificial light. Standard lights create artificial light that has a uniform displacement and intensity when cast from the fixture. The light source in the lighting fixture family is defined in the Family Editor. (Lighting families are not covered in this book.)

Photometric Lights Artificial light that mimics natural light. Photometric lights utilize real-world data to control the lighting parameters such as hotspot, falloff, and so on, rather than just having light coming out at the same intensity. The light source in the lighting fixture family is defined in the Family Editor and is not covered in this text.

Light families that were created in a previous version of Revit (pre-2009) will need to be manually upgraded. Open these fixtures in the Family Editor and then load them into Revit.

For artificial light, lighting fixtures need to be added to the building model. Those can be organized into light groups if required. Before rendering, individual lighting fixtures or light groups can be turned on or off to achieve the desired result. This is explained in the section "Setting Up Interior Lighting" later in this chapter.

Displaying Light Sources

When setting up lights within a project for rendering, it can be very useful to see the pattern of light for each light source in the view. By default, light sources are not displayed in the view (Figure 11.11). To display light sources, do the following:

Figure 11.11

By default, light sources are not shown in the view.

1. After closing the Rendering dialog box, open the Visibility/Graphic Overrides dialog box.

2. In the Model Categories tab's Lighting Fixtures category, select the Light Source check box (Figure 11.12).

3. Change the displayed color or the light sources within the Object Styles dialog box, as you would with other model categories.

4. Click OK to close the Visibility/Graphic Overrides dialog box. The light sources will now be displayed (Figure 11.13).

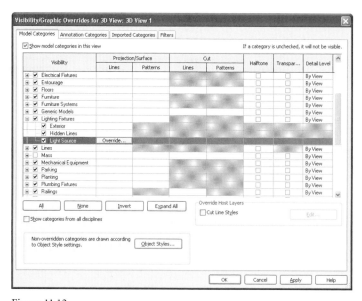

Figure 11.12

Visibility/Graphic Overrides dialog box with light sources enabled

Figure 11.13

Light sources shown in the view

Setting Up Exterior Lighting

The overall workflow of setting up exterior lighting of 3D views in Revit is based on the concept of defining a location and date/time to allow Revit to determine the resulting exterior lighting.

Exterior lighting of 3D views is defined using the Sun Settings feature located on the Additional Settings drop-down on the Manage tab of the ribbon (Figure 11.14).

Figure 11.14

The Additional Settings drop-down appears on the Manage tab.

Alternatively, Sun Settings can also be accessed via the Rendering dialog box and the Graphics Display Options dialog box.

The Sun Settings dialog box (Figure 11.15) lets you define exterior lighting based on a geographic location when you select Still, Single Day, or Multi-Day. You can also directly define the sun altitude and azimuth by selecting Lighting as a mode for Solar Study.

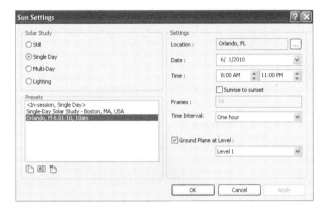

Figure 11.15

Sun Settings dialog box

Using the Still Solar Study mode, you can use the Location, Date, and Time options to define the exterior lighting of the view (Figure 11.16). You can set Location in one of two ways:

• You can set it on the Location tab of the Location Weather And Site dialog box by defining the project address and using either the Default City List or Internet Mapping Service to retrieve the required location data.

Figure 11.16

Location setting

• You can set it using the Site tab of the Location Weather And Site dialog box (Figure 11.17), which will refer to any site already defined in the project.

Figure 11.17

Location Weather And Site dialog box, Site tab

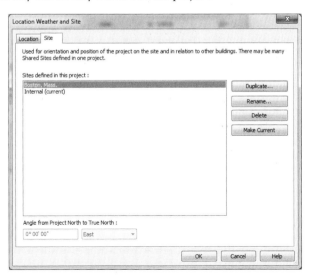

The Sun Settings dialog box will also allow you to specify a ground plane for shading purposes at any level defined in the model (Figure 11.18). This feature is useful for displaying ground shadows in situations where no building site (topography) has been defined in the model.

When you select Ground Plane At Level, the software casts shadows on the specified level in 2D and 3D shaded views. See Figure 11.19. When you deselect this option, the software casts shadows on the toposurface, if one exists.

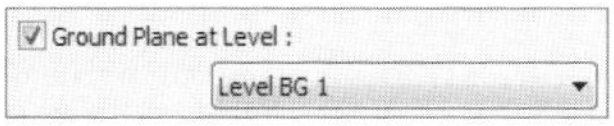

Figure 11.18

Ground Plane At Level setting

Figure 11.19

Topography turned off with Ground Plane At Level enabled

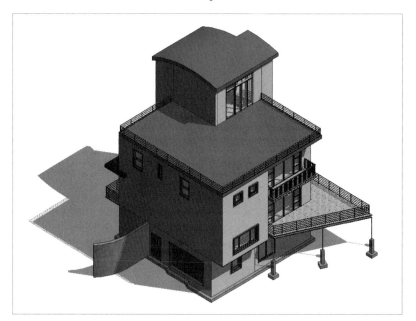

Use the Ground Plane At Level setting only in shaded views, such as the Realistic shaded mode used for real-time rendering. If you want to display shadows on a ground plane using the Revit Rendering tool, a toposurface must exist in the model.

Setting Up Interior Lighting

To set up interior lighting, you must add lighting fixtures to the model. A lighting fixture is a family-based model element (Figure 11.20) that emits light from one or more light sources.

Revit provides a variety of predefined lighting fixtures as families. These range from wall lights, ceiling lights, and table and floor lamps to exterior artificial lighting fixtures such as garden and street lights. Also, you can design individual lighting fixtures in the Family Editor and added them to the model. Additional lighting fixture families are available from the Revit Web Content Library as well as other Revit content providers.

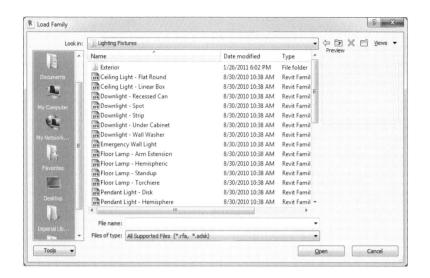

Figure 11.20

The Lighting Fixtures folder selected in the Load Family dialog box

Best Practices for Placing Lighting Fixtures in the Model

Because lighting fixtures are family-based model elements, placement is similar to any other family-based Revit component. However, it may be necessary to adjust view settings so you can see the lighting fixtures when placing them in a view.

To make sure lighting fixtures display in the view where you are placing them, open the Visibility/Graphic Overrides dialog box for the view (Figure 11.21) and ensure that the Lighting Fixtures category is checked.

Figure 11.21

Make sure Lighting Fixtures is checked in the Visibility/ Graphic Overrides dialog box.

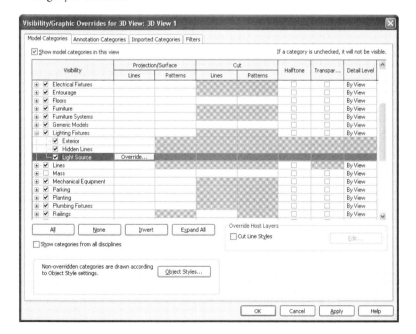

You must also select the appropriate view for placing lighting fixtures. Depending on the lighting fixture family, the fixture can be either work-plane based or based on walls, ceilings, faces, or floors. Placing a lighting fixture that is ceiling based, for example, will require a ceiling to be present in the model. It will also be most appropriate to use a reflected ceiling plan to place ceiling-based lighting fixtures.

Similarly, when placing a tabletop lamp, you may have to use a section or interior elevation view to ensure that the lighting fixture is actually placed on the tabletop and not on the floor underneath.

Wall-based lighting fixtures can easily be placed in floor plan views. We recommend that, depending on the placement height and cut plane height of the view, you use an interior elevation of the wall on which the lighting fixtures are placed to determine their appropriate layout.

Changing Lighting Fixtures

Since lighting fixtures are family based, instance and type parameters displayed for a lighting fixture depend on how the family was created. In the Photometrics section of the family's Type Properties dialog box (Figure 11.22), you'll find a standard set of parameters that will influence the way a lighting fixture will affect a rendering of a 3D view using artificial lighting. To access the type properties, in the Properties palette select the family and click Edit Type.

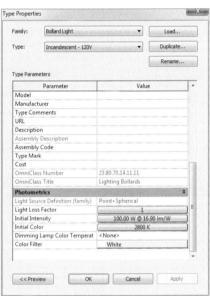

Figure 11.22

Type Properties dialog box

Controlling the Brightness of an Artificial Light Source

In a project environment, you can change the brightness of a light source by using a number of methods, as explained in the following sections.

Changing the Initial Intensity of the Light Source

Initial Intensity is a type parameter of every light source (Figure 11.23). For example, using this parameter you can change a light source so that it uses a 100 watt bulb rather than a 60 watt bulb. Do so by specifying 100 W in the Wattage field of the Initial Intensity dialog box.

Figure 11.23

Initial Intensity dialog box

Changing the Light Loss Factor

The Light Loss Factor setting is used to enhance or reduce the light output in order to reflect environmental factors in the project. Factors such as temperature and dust affect the way light is distributed in a model. The Light Loss Factor setting (Figure 11.24) allows you to fine-tune a scene to account for these factors. By moving the slider in the Light Loss Factor dialog box to the right, you'll make the scene more brightly lit by that light fixture. Moving the slider to the left will reduce the distribution of light from that fixture, resulting in a scene that's less brightly lit.

Figure 11.24

Light Loss Factor dialog box

Dimming the Light Using the Artificial Lights Feature

The Artificial Lights feature allows you to dim individual light sources to create mood lighting in a rendered image. Use the Artificial Lights feature provided in the Lighting section (Figure 11.25) of the Rendering dialog box.

Figure 11.25

Lighting section in the Rendering dialog box

> Artificial Lights will only become available when you select a lighting scheme that uses artificial lights. It will be grayed out if you've selected Sun Only for an exterior or interior lighting scheme.

The Artificial Lights dialog box (Figure 11.26) differentiates between Grouped Lights and Ungrouped Lights. You can turn both Grouped Lights and Ungrouped Lights on or off or assign them a dimming value.

We have already touched on a few of the settings in the Rendering dialog box for lighting, and we will go into a little more detail here. When setting up your rendering options, the first step is to choose between exterior and interior schemes. With each scheme, you can pick from three options (Figure 11.27):

- Sun Only
- Sun And Artificial
- Artificial Only (When this option is selected, Revit will calculate only the lights that are included in the selected option.)

Figure 11.26

Artificial Lights dialog box

Figure 11.27

Lighting scheme options

If you choose a scheme that uses the sun, you can then access the Sun Settings dialog box by clicking the Browse button (Figure 11.28)  to the right of Sun Setting.

Grouping Lights

When you are rendering, Revit will calculate lighting for every light source you have in your project, regardless of the location. For that reason, you want to use the Artificial Lights dialog box to manage your individual lights. Depending on the number of lights in your project, taking advantage of these options can dramatically improve your lighting performance.

The Artificial Lights dialog box (Figure 11.26) is broken up into two areas:

- The left side of the dialog box lists all the lights in the project. In this list, you can specify what lights are on and off and control the dimming of the lights.

- The right side contains two groups: Fixture Options to add or remove lights to a group and Group Options for creating and managing groups.

As you can see in Figure 11.26, you have several lights throughout the project. You need to organize these lights in order to improve rendering performance and better manage your scenes. In the following steps, we will walk you through creating the three new groups—Kitchen Strip Lights, Kitchen Can Lights, and Bedroom Lights—and then you will move your light fixtures into these groups.

1. In the Rendering dialog box, click the Artificial Lights button after choosing a lighting scheme that utilizes artificial lights.

   If the Artificial Lights button is grayed out, then your lighting scheme does not include artificial lights.

2. In the Artificial Lights dialog box, click New under Group Options to create a new group (Figure 11.29).

3. Name the group **Kitchen Recessed Lights**.

4. Repeat steps 2 and 3 to create groups for Kitchen Can Lights and Bedroom Lights.

Now that you have created your groups, you can start moving the ungrouped lights into their respective groups:

Figure 11.29

New Light Group dialog box

1. Open a project view that displays the light fixtures you want to assign to a light group. This is typically going to be a plan view. The 3D perspective view will not work for this operation.

2. Select the light fixtures.

3. On the Options bar (Figure 11.30), set Light Group to the group you want to move the selected lights into.

Figure 11.30

When light fixtures are selected, the Options bar provides a method to assign them to a light group.

Revit will then prompt you with a dialog box letting you know that "You are about to move all selected lights into a new light group: *Light Group Name.*"

4. At the prompt, click OK to move the lights.

To remove lights from a light group:

1. With the lights selected, click None on the Options bar for Light Group.

2. At the prompt, click OK.

Another method for adding and removing lights to a light group is using the Artificial Lights feature in the Rendering dialog box while in a 3D view:

1. In the Artificial Lights dialog box, select the lighting fixtures under Ungrouped Lights.

2. In the Fixture Options section, click Move To Group.

3. In the Lights Group dialog box, select the light group where you want to place the lights.

4. At the prompt, click OK to move the lights.

The main drawback to using this method is you may not be able to determine which light you are selecting. For example, in Figure 11.29, lights numbered 24 through 27 are table lamps used in several different rooms. Although you have a light name, you do not know the location. So if you are trying to complete a rendering in one room, you may inadvertently place a light in the wrong light group. To remove lights from a light group, you follow the same steps but choose lights from the Grouped Lights list and then click Remove From Group.

Figure 11.31

Artificial Lights dialog box

The final way you can add or remove a light in a light group is by using the Light Group Editor:

1. In a project view (such as a reflected ceiling plan), select the light fixture.

2. On the Options bar, select Edit/New from the Light Group drop-down. The Artificial Lights (Figure 11.31) dialog box will open and you can add the lighting fixture to, or remove it from, a group.

If you select a light that is not part of a light group, the Edit/New button on the Options bar will not be available. You can, however, add that light to a light group.

If you select multiple lights that are part of different light groups, again the Edit/New button will not be available. You will have to edit your selection set to contain only lights in a common light group.

Editing Lights in Groups

Once Revit is in the Light Group: Edit mode, the Light Group panel (Figure 11.32) is active and will appear below the Options bar.

Revit will now differently display lighting fixtures to indicate whether or not they belong to a light group:

- Light fixtures that are not assigned to a light group display normally.

- Light fixtures that are associated with the active light group are displayed in green.

- Light fixtures that belong in another light group and model elements are displayed at halftone.

Figure 11.32

When editing a light group, use the Light Group panel floating toolbar to add or remove lights from the light group.

To add light fixtures to a group:

1. Click the Add button in the Light Group panel.

2. Select each light fixture that you want to add to the group.

   When you select and add a light fixture, Revit will display that fixture as green, indicating that it has been added to the group.

To remove a fixture from a group:

1. Click the Remove button.

2. Select the fixture or fixtures.

3. Click Finish.

If necessary, you can open other project views to add or remove light fixtures to light groups.

Using Groups to Control Lights

Now that you have created your light groups, you have the ability to more efficiently manage your lights. In the next example, we will demonstrate how to turn lights on and off.

Figure 11.33 shows the 3D scene and the Artificial Lights dialog box. If you want to turn off a group of lights, you need to deselect the check box next to the group name. Selecting the check box turns the lights on. If you want to turn individual lights on or off, then deselecting or selecting the check box will accomplish that.

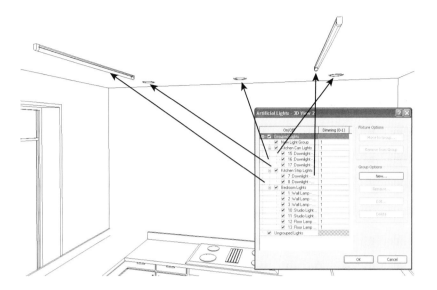

Figure 11.33

The arrows indicate which lights are assigned to which light group.

The next option to the right of the light name is the Dimming field. The Artificial Lights dialog box lets you specify a value for dimming a particular light source or light group in the model (Figure 11.34). The value can range from 0 to 1, with 0 meaning that the light is effectively turned off and 1 meaning that the light is effectively not dimmed. When specifying a value for dimming a light group, all lights belonging to this group will inherit the value for dimming.

If required, the value for dimming any individual light source within a group can still be manually overridden by specifying a different value for the light without affecting the setting of any other light in the group (Figure 11.35).

Figure 11.34

Dimming grouped lights using the Artificial Lights dialog box

Figure 11.35

Overriding dimming

Advanced Settings for Lighting Fixtures

Advanced settings for changing lighting fixture type properties that affect rendering can be accessed via the Photometrics parameter group of the light fixture's Type Properties dialog box (Figure 11.36).

The settings that determine the way a light source affects rendering of a 3D view of the model are Light Loss Factor (Figure 11.37), Initial Intensity, Initial Color, Dimming Lamp Color Temperature Shift, and Color Filter.

Light Loss Factor Light Loss Factor refers to a value to calculate the amount of light lost due to environmental factors such as dust and ambient temperature.

Initial Intensity Initial Intensity defines the brightness of the light before environmental factors reduce or change the quality of the light (Figure 11.23). Initial intensity can be defined by these options: Wattage, Luminous Flux, Luminous Intensity, or Illuminance At A Specified Distance.

Note that in photometry, Luminous Flux is the measure of the perceived power of light. Illuminance is the total luminous flux incident on a surface per unit area. Stated differently, Illuminance is the surface density of the luminous flux.

Initial Color Initial Color is the color of the light source before it is affected by color filters and environmental factors. The Initial Color dialog box (Figure 11.38) offers a range of preset curves that determine the color shift when dimming the light source based on the type of light source used.

Dimming Lamp Color Temperature Shift Dimming Lamp Color Temperature Shift defines whether the color and intensity of a dimmed light source change based on predefined curves. Incandescent light, for example, usually changes to a warmer, more yellow tone when dimmed.

Color Filter Color Filter defines a color used to change the light emitted from the light source (Figure 11.39). It allows you to further change the color tone of the light emitted by the light source.

Figure 11.38

Initial Color dialog box

Figure 11.39

Initial Intensity dialog box

Best Practices for Using Artificial Lighting When Rendering a 3D View

Using multiple artificial light sources to illuminate a 3D view for rendering purposes can be resource intensive. The more artificial light in a model, the longer the actual rendering process will take to produce the final image. Before rendering the view, make a thorough check of the lighting fixture placement to ensure it will lead to the desired result. You can do so by utilizing Shaded or Realistic visual styles for the view. This enables you to plan the appropriate number of artificial lights and set the required spacing, angle, and setback values. Shaded or Realistic visual styles allow you to roughly predict the final outcome of the rendering before starting the rendering process.

As a rule of thumb, an interior view using several artificial lights will take longer to render than an exterior view using Exterior: Sun Only as a source lighting scheme in the Rendering dialog box. The same exterior view will take longer to render when no natural light is present and artificial lights are used to illuminate the scene, such as in a nighttime view of the model.

The actual light shape setting of a particular lighting fixture family can also affect rendering times. Generally, point light shapes render faster than line, rectangle, and circle lights.

Setting the Background

You are almost done. You need to review and adjust a few more settings in the Rendering dialog box, so let's look at the Background option. This option allows you to create a custom background. In this section, we will discuss how you can control the background of your rendering.

To define a custom background, do the following:

1. From the View tab's Render panel, click the Style drop-down in the Background section.

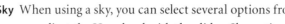

Figure 11.40

Background style options

You can choose from three styles for creating a background (Figure 11.40):

Sky When using a sky, you can select several options from the drop-down. Then you can adjust the Haze level with the slider. Sky options are based on actual colors that are physically correct. When the scene time (2 PM, 8 PM, 3 AM) changes, the sky color will change to accurately reflect the sky conditions at that time of the day. Figure 11.41 shows a rendering using the Sky: Few Clouds option.

Color You can also use a simple color as the background. Click the color swatch to select a different color. Figure 11.42 shows a rendering using the Color option.

Figure 11.41

Rendered image using the Sky: Few Clouds option

Figure 11.42

Rendered image using the Color option

Image The last option lets you specify an image. You will need to select a BMP, JPEG, PNG, or TIFF file. After selecting the image, you will be able to adjust the image scale and the offset. Figure 11.43 shows a rendering using an image of a sky background.

Figure 11.43

Rendered image using the Image option

2. To specify an image for the background, in the Rendering dialog box set Style to Image (Figure 11.43).

3. Click the Customize Image button.

4. In the Background Image dialog box, click the Image button (Figure 11.44).

5. Navigate to the location where you stored your image file, select the image, and click Open.

6. Back in the Background Image dialog box, specify the Scale and Offset values, and click OK.

With the background settings, you can quickly and easily add a custom background to your rendered image.

Adding and Adjusting Materials

With your lights set, you can now move on to adjusting materials, the third phase in your rendering workflow. Revit ships with a library of materials specifically for creating architectural renderings. You can also modify this library to create new materials to meet your specific project needs. Materials are what you use to define the appearance and characteristics of your model. You use materials to define the following:

Figure 11.44

Background Image dialog box

- Color that displays in a shaded project view
- Color and pattern that displays on the surface of an element
- Color and fill pattern that displays when the element is cut
- Render appearance that displays in a rendered image and in a realistic view
- Data about the materials description, manufacturer, cost, and keynotes
- Structural information about the material

Revit provides several methods for applying materials to building elements. Materials can be assigned to Revit elements as type or instance properties when you place them in your building project or when you are creating or editing families. Some elements such as walls, floors, and ceilings need to have materials applied when you are defining the layers of those assemblies.

Figure 11.45

Materials button on the Manage tab's Settings panel

Before you get into placing or replacing materials in your building project, let's explore the Materials dialog box. To open this dialog box (Figure 11.45), click the Materials button on the Manage tab's Settings panel.

The Materials dialog box provides you with the means to search your current materials and to create and edit existing materials. The dialog box is broken up into two main parts:

- The left side allows you to search, create, rename, and delete materials. To search for materials by name, use the search field at the top.

- The right side allows you to define shader rules and settings that define a specific material. This is broken up into four tabs and includes graphic properties, rendering appearance properties, identity values, and physical characteristics.

As you define new materials in Revit, you will notice that the shader rules and settings can vary depending on the type of material you are trying to define. Figure 11.46 shows the Render Appearance settings for Steel and Concrete.

Figure 11.46

Render Appearance settings for Steel (left) and Concrete (right)

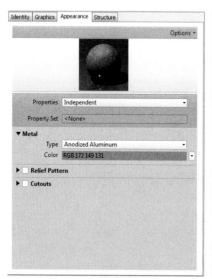

To assign or replace a material in your project, the first thing to do is search the existing library to see whether you are lucky enough to find a material that will suit your needs. Although you have a large collections of materials to choose from, chances are you are going to have to modify or create new materials in your project. The next steps will walk you through the process of modifying or creating a new material. In the following example, you are going to create a new teak wood material:

1. On the Manage tab's Settings panel, click Materials.

2. From the list on the left side of the dialog box, select the Wood – Cherry material.

3. At the bottom-left side, click the Duplicate button.

   Revit will display a dialog box asking you to provide a new material name.

4. Enter **Wood – Teak**, and click OK.

5. On the left side of the dialog box, select the new Wood – Teak material.

6. On the right side of the dialog box, click the Appearance tab (Figure 11.47).

   You are not going to make any changes at this time on the Appearance tab.

7. On the left side of the Materials dialog box, click the Appearance Property Sets tab (Figure 11.48).

8. On the left side of the Appearance Property Sets tab, scroll down to Wood and click on it.

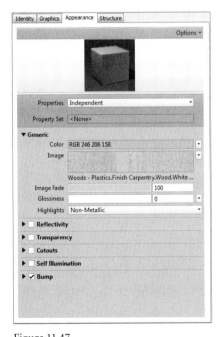

Figure 11.47

Appearance tab for the newly created Wood – Teak material

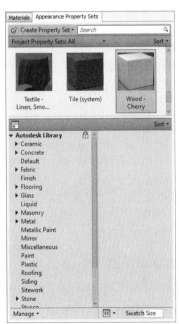

Figure 11.48

The Appearance Property Sets tab displays predefined ProMaterials that ship with Revit.

9. On the right side of the Appearance Property Sets tab, scroll down and select the material Teak – Natural Polished.

10. Click the Swatch Shape drop-down (Figure 11.49) to change the scene in which the material will be previewed on the Appearance tab.

11. Click OK to close the Materials dialog box.

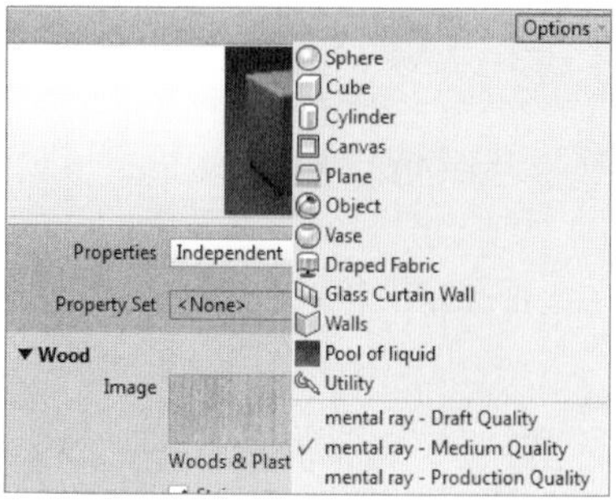

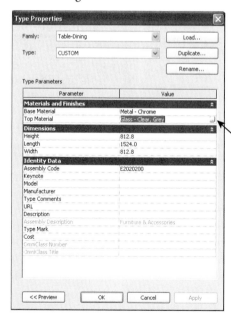

Figure 11.49

Swatch Shape drop-down

Assigning a Material to an Element

Now that you have created a new material, you need to assign it to an element in your model. In the sample project file, you will assign the newly created Wood – Teak material to the countertop located in the kitchen.

1. Open the source file `rac_basic_sample_project.rvt`.

2. Save the file as **materials.rvt**.

3. Switch to the Level 2 floor plan view.

4. Zoom into the kitchen area in the center of the building.

5. Select the Table-Dining CUSTOM table.

    If you are having trouble selecting the tabletop, remember to use the Tab key to cycle through the elements your cursor is hovering over.

6. On the Properties palette, select Edit Type.

7. In the Type Properties dialog box (Figure 11.50), go to the Materials And Finishes section and click the Browse button for Top Material. This will take you to the Materials dialog box.

8. In the Materials dialog box, scroll or search for the material Wood - Teak in the Material Class: Wood and select it.

Figure 11.50

Click Browse to choose a new countertop material.

9. Click OK to close the Materials dialog box.

Notice that the countertop material has been changed to Wood – Teak.

10. Click OK to close the Type Properties dialog box.

Applying a Material with the Paint Tool

Another method you can use to apply a material to an element is the Paint tool. This tool allows you to "paint" a material on the selected face of an element or family. The Paint tool can come in handy early in the design phase when you are not overly concerned about the layers of an element and just want to see a down-and-dirty finish. Elements that you can paint are walls, roofs, massing, floors, and families. To paint a surface, follow these steps:

1. On the Modify tab's Geometry panel, click the Paint drop-down ⬚ ▾. Select the Paint tool.

The Materials dialog box will open, allowing you to select a different material.

2. In this dialog box (Figure 11.51), select the material you want to apply by clicking on one of the swatches displayed.

3. Move the cursor to the face of an element and highlight it.

If you have trouble selecting the face of the element, remember to use the Tab key to cycle through the various elements or faces. Also keep an eye on the status bar, which will indicate whether you have already painted a face.

4. Click to paint the material to the face.

5. When you are finished with applying the material, click the Done button in the Materials dialog box to close it.

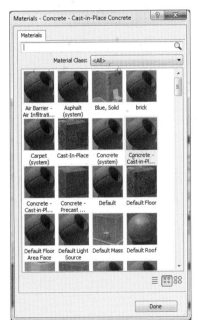

Figure 11.51

Select the material you want to apply.

Editing Materials

The following sections cover some of the advanced aspects of creating and adjusting materials.

Getting Started: Accessing the Materials Dialog Box

To access the Rendering settings of materials in Revit, click the Materials button on the Manage tab's Settings panel.

Here the currently utilized Render Appearance for any material will be displayed in a preview picture. Clicking the Appearance tab on the right side of the Materials dialog box will display the currently used setting for the selected material (Figure 11.52).

Figure 11.52

Appearance tab in the Materials dialog box

Depending on which Render Appearance is currently active for the material selected, various detailed settings can be accessed on the bottom half of the Appearance tab. Clicking the Appearance tab will expose the Appearance Property Sets tab on the left side of the dialog box.

Changing the Render Appearance

Render Appearances in Revit are based on material presets that are installed by default. The presets on the Appearance Property Sets tab of the Materials dialog box allow you to change the Render Appearance of the material selected.

The Render Appearance library consists of a variety of materials typically used in a building project. Materials are grouped into categories such as Ceramic, Metal, and Stone. Depending on the material group a material belongs to, it will have different parameters that you can alter to fine-tune the material preset. For example, a material from the Ceramic group (Figure 11.53) will allow you to change the type of ceramic, Finish Bumps, and Relief Patterns, whereas a material from the Metal group will allow you to change the type of metal, the Relief Pattern, and Cutouts.

If you require maximum flexibility to create a new material, select material templates in the Default category. The materials of this category are the basic templates of any material in the Render Appearance Library. By using the Generic material in the Default group, you can change any setting of any material template.

Previewing Materials

A preview of the material appears in the Materials dialog box. You can adjust the type, size, and quality of this preview by using the Options drop-down located above the preview image:

1. Open the Materials dialog box and select a material.

2. Click the Appearance tab.

3. Click the small arrow besides the Options button located right above the material preview image.

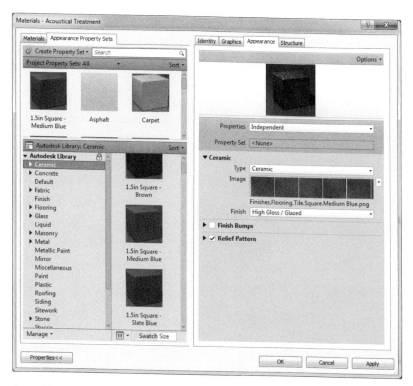

Figure 11.53

Materials dialog box with material from Ceramic group selected

4. Select preview object options such as Cube, Plane, or Vase.

5. Check how the material preview will update.

The material preview options are most useful when you need to get an initial idea of how the material will look like before applying it to an object and rendering the image. Different objects are more suitable for particular material types than others. So, for example, when you create a highly reflective material and want to check its appearance, you will most likely want to use a curved object such as the Cylinder or the Square to be able to predict the reflections the object will show. On the other hand, when adjusting a material used as a wall paint, you may want to choose the Walls or Plane object.

Understanding the Settings

Let's take a closer look at the individual settings you can use for creating materials:

Generic This is the starting point for creating a new material. Settings in the Generic section (Figure 11.54) will determine the basic appearance of the material. They allow you to specify a base color as well as a texture for the material. Textures can either be bitmaps or one of the procedural

Figure 11.54

Generic settings on the Appearance tab

textures that can be adjusted for the specific material. When using a texture, parameters such as Image Fade, Glossiness, and Highlights can also be set individually.

Reflectivity When enabled, Direct and Oblique reflectivity can be individually set for the material (Figure 11.55). Direct and Oblique reflectivity values can also be set by using image files—again the Materials dialog box offers a choice of bitmaps or procedural textures.

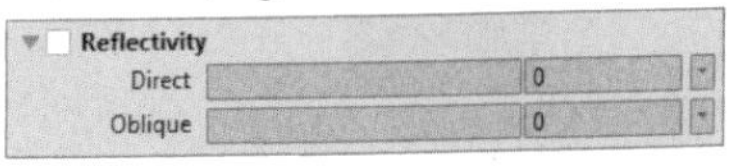

Figure 11.55

Reflectivity settings on the Appearance tab

Transparency Transparency specifies the amount of light that strikes the surface at a 90-degree angle and bounces off. Translucency specifies the amount of light that strikes the surface at a very shallow angle (close to 0 degrees) and bounces off (Figure 11.56).

You can specify the Amount setting for Transparency by using the slider control. In addition, the Materials dialog box lets you use an image—either a bitmap or procedural texture—to control transparency of the material (Figure 11.57).

Once you select an image, you can fine-tune it using the controls for Image Fade, Translucency, and Refraction (Figure 11.58).

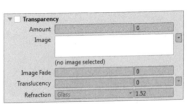

Figure 11.56

Transparency settings on the Appearance tab

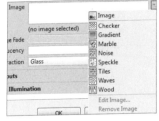

Figure 11.57

Image settings on Materials dialog box

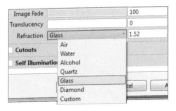

Figure 11.58

Extended Image settings on the Appearance tab

Figure 11.59

Cutout applied to sample material

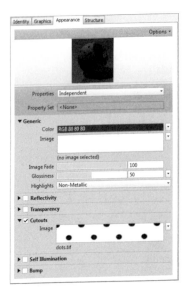

Cutouts Cutouts allow you to punch holes into a material (Figure 11.59). They can only be based on image files; again, the Materials dialog box in Revit will let you use a bitmap file or a procedural texture to define the cutout. Cutouts are most helpful when it comes to creating a material such as wire fences or punched holes in sheet metal. They allow you to create the image of complex geometry without having to actually create the physical geometry.

Self Illumination Self Illumination allows the material to emit light (Figure 11.60). The parameters for Self Illumination are Filter Color (either an RGB value or an image), Luminance, and Color Temperature.

Bump Bumps add a surface texture to the material (Figure 11.61). The Materials dialog box lets you specify an image—either a bitmap or a procedural texture preset—as well as tune the amount of bump mapping on the material.

Figure 11.60
Self Illumination settings

Figure 11.61
Procedural bump map settings

Creating a Punched-Out Sheet Metal

In the following exercise, you will create the material for a punched sheet of aluminum metal (Figure 11.62):

1. Open the Materials dialog box, select the Default material, and create a new material by clicking the Duplicate button.

2. Name the material **Punched Out Aluminum Sheet**.

3. Select the Appearance tab and then click the Appearance Property Sets tab on the left side of the Materials dialog box.

4. In Autodesk Library, select Default; right next to it, scroll down to and select the Metal template material in the Default group.

5. From the Metal settings, select Aluminum Frame – Painted White, which is the third material from the top in the Metal material library category.

6. On the Appearance tab on the right side of the Materials dialog box, click the Cutouts check box.

7. From the Type drop-down, click Custom to use the sample image `dots.tif` provided.

Figure 11.62
Punched-out aluminum material

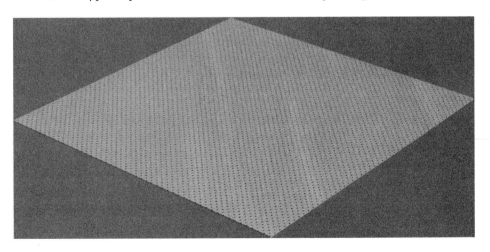

8. Click into the Image text box.

9. Navigate to the sample image `dots.tif` and open the file.

10. Apply the material to any suitable geometry (Figure 11.62) and test-render the new material.

Adding Entourage and Plants

Depending on the purpose of the rendering as well as whether the rendering is an indoor scene or an outdoor scene, additional objects commonly referred to as *entourage* may be required.

Revit has a dedicated family category named Entourage. These are model objects ranging from cars to people to furniture objects. Commonly objects found in the `Entourage` folder of families installed with Revit utilize ArchVision RPC content technology. Those objects will appear in a simplified representation in the model itself but use highly detailed image-based representations when being rendered. In addition to the sample RPC-based entourage families installed with Revit, additional RPC content can be purchased from ArchVision.

As with Entourage families, Revit also installs a set of Planting families that are based on ArchVision RPC rendering technology (Figure 11.63).

Figure 11.63

Entourage and Planting added to the scene

Note that both Entourage and Planting are model-based Revit families that can be created and changed in the Family Editor. Besides using ArchVision RPC-based content, you can create objects for planting and entourage by using Revit geometry or by importing geometry such as DWG or DXF files. However, detailed and complex models of cars and plants will significantly increase the file size and overall performance of the model. In scenarios where custom-made detailed planting and entourage is utilized, it is advisable to use dedicated worksets for those objects or use file linking to load these objects on demand into the model when rendering.

Settings for Rendering Quality

In addition to the basic settings for rendering your image, the Rendering dialog box provides advanced settings for controlling the output before and after the rendering process.

You can access a number of preset quality settings using the Setting drop-down in the Quality group of the Rendering dialog box. Presets include Draft, Low, Medium, High, and Best (Figure 11.64). There is also a Custom (View Specific) setting that you can modify using the Edit feature.

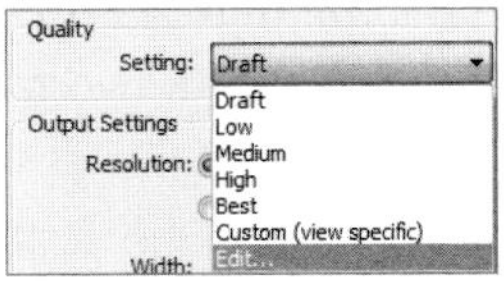

Figure 11.64

Quality settings in the Rendering dialog box

Clicking the Edit option will bring up the Render Quality Settings dialog box (Figure 11.65). Take one of the presets, make adjustments, and then copy it to the Custom setting. Once this is done, you can choose Custom in the Setting drop-down and the settings will be stored with the 3D view to be rendered.

The various adjustments that you can make in the Advanced Rendering Settings of the Render Quality Settings dialog box are described in the following sections.

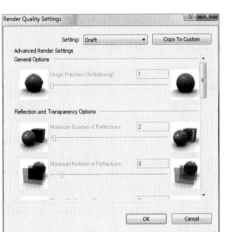

Figure 11.65

Render Quality Settings dialog box

Image Precision

Image Precision (Antialiasing), shown in Figure 11.66, is a software technique for diminishing jaggies, the stairstep-like effect that can sometimes be seen along diagonal edges and round objects in a rendering.

Antialiasing reduces the prominence of jaggies by surrounding the stairsteps with intermediate shades of color. The higher the Antialiasing value, the fewer jaggies you'll see. However, edges become blurry when you set the value too high.

Figure 11.66

Image Precision (Antialiasing)

Reflection and Transparency Options

Reflections as well as transparency are the keystones to achieving realistic quality in a rendered image. An image with low-quality settings for reflections and transparency will be perceived as artificial; higher-quality settings will make your image look more realistic but also contribute largely to longer rendering times. Let's look at the available options:

Maximum Number Of Reflections This value determines how many times a ray of light is bounced back and forth between reflecting objects. The higher the value, the more accurate the image will appear; however, this accuracy comes at the cost of rendering time (Figure 11.67).

Maximum Number Of Refractions This value is similar to the Maximum Number Of Reflections setting. Refraction occurs when waves travel from a medium with a given refractive index to a medium with another at an angle. At the boundary between the media, the wave's phase velocity is altered, usually causing a change in direction (Figure 11.67).

Blurred Reflections Precision This value determines the smoothness of edges or surfaces in blurred reflections. The higher the value, the smoother the edges or surfaces will appear (Figure 11.67).

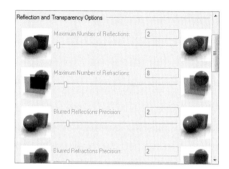

Figure 11.67

Reflection and Transparency options in the Render Quality Settings dialog box

Blurred Refractions Precision Similar to the Blurred Reflections Precision setting, this value affects the smoothness of objects seen in blurred refractions, such as objects seen through glass or other transparent media (Figure 11.67).

Shadow Options

When Soft Shadows are turned on, Soft Shadow Precision controls the smoothness of shadow edges. When Soft Shadows are disabled, the edges of shadows will appear sharp (Figure 11.68).

Figure 11.68

Shadow options in the Render Quality Settings dialog box

Indirect Illumination Options

Indirect illumination is a technical term that refers to light that is not directly emitted from light sources in your scene. This includes ambient light as well as light reflected from objects in your scene. Indirect Illumination Options allow you to control the amount of indirect light that will illuminate your scene (Figure 11.69).

Compute Indirect And Sky Illumination When turned on, this setting allows you to include light from the sky and light that bounces off other objects.

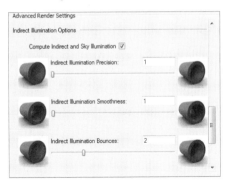

Figure 11.69

Indirect Illumination Options in the Render Quality Settings dialog box

Indirect Illumination Precision Indirect Illumination Precision is the level of detail that is visible in indirect light. A higher value creates more detailed indirect illumination and shadows. Higher precision causes smaller subtle effects that can usually be seen in corners or below objects.

Indirect Illumination Smoothness If indirect illumination displays as an irregularly shaped spot, stain, or colored or discolored area, you can try to amend this by changing the settings for Indirect Illumination Smoothness. Again, a higher value causes smaller subtle effects that can usually be seen in corners or below objects.

Indirect Illumination Bounces This setting determines the number of times that indirect light bounces off objects in the scene. It controls the amount of realism in indirect lighting. When this option is set to a higher value, light can penetrate further into a scene, resulting in more physically correct lighting and a brighter scene.

Daylight Portal Options

These settings (Figure 11.70) only apply to interior views that include daylight for rendering purposes.

Windows This setting controls whether Revit rendering will calculate window glass areas as daylight portals—in other words, whether sunlight will penetrate through a windows glass pane.

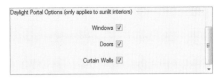

Figure 11.70

Daylight Portal Options in the Render Quality Settings dialog box

Doors Similar to Windows, this setting determines whether sunlight will penetrate through a door's glass pane, if applicable.

Curtain Walls This setting determines whether light will penetrate through transparent curtain wall panels.

The Daylight Portal settings are especially important when you are creating interior renderings using exterior illumination. An example is when you want to display an interior scene on a bright day lit only by the light that penetrates through the windows. To obtain a high-quality result for your rendering, you need to enable daylight portals when attempting to render an interior scene using exterior illumination.

Real-Time Rendering

Figure 11.71

Visual Styles pop-up on the View Control bar

Real-time rendering utilizes the Realistic visual style in Revit. The realistic visual style displays material appearances in the model view in real time. Shadow and depth settings can also be applied and are recognized by the Realistic visual style. No explicit rendering command is needed since the view will always update in real time.

To invoke real-time rendering, you'll need to specify the Realistic visual style in the Visual Styles flyout on the View Control bar (Figure 11.71).

In order to be able to see material textures applied to objects in the Realistic visual style, select the Use Hardware Acceleration (Direct3D®) option. If hardware acceleration is not available or turned off, the Realistic visual style will look the same as the shaded visual style.

To check if Hardware Acceleration is turned off, choose Application → Options, and in the Graphics tab, under Graphics Mode select Use Hardware Acceleration (Direct3D), as shown in Figure 11.72.

Figure 11.72

Select Use Hardware Acceleration (Direct3D®).

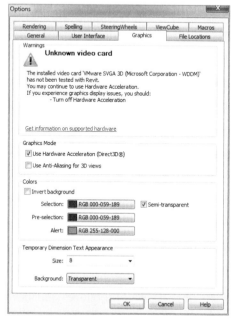

Settings for Real-Time Rendering determining the quality of a real-time rendering using the Realistic visual style can be accessed from the Graphic Display styles available in the Visual Styles pop-up on the View Control bar, shown earlier in Figure 11.71. To invoke the Graphic Display Options dialog box, select Graphic Display Options on the View Control bar. Here are the available settings:

Model Display Surfaces should be set to Realistic for real-time rendering purposes (Figure 11.73). Using the two checkboxes located below the Surfaces drop-down, Show Edges can be turned on or off, and Surfaces can be set to Ghosted (semi transparent). As with all visual styles in general, Silhouettes can be set to any line style available in the Revit project. For the purpose of real-time rendering, we do not recommend selecting either Show Edges or Ghost Surfaces.

Shadows Shadows can be turned on or off; in addition, Show Ambient Shadows allows you to simulate the blocking of diffused (ambient) light.

Lighting Sun Settings allow you to specify exterior illumination depending on place and time or by azimuth and altitude. Sun And Shadow Intensity can be adjusted directly for the visual style using the sliders for Sun, Ambient Light, and Shadows.

Background Background allows you to specify a gradient background if desired. You can individually define colors for Sky, Horizon, and Ground (Figure 11.74).

Save as View Template Save as View Template allows saving the current settings as a view template that then can be applied to other 3D views.

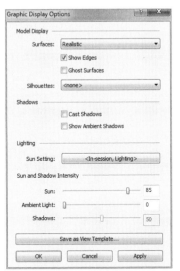

Figure 11.73

Graphic Display Options dialog box

Figure 11.74

Gradient option in the Graphic Display Options dialog box

Figure 11.75 shows the model displayed with the Realistic visual style set for surfaces, Silhouettes set to Medium Lines, Shadows enabled, and Background set to use a gradient background (Figure 11.75).

Figure 11.75

Example of the Realistic visual style

Exporting a Model for Rendering in an External Application

For exporting a model to be rendered in an external application, Revit offers the FBX data exchange format. The benefit of using FBX data exchange is that many of the settings done for a 3D view to be rendered will be utilized in an external application, such as 3ds Max, that supports FBX data exchange. This approach eliminates the need to reapply materials and lighting settings in the external application.

To export a model using the FBX interface, follow these steps:

Figure 11.76

Choose Export → FBX from the Application menu.

1. From the Application menu, select Export → FBX.

2. In the Export 3ds Max (FBX) dialog box, provide a name for the file.

3. Click Save (Figure 11.76).

No further adjustments or settings need to be done upon export.

When importing the FBX file into applications such as 3ds Max, settings for materials, lighting, and camera (the original camera location of the 3D View the FBX file was exported from) will be preserved (see Figure 11.77 and Figure 11.78). To import the FBX file into 3ds Max, you need to go to the 3ds Max Application menu and select Import → Import.

Figure 11.77

Model taken into 3ds Max

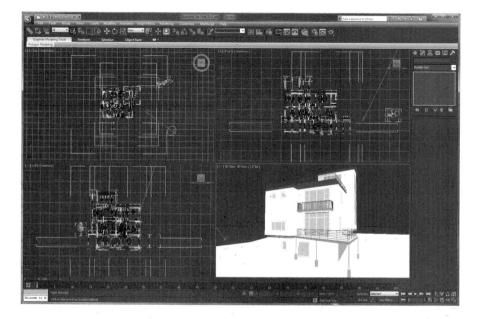

Figure 11.78

Rendering done in
3ds Max

CHAPTER 12

Working with Other Files

Although Autodesk Revit Architecture is entirely
capable of working as a stand-alone platform that can be used to bring a project from
conceptual design through construction documentation, there are many times where
interacting with other file formats will be necessary or advantageous.

Working with other Revit models, CAD files, or raster images is routinely required
on many projects. Revit has functions for linking, importing, and exporting multiple
file formats. Revit project files can be linked into one another for modeling and scheduling purposes or can be permanently combined. CAD files can be linked in and used as a
background to begin a new project, for site plans, or as final construction details. Raster
images can be used for project or company logos, for onscreen display, or for photorealistic renderings.

This chapter covers the following topics:

- **Linking Revit models**

- **Controlling display**

- **Working with CAD files**

- **Exporting DWF files**

- **Using raster files**

Linking Revit Models

Revit project .rvt files, also referred to as *Revit files*, are commonly linked together to form a complete *building information modeling* (BIM) process of the building project. Architectural designers will link the Revit Structure and Revit MEP models into the architectural project model to help coordinate the design and review model changes. Architectural models will often be linked on large projects to form one complete architectural building model. Once models are linked, issue documents, as well as schedules and sheet lists, can be produced from one master file that includes the host file and any linked files if desired.

Figure 12.1

Link Revit tool

In addition to project coordination, a Revit project file linked into a host Revit project file can be used when generating schedules, checking for model interferences, and creating views of the assembled building model.

Also, the linked file can be monitored so that the user is alerted to any changes that have been made in the linked file. When creating final documentation, elements contained in the linked file may be intelligently tagged in the host file.

The Link Revit tool (Figure 12.1) on the Link panel in the Insert tab allows .rvt project files to be loaded into the current .rvt project file. Once the Link Revit tool is selected, the Import/Link RVT dialog box opens. Figure 12.2 shows all of the lower flyouts expanded.

Figure 12.2

Import/Link RVT dialog box expanded

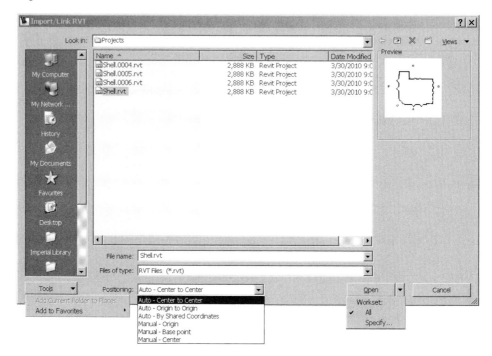

The top portion of the Import/Link RVT dialog box offers typical Microsoft Windows control and navigation options. The left portion of the dialog box contains a Places list where frequently visited folders can be accessed. The lower portion of the dialog box, shown expanded, has option settings that can be used to control the Revit files being linked.

These are the Positioning options in the Import/Link RVT dialog box:

Auto – Center To Center This option aligns the geometric centers of both the linked file and the host file. The alignment occurs in all three coordinates, *X*, *Y*, and *Z*.

Auto – Origin To Origin This option aligns the 0,0,0 base points of both files. This is the most commonly selected method.

Auto – By Shared Coordinates If the project uses shared coordinates, this option will align the linked file with the shared coordinate system and maintain the relative positions of the two files. This is useful for assembling sites and campus and condominium types of projects.

Manual – Origin The origin of the linked file will be located at the cursor and will be placed at the insertion point selected in the host file.

Manual – Base Point The base point of the AutoCAD file will be located at the crosshairs and will be placed at the insertion point selected in the host file.

Manual – Center The file will be centered on the cursor and will be placed at the insertion point selected in the host file.

If the file being linked into the host model was saved in an earlier version of Revit software, a project upgrade notification dialog box will display. The linked file will be temporarily upgraded to match the release of the current software. This message will be displayed each time the file is linked in. The linked file will need to be opened and saved in the current format to eliminate this message permanently.

A linked Revit file may be selected and edited only as one object (Figure 12.3). Individual elements of the linked file may not be edited or moved within the linked file. Editing of the link is limited to display, properties, location, and orientation. Once the file has been linked into the host, it can be moved and rotated as necessary. Linked files may also be copied, which will create an additional instance of the linked file.

To ensure that the linked file is not later accidentally moved, select the linked file, and choose the Pin tool 📌 on the Modify panel to lock the file in place.

Individual elements within the linked file can be selected using the Tab key to highlight the individual elements prior to selecting the element (see Figure 12.4). The properties of the selected element can be viewed in the Properties dialog box, but they can't be altered and will appear gray (Figure 12.5).

Figure 12.3

**Linked Revit
file selected**

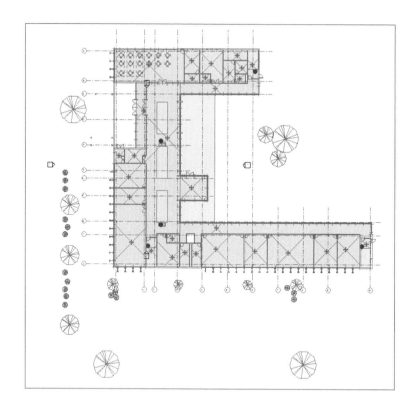

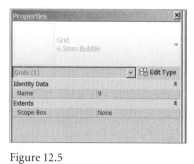

Figure 12.5

Properties of selected element

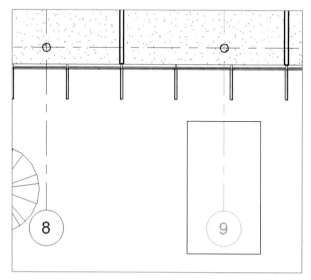

Figure 12.4

Individual grid element selected

To convert a linked Revit file from a link to an import, you use the Bind Link command:

1. Select the linked Revit model.

2. Choose Bind Link from the Link panel on the ribbon.

This command will convert the linked Revit model to a model group within the host file. Once the command is chosen, the Bind Link Options dialog box will open (Figure 12.6). Three options are available within the Bind Link command.

Include Attached Details This option includes any detail groups that exist in the linked file and creates matching detail groups in the host file. This option is the only option selected by default.

Include Levels This option creates uniquely named levels in addition to any levels already present in the host file.

Include Grids This option creates uniquely named grids in addition to any grids already present in the host file.

Binding a large Revit model may take quite a bit of time. Revit will display a warning alerting you to the potential time involved and ask you to consider linking. Select Continue to bind the link.

Figure 12.6
Bind Link Options dialog box

Controlling Display

The display of linked Revit models can be controlled from within the host file. Changes to the display of the linked models made within the host file will not alter the linked files but will only affect how the linked files display within the host file.

Visibility/Graphic Overrides

Once a Revit file is linked into a host, opening the Visibility/Graphic Overrides dialog box (we'll refer to this as Visibility/Graphic) will activate an additional tab named, appropriately, Revit Links, as shown in Figure 12.7.

Visibility	Halftone	Underlay	Display Settings
☑ Intro_to_ARA.rvt	☐	☐	By Host View
☑ Project1.rvt	■	■	By Host View

Visibility	Halftone	Underlay	Display Settings
☑ Intro_to_ARA.rvt	■	■	By Host View
☑ 3 (<Not Shared>)	☐	☐	Not Overridden
☑ Introduction to revit.rvt	☐	☐	By Host View
☑ (<Not Shared>)	☐	☐	Not Overridden
☑ Renamed (<Not Shared>)	☐	☐	Not Overridden

Figure 12.7
Revit Links tab and a linked file with multiple instances

Open Visibility/Graphic by clicking the button in the Properties palette (Figure 12.8) or by pressing VV or VG on the keyboard.

Figure 12.8

Visibility/Graphic Overrides palette button

Each linked Revit file will have a line showing the filename. The line with the filename is considered the primary, or *parent*. You can expand this line by clicking the plus sign to the left of the filename to show the instances of the linked file, also known as *children*. Any changes to the visibility settings of the parent will translate to all children unless the child file has been overridden. One instance will be shown after a Revit file is linked into a host. If the linked file is linked in again or copied within the model, additional child line items will appear, one for each instance of the linked file (see Figure 12.7). Children can be renamed by selecting the individual child and typing the desired name in the Properties palette. This chapter will focus on the settings as they apply to the primary linked file, but the majority of the settings may be applied individually to each instance.

The parent or children of linked files can be displayed in either halftone or as an underlay by selecting the appropriate check box (see Figure 12.7).

Halftone Displays the entire linked file using a medium shade of gray. This is suitable when the linked file needs to be used as a background in the view.

Underlay Displays the entire linked file using a medium shade of gray. This is suitable when the linked file needs to be used as a background in the view. In addition, when using the Underlay setting, links can be exported to the DWG file format and placed on a specific layer with a specific color, for example AutoCAD color 8.

Halftone and Underlay Combined When you select both the Halftone and Underlay boxes, the linked file will display in a lighter shade of gray than either the Halftone or Underlay settings used alone. This will not affect the export to DWG using Underlay.

To apply display changes only to one instance of the linked file, click the Not Overridden button in the Display Settings column beside that instance, and then click the Not Overridden button (Figure 12.9) that appears. Note that one instance is automatically listed for the initial link, even though it has not been duplicated. The display settings can be made at the parent level or the instance level, but it may be slightly easier to make the changes at the parent level.

When you click the Not Overridden button shown in Figure 12.9, a dialog box named RVT Link Display Settings (Figure 12.10) will open, offering the Override Display Settings For This Instance check box. Once this is selected, the settings you changed will apply only to the particular instance selected.

Figure 12.9

Not Overridden instance button

Visibility	Halftone	Underlay	Display Settings
☑ Floor.rvt	☐	☑	Custom
☑ Plan (<Not Shared>)	☐	☑	Not Overridden

In Visibility/Graphic, at the parent link level, clicking the By Host View button (Figure 12.11) will display four additional tabs for controlling the display of the linked file:

Figure 12.10

Override Display Settings For This Instance check box

- Basics
- Model Categories
- Annotation Categories
- Import Categories

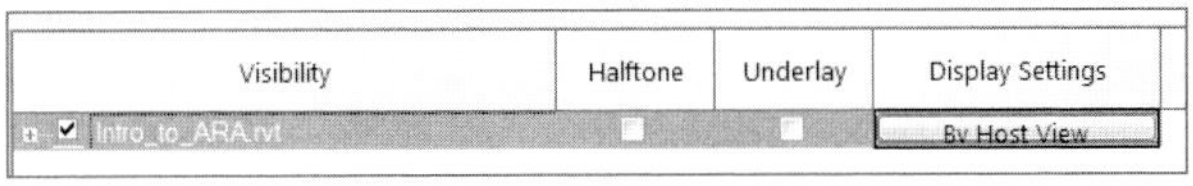

Figure 12.11

By Host View button

RVT Link Display Settings Basics Tab

The Basics tab shows three options (Figure 12.12) for displaying the linked file: By Host View, By Linked View, and Custom.

Figure 12.12

Display options

BY HOST VIEW

The default Visibility/Graphic setting for the linked Revit file is By Host View. The By Host View setting uses the same display settings as the Model Categories tab (Figure 12.13) in the host file so that the same elements are displayed in the link as in the host. For example, if the Walls check

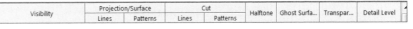

mark is cleared so that walls do not display in the host file, the walls in the link file also do not display. With the exception of the Visibility check box and the Halftone check box on the Revit Links tab, the entire display is controlled on the Model Categories tab.

Figure 12.13

Model Categories tab

Note that annotations contained in the linked Revit file will not display using By Host View.

The model category settings controlled using By Host View are as follows:

- Visibility
- Line
  - Weight
  - Color
  - Pattern
- Pattern
  - Visible
  - Color
  - Pattern
- Halftone
- Ghost Surfaces
- Transparent
- Detail Level

BY LINKED VIEW

Choosing the By Linked View setting allows the user to select a view from the linked file (Figure 12.14) and displays the settings from that view in a view in the host file. The view selected can be any view in the linked file regardless of level as long as the view selected is the same type as the view in the host file. For example, a floor plan or plan view in the linked file will display in a floor plan or plan view in the host file, and a ceiling plan view from the linked file will display in any ceiling plan view in the host file.

The By Linked View setting displays the annotations from the linked file so that it can be used as a reference or for printing. Callout tags and bubble heads from the linked file do not display in the host regardless of which display settings are chosen. The callouts and bubble heads from the linked file reference views and sheets that exist in the linked file and not in the host file, which would cause misleading and erroneous references. You can directly add sections and elevations in the host file using standard view commands and then adjust the display of the linked model to meet the needs of the view.

Figure 12.14

By Linked View settings in the RVT Link Display Settings dialog box

Expand the Linked View list box to see a list of views in the linked file that can be displayed in the current view. These views will display the linked file using the same settings as were used in the linked file.

CUSTOM

Using the Custom setting (Figure 12.15) gives you the most complete control of the display of the linked file. You can adjust the display of the linked file as needed to meet the needs of the view in the host file. Individual model, annotation, and linked categories can be changed, and the display of individual worksets can be toggled on or off using the appropriate tab and selecting custom on that tab.

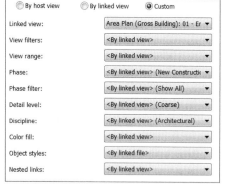

These settings alter the display of the linked file only and do not affect any elements native to the host file.

Many of the settings available on the Basics tab are dependent on the linked view chosen in the Linked View list box. The View Filters and Color Fill options are based on the current status of the linked view from the linked file. The color fill or filter must be active in that view in the linked file in order to be able to display that view in the host file.

Figure 12.15

Custom options on Basics tab

The Custom option allows you to set these values:

Linked View This determines what options are available. This setting allows the view from the linked file to be displayed in the host using all settings, filters, and color fills from the linked view.

View Filters If the view filter is active in the current view, this setting will control whether any host file view filter, view filter from the linked file, or no filter is used to alter the display of the linked file.

View Range This controls whether the view range of the host view or the view range from the linked view is used to display the linked file.

Phase This allows you to select the phase currently set in the host view properties or any phase available in the linked file for control of the display of the linked file.

Phase Filter This allows you to select the phase filter currently set in the host view or any phase filter available in the linked file for control of the display of the linked file.

Detail Level You can choose Coarse, Medium, or Fine for the linked file view, as well as By Linked View and By Host View.

Discipline You can select By Host View, By Linked View, or any standard discipline setting, including the following:

- Architectural
- Structural
- Mechanical
- Electrical
- Coordination

Color Fill You can apply color fills active in either the linked file view or the host file view to the linked file view using this setting. Note that color fills need to be created and active in order to apply this setting.

Object Styles You can assign object styles from the linked file or from the host file to the linked file using this setting.

Nested Links When the linked file has other Revit linked files nested within it, this setting controls whether the view settings of the linked file (By Parent Link) or the view settings of the nested link (By Linked View) are displayed.

RVT Link Display Settings Categories Tabs

You can use the Model, Annotation, Analytical Model, Import Categories, and Worksets tabs to tailor the display of the elements within the linked file using similar commands as those that exist in the host file views under Visibility/Graphic Overrides. Refer to Chapter 6 "Visibility Controls," for additional information about these settings.

On the Basics tab, select the Custom option; the categories tabs cannot be used to adjust the link display unless you are using the Custom setting.

The radio button, at the top center of the dialog box, is set to By Host View by default. You can choose from three possible options:

By Host View Matches the settings used in the Visibility/Graphic settings of the host view.

By Linked View Matches the settings used in the Visibility/Graphic settings of the linked view. This setting will be available only if there is a view selected on the Basics tab in the Linked View list.

Custom Allows full control of each setting within the categories list. Elements within the linked file respond to the settings selected here and override the view's Visibility/Graphic settings.

Worksets

If the linked file is a worksharing-enabled file, an additional tab will be displayed named Worksets (Figure 12.16). Two settings are available in the list box at the top of the dialog box, By Host View and Custom.

Figure 12.16

RVT Link
Display Settings
Worksets tab

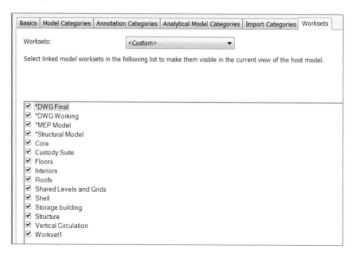

By Host View Worksets in the linked file that have identical names to worksets in the host file assume the on/off display setting of the host view. If no identical name exists, the elements in the linked workset will be set to display.

Custom This allows independent on/off display control of the elements on that workset in the linked file.

Managing Links

Linked files are automatically reloaded when the host file is reopened, which ensures that the linked file displayed is the most recent version. If the linked file is not found when opening the host file, Revit will display an error message to that effect (Figure 12.17).

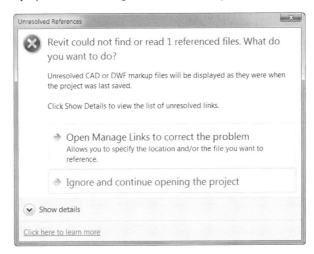

Figure 12.17

**Unresolved Refer-
ences dialog box**

Linked Revit files will not display if the reference is unresolved, while CAD and DWF linked files will display as they were last shown in the host file.

When working on a Revit project, it will be necessary to sometimes manage links using the tools available in the Manage Links dialog box. These tools allow the user to control reloading, unloading, removing, and repathing of the linked file.

You can open the Manage Links dialog box from the Manage tab on the Manage Project panel. It is also available on the Insert tab's Link panel. Four tabs are available in the Manage Links dialog box:

- Revit
- CAD Formats
- DWF Markups
- Point Clouds

Managing Revit Links

On the Revit tab (Figure 12.18), the name of each linked Revit file is shown. Each column shows information about the linked file, and selecting the filename in the Linked File column allows you to make changes to the file. Some columns report information only, while others can be selected to make changes to the linked file's behavior, as shown in Table 12.1.

NAME	PURPOSE	USE
Linked File	Filename.	Select the filename to make changes to the link settings for that link.
Status	Identifies whether file is currently loaded into the project.	Read-only setting that will display Loaded, Unloaded, or Not Found. Not Found indicates an unresolved reference. The saved path column can be used to repath the link.
Reference Type	Overlay or Attachment will be listed. Overlay is the default type. When a file is linked into another as an overlay, the linked file shows only in the host file and not in any subsequent hosts of the current host.	Clicking Overlay in this column will allow the link to be toggled between Overlay and Attachment.
Positions Not Saved	Shows whether the file's coordinates have been saved in the shared coordinate system. This check box indicates that changes to the linked file coordinate system have been made but not saved back to the file.	Read-only.
Saved Path	Displays the path where the linked file was found. (The filename is displayed only if the linked file is stored in the same folder as the host.)	Read-only.
Path Type	Path type listing. The default type is Relative.	Clicking the Path Type listing allows the path type to be toggled between Relative and Absolute.
Local Alias	Displays the path of the workshared linked file.	If the linked file is a local copy of a central file, the path of the local file will be displayed here. The path of the central file will be displayed in the Saved Path column.

Figure 12.18

Manage Links dialog box Revit tab

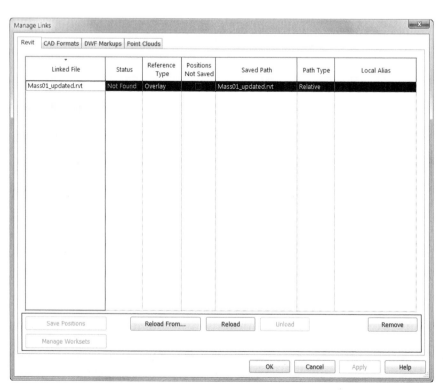

Project Gallery

On the following pages, you will find a combination of images from a few architectural firms rendering in Autodesk Revit Architecture or using the model geometry from Revit Architecture and rendering in other applications. We hope you gain some inspiration from these images.

Joint Base Andrews Ambulatory Care Center

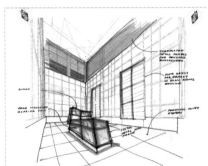

COURTESY: RLF (ROGERS, LOVELOCK, AND FRITZ). RLF ARCHITECTURE | ENGINEERING | INTERIORS. PROGRAM UTILIZED: REVIT.

The Joint Base Andrews Ambulatory Care Center project was given strict criteria by the client in initiating its exterior design. Several iterations were examined and presented to the client through an interchange between sketch and Revit modeling. Sketching was a quick means of conveying the concept, and Revit allowed for a defined study of materiality and daylighting.

The concept for the Joint Base Andrews Ambulatory Care Center project focused on filtering the interior of the building with natural light for the benefit of its occupants. This was accomplished by providing transparent exterior walls, as well as a series of light wells that perforated the interior organization of the main building to maximize daylighting. From initial sketch concepts, Revit was used as a tool to experiment with materiality and scale through section and several three-dimensional techniques.

JE Dunn Headquarters, Kansas City, MO
Architect: 360 Architecture

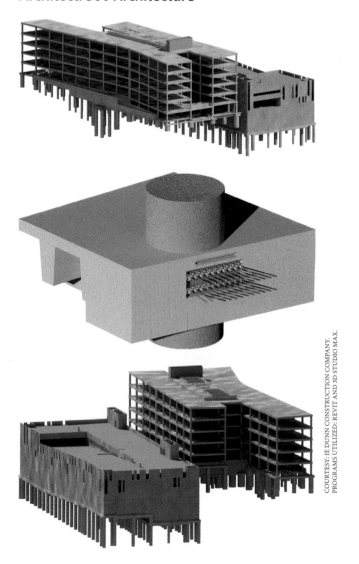

TOP: The JE Dunn Headquarters building is a five-story concrete pan deck system with an adjacent six-level structural precast parking garage. Revit Structure was used extensively during construction to increase productivity of the concrete work put in place, as well as trade coordination where attachments were made to the structure. **MIDDLE:** This is an example of trade-to-trade coordination between curtain wall connections and post-tension anchors. **BOTTOM:** Revit Structure was used on the JE Dunn Headquarters parking garage to do a shop drawing review of the precast structure as well as quality control for the layout of critical precast embeds and connections.

Morrison Architects

COURTESY: MORRISON ARCHITECTS. PROGRAM UTILIZED: REVIT

Contemporary home designed to be energy efficient. **TOP LEFT:** Pool side view **TOP RIGHT:** Interior atrium view looking at sitting area **BOTTOM:** Courtyard overlooking pool

Morrison Architects

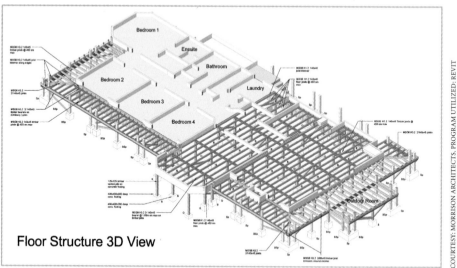

Floor Structure 3D View

COURTESY: MORRISON ARCHITECTS. PROGRAM UTILIZED: REVIT

Villa renovation with contemporary addition but in keeping with features of an old villa home. TOP: Perspective view looking toward veranda extension and new outdoor room BOTTOM: 3D framing and floor structure

Morrison Architects

Energy-efficient new home overlooking Auckland Harbor. Four split levels, including basement, featuring outdoor room with fireplace and cantilevered deck over swimming pool, full height joinery. **TOP LEFT:** High angle view looking toward deck and outdoor room **TOP RIGHT:** Lower garden area **BOTTOM:** Front entry

Morrison Architects

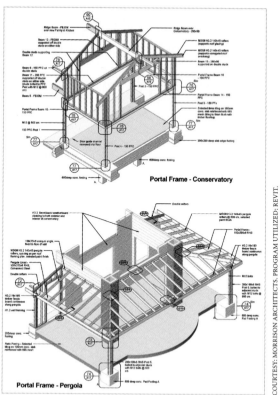

Bungalow renovation with contemporary additions. Featuring new outdoor room with roof glazing and pergola to back of house. **TOP LEFT:** Interior rendering of kitchen and living room **BOTTOM LEFT:** Interior rendering of kitchen. **TOP RIGHT:** 3D framing of outdoor room and pergola

Fort Irwin Hospital Replacement, Fort Irwin, CA
Architect: RLF/Ellerbe Becket Joint Venture

This 216,000-square-foot healthcare facility includes an inpatient community hospital, an outpatient clinic, central energy plant, and ambulance shelter. The facility is located in the High Mojave Desert, and the surrounding rocky landscape creates a unique design environment. Using Revit platforms for architecture, structure, and MEP, the team is using building information modeling (BIM) to meet milestones dictated by the project's aggressive schedule. The project team is currently validating lifecycle costs for sustainable and renewable solutions to meet its targeted goal of LEED-Gold (Leadership in Energy & Environmental Design).

Fort Irwin Mechanical Penthouse Studies

COURTESY: RLF (ROGERS, LOVELOCK, AND FRITZ). PROGRAM UTILIZED: REVIT. RLF ARCHITECTURE | ENGINEERING | INTERIORS. PROGRAM UTILIZED: REVIT.

The Revit multiple-discipline platforms for architecture, structure, and MEP create opportunities to dissect designs and interface, allowing instant validation of concepts. This is an early design effort between disciplines reviewing the functional requirements of mechanical systems while analyzing both the aesthetics and constructability of the building envelope.

Morrison Architects

COURTESY: MORRISON ARCHITECTS. PROGRAM UTILIZED: REVIT.

Three-story house renovation with multiple outdoor living areas. Mix use of weatherboard on timber frame and plaster over concrete block. **TOP LEFT:** Garden looking back toward front entry **TOP RIGHT:** Interior rendering of living room **BOTTOM:** Upper deck looking back into living room

Morrison Architects

Rest home renovation. **TOP:** Front entry **MIDDLE:** Front entry
BOTTOM: Front entry

Morrison Architects

COURTESY: MORRISON ARCHITECTS. PROGRAM UTILIZED: REVIT.

Bungalow alteration and addition. Gable roofs in keeping with the existing house and surrounding neighboring homes. Ivy walls to main level.

TOP: View from rear yard looking back toward house
MIDDLE: View toward front entry **BOTTOM:** Street view

Altman Beauchene Architects

TOP: Looking south into the project **MIDDLE:** Plan view rendering of the site. **BOTTOM:** Looking north into the project

Daniel Hernandez, Advanced Dipl. Arch.

BANQUET HALL DESIGN, PROJECT RENDERINGS, EXTERIOR VIEWS

The exterior of this banquet hall is made up of brick, concrete blocks, precast concrete brackets, quoins and paneling. The exterior pot lighting in the soffit lends a dramatic feel to this building, as well as lighting the adjacent sidewalk to the connected parking lot.

BANQUET HALL DESIGN, PROJECT RENDERINGS, INTERIOR VIEWS

This traditional style building is framed using large steel beams and columns to allow larger open spaces and flexibility for hosting large parties and events without structural columns taking away from the space. The steel framing is encased in wood paneling to lend a richer look and elegance to the space. Soft lighting directed up toward the high arched ceilings brightens up the rooms without an excess amount of visible lighting fixtures, making the enormous chandelier a focal point.

E. E. & A. Designs

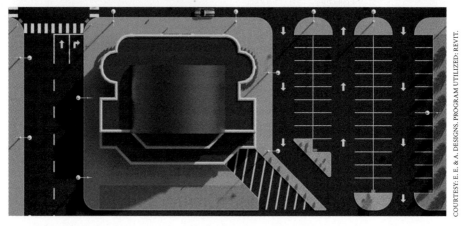

This is a project called Dover Theatrics located on the southeast corner of Queen Street and Loockerman Street. The building is a theater and museum. **TOP LEFT:** Northeast perspective **TOP RIGHT:** Front hallway **BOTTOM:** Site

Highplans

COURTESY: HIGHPLANS. PROGRAM UTILIZED: REVIT.

COMMERCIAL PROPERTY, PROJECT RENDERINGS

A small block of commercial units with apartments above. There is an open walkway to the apartments covered by the louvres. The rendering was completed to show the planners that the apartments could be added but concealed.

Osborn Architects

JPL MISSION OPERATIONS CENTER, PROJECT RENDERINGS

Osborn was selected by Jet Propulsion Laboratory (JPL) to provide schematic design services for its new 130,000-square-foot six-story $80 million Mission Operations Center. Occupying a strategic corner location, the new facility is sited through a comprehensive campus master plan. The current and future building placement allows a new performative landscape that conducts people and water through the steep terrain of the JPL campus. The new associated plazas and landscapes further enhance the ecological character and human habitation of the site through chaparral plantings, woodland groves, and outdoor meeting decks.

The proposed building animates the site with the movement of the sun and the creation of shadow, while movement of people through exposed stairs further activates the facades. As the sun goes down, the emergence of light from within the building will communicate its active function. While in this early stage, the design has pursued some elemental strategies to assist in achieving a LEED-Silver rating through the careful siting, sun control, and energy production strategies. **TOP LEFT:** Exterior rendering **TOP RIGHT:** Exterior rendering **BOTTOM:** Mars interior

Here are the actions of the various buttons at the bottom of the Manage Links dialog box:

Remove Removes the link, and any association to it, from the host file. Note this command cannot be undone, and the file would have to be linked in again if it was needed.

Unload Unloads the link from the host file but maintains the link association.

Reload Reloads linked files. The files may need to be updated so that the most current linked file is displayed or a linked file that has been unloaded is reloaded. Linked files automatically reload only when you open the host file. If any changes have been saved to the linked file, they will not display in the host file until the linked file is reloaded.

Reload From Used to restore links that are unresolved. Navigate to the new location of the linked file, and select the file.

Save Positions Allows the user to save positions to the selected linked file. If the linked file is moved and the positions are not saved, the file will revert to its last saved position when reopened.

Manage Worksets Opens the Manage Worksets dialog box. Worksets can be manually opened or closed in the Worksets dialog box. Worksets that are not opened do not display and are not loaded into the current session. This improves computer performance by reducing the size of the working model memory footprint.

Managing CAD and DWF Links

In addition to the commands listed earlier, linked CAD files have two additional commands available in the Manage Links dialog box:

Preserve Graphic Overrides This box is selected by default. When selected, any changes made to the graphic display of the linked CAD file are saved when the file is saved and subsequently reopened.

Import The linked CAD file is converted from a link to an import and is imported into the host file.

The DWF Markups tab has two additional commands that affect markup DWF files:

Save Markups Saves any changes made to the DWF markup file in Revit to the DWF file for review in Autodesk Design Review.

Located In Displays the sheet or sheets that a DWF linked file is linked to. Linked DWF files can be linked to more than one view.

Managing Point Clouds

The *Point Clouds* tab has a smaller set of commands available than for the other types of linked files. Point cloud files are created by using laser scanners to scan existing environments and buildings.

Remove Removes the link, and any association to it, from the host file. Note this command cannot be undone, and the file would have to be linked in again if it were needed.

Unload Unloads the link from the host file but maintains the link association.

Reload Reloads linked files. The files may need to be updated so that the most current linked file is displayed or a linked file that has been unloaded is reloaded. Linked files automatically reload only when you open the host file. If any changes have been saved to the linked file, they will not display in the host file until the linked file is reloaded.

Reload From Used to restore links that are unresolved. Navigate to the new location of the linked file, and select the file.

Tagging Linked Revit Models

This release of Revit can tag certain elements within linked files, allowing you to generate fully coordinated documentation models from a single file created from individual linked files. Most linked model element tags and symbols can be placed in the host file with the exception of the following types:

- Space tags
- Zone tags
- Path reinforcement span symbols
- Area reinforcement span symbols

Tagging elements is accomplished using the Tag By Category command (see Figure 12.19) or the Tag All Not Tagged command. When using the Tag All Not Tagged command, select the Include Elements From Linked Files check box to tag elements from the linked file. The process of adding tags is the same as adding tags for elements that exist directly in the host file.

Figure 12.19

Tag By Category

The different behavior will appear when elements in the linked file are deleted that have been previously tagged in the host file. Tags that read information from elements directly in the host file will always be up to date. If the properties of the element they are tagging are changed, the tag will update; and if the element that they are tagging is deleted from the model, they will be deleted automatically (see Table 12.2). Tags hosted by elements in linked files behave differently than tags hosted by elements in the host file depending on the status of the linked file and the types of changes made to the linked tagged element.

ACTION	TAG BEHAVIOR	REPAIR PROCEDURE
Properties of the linked elements are changed in the linked file.	Tags automatically update when linked file is reloaded.	None required.
Linked element is deleted from the linked file.	When file is reloaded, a warning message is displayed (Figure 12.20). Tags display question marks indicating that they have become orphaned. Orphaned tags displaying a question mark will print and not automatically be prevented from printing.	Use the Reconcile Hosting command to review and repair the orphaned tags.
Linked file is unloaded from the host file or unresolved.	Tags do not display in the host file.	Upon reloading the unloaded link, the tags reappear and display the correct information.
Linked file is removed from host or deleted from host.	Tags are deleted from host file.	Tags will need to be reapplied to the elements once the file is relinked into the host.

Table 12.2

Linked tag behaviors

Figure 12.20

Missing element warning

Reconcile Hosting Tool

Once a warning has been displayed alerting you to the fact that an element is missing from the linked file, start the Reconcile Hosting tool from the Collaborate tab's Coordinate panel.

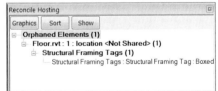

The Reconcile Hosting browser (Figure 12.21) is a modal window that allows you to work on the model while keeping the browser open and accessible. The browser displays the number of orphaned elements, the linked filename that the missing elements are reported from, the category of tag that is missing, and the individual lines for each orphaned tag.

Reconcile Hosting

Figure 12.21

Reconcile Hosting browser

There are three options buttons at the top of the browser:

Graphics The Graphics option (Figure 12.22) provides tools to change the line weight, line color, and line pattern of the orphaned tags to make them easier to view on the screen.

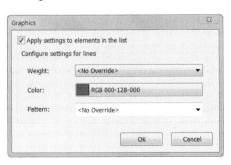

Figure 12.22

Graphics settings

Sort The list of orphaned tags can be sorted by link and then by category, or it can be sorted by category and then by link.

Show After selecting an orphaned tag or tags from the Reconcile Hosting browser, selecting Show will zoom the view centered on the orphaned tags (Figure 12.23).

Figure 12.23

Result of Show

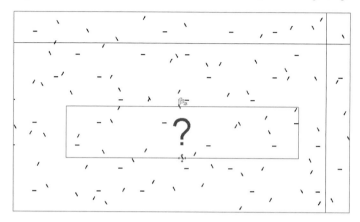

Orphaned tags can be deleted either individually or as a group and, if appropriate, can be relinked to a different object individually. Right-clicking the linked filename in the Reconcile Hosting browser or right-clicking the tag category offers a Delete command to remove all the orphaned tags at one time.

Right-clicking one individual orphaned tag allows the user either to delete the tag or to select a new host (Figure 12.24). If you choose Pick Host, you will be able to select a new host. The host must be the same Revit category as the previously deleted host.

Figure 12.24

Context menu options

You can select multiple individual orphaned items by choosing one item, pressing the Shift key, and then selecting an additional item in the list. Not only will the two items be selected, but all the items in between will be selected. Regardless of how multiple items are selected, the only option is to delete the tags.

Working with CAD Files

Revit supports the import and export of CAD file formats (listed in Table 12.3) for a variety of uses in both 2D and 3D formats. Files can be imported for use in site plan views, as backgrounds for beginning a model, for detail drawings, or for use in three-dimensional massing models for massing studies and element creation.

FORMAT	IMPORT	EXPORT
DWG	All versions	2000, 2004, 2007, 2010
DXF	All versions	2000, 2004, 2007, 2010
DGN	Version 7	Version 7
SAT	Version 6	Version 6
SKP	All versions	None

Table 12.3

File formats supported

Linking or Importing DWG

Revit Architecture offers many tools for working with DWG files. These tools are available regardless of what application was used to create the files. Many CAD applications and other BIM applications by default create file formats not listed in Table 12.3. These applications may have the capability of creating DWG files. DWG files would provide an easy method of bringing in files from various other applications.

All the CAD files listed in the table can be linked or imported into the Revit model. Linking is generally the preferred approach because it is easier to remove the file and not leave behind any unwanted artifacts or element types. In addition, linked files will be updated if the linked file changes. Regardless of which method is selected, the conversion of line weights is identical.

Choose Link CAD or Import CAD on the Insert tab's Link or Import panel (Figure 12.25). The dialog box that opens has the same positioning settings as outlined in the "Linking Revit Models" section earlier in this chapter.

Figure 12.25

CAD-specific settings

Choose the type of file to load from the Files Of Type list:

- DWG – AutoCAD-based products
- DXF – AutoCAD exchange format
- DGN – MicroStation-based products
- SAT – Standard ACIS text
- SKP – SketchUp

Selecting the Current View Only check box limits the display of the linked or imported CAD file to the view that was active when the file was brought into the project file. If this box is not selected, the CAD file will be visible in *all* views, including 3D views and elevations. This will require the user to manage the display of the CAD file in many views. Selecting this check box will produce a much cleaner Revit project environment and eliminate the need to change the display settings in all of the other views in the host project so that the linked or imported file will not display.

Your choices for the Colors setting are as follows:

Black And White This option will make the import appear the same as default Revit objects and discard the colors from the import. This is the preferred method of linking and importing for printing purposes.

Preserve This option retains the colors from the imported file and displays those colors in the Revit project.

Invert This option inverts the colors of the imported file. This may be helpful for some files if they were originally created with colors that displayed well on a dark background but are difficult to see on the default light Revit background.

For the Layers setting, you can choose from these options:

All This loads all the layers of the imported file regardless of their current state.

Visible This loads only the layers currently visible in the imported file.

Specify Once the import/link is started, a list box will appear allowing the user to choose the specific layers to load. This is the most efficient method of loading the file but may require the user to be familiar with the file.

Under Import Units, these values are available:

Auto-Detect This reads the units of the import/link file and adjusts the file scale to match the current Revit project. This usually works well with recent DWG files but may not with older DWG files and DGN files.

Units Choose the units that the CAD file was drawn in.

Custom Factor Set a scale factor to be applied upon loading the CAD file.

The Place At setting assigns the import/link file to a specific level of the Revit project. The Orient To View check box aligns the import or link with the current view.

Import Settings: Line Weights

Line weights of imported DWG and DXF files are controlled by a customizable text file. This file can be adapted for various files received from different consultants or internal files. The files can be saved and made active whenever necessary in order to automatically change the line weights of the objects in the linked or imported DWG or DXF file. In addition, the version that the DWG file was created in will affect the import line weights, as shown in Table 12.4.

FILE TYPE	SOURCE FILE PLOT TYPE	INSERTION METHOD	REVIT LINE WEIGHT
DWG	STB (Named Plot Styles)	Link	Line weight by AutoCAD layer line weight.
			Object line weight overrides are retained.
DWG	STB (Named Plot Styles)	Import	Line weight by AutoCAD layer line weight.
			Object line weight overrides are retained.
DWG	STB (Named Plot Styles)	Exploded	Line weight by AutoCAD layer line weight.
			Object line weight overrides are discarded, and the objects revert to the layer line weight.
DWG	CTB (Color Table Plot Styles)	Link	Line weight by AutoCAD layer color.
			Object line weight overrides are discarded.
			Object color overrides are discarded.
DWG	CTB (Color Table Plot Styles)	Import	Line weight by AutoCAD layer color.
			Object line weight overrides are retained.
			Object color overrides are discarded.
DWG	CTB (Color Table Plot Styles)	Exploded	Line weight by AutoCAD layer color.
			Object line weight overrides are discarded, and the objects revert to the layer color line weight.
			Object color overrides are discarded.
DXF	Release 12	All	Object line weight by color.
DXF	R2000 & Newer	All	Object line weight by color.
			Object line weight overrides are retained.

Table 12.4

Imported DWG/ DXF line weight conversion

You can access the import line weight settings on the Insert tab's Import panel. The small dialog box launcher arrow (Figure 12.26) at the bottom-right corner of the panel will open the Import Line Weights dialog box (Figure 12.27).

Figure 12.26

Insert panel and arrow

Figure 12.27

Import Line Weights dialog box

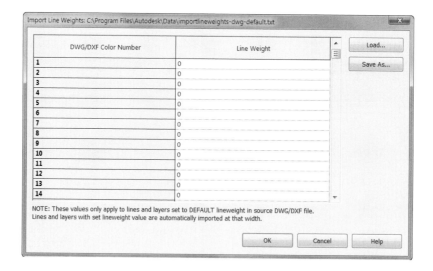

The left column lists 255 AutoCAD colors and will convert the lines, polylines, arc, circles, and so on of that color or the layer line weight to the Revit line weight chosen in the right column. The line weights are controlled in the standard Revit Line Weights dialog box (accessed via the Manage tab's Additional Settings button).

At the top right of the Import Line Weights dialog box are two buttons. The Load button allows you to load a previously saved file to make those settings active, and Save As allows you to save the current settings for future use. Common custom file uses are for internal detail drawings or to match the standards of a repeat client. The default path for Windows 7 is

```
C:\program Files\Autodesk\Revit Architecture 2012\Data
```

Five preconfigured import standards are stored in the Data folder and ship with the program:

```
importlineweights-dwg-AIA.txt
importlineweights-dwg-BS1192.txt
importlineweights-dwg-CP83.txt
importlineweights-dwg-default.txt
importlineweights-dwg-ISO13567.txt
```

Any import standard that is set as active, or created, will remain active until another is set active.

Fonts

TrueType fonts are displayed in Revit using the same font as the original text as long as the font exists on the host computer. For SHX fonts, Revit displays text in a linked file and matches the font as closely as it can when the DWG file is inserted into the Revit file. For imported files, Revit automatically creates a text family type and assigns a font to the imported text. To control the fonts of SHX-based text being imported into Revit, edit the Shxfontmap.txt file. This file is located in the Data folder of the Revit installation directory.

Here is an example of two additional lines added to the file:

```
Txt.shx     Arial
Romans.shx   Arial
```

The SHX font name and its extension are listed in the left column, and after a tab, the Windows TrueType font name is listed in the right column. Edit the file as needed and save the changes. Revit does not need to be restarted; the file is read during each import or link.

Display Control

The display of imported or linked DWG files is controlled using the Visibility/Graphic Overrides display settings. The Imported Categories tab (Figure 12.28) displays all linked and imported CAD files in the current project. Each file can be expanded to display a list of layers, or levels. The file can be set to display or not by selecting the check box to the left of the filename, or it can be set to display differently by overriding the settings for Projection/Surface. Similar to other elements in Revit, the line weight, color, and line patterns can be changed per view.

Figure 12.28

Imported Categories tab

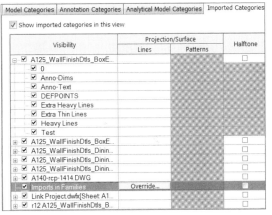

Exporting DWG

The capability to customize the export of DWG files offers multiple benefits to Revit users. Often you will be involved with either consultants or clients who prefer a DWG file as a working file or as part of the package of deliverable files. The options discussed in the following sections allow you to customize the exported file to meet the receiver's standards.

You can access the Export settings by clicking the application menu and selecting Export → Options → Export Setups DWG/DXF. This opens the Modify DWG/DXF Export Setup window. This window has a Select Export Setup panel and eight tabs for configuring the DWG/DXF file export (Figure 12.29).

Export Setups DWG/DXF

Figure 12.29

Modify DWG/
DXF Export Setup
window

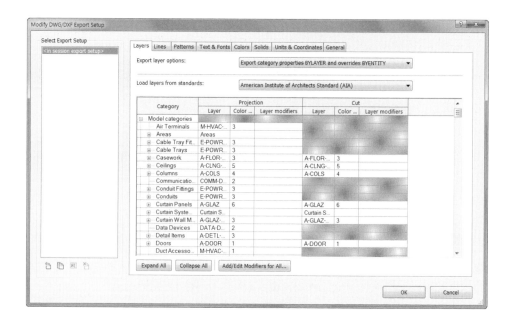

Figure 12.29

Modify DWG/
DXF Export Setup
window

Select Export Setup Panel

The Select Export Setup panel lists all export setups that have been created in this project. Export setups are project specific but can be shared among different projects using the Transfer Project Standards tool. Export setups can also be saved in a template file for use on any new projects based on that template.

Figure 12.30

Export Setup
buttons

At the bottom of the panel are four buttons (Figure 12.30) that allow the user to create a new export setup, duplicate an existing export setup, rename an existing export setup, or delete an existing export setup. An export setup stores all of the settings from all of the tabs in the Modify DWG/DXF Export Setup window. When editing an export setup, select the previously saved export setup in the panel, and any changes made to settings will be automatically saved to the export setup.

New Export Setup Creates a new export setup using the default settings and prompts you for a name.

Duplicate Export Setup Copies the selected existing export setup and prompts you for a name.

Rename Export Setup Prompts you for a new name for the selected export setup.

Delete Export Setup Deletes the selected export setup without a prompt. The delete can be undone only by exiting the Modify DWG/DXF Export Setup window and selecting Undo, which will roll back all operations that were performed during the previous use of the window.

Layers Tab

Customizing the layers generated in the DWG file provides a means to create DWG files that meet a specific client or deliverable requirement.

Export Layer Options The Export Layer Options list box has three options, as outlined in Table 12.5.

Table 12.5

Export Layer Options

OPTION	RESULT
Export Category Properties BYLAYER And Overrides BYENTITY	All objects of the category are placed on the same layer. Elements with display overrides on them are also placed on the same layer but with overrides by object.
Export All Properties BYLAYER, But Do Not Export Overrides	All objects are placed on the same layer with properties set to BYLAYER.
Export All Properties BYLAYER, And Create New Layers For Overrides	All properties are set to BYLAYER, overridden objects placed on a new layer.

Load Layers From Standards Four layer standards ship with Revit Architecture, and an option is available to load preexisting custom layer standards text files created in prior versions of Revit products. The ability to save layer standards text files no longer exists; export setups replaced that function.

LAYER NAMES AND COLORS

The middle area of the tab window contains a matrix of all the categories and subcategories available from the Revit file (Figure 12.31). This includes all objects from Revit Architecture, Revit Structure, and Revit MEP. In addition, any imported DWG files will be listed, with each layer having its own subcategory line.

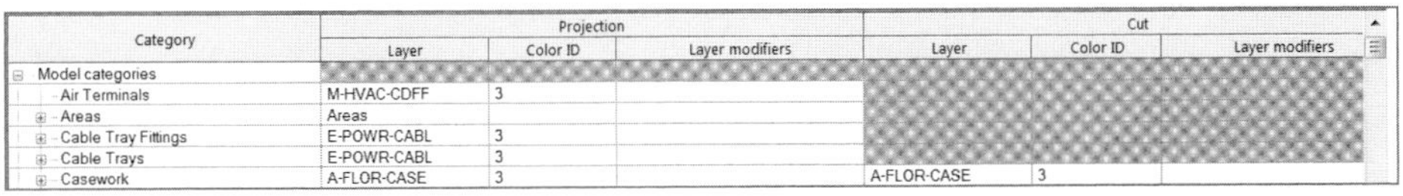

Figure 12.31

Export layer list

Layer names can be edited by clicking in the Layer column and typing the desired layer name. For color selection, you can type a color number (1–255) in the Color ID column. You can do this for both the projection lines and the cut lines.

LAYER MODIFIERS

There are Modifier columns for Projection and Cut.

The list of modifiers (Figure 12.32) is predefined and cannot be added to or removed from. Layer modifiers allow additional information to be included in the layer names of the exported file. Modifiers may be grouped into the following general categories:

- Automatic: Level, View Type
- Project Specific: Workset, Phase Created

- Informative: Function, Structural Usage
- User Custom: Custom1, Underlay

Figure 12.32

Layer Modifiers list

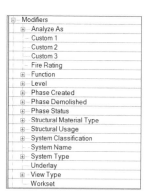

Modifiers can be applied to individual categories or to multiple categories at once. Some modifiers can be applied to all categories by clicking the Add/Edit Modifiers For All button below the matrix.

The Add/Edit Layer Modifiers window that appears has a panel on the left that contains modifiers available to be added to all categories. Choose the desired modifier from the left panel and click the Add Modifier button in the center of the window, shown in Figure 12.33, to add it to the list on the right.

Figure 12.33

**Add/Edit Layer
Modifiers**

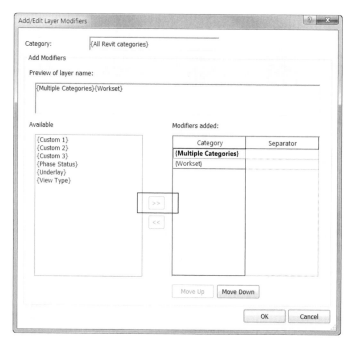

You can add separators to the layer name by typing the desired separator after the modifier where you want it to appear. In this example (Figure 12.34), we placed a hyphen

Figure 12.34

Name separator

Modifiers added:		
Category		Separator
{Multiple Categories}		-
{Workset}		

Figure 12.35

**Resulting
layer name**

after the {Multiple Categories} modifier and the layer in the exported DWG file reads as A-WALL-Shell (Figure 12.35). Modifiers display only at the time they are added to the window. Once you click OK to close the window, the modifiers will not display upon subsequent opening of the window, however they will still be in

- A-WALL-PATT-Storage building
- A-WALL-Shell
- A-WALL-Storage building
- A-WALL-Vertical Circulation

place and will be visible when you edit individual categories and in the Modifier column in the matrix.

Even though the separator is not visible in the window, upon reopening the Add/Edit Layer Modifiers window you will still be able to edit the separator.

To add layer modifiers to individual categories, select the category, or multiple categories if desired, click in the Modifier column to display the Add/Edit Modifier button, and pick the button (Figure 12.36). The same Add/Edit window will open; you can add modifiers to only the selected categories. Note that the separator will appear in this window because it is specific to the category selected. You will need to add the modifier(s) to both the Projection and the Cut columns where applicable.

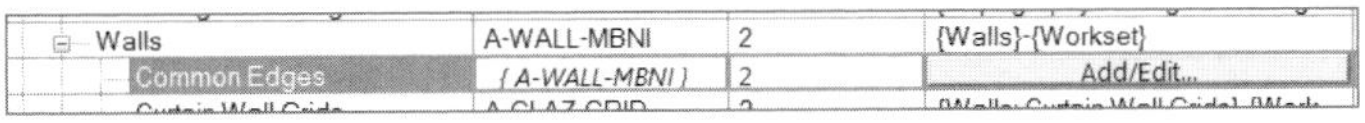

Figure 12.36

Add/Edit button modifier

In order to export linked Revit files that have been set to display as Underlay and have them created on their own layer and color, set the linked file to display as Underlay in the Visibility/Graphic Overrides window by checking the Underlay box. Then choose the Layers tab of the Modify DWG/DXF Export Setup window and set the Underlay modifier to the desired color and layer name (Figure 12.37). Make sure that you select Export All Properties BYLAYER, But Do Not Export Overrides, and perform the export.

Figure 12.37

Resulting layer in DWG file

Lines Tab

The Lines tab lets you specify how line patterns in Revit are converted when exported (Table 12.6). There are three settings that control how lines are exported to DWG: the linetype scale setting, the .lin file to use for linetypes, and the individual mapping of specific line patterns.

OPTION	RESULT
Scaled Linetype Definitions	This option exports linetypes based on the previously scaled by view scale. This option preserves graphical intent.
Modelspace (PSLTSCALE = 0)	Sets the LTSCALE parameter to view scale and the PSLTSCALE variable to 0.
Paperspace (PSLTSCALE = 1)	Sets both LTSCALE and PSLTSCALE to 1

Table 12.6

Export Layer Options

Load DWG Linetypes From is used to point to a specific file to use for this export setup. You can then convert a Revit line pattern to any specific linetype available in the .lin file specified in the dropdown list. This includes complex linetypes. Once you've selected the .lin file, choose a pattern from the Revit Line Patterns column on the left and select the linetype to map to in the right column. Individual or multiple selections can be mapped in one step. If you don't choose a mapping, the export will use the default Automatically Generate Linetypes method as in prior releases of Revit. Clicking the Reset All button will set all of the mapping back to the default, Automatically Generate Linetypes.

Patterns Tab

The Patterns tab lets you specify how Revit fill patterns are converted when exported to DWG files. There are two settings available. You can specify a specific .pat file to use for the DWG hatch patterns and then choose the Revit fill patterns to map to specific DWG hatch patterns. Clicking the Reset All button will set all pattern mappings back to the default, Automatically Generate Hatch Pattern, as used in prior releases of Revit.

Note that you must choose the pattern type of Model or Drafting to see those particular patterns in the list.

Text & Fonts Tab

Two settings are available here that control how text is exported from Revit to DWG. The Text Treatment During Export setting has two options:

Exact (Formatting Intelligence Will Be Lost) Text will appear exactly as exported but will lose bulleting and numbered list functionality.

Approximate (Formatting Intelligence Will Be Maintained) Text appearance may vary, but functionality will be retained.

Once you choose the export setting, specific text fonts in Revit can be mapped to specific text fonts in the DWG file. The font list is generated from the operating system font list and shows only fonts that are compatible with Revit. Text in the DWG file will be created using the specified font but will use the standard text style.

Clicking Reset All changes all text mapping back to the Automatically Map Font default setting.

Colors Tab

Here you can select whether colors in the DWG file are created using Index Color or True Color:

Index Color Objects will be exported to DWG and use the index colors. Object and layer colors will be based on the closest index color and may not exactly match.

True Color Objects will be exported using true colors and will match the Revit object color exactly.

Solids Tab

When you export 3D views from Revit, the resulting DWG file will be a 3D model. 3D models will be exported as meshes or solids based on the selection in this tab.

Polymesh Exports geometry as polymeshes.

ACIS Solids Exports geometry as ACIS solids unless geometry is already a polymesh. (Toposurfaces are an example.)

Units & Coordinates Tab

This tab determines what the unit setting in the DWG file will be set to and also whether the Revit model is exported using the Project Internal coordinates or the active Shared coordinates.

Project Internal This exports the DWG files based on the Revit origin and matches that to the DWG origin.

Shared This exports the geometry based on the active shared coordinate system. This is accurate only for views that do not export from sheet views.

General Tab

Settings on the General tab allow you to include room and area information or to preset layers to be non-plottable in the DWG file.

Room and Area Boundaries If Export Rooms And Areas As Polylines is checked, all rooms and areas will be exported onto a single layer each as closed polylines.

Non-plottable Layers Checking this option and adding the appropriate text to the window will make any layers containing that text non-plottable. This could also be used with one of the custom modifiers to make specific category layers non-plottable.

Default Export Options These are the default settings for exporting files, but you can override them on a case-by-case basis.

Export Views On Sheets And Links As External References Checking this option creates more files because the output will generate page setup files in addition to the DWG files. What works best may be up to the firm receiving the files to decide.

Export To File Format Select the desired output file format; the choices are AutoCAD 2010, 2007, 2004, and 2000.

This completes our discussion of export setup creation. Export setups can and should be a part of your template or templates so that multiple users can perform exports quickly and consistently.

Exporting DWG Files

Once the export setup is complete, to export the DWG files select the Application menu → Export → CAD Formats → DWG to open the DWG Export window (see Figures 12.38 and 12.39).

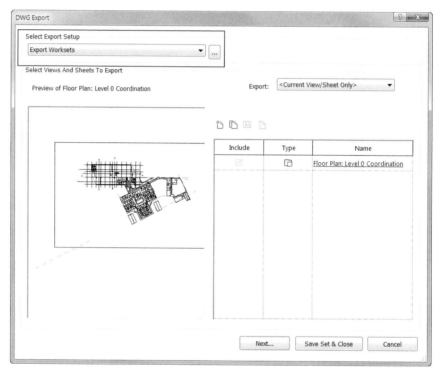

You will use this window to assign an export setup to the DWG files and to select which views will be exported.

EXPORT SETUPS

In the DWG Export window, select any preconfigured export setups from the drop-down list. If no export setups have been created, <In Session Export Setup> will be the only option available and will use the most recent settings. You may also click the browse button at the right end of the Select Export Setup drop-down list to open the Modify DWG/DXF Export Setup window. Then you can either make changes to the setup or create new setups. There is no difference in the use of the window when opening it using this method.

VIEW SELECTION

Views, sheets, or both can be exported to DWG or DXF files. The default setting in the Export list box is Current View/Sheet Only, and it will export a single view, or sheet, to a DWG file.

Opening the Export list box allows the user to select In Session View/ Sheet Set for the export instead of the Current View/Sheet Only selection (Figure 12.40). This offers additional options and settings to control the export of views and sheets (Figure 12.41).

Figure 12.40

In Session View/ Sheet Set

From the Show In List drop-down list, choose the types of views, sheets, or a combination of both that you want to see displayed in the panel options:

Views In The Set Displays all views in a previously saved set.

Sheets In The Set Displays all sheets in a previously saved set.

All Views And Sheets In The Set Displays all views and sheets in a previously saved set.

Views In The Model Displays all views in the project.

Sheets In The Model Displays all sheets in the project.

All Views And Sheets In The Model Displays all views and sheets in the project.

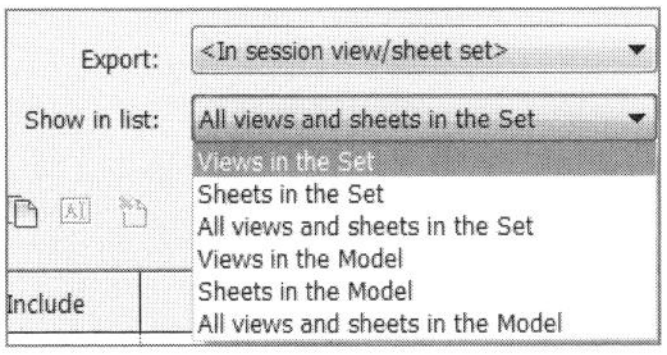

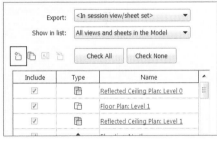

Figure 12.41

Selection options

Choose one of the options, and the panel below the options will fill in with views and/ or sheets (Figure 12.42). You can select Check All or Check None, or you can select views or sheets individually to add or remove them from the selection.

Once you have selected a set of sheets to be exported, you can group the selection set into a new set. (This is optional but can save time when the same set of views will be exported repeatedly during a project.) The New Set button is highlighted in Figure 12.42. Click the button and then type a name for the set to save the selection for future use. Some common uses are to save all plan sets, all elevations, full sets, and so on.

Once you've named the set, select the views that you would like included in the set. Saves to the set are automatic. Once created, the set will be available for selection in the Export list box for this and for future exports. The set appears as shown in Figure 12.43.

Figure 12.42

Sheet/view selection

After the views and sheets have been selected, click Next at the bottom of the DWG Export dialog box. The Export CAD Formats dialog box (Figure 12.44) allows you to provide a name for the exported file, a prefix to the filename for multiple files, and where the exported files are to be saved.

Figure 12.43

Saved selection set

Figure 12.44

Export CAD Formats dialog box

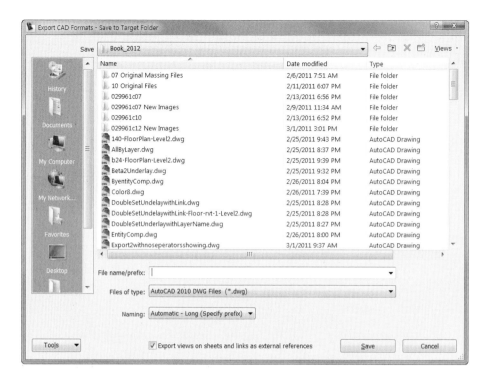

The Naming options are as follows:

Automatic – Long (Specify Prefix) Manually specify a prefix in the File Name/Prefix field or accept the default, which uses this format:

Revit Sheet/View: Project Name-View Type-View Name

(The prefix name cannot be blank.)

Automatic – Short Revit Architecture determines the name of the file automatically. The format is as follows:

Revit Sheet: Sheet Name or Revit View: View Type-View Name

Manual This is available only when exporting Current View/Sheet Only export settings. The complete filename can be entered manually.

You also have the option to override in which DWG format the files will be exported, which was set in the export setup. Choose the appropriate format for this export only from the Files Of Type list box. DWG files are always forward compatible, meaning that an older-format DWG file can be opened in a newer software release, but an older software version will not open a DWG file saved in a newer format.

You can also choose to override the export option for Xrefs that was set in the export setup, again for this export only.

Importing and Exporting DGN Files

DGN files can be linked, imported, and exported like DWG and DXF files. Unlike DWG/DXF files, no customization settings are available when importing a DGN file; customization settings are available that control the output when exporting a Revit model to DGN.

DGN files link to Revit and display exactly as they were displayed in MicroStation except for the color overrides chosen during the link process. Imported DGN files display exactly as displayed in MicroStation except the line weights will be lost during the import.

Most 3D elements from DGN are supported for Revit linking and importing with the exception of cones, B-spline surfaces, and smart solids.

Exporting a DGN file from a Revit file allows the user to choose various level and template settings that will help tailor the DGN file to the user's needs.

To export to DGN, choose the Application menu ➤ Export ➤ CAD Formats and then select the file type DGN to open the DGN Export Settings window (see Figure 12.45).

The Views/Sheets tab (Figure 12.45) offers the same selection and saving options as explained in the "Exporting DWG" section earlier in this chapter. Refer to that section for an explanation of how to save sets for future use. All sets created for export whether through DWG export or DGN export are available for either export operation.

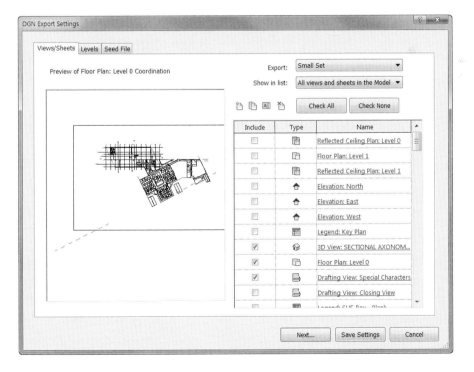

Figure 12.45

DGN Export Settings' Views/Sheets tab

The DGN Levels tab (Figure 12.46) will let the user customize the output to match an existing standard or a client standard by picking the Level Settings button

Figure 12.46

**DGN Level
Settings Window**

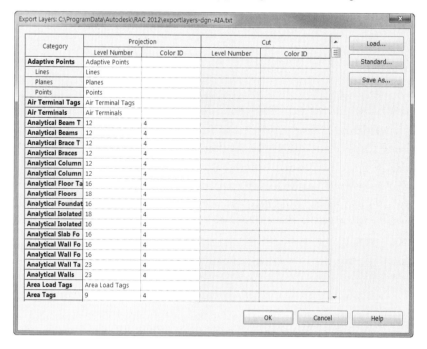

To set the level color and level names for the export, do the following:

1. Click the Layer Settings button on the Levels tab.

    The left column of the dialog box that opens lists all the categories and subcategories available from the Revit file. This includes all objects from Revit Architecture, Revit Structure, and Revit MEP. In addition, any imported CAD files will be listed, with each level having its own subcategory line.

2. Select Level Numbers in the left column, and type a color ID number (1–255) in the far-right column.

    Do this for both the projection lines and the cut lines. You can export the settings by clicking the Save As button at the top right of the dialog box. Clicking the Load button will load previously saved export settings files, and clicking the Standard button will bring up a list of predefined export settings files. Selection sets that you have saved for DWG/DXF export and any that have been saved for DGN export will be available for selection.

3. Once you've created an export standard, click OK at the bottom of the Export Layers dialog box.

    These settings are also accessible from the Application Menu → Export → Options location.

4. Select the Seed File tab, shown in Figure 12.47, to enable a DGN template (a Micro-Station seed file).

5. Select the Use DGN Seed File For Export check box.

6. Click the browse button to the far right of the list box to browse for a suitable DGN template file.

7. Click Next at the bottom of the dialog box to start the export process.

Figure 12.47

DGN Seed File tab

DGN files are saved one view or sheet to a file in the selected folder. The naming options are identical to the DWG naming options noted earlier.

Exporting DWF Files

DWF and DWFx files (Drawing Web Format; see Table 12.7) can be used to share designs with clients, consultants, or anyone else who would need access to the design information and project data. Both DWF and DWFx files can be exported in 2D or 3D formats depending on the intended use for the file. 2D DWF files can be used to review design data, to perform quantity takeoffs (requires additional software, such as QTO), and to function as backgrounds in CAD designs or to plot the design set remotely, even to scale if desired. Parameters and properties associated with model elements can also be included in the file. 3D DWFs can be used for presentations and model review. Design Review, which installs along with Revit and is available as a download from Autodesk, will display both types of DWF and DWFx files. In addition, the Microsoft XPS viewer will display DWFx 2D files. The XPS viewer is included with Windows Vista and Windows 7 and is available for download for Windows XP.

> DWFx files are slightly larger because of their support of the XPS viewer.

FILE TYPE	VIEWER
DWF	Design Review Viewer: Full 2D and 3D support, password protection, parameter information
DWFx	Design Review Viewer: Full 2D and 3D support, password protection, parameter information
	XPS Viewer: Parameter information support, no 3D support, no password support

Table 12.7

DWF format comparison

The export command for DWF files is available by choosing the Application menu → Export → DWF/DWFx (Figure 12.48). The type of view or views that you select for export will determine the type of DWF file that is exported. Any 2D views will be exported as 2D DWF files or views within a file, while any 3D views will be exported as 3D DWF files or 3D views within a DWF file. Both types of views can exist within one file.

Figure 12.48

**Exporting
DWF/DWFx**

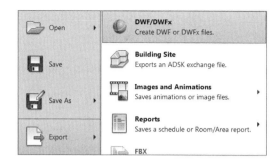

The DWF Export Settings dialog box is shown in Figure 12.49 open to the Views/ Sheets tab. The Views/Sheets tab has the same capabilities and functions as it does in the CAD export commands. It also shares the same saved sets as the CAD file export. Please refer to that section for additional information.

Figure 12.49

**DWF Export
Settings dialog box**

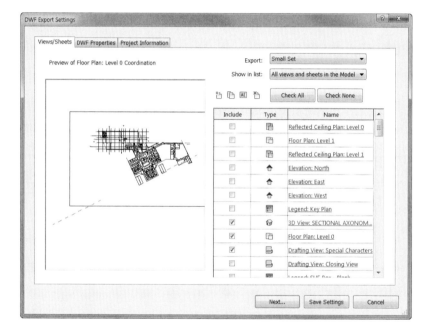

The DWF Properties tab (Figure 12.50) controls how the DWF file is exported, including what is placed in the file during import, what the quality level is, whether properties are exported in addition to the geometry and annotations, and how rooms and areas are exported.

Element Properties Controls whether element properties (parameters) are included in the export. This includes both type and instance properties.

Rooms And Areas In A Separate Boundary Layer Exports room and area boundaries to a separate layer. This allows the room and area data to be more easily viewed separately from the file geometry.

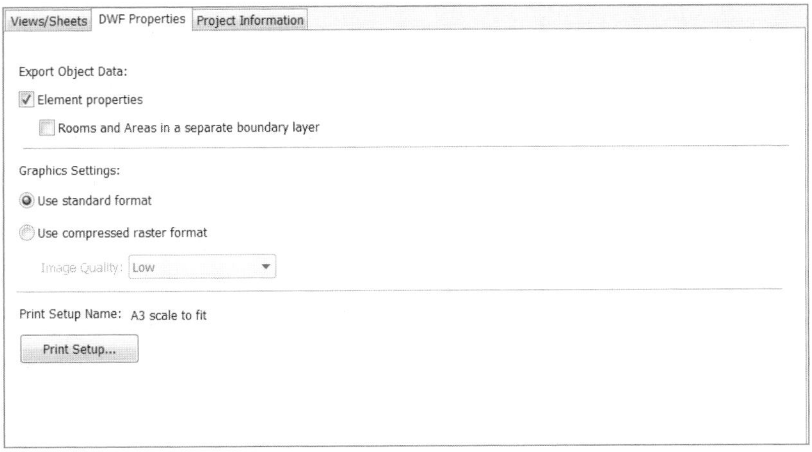

Figure 12.50

DWF Properties tab

Use Standard Format Exports images as PNG files.

Use Compressed Raster Format Exports images in compressed .jpg format. This typically produces a smaller file size. Select from Low, Medium, and High quality settings from the Image Quality list box.

Print Setup This button opens the standard Revit Print dialog boxes where you can set the printing preferences. This information—sheet size, placement, center, and so on—is embedded in the DWF file and will be available to the recipient so that the sheets can be printed exactly as expected, if the user printing the files has the equivalent plotter.

The Project Information tab displays the standard project information dialog box that is also available from the Manage tab on the ribbon. You can make changes to project information in this dialog box as part of the export process if you need to.

> Any changes made on this Project Information tab will also change the project information on the Manage tab and not be restricted to the DWF export.

Saving DWF Settings

At the bottom of all three tabs in the DWF Export Settings dialog box is the option to save settings. Clicking this button saves any settings you have selected during the export setup process and exits the Export command. The settings are retained exactly as they were chosen. They include sheet and view choices, DWF properties, and project information.

When you click Next, the Save To Target Folder dialog box opens (Figure 12.51), allowing you to save the file to the desired directory and additionally control the type of file created and whether the file is a single sheet or view per file or a combined set of sheets and views per file. Click the OK button to proceed with the export process.

Figure 12.51

**Save To Target
Folder**

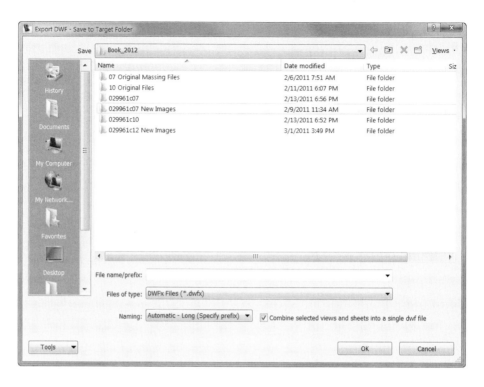

Options available in the Export DWF – Save To Target Folder dialog box are as follows:

Files Of Type   Choose either DWF or DWFx. See Table 12.7 for additional information.

Naming   There are three possible naming schemes:

Automatic – Long (Specify Prefix)   Defaults to the project name and then appends the view name to the project name. This allows you to type a specific filename to replace the project name and then appends the name of the first view exported to the typed filename.

Automatic – Short   Uses the view or sheet name from the Revit project.

Manual   This is available only when exporting Current View/Sheet Only export settings. The complete filename can be entered manually.

Combine Selected Views And Sheets Into A Single DWF File   When selected, this produces a single file that has all the views and sheets selected for export included in it. When deselected, the export creates a single file per view or sheet selected for export.

Linking DWF

When used in conjunction with Autodesk Design Review, Revit-exported DWF files can be linked back into a Revit project and allow the user to track markups and revisions to the project sheets without using paper. The process is to export the Revit sheet views to a DWF file. Once the DWF file is created, you can add in markups and comments using Autodesk Design Review software (see Figure 12.52).

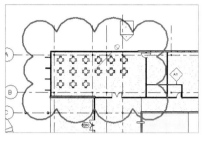

Figure 12.52

Markup and properties created in Autodesk Design Review

Design Review Round Trip Procedures

Once the review is finished, save the DWF file. Then link the DWF file back into the Revit project file from which it was exported. You'll find the Link DWF Markups command on the Insert tab of the Link panel. The DWF is linked into the project file as an Import Symbol Markup Object.

DWF sheets will automatically be placed on the correct sheet in the Revit project as an import symbol. If there are sheets in the DWF file that do not have markups, a notification window will be displayed alerting you. The sheets in the pages in the DWF file that have markups will appear in the Link Markup Page To Revit Sheets window (Figure 12.53). The linked views will automatically be associated with the correct sheet. If the sheet has been renamed, you can manually select the sheet to link the DWF view to. Once the sheets are linked into the project, any markups and notes can be reviewed, commented on, and re-exported for further review (Figure 12.54).

DWF
Markup

Figure 12.53

Link Markup Page To Revit Sheets

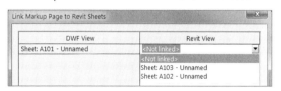

Figure 12.54

Markup and comments in Revit sheets

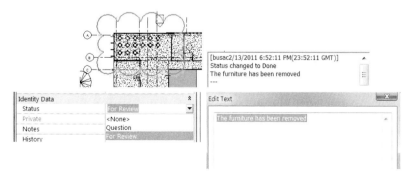

Using Raster Files

Raster files can be incorporated into Revit project files and also into Revit family files, such as title blocks. Multiple file formats are supported: BMP, JPEG, PNG, and TIFF.

The raster file will be included in the Revit project file once it is inserted and will not need to be sent separately when sharing the project file or any titleblock family files.

1. Import the image using the Image command on the Insert tab's Import panel.

2. Navigate to the folder that contains the image, and select the image.

3. Click Open, and you are returned to the Revit project.

4. The image will be centered on the cursor; click to place the image.

5. Once the image is placed, you can adjust the size of the image as follows:

    a. Select the image.

    b. Grip edit by dragging the corners or by selecting the image and changing the properties in the Properties palette.

To remove all instances of an image, follow these steps:

1. Choose Manage Images from the Insert tab's Import panel.

2. Select the image from the list.

3. Choose Delete.

    This will delete all instances of the image.

Images can be copied within a project using the standard Revit Copy command. If an image has been copied and only a single instance needs to be deleted, do the following:

1. Open a view that displays that image.

2. Select the image.

3. Press the Delete key, or right-click and choose Delete from the context menu.

Any other instances that exist in the project will remain. To fully remove an image from the project, either individually delete all instances or use the Manage Images command.

CHAPTER 13

Rooms and Areas

In this chapter, we will discuss creating rooms and areas in Autodesk Revit Architecture.

You create rooms to extract information from the model, add user-defined information, or automatically calculate spaces about the building model. The room element is a *nongraphic* element in the model that represents a defined space in the model. The Revit Room object is not visible on your printed sheets, but it does contain information about the space it is located in. You also use rooms to create schedules, such as a room finish schedule.

You use areas to create area calculations. Rooms and areas are not interchangeable, so if you want to create an area calculation, you need to create an area plan and add an area schedule.

This chapter covers the following topics:

- ▪ **Defining rooms and creating room schedules**
- ▪ **Creating area plans**

Defining Rooms and Creating Room Schedules

In this section, you will create rooms to define spaces in your project, such as offices, hallways, and conference rooms. You can assign data to the room elements, including the room name, number, finish data, and so on. You can then use this information to generate room schedules, generate reports, and perform calculations. You can also tag the room to display information such as the room name, number, and square footage.

Rooms are model elements like doors, walls, and windows, but you can add rooms to the model graphically in a plan view or create them in a schedule view. When you create rooms in a schedule, you are creating unplaced rooms. This is not the same as using the Room tool in a plan view. One reason to create rooms in a schedule view is to predefine a listing of the rooms you need in a building program. As you lay out your building program and add rooms to the plans, you can use all the predefined information.

When you place rooms, you need to associate them with a *bound* space. A space is bound when three or more walls or room separation lines enclose that space. Revit provides you with options to specify whether a wall is bounding or nonbounding. You might use this option if you do not want half-height walls or movable partitions to divide a space. Room separation lines allow you to subdivide a room into two or more different areas.

In this exercise, you will define several rooms and then use room separation lines to further define the room:

1. Open the source file `Dataset_13_01.rvt`, available among the book's companion download files at www.sybex.com/go/introducingrevit2012.

2. Save the file as **Add_rooms.rvt**.

3. In the Project Browser, make the 02 – Ground Floor floor plan view active.

4. On the Home tab's Room & Area panel, click the upper portion of the Room button.

   The Room button is a split button, with the top portion for creating a room and the lower portion for creating either a room or a room separation line.

   When placing a room, you have a number of options to consider in the ribbon and Options bar (Figure 13.1). Most of the options on the ribbon should be familiar to you from working with other tools.

   The ribbon has two options:

   Highlight Boundaries This button highlights all options that can be used as a boundary for rooms.

Figure 13.1

Modify | Place Room tab and Options bar for placing a room

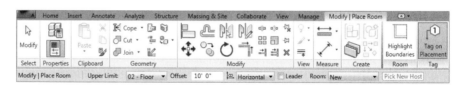

Tag On Placement When selected, this button adds a room tag to the rooms as they are added to the project. If this option is not selected, then room tags will not be added when rooms are added to the project.

Use the Highlight Boundaries option when you want to quickly see what the room boundary options are on the plan drawing. This can help you determine whether you need to use room separation lines to further divide an area.

The options on the Options bar are as follows:

Upper Limit and Limit Offset These define the upper boundary of the room. Upper Limit is the level from which to measure the upper boundary of the space. Limit Offset is the distance at which the upper boundary of the space occurs, measuring from the Upper Limit level.

Tag Orientation When Tag On Placement is selected, this option sets the orientation of the tag to horizontal, vertical, or model.

Leader This option adds a leader to your tags.

Room This option provides a listing of rooms that have not yet been placed in the model. If there are no unplaced rooms in the model, then the only choice displayed will be New, which will create a new room.

5. In the Modify | Place Room tab's Tag panel, activate the Tag On Placement option. You will use the default settings on the Options bar.

6. Move your mouse pointer over the southwest room. This is the room to the left of the kitchen and pantry.

    Notice that there is an *X* in the room; the room tag is being displayed, and the outline of the room boundary is highlighted (Figure 13.2).

7. Click in the space to create the room and its tag.

8. Hit the Esc key once to exit out of the Room tool.

    To change the properties of a room, you need to select it. You can accomplish this in a couple of ways:

    • Move your mouse pointer within the room until your mouse pointer finds the *X*.

    • Move your mouse pointer to the edge of a boundary wall, press the Tab key, watch the status bar until the room is selected, and then click the mouse.

    The room is then selected, and you can edit the parameters of the room.

9. Select the room you just placed.

10. In the Properties palette, name the room **Laundry**, and assign the room number **GF-04**.

Figure 13.2

The *X* appears when
you are placing a
room.

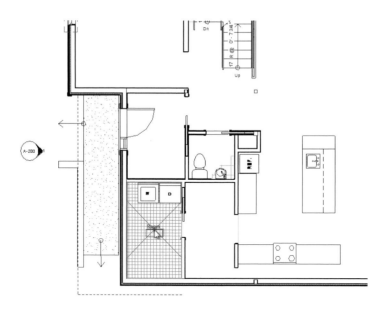

Figure 13.2

The *X* appears when
you are placing a
room.

While the Room tool is active, existing rooms will display an X through the room. This is a visual cue indicating which spaces have not been assigned rooms.

Notice that when you place rooms, Revit will automatically attempt to align tags. You might have also noticed that Revit will automatically number each room sequentially. Although it is a simple process to renumber rooms, you can save yourself some time if you plan your placement of rooms to allow Revit to number the rooms for you.

11. Repeat steps 4 and 10 to create rooms for the Pantry, Restroom, and Entry, as shown in Figure 13.3.

Figure 13.3

Adding rooms as
indicated

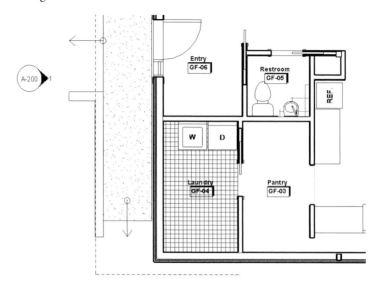

Room Separation Lines

In Revit, you have the ability to create spaces that you can use to define rooms without using walls. You can do so by using room separators. You can also use the Room Separation Line tool to further divide a space if necessary. A *room separation line* is a line that you draw in a view to define an area that is used for different purposes. For example, you may have a large room that needs to be labeled as two different rooms and using a wall to divide the spaces is not desired. A room separation line can be used to subdivide the space and Room objects can be placed in each area. Room separation lines are visible in plan views, 3D views, and perspective views. In the next example, you will use the Room Separation Line tool to define an existing space.

1. If you completed the previous section, continue using that file. Otherwise, open the source file Dataset_13_02.rvt, available among the book's companion download files at www.sybex.com/go/introducingrevit2012.

2. Save the file as Room_Separation.rvt.

3. Open the floor plan 02 – Ground Floor.

4. Using the Room tool from the Room & Area panel of the Home tab, click on the top portion of the Room split button and, using Figure 13.4 as a reference, create a room.

5. Name the room **Living Room** with a room number of **GF-07**.

Clicking on the room element for the Living Room (Figure 13.5) shows a room that extends into the kitchen area, dining room, hallway, and study. In the steps that follow, you will use the room separation line to subdivide the room for the kitchen, dining room, hallway, and study. Although you could use drafting lines to divide the space, you want to use the Room Separation Line tool for scheduling purposes and to ascertain its area.

1. Zoom into the southeast corner of the building to the area to the right of the Restroom and Pantry.

> Room separation lines do not print.

2. On the Home tab's Room & Area panel, click the lower portion of the Room split button, and select Room Separation Line.

3. Using Figure 13.6 as a reference, draw four room separation lines to subdivide the one large room into several smaller rooms.

Figure 13.4

Creating a room element for the Living Room

Figure 13.5

Large room that needs to be sub-divided for other distinct spaces

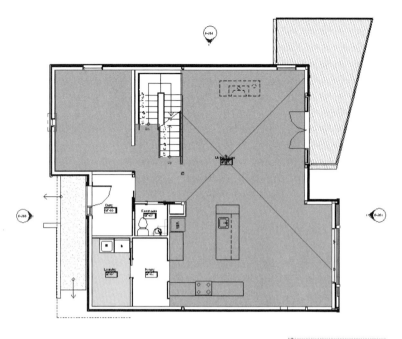

Figure 13.6

Using room separation lines to define new spaces for rooms

4. Press Esc twice to end the Room Separation Line tool.

Notice that the previously defined room has not been split into multiple rooms (Figure 13.7). The original room has been constrained in size, and the other side of the room separation line is a space without a room. What you need to do now is add additional rooms for our other spaces.

5. Using Figure 13.8 as a reference, create rooms for the following:

   · Dining Room, GF-01

   · Kitchen, GF-02

   · Hallway, GF-08

   · Study, GF-09

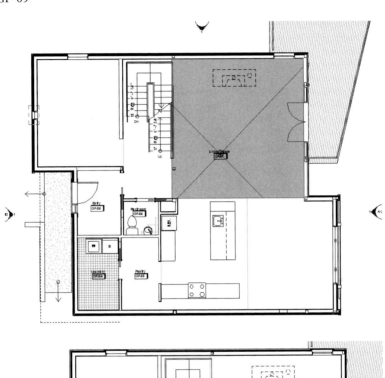

Figure 13.7

Completed subdivided room

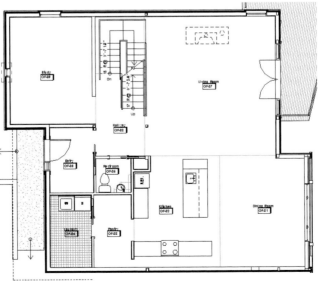

Figure 13.8

Ground floor rooms defined

Room Schedules

As you add rooms to your model, you will want to create a room schedule to organize and display room information such as room name, number, finishes, occupant, the department the room is assigned to, and so forth. In this section, you are going to create a basic room schedule. In Chapter 14, "Tags, Schedules, and Keynotes," we will cover schedules in more detail.

1. If you completed the previous section, continue using that file. Otherwise, open the source file `Dataset_13_03.rvt`, available among the book's companion download files at www.sybex.com/go/introducingrevit2012.

2. Save the file as **Room_Schedule.rvt**.

3. Click the View tab, go to the Create panel, click the Schedules drop-down, and select Schedule/Quantities.

4. In the New Schedule dialog box, select Rooms from the category list.

5. Make sure the name is set to Room Schedule and that the Schedule Building Components radio button is selected. The Phase option should be set to New Construction, as shown in Figure 13.9.

6. Click the OK button to close the New Schedule dialog box and open the Schedule Properties dialog box.

7. On the Fields tab, move the following items in order from the Available Fields section to the Scheduled Fields section, as shown in Figure 13.10.

   - Name
   - Number
   - Base Finish
   - Floor Finish
   - Wall Finish
   - Ceiling Finish
   - Department
   - Comments

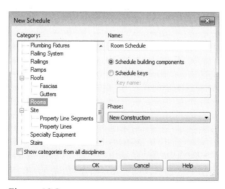

Figure 13.9

New Schedule dialog box

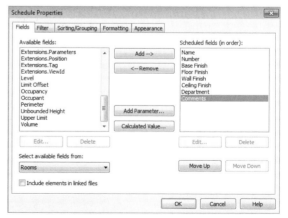

Figure 13.10

Adding fields to the room schedule

To accomplish this, either select the field in Available Fields and click the Add button, or double-click the field to add it to the Scheduled Fields section.

8. Click the Sorting/Grouping tab, and set Sort By to Number.

9. Click OK to close the Schedule Properties dialog box. A schedule will be created, as shown in Figure 13.11.

Now that you have a basic room schedule, you can add, edit, or delete values for the various fields. You can do so by clicking in the individual fields and entering the appropriate data. This process can be very time-consuming, since Revit permits you to edit only one field at a time.

Figure 13.11

Room schedule

Name	Number	Base Finish	Floor Finish	Wall Finish	Ceiling Finish	Department	Comments
Family Ro	001	B	B.F.	P.G.	P.G.		
Mech. Ro	003	A	B.P.	P.G.	P.G.		
Bathroom	002	C	T.C.	P.G.	P.G.		
Living Ro	102	B	B.F.	P.G.	P.G.		
Kitchen	103	B	B.F.	P.G.	P.G.		
Entry Hall	100	C	T.C.	P.G.	P.G.		
Study	108	C	T.C.	P.G.	P.G.		
Laundry	106	C	T.C.	P.G.	P.G.		
Lobby	105	C	T.C.	P.G.	P.G.		
WC	101	C	T.C.	P.G.	P.G.		
Dining Ro	104	B	B.F.	P.G.	P.G.		
BEDROO	FF-02	B	B.F.	P.G.	P.G.		
READING	FF-01	B	B.F.	P.G.	P.G.		
BATHRO	FF-03	C	T.C.	P.G.	P.G.		
BATHRO	FF-04	C	T.C.	P.G.	P.G.		
CHAMBR	205	B	B.F.	P.G.	P.G.		
BEDROO	FF-06	B	B.F.	P.G.	P.G.		
ATELIER	301	B	B.F.	P.G.	P.G.		
Laundry	GF-04						
Pantry	GF-03						
Restroom	GF-05						
Entry	GF-06						
Living Ro	GF-07						
Dining Ro	GF-01						
Kitchen	GF-02						
Hallway	GF-08						
Study	GF-09						

Key Schedules for Rooms

As you work on your building project, you are going to find that some of your schedules, such as rooms, doors, and windows, will contain a great deal of information. Depending on the size of your project, you could be dealing with anywhere from a few dozen rooms to several hundred. Rather than having to manually enter information such as wall and floor finish for each room separately, it would be much easier if you could find a method to automatically fill in this information. Using key schedules, you can create a list of styles that you predefine to use in your schedules.

For example, you may have a project with finishes that apply to many of the rooms or many different doors that share the same type of hardware. Rather than assigning this information to each individual element, you can use key schedules to automatically fill in the fields.

In the following example, you will create a key schedule to aid in assigning finishes to the rooms in the example project:

1. If you completed the previous section, continue using that file. Otherwise, open the source file `Dataset_13_04.rvt`, available among the book's companion download files at www.sybex.com/go/introducingrevit2012.

2. Save the file as `Room_Key_Schedule.rvt`.

3. Click the View tab, go to the Create panel, click the Schedules drop-down, and click Schedule/Quantities.

4. In the New Schedule dialog box, select Rooms from the Category list.

5. Set Name to **Key - Room Style Schedule**. The Schedule Keys radio button should be selected, and set Key Name to **Room Style**, as shown in Figure 13.12.

Figure 13.12

New Schedule dialog box for creating a room key schedule

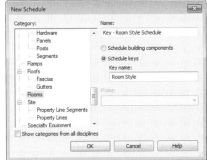

Revit does not provide a great deal of flexibility in organizing schedules. In step 5, we added the prefix "Key -" to the name of the key schedule to differentiate the key schedule from other schedules in the project.

6. Click OK to close the New Schedule dialog box. The Schedule Properties dialog box will open.

    In the Schedule Properties dialog box, the key name is automatically added to the Scheduled Fields list. You need to add the fields that you want to predefine in the style.

7. On the Fields tab, add the following items in order from the Available Fields section, as shown in Figure 13.13:

    - Base Finish

    - Floor Finish

    - Wall Finish

    - Ceiling Finish

Figure 13.13

Schedule properties for the room key schedule

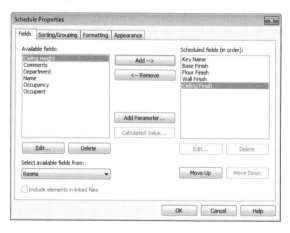

Either select a field and click the Add button, or double-click the field to add it to the Scheduled Fields section.

8. Click OK to close the Schedule Properties dialog box.

9. On the Modify Schedule/Quantities ribbon tab's Rows panel, click the New button to create a new row.

    In each row you are going to create new values. Specifically, you will create rows for several of the rooms and then apply the finishes associated with each room type.

10. Using Figure 13.14 as a reference, create rows and key values for the room names Bathroom, Bedroom, and Utility.

11. Fill in the appropriate information for each of the key values.

Now that you have created your key schedule, you need to apply it to your room schedule.

Room Style Schedule				
Key Name	Base Finish	Floor Finish	Wall Finish	Ceiling Finish
Bathroom	BS-06	FF-03	WF-2F	CF-31
Bedroom	BS-01	FF-03	WF-1F	CF-31
Utility	BS-04	FF-02	WF-5F	CF-02

Figure 13.14

Room style schedule

12. In the Project Browser, open the room schedule that you created earlier in this section, open one of your own room schedules, or create a new schedule.

13. In the Properties palette, click the Edit button to the right of Fields.

14. In the Available Fields list, locate the Room Style field that you created in step 6.

Figure 13.15

Adding the key named Room Style to the room schedule

15. Select the field and click the Add button, or double-click the field to add it to the Scheduled Fields section and use the Move Up button to position it between Number and Base Finish (see Figure 13.15).

16. Click OK to close the Schedule Properties dialog box.

17. In the schedule, locate Bathroom FF-02. In the Room Style cell for the room named Bathroom with a room number of FF-02, click in the cell (Figure 13.16). A drop-down menu will appear; select Bathroom.

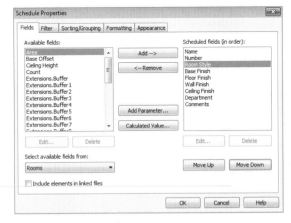

Notice that, after you change the Room Style cell from none to Bathroom, the cells for Base Finish, Floor Finish, Wall Finish, and Ceiling Finish are automatically filled in. If you were to return to the key schedule and edit the values in there, the room schedule would automatically update.

Figure 13.16

Selecting a room key style (top) populates the room finish information (bottom).

The main drawback to using a key schedule is that once you apply a key value to a schedule row, you will not be able to modify any of the fields defined in the key schedule. For example, in the previous example of room FF-02, when you apply the key value you will not be able to edit the wall finish in the room schedule. You can, however, make changes in the key schedule and those changes will automatically update in the room schedule.

Creating Area Plans

You use area plans to show different spatial relationship–based area schemes and levels in the model. If you need to perform basic square footage calculations, you can query the area of the room elements in your project. These rooms provide basic finished area, volume, and finish designations. For more detailed calculations, you use area plans. Area plans use area boundary lines and area elements to define areas. You can create multiple area plans for every area scheme and level. In the following steps, you will create an area plan:

1. If you completed the previous section, continue using that file. Otherwise, open the source file Dataset_13_05.rvt (mDataset_13_05.rvt), available among the book's companion download files at www.sybex.com/go/introducingrevit2012.

2. Save the file as Area_Plan.rvt.

3. On the Home tab's Room & Area panel, click the Area button drop-down and click Area Plan.

4. In the New Area Plan dialog box, choose Gross Building from the Type drop-down list.

5. Choose 02 – Ground Floor for the area plan view.

6. Click OK to close the New Area Plan dialog box.

   A new gross building area plan is created. The floor plan will have a purple boundary around the exterior walls. You will then use the Area Boundary Line tool, which is similar to the Room Boundary Line tool, to manually add additional boundary lines to create regions that you wish to measure.

7. On the Home tab's Room & Area panel, click the Area tool drop-down again and choose Area Boundary Line to create boundary lines.

8. Using Figure 13.17 as a reference, create the additional area boundary lines indicated by the arrows.

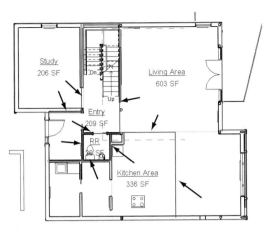

Figure 13.17

Creating additional room boundary lines

Figure 13.18

Preliminary area plan with legend

9. On the Home tab's Room & Area panel, click the Legend button.

10. Place the legend in the upper-right corner of the view, as shown in Figure 13.18.

11. In the Choose Space Type And Color Scheme dialog box (Figure 13.19), set Space Type to Areas (Gross Building), and set Color Scheme to Scheme 1.

12. Click OK to close the Choose Space Type And Color Scheme dialog box.

    In the next few steps, you will adjust the color scheme legend.

13. Select the legend.

14. On the Modify | Color Fill Legends tab's Scheme panel, click the Edit Scheme button.

    This will open the Edit Color Scheme dialog box (Figure 13.20), in which you can adjust or create new color schemes. In the next example, you are going to create a new scheme and change the color scheme to be based on the area of the room rather than the name.

15. In the Schemes section, select Scheme 1.

16. At the bottom of the Schemes section, click the Duplicate ⧉ button and name the new scheme **Gross Building Area**.

17. In the Scheme Definition area, change the title to **Gross Area Legend**.

Figure 13.19

Selecting Space Type and Color Scheme

Figure 13.20

Edit Color Scheme dialog box

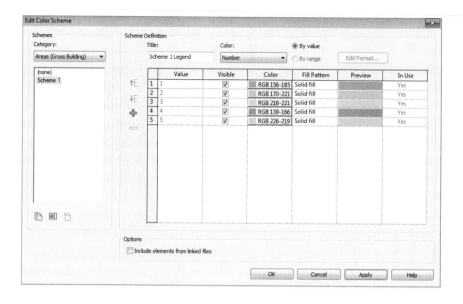

18. In the Color drop-down, select Area.

    The Colors Not Preserved dialog box will open. This dialog box warns you that any changes you make will not preserve your color scheme.

19. Click OK to accept the warning.

20. Click the By Range radio button. Doing so will allow you to create a color scheme based on an area.

    You now have a color scheme that will color by area elements based on their area. In this example, you have two colors, one for areas that are smaller than 20 SF (2 SM) and one for rooms greater than 20 SF (2 SM). Let's add a third option that will color areas that are less than 150 SF (14 SM), areas that are between 150 SF (14 SM) and 300 SF (28 SM), and finally areas that are greater than 300 SF (28 SM).

21. Click in one of the rows, and then click the green + to add a new value.

    Revit automatically creates a new value for you. The color scheme will now show three options. You can now make changes to the legend caption, color, and fill patterns.

22. Using Figure 13.21 as a reference, do the following:

    • In the third row, change the At Least option to 300 SF (28 SM).

    • In the second row, change the At Least option to 150 SF (14 SM).

23. Click OK to return to the model.

24. Press the Esc key to deselect the legend. Your area plan should look like Figure 13.22.

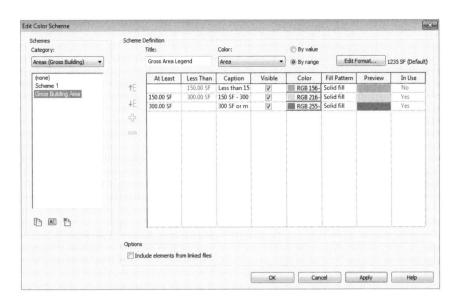

Figure 13.21

Enter these settings in the Edit Color Scheme dialog box.

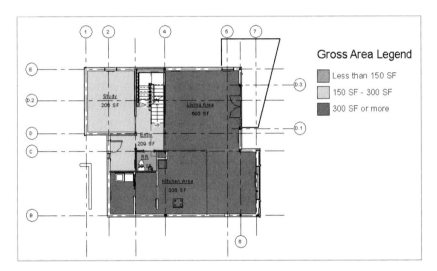

Figure 13.22

Finished area plan

Identifying Rentable Areas

Now that you have defined the gross areas, you can move on to calculating the *rentable areas*. You will follow the same procedures to create a rentable area as you did for creating a gross area plan. The main difference between creating a gross area plan and a rentable area plan is that Revit will draw an area boundary on the inside of the exterior walls for a rentable area, whereas with the gross area, the lines were drawn on the outside of the exterior walls.

1. If you completed the previous section, continue using that file. Otherwise, open the source file Dataset_13_06.rvt, available among the book's companion download files at www.sybex.com/go/introducingrevit2012.

2. Save the file as `Rentable_Plan.rvt`.

3. On the Home tab's Room & Area panel, click the Area button drop-down and click Area Plan.

4. In the New Area Plan dialog box, choose Rentable from the Type drop-down list, and choose 02 – Ground Floor for the area plan view. Click OK to close the dialog box.

   A new rentable building area plan is created. The floor plan will have a purple boundary around the exterior walls. Note that because you have created a rentable plan, the boundary lines are on the inside of the exterior walls.

5. On the Home tab's Room & Area panel, click the Legend button.

6. Place the legend in the upper-right corner of the view.

   The Choose Space Type And Color Scheme dialog box will open.

7. Set Space Type to Areas (Rentable), and set Color Scheme to Scheme 1. Click OK to close the dialog box.

   In the next few steps, you are going to modify the area that Revit automatically created. In this example, you want to make sure you are not going to calculate common spaces (such as the stair cores) within the building. You will use the Area Boundary Line tool to define these spaces. This tool works in a similar way as the Room Separation Line tool.

8. From the Home tab's Room & Area panel, click the Area button drop-down and click Area Boundary Line.

9. Using Figure 13.23 as a reference, define boundaries using the Area Boundary Line tool.

Figure 13.23

Defining boundaries around the common spaces in your project

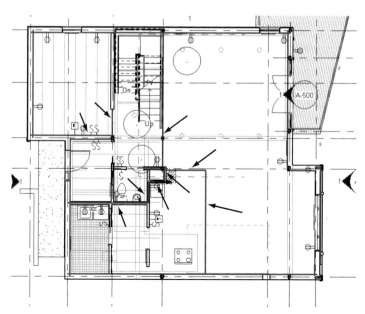

In the next step, you need to create areas for the new spaces that you created.

10. From the Home tab's Room & Area panel, click the Area button drop-down and click Area.

11. Using Figure 13.24 as a reference, create an area for each of the spaces to be defined as an area. This is going to be the rentable space.

12. Select this area.

13. In the Properties palette, make sure that Area Type is set to Floor Area, as shown in Figure 13.24.

Figure 13.24

Defining the area type for a selected area

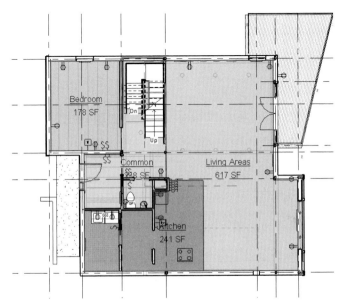

Just as with the gross area plan, you can edit the rentable area legend to alter the rentable area plan to suit your needs.

Whether you are creating gross building or rentable area plans, you can schedule these area plans.

CHAPTER 14

Tags, Schedules, and Keynotes

In this chapter, we will discuss using tags to label building elements in your projects, using schedules to view and examine your project, and using text to annotate it. Tags are 2D symbols with unique properties used to represent each building element. A tag works by pulling parameters from an element. Tags are also dynamic; as the building is updated and values change, the information in the tag is updated automatically.

Schedules provide another view in which you can examine and edit your building project. Schedules list parameters for the elements in your building project. The schedules are dynamic and allow you to make changes to data stored in element parameters, calculate values, or even alter model geometry. Schedules are a powerful tool often overlooked by new users.

Autodesk Revit Architecture offers a number of methods for annotating the various building components in your building project. One of these methods is to use keynoting. Keynoting provides a method of annotating the types of materials, elements, and user-defined elements included in your building project. You add keynotes to model views. The benefit of keynoting is that it will save you time when you are documenting and coordinating the various building elements used in a building project.

This chapter covers the following topics:

- **Adding tags**

- **Creating schedules**

- **Working with keynotes**

Adding Tags

Tags are annotation elements, and they have some of the same characteristics as annotations. Tags are view-specific. When you place a tag in one view, that tag will not be visible in any other views. When you place a tag, it will automatically try to align with other tags in the view. Tags will also scale with the view.

Revit includes a number of predefined tags, but not all tags are loaded automatically in the default template. You can load additional tags, and Revit lets you customize the tag to display any element parameter required. Figure 14.1 shows some of the various types of predefined tags.

Figure 14.1

**Different uses
of tags**

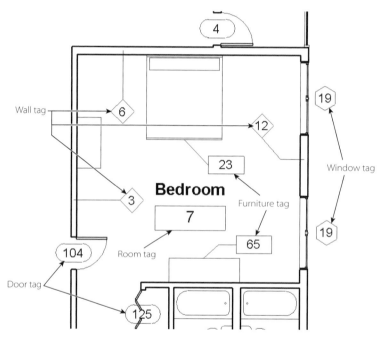

Loading Tags

Out of the box, Revit ships with several predefined tag annotation families. You can customize these tags to meet your specific graphical needs. Depending on the template, your project may need to have additional tags loaded. To load new tags, follow these general steps:

1. Start a new project using the default template or open one of your existing files.

2. On the Annotate tab's Tag panel, expand the panel and choose Loaded Tags.

   The Loaded Tags dialog box will now be displayed (Figure 14.2). The Category column lists the various Revit element categories. The Loaded Tags column lists any of the loaded tags in your project. At the bottom-left corner of the dialog box you'll see a Show Categories From All Disciplines check box. By default, the Category column will display only Revit Architecture element categories. If you select the Show Categories From All Disciplines check box, the Category column will display all the element categories for architecture, structural, and MEP elements.

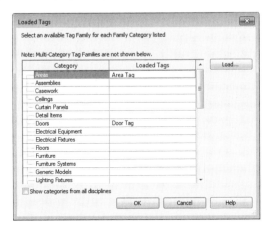

Figure 14.2

Loaded Tags dialog box

3. Click the Load button to select additional tags to load.

4. Navigate to the Annotation folder of your Revit content library, and begin by selecting your tag families.

   For Windows 7 users the file can be found at:

   ```
   C:\Users\All Users\Autodesk\RAC 2012\Libraries\US Imperial\US Imperial\
   Annotations\
   ```

   For metric users:

   ```
   C:\Users\All Users\Autodesk\RAC 2012\Libraries\US Metric\Annotations\
   ```

   You can select multiple tag files by holding either the Shift or the Ctrl key while selecting the families.

5. When you have finished selecting tags, click the Open button, and then click OK in the Loaded Tags dialog box.

   If you load a family that already exists in the project, a dialog box will open warning you of this.

Using Tags

For some elements such as doors and windows, when you place the element, there is an option to automatically place a tag. You just click Tag On Placement on the Modify | Place Door or Modify | Place Window tab to automatically tag the element (Figure 14.3). For other elements such as walls and furniture, you can place a tag only after the wall or furniture has been placed. In the next steps, we will walk you through tagging elements.

You can find the tools to place tags on the Annotate tab's Tag panel (Figure 14.4). You are provided with seven tagging options:

Tag All Not Tagged If you have multiple elements in a view that do not have tags, Tag All Not Tagged allows you to apply tags to untagged elements in one operation.

Figure 14.4

Tagging options

Tag By Category This option allows you to tag elements by category or type.

Multi-Category Tag This option allows you to tag elements across different family types.

Material Tag This option identifies the type of material used for an element or a layer of an element.

View Reference This option displays the sheet and detail number of a view that has been split by a matchline. Note that this tool is active only in views with dependent view relationships.

Area Tag This option displays the total area within an area boundary.

Room Tag This option displays the name and number of a room.

Loaded Tags This option displays a dialog box listing the tags that will be used for each element category.

Keynote This option tags the selected element using the keynote specified for the selected element type.

Keynoting Settings This option specifies the location of the keynote table and the numbering method for keynotes.

Now that we have discussed the Tag options, let's take a closer look at some of these options.

Tag By Category

The Tag By Category option allows you to tag elements either by category or by type. To place tags using the Tag By Category tool, follow these steps:

1. Open a view in which you want to tag elements.

2. On the Annotate tab's Tag panel, click Tag By Category.

3. On the Options bar, set the Orientation value of the tag to either Horizontal or Vertical, and set the desired leader options.

4. Move your mouse pointer over an element to tag.

   Revit will provide a preview of the tag and tag value.

5. Click to place the tag.

Tag All Not Tagged

As you work on your building project, you will find that it can be time-consuming to individually tag each element in the project. The Tag All Not Tagged tool enables you to apply tags to all untagged element in a view in a single operation. It is a great tool for ensuring that you have tagged all the elements in a view. The main drawback to this tool is that you have little control over the placement of the tags.

To place tags using the Tag All Not Tagged tool, follow these steps:

1. Open a view in which you want to tag elements.

2. On the Annotate tab's Tag panel, click the Tag All Not Tagged button.

   The Tag All Not Tagged dialog box (Figure 14.5) opens. This dialog box provides several options:

   - You can tag all objects in the current view.
   - You can tag only the selected objects in the current view.
   - You can tag elements in linked files.
   - You can add a leader to the tag.
   - You can specify the orientation of the tag.

   You can also specify what elements to tag:

   - To tag all visible elements in the current view that do not have tags, select the radio button All Objects In Current View.
   - To tag only the elements you have selected, select Only Selected Objects In Current View. To use this option, you must first select the objects prior to initiating the Tag All Not Tagged tool.

   If you have multiple tag styles loaded, you have the ability to select the tag style.

3. Select the tag categories you want to use.

   In Figure 14.5, we have multiple tag categories to choose from (room, wall, doors, etc). You may decide that you want to tag only walls and doors. To select just these categories, press the Shift or Ctrl key while selecting categories.

4. Set the Leader and Orientation options.

5. Click OK to close the dialog box and place the tags.

Figure 14.5

Selecting door tags in the Tag All Not Tagged dialog box

Material Tag

In the previous example, the Tag All Not Tagged tool reads the instance or type description of an element and generates a tag. The Material Tag tool allows you to generate a tag based on the type of material used for either an element or a layer of an element. This tool pulls the tag information from the Description line in the material definition (Figure 14.6). For example, if you are tagging a wall by material (Figure 14.7), you will be able to tag the materials used in the wall assembly. Doing so allows you to tag the CMU, sheathing, and studs separately.

Figure 14.6

Material description example

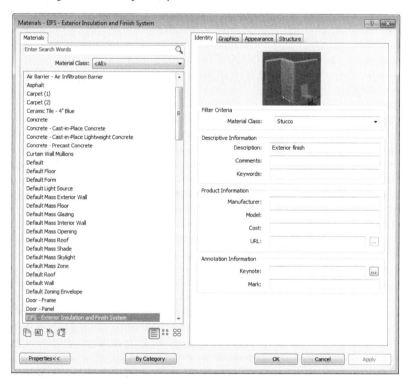

To place tags using the Material Tag tool, follow these steps:

1. Open a view in which you want to tag elements.

2. Click the Annotate tab's Tag panel, and click Material Tag.

   The Options bar provides several options that you can set, such as Horizontal or Vertical tag orientation. You can also create a leader to the tag.

3. Move your mouse pointer over the element to highlight the material that you want to tag. Revit will provide a preview of the tag for the element your mouse pointer is over.

If your material tag is displaying a question mark (as in Figure 14.7), the material description is not being read.

   a. First, make sure that the view detail level is set to either Medium or Fine. If it is set to Coarse, the material is not visible, and the tag will not display.

   b. Next, check the Description field of the Identity tab for the element's material (shown in Figure 14.6).

      Or after the tag is placed, you can double-click the question mark, and you can manually type in a material description. This is after step 4.

4. To place the tag, click the element.

   If you elected to create a leader, you will need to click again to place the leader before the tag is created.

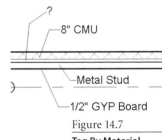

Figure 14.7

Tag By Material example with a blank material definition

Tagging 3D Views

Revit Architecture 2012 provides an option to tag elements in 3D views. In the following steps, you are going to open a 3D view and tag elements in the project:

1. From the book's companion download files (available at www.sybex.com/go/ introducingrevit2012), open Dataset_14_01.rvt.

2. Open the 3D View, {3D}.

   In order to tag elements in 3D views, you must first lock the 3D view so that the orientation cannot be changed. Tags can only be placed in 3D views that have been locked. There is a new Lock/Unlocked 3D View button (Figure 14.8) on the View Control bar that enables the tools for controlling the locking and unlocking of 3D views. The button provides three options:

   Save Orientation And Lock View This option locks the view at the current orientation and the ViewCube tool is disabled.

   Restore Orientation And Lock View When this option is used on an unlocked view, the reoriented view can be restored to its previously locked orientation. Any tags or keynotes placed in the view will be displayed.

   Unlock View This option unlocks the current view so that the view orientation can be changed. Any tags or keynotes in the view will disappear.

3. Click the Lock/Unlocked 3D View button and select Save Orientation And Lock View.

   The Rename Default 3D View To Lock dialog box opens.

Figure 14.8

The View Control bar in a 3D view with Lock/Unlocked 3D View button options

4. In the Rename Default 3D View To Lock dialog box, name the new view **3D Annotated View**.

Note that the original view name has been changed.

5. Using Figure 14.9 as a reference, add the tags to the model.

Figure 14.9

3D views with tags

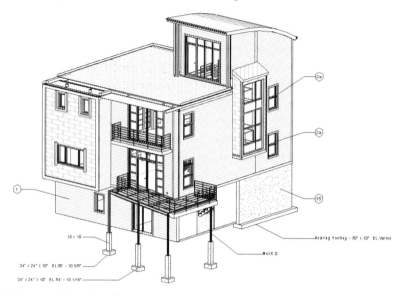

6. Save and close the file.

When tagging 3D views, keep the following things in mind:

- You are not able to "lock" the default 3D view, {3D}. If you try to lock the {3D} view, a dialog box will appear asking you to rename the view. This applies only to the {3D} view.

- The Tag and Keynote tools on the Tag panel of the Annotate tab will appear enabled for all 3D views. If you attempt to use a Tag or Keynote tool in an unlocked 3D view, a dialog box will warn you that you need to lock the view first.

- Material, area, room, and space tags cannot be used in 3D views.

- Tags and keynotes cannot be placed in perspective 3D views.

- Using the Tag On Placement option may not work in all cases.

Creating Schedules

As previously mentioned, Revit is a database, and it provides you with the ability to view your data in different forms. Sometimes that means looking at the geometry in a plan, section, detail, or 3D view. You also have the ability to look at your building project through a schedule. Schedules allow you to view information about your building project in a tabular display of information.

Figure 14.10 shows an example of a door schedule that is dynamically updated as changes are made to the model. The information from the schedule is read from the element properties in the project. Information can be displayed for each item or type and can include such information as size, material, finish, fire rating, cost, level, description, and comments. If this information is changed in the model, the schedule automatically updates. If you change the information in the schedule, the model is updated.

Figure 14.10

Door schedule example

| Type Mark | LEAF TYPE | DOOR SIZE | | DOOR | | FRAME | | DETAIL | | | Fire Rating | Electronic Access Control | Comments |
		Width	Height	Mat'l	Style	Mat'l	Style	Head	Jamb	Sill			
D39	DOUBLE	6' - 0"	7' - 0"	H	F	H	S	A3/A-623	A4/A-623	B2/A-623			
D58	DOUBLE	6' - 0	7' - 11 3/					B3/A-623	B4/A-623	B2/A-623			
D71	SINGLE	3' - 0"	7' - 0"	H	G	H	S	A3/A-623	A4/A-623	B2/A-623			
D72	SINGLE	3' - 0"	7' - 0"	H	F	H	S				UNRATED		
F2	SINGLE	3' - 0"	7' - 0"	W	F	H	S				20 MIN		
F13	SINGLE			AG	FG	A	-	B3/A-623	B4/A-623	B2/A-623			
F15	SINGLE	3' - 0"	7' - 0"	W	F	H	S	A5/A-623	B1/A-623	B2/A-623	60 MIN		
F16	SINGLE	3' - 0"	7' - 0"	W	N	H	S	A3/A-623	A4/A-623	B2/A-623	60 MIN		
F17	SINGLE	3' - 0"	7' - 0"	W	N	H	S				20 MIN		
F18	DOUBLE	6' - 0"	7' - 0"	W	N	H	S	A3/A-623	A4/A-623	B2/A-623	20 MIN		
F20	DOUBLE	6' - 0"	7' - 0"	W	F	H	S	A5/A-623	B1/A-623	B2/A-623	45 MIN		Mechanical
F21	SINGLE	3' - 0"	7' - 0"	W	F	H	S	A3/A-623	A4/A-623	B2/A-623	45 MIN		
F25	DOUBLE	6' - 0"	7' - 11 3/					B3/A-623	B4/A-623	B2/A-623	45 MIN		
F27	SINGLE	3' - 0"	7' - 10"	AG	FG	A	-	B3/A-623	B4/A-623	B2/A-623	20 MIN		1-HR DELUGE
F32	DOUBLE	5' - 0"	7' - 0"			H	S	A1/A-623	A2/A-623	B2/A-623			
F33	SINGLE	3' - 6"	7' - 0"	W	F	H	S	A5/A-623	B1/A-623	B2/A-623	60 MIN		
N2	SINGLE	3' - 0"	7' - 0"	W	N	H	S	A3/A-623	A4/A-623	B2/A-623	60 MIN		

Schedules can be created at any stage of a project, and the data in the schedule can be filtered and sorted to suit your needs. As the project progresses, changes to the project will be instantly reflected in the schedules. You can also change the format of the schedule when you place it on a sheet.

Revit has seven types of schedules:

Schedules These are the most common schedule you will create. They can be used to extract quantities from the model. Some examples are door, window, and room schedules.

Key Schedules These schedules list styles that you predefine for use in schedules. An example is a room schedule, where there might be some finishes that apply to many rooms. Key schedules make it easy to automatically fill in fields in the schedule rather than entering data in each field of the schedule.

Material Takeoffs These schedules list all the materials and subcomponents of Revit families and allow for a more comprehensive level of detail for each assembly.

Annotation or Note Block Schedules These schedules list the notes that are applied to elements and assemblies and list the annotation symbols used in the project.

Revision Schedules These schedules list revisions in the project.

View Lists These schedules list all the views in the Project Browser and their properties.

Drawing Lists These schedules list all the sheets in the project.

Creating a Component Schedule

The following steps describe how to create a basic schedule in Revit. In this particular schedule, you are going to create a basic window schedule:

1. From the book's companion download files (available at www.sybex.com/go/introducingrevit2012), open Dataset_14_02.rvt.

2. In the View tab's Create panel, click the Schedules drop-down, and click Schedules/Quantities to open the New Schedule dialog box.

   You can also create a new schedule or legend view by right-clicking on the Schedules/Quantities or Legends node in the Project Browser.

   The New Schedule dialog box (Figure 14.11) displays the various categories of building elements in the Category list. By default, it will display elements specific to Revit Architecture. Selecting the Show Categories From All Disciplines option will display element categories from Revit Structure and Revit MEP as well.

   You select the desired category to create a schedule. For example, to create a door schedule, you can select Doors from the Category list. When you select a category, the category name is displayed in the Name text field. You are going to create a window schedule in this exercise.

3. In the New Schedule dialog box, select Windows under Category.

4. Under Name, name the schedule **Window Schedule**.

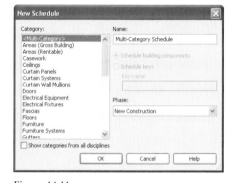

Figure 14.11
New Schedule dialog box

   Click the Schedule Building Components radio button if you want to create a schedule of the building elements. The Schedule Keys radio button is used to create a key schedule. The Phase drop-down lets you set up the phase of the construction.

5. Click OK to close the New Schedule dialog box. The Schedule Properties dialog box opens.

   The Schedule Properties dialog box (Figure 14.12) provides options for specifying the information that will be included in the schedule and how it will be displayed. There are five tabs to help you manage this:

   Fields This tab allows you to select parameters that will be used in your schedule. This tab will determine which fields will actually be reported in the schedule. Select the field in the left column, and click the Add button. Note that the field's order will determine the column order in the schedule. The top field will be the far-left column in the schedule, and so on.

Filter The Filter tab allows you to narrow your schedule and show only specific information by filtering the schedule. In this chapter's example, you will filter your walls based on their function. You only want to schedule the exterior walls and therefore not show the interior ones.

Sorting/Grouping This tab is where you will work on controlling how the information is organized. For example, you have a multilevel project and want to create a door schedule for the entire project. You can sort and group the schedule so that the doors are grouped by level and sorted by their mark number.

Formatting The Formatting tab controls an individual field's behavior. You can, for example, decide to change the actual name displayed in the schedule.

Appearance This tab controls how the schedule will look once placed on a sheet. It doesn't affect how the view displays but only how the final prints look.

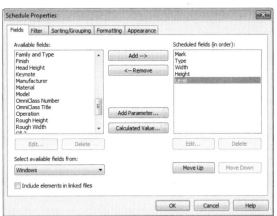

Figure 14.12

The Schedule Properties dialog box

On the Fields tab, add the settings shown in Figure 14.12 to your schedule.

6. In the Available Fields list, select Mark.

7. Click the Add button to add Mark to the Scheduled Fields (In Order) list.

   You can also double-click the parameter to add it to the Scheduled Fields (In Order) list.

8. Repeat steps 6 and 7, but add Type, Width, Height, and Level.

   On the Sorting/Grouping tab, you will be sorting by the Mark number, as shown in Figure 14.13.

9. On the Sorting/Grouping tab, set the options as follows:

   • Set Sort By to Mark.

   • Select Ascending to sort the Mark number by ascending order.

   • Make sure that Header is not selected. This will place the Mark number on top of the column.

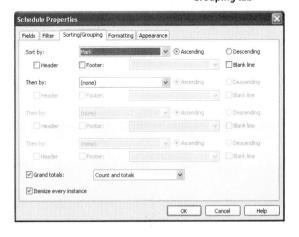

Figure 14.13

Schedule Properties dialog box, Sorting/Grouping tab

- Make sure that Footer is not selected.

- Select Grand Totals, and then select Counts And Totals. This will give you an overall count and totals for all doors used in the project.

10. Click OK, and you will be taken to a view of the schedule (Figure 14.14).

11. Save the file for use in the following sections.

Window Schedule				
Mark	Type	Width	Height	Level
1	36" x 66"	3' - 0"	6' - 0"	Ground Floor
2	96" x 48"	8' - 0"	4' - 0"	Ground Floor
3	36" x 60"	3' - 0"	5' - 0"	First Floor
4	14" x 48"	1' - 2"	4' - 0"	First Floor
5	36" x 60"	3' - 0"	5' - 0"	First Floor
6	36" x 60"	3' - 0"	5' - 0"	First Floor
7	30" x 46"	2' - 6"	3' - 10"	Basement
8	24" x 36"	2' - 0"	3' - 0"	First Floor
9	24" x 36"	2' - 0"	3' - 0"	First Floor
10	36" x 60"	3' - 0"	5' - 0"	Ground Floor
11	14" x 48"	1' - 2"	4' - 0"	First Floor
12	14" x 42"	1' - 2"	3' - 6"	Ground Floor
13	14" x 48"	1' - 2"	4' - 0"	First Floor
14	36" x 18"	3' - 0"	1' - 6"	Ground Floor
15	24" x 24"	2' - 0"	2' - 0"	Second Floor
16	24" x 24"	2' - 0"	2' - 0"	Second Floor
17	24" x 24"	2' - 0"	2' - 0"	Second Floor
17				

Figure 14.14

Sample door schedule

Modifying a Component Schedule

Once you've created your schedule, you often need to either refine the fields in the schedule or add information to it. To modify a schedule, first access the necessary options by doing one of the following:

- When in a schedule view: from the Properties palette, select any of the five schedule tabs under Other.

- When in a sheet view:

  a. Select the schedule.

  b. Right-click and select Edit Schedule.

  c. From the Properties palette, select any of the five schedule tabs under Other. Right-click anywhere, and select View Properties.

Exporting Schedules

You can export schedules to various formats to facilitate communications with other parties. To export a schedule, use the following steps:

1. Go to the schedule view you want to export.

2. Click the Application menu, and choose Export → Reports → Schedule.

3. Browse to the desired folder, enter a name, and click the Save button.

Schedules export as delimited text files (.txt) that can be later opened in spreadsheet programs such as Microsoft Excel.

4. In the Export Schedule dialog box, under Schedule Appearance, select Multiple Rows, As Formatted to keep the look of the schedule the same.

5. Select Export Group Headers, Footers And Blank Lines.

6. In the Output Options, select (Tab) as the Field Delimiter and the quotes (") as the text qualifiers.

7. Click OK.

Material Takeoff

Using Revit, you can quantify specific materials. Quantifying material is slightly different from a component schedule because it lists a specific material and some of its properties along with the component's properties. In this example, you will list the Gypsum Wall Board material from your example file. You will continue using `Dataset_14_02.rvt` from the previous example. If you are just starting at this point, from the book's companion download files (available at `www.sybex.com/go/introducingrevit2012`), open `Dataset_14_02.rvt`, and then follow these steps:

1. On the View tab's Create panel, click Schedules, and then click Material Takeoff.

2. In the New Material Takeoff dialog box, select Walls as the category. Click OK.

3. In the Material Takeoff Properties dialog box, add the following fields (Figure 14.15):

    *   Function

    *   Family And Type

    *   Structural Usage

    *   Material: Name

    *   Material: Area

    *   Material: Cost

4. On the Filter tab, set the Filter By fields as follows:

    *   Material: Name, Equals, and Finishes – Interior – Gypsum Wall Board

    *   Function, Equals, and Interior

    *   Structural Usage, Equals, and Bearing (as shown in Figure 14.16)

5. On the Sorting/Grouping tab (Figure 14.17), set the options as follows:

    *   Set Sort By to Function.

    *   Select Footer, and select Totals Only.

    *   Select Blank Line.

    *   Select Grand Totals, and select Totals Only.

    *   Select Itemize Every Instance.

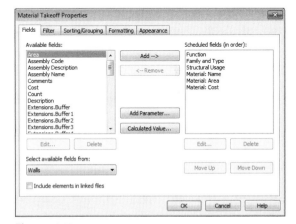

Figure 14.15

Field listing for material takeoff example

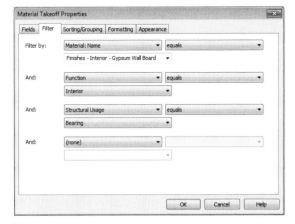

Figure 14.16

Filtering for Gypsum Wall Board material

Figure 14.17

Sorting/Grouping tab for material takeoff example

Material Takeoff Properties

Fields | Filter | Sorting/Grouping | Formatting | Appearance

Sort by: Function ⊙ Ascending ○ Descending
☐ Header ☑ Footer: Totals only ☑ Blank line

Then by: (none) ○ Ascending ○ Descending
☐ Header ☐ Footer: ☐ Blank line

Then by: (none) ○ Ascending ○ Descending
☐ Header ☐ Footer: ☐ Blank line

Then by: (none) ○ Ascending ○ Descending
☐ Header ☐ Footer: ☐ Blank line

☑ Grand totals: Totals only

☑ Itemize every instance

OK | Cancel | Help

6. On the Formatting tab, select Material: Area, and check Calculate Totals.

7. Select Structural Usage, and check Hidden Field to hide the field in the schedule.

8. Click OK and save the settings.

Figure 14.18 shows the takeoff schedule.

Figure 14.18

Wall Material Take-off schedule

Wall Material Takeoff				
Function	Family and Type	Material: Name	Material: Area	Material: Cos
Interior	Basic Wall: Siding Wall 2	Finishes - Interior - Gypsum Wall Board	239 SF	
Interior	Basic Wall: Siding Wall 2	Finishes - Interior - Gypsum Wall Board	705 SF	
Interior	Basic Wall: Interior - 4 1/2"	Finishes - Interior - Gypsum Wall Board	307 SF	
Interior	Basic Wall: Interior - 6 1/2"	Finishes - Interior - Gypsum Wall Board	37 SF	
Interior	Basic Wall: Stone Facade	Finishes - Interior - Gypsum Wall Board	750 SF	
Interior	Basic Wall: Siding Wall 2	Finishes - Interior - Gypsum Wall Board	444 SF	
Interior	Basic Wall: Siding Wall 2	Finishes - Interior - Gypsum Wall Board	175 SF	
Interior	Basic Wall: Siding Wall 2	Finishes - Interior - Gypsum Wall Board	177 SF	
Interior	Basic Wall: Interior - 6 1/2"	Finishes - Interior - Gypsum Wall Board	242 SF	
			3075 SF	
			3075 SF	

You now have a list of all the walls that contain the Gypsum Wall Board material and the associated area. The last step will be to add a cost and multiply that cost by the area to have a total cost:

1. In the Properties palette, click the Fields Edit button.

2. Click the Calculated Value button to create the formula.

3. Enter **Total Cost** as the name (Figure 14.19).

4. Select the Formula radio button.

5. Set Discipline to Common.

6. Set Type to Currency.

7. Insert (**Material: Area / 1 SF**) * **Material: Cost** in the Formula field.

8. Click OK.

Calculated Value

Name: Total Cost

⊙ Formula ○ Percentage

Discipline: Common

Type: Currency

Formula: rial: Area / 1 SF) * Material: Cost ...

OK | Cancel | Help

Figure 14.19

Creating a calculated value

In the next step, you need to divide the Material: Area value by a single unit (1 SF) to allow Revit to multiply the values. *Revit can only multiply the same value type or numbers.*

Figure 14.20

Changing the field format

9. On the Formatting tab, select Total Cost, and check Calculate Totals.

10. Click Field Format, and deselect Use Default Settings.

11. Change the Unit Symbol field to $ (Figure 14.20).

12. Click OK in each dialog box. This will bring you back to your schedule.

13. In any of the empty fields under the Material: Cost column, type the value **1.25** for the cost.

Since all walls are using the same material, Revit will fill in all the values automatically. It will then multiply the area by the cost and give you a total per function and a grand total for the project (Figure 14.21).

Figure 14.21

Completed wall takeoff schedule

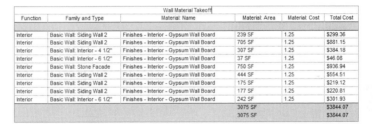

Function	Family and Type	Material: Name	Material: Area	Material: Cost	Total Cost
Interior	Basic Wall: Siding Wall 2	Finishes - Interior - Gypsum Wall Board	239 SF	1.25	$299.36
Interior	Basic Wall: Siding Wall 2	Finishes - Interior - Gypsum Wall Board	705 SF	1.25	$881.15
Interior	Basic Wall: Interior - 4 1/2"	Finishes - Interior - Gypsum Wall Board	307 SF	1.25	$384.18
Interior	Basic Wall: Interior - 6 1/2"	Finishes - Interior - Gypsum Wall Board	37 SF	1.25	$46.08
Interior	Basic Wall: Stone Facade	Finishes - Interior - Gypsum Wall Board	750 SF	1.25	$936.94
Interior	Basic Wall: Siding Wall 2	Finishes - Interior - Gypsum Wall Board	444 SF	1.25	$554.51
Interior	Basic Wall: Siding Wall 2	Finishes - Interior - Gypsum Wall Board	175 SF	1.25	$219.12
Interior	Basic Wall: Siding Wall 2	Finishes - Interior - Gypsum Wall Board	177 SF	1.25	$220.81
Interior	Basic Wall: Interior - 6 1/2"	Finishes - Interior - Gypsum Wall Board	242 SF	1.25	$301.93
			3075 SF		$3844.07
			3075 SF		$3844.07

14. Save the file for use in the next section.

Working with Keynotes

Keynotes are annotation tags that allow you to apply a specific numbering to elements in your building project. Unlike a note created using a text tool, keynotes are a shorthand alphanumeric descriptor for elements in your projects. Why would you use keynotes? Keynotes help ensure consistency in your document set.

Figure 14.22 shows the same detail using both keynotes and text notes to call out elements of your building project. Because text notes are created by each user, in a document set there is a chance for deviation in the descriptions. Keynoting prevents that, as long as the correct keynote is assigned to the element. Using keynotes with a keynote legend requires less room in your details than typical drawing notes. When used effectively, keynoting can simplify your annotation process.

Figure 14.22

Detail with (top) keynotes and (bottom) the text notes

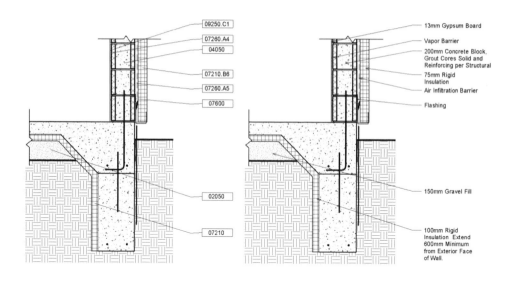

Assigning a Keynote Text File to the Project

A keynote parameter needs to be assigned to your model elements, detail components, and materials in order for the keynote system to tag properly. This keynote parameter will then reference the more detailed description in a keynote text file (Figure 14.23), so you must first associate your project with this keynote text file.

You will continue using Dataset_14_02.rvt. If you are just starting at this point, open the source file from the book's companion download files (available at www.sybex.com/go/introducingrevit2012), and open Dataset_14_02.rvt. Save the file as **Scheduling14kn.rvt**. To associate the keynotes text file, follow these steps:

1. Expand the Annotate tab's Tag panel and select Keynoting Settings.

   This opens the Keynoting Settings dialog box (Figure 14.24).

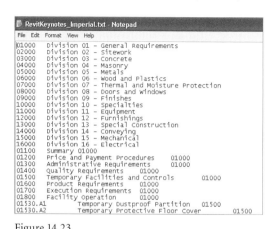

Figure 14.23

Partial view of the keynote text file

Figure 14.24

The Keynoting Settings dialog box

2. Make sure that you have a keynote text file associated with the project. If you don't, click the Browse button and navigate to the keynote file. If Revit Architecture 2012 was installed using the default location, the keynote text file will be found in the US Imperial or US Metric folder location.

For Windows 7 users, the file can be found at:

`C:\ProgramData\Autodesk\RAC 2012\Libraries\US Imperial\RevitKeynotes_Imperial_2004.txt`

For metric users:

`C:\ProgramData\Autodesk\RAC 2012\Libraries\US Metric\RevitKeynotes_Metric.txt`

3. If you have a specific keynoting file you are using for a project, make changes to the Path Type field, setting it to Absolute or Relative.

4. For Numbering Method, select By Keynote.

The Keynoting Settings dialog box provides you with the following options:

Full Path This option displays the entire path of the keynote file.

Saved Path This option displays the filename of the loaded keynote file.

View This option opens the Keynotes dialog box so that you can view the contents of the keynote file.

Absolute (Path Type) This option identifies a specific folder located on your local computer or a network server. The path is stored in the Uniform Naming Convention (UNC) format, such as *servername**share**folder**folder*\keynote.txt.

Relative (Path Type) This option looks for the keynote file where the project file or central model is located. If the file is moved to a new location, Revit expects to find the keynote file in this new folder location as well.

At Library Locations (Path Type) This option looks for the keynote file in the location of the stand-alone installation or network deployment specified.

By Keynote (Numbering Method) This option specifies that the actual keynote number is used in the tag (Figure 14.25), in the 16-division CSI format.

By Sheet (Numbering Method) This option numbers keynotes according to their order of creation on a particular sheet (Figure 14.26). With this system, it is possible that the same keynote could be a different number on a different sheet. Note that when this method is used, the value for the keynotes will be displayed only when the view that the keynotes were created on is placed on a sheet.

Now that you have assigned the keynote file to the project and the keynoting method, you can assign keynotes to model elements.

Figure 14.25

Imperial keynotes, numbered by note

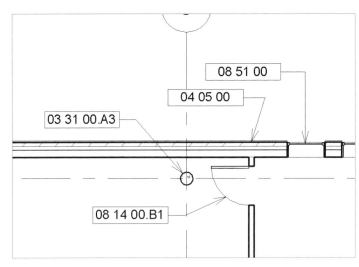

Figure 14.26

By Sheet keynotes

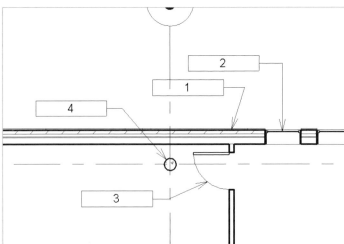

Assigning Keynotes to Model Elements

Assigning keynotes to your model elements, detail components, and materials is the most time-consuming part of using keynotes. This is because you have to assign a value to the Keynote Type parameter for each type (element, detail component, material) that you want to keynote in your project if this has not already been done to families in your Revit content library. The Keynote parameter is a type parameter. To assign a keynote to an element, follow these steps:

1. Click OK to close the Keynote Settings dialog box.

2. Select the element, and edit the type properties.

3. Click the browse button [...] in the Keynote field (Figure 14.27).

4. This takes you to the Keynotes dialog box (Figure 14.28). Select the appropriate keynote for the element you have selected.

5. Click OK to close the Keynotes dialog box.

6. Click OK to apply the selected keynote to the element type properties.

Creating Keynotes

To create a keynote, you are going to follow the same general guidelines that you use when placing tags in the "Using Tags" section of this chapter. With keynotes, though, you have three options:

Element When you select an element, the keynote assigned to the type properties is used. If you select an element that does not have a keynote assigned to it, the Keynote Listing dialog box is displayed, allowing you to assign a keynote.

Material When you select an element, the keynote assigned to the material that was assigned to the selected element is used. If you select a material that does not have a keynote assigned to it, the Keynote Listing dialog box is displayed, allowing you to assign a keynote.

User When you select an element, the Keynote Listing dialog box is displayed, allowing you to assign a keynote. This occurs even if the element already has a keynote assigned to the type property.

As you work on keynoting, you may decide that you need to switch from By Keynote to By Sheet, or vice versa. This is not a problem as long as you remember that Revit will allow you to use only one method at a time per project. To change the numbering method, open the Keynoting Settings dialog box, and change Numbering Method to the desired method.

Creating a Keynoting Legend

The last piece of the keynoting tool that we need to cover is the keynoting legend. This feature will provide the legend for all of your keynotes. To create a keynote legend, do the following:

1. On the View tab's Create panel, click Legends and then Keynote Legend.

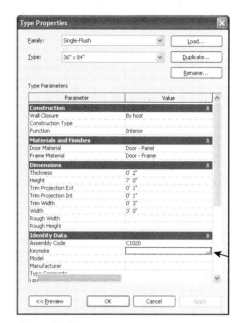

Figure 14.27

Type properties for a door

Figure 14.28

View of the keynote text file within Revit

The New Keynote Legend dialog box will appear, prompting you to name the legend.

2. Provide a unique name for the legend, and then click OK.

You are then taken to the Keynote Legend Properties dialog box. Revit has taken care of setting all the properties for the legend with one exception: You have the ability to specify whether you want to filter keynotes by sheet (Figure 14.29).

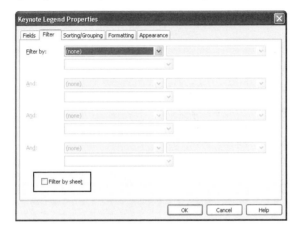

Figure 14.29

Filtering keynotes in the Keynote Legend Properties dialog box

3. Select this option to place all your keynotes into a single legend that you can place on multiple sheets.

When you place the legend on a sheet, only those keynotes that appear on the sheet will be shown in the legend.

Customizing the Keynote File

To customize a keynote file, you just have to edit a tab-delimited text file (with the file extension .txt). Although you can use Notepad or a similar text editor, we prefer to use Microsoft Excel (Figure 14.30). The formatting of the file is much easier to work with in Excel than in Notepad or a similar product.

Open RevitKeynote_Imperial.txt (or RevitKeynote_Metric.txt). You can find this file in the root directory of your Revit content library.

For Windows 7 users, the file can be found at:

C:\ProgramData\Autodesk\RAC 2012\Libraries\US Imperial\RevitKeynotes_Imperial_2004.txt

For metric users:

C:\ProgramData\Autodesk\RAC 2012\Libraries\US Metric\RevitKeynotes_Metric.txt

Figure 14.30

Keynote file opened in Excel for editing

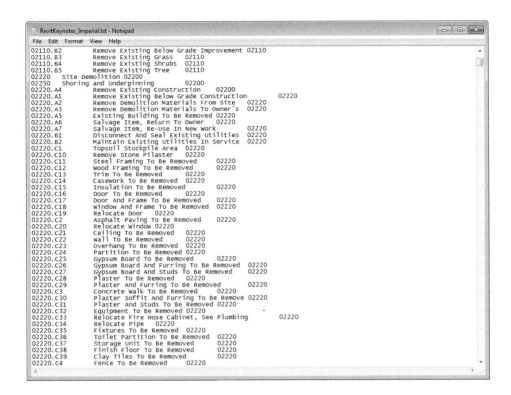

The keynote file is broken up into three columns:

- The keynote number for each keynote.

- The actual keynote.

- The reference section that the keynote falls under. When you open the TXT file in Excel, this column will be labeled User Notes.

In Figure 14.30, refer to keynote 02220.B1 in the RevitKeynote_Imperial.txt file. This is the keynote for Disconnect And Seal Existing Utilities. The third column entry for this entry is 02220. This means that this particular keynote falls under section 2220 Site Demolition.

If you are going to add new entries to the keynote text file, we recommend that you place them in front of the entries provided by Autodesk. In Figure 14.31, we have opened the RevitKeynotes_Imperial.txt file in Excel for editing. We have added four new rows. The first row creates a new User Notes division. Rows 2 through 4 are new keynotes.

Figure 14.31

User-modified keynote file

	A	B	C
1		0 Division 00	User Notes
2		1 BIM Standards and Procedures	0
3		2 Site Preparation	0
4	0002.A1	Clear Debris	2
5		1000 Division 01 - General Requirements	
6		2000 Division 02 - Sitework	
7		3000 Division 03 - Concrete	
8		4000 Division 04 - Masonry	
9		5000 Division 05 - Metals	
10		6000 Division 06 - Wood and Plastics	
11		7000 Division 07 - Thermal and Moisture Protection	
12		8000 Division 08 - Doors and Windows	
13		9000 Division 09 - Finishes	
14		10000 Division 10 - Specialties	
15		11000 Division 11 - Equipment	
16		12000 Division 12 - Furnishings	
17		13000 Division 13 - Special Construction	
18		14000 Division 14 - Conveying	
19		15000 Division 15 - Mechanical	
20		16000 Division 16 - Electrical	

Whether using Excel or a text editor, make sure that you save the file as a TXT file in a tab-delimited file format. After you have made your edits and saved the file, reassociate it with your project or template, and you can use those new definitions.

CHAPTER 15

Detailing

This chapter concentrates on detailing functions such as detail components and detail lines. We'll also cover how to create a typical details library so that you can systematically develop, store, and reuse your Autodesk Revit Architecture drafting views in a standardized fashion. Since drafting views have no connection to the model, they can be saved and inserted from project to project.

This chapter covers the following topics:

- **Understanding detail and drafting views**
- **Component symbol fundamentals**
- **Detailing tools**
- **Creating and managing detail libraries**

Understanding Detail and Drafting Views

Detail views are those that are directly cut from the model and show modeled elements, whether they are section, elevation, or plan views. Within those views, you must configure the display accordingly, and you most likely will add 2D elements to complete the section or detail.

Drafting views, on the other hand, have no connection to the model. The elements used in these views are completely 2D (see Figure 15.1) and are essentially like doing 2D CAD in AutoCAD or MicroStation. In fact, once you get proficient in using Revit detailing, you will find that it can be as fast or faster to do than if you are working in comparable 2D programs.

In both of these view types, you can add additional nonmodeled elements such as detail lines, filled regions, and detail components in order to finish it.

This prompts the question: *How much should be modeled and how much should be done with 2D elements?* You will quickly find as you learn this process that not everything can be modeled and that you must take great care in choosing how much is appropriate in any particular situation. Otherwise, you will find your fee getting burned up quickly on elements that make little difference to the overall model.

Since detail views are actual cuts through the model, they can easily change as the design process continues, which can be very disconcerting. You think you have finished a detail view and then come back a few weeks later only to find that modeled elements have moved and the whole view needs to be reworked. If you have placed drafting elements into the view, they probably did not move with the modeled elements and so must be repositioned. Drafting views, on the other hand, have no modeled elements, so this problem does not occur.

One important way to keep the modeled elements together with view-specific detail components is to actually embed the 2D components into the model family. That is a more advanced way to approach detailing. Another way to avoid this situation is to use the Freeze Drawing extension. If you have a subscription contract with Autodesk, you can download the Extensions for Revit for free from the Autodesk website. The Freeze Drawing extension turns a detail view into a drafting view, so it is independent of the model. The view is actually exported to AutoCAD in the background and then re-imported as a drafting view. If you want to create a typical detail, you will find that this function will work well for you. The downside is that the detail view is divorced from the model, and any updates to the model will not be reflected in it.

Figure 15.1

Drafting view of a curtain wall jamb

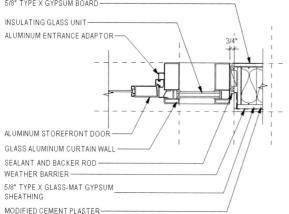

5/8" TYPE X GYPSUM BOARD

INSULATING GLASS UNIT

ALUMINUM ENTRANCE ADAPTOR

3/4"

ALUMINUM STOREFRONT DOOR

GLASS ALUMINUM CURTAIN WALL

SEALANT AND BACKER ROD

WEATHER BARRIER

5/8" TYPE X GLASS-MAT GYPSUM SHEATHING

MODIFIED CEMENT PLASTER

This is a very important point to consider. It is easy to get into this habit in the final phases of design, when schedules are tight and you have lots of detailing to finish. You start quickly creating drafting views for your details and then realize they do not reflect what the model looks like. It could take considerable time to adjust the model, so you decide to just correct the drafting views and not the model. That is a slippery slope, since the more you do it like that, the more your model loses its integrity. So, you must be very mindful of the mix of modeled and detail items and strive for consistency.

What tools are available for this task of creating finished views? The following sections will walk you through the basics and introduce you to the way this process works and to those tools you will be using time and again as you work to complete your projects.

Component Symbol Fundamentals

Revit Architecture comes with a full library of useful 2D component symbols, and you can create your own as well. As you do more and more projects, you can and should build a library of component symbols that conform to your company standards and that can then be used over and over again. Managing and categorizing them for easy use should be a priority.

You will use three different types of component symbols for your detailing needs:

- Detail components
- Repeating details
- Legend components

The tools are located on the Component drop-down of the Detail panel of the Annotate tab. These are not to be confused with the Component tool that is on the Home tab. That tool inserts three-dimensional modeled elements such as furniture and trees into the project.

Detail Components

Detail components are 2D representations of modeled elements, such as concrete masonry units in sections that can be used in your detailing views. The components appear only in the view in which they are placed. Revit Architecture ships with a large library of detail components that can be loaded into your project as required. In Figure 15.2, you can see a finished slip joint at metal panel/plaster plan detail. The panel head joint detail item is copied and shown at the bottom of the figure.

What detail components are you able to use in this detail?

- The panel head joint
- The gypsum sheathing
- The slip joint
- The 6″ interior studs

Figure 15.2

The slip joint at metal panel/plaster plan detail

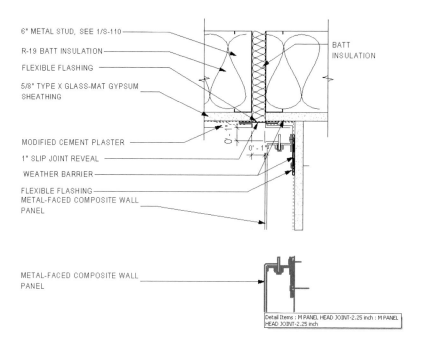

6" METAL STUD, SEE 1/S-110

R-19 BATT INSULATION

FLEXIBLE FLASHING

5/8" TYPE X GLASS-MAT GYPSUM SHEATHING

MODIFIED CEMENT PLASTER

1" SLIP JOINT REVEAL

WEATHER BARRIER

FLEXIBLE FLASHING
METAL-FACED COMPOSITE WALL PANEL

BATT INSULATION

METAL-FACED COMPOSITE WALL PANEL

Detail Items : M PANEL HEAD JOINT-2.25 inch : M PANEL HEAD JOINT-2.25 inch

Added to that are some detail lines, the batt insulation, dimensions, and text. With that, you will have the entire detail completed and ready for insertion onto your sheet. In the following sections of this chapter, you will examine these items more closely.

The components are classified in the *Construction Specifications Institute (CSI) format* so that you can easily browse to your exact component in the detail component libraries. Within the particular folder, you will find component families for Top, Side, and Sectional views of the element. These elements can be used in detail views cut from the model as well as in your drafting views. As an example, let's load a CMU block module into a project by doing the following:

1. From the book's companion download files (available at www.sybex.com/go/introducingrevit2012), open Dataset_15_01.rvt, and browse to Section 1 if it's not there already.

   You will see two generic modeled wall elements: one wood and one CMU.

2. On the Load From Library panel of the Insert tab, click Load Family.

3. Click Detail Components in the Imperial (or Metric) Library.

4. Click Div 04-Masonry.

5. Within the Masonry folder, select the 042200-Concrete Unit Masonry folder.

6. Double-click the Fluted CMU-8 Flutes-Section family, and it will be loaded into the project.

FINDING DETAIL COMPONENTS

Components that do not exist in the shipped libraries can be created, and you can also find many of them on the Web in such places as the Autodesk Seek site or a particular manufacturer's site. More and more manufacturers are seeing the benefit of creating full libraries of their products, so be sure to look for them. There's no reason to "reinvent the wheel."

Now that the detail component has been loaded into your project, let's examine the basic process of inserting the component into a detail. As you have been learning, Revit families can have any number of specific types. In the case of the Fluted CMU family just loaded, there are 13 different types already created within the family, depicting different widths of CMU wall. You can add more types if required. In the current example, you are adding the component to an 8″ masonry wall, so you will use an 8″ × 8″ × 16″ type.

To add a component to your view, do the following:

1. On the Detail panel of the Annotate tab, click Detail Component in the Component drop-down.

   The Type Selector in the Properties palette will list all the loaded components (see Figure 15.3).

2. In the list, highlight the Fluted CMU-8 Flutes-Section 8″ × 8″ × 16″ type, and drag it onto your model.

3. Place the component over the modeled wall element.

4. Lock the component into place by closing the blue padlocks (see Figure 15.4).

After you place components into your detail, you can move them either to the front or to the back of the view (called setting the *draw order*) so that they will display correctly in the detail. To alter the draw order of a particular component, highlight it and, on the Arrange tab, select which way, frontward or backward, you want to move it.

That is the basic approach to loading and placing a component into your project.

Repeating Details

A *repeating detail*, as its name implies, uses a single component and repeats it along a linear path at a defined spacing. Repeating details are very useful and can save considerable amounts of time and effort if used appropriately. Masonry block walls are a good example of how this can be used to create a detail. The masonry block unit is specified

Figure 15.3

Selecting a component from the Type Selector

Figure 15.4

Adding the component over the modeled wall

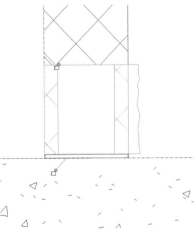

along with the vertical spacing of the block. Best practice is to identify any repetitive elements that you will be using frequently in your details and turn them into a repeating detail.

To add a new repeating detail to your project, the general procedure is as follows:

1. On the Annotate tab's Detail panel, click the Component drop-down, and choose Repeating Detail Component.

2. Select a detail component from the Type Selector in the Properties palette.

3. Click Edit Type.

4. Specify the component in the Detail parameter.

5. Specify the Layout type.

6. Specify the Spacing value for the repeating pattern.

7. Click OK to exit.

If no type exists, you will need to make one. So, let's create one in the following exercise. To make a new CMU block a Repeating Detail type, do the following:

1. Open `Dataset_15_02.rvt`, (`mDataset_15_02.rvt`) and go to Section 1.

2. On the Annotate tab's Detail panel, click the Component drop-down, and choose Repeating Detail Component.

3. Click Edit Type in the Properties palette and then Duplicate in the Type Properties dialog box.

4. Name the new repeating detail **CMU 8 × 8 × 16 Split Face** (**M_Split Face CMU-Section**), and click OK.

5. In the Type Properties dialog box, select Fluted CMU-8 Flutes-Section: 8″ × 8″ × 16″ (200 × 200 × 400mm) from the Detail drop-down.

6. Set the Spacing to **0′ 8″** (**200mm**).

7. Click OK to close the Type Properties dialog box.

Your Type Properties dialog box should look like Figure 15.5.

Figure 15.5

Type Properties dialog box for a Repeating Detail type

Back in Section 1, you can now draw an instance of the CMU repeating detail.

8. Click to place the first block.

9. Move your mouse pointer and click at the end of the repeated units.

Your detail should look something like Figure 15.6.

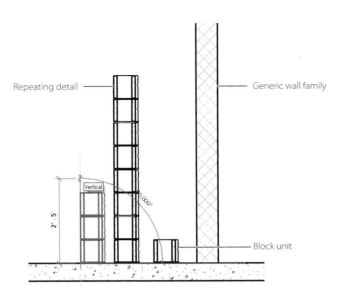

Figure 15.6
Repeating details

Legend Components

Legend components, as the name indicates, are symbols used for creating legends. Virtually all projects require one. Legend component symbols are 2D representations that depict an annotation or modeled element in your project. Examples of this type of element are north arrows, scale bars, and wall types (see Figure 15.7). Regardless of the scale of the particular view you are working on, the symbols will maintain the same size when printed. They are scale independent. For an actual example of a legend, see Chapter 2, "Views."

Suppose you want to create a graphical legend of door types that you have added to your project. If you use an instance of the actual family as a symbol, that element will be counted as being part of the project when scheduled.

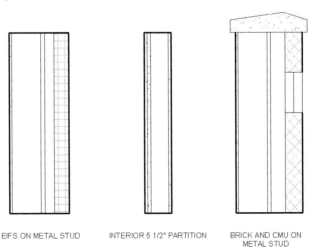

Figure 15.7
Wall types in elevation used as legend components

EIFS ON METAL STUD   INTERIOR 5 1/2" PARTITION   BRICK AND CMU ON METAL STUD

Of course, you do not want that counted because it is not really part of the building you are designing. So when you create a legend instead of using a real wall segment, you drag a legend component symbol of the family into the legend. Once you have placed it, you can configure it to show a plan or elevation view, and it can be shown in coarse, medium, or fine mode.

Legends are the only graphic views that can be placed onto multiple sheets. Annotation symbols, materials, phasing graphics, line styles, and model items like doors, detail, and model groups all can have legend symbols. Creating one is a fairly straightforward thing to do.

Follow these steps to make a component legend:

1. On the View tab, choose the Create panel, click the Legends button, and select Legend from the drop-down list.

2. Give the legend a name, and give it a scale.

3. Click the Component drop-down on the Annotate tab.

4. Select Legend Component from the drop-down list.

5. On the Options bar, highlight the symbol you want from the drop-down list in the Family Type listing (see Figure 15.8).

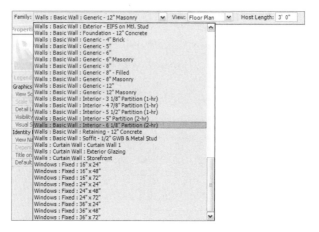

Figure 15.8

The Legend compo-
nent's Options bar

6. Select the view type to display—Plan, Section, or Elevation—depending on the symbol type.

7. Specify a Host Length on the Options bar for the legend symbol.

8. Place the component in the view.

9. Add any other detail or group components to the view.

10. Create descriptive text next to each item.

11. The Legend view can now be dragged onto a sheet. Sheets are discussed later in Chapter 16.

Those are the basics for component symbols. Of course, as you learned previously, you can create detail groups that allow you to assemble and associate a set of detail components that you will use more than once in your project. Once the group is created and named, you can locate it in the Group area at the bottom of the Project Browser for easy insertion by dragging it into your views. For more information, refer to Chapter 10, "Groups."

The next section will introduce you to more of the detailing tools that Revit Architecture provides so you can create great-looking and accurate details.

Embedding Detail Components in Modeling Families

As you progress in learning Revit Architecture, you will want to create your models in such a way that the views derived from the cut sections and elevations are as complete as possible without adding a lot of view-specific 2D entities such as lines and detail components. It is the most efficient way to proceed with your virtual design since you will not have to then manage all those detached entities as the model flexes during the design process. You will find that having to constantly edit and relocate elements is a time-consuming task.

One important way to accomplish this goal is to embed your detail components into the modeled families. What do we mean by that? This is a way to keep the detail elements with the modeled elements as they move during the design process. The design development phase can see your model changing constantly and dramatically.

Let's look at the example of a 2×6 (40×150mm) wood-bearing wall in a section view and see how this cut of the wall was developed in order to display this way (see Figure 15.9). This will give you a better understanding of some of the more advanced techniques you need to learn to be a power user of Revit.

In this example, you will add detail components into the wall family type so that the top and bottom plates are automatically shown when you cut the section. First, you go to the profile family to create a profile with an added detail component inserted into it. Then, you go to the wall definition and apply that profile as a sweep. It is a two-step process that sounds more onerous than it actually is.

The general procedure to complete this process is as follows. First you create the required profile for the 2×6 (40×150mm) flat stud plate.

1. Start a new project or work with an existing project.

2. On the Application menu, choose New → Family.

3. Choose `Profile.rft` (`Metric Profile.rft`) as the template type, and then click Open.

4. On the Insert tab's Load From Library panel, click the Load Family button.

5. In the US Imperial library section, select Detail Components, and then browse to the `Div 06-Wood And Plastic` folder.

Figure 15.9

Wood-bearing wall type with embedded profiles for top and bottom wood plates and bolts

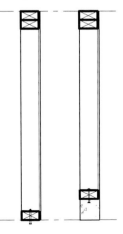

6. Browse and select 061100 – Wood Framing, and then choose Nominal Cut Lumber – Section.

7. Click Open, and then select the 2×6 (40×150mm) component. Click OK to exit.

8. Go to the Ref. Level plan and zoom extents so you see the reference planes.

9. On the Home tab's Detail panel, click Detail Component.

10. Place the 2×6 (40×150mm) component at the intersection of the reference planes.

    Now that you have inserted the component, you will place and lock profile lines around it:

11. Select the 2×6 (40×150mm) component, and rotate it 90°.

12. Center the 2×6 (40×150mm) component on the vertical reference plane.

13. Align the bottom line of the 2×6 (40×150mm) with the horizontal reference plane.

14. On the Home tab's Detail panel, select the Line tool.

15. Now draw profile lines at the exterior edges of the 2×6 (40×150mm) component by using the Rectangle tool from the Draw panel.

16. Lock them to the component by closing the blue padlocks.

17. Select the detail component, and then click Visibility Settings on the Visibility panel of the Modify | Detail Items tab.

18. Deselect Coarse by deselecting the box, and then click OK.

19. On the Application menu, click Save, and save the profile file as `2x6 (40x150mm) Plate`.

20. Click Load Into Project on the Family Editor panel of the Modify tab, and load the profile into your project file.

The profile with the embedded detail component is now complete and ready to be used in the wood wall family. As you can see, the process is not too difficult to accomplish.

In the final part of the process, you will add the profile you just created with the embedded component into the wall family definition as a sweep.

1. Switch to a plan view.

2. On the Build panel of the Home tab, click Wall from the Wall drop-down.

3. In the Properties palette, change the wall type to Generic 6″ (150mm), and click Edit Type.

4. Click the Edit button in the Structure Value field.

5. Click the Preview button in the Edit Assembly dialog box.

6. In the View list, choose Section: Modify Type Attributes in order to get a sectional view of the wall.

7. Click the Sweeps button, and then click the Add button in the Wall Sweeps dialog box.

8. Select 2×6 (40×150mm) Plate for the profile name in the Profile field.

9. Finally, change the offset value to **–3″** (**–75mm**) and click Apply.

   You should see the profile at the bottom of the wall in the section preview.

10. Click OK until you exit all the dialog boxes.

The basic procedure is now competed. Did you get all the way through it? Now let's look at an instance of the wall:

1. Go to a plan view.

2. Draw a wall segment.

3. Create a section through it.

   Remember that you set the Visibility so that the component does not show in Coarse detail level, so make sure the section is in Medium or Fine mode.

4. Move the wall in the section, and notice that the bottom plate moves with it.

   That is just what you were trying to accomplish.

Now that you have completed that, for added practice return to the wall definition family and add two top plates to the wall definition in the same manner as you have just done.

This is just one example of how using embedded components can make your modeling life much easier. Did you also notice in Figure 15.9 that there is a bolt into the concrete? That is another detail component that was added to the profile. Can you add that one into your wall definition too?

Now that you have an idea of how to use component elements, let's next explore the major detailing tools that you will be using as you work in Revit Architecture.

Detailing Tools

Detail lines are those that you use for basic 2D drawing purposes. You use them to complete detail views and, of course, for most of your drafting view lines. Detail lines can add important information that might not be necessary to model. As opposed to model lines, which appear in all views, detail lines are view-specific. One warning to consider is that overusing 2D linework rather than modeling elements means that your 3D model will correspondingly lose its integrity. Too much "faking" by using 2D linework because you are rushed for time or do not know how to model an element is not a good practice.

By default Revit comes with a set of existing line styles. Some of these types cannot be removed; you can identify these easily because they have brackets around their names. You can also create new line types easily. Best practice is to create a set of line styles that corresponds to your company's standards and add the set to your template file.

Detail Lines

To add linework to your detail, follow these general steps:

1. On the Detail panel of the Annotate tab, click the Detail Line tool (or use the shortcut DL).

2. After the Modify | Place Detail Lines tab appears, select a line style from the Line Style panel (see Figure 15.10).

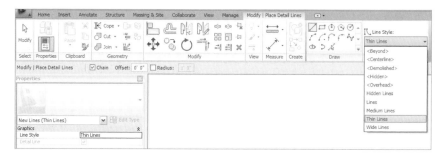

3. Select a line tool from the Draw panel such as a Rectangle, Arc, or Spline.

4. Sketch the line as required.

The Pick Lines option is important to use when you are doing linework because it allows you to draw by selecting existing geometry or linework, which can save considerable time and effort as you work.

Use this mode by selecting the green line in the Draw panel with the mouse pointer. You then select an existing line or edge in the view, and it will be duplicated, but with the line type that you have selected from the Line Style panel.

Temporary dimensions aid you in placing the linework (see Figure 15.11). As you draw the line, drag the cursor in the direction you want to draw, and start typing. That will allow you to specify the exact length of the line you are drawing within the temporary dimension box.

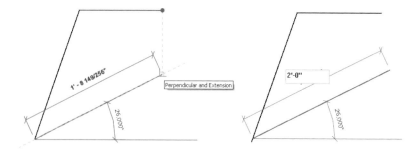

That is basically how lines are placed in the project. Next you'll learn how to edit them after they are in the view.

Editing Detail Lines

Once you start adding lines in your views to create geometry, you will need to edit them in many ways such as by moving, copying, and trimming. Those commands are located on the Modify panel of the Modify tab. The Modify commands work for some modeled elements as well. For instance, you can trim two walls together or two structural beams together. Figure 15.12 shows a spline before and after its geometry has been edited. First you highlight the line, which will show grips in blue that can be dragged to new positions. In this case, the open circles can be dragged to alter the spline angles. The filled blue grips at either end will extend the spline segment. Of course, different line types will have different grips or snap points that can be dragged.

Figure 15.12

Editing the spline by dragging the blue open grips

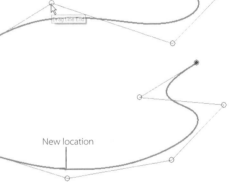

New location

That was not too difficult, was it? Now let's see how to create a new line style for your project. Creating a new line style is not a difficult task. The more important task is to develop a good system of line definitions. Perhaps you use the National CAD Standards AIA layering system in AutoCAD. You can re-create the same names in Revit for easy translation of details back and forth between Revit and AutoCAD. To create new line styles, you specify several parameters: a line weight, a line color, and a line pattern.

To edit an existing line style or add a new one, do the following:

1. Click Additional Settings on the Settings panel of the Manage tab.

2. Click Line Styles in the drop-down menu to access the Line Styles dialog box.

3. Either edit the existing line style (the weight, color, or pattern), or click the New button to create a new line type (see Figure 15.13).

Figure 15.13

Creating a new line type via the Line Styles dialog box

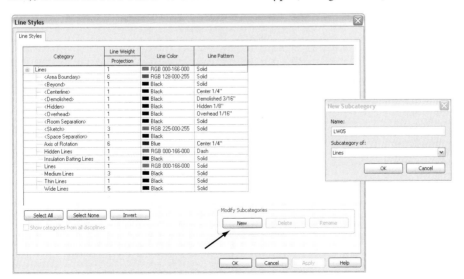

The next section looks at plotting issues related to line widths that might need adjusting depending upon your plotter type.

Line Weight Plotting

As you have seen, each line style has an associated line weight assigned to it. For different view scales, the weight can be adjusted so you can control the look of your plotted output better. This will take some experimentation on your part since it depends a lot on which brand of plotter you are using to plot your project. All the plotters act a little bit differently, necessitating some adjustment to these values. Model line weights, perspective line weights, and annotation line weights can all be controlled in this way.

The Line Weights dialog box (see Figure 15.14) is opened by going to the Manage tab and then clicking Line Weights on the Additional Settings drop-down on the Settings panel. Once you are in the dialog box, you can adjust the values in three tabs:

- Model Line Weights
- Perspective Line Weights
- Annotation Line Weights

In the Model Line Weights tab, if you click the Add or Delete button you can also add new scales to the list that might not be there by default or delete those you might want to remove.

Figure 15.14

The Line Weights dialog box

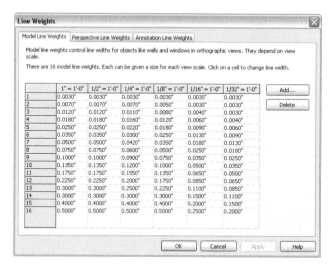

Line Patterns

Line patterns are used to create the different line styles such as Hidden and Centerline that you will use when documenting your projects. Many line patterns are already created for you, and you probably will not need to create new ones too often. Open the Line Patterns dialog box by going to the Manage tab's Settings panel. In the Additional Settings drop-down, select Line Patterns. Each pattern is a set of dots, dashes, and spaces with specified lengths (see Figure 15.15). You can edit the existing patterns and create new patterns that you might require as needed.

Figure 15.15

The Line Patterns dialog box

Overriding Lines with the Linework Tool

The line styles that you have learned to use for detailing lines in your 2D drafting views also have an important function to play for lines of detail views that contain modeled elements. Using the Linework tool, you can quickly override any line that is displayed in order to emphasize or possibly deemphasize it in some way. With the Linework tool, you can override the line style of most model lines if they do not display as you prefer. The override is applied only for the current view that you are working in even though the modeled element may show up in other views. You might want to emphasize a line by making it heavier, or you might want to make it invisible. You can do this with the Linework tool.

You can find the Linework tool on the Modify tab in the View panel. To edit a line using the Linework tool:

1. Simply select a line type from the Line Styles drop-down list.

2. Select a line in the view that you want to change.

Be aware, though, that the Linework tool does not work on detail components, dimensions lines, models lines, or detail lines.

> **BE CAREFUL USING THE LINEWORK TOOL**
>
> In practice, the Linework tool can be quite finicky and unpredictable. You will find quite often that once you change a particular line with the Linework tool, you will come back a few days later and find it has reverted to its original appearance. Also, getting your modeled elements to display correctly can be quite challenging. Display issues take up a considerable amount of time while you are working on a project, and it can be very tempting to just use the Linework tool to correct those issues. Best practice is to minimize that usage and to work diligently to resolve your display issues in other ways.

Representing Insulation

Surely insulation is not something that is readily modeled, so the task falls to 2D detailing in most cases. The Insulation family has two parameters:

- Insulation Width
- Insulation Bulge To Width Ratio

As with most other Revit families, you can create different types by varying these parameters (see Figure 15.16). Once an instance is placed into your project, you can stretch or compact the instance by moving the grips at each end.

Figure 15.16

**Three types of
Insulation**

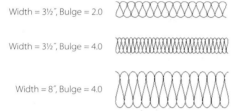

Width = 3½", Bulge = 2.0

Width = 3½", Bulge = 4.0

Width = 8", Bulge = 4.0

The general approach to adding insulation to your detail is as follows:

1. Select the Insulation tool from the Detail panel on the Annotate tab.
2. On the Options bar, set the following:
   - The width
   - An offset distance for placement
   - Whether the insulation is to be drawn to the center, near side, or far side
3. Simply click at the starting point and then at the end point to draw the instance of insulation.

Filled Regions

Filled regions are hatch patterns that can be added to your details. A continuous boundary of lines is sketched and then filled with a pattern of your choosing. The boundary lines for the filled region can be invisible or any combination of line types. For instance, if you were creating an earth hatched area, you might want the top boundary line to represent the finish grade, so you would make it a solid line, while the other boundary lines remain invisible (see Figure 15.17). By default Revit comes with a set of defined patterns. You can add to this set by importing pattern files from AutoCAD or by creating your own patterns.

Here is the general process for creating a filled region in a detail view:

1. On the Annotate tab's Detail panel, click Filled Region on the Region drop-down.
2. Use the Draw tools on the Modify | Create Filled Region Boundary tab to create your region boundary.

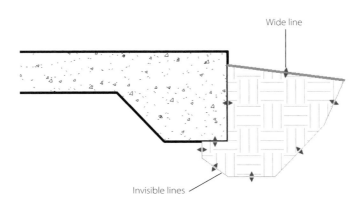

Figure 15.17

Earth hatching added to detail

Use Invisible Lines for your boundary where you do not want to see them in the final pattern.

3. In the Type Selector, select the Filled Region pattern that you would like to use.

4. Click the green check mark in the Mode panel to finish the geometry.

If you need to change the Filled Region pattern after the region was created:

1. Highlight the geometry.

2. In the Properties palette's Type Selector, select an existing fill type for the bounded region.

If the pattern that you want to use does not exist, you can create your own. Filled regions are just another Revit family, and different types can be created. To create an Earth fill type, do the following:

1. On the Annotate tab, click Filled Region on the Region drop-down.

2. On the Properties palette, click Edit Type.

3. In the Type Properties dialog box, click Duplicate.

4. Give the new fill pattern the name **Earth Hatch**.

5. In the Type Properties dialog box, click the ellipsis button in the far right end of the Fill Pattern Value box.

6. Select Earth in the list of patterns in the Fill Patterns dialog box, and then click OK.

7. Give the pattern a line weight and color, and specify whether it should be transparent or opaque.

8. Click OK, and the new pattern is complete and ready for use in your filled regions.

But what if the fill pattern does not exist? New patterns can be created. With the Simple option, you define an angle and line spacing and whether the pattern will be parallel lines or a crosshatch pattern. Or you can import patterns from the AutoCAD acad.pat file. To add a new fill pattern, do the following:

1. On the Manage tab, click Fill Patterns in the Additional Settings drop-down.

Figure 15.18

Selecting or creating a new fill pattern

2. In the Fill Patterns dialog box (see Figure 15.18), click the New button.

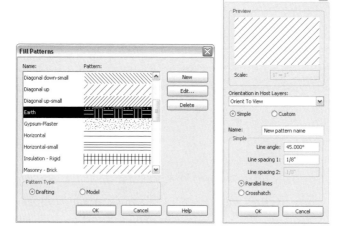

3. In the New Pattern dialog box, select the Simple or Custom option.

4. Define the values for the Simple option or import a pattern for the Custom option.

5. Click OK, and exit the dialog boxes.

WHY DON'T MY DETAILS LOOK LIKE I WANT THEM TO?

Display issues are a constant concern when you are creating your construction documents. You will discover as you learn to model that a good amount of your time (and fee) is spent getting the detail views that you have derived from the model to appear correctly. It can be a very frustrating task. At times there is just no way to get it to look the way you want it to look.

The Masking Regions tool allows you to hide problem areas. You can leave it that way, or you can draw over the masking region with 2D lines in order to "fake" what you think you should be showing. It is not good practice, though, to overdo faking the detail view. You need to concentrate on maintaining the integrity of the model as much as possible. Remember that your plan, section, and elevation views are derived from the model. As you fake more and more on your details, you are giving up on the integrity of the model. Eventually this will lead to disaster because your model becomes a false representation of the design.

Masking Regions

Masking regions are a special variety of filled region used to hide problem areas (see Figure 15.19). Masking regions can be used to mask detail elements or modeled elements. To add a masking region, do the following:

1. On the Annotate tab, click the Detail panel, and choose Masking Region on the Region drop-down.

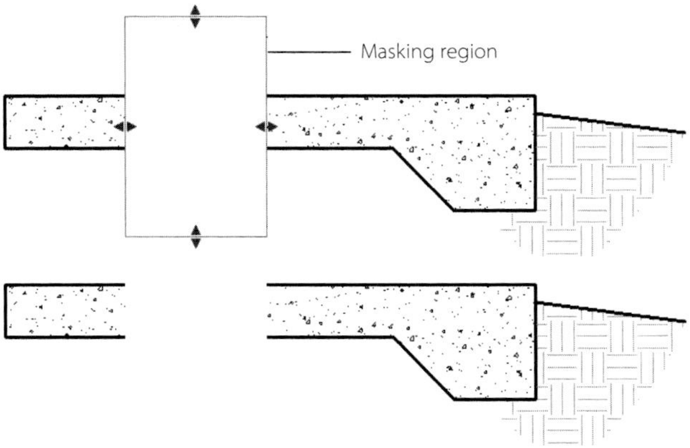

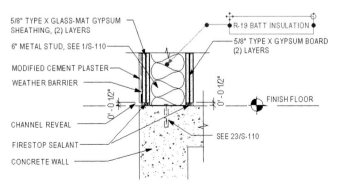

Figure 15.19

Masking region covering a portion of the detail

2. In Sketch mode, draw the boundary of the masking region.

   Boundary lines can be of any line type desired. Closed boundaries can be added within the outer boundary to further refine the masked area.

3. Complete the masking region by clicking the green check mark in the Mode panel.

   After completion, you can highlight the region and adjust its boundaries by dragging the blue grips.

No discussion of detailing would be complete without learning how to add text notes, so let's look at how this tool is used in Revit Architecture.

Adding Text

In Chapter 3, "Constraints and Dimensions," you learned the basics of how dimensioning can be added. In Chapter 14, "Tags, Schedules, and Keynotes," you learned how to apply tags to elements and how those tags can then be scheduled as necessary to help document your project. Best practice is to tag elements as much as possible in any view that needs to be documented. This gives you the maximum flexibility since the tag value changes automatically when the type of element is updated. But there are many situations where you must use text notes; see Figure 15.20, which has a mix of tags and text notes.

Figure 15.20

Some annotations are tags, and some are text.

In this section, you will learn about the mechanics of the Text tool in Revit Architecture. The text function comes with full formatting capabilities (see Figure 15.21), including the following:

- Leader segments can be added as one line, two lines, or a curved line.
- The leader location in relation to the note has six different options.
- Notes can be aligned left, center, or right.
- Lists are supported in the notation—bullets and numbering.
- Word wrapping is supported.
- Text can be boxed.
- Spelling can be checked and corrected.
- Find and replace can be done on the body of the note.

Figure 15.21

The Modify | Place Text tab

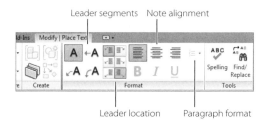

Text, like other detailing elements, is view-specific except in dependent views. Now that you see some of the capabilities of the Text tool, you'll learn how to add a note to your view.

Adding a Text Note to Your View

Adding a notation is not at all difficult, and it is very dynamic in that the tool stays active while you rotate or move the note. To add a text notation to a view:

1. Click the Text tool on the Text panel of the Annotate tab, or click the Text button on the Quick Access toolbar.

2. Create a leader first if you need one.

   There are quite a few leader placement options so that you can add the leader to the top, middle, or bottom of the note. The last pick for the leader line placement (or the first pick if there is no leader) will set the upper left-hand corner of the text box.

3. Once the box is established, type the text string into the box.

4. After you complete the text, click outside the box somewhere in the drawing area to complete the insertion.

When you highlight the text note, several controls become available (see Figure 15.22). The text box can be dragged to a new position. It can also be rotated. The blue solid grips will stretch the note box. When you do that, the text inside the box will wrap as necessary to fit the new box size, as long as you have not added hard returns into the text string. There is also a leader segmentation grip so you can make two lined leader segments and control their lengths.

If you need to edit the text string, simply highlight the text note and then click into the text area, which becomes active. You make your changes to the text string and then exit by clicking outside it in the drawing area.

Figure 15.22

Text note with text box editing features displayed

Creating and Editing Text Styles

Revit Architecture uses Windows TrueType fonts. You will find it necessary to make many different types of text styles since very few are there by default. In the following exercise, you'll make a new style for ⅛″ (2.5mm) text notes using a Times New Roman font (see Figure 15.23).

Figure 15.23

Type Properties dialog box

1. On the Annotate tab, click the small arrow on the bottom right of the Text panel.

   That will display the Type Properties dialog box.

2. Click Duplicate, and then name the new text style ⅛″ **(2.5mm)**
   Times New Roman.

3. Click OK to return to the Type Properties dialog box.

4. Set the options as follows:

Background	Transparent
Leader Arrowhead	Arrow Filled 20 Degree
Text Font	Times New Roman
Text Size	1/8″ (2.5mm)

5. Click OK to finish.

   To edit text styles:

1. Select the Text tool.

2. In the Properties palette, select the type you want to edit.

3. Select Edit Type, and make the corrections.

4. Click OK, and the change is complete.

Preparing General Notes

General notes are the big text item that you usually will face in a project. Yes, there are plenty of small notations on plans and details, but they do not compare to your general notes, which are usually a sheet or two at the front of your document set. These take all the formatting capabilities you'd expect from a full-blown word processor such as Microsoft Word. We will offer two approaches for adding general notes.

Most general note sets consist of specific sections. One good approach to preparing and reusing them is to make each general note section in its own drafting view. Within the drafting view, create the section text in one text box. That way, you can control the formatting more easily. Drag the sections onto the sheet as needed. From job to job, different sections can be taken on or off the sheet as they are required.

As you will see in the next section on detail libraries, you will be able to import the sheet of notes, or any individual drafting view, into your new projects. You might even consider keeping a specific Revit file with all your general notes there so you can easily manage them and access them on new projects.

There is another approach to preparing and managing general notes on a sheet. If you have a subscription to Autodesk, you will find a general notes creator in the extensions. Microsoft Word documents with full formatting can be imported. The tool then manages the notes in rows and columns of your choosing, making the tedious layout work on the sheet easier to handle.

Creating and Managing Detail Libraries

The discussion of drafting views cannot be complete without investigating how these details can be managed as a set of typical details. How can you use your current details in Revit? Do they all need to be redrawn? The answer is that with some preparation, you can import your current set of 2D details directly into drafting views. If you are transitioning from 2D AutoCAD or MicroStation, you probably already have a set of typical details, and you will not want to draw them again. As you begin your company's transformation into the BIM process, you might want to put off this task. Consider what might be a good implementation timeline for implementing portions of your new BIM system.

Your drafting staff will learn this new technology at differing speeds, so it is necessary to keep work for them in AutoCAD until they can improve their skills in Revit. It can be quite overwhelming to try to transition your whole drafting system at one time. Once you build up experience with the new modeling workflow, you will want to have the whole project in Revit, typical details and all.

You can take three approaches:

- Leave the typical details in AutoCAD:
  - Create a blended construction document set for your project, with some work done in Revit while the typical detail sheets remain in AutoCAD.

- One downside is that you need to plot the project from two platforms, so you will need to maintain two title sheets.
- Import/link the details into Revit as blocks without exploding them:
  - In this case, you will do any drafting corrections and additions to the blocks in AutoCAD.
  - The details will be linked into the Revit file so that they automatically update to reflect those changes.
  - This has the advantage that you will then be able to plot your entire project in Revit. The sheets will also have a similar look to them.
- Create the details from scratch in Revit:
  - Though initially more time-consuming to complete, this approach is direct and eliminates the need to touch up the details that have been imported.
  - Selectively prepare typical details using the Freeze Drawing tools from the subscription Revit Extension tools to show the actual conditions you encounter, using the modeled elements as your guide.

When you first import the detail, it is still a block, and an import filter is used to map the AutoCAD layer names to the line styles in Revit. After insertion, you can partially or fully explode the block in the drafting view in order to work on it. The importation process, though, has several issues that you will want to consider so you can create an accurate, clean detail once you have completed it:

- Line styles are created in Revit with the name of the AutoCAD layer if there is no corresponding line type that already exists.
- Hatch patterns become fill patterns, but the names of the patterns end up being long and odd sounding.
- If you partially explode the imported details, elements such as hatch patterns and nested blocks in the original details will not be exploded. If you fully explode the details, the hatch patterns become individual line segments. Having so many small lines can create performance issues.
- Leaders lose their arrows.
- Special AutoCAD characters are not supported.
- It is best practice not to explode the DWGs in the production files. Rather, explode and clean up AutoCAD detail DWGs in a separate throwaway file first and then bring them into the project file. That will keep your production file clean of unwanted line style, hatch pattern, and text style definitions.

Once you start building up a set of typical detail drafting views in Revit, you will need a way to import and export them from your projects. The Save To Library and Insert

From File tools accomplish these tasks and will be discussed in the following sections. These tools work only for views that have no modeled elements in them.

Saving to a Library

The Save To Library tool allows you to save families, groups, drafting views, and sheets from your project. Let's step through the general process of saving a drafting view:

1. Click Save As on the Application menu.

2. Choose Library → View.

3. In the Save Views dialog box (see Figure 15.24), select the box next to the sheet or view names you want to export.

Figure 15.24

Saving drafting views and sheets with the Save To Library option

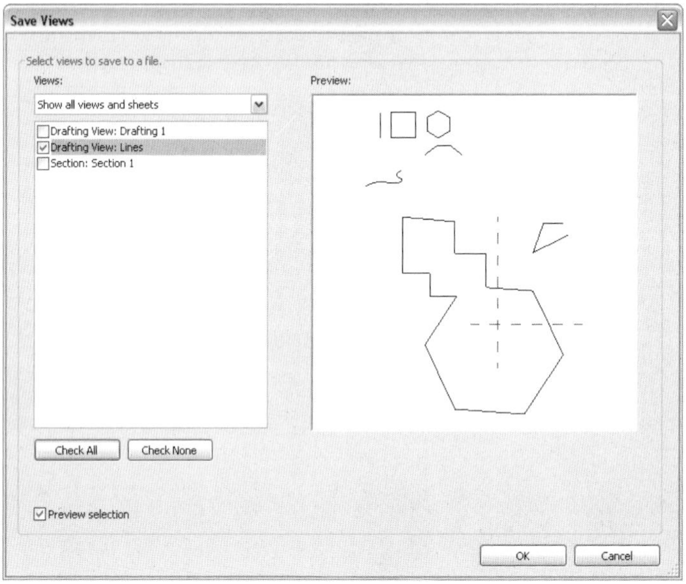

4. Browse to the folder where you want to store the view.

5. Click Save. This process will create a new RVT file.

> When you select an entire sheet to export, each drafting view is separately created as well.

Inserting from a File

The Insert From File tool is the reverse process of exporting the detail. Details can be inserted from any other Revit file where they may reside. You can choose a whole sheet or an individual view to import. The general process to insert the detail is as follows:

1. Click Insert From File on the Import tab of the Insert tab, and then click Insert Views From File.

2. Browse to the folder, and then select the .RVT file.

3. Select the sheet or views that are listed in the Insert Views dialog box (see Figure 15.25) that you want to insert.

4. Click OK.

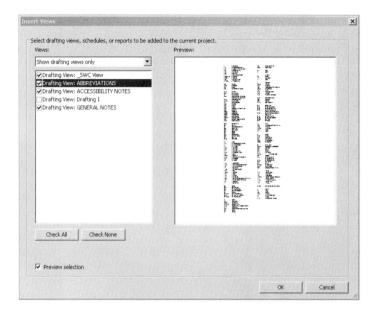

Figure 15.25

Inserting drafting views with the Insert From File option

It is really as simple as that. One good approach is to create a Revit project file that contains only your typical detail sheets and drafting views. On each of the sheets, various details will have reference bubbles pointing to details on other sheets. You can reference those to the other sheets so that if the drawing numbers change in your project, those references will automatically update.

CHAPTER 16

Sheets

This chapter will walk you through the process of creating, managing, and printing sheets. In our industry, sheets are still the end result of a project. They need to be signed and stamped as legal documents and therefore are a very important part of the process.

You will also learn how to organize sheets. This will help you keep your Autodesk Revit Architecture project better organized so that the whole team can function within your organization in a timely manner.

This chapter covers the following topics:

- **About titleblocks and sheets**
- **Setting up sheets**
- **Organizing sheets**
- **Exporting sheets and DWF**

About Titleblocks and Sheets

When it comes time to print your drawings in Revit, you need to create sheets. These are the individual pages in your construction document set. On these sheets you will drop views such as plans, elevations, sections, details, and so on. You will have one sheet for each construction document page, but you can have multiple project views or schedules on each sheet view. It is important to note, though, that once you place a view (plan, section, detail, schedule, and so on) on your sheet, you can't place that view on another sheet.

To help define your sheets, you will want to create a *titleblock*. Titleblocks define the size and appearance of a drawing sheet. Titleblocks are families; you use the Family Editor to create them. In the titleblock you can specify the sheet size, add borders or logos, and add intelligent labels to control the display of information.

Revit includes several titleblock families that can be used to create custom titleblocks to suit your project needs. Your organization probably has existing titleblocks from other CAD programs that you'll want to continue to leverage. In this chapter, we will walk you through the steps of creating a new titleblock and using existing CAD data as an underlayment to speed the titleblock-creation process.

Creating a Titleblock

The titleblock is the template for the sheets. Table 16.1 describes the various Revit elements that are used to define the titleblock.

Table 16.1

Titleblock elements and tools

ELEMENT/TOOL	DESCRIPTION
Family types	Allow you to define different properties of the family. For example, you might have one titleblock family that contains different types for the various titleblock sizes and usage.
Lines	Used to create the border and lines that divide the titleblock into different areas.
Symbols	2D drawing symbols such as a north arrow or a company logo that has been created with Revit geometry.
Masking region	Used to mask or hide a region in the family.
Filled region	Used to create a 2D view–specific graphic.
Dimensions	Used to show and control distances between the various titleblock elements.
Text	Adds text to the titleblock. Text can be modified only when in the Family Editor.
Reference lines	Used as reference geometry and can be used to align other titleblock elements. Do not print.
Labels	Data field that is used to display specific parameters when the titleblock is loaded into the project. Unlike text, a label will change as the project parameter associated with it changes. Typical label parameters are Project Name, Project Number, Sheet Name, Sheet Number, and Scale.
Images	Allow you to place an image such as your company logo into the titleblock.

In this exercise, you will create a very basic titleblock using CAD geometry as an underlay:

1. Go to the Application menu, and choose New → Family (Figure 16.1).

2. Open the `Titleblocks` folder.

3. Select `D - 36 × 24.rft (A1.rft)`, and then click Open.

Figure 16.1

Creating a new family

The Family Editor is now opened. In the drawing area, you are presented with a blank canvas with the exception of four lines that represent the extents of your 36″×24″ sheet (420×297mm). In the next sequence of steps, you will import the CAD file of your company titleblock to use as your underlay.

4. On the Insert tab's Import panel, click Import CAD.

5. Browse to the source file `Titleblock.dwg` (`mTitleblock.dwg`), available from the book's companion download files (available at www.sybex.com/go/introducingrevit2012), as shown in Figure 16.2.

Figure 16.2

Import CAD Formats dialog box

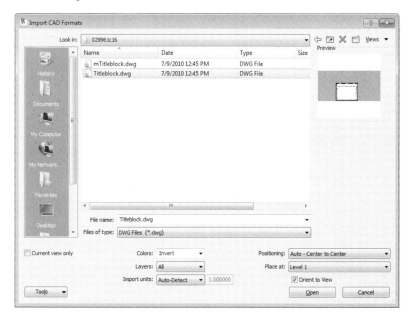

6. In the Import CAD Formats dialog box, set Import Units to Inch, and click Open.

Now that you have imported the CAD file (Figure 16.3), you can trace the CAD lines using Revit lines. This will create the framework of your titleblock.

Figure 16.3

Titleblock with imported CAD file

7. On the Home tab's Detail panel, click the Line tool.

8. On the Modify | Place Line tab's Draw panel, click the Pick Lines tool.

9. Select each of the lines in the CAD file to create Revit lines.

Once you have created your Revit lines, you have the framework of your titleblock, and you can start adding text to identify the different sections. In the next steps, you will

Figure 16.4

Text tool used to create static text

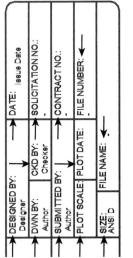

use the Text tool to create static information to display information such as the identifier for the Date, Plot Scale, CKD BY, File Number, and other fields (Figure 16.4). Later you will use labels to provide the display parameter information for the previously listed fields.

If you did not complete the previous steps, you can open the `Titleblock Add Text.rfa` (m `Titleblock Add Text.rfa`) family from the book's companion download files (available at www .sybex.com/go/introducingrevit2012) to continue with this section. In this section, we are going to create the static text needed in the titleblock. The sample file has an imported CAD file that we are using as a background for the placement of our text object. When you open the sample file, the CAD file elements are colored green.

1. On the Home tab's Text panel, click the Text tool.

2. In the Properties palette, click the Edit Type button. You are going to create a new text type.

3. In the Type Properties dialog box, click the Duplicate button.

4. Name the new text type **1/16″ Arial (25mm Arial)**.

5. Change the text size to 1/16″ (25mm).

6. Click OK to close the Type Properties dialog box.

   Using Figure 16.4 as a reference, you will create Revit text for each text item indicated.

7. Select a left attachment point and a right attachment point for text insertion.

8. Make sure that the alignment on the Modify | Place Text tab's Format panel is set to Align Left.

9. Add text for the field descriptions using the move and rotate tools to position the text correctly. Use Figure 16.4 as a reference, or create text for the indicated green-colored text in the imported CAD file.

When creating a titleblock, it may also be necessary to import an image file of your company or client logo. Revit provides you with a simple means for handling this task:

1. On the Insert tab's Import panel, click Image. This will open the Import Image dialog box.

2. Navigate and open `CompanyLogo.jpg` from the book's companion download files (available at `www.sybex.com/go/introducingrevit2012`).

3. Place this logo in the top-right box in your titleblock.

4. Repeat steps 1–3, and load `ProjectLogo.jpg` from the book's companion download files (available at `www.sybex.com/go/introducingrevit2012`).

5. Place this just below the project title.

> Limit the number of images that you import into your project. Revit provides a means for managing imported images. You can manage images from the Insert tab's Import panel by clicking the Manage Images button. The Manage Images dialog box lists all the images used in the project, including any rendered images. Using this dialog box is the only way you can delete an image from the project. Selecting and deleting an image in a view does not remove the image from the project, only from that view.

Now that you have created your field description text, you can use the Label tool to fill out the information. You use labels to read information from the project and automatically display that information. These are some examples of data that you can use for display information:

- Project name
- Sheet name
- Sheet number
- Scale

If you did not complete the previous steps, you can open the `Titleblock Add Label.rfa` (`m Titleblock Add Label.rfa`) family from the book's companion download files (available at www.sybex.com/go/introducingrevit2012), to continue with this section.

1. On the Home tab's Text panel, click the Label tool.

2. In the Properties palette, click the Edit Type button. You are going to create a label type.

3. In the Type Properties dialog box, click the Duplicate button.

4. Name the new label style **1/16″ Arial (25mm Arial)**.

5. Change the text size to 1/16″ Arial (25mm Arial).

6. Click OK to close the Type Properties dialog box.

7. In the Properties palette, click the Edit Type button.

   You are going to create another label type.

8. In the Type Properties dialog box, click the Duplicate button.

9. Name the new label style **5/16″ Arial Bold (125mm Arial Bold)**.

10. Change the text size to 5/16″ Arial (125mm Arial).

11. Check the Bold check box option.

12. Click OK to close the Type Properties dialog box.

    In the next steps, you'll create a label that will populate your titleblock with the sheet number.

13. Click a point for the location for the sheet number. This will cause the Edit Label dialog box to open (Figure 16.5).

14. In the Category Parameters section, click the Sheet Number parameter.

15. Click the Add Parameter(s) To Label icon to add it to the Label Parameters list.

Figure 16.5

Steps for creating a label for a titleblock

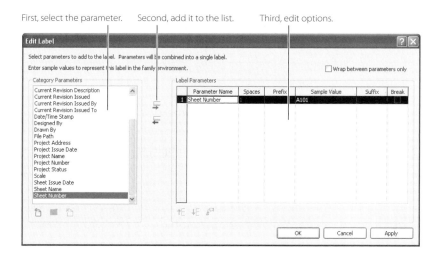

16. Click OK to close the Edit Label dialog box.

17. Hit the Esc key twice to exit the Edit Label tool.

18. In the Properties palette, set Horizontal Alignment to Center.

19. Move the label you just created to properly position it.

> In the Edit Label dialog box, you can add more than one parameter to a single label. Sheet Number is a good example of where you need to utilize only a single parameter. Project Location, which could consist of a street address, city, state, zip code, and phone number, is a good example of where you could utilize multiple parameters.

In the next steps, you will use the 1/16″ (25mm) Arial label to create a label for the view scale.

20. On the Home tab's Text panel, click the Label tool.

21. In the Properties palette, make the 1/16″ (25mm) Arial label.

22. Locate the PLOT SCALE: description field in the titleblock, and click below that.

This is where you will display the scale of the sheets. The Edit Label dialog box will open.

23. In the Category Parameters section, click the Scale parameter.

24. Click the Add Parameter(s) To Label icon to add it to the Label Parameters list.

25. Click OK to close the Edit Label dialog box.

26. Hit the Esc key twice to exit the Edit Label tool.

27. In the Properties palette, set Horizontal Align to Left.

28. Move and rotate the label you just created to properly position it.

29. Save the file on your local computer.

> When you load the titleblock into your project and create a sheet, if you have only one view on the sheet, the scale of that view will be displayed. If you have multiple views in a sheet, the Scale parameter will display as indicated.

When you create a titleblock, you may need to display information in which Revit does not have a predefined parameter in the Category Parameters list, as shown in Figure 16.5. An example of this might be CONTRACT NO. You could populate the titleblock with the contract number by using the Text tool, but in the next example, you are going to use the Label tool. This will enable you to populate this information by filling out the Project Information fields. This information can be modified within a project by selecting the Manage tab's Settings panel and clicking Project Information. In the next section, you will create a shared parameter that will allow you to create the CONTRACT NO label.

Shared Parameters and Titleblocks

To accomplish this, you need to create something called a *shared parameter*. Shared parameters are parameters that you can create to add to your families or project and then share that parameter data with other families or projects. These shared parameters will allow you to add specific information that is not already defined in the family file or

Figure 16.6

**Edit Shared Param-
eters dialog box**

project template. We are just going to skim the surface of shared parameters. Consult the online help for more information on using shared parameters.

The first thing you need to do is create a shared parameter file:

1. On the Manage tab's Settings panel, click Shared Parameters.

   This will open the Edit Shared Parameters dialog box (Figure 16.6).

2. Click the Create button to create a new shared parameter file.

3. In the Create Shared Parameter File dialog box, specify a filename and location to which to save your file.

4. Click the Save button to create your Shared Parameter text file.

5. In the lower-right corner of the dialog box, under Groups, click the New button.

6. In the New Parameter group, specify **Titleblock** for the New Parameter Group name.

7. On the middle-right side of the dialog box, under Parameters, click the New button.

8. In the Parameter Properties dialog box, enter the following information:

   - Name: **Contract Number**
   - Discipline: **Common**
   - Type of Parameter: **Text**

9. Click OK twice to close the Parameter Properties and Edit Shared Parameters dialog boxes.

Now that you've created your shared parameter for the contract number, you need to tie that to your label. Often it is easier to copy an existing label and modify the copy. We will demonstrate that method:

1. Locate the Plot Scale label that you created in the previous steps, and select it.

2. On the Modify | Label tab's Modify panel, click the Copy button.

3. Select the start and end points (Figure 16.7).

4. To edit a label, select it, and click Edit Label from the Label panel.

5. In the Edit Label dialog box, remove Scale by selecting it and clicking the Remove Parameter From Label button (red arrow pointing left).

   Because the Category Parameters section does not have a Contract Number parameter, you need to create this parameter.

6. At the bottom of the Category Parameters section, click the Add Parameter button.

7. In the Parameter Properties dialog box, click the Select button. This will allow you to select a shared parameter.

8. In the Shared Parameters dialog box, in the Parameter Group section, make sure that Titleblock is selected.

9. Under Parameters, make sure that Contract Number is selected.

10. Click OK twice to close the Parameter Properties and Shared Parameters dialog boxes.

    Notice that in the Category Parameters section, Contract Number has been added.

11. In the Category Parameters section, click the Contract Number parameter.

12. Click the Add Parameter(s) To Label icon to add it to the Label Parameters list.

13. Click OK to close the Edit Label dialog box.

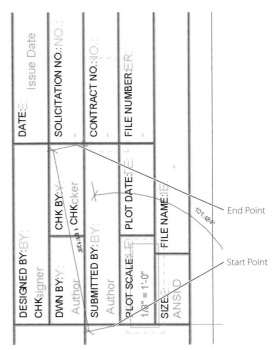

Figure 16.7

Copying the label

At this point you can change properties such as the justification for the labels and their positioning. One last thing to consider is the width of the label. When the information is larger than the width of the label, Revit will automatically wrap it and add a line below. To control the width, simply select the label and drag the blue dots on each side to the appropriate location.

You can experiment with adding additional text, images, or labels to the titleblock. When you have finished using the CAD file as a background, it is very important that you remove it from the family. Leaving the CAD geometry in the Revit family increases the file sizes and requires you to make additional visibility changes to hide the imported file. Once you have added the remaining labels, you can delete the imported CAD file; follow these steps:

1. Select the imported CAD file.

   Since you have Revit geometry on top of an imported CAD file, selecting might be difficult. Remember to use the Tab key to cycle through elements that your mouse pointer is hovering over.

2. With the imported CAD file selected, hit the Delete key.

3. Save the titleblock using the name `Titleblock SP.rfa (mTitleblock SP.rfa)`.

Loading and Testing a Titleblock

Now that you have created the titleblock with a shared parameter, you need to load it into a project for testing. You will start by opening and loading your titleblock family and setting up the shared parameters to populate the titleblock labels.

1. From the book's companion download files (available at www.sybex.com/go/introducingrevit2012), open Dataset_16_01.rvt (m Dataset_16_01.rvt).

2. Load Titleblock SP.rfa into the project:

    *   If you did not complete the previous steps, you can load the Titleblock SP.rfa family from the book's companion download files (available at www.sybex.com/go/introducingrevit2012). From the Insert tab's Load From Library panel, click the Load Family button and open the Titleblock SP.rfa family.

    *   If you have been following along, save the titleblock with the name **Titleblock SP.rfa**. On the Home tab's Family Editor panel, click Load Into Project. If you have multiple projects or families open, make sure you select Advanced Sample Project.

3. In the Project Browser under Sheets (All), double-click sheet 000 – Cover. This will open the sheet in the drawing window.

4. Select the titleblock, and then in the Properties palette change the type to Titleblock SP.

    When you do this, the upper-left 3D view, project title, and drawing list will no longer fit inside the titleblock.

5. In the drawing area, move the text, schedule, and drawing view so that they fit into the schedule.

In the next steps, you point to a sample shared parameter file created for this section. The text file has shared parameters for Contract Number, Plot Date, Issue Date, and Project Title. Whenever you're working on a project and shared parameters, you will want to make sure that the project is pointing to the correct shared parameter file that you created earlier and then tie those shared parameters to the project.

1. From the Manage tab's Settings panel, click Shared Parameters. This will open the Edit Shared Parameters dialog box (Figure 16.8).

Figure 16.8

Edit Shared Parameters dialog box

2. Click the Browse button, and navigate to the `C16-SP.txt` file from the book's companion download files (available at www.sybex.com/go/introducingrevit2012).

3. Click Open to open the `C16-SP.txt` file.

4. Click OK to close the Edit Shared Parameters dialog box.

    You will now tie the shared parameters to your project parameters.

5. On the Manage tab's Settings panel, click Project Parameters.

    This opens the Project Parameters dialog box (Figure 16.9), which lists all the project-specific parameters that are available to elements within the project.

Figure 16.9

Project Parameters dialog box after adding shared parameters

6. Click the Add button.

    This will open the Parameter Properties dialog box (Figure 16.10), where you can define project parameters that are specific to the project.

7. Under Parameter Type, click the Shared Parameter radio button, and click the Select button.

    This takes you to the Shared Parameters dialog box, where you can select which shared parameters you want to use to create a project parameter.

8. Verify that the Parameter group is set to Titleblock.

9. Select the Contract Number parameter, and click OK to close the Shared Parameters dialog box.

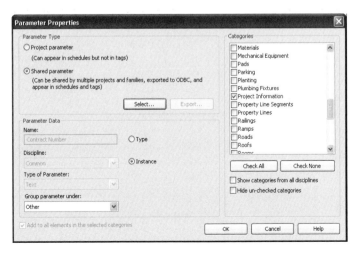

Figure 16.10

Using the Parameter Properties dialog box to create our shared parameter

10. In the Parameter Properties dialog box, set the following:

- Set Group Parameter Under to Other.

- Click the Instance radio button.

- Under Categories, select Project Information.

11. Click OK to close the Parameters Properties dialog box.

   In the previous step, you set the Contract Number parameter to display in the Other parameter group, you set the Contract Number parameter to be an Instance parameter, and you assigned the Contract Number parameter to be associated with the Project Information category.

12. Repeat steps 5–11 for Issue Date, Plot Date, and Project Title.

13. Click OK to close the Project Parameters dialog box.

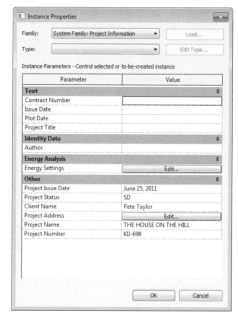

Figure 16.11

Project Information dialog box

The new parameters can now be used to populate your titleblock. To add data to these parameters, you need to open the Project Information dialog box (Figure 16.11). You can do this by going to the Manage tab's Settings panel and clicking the Project Information button.

Placing a Revision Schedule

Now that you have a basic titleblock framework complete, you can enhance it by including a revision schedule. Revit provides you with some flexibility in regard to the information you display.

The revision schedule is placed directly within the titleblock. It behaves exactly like a regular schedule and will read the revision and sheet issue information from the project.

The first thing you need to do is create a revision schedule:

1. Open the `Titleblock RS.rfa` (`mTitleblock RS.rfa`) family from the downloads that accompany this book (available at www.sybex.com/go/introducingrevit2012).

2. In your titleblock family, from the View tab's Create panel, click the Revision Schedule button.

   This will open Revision Properties dialog box (Figure 16.12).

The first tab, Fields, allows you to select the fields that you want to use in your revision schedule. This example will use the following:

- Revision Number
- Revision Description
- Revision Date
- Issued by

On the right side of the dialog box under Scheduled Fields (In Order), there is an extra field called Revision Sequence. You need to remove this from the schedule.

3. Select the Revision Sequence field.

4. In the top middle of the dialog box, click the Remove button.

   This will remove the Revision Sequence field from the schedule.

5. Select the Issued By field in the Available Fields listing, and then click the Add button.

6. Use the Move Up and Move Down buttons to reorder the scheduled fields as shown in Figure 16.12.

7. Click the Sorting/Grouping tab.

   Here, you can use parameters to sort/group your schedules. In this example, you will sort by revision number to keep your revisions organized.

8. As shown in Figure 16.13, in the drop-down field next to Sort By, select Revision Number.

9. At the bottom of the dialog box, select the Itemize Every Instance check box.

   This will ensure that all instances of an element in individual rows are displayed.

   The next tab is the Formatting tab (Figure 16.14). This allows you to replace the default name for the column header.

10. This schedule will be labeled as a revision schedule, so remove the word *Revision* from all three fields.

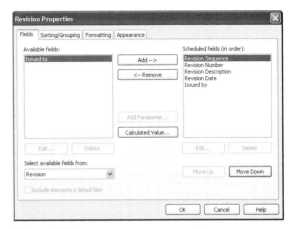

Figure 16.12

Revision Properties dialog box

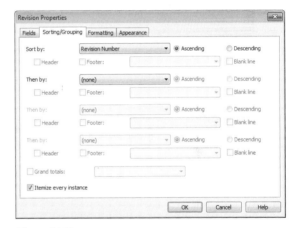

Figure 16.13

Revision Properties: Sorting/Grouping tab

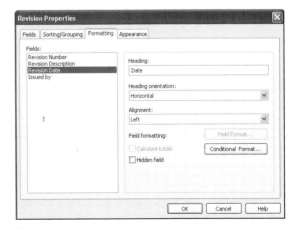

Figure 16.14

Revision formatting

11. Edit the Heading field and the Alignment drop-down for each field, as shown in the following list:

Field	Heading	Alignment
Revision Number	Rev	Left
Revision Description	Descrip	Center
Revision Date	Date	Right
Issued by	IB	Right

The next tab is the Appearance tab (Figure 16.15). This allows you to change the display of your revision schedule. In this example, you are going to turn off the grid lines and outlines of the schedule and use bold for the body text.

Figure 16.15

Using the Appearance tab to adjust the appearance of the revision schedule

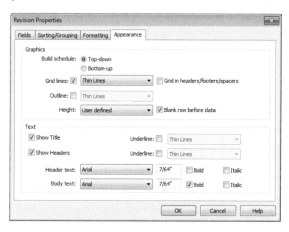

12. In the Graphics section of the dialog box, deselect the Grid Lines check box; this will prevent grid lines from being drawn.

13. Also deselect the Outline check box.

14. In the Height section, click the drop-down box and change the listing to User Defined.

15. In the Text section of the dialog box, to the right of Body Text, select the Bold box.

16. Change the Header Text and Body Text sizes to 7/64″ (180mm).

    This will ensure that the revision schedule rows fit with the titleblock revision schedule geometry.

17. Click OK to close the Revision Properties dialog box.

    You will then be taken to a view of the revision schedule. Because you are working with a titleblock family in the Family Editor, there will be no information to display.

18. Close the Revision Schedule view.

You have made some basic changes to your revision schedule, including changing the fields that are displayed, how the information will be sorted, the formatting of the data, and how the schedule will look. You can now place the revision schedule on the sheet.

19. In the Project Browser, expand Views (All).

20. Under Schedules, select and drag the revision schedule from the Project Browser onto the sheet.

21. Click and place the revision schedule just below your company logo.

22. Select the revision schedule.

23. On the Options bar, in the Rotation On Sheet drop-down, select 90° Counterclockwise.

24. Use Figure 16.16 as a reference to move the schedule.

    You will notice that the revision schedule won't snap to anything, so you will need to approximate the placement.

25. Start by placing the left side. Remember that you can nudge it using the arrow keys on the keyboard.

26. To adjust the widths of the columns, select the revision schedule (Figure 16.17) and drag the blue triangles at the top of the schedule to align with the grid lines in the titleblock.

    You also need to define the overall height of the revision schedule.

27. Drag the blue triangles up to meet the bottom of the revision schedule area in the titleblock. This will define the bottom boundary.

    You have finished creating the titleblock.

28. Save the family by going to the Application menu and selecting Save As → Family.

29. Navigate to a location where you plan on storing your company-created families (this is typically a network drive), and name the file `D - 36x24.rfa (A1.rfa)`.

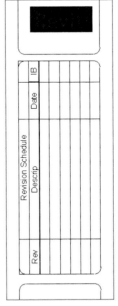

Figure 16.16

Revision schedule placed in the titleblock

Figure 16.17

Adjusting the schedule column widths

Setting Up Sheets

In this section, you'll look at how to create new sheets and how the page setup works. You'll learn to manage sheets to keep a project organized and easy enough for all team members to follow.

Creating New Sheets

To create a new sheet, you first need to load the titleblock. Revit provides multiple methods for loading families into a project. One of the easiest is to drag the family into Revit from Windows Explorer. You can also use the Load Family tool.

1. From the book's companion download files (available at www.sybex.com/go/introducingrevit2012), open Dataset_16_02.rvt (mDataset_16_02.rvt).

2. Save the file to your local computer and name it **CreateSheets16.rvt**.

3. From the Insert tab's Load From Library panel, click the Load Family button.

4. From the book's companion download files, load the E1 30 x 42 Horizontal.rfa (A0 840 x 1190 Horizontal.rfa) family.

5. Adding a sheet can be done in several ways. Use *one* of these two methods:

   - On the View tab's Sheet Composition panel, click the Sheet button.

   - In the Project Browser, scroll down and right-click Sheets (All), and select New Sheet.

   Either of these actions will open the New Sheet dialog box, where you can select the titleblock you are going to be using. Make sure that E1 30 × 42 Horizontal : E1 30 × 42 Horizontal (A0 840 x 1190 Horizontal : A0 840 x 1190 Horizontal) is selected. (In either method, if you don't see the titleblock, then you will need to load it. Click Load and resume with step 4.)

6. Click OK in the New Sheet dialog box to create a new sheet.

   The first sheet is now created and displayed in the drawing window. Notice that Revit automatically gives the sheet a default name and number. Chances are this is not what you want to use. To modify that information:

7. Right-click the sheet in the Project Browser, and select Rename.

   This will open the Sheet Title dialog box, where you can change the sheet name and number.

8. Change the sheet number to **A-103**; change the sheet name to **First Floor Plan**.

   In the next step, you are going to close the Sheet Title dialog box. Prior to doing this, in the drawing window and Project Browser, notice the current sheet name and number. When you click OK, Revit will rename everything for you automatically.

9. Click OK to close the Sheet Title dialog box.

10. Repeat steps 5–7, creating another sheet:

    - Sheet number: **A-104**

    - Sheet name: **Second Floor & Roof Plan**

Now let's update the Project Name value. Revit Architecture again provides you with multiple methods to accomplish this:

- Click the Project Information button on the Settings panel of the Manage tab.
- Select the titleblock, and then click the Project Name value; this allows you to directly edit the text.

1. Using either of those methods, change the following information:
    - Project Name: **Stanley Beach House**
    - Project Number: **100.5698 AB JX**
    - Project Issue Date: **July 10, 2011**
    - Client Name: **Green Development**
2. Now go to the Manage tab's Settings panel and click Project Information.
3. Verify the value for Project Name (Figure 16.18).

    That confirms that the information is bidirectional.

Figure 16.18

Editing the project information in the titleblock updates the Project Information parameters, and vice versa.

Adding Views on the Sheets

The next task is to place views on sheets, for which Revit provides two methods. The first process is actually really simple: drag and drop a view from the Project Browser onto the sheet.

1. In the Project Browser, make sheet A103 – Overall First Floor Plan active.
2. Under Floor Plans, drag the First Floor floor plan onto the sheet.

3. When your mouse pointer is in the drawing window, release the left mouse button.

   Your cursor will change to a preview of the extents of the view. You use this as a reference.

4. Locate where you would like to place the sheet within the titleblock and click.

   The second method is just as easy:

1. In the Project Browser, make sheet A-104 – Second Floor and Roof Plan active.

2. On the View tab's Sheet Composition panel, click the View button. This opens the Views dialog box (Figure 16.19).

3. Within the dialog box, select the Second Floor plan view.

4. Click the Add View To Sheet button.

5. Using the extent of the view as a reference, place the view on the sheet.

6. On the View tab's Sheet Composition panel, click the View button. This opens the Views dialog box.

7. Within the dialog box, select the Roof plan.

8. Using the extent of the view as a reference, place the view on the sheet.

Figure 16.19

Adding views to a sheet using the Views dialog box

Notice that Revit automatically creates a viewport with a view title and fills the value for Scale in the titleblock.

Since your view was set at $1/4″ = 1′- 0″$ (1:50), Revit automatically sized the view appropriately, but if you need to use a different one, there are several ways you can change the view after placement:

- You can go back to the Floor Plan: First Floor and change the scale directly in the view.

- You can click the Floor Plan: First Floor view in the Project Browser and in the Properties palette change the View Scale value.

- You can right-click the view on the sheet and select Activate View. You will still be working in the context of the sheet, but you will work as if you were back to the Floor Plan: First Floor view, giving you access to the scale. (To return to the sheet, right-click again and select Deactivate View.)

To change the location of the view title, simply select it and drag it. If you have more than one view on the sheet, the view title will snap to the other ones for easier alignment.

To change the length of the line in the view title, you need to select the viewport, not the view title. You will then see blue dots at each end of the view title.

Adjusting the Crop Region

In this section, we'll discuss crop regions. Crop regions define the boundaries of a project view. For example, in Figure 16.20 two elevation views are shown. The top view does not have a crop region defined, and view extents are defined by the geometry in the model. The bottom view, however, has had a crop region defined so that you limit and define how much of the view will be displayed. In the following section, you'll create two new views for your building elevations and then drop elevation views onto the sheets. Then use the crop region function to alter the extents of the view.

Figure 16.20

Sheet with one view's extents spilling outside the sheet

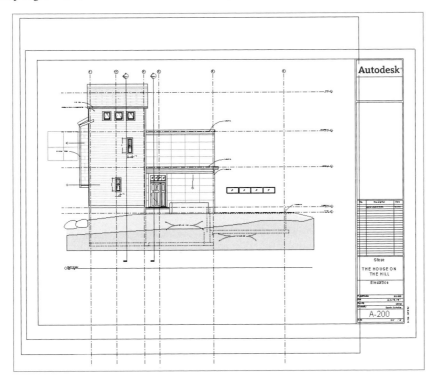

1. From the View tab's Sheet Composition panel, click the Sheet button.

2. In the New Sheet dialog box, make sure that E1 30 × 42 Horizontal : E1 30 × 42 Horizontal (A0 840 x 1190 Horizontal : A0 840 x 1190 Horizontal) is selected.

3. Rename the new sheet **Elevation**.

4. Change the sheet number to **A-200.**

5. Make sheet number A-200 active.

6. Add the North Elevation (Building Elevations) to sheet A-200.

7. Select the view, and in the Properties palette set the view scale to 3/8″ = 1′-0″ (1:50).

Notice in Figure 16.20 that the North Elevation grid lines spill over the extents of the titleblock. You will use the crop region function to alter the extents of the North Elevation.

8. Right-click and select Activate View. You can also make the view active by clicking the Activate View button from the Viewport panel on the Modify | Viewports tab.

9. In the Properties palette under Extents, select the check boxes for Crop View, Crop Region Visible, and Annotation Crop. The crop region can also be turned on and off by clicking the Show Crop Region button on the View Control bar.

Figure 16.21 shows an example of a crop region with the model and annotation crop regions turned on. Crop regions have two main components:

Model Crop Crops model elements, detail elements, section boxes, and scope boxes at the model crop boundary. Visible crop boundaries of other related views are also cropped at the model crop boundary.

Annotation Crop Crops annotation elements when they touch any portion of the annotation element. For example, if you have a tag and the annotation crop is crossing that tag, then the tag information will not be displayed. This is done to prevent partial annotations.

Figure 16.21

Crop region control

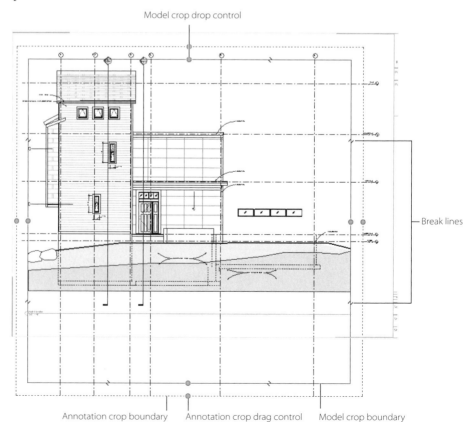

10. To adjust the crop region, drag the blue control grips until the West elevation has similar extents to the East elevation.

    If you want to specify an explicit size for the crop region, then click the Size Crop button on the Crop panel on the Modify | Views tab. This provides you with options to control the width and height of the model crop and to adjust the annotation crop offsets from the model crop.

11. When you have finished, right-click in the drawing area, and select Deactivate View.

12. Adjust the view title so it is appropriate for the new view extents.

13. Make sheet A-201 active.

14. Add the North and South elevations (building elevations) to the sheet, placing the North elevation above the South.

15. Adjust the model crop and view title as needed.

> The crop region won't print by default.

Aligning Views on the Sheets

In this section, we'll discuss using the Guide Grid tool to aid in aligning views on sheets. This tool provides a method to help align views on different sheets.

1. From the book's companion download files (available at `www.sybex.com/go/ introducingrevit2012`), open `Dataset_19_03.rvt` (m. `Dataset_19_03.rvt`).

2. Save the file and call it `GuideGrids16.rvt`.

3. Create two new sheets and name them **A100** and **A101**.

   You are now going to add guide grids to the sheets to align views on different sheets so they appear in the same location from sheet to sheet.

4. On sheet A100 drag and drop the First Floor floor plan to the sheet and change the view scale to 1/4″ = 1′-0″ (1:50).

5. On sheet A101 drag and drop the Second Floor floor plan to the sheet and change the view scale to 1/4″ = 1′-0″ (1:50).

6. From the View tab's Sheet Composition panel, click the Guide Grid button.

   This will open the Guide Grid Name dialog box.

7. Enter **Plans** for the guide grid name, and click OK to close the Guide Grid Name dialog box; the guide grid is created.

   Revit will allow you to create multiple guide grids in a project. You may want to create several guide grids for plans, sections, details, and so on. Guide grids can be shared between sheets, and once created, they are instance properties for the sheet.

Figure 16.22

Guide grid that has been selected with extent controls

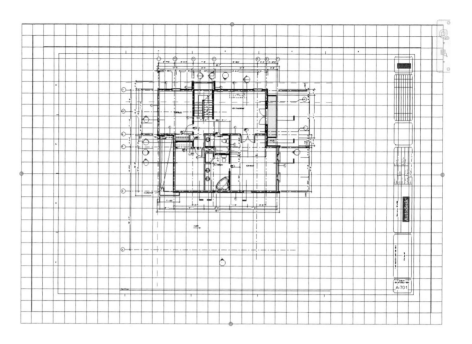

8. Click and drag the extent controls (blue dots) to resize the guide control to fit within the view area of the titleblock (Figure 16.22).

   With the grid in place, you can now use the Move tool to reposition your views. Crop regions and datums (such as elevations and grid lines) can be used as reference points to be moved into alignment with the guide grid lines.

   By default the guide grid spacing is set to 1″ (25mm). For these purposes, you can increase the spacing of the grids to help you align views on other sheets. If you change the guide grid space to 6″ (150mm), you will have an easier time.

9. Select the guide grid.

   When trying to select the guide grid, you won't be able to click one of the grid lines. Instead, move your mouse pointer to the extents of the guide grid, and hit your Tab key to cycle through the possible selections. When the status bar indicates that you have preselected a guide grid, click the mouse button to select it.

10. In the Properties palette, set the Guide Spacing to 3″ (75mm), and click the Apply button at the bottom of the palette.

11. Select the floor plan viewport, and click the Move button from the Modify | Viewports tab's Modify panel.

12. For the basepoint, select the intersection of grid lines 1 and E.

13. For the move endpoint, select a guide grid location. Use Figure 16.23 as a reference.

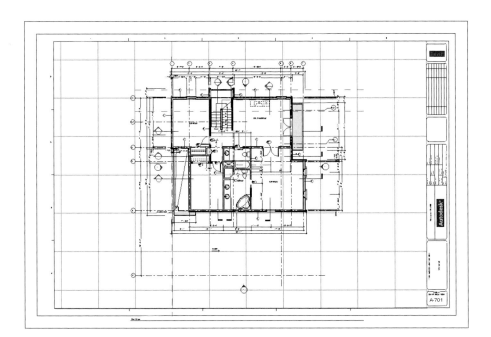

Figure 16.23

Using the guide grid to align a view

14. Make sheet A101 active.

15. In the Properties palette for the sheet, scroll to the bottom of the list.

16. Under Other, set the Guide Grid option to Plans. The sheet will now display the guide grid.

17. Again, select the viewport, and click the Move button from the Modify | Viewports tab's Modify panel.

18. Repeat steps 12 and 13.

Organizing Sheets

As your building project develops, you are going to be creating many different views for plans, sections, elevations, details, schedules, and so on. These views will then be dropped on the sheet. Revit makes it possible for you to organize your sheets in a logical manner—for example, by type (Floor Plan, Elevations, and so on). This helps once again to keep your project well organized. In this section, you can use one of your own project files or follow along using the source file.

To organize the sheets, you will need to use a project parameter:

1. From the book's companion download files (available at www.sybex.com/go/ introducingrevit2012), open Dataset_19_04.rvt.

2. On the Manage tab's Settings panel, click the Project Parameters button.

3. In the Project Parameters dialog box, click Add to create a new one.

4. In the Parameter Properties dialog box (Figure 16.24), set the values as follows:

> Parameter Type: Project Parameter
>
> Parameter Data | Name: Sheet Classification
>
> Parameter Data | Discipline: Common
>
> Parameter Data | Type of Parameter: Text
>
> Parameter Data | Group Parameter Under: Identity Data
>
> Parameter Data: Instance radio button
>
> Categories: Sheets

5. Click OK twice to close the dialog boxes.

6. In the Project Browser, click sheet A100 to highlight it.

   In the Properties palette under the Identity Data section, you will see your newly created parameter called Sheet Classification.

7. Enter **Floor Plan** as the value, and click Apply (Figure 16.25).

Figure 16.24

Creating a project parameter

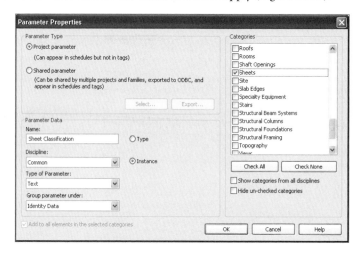

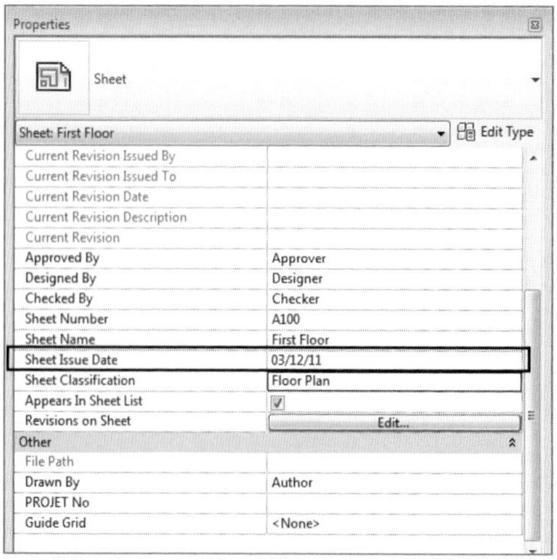

Figure 16.25

Setting the Sheet Classification parameter

Now that you've identified the view, you need to set the Project Browser to display that new level of organization.

1. In the Project Browser, right-click Sheets (All), and select Type Properties.

2. In the Type Properties dialog box, change the Type from All to Drawn By.

   You need to do that because you can't duplicate the All type.

3. Click Duplicate, and enter **Sheet Classification** (Figure 16.26).

4. Click the Edit button to the right of Folders.

5. In the Browser Organization Properties dialog box, set the following:

   - Set Group By to Sheet Classification.
   - Set Then By to <None>.
   - Set Sort By to Sheet Number.
   - Select the Sort By: Ascending radio button (Figure 16.27).

6. Click OK twice.

Now all sheets are stored under a Sheet Classification. Notice that all the sheets that do not have the Sheet Classification set yet are stored under ??? (Figure 16.28). Simply set the Sheet Classification value for the remaining sheets.

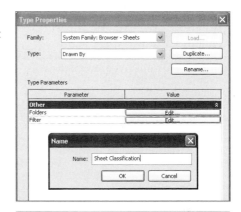

Figure 16.26

Organizing the sheets by their classification

Figure 16.27

Organizing the folder hierarchy

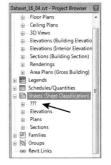

Figure 16.28

Uncategorized sheets show question marks.

Building a Sheet List

Before you move to printing, you will create a *sheet list* of all the sheets in your project to place on the title page:

1. On the View tab's Create panel, click the Schedules drop-down button, and select Sheet List.

    This will open the Sheet List Properties dialog box.

2. In the Sheet List Properties dialog box under the Fields tab, add two fields to the Scheduled Fields list (Figure 16.29): Sheet Number and Sheet Name.

Figure 16.29

Adding the sheet parameters

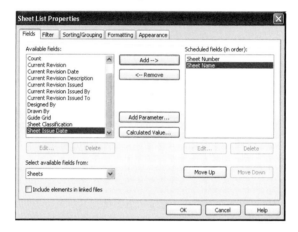

3. Under the Sorting/Grouping tab (Figure 16.30), do the following:

    a. Set Sort By to Sheet Number.

    b. Select Grand Totals, and set it to Count And Totals.

    c. Make sure Itemize Every Instance is selected.

4. Click OK to close the Sheet List Properties dialog box.

    The schedule now displays the list of the sheets sorted by number and shows a total of sheets.

Figure 16.30

Sorting the sheet list

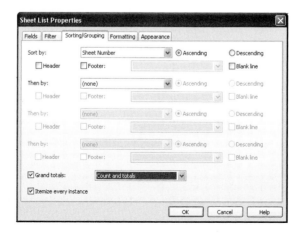

5. Create a new sheet called **Sheet A-000 - Title Page**.

6. Drag the schedule called Sheet List from Schedule/Quantities in the Project Browser into the drawing sheet (Figure 16.31).

Figure 16.31

Placing the sheet list on the title page

Exporting Sheets and DWF

Although Revit provides many great tools for modeling in 3D, in the end you are still creating 2D sheets to review, print, sign, and seal. In a perfect world, you could print sheets on paper and not have to worry about the cost or environmental issues related to using paper. To reduce waste and improve communications, Autodesk has provided the Design Web Format (DWF) file format. With DWF files, you can export 3D models and sheets in a lightweight file format that can be read and marked up in a free application called Design Review. DWF files are a great way of communicating your designs to your clients or even other consultants. They are lightweight, easy to work with, and really reliable.

DWF files let you share design information securely and easily. Using the DWF format, you can avoid unintended changes to project files, and you can share project files with clients and others who do not have Revit Architecture. DWF files are significantly smaller than the original RVT files, making them easy to send by email or post to a website.

DWFx files contain the same information as DWF files but can be opened and printed using the free Microsoft XPS viewer.

> To view a DWF, the other party will need the free DWF viewer called Design Review, which can be downloaded from the Autodesk website (www.autodesk.com).

A great use for DWF files is to review projects. They can be used to mark up the project without using a single sheet of paper. Once the files get marked up by a project manager, they can then be relinked into Revit for an easy workflow. Markups will appear exactly on top of the proper sheet. To create a DWF, follow these steps:

1. Choose the Application menu, and select Export → DWF/DWFx.

   This will open the DWF Export Settings dialog box (Figure 16.32). The left side of the dialog box shows a preview of the selected sheet, while the right side allows you to manage the export settings.

   The first step is to select what you want to print. Generally speaking, you will export sheets rather than views. Your sheets will contain all the relevant views. If you were to export sheets and views, each view that has been placed on a sheet would be a duplicate. Your building project also probably contains many views that are used to help construct your building project and that were never intended to be used in your construction documents.

Figure 16.32

DWF Export Settings dialog box

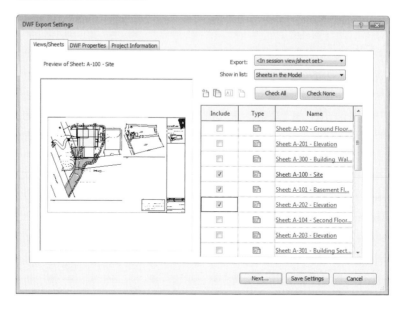

2. In the DWF Export Settings dialog box, on the Views/Sheets tab, click the Export drop-down. Select <In Session View/Sheet Set>.

3. Under Show In List, select Sheets In The Model.

   This will display all the current sheets that have been created in the model.

   You can click the Check All button to select all the sheets, or you can individually select them by selecting the Include check box for each required sheet. (Clicking a column header will allow you to sort the sheets using that header.)

4. Click the check box for sheets A-100, A-101, and A-202.

5. Make changes as needed using the following features:

   DWF Properties Tab Allows you to manage the level of information that will be embedded into the DWF (Figure 16.33). Under Export Object Data, the Element Properties check box will allow the recipient to see the instance and type properties of the elements in the exported views. The Rooms And Areas In A Separate Boundary Layer check box exports the room and area properties to a layer separate from the geometry. This allows you to view individual rooms and room data when you are exporting a project or a view for use with facility management software.

   Graphics Settings Option Allows you to select which graphic format to use when exporting images. The Use Standard Format radio button exports images as PNG files; the Use Compressed Raster Format option exports images using a compressed JPG format.

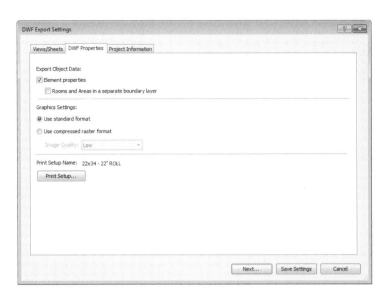

Figure 16.33

**DWF Properties tab
of the DWF Export
Settings dialog box**

Print Setup Button Allows you to control print settings. The print settings (Figure 16.34)
are similar to those used by other Windows applications.

Project Information Tab Allows you to make changes without having to go back to the
project (Figure 16.35). This is handy if you need to adjust a check or issue date.

6. When you have made all the adjustments to the DWF Export Settings dialog box,
   click the Next button to continue the export.

   You will be prompted with the Export DWF dialog box.

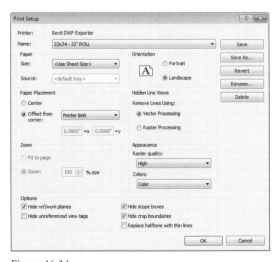

Figure 16.34

Print Setup dialog box

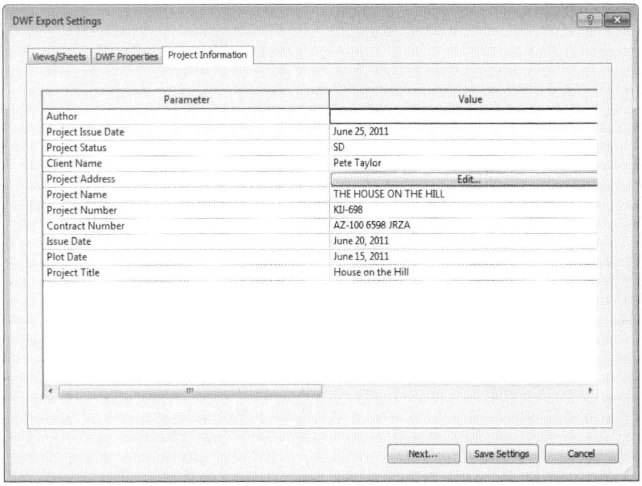

Figure 16.35

The Project Information tab

7. Browse to a location and give the file a name. The default is the project name. The naming can be as follows:

    Automatic—Long (Specify Prefix) Manually specify a prefix in the File Name/ Prefix field or accept the default, which uses this format: Revit Sheet/View: Project Name-View Type-View Name.

    Automatic—Short This format is Revit Sheet: Sheet Name or Revit View: View Type-View Name.

The "Combine selected views and sheets into a single dwf file" check box allows you to create either individual DWF files or a multisheet DWF file. If you plan to have only one project manager review the set, then you can select the option. On the other hand, if you plan on having multiple reviewers, you're better off deselecting it so that all those people can access the files at the same time (which is impossible to do with only one file).

You can also create sets to be able to easily retrieve sheets later. To do so, click the New Set button at the top left of the list of sheets (Figure 16.36), give the set a name, and follow the previous steps to complete your selection. Then click OK to save the set in the project.

Figure 16.36

The New Set button in the DWF Export Settings dialog box

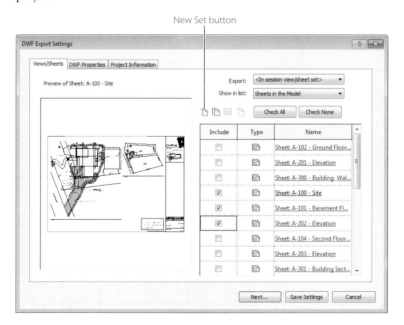

CHAPTER 17

Design Options

When working with multiple design alternatives, it can be frustrating to wait for a decision and then have to apply that decision to the progressing documentation. When using traditional CAD software, there are no specialized tools when you are dealing with design options. Fortunately, you get a purpose-built tool within the Autodesk Revit Architecture platform called design options. With this toolset, you can start design alternative(s) at any time and apply the chosen design direction directly to the model—all views, tags, and schedules are coordinated instantly.

This chapter covers the following topics:

- **Design options terminology**
- **Setting up design options**
- **Editing design options**
- **Showing design options in various views**
- **Adding tags and annotations in design options**

Design Options Terminology

During the design process, you work on the design of a building with a particular outcome in mind and use the model to flesh out the ideas that everyone involved has for the building. At some point, you will need to explore (or be asked to create) alternative solutions to part of the building. It is at this point that design options become important. Before we go further, it is helpful to understand some of the terminology used in relation to design options:

Main Model The main model encompasses the Revit model without any variations or alternatives. Before any design options are created, everything is part of the main model.

Design Option Set The design option set is a collection of alternatives that address a particular design issue. A design option set uses a portion or area within the project where alternatives are being considered.

Design Option A design option is one possible solution to the design issue. Each design option set will have at least one option. For it to be useful, you should have two or more showing alternatives. Each design option is specific to the issue addressed in the option set. You can have only one primary option (defined shortly) per set.

Dedicated View After you have created a design option, each model view adds a Design Option tab in the Visibility/Graphic Overrides dialog box. You can dedicate a view to a specific design option for each design option set using the Design Options tab in the Visibility/Graphic Overrides dialog box. When this view is active or added to a sheet, the options you have dedicated are always shown along with the main model.

Primary Option The primary option is the one favored by you or your client in the option set and shares a closer relationship to the main model than secondary options. Typically, the primary option is the one most likely to be accepted in the final design. Elements in the main model can reference elements in the primary option, and vice versa. By default, each view inside Revit is set to display both the main model and the primary option.

Secondary Option The secondary option is another possible alternative to the primary option within the same option set. You can have one or more secondary option(s) within a design option set. Elements in the secondary option can reference elements in the main model; however, elements in the main model cannot reference elements in the secondary option.

Automatic Display When design options are enabled, each view displays the main model and the primary option, if no options are being edited. By default, the visibility of a design option is set to automatic, which shows the primary option, and the visibility can be adjusted to show secondary options by going to the Visibility/Graphic Overrides dialog box. You can control the visibility of design options within the model for the following views: plan, elevation, 3D, and drafting. If you are editing an option, the view displays the main model and the option you are editing.

To be clear, we are not talking about wholesale design changes to the entire model (for example, a design with a large circular footprint versus a design with a large rectangular footprint). Completely different building design solutions are better represented in different Revit model files. Instead, we are talking about design options to parts/portions within the overall design. The following are some examples:

- Alternative entry designs
- Interior departmental plan layouts
- Furniture design/layout
- Exterior façades
- Predefined, repeatable layout configurations
- Quantify metrics/values with schedules
- Roof configurations

Figure 17.1 shows examples of two design options within the building's exterior curtain wall.

In other CAD systems, having multiple design options means having multiple files or one file with multiple copies of the same geometry. A change to one does not mean the others change. Inconsistencies are inherent in this type of process, and errors are common. Revit addresses this issue by allowing you to develop and document multiple design options simultaneously as the rest of the design moves forward. Revit can synchronize these alternatives with the design once a decision has been made on which to keep and which to remove, and the project can move forward without the need for manual intervention.

Figure 17.1

Two design options for a curtain wall

Setting Up Design Options

You can access the design options in one of two ways. You can select the Manage tab and click Design Options (see Figure 17.2), or, new in Revit 2012, you can click the Design Options button in the status bar along the bottom of the screen.

When creating design options, you begin by defining an *option set*, which is a grouping of options. It is good practice to keep your option sets isolated to a specific task or area within the model. An option contains the model data/objects that show each alternative or competing design option/scheme.

To get started, you will create two new option sets in this section:

1. From the book's companion download files (available at `www.sybex.com/go/introducingrevit2012`), open `Dataset_17_01.rvt`.

2. On the Manage tab → Design Options panel, click the Design Options button.

3. In the Option Set area, click New.

4. In the Option area, click New to add second and third options (see Figure 17.3).

   Within each area you can rename the option sets to something more descriptive. To do this:

   a. Highlight the option set or option.

   b. Choose Rename from the appropriate section.

   In Figure 17.4, the Design Options dialog box shows the design options renamed with an option set called Front Entry. Within the option set are multiple alternative design options

Figure 17.3

Design options with an option set defined

of differing configurations. In the Front Entry set, you will be exploring three schemes:

- French Doors is the primary option.

- Single Door w Sidelight and Single Door w Sidelights are the secondary options.

You can have multiple options under each option set, but only one entry within each option set can be considered the *primary*, or top, choice until a decision has been made to eliminate the others.

5. Click the Option Set 1 text to highlight it, and click the Rename button under Option Set on the right side of the dialog box.

6. Rename the option set **Front Entry** and click the OK button to close the Rename dialog box.

7. Click the Option 1 (primary) text and click the Rename button under Option on the lower-right side of the dialog box.

8. Rename the option **French Doors** and click the OK button to close the Rename button.

9. Repeat steps 7 and 8 to rename Option 2 **Single Door w Sidelight** and Option 3 **Single Door w Sidelights** (Figure 17.4).

10. Click the Close button to close the Design Options dialog box.

11. Save the file to your local desktop.

Figure 17.4

Renaming the options to Front Entry

> The default names of design option sets are Option Set 1, Option Set 2, and so on. You will find it easier to rename these from the start to something more descriptive. Unfortunately, you cannot simply select the option set from the "white area" of the dialog box. To rename, you will need to select your option set, click the Rename button in the Option Set section on the right, and rename it in the Rename dialog box.

Editing Design Options

Now that you have the design option set and design options created, it is time to create and/or add elements to each set. In the following section, we are going to create three design options for a new front entry. This will allow us to demonstrate some of the functionality of Revit's design options tool.

When working with design options, chances are that you are going to be working on a building project, and the designer, owner, or some other stakeholder is going to want to see different options in addition to the original design. Revit provides a tool that allows you to move building elements to option sets.

To move existing elements to an option, you need to be working in the main model. You can determine if you are working in the main model by looking at the Active Design Options list. On the Manage tab, Design Options panel, just above the Design Options panel text is the Active Design Options drop-down. This displays either Main Model or the name of the design option you are working in. This information can also be found in the right-most drop-down on the status bar.

1. From the book's companion download files (available at www.sybex.com/go/introducingrevit2012), open Dataset_17_02.rvt or continue using the file from the previous section.

2. On the Ground Floor, select the wall to the left of the Entry Hall.

   It is a Basic Wall Stone Façade and has a wall tag mark number of 6.

3. On the Manage tab, Design Options panel, click the Add To Set button (Figure 17.5).

   This will open the Add To Design Option Set dialog box.

Figure 17.5

Design Options panel

4. Verify that each of the three options is checked.

5. Click the OK button to close the Add To Design Option Set dialog box.

   We are adding the wall to each design option because we are going to be adding different doors for each option. Since doors need to be hosted, we need to include the wall into the design option. If we do not include the wall, then we will not be able to add the door as part of the design option.

   In the next steps, we will start adding doors to the different design options. We will first add a French door to the French Doors option.

   When working with design options, note that elements that are not part of the current design option are grayed out.

6. On the status bar, the far right pull-down menu (Figure 17.6) allows you to set the current design option. Select French Doors (primary).

Figure 17.6

Changing the design option via the status bar

7. From the Home tab → Build panel, click the Door button.

8. In Type Selector, select Single French Door – Milette 305 32″ × 80″.

9. Place the door as shown in Figure 17.7.

10. Change the door tag number to **101**.

11. Repeat steps 5–9, placing the Masonite Royal Mahogany w Sidelight 36″ × 80″ door on the Single Door w Sidelight option.

12. Repeat steps 5–9, placing the Single-Raised Panel with Sidelights 36″ × 80″ door on the Single Door w Sidelights option.

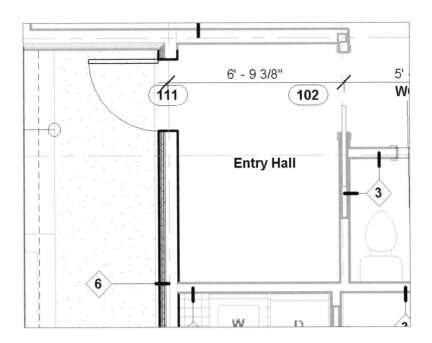

Figure 17.7

Placing the French door in the French Door design option

You will know that you are editing a design option in one of two ways:

- The first way is graphically. In the plan, elevation, 3D, and drafting views, the existing geometry that is part of the main model will be displayed as ghosted.

- In the status bar, the far-right white area will show the name of the design option that is being edited.

You can edit or make adjustments to a design option at any time by returning to the Design Options dialog box or using the Active Design Option drop-down on the status bar.

13. Switch to the main model.

14. Save and close the file.

Moving Between Option Sets

More often than not, you will find that you want to move back and forth between multiple option sets. While you are editing the selected option set, the status bar next to the Design Options button shows the other options available in the drop-down menu. By changing from one option to another, any geometry that was created in the previously selected option that does not exist within the newly selected option will not be shown. These design options are independent of each other, and the geometry exists only within the individual options themselves.

If you have finished editing a design option or just want to get back to working with the main model, you can choose Main Model from the status bar's Design Options drop-down menu. This is the same as opening the full Design Options dialog box, clicking Finish Editing, and then clicking Close.

On the status bar when a design option is being edited, you will notice a small Exclude Options (Figure 17.6) or Active Only check box. When the Active Only check box is selected, any geometry within the main model is ignored while picking or windowing. With the Active Only box deselected, the main model will still be ghosted, but all the geometry within it can now be selected.

If you are in the main model, the status bar's Design Options area will show an Exclude Options check box instead. This plays a similar role to Active Only except in reverse: within the main model with this selected, Revit will not allow any design options displayed from accidentally being selected. Deselecting this will allow you to select objects with a design option.

When at least one or more design option sets are created, the status bar's Design Options area adds another useful item, Add To Set (see Figure 17.8). This is grayed out unless you have at least one or more objects selected.

Figure 17.8

Design Options Add To Set

A common use in deselecting the Active Only check box and clicking the Add To Set button on the status bar is when there are objects that you would like to copy from the main model to include in one or more design options. As an example, let's take a furniture layout that was originally done in the main model and now consider different layout configurations.

Our sample project has a design option set called First Floor Bedroom. This option set has two design options, Option 1 and Option 2. Option 2 has a bedroom layout. Option 1 is empty, and in the following section we are going to move the objects from the main model into Option 1.

1. From the book's companion download files (available at www.sybex.com/go/introducingrevit2012), open Dataset_17_03.rvt.

2. Zoom into the bedroom in the northeast corner of the building.

3. Select the furniture (bed, two nightstands, entertainment center, and chair) to move from the main model (making use of picking, windowing, and/or filters), and place it within one or more of the design options created earlier. To do this:

   a. With the objects selected, click the Design Options status bar's Add To Set button.

   b. In the Add To Design Option Set dialog box (see Figure 17.9), choose which design option set this should be part of and which design option (one or more) you want to move the selected objects into.

This step will remove the geometry from the main model and place it within one or more design options as selected.

If geometry already exists that you want to move into a design option set, take advantage of the features that Revit offers to pick, select, and filter, including the Exclude Options and Active Only check boxes on the status bar.

4. Save the file to your local desktop.

Figure 17.9

Add To Design Option Set dialog box

Showing Design Options in Various Views

Now that you understand and have created design option sets and defined the design options, it is time you take this knowledge and show it graphically in different views. Once you've decided which design option you want to keep, you will merge this into the main model by accepting the primary option.

> Keep in mind that the process for working with all views and showing the different design options is similar.

Duplicating the View

You will be using the floor plan in this example. Within the floor plan that you want to work with, you will see the main model as well as the primary design options by default. You will set up the views to show the other design options by first duplicating the view as many times as you need to match the number of design options you want to show.

1. From the book's companion download files (available at `www.sybex.com/go/ introducingrevit2012`), open `Dataset_17_02.rvt` or continue using the file from the previous section.

2. In the Project Browser, select the Ground Floor floor plan, right-click, and choose Duplicate With Detailing (to include a copy of the annotation).

3. Rename the view **Ground Floor – French Door**.

4. Repeat steps 2 and 3 to create additional views for Ground Floor – Single Door w Sidelight and Ground Floor – Single Door w Sidelights.

5. Make the Ground Floor – French Door active.

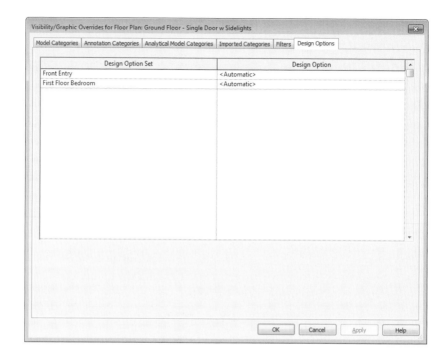

6. Type **VG** on the keyboard to open the Visibility/Graphic Overrides (VG) dialog box and switch to the Design Options tab (Figure 17.10).

   On the Design Options you will see each of your design option sets listed. To the right of each option set is a drop-down that allows you to select a particular design option.

7. In the Design Option drop-down for Front Entry, select French Doors. This sets the design option French Doors for this view.

8. Click OK to close the Visibility/Graphic Overrides dialog box.

9. Repeat steps 6–8, making the Ground Floor – Single Door w Sidelight option active and setting the Design Option in VG to Single Door w Sidelight.

   Figure 17.11 shows three examples of the main model with different design options.

10. Repeat this process to create the required presentation drawings showing multiple design options, plans, schedules, and 3D views, and place them on sheets for presentation.

11. Save the file.

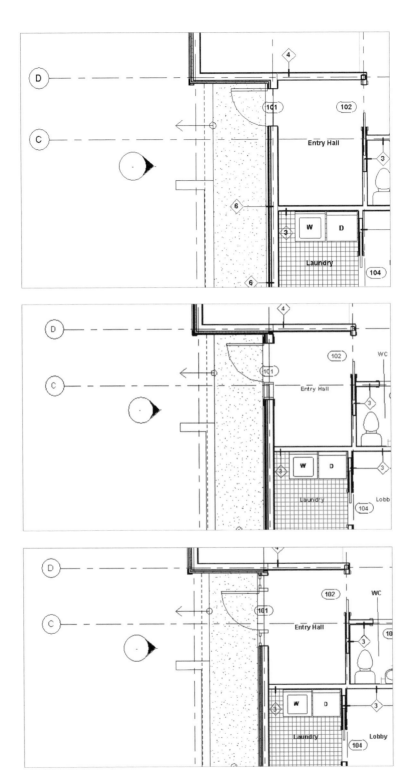

Figure 17.11

Floor plans with alternative design options

To tell *schedules* which design option to display, you cannot use the shortcut key VG; rather, open the properties, and on the Visibility/Graphics Overrides line under Graphics, click Edit (Figure 17.12). Then select the appropriate design option (Figure 17.13).

Figure 17.12

Displaying design options by editing the Visibility/Graphics Overrides properties of a schedule

Figure 17.13

Visibility for Schedule design options

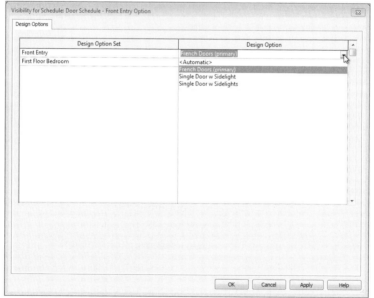

Setting the Primary Option

When you've decided which design option to proceed with, you should set that choice as the primary option. If it is currently a secondary option, you can elevate it to the primary option status in the Design Options dialog box as follows:

1. From the book's companion download files (available at www.sybex.com/go/introducingrevit2012), open Dataset_17_02.rvt or continue using the file from the previous section.

2. Switch to the First Floor floor plan.

3. From the Manage tab → Design Options panel, click the Design Options button.

4. In the First Floor Bedroom option set, click Option 2.

5. In the lower left-hand corner of the Design Options dialog box, choose Make Primary from the Options section.

Once you've designated your choice for the project as the primary option, you can click the Option Set name to accept the primary option. Click Accept Primary to remove the objects within from the design option, place them within the main model, and coordinate them through the documentation set, and any other design options within it will be deleted with a warning, as shown in Figure 17.14.

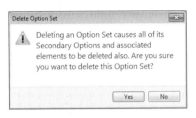

Figure 17.14

Warning from the Accept Primary command

6. Select the First Floor Bedroom option set.

7. On the right side of the dialog box, click the Accept Primary button.

If you click Accept Primary for a design option set that has views associated with it, a second dialog box will open like the one shown in Figure 17.15, asking if you want to delete views associated with the option(s) that are being deleted.

Figure 17.15

Delete Dedicated Option Views example

Adding Tags and Annotations in Design Options

It is straightforward to add room tags after the design options are created. Although it does not always happen in that order, it does illustrate what Revit is ultimately looking for. So, in this section, you will start with the methodology that Revit prefers and then learn how to proceed when you already have rooms created when you create design options.

If the rooms are created *before* you introduce design options, keep these two tips in mind:

• Be sure to use the Duplicate With Detailing option to create the views. That way, the room tags are already shown in each view.

• When adding elements to the first option, be sure to select the room tags. That way, they (and the room boundaries) will not be part of the main model. If you miss one (or more), there will be some confusion when you create the second option. Otherwise, everything else works the same.

After design options are created, following these steps when placing them:

1. Make sure you are *not* editing any design option.

2. Start with the view that shows your primary design option and the main model.

3. Add the first room tag to the plan (this is assuming that the first room is the same in both designs).

4. Edit the room number to the desired number. This establishes a pattern for Revit to follow.

5. Proceed by tagging all the rooms that are the same in both design options.

6. Next, click the Edit Selected button for your first design option.

7. Now add room tags to the rooms created by the walls in the primary design option.

   At this point, you should have the plan tagged. Everything looks good. But this is where it gets tricky.

8. Finish editing the first option, and return to the main model.

9. Open the view for Option 2.

10. Place a room tag in one of the rooms that is the same in both options.

    It should pick up the number you gave it in the Option 1 view. Because it is the same "room," it wasn't tagged.

11. Proceed to tag all the rooms that are the same in both options.

    If you accidentally tag a room that overlaps with a room in Option 1, you will get a warning. Don't panic. Just delete the tag you placed. When you get the warning that says it can be ignored, don't ignore it!

12. When you're ready to tag the rooms formed by walls in Option 2, click the Edit Selected option, and add tags within the view.

    The same warning will show up if you attempt to tag a room that is not part of the design option (in other words, it is the same in both options). You will be able to renumber the tags in a design option to follow the numbering scheme of the main model.

So, when you think about it, it really makes sense. If you want to tag a room common to both design options, do it in the main model when *not* editing a design option. When you want to tag a room created by a design option, do it while editing *that* design option. This is what Revit is expecting.

For the numbering of room tags, the last value used influences the pattern of the next values. For example, if you started with Room 101, the next room would be 102, and so on, unless you manually changed a value and then started the next room tag. This is useful when trying to match the numbering scheme of the main model. Also, when working with design options, you can have duplicate numbers provided they are not in the main model. Because the two design options cannot coexist in the same option, Revit does not see them as duplicated.

Here are some more considerations related to including rooms in options:

- Rooms can be placed in each design option independently. The room bounding areas and room separation lines in that option, in the main model, and in primary options of other option sets define the boundary. Revit ignores walls and room separation lines in secondary options of other option sets.

- To assign different room properties, such as occupancy, in different options, the room must be included in that option where you want to show room properties such as occupancy.

- If the shape, size, or location of a room varies in different options of one option set, then the room must be included in that option set.

- If the shape, size, or location of the room is the same in different options and you want properties assigned to the room to be the same for all options, keep the room in the main model.

- If you place a room in an area that already has a room assigned to it, you will get the following error: Option Conflict.

Tagging doors and windows is a bit different. The tags for these elements are visible and editable whether or not you are editing a design option. In other words, they are not part of any design option. This is why when you select objects and try to add them to a design option, if you have included door and window tags (and some other elements as well), you receive a warning.

Using annotation tools (such as Text, Detail Lines, Regions, Detail Groups, and Insulation), you can interact with the design options and views. While editing a design option, you can place an annotation, and although it may seem like you are adding this to the design option itself, Revit is actually placing this in the active view in the main model and not as part of the design option.

Dimensions behave like the previous annotation elements. Where they differ is that when the design option displayed within the view is changed, dimensions that are associated to geometry within that design option will no longer be displayed unless that design option is visible within the view.

CHAPTER 18

Phases

Phases in Autodesk Revit Architecture are distinct and separate milestones for the life of your project. For example, Existing, Demolition, and New Construction can be used to represent either a specific period or the status of the project at a specific milestone. Revit projects always have at least one phase and by default Existing and New Construction are already created. By default, any object created is placed in the New Construction phase. These default phases can be renamed, and you can add additional phases to your project.

Phases are commonly used when you have an existing building that is undergoing some refurbishment. Phases are used to differentiate among the existing, demo, and new construction. Phases are also used when you have a project that is going to be built in multiple stages and you need to document the sequence of construction. Revit displays objects belonging to different phases with different user-definable line types.

When it comes to *phasing*, it is very difficult to keep track of what part will remain and what part will be demolished. In traditional file-based CAD systems, it is a logistics and training nightmare to keep things working smoothly. Fortunately, Revit has phasing tools specifically for this purpose. With this tool set, you can use phases applied to the elements and components in the model, and all views and schedules are coordinated instantly.

This chapter covers the following topics:

- Phasing tools
- Phases
- Infill elements
- Demolishing elements
- Rendering and existing phases

Phasing Tools

When working with phasing-related data, if one phase could be finished and become the "existing" phase before the next phase work begins, that would be ideal. But more often than not, you will find yourself working on multiple phases all at the same time. In a traditional CAD platform, this causes you to keep multiple copies of multiple files and in most cases track these files manually. If one file changed, that change would have to be manually propagated to the "copied" files. Not only that, but you must add company naming standards, external reference structures, multiple floors, multiple buildings, submittal requirements (for example, multiple buildings but a single submittal), and more to the mix. In short, it's a lot of work.

Within the Revit platform, you can use the phasing-related tools. If you have been following along with the examples in the book or if you've used Revit prior to this, you may not have even realized that you were already taking advantage of some of the phasing-related tools. Figure 18.1 shows the first phase of a multiple-phase project, and Figure 18.2 shows the progression of the original warehouse that was converted and expanded to office space. Later a new upfit was done to open up the interior layout (Figure 18.3).

Figure 18.1

Existing warehouse footprint

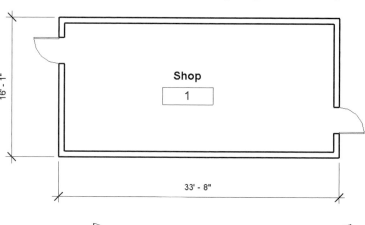

Figure 18.2

Warehouse expansion to office space (note existing structure ghosted on the bottom left)

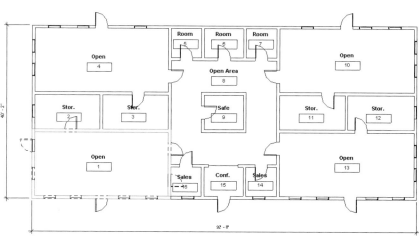

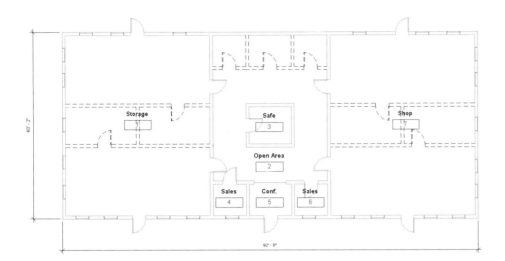

Figure 18.3

Office space new owner upfit (note removal of previous walls and elements displayed with dashes)

You can find the phasing-related tools on the Manage tab. Click the Phases button, and you are offered a dialog box with three tabs. The first tab, Project Phases (Figure 18.4), allows you to create as many new phases as you need for this project, give them a description, and arrange the order from past to future. You also have the ability to combine phases.

Phases

Demolish

Phasing

Figure 18.4

Project Phases tab with options

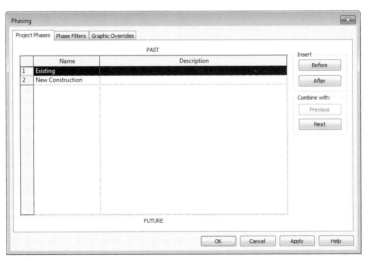

The Phase Filters tab allows you to control what is visible in a view based on its selected phase assignment (Figure 18.5).

Phase filters control the display settings for the four Graphic Overrides states: New, Existing, Demolished, and Temporary. For each state, the filter can apply one of three settings in the drop-down:

By Category This will display elements using the default style settings from the Manage ➔ Settings ➔ Object Styles dialog box or from any graphic overrides that may have be applied to the view.

Figure 18.5

Phase Filters tab with default options. These allow you to control what is displayed in the view.

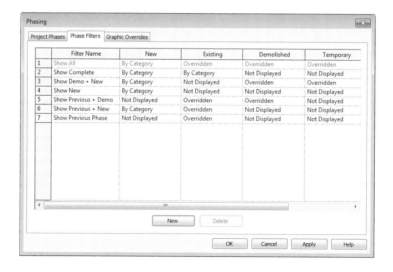

Overridden This will use the override settings as defined on the Graphic Overrides tab.

Not Displayed This will not display any matching elements within the view.

You can edit the existing phase filters as well as create your own. We will focus on taking advantage of the ones provided out of the box in the templates, which use the following phase filters:

Show All Will display New, Existing, Demolished, and Temporary elements in the current phase. Elements that have been demolished in prior phases will not be shown. This filter cannot be deleted.

Show Complete Will display New and Existing together.

Show Demo + New Will display New and Demolished elements.

Show New Will display New elements.

Show Previous + Demo Will display Existing and Demolished elements.

Show Previous + New Will display New and Existing elements.

Show Previous Phase Will display Existing elements.

The Graphic Overrides tab provides four states (Figure 18.6) that can be used to describe and graphically convey an element at any point in time. Although you can edit some of their properties, you are unable to delete from or add to the ones provided in this list. The four states are as follows:

Existing Relative to the active phase, these are elements created in a phase previous to the one you are currently working in.

Demolished These are elements created in an earlier phase and demolished within the current phase.

Figure 18.6

The Graphic Overrides tab allows you to control the appearance of a phase representation in a view, based on its phase assignment.

New These are elements created within the current phase.

Temporary This is used for elements that are created and demolished within the same phase.

Phases

Phases provide the ability to represent key periods in the life of the project. In the out-of-the-box templates, two phases exist by default: Existing and New Construction. The default current phase is New Construction. This means that everything created is assigned to this phase until it is either demolished using the Demolish tool or reassigned to another phase. The Existing phase is used if you are working on a remodeling project and you need to show which elements are existing and which are new.

You can create as many phases as necessary and assign building elements to these phases. Every element in Revit exists within a period defined by two phasing parameters. These are the phase in which an element is created and the phase in which it is demolished. The Phase Demolished parameter can be set to None, which is the default for any new element that is created. Figure 18.7 shows that the wall was created in Phase 2012 and is not currently set for demolition during any of the planned project phases.

You can also create duplicate views and assign different phases and phase filters to these views.

Figure 18.7

Properties palette's Phasing properties

Defining Project Phases

If you are working on a project that will utilize Revit Phases, it is very important to define those phases before you do anything else. This is because every view in Revit has a Phase property associated with it. Phases can be created at any point in the project; it is just simpler to set up views at the beginning of the project. In this section, we are going to define project phases. Figure 18.8 shows the Project Phases tab of the Phasing dialog box.

Figure 18.8

Phasing dialog box showing the Project Phases tab

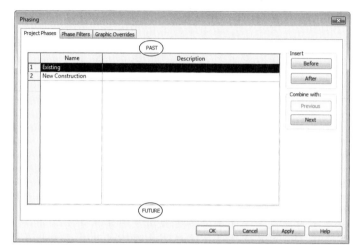

The important item to note about the Phasing dialog box is that phases will be listed from PAST to FUTURE in the dialog box. This system allows us to create a timeline of our project and see how phases are related to one another. By default two phases are created for us, called Existing and New Construction.

NAMING CONVENTIONS FOR PHASES

There is a lot of debate within the Revit community of how phases should be named. One camp believes that using naming conventions such as Existing, West Wing Construction, East Wing Remodel, and the like is the preferred method. Another camp believes that naming phasing Phase 1, Phase 2, and so on is better because it is more specific about a milestone or period. We recommend a hybrid approach using the Phase # + *Description of Phase* format. An example would be Phase 3 – Lobby Renovation. Regardless of the naming convention, it is important to always have the first phase at the top of the list and the last phase of the project at the bottom.

In this section, we are going to create three phases. We will rename the two phases already found in the project and create a new phase.

1. From the book's companion download files (available at www.sybex.com/go/introducingrevit2012), open Dataset_18_01.rvt.

2. On the Manage tab, choose the Phasing panel and click the Phases button. This opens the Phasing dialog box.

3. In the Phasing dialog box, click Existing in the Name column and rename it **Phase 1 – 1994 Construction**.

4. In the Name column, rename New Construction to **Phase 3 – 2014 Construction**.

   In the next step, we are going to create a new phase called Phase 2 – 2012 Construction.

5. With the Phase 3 – 2014 Construction phase name active, on the right side of the Phasing dialog box, click the Before button under Insert to create a new phase before Phase 3 – 2014 Construction.

6. Rename the newly created phase **Phase 2 – 2012 Construction**.

Assigning a Phase to a View and Element

Each project view has both a Phase and a Phase Filter property to control visibility. Because phasing visibility settings are view specific, you can create phased views with preassigned phase filters in your template as a starting point for the project. Figure 18.9 shows the location of the Phasing properties for the view.

When elements are first created and components placed, their Phase property matches that of the view in which they are created or placed. For example, if the current view phase is set to Phase 3 – Construction and you draw a wall, that wall will then inherit a Phase Created property of Phase 3 – Construction. This is useful when you have a project with phases already defined and now need to add elements or components within the view, select the view with the appropriate phase setting, and create or place as needed.

In this section we are going to create plan views that show the Phase 1 – 1994 Construction, then the Phase 2 – 2012 Construction, and finally the Phase 3 – 2014 Construction views. When we work in these views, any elements that are created will have their Phase Created parameter set based on the active view.

1. From the book's companion download files (available at www.sybex.com/go/introducingrevit2012), open Dataset_18_02.rvt.

2. In the Project Browser, right-click the Level 1 floor plan and select Duplicate View → Duplicate, to create a new view.

3. Name the duplicated view **Level 1 – 1994 Construction**.

Figure 18.9

Properties palette's Phasing properties

4. In the Project Browser, right-click the Level 1 floor plan and select Duplicate View → Duplicate to create another new view.

5. Name the duplicated view **Level 1 – 2012 Construction**.

6. In the Project Browser, right-click the Level 1 floor plan a third time and select Duplicate View → Duplicate to create a third new view.

7. Name the duplicated view **Level 1 – 2014 Construction**.

   With the views created, we can now set the Phasing properties for the view.

1. Make the Level 1 – 1994 Construction view the current view.

2. In the Properties palette for the view, scroll to the bottom on the dialog box, where you will find the Phasing parameters for this view.

   Views have two parameters for controlling phasing: Phase Filter and Phase (Figure 18.10). The Phase Filter parameter allows us to control what is visible in the view. There are eight Phase Filter options, with four Phase Status options (Figure 18.11).

Figure 18.10

View Phasing parameter options

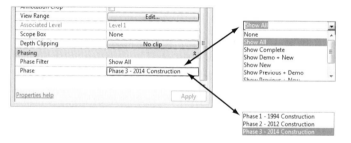

Figure 18.10

View Phasing parameter options

In the Phasing dialog box, the Graphic Overrides tab lists the four statuses that any element Revit can have at any time:

Existing Element was created in an earlier phase of the project and continues to exist in the current phase.

Demolished Element was created in an earlier phase of the project and is demolished in the current phase.

New Element was created in the current phase.

Temporary Element was created and demolished during the current phase.

Phase filters are rules that you can apply to a view to control the display of elements based on their phase status (New, Existing, Demolished, or Temporary). Following is a list of the default phase filters:

Show All Shows all New, Existing, Demolished and Temporary elements.

Show Complete Shows both the existing and new construction phases.

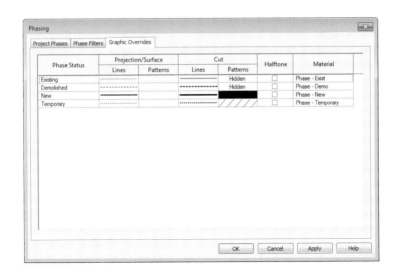

Figure 18.11

Graphic Overrides tab of the Phasing dialog box

Show Demo + New Shows Demolished elements and all New elements.

Show New Shows all New elements.

Show Previous + Demo Shows all Existing elements and Demolished elements.

Show Previous + New Shows all elements.

Show Previous Phase Shows elements from the previous phase.

3. Set the Phase Filter to Show All.

4. Set the Phase to Phase 1 – 1994 Construction.

   Our Level 1 – 1994 Construction floor plan has now been set up so that only the Phase 1 – 1994 Construction phase will be displayed. We will not set up views for Phase 2 and Phase 3.

5. Make Level 1 – 2012 Construction active.

6. Set the Phase Filter to Show All.

7. Set the Phase to Phase 2 – 2012 Construction.

8. Make Level 1 – 2014 Construction active.

9. Set the Phase Filter to Show All.

10. Set the Phase to Phase 3 – 2014 Construction.

    Now that our views are created, we can assign Phase properties to the elements in the project.

11. Save the file to your local computer and close any open views.

    With our views set up, we can now assign phasing properties to model elements.

Figure 18.12

Selecting room in the middle of the building

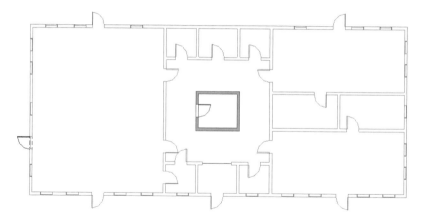

In a perfect world, we would be able to set up our phases prior to doing any modeling. However, more often than not, we will find elements or components in the project where the phasing needs to be adjusted at some point. This could be because someone unfamiliar with the project phasing setup comes in to assist on the project, because of components or elements that are now going to be part of the project sooner/later than originally planned, or because of another reason. To change the Phasing property, do the following:

1. From the book's companion download files (available at www.sybex.com/go/ introducingrevit2012), open Dataset_18_03.rvt, or continue using your file from the previous step.

2. Using Figure 18.12 as a reference, select the four walls and door in the center of the building.

3. In the Properties palette, change the Phase Created property to Phase 2 – 2012 Construction (Figure 18.13).

   Making this change will instantly update the project model and visually change it to match the graphic designations, as defined earlier.

4. Save and continue on to the next section.

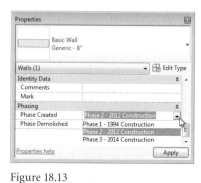

Figure 18.13

Properties palette showing the Phasing properties

Phase Properties of Schedules

You can filter and phase a schedule just like you can a view, in the properties of the schedule. You accomplish this by assigning the Phase Filter and Phase properties for the view. In this section, we will create a door schedule for each phase of the project.

1. In the Project Browser, right-click the Schedule/Quantities button and select New Schedule/Quantities.

2. Using Figure 18.14 as a reference, set the schedule category to Doors.

3. Name the schedule **Door Schedule for Phase 1 – 1994 Construction**.

4. Set the Phase to Phase 1 – 1994 Construction.

5. Click OK to close the New Schedule dialog box.

6. In the Schedule Properties dialog box, add the following in order to the Scheduled fields:

> Mark
>
> Width
>
> Height
>
> Thickness
>
> Type

7. Click the Sorting/Grouping tab.

8. Set Sort By Value to Mark.

9. Switch to the Formatting tab.

10. In the fields list, highlight Mark.

11. In the heading, change the text to **Door Number**.

12. Click OK to close the Schedule Properties dialog box (Figure 18.15).

When you create a new schedule, it is important to set the Phase property to match the desired report, as we did in step 4.

In your multiple-phase project, you can create duplicate views of the schedule to keep the same formatting and assign different phases and filters as desired to display your information.

Figure 18.14

Creating a phase-aware door schedule

Figure 18.15

Phase 1 – 1994 Construction door schedule

Door Schedule for Phase 1 - 1994 Construction				
Door Number	Width	Height	Thickness	Type
1	3' - 0"	7' - 0"	0' - 2"	36" x 84"
4	3' - 0"	7' - 0"	0' - 2"	36" x 84"
5	3' - 0"	7' - 0"	0' - 2"	36" x 84"
6	3' - 0"	7' - 0"	0' - 2"	36" x 84"
7	3' - 0"	7' - 0"	0' - 2"	36" x 84"
8	3' - 0"	7' - 0"	0' - 2"	36" x 84"
9	3' - 0"	7' - 0"	0' - 2"	36" x 84"
11	3' - 0"	7' - 0"	0' - 2"	36" x 84"
12	3' - 0"	7' - 0"	0' - 2"	36" x 84"
13	3' - 0"	7' - 0"	0' - 2"	36" x 84"
14	3' - 0"	7' - 0"	0' - 2"	36" x 84"
15	3' - 0"	7' - 0"	0' - 2"	36" x 84"
16	3' - 0"	7' - 0"	0' - 2"	36" x 84"
17	3' - 0"	7' - 0"	0' - 2"	36" x 84"
18	3' - 0"	7' - 0"	0' - 2"	36" x 84"
19	3' - 0"	7' - 0"	0' - 2"	36" x 84"
21	3' - 0"	7' - 0"	0' - 2"	36" x 84"

When naming your schedules, you will find it helpful to include the name of the phase as part of the schedule name. You can do this by editing the View Name in the Schedule Properties palette, for example, Door Schedule for Phase 1 – 1994 Construction and Door Schedule for Phase 2 – 2012 Construction. Doing this will make it easier for you and others on the project to know what the schedule is reporting without having to check the view properties.

Phase-Specific Room Boundaries

All rooms are phase-specific in a project. When you add a room to a plan view or create a room by adding a row to a room schedule, the room is automatically assigned the specified phase of the view. Once you place a room in the project, the phase properties of the room can't be changed.

For example, if we place a room in a view that has the Phase set to Phase 2 – 2012 Construction, then all rooms placed there are assigned to the Phase 2 – 2012 Construction phase. These rooms will not display when you switch to another view that is using a different phase. If you want a room to be associated with a different phase, then that room needs to be added in the view with the desired phase set.

If you need to carry rooms over to future phases, say from Phase 1 to Phase 2, Phase 3, and so on, then:

1. Copy the room using the Copy to Clipboard command.

2. Switch to the desired future phase view.

3. Use the Paste Aligned / Current View command.

As the project progresses, you can report room areas for different phases. Also, the same room name and number can exist in the same or different locations of the model, provided they are in different phases. We recommend that you do not switch the phase in the same plan view but rather make duplicate plan views with dedicated phases.

You can make edits to room-bounding elements in one phase without affecting other phases. For example, you can delete room-bounding walls in one phase and, provided those walls do not exist in other phases, not impact the room boundaries defined in other phases. Revit ignores any room-bounding elements that do not exist in the active phase in which you are working.

Rooms become part of the phase as you place them in the view. Figure 18.16 shows the Phase 1 – 1994 Construction, Level 1 floor plan.

Compare Figure 18.16 with Figure 18.17, and notice that room tags occupying the same space can have different names and/or numbers. You can also have the same room numbers in a different phase in the same or different locations.

Figure 18.16

Phase 1 – 1994 Construction, Level 1 floor plan

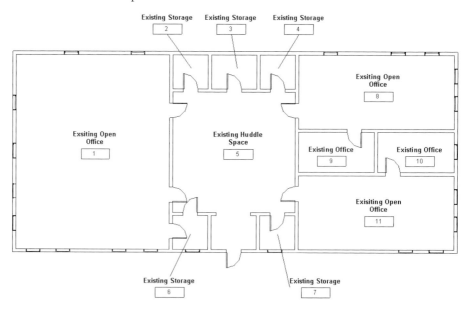

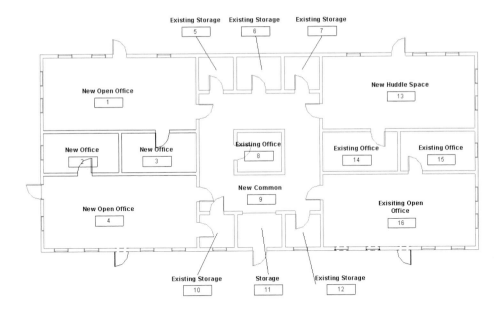

Figure 18.17

Phase 3 – 2014 Construction, Level 1 floor plan

You can find an example of a room in a phased project among the files you downloaded at the book's companion web page (www.sybex.com/go/introducingrevit2012). Look for Dataset_18_04.rvt.

Infill Elements

Infill elements used to occupy the spaces of demolished walls or doors occur when a hosted element and its host do not have the same values for Phase Created and Phase Demolished. In the first image in Figure 18.18, you see a previous phase that contains a wall and a door. In the second image, which is a later phase, the door has been demolished, a window has been placed in the same location, and Revit infills the wall where the door is being removed. When Revit places an infill, you cannot drag, move, mirror, rotate, copy, or paste the element.

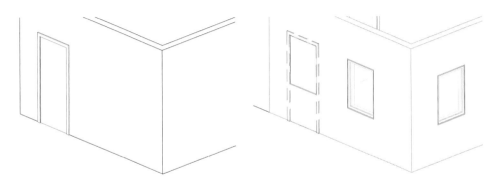

Figure 18.18

Revit infill of the wall when existing door is demolished and a new window is placed in the view

Take note when an item is demolished and an infill placed; that infill will behave just like the host elements in that you can place a new element within or overlapping that area.

Also keep in mind that infill elements for roofs and floors project down from the top face, and infill elements for ceilings project up from the bottom face.

Infill Elements for Earlier Phases

If you place an insert into a host in a phase later than the host's creation phase, Revit creates an infill element for earlier phases.

Where you have an existing shell drawn for your project, place a door or window in the exterior with the view phase set to a future phase (Figure 18.19 top). Open a view with an earlier phase, and you will find an infill element in the area where the door or window will be created in the future (Figure 18.19 bottom).

Figure 18.19

Revit infill added to the host object in an earlier phase of the project

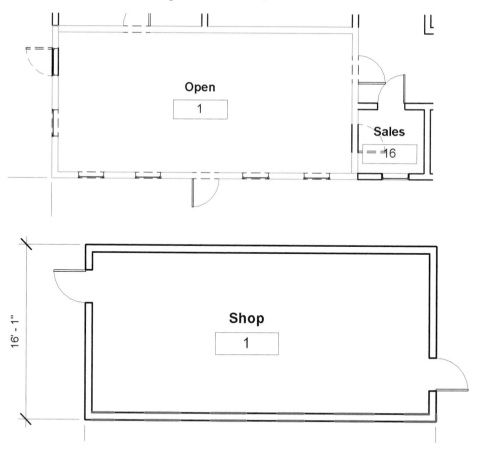

Demolishing Elements

When you think about demolition, you probably consider this to be a phase or specific milestone of the project. After all, if you are working on a renovation project, you probably create demolition plans for the project. Revit, however, does not consider demolishing to be a phase; it is more of an object state.

We have referred to the use of the Demolish tool with phasing. To use this tool, you model the existing project using elements and tools outlined in the book as normal, including the elements that you want to demolish. You do this because the demolition work isn't really a phase *per se* but more a parameter of an element.

When the modeling is completed, you are ready to indicate what will be demolished. To do this, follow these steps:

1. Open a view that has the element you want to demolish.

2. Click the Demolish button, as shown on the Manage tab's Phasing panel.

3. Select the elements that are to be demolished.

Revit will then automatically change the element properties to the proper Phased Demolished value.

Figure 18.20 shows a project underway using phases: An older phase is half-toned per the phase filter, while the demolition is dashed.

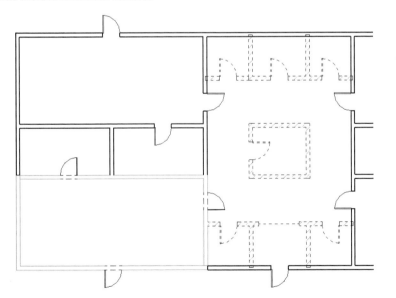

Figure 18.20

Floor plan showing demolished walls

DEMOLISHING PART OF A WALL

If only part of a wall is to be demolished, do the following:

1. Select the wall to be split.

2. From the Modify | Walls tab, choose the Modify panel, and click the Split Element button to break the wall as necessary.

3. Demolish the appropriate part.

Notice that if you demo a wall that contains a door or a window, the door or window is demolished as well.

Rendering and Existing Phases

When rendering in Revit, the phase that elements are assigned to can affect the final rendered output. A common occurrence is when you are displaying elements from an earlier phase in the view of a newer phase. This is based on the phase filter, which can override existing objects to display using an alternative material (the default override is the Phase – Exist material) from the one assigned to the object. By default, some of the phase filters use the Overridden value (see Figure 18.21).

Figure 18.21

Phase Filters settings

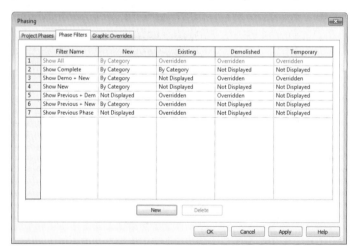

Figure 18.22 shows what happens when the Phase Filter property is set to Show All. To render the view without the phase filter, you can temporarily change the Phase Filter setting to None for the view and then render. This will use the default materials that were applied to the objects, as shown in Figure 18.23.

You can find an example of rendering a phased project among the files you downloaded at the book's companion web page (www.sybex.com/go/introducingrevit2012). Look for Dataset_18_05.rvt.

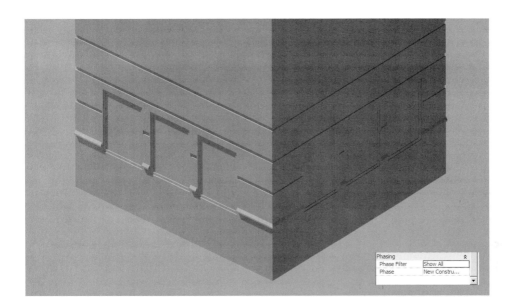

Figure 18.22

**Rendered image
with Phase Filter
set to Show All**

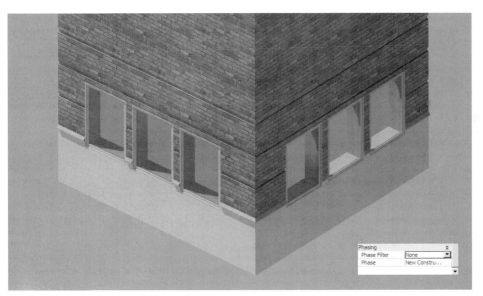

Figure 18.23

**Rendered image
with Phase Filter
set to None**

CHAPTER 19

Autodesk Revit Architecture for Interiors

An interior designer can use a number of tools in Autodesk Revit Architecture to streamline and improve the production process. In this chapter we will discuss using Revit to create your programming documents to verify that your proposed spaces meet the project's programming requirements. We will also cover how to use Revit to efficiently create finish schedules using key schedules, which help automate the process of populating repetitive data. Because a finish schedule is sometimes not adequate to properly detail all the finishes, we will demonstrate how to use elevations and plans to show this information.

Revit provides a tool to create a framework for documenting your design and project, but it cannot draw it for you. The strength of Revit lies in its handling of repetitive tasks, calculating and tabulation, and coordination. You still need to provide the design and clearly communicate your design to the builder.

This chapter covers the following topics:

- **Creating the programming document**
- **Finish and key schedules**
- **Finish elevations and plans**

Creating the Programming Document

The initial phase of a typical project starts with a programming document. This document summarizes the types of spaces required along with the amount of space needed, usually expressed as square feet. When starting a project in Revit, you can take the information gathered in the programming phase of the process and transfer the data to a schedule in Revit.

As the project takes shape as a floor plan, you can use this schedule as your guideline to keep the square footage and space requirements in check. The program can start out very simple as blocks of space—departments, for example—to demonstrate how they fit into a particular building layout.

The program schedule can be expanded to include more detailed information as your space planning progresses. The schedules utilize the same expressions found in Excel. Setting up a room schedule that includes square footage counts can also be utilized to represent BOMA (Building Owners and Managers Association) plans, occupant loads, and plumbing fixture counts.

The sample file we are using is a commercial building that is large and repetitive, which is good for demonstration purposes.

Starting a Schedule

To begin a program schedule, we'll start a new schedule and select Rooms as the category.

1. From the book's companion download files (available at `www.sybex.com/go/introducingrevit2012`), open `Dataset_19_01.rvt`.

2. From the View tab → Create panel, select Schedules → Schedule/Quantities.

   This will open the New Schedule dialog box (Figure 19.1).

3. In the New Schedule dialog box, select Rooms in the Category list.

4. Change the Name entry as shown in Figure 19.1 to **Programmed Area**, and click OK to create the schedule.

   This will open the Schedule Properties dialog box (Figure 19.2).

Figure 19.1

**Creating a new
Room schedule**

5. In the Fields tab of the Schedule Properties dialog box, select the following fields in order from the Available Fields area of the dialog box, and click the Add button to schedule these fields:

Department

Area

In the next steps we need to create a new Project parameter called Program Area for calculating square footage.

6. In the Schedule Properties dialog box, click the Add Parameter button.

This will open the Parameter Properties dialog box (Figure 19.3).

7. Make sure that Parameter Type is set to Project Parameter.

8. Under Parameter Data enter **Program Area** in the Name field.

9. Set the Type Of Parameter field to Area.

10. Set the Group Parameter Under field to Analysis Results.

11. Click OK twice to close the Parameter Properties and Schedule Properties dialog boxes, and your schedule will generate itself.

12. In the schedule, click the Area field and change it to read **Actual Area** (Figure 19.4).

Since no rooms have been placed in the floor plan yet, the actual area does not exist.

13. On the Modify Schedule | Quantities tab of the ribbon choose the Rows panel and click the New Row button.

14. In the cell under Department, type **Administration**.

15. In the cell under Program Area, type **3035 SF**.

16. Repeat steps 13–15 for the departments and program areas in the following table:

DEPARTMENT	PROGRAM AREA
Accounting	5500 SF
Engineering	6200 SF
HR	800 SF
IT	2500 SF

The next step is to create a column to set up totals for each row.

17. In the Properties palette for our Programmed Area schedule, click the Edit button next to Formatting.

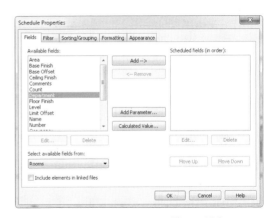

Figure 19.2

Schedule Properties dialog box

Figure 19.3

Project parameter for calculating square footage

Programmed Area		
Department	Actual Area	Program Area
Accounting	Not Placed	
Engineering	Not Placed	
HR	Not Placed	
IT	Not Placed	

Figure 19.4

Create a project parameter for calculating square footage.

18. Select Area in the Fields list of the Schedule Properties dialog box, and check the Calculate Totals check box, as shown in Figure 19.5.

Figure 19.5

Calculate Totals for Area

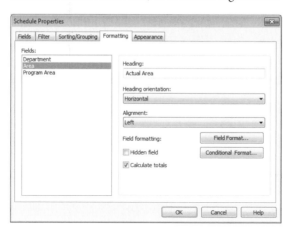

19. Repeat step 18 for Program Area.

20. On the Sorting/Grouping tab, check the Grand Totals check box and set Grand Totals to Totals Only.

21. Save your file.

Creating a Space Plan

In the following section, we are going to create a space plan. A space plan is a preliminary graphic representation of project's space requirements. Typically these space plans show walls, doors, and room sizes. Now that your program is set up in a schedule format, go to your floor plan.

1. From the book's companion download files (available at www.sybex.com/go/introducingrevit2012), open Dataset_19_02.rvt or continue using the file from the previous section.

2. Open the Level 1 floor plan.

3. On the Home tab's Room & Area panel, click the Room button. The Modify | Place Room tab will appear.

4. Open the Options bar, click the drop-down list for Room (Figure 19.6).

    The rooms from the program schedule will automatically be listed.

Figure 19.6

Listing of Rooms from the program schedule

5. Using Figure 19.7 as a reference, select Administration from the drop-down list and place it on the floor plan.

The newly placed room will fill up the entire plan except for the core elements.

Figure 19.7

Administration space

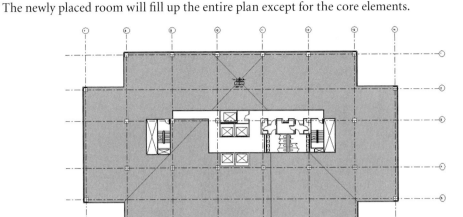

In the next step, we are going to add room separation lines to subdivide the open areas.

6. Go back to Home tab's Room & Area panel. Select Room Separation Line from the Room button pull-down.

7. Using Figure 19.8 as a reference, draw the following room separation lines and add the remaining rooms to the floor plan. Note that the room separation lines have been enhanced to make them stand out.

8. Switch views to the Programmed Area schedule.

9. Save your file to the desktop.

Figure 19.8

Using room separation lines to define spaces for rooms

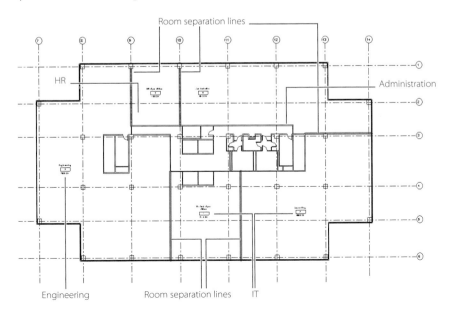

Notice that the Actual Area column now displays the actual square footages. To further analyze the program schedule, in the next steps we will add a Calculated Value column to show the delta, or difference, between the actual and programmed areas.

1. From the book's companion download files (available at www.sybex.com/go/ introducingrevit2012), open Dataset_19_03.rvt or continue using the file from the previous section.

2. In the Properties palette for the Programmed Area schedule, click the Edit button for the Fields category.

3. Click the Calculated Value button to bring up the Calculated Value dialog box.

4. For the Name field, enter **Difference**.

5. Make sure the default radio button, Formula, is selected.

6. Change the Type to Area.

7. To set up the formula, click the browse button ….

   This will open the Fields dialog box, which allows you to select field names to add to the formula.

8. Select Area from the list, and click OK.

9. Enter a minus sign.

10. Click the browse button … again, select Program Area, and click OK.

    This creates a formula for the actual area minus the Program Area, as shown in Figure 19.9.

11. Click OK to return to the Schedule Properties dialog box (Figure 19.2).

    In the next steps, we are going to create a new field that will calculate the percentage difference for our actual and program areas.

Figure 19.9

Creating a formula to show the difference between the actual and programmed areas

12. Click the Calculated Value button to bring up the Calculated Value dialog box.

13. For Name, enter **Percent Difference**.

14. Make sure the default radio button, Formula, is selected.

15. Change the Type to Number.

16. For the formula, enter **Difference / Program Area** using the browse … button as before. Click OK.

    This creates the formula Difference / Program Area, as shown in Figure 19.10.

17. Click OK to close the Calculated Value dialog box.

Our schedule now has Difference and Percent Difference columns. Our Percent Difference column, though, is not displaying as a percentage.

If you started this section using your file from the previous section, the actual square footage values may vary depending on the placement of your room separation lines.

18. To change to Percentage Difference column to read as a percentage, select the Formatting tab in the Schedule Properties dialog box.

19. Highlight Percent Difference, and click the Field Format button.

20. Uncheck the Use Default Settings box.

21. Change Units to Percentage, Rounding to 1 decimal place, and Unit Symbol to %.

22. Click the OK button twice to close the Formatting tab and the Schedule Properties dialog box.

23. Save and close the file.

Room bounding allows a wall to either be detected by rooms or ignored. This is useful for instances such as plumbing chases, alcoves, or when toilet partitions are created with the Wall tool.

Figure 19.10

Creating a formula to show the percentage difference between the actual and programmed areas

We now have a basic Programmed Area schedule (Figure 19.11). Using the basic department floor plan, the layout can be adjusted using the room separation lines so that the actual square footage matches the program square footage, using the schedule as a guide. A helpful tool while adjusting the room separation lines is to turn on the Show Area check box for the room tag graphics. This will provide real-time feedback as the room separation lines are moved.

Programmed Area				
Department	Actual Area	Program Area	Difference	Percentage Difference
Accounting	4556 SF	5500 SF	-944 SF	-17.2%
Engineering	7039 SF	6200 SF	839 SF	13.5%
HR	1100 SF	800 SF	300 SF	37.5%
IT	2114 SF	2500 SF	-386 SF	-15.4%
Adminstration	4013 SF	3035 SF	978 SF	32.2%
	18822 SF	18035 SF		

Figure 19.11

Programmed Area schedule

Refining the Space Plan

The program schedule can be edited to break the departments into specific rooms. The next step is to expand the program schedule to show more detailed information.

1. From the book's companion download files (available at www.sybex.com/go/introducingrevit2012), open Dataset_19_04.rvt.

We are using this file because we have added additional room separation lines to define spaces to see if the room we define will meet the program requirements.

2. Open the Programmed Area schedule.

   To see the square footage breakdown for each department, we will edit the sorting and grouping of the schedule.

3. In the Properties palette, click the Edit button for Sorting/Grouping.

4. Sort by Department, and put a check mark next to Header and Footer.

5. Change the Footer sort group to Totals Only.

6. Click OK to close the Schedule Properties dialog box to update the Programmed Area schedule (Figure 19.12).

Figure 19.12

Sorted and grouped Programmed Area schedule

Department	Room Name	Actual Area	Program Area	Difference	Percentage
Accounting					
Accounting	Accounting Open Office	3737 SF	3300 SF	437 SF	13%
Accounting	Accounting Office	167 SF	170 SF	-3 SF	-2%
Accounting	Accounting Office	181 SF	170 SF	11 SF	7%
Accounting	Accounting Office	171 SF	170 SF	1 SF	1%
Accounting	Accounting VP Office	213 SF	225 SF	-12 SF	-5%
		4470 SF	4035 SF		
Administration					
Administration	Administration Open Office	3432 SF	5000 SF	-1568 SF	-31%
Administration	Exec VP	254 SF	250 SF	4 SF	2%
Administration	Pres Office	328 SF	325 SF	3 SF	1%
		4013 SF	5575 SF		
Engineering					
Engineering	Engineering Open Office	6197 SF	6200 SF	-3 SF	0%
Engineering	Eng Office	285 SF	170 SF	115 SF	68%
Engineering	Eng Office	250 SF	170 SF	80 SF	47%
Engineering	Eng Office	154 SF	170 SF	-16 SF	-10%
Engineering	Eng Office	160 SF	170 SF	-10 SF	-6%
		7046 SF	6880 SF		
HR					
HR	HR Open Office	605 SF	800 SF	-195 SF	-24%
HR	HR Office	147 SF	170 SF	-23 SF	-13%
HR	HR Office	143 SF	170 SF	-27 SF	-16%
HR	HR VP Office	197 SF	250 SF	-53 SF	-21%
		1093 SF	1390 SF		
IT					
IT	IT/Tech Open Office	2200 SF	2500 SF	-300 SF	-12%
		2200 SF	2500 SF		
		18821 SF	20380 SF		

7. Save the file to your computer.

Conditional Formatting

To help analyze the program schedule, *conditional formatting* can be applied when an area exceeds a certain value. Conditional formatting in schedules will allow us to visually identify parameters that meet or do not meet specific conditions that we indicate. In this next example, we will create conditional formatting criteria to highlight the cells that have a value either greater than 10% or less than -10% of the program requirement for area.

1. From the book's companion download files (available at www.sybex.com/go/introducingrevit2012), open Dataset_19_05.rvt or continue using the file from the previous section.

2. Open the Programmed Area schedule.

3. In the Properties palette, click the Edit button for Formatting.

4. Highlight Percentage Difference, and click the Conditional Format button.

5. In the Condition Formatting dialog box, set Test to Not Between and set Value to 10% and -10%.

6. Change Background Color to yellow (Figure 19.13).

7. Click the OK button twice to close the Conditional Formatting and Scheduling Properties dialog boxes.

   This condition will highlight any areas that are more than 10% over or under the program requirement (Figure 19.14).

8. Save and close the file.

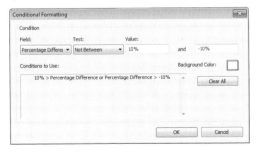

Figure 19.13

Conditional Formatting dialog box

Figure 19.14

Programmed Area schedule with highlighted areas more than 10% over or under the program requirement

		Programmed Area			
Department	Room Name	Actual Area	Program Area	Difference	Percentage
Accounting					
Accounting	Accounting Open Office	3737 SF	3300 SF	437 SF	13%
Accounting	Accounting Office	167 SF	170 SF	-3 SF	-2%
Accounting	Accounting Office	181 SF	170 SF	11 SF	7%
Accounting	Accounting Office	171 SF	170 SF	1 SF	1%
Accounting	Accounting VP Office	213 SF	225 SF	-12 SF	-5%
		4470 SF	4035 SF		
Administration					
Administration	Administration Open Office	3432 SF	5000 SF	-1568 SF	-31%
Administration	Exec VP	254 SF	250 SF	4 SF	2%
Administration	Pres Office	328 SF	325 SF	3 SF	1%
		4013 SF	5575 SF		
Engineering					
Engineering	Engineering Open Office	6197 SF	6200 SF	-3 SF	0%
Engineering	Eng Office	285 SF	170 SF	115 SF	68%
Engineering	Eng Office	250 SF	170 SF	80 SF	47%
Engineering	Eng Office	154 SF	170 SF	-16 SF	-10%
Engineering	Eng Office	160 SF	170 SF	-10 SF	-6%
		7046 SF	6880 SF		
HR					
HR	HR Open Office	605 SF	800 SF	-195 SF	-24%
HR	HR Office	147 SF	170 SF	-23 SF	-13%
HR	HR Office	143 SF	170 SF	-27 SF	-16%
HR	HR VP Office	197 SF	250 SF	-53 SF	-21%
		1093 SF	1390 SF		
IT					
IT	IT/Tech Open Office	2200 SF	2500 SF	-300 SF	-12%
		2200 SF	2500 SF		
		18821 SF	20380 SF		

Analysis

In Chapter 13 we discussed how area plans show spatial relationships based on area schemes and levels in your model. In this section we are going to use schedules to perform occupant and minimum plumbing fixture count analysis.

Occupant Load

The following steps use schedules to calculate occupancy loads based on the 2009 IBC Table 1004.1.1.

1. From the book's companion download files (available at www.sybex.com/go/introducingrevit2012), open Dataset_19_06.rvt.

We are using this file because we have added additional room separation lines to define spaces to see if the room we define meets the program requirements.

2. Switch to the Key – Occupancy Per 2009 IBC Table 1004.1.1 schedule.

This is a key schedule that was created from, and is based on, the 2009 IBC Table 1004.1.1 for Occupant Load. Later in this chapter we will go into more detail on creating a key schedule. This key schedule contains the code information from the IBC Table. The table has three fields:

Occupancy Type Describes the use of the room

S.F. Per Person Required square footage per person

Occupancy S.F. Type Either net or gross square footage

If your project requires the 2006 IBC Table 1004.1.1 for Occupant Load, then duplicate the key schedule for 2006 IBC and modify the values as required.

The next step is to create a calculating room schedule.

3. From View tab → Create panel → Schedules drop-down button, click the Schedule/Quantities button to open the New Schedule dialog.

4. For the Category, select Rooms.

5. Name it **Occupancy Tabulation per 2009 IBC Table 1004.12**.

6. Make sure that Phase is set to New Construction, and click OK to close the New Schedule dialog box.

7. Add the following fields to be scheduled:

Number

Name

Occupancy

Area

S.F._Per_Person

8. Click the Calculated Value button to add a calculated value.

9. Next to Name, type **Persons** for the name of the calculated value.

10. Make sure the Formula radio button is enabled.

11. Set Discipline to Common.

12. Set Type to Number.

13. Type the following for the formula: (**Area / S.F._Per_Person / 1' ^ 2**). Use Figure 19.15 as a reference.

14. Click OK to close the Calculated Value dialog box.

> Parameter names are case sensitive. "PERSONS" and "persons" are not valid usages if the parameter name is defined as "Persons."

15. Switch to the Formatting tab of the Schedule Properties dialog box.
16. Select the Persons field, and check the Calculate Totals box.
17. Repeat step 16 for S.F._Per_Person.
18. Switch to the Sorting/Grouping tab of the Schedule Properties dialog box.
19. Change Sort By to Number.
20. Select the Grand Totals check box, and select Totals Only at the bottom of the dialog box.
21. Select the Itemize Every Instance check box.
22. Click OK to return to the schedule.

    In the schedule, notice that for the Occupancy column there are numerous (none) values (Figure 19.16).

23. Click the far right-hand side of the (none) field in the Occupancy column for room number 100.

    This will open a drop-down menu that will allow you to select from a list of the Occupancy Type values from our Key - Occupancy Per 2009 IBC Table 1004.1.1 schedule.

24. Select the appropriate value for each room in the schedule. Figure 19.17 is provided as a reference.

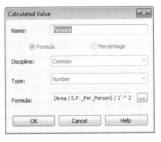

Figure 19.15

Completed calculated value for the Persons schedule field

Occupancy Table per 2009 IBC Table 1004.12

Number	Name	Occupancy	Area	S.F._Per_Per	Persons
100	Reception	(none)	782 SF		
101	Closet	(none)	66 SF		
102	Coffee	(none)	72 SF		
103	Hall	(none)	314 SF		
104	Administr	(none)	944 SF		
105	VP HR Of	(none)	242 SF		
106	Admin Sm	(none)	242 SF		
107	Exec VP	(none)	242 SF		
108	Pres Offic	(none)	348 SF		
109	Huddle	(none)	159 SF		
110	Supply	(none)	139 SF		
111	Print Roo	(none)	327 SF		
112	Hall	(none)	435 SF		
113	Admin Co	(none)	352 SF		
114	Large Co	(none)	497 SF		
115	Eng Conf	(none)	352 SF		
116	Coffee	(none)	86 SF		
117	Huddle	(none)	146 SF		
118	Engineeri	(none)	1618 SF		
119	VP Engin	(none)	186 SF		

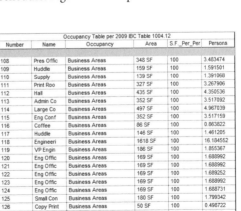

Figure 19.16

Partial view of the schedule Occupancy Table per 2009 IBC Table 1004.12

Occupancy Table per 2009 IBC Table 1004.12

Number	Name	Occupancy	Area	S.F._Per_Per	Persons
108	Pres Offic	Business Areas	348 SF	100	3.483474
109	Huddle	Business Areas	159 SF	100	1.591501
110	Supply	Business Areas	139 SF	100	1.391068
111	Print Roo	Business Areas	327 SF	100	3.267906
112	Hall	Business Areas	435 SF	100	4.350536
113	Admin Co	Business Areas	352 SF	100	3.517092
114	Large Co	Business Areas	497 SF	100	4.967039
115	Eng Conf	Business Areas	352 SF	100	3.517159
116	Coffee	Business Areas	86 SF	100	0.863822
117	Huddle	Business Areas	146 SF	100	1.461205
118	Engineeri	Business Areas	1618 SF	100	16.184552
119	VP Engin	Business Areas	186 SF	100	1.855367
120	Eng Offic	Business Areas	169 SF	100	1.688992
121	Eng Offic	Business Areas	169 SF	100	1.688992
122	Eng Offic	Business Areas	169 SF	100	1.689252
123	Eng Offic	Business Areas	169 SF	100	1.688992
124	Eng Offic	Business Areas	169 SF	100	1.688731
125	Small Con	Business Areas	180 SF	100	1.799342
126	Copy Print	Business Areas	50 SF	100	0.498722
127	Hall	Business Areas	908 SF	100	9.07919
128	Sales Offi	Business Areas	169 SF	100	1.688992
129	Sales Offi	Business Areas	169 SF	100	1.68901
130	Sales Offi	Business Areas	169 SF	100	1.688992
131	VP Sales	Business Areas	185 SF	100	1.853988
132	Sales Op	Business Areas	1224 SF	100	12.238962
133	Sales Con	Business Areas	431 SF	100	4.309943

Figure 19.17

Partial view of the schedule Occupancy Table per 2009 IBC Table 1004.12 with Occupancy values defined

When you select the value, the schedule will automatically fill in the appropriate S.F._Per_Person value and calculate the Persons value for that room.

25. Save the file to your local desktop.

Plumbing Fixture Load

In the next example, we are going to take the code example a step further by creating schedules to calculate the minimum number of plumbing fixtures required.

1. From the book's companion download files (available at www.sybex.com/go/ introducingrevit2012), open Dataset_19_07.rvt or continue using the file from the previous section.

2. Find the SCHEDULE - Occupancy Tabulation per 2009 IBC Table 1004.12 schedule in the Project Browser.

3. Right-click the schedule name, and select Duplicate View → Duplicate.

4. Right-click the new schedule name in the Project Browser, and click Rename.

5. Rename the schedule **Minimum Plumbing Facilities Per Table 2902.1 Business**.

6. In the Properties palette click the Edit button to the right of the Fields list.

7. Create the following calculated values (Calculated Value Name | Type | Formula):

   Men | Number | Persons / 2

   WC_Men | Number | if((Men < 50), (Men / 25), (2 + (((Men − 50)) / 50)))

   Lav_Men | Number | if(Men < 50, Men / 40, (2 + (Men − 50) / 80))

   Women | Number | Persons / 2

   WC_Women | Number | if((Women < 50), (Women / 25), (2 + (((Women − 50)) / 50)))

   Lav_Women | Number | if(Women < 50, Women / 40, (2 + (Women − 50) / 80))

   DF | Number | (Men + Women) / 100

   Service Sink | Number | 1

8. In Formatting tab, make Area and S.F._Per_Person hidden fields.

9. Remove the following fields from the schedule:

   Number

   Name

   Occupancy

10. Make the following fields calculated totals:

   S.F._Per_Person

   Persons

Men

WC_Men

Lav_Men

Women

WC_Women

Lav_Women

DF

Service Sink

11. Switch to the Formatting tab.

12. Click the Field Format button and uncheck Use default setting.

13. Set the Units to Fixed.

14. Make sure that Rounding is set to "0 decimal places" and click OK to close the Format dialog box.

15. Repeat steps 11 – 14 for:

Women

Men

16. Switch to the Sorting/Grouping tab.

17. Uncheck Grand Totals and Itemize every instance.

18. Click OK to close the Schedule Properties dialog box.

The schedules will now self-calculate if your project in the room occupancy schedule has been filled out (Figure 19.18).

Minimum Plumbing Facilities Per Table 2902.1 Business								
	Men			Women				
Persons	Men	WC_Men	Lav_Men	Women	LAV_Women	WC_Women	DF	Service Sink
183	92	3.665676	2.291047	92	2.291047	3.665676	1.832838	51

Figure 19.18

Completed Minimum Plumbing Facilities Per Table 2902.1 Business

19. Find the Minimum Plumbing Facilities Per Table 2902.1 Business schedule in the Project Browser.

20. Right-click the schedule, and select Duplicate View → Duplicate.

21. Right-click the new schedule in the Project Browser, and click Rename.

22. Rename the schedule **Minimum Plumbing Facilities Per Table 2902.1 Mercantile**.

23. In the Properties palette, click the Edit button to the right of the Fields listing.

24. Create the following (Name | Type | Formula):

Men | Number | Persons / 2

WC_Men | Number | Men / 500

Lav_Men | Number | Men / 750

Women | Number | Persons / 2

WC_Women | Number | Women / 500

Lav_Women | Number | Women / 750

DF | Number | (Men + Women) / 1000

Service Sink | Number | 1

25. In Formatting tab, make Area and S.F._Per_Person hidden fields.

26. Make the following fields calculated totals:

S.F._Per_Person

Men

WC_Men

Lav_Men

Women

WC_Women

Lav_Women

DF

Service Sink

27. Click OK to close the Schedule Properties dialog box.

The schedules will now self-calculate if your project in the room occupancy schedule has been filled out (Figure 19.19).

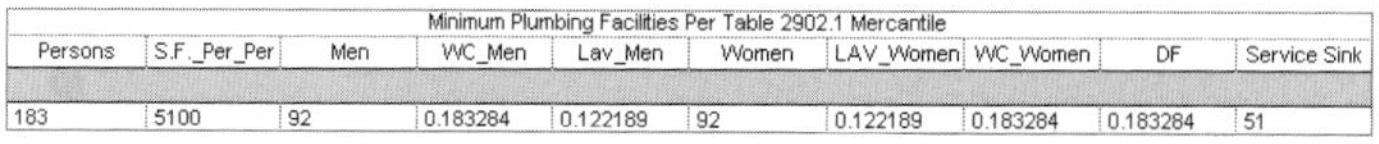

Figure 19.19

Completed Minimum Plumbing Facilities Per Table 2902.1 Mercantile

Minimum Plumbing Facilities Per Table 2902.1 Mercantile									
Persons	S.F._Per_Per	Men	WC_Men	Lav_Men	Women	LAV_Women	WC_Women	DF	Service Sink
183	5100	92	0.183284	0.122189	92	0.122189	0.183284	0.183284	51

28. Save your file to the desktop.

A completed version of this exercise can be downloaded from the book's companion files (available at www.sybex.com/go/introducingrevit2012); open Dataset_19_07_Complete.rvt.

Finish and Key Schedules

When rooms are straightforward (paint, base, carpet) and the project is orientated in a linear fashion or your rooms are mostly rectangles, creating a simple room finish schedule, as discussed in Chapter 14, is a snap. Inputting all this finish information can be time consuming. Instead, you can use key schedules, which are essentially nothing more than schedules of keys that you can use in other schedules. These can help expedite your work and be a time saver when the design changes. In that chapter, we also discussed scheduling walls based on their cardinal direction (North, South, East, or West).

Basic Finish Schedule

In this section we create a schedule of room finishes that could be used for a wide variety of applications, including estimating costs and quantities of materials required.

To create a new finish schedule, follow these steps:

1. From the book's companion download files (available at www.sybex.com/go/introducingrevit2012), open Dataset_19_08.rvt or continue using the file from the previous section.

2. On the View tab's Create panel, click the Schedules drop-down button and select Schedule/Quantities.

3. In the New Schedule dialog box, select Rooms from the Category list.

4. Name the schedule **Finish Schedule**.

5. Click the OK button to close the New Schedule dialog box.

6. In the Schedule Properties dialog box, select Name from the Available Fields list.

7. Click the Add button to move it to the Schedule Fields list.

8. Repeat steps 6 and 7 for the following fields:

   Number

   Floor Finish

   Base Finish

   Wall Finish

   Ceiling Finish

9. Click OK to close the Schedule Properties dialog box and to create the room Finish Schedule (Figure 19.20).

10. Save your file to the desktop.

Figure 19.20

Finish Schedule

Finish Schedule					
Name	Number	Floor Finish	Base Finish	Wall Finish	Ceiling Finish
Administration Open	1				
Accounting Open Offi	2				
Engineering Open Offi	3				
HR Open Office	4				
IT/Tech Open Office	5				
Sales Open Office	6				
Break	7				
IT Server	8				
HR Conference	9				
Coffee	10				
Closet	11				
Small Conference	12				
Sales Conference	13				
Acct Conference	14				
VP Acct Office	15				
Acct Office	16				
Acct Office	17				
Acct Office	18				
HR Office	19				
HR Office	20				
VP HR Office	21				
Admin Sm Conf	22				
Exec VP	23				
Pres Office	24				
Admin Conference	25				
Large Conference	26				

If your room schedule does not display any rooms, then it is possible that the room schedule is not showing the correct phase. In this example, in the Properties palette, make sure that Phase is set to Programming 1.

After creating the schedule, you can further organize it by sorting by room numbers and, if applicable, by level. The previous steps provided us with a very basic, very simple schedule.

Key Schedules

Rather the manually filling in repetitive information for rooms, a room-style key schedule will populate your schedule for you. This allows for changing large quantities of room finishes quickly.

In the following steps we are going to edit the original room Finish Schedule and add the newly created room style.

1. If you are continuing from the previous lesson, you can continue to use that file, or from the book's companion download files (available at www.sybex.com/go/introducingrevit2012), open Dataset_19_09.rvt.

2. On the View tab's Create panel, click the Schedules drop-down button and select Schedule/Quantities.

3. In the New Schedule dialog box, select Rooms from the Category list.

4. Name the schedule **Room Style Schedule**, and click the radio button for Schedule Keys.

5. Enter **Room Style** in the Key Name field, and click the OK button (Figure 19.21).

   The Schedule Properties dialog box will appear.

6. Select Floor Finish from the Available Fields list and then click the Add button.

7. Repeat step 7 for

   Base Finish

   Wall Finish

   Ceiling Finish

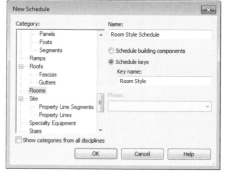

Figure 19.21
Creating a room-style key schedule

8. Click OK to close the Schedule Properties dialog box.

   The key schedule is automatically created.

9. Using Figure 19.22 as a reference, add the finish information for each room-style type by clicking the New Row button on the Modify Schedule | Quantities tab → Rows panel on the ribbon.

10. Select Finish Schedule.

11. In the Finish Schedule Properties palette, click the Edit button for Fields.

12. In the list of Available Fields, select Room Style, and click the Add button to add it to the Scheduled Fields list.

Room Style Schedule				
Key Name	Floor Finish	Base Finish	Wall Finish	Ceiling Finish
Break/Copy	VCT-1	Rubber-1	Paint-4	ACT-3
Conference	Carpet-3	Wood-1	Paint-3	ACT-3
Executive Of	Carpet-1	Wood-1	Paint-2	ACT-3
Office	Carpet-1	Rubber-2	Paint-2	ACT-2
Open Office	Carpet-2	Rubber-1	Paint-1	ACT-1

Figure 19.22
Completed Room Style Schedule

13. With Room Style selected in the Scheduled Fields list, click the Move Up button to make Room Style the third field listed, and click OK to close the Schedule Properties dialog box, as shown in Figure 19.23.

    With the key schedule created, we can now populate the Floor, Base, Wall, and Ceiling finishes by selecting the appropriate Room Style in the Finish Schedule.

14. In the Finish Schedule, locate the cell for the Room Style in the Accounting Open Office.

15. Click in the cell, and from the drop-down list, select Open Office.

    Notice that after you select Open Office, the finish information for Floor, Base, Wall, and Ceiling is added.

16. Using Figure 19.24 as a reference, set the Room Style for the other rooms.

17. Save your file to the desktop.

Adding Cardinal Direction to Walls

A missing component for most projects is the ability to schedule wall finishes for North, East, South, and West walls. These are added through Shared Parameters under the Manage tab of the ribbon. Once your shared parameters are defined, you can add them into the Project Parameters dialog box.

The first thing we are going to do is create a shared parameter file. Keep in mind that when editing or adding data to the shared parameter file, this information should be coordinated with your office BIM manager because it will affect all users and may cause problems with projects.

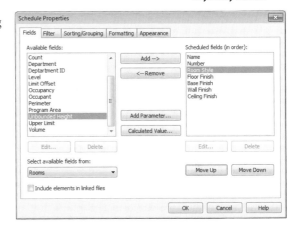

Figure 19.23

Finished Schedule Properties dialog box with the Room Style key added

Finish Schedule

Name	Number	Room Style	Floor Finish	Base Finish	Wall Finish	Ceiling Finish
Accounting Open Office	2	Open Office	Carpet-2	Rubber-1	Paint-1	ACT-1
Engineering Open Office	3	Open Office	Carpet-2	Rubber-1	Paint-1	ACT-1
HR Open Office	4	Open Office	Carpet-2	Rubber-1	Paint-1	ACT-1
IT/Tech Open Office	5	Open Office	Carpet-2	Rubber-1	Paint-1	ACT-1
Sales Open Office	6	Open Office	Carpet-2	Rubber-1	Paint-1	ACT-1
Break	7	Break/Copy	VCT-1	Rubber-1	Paint-4	ACT-3
IT Server	8	Office	Carpet-1	Rubber-2	Paint-2	ACT-2
HR Conference	9	Conference	Carpet-3	Wood-1	Paint-3	ACT-3
Coffee	10	Break/Copy	VCT-1	Rubber-1	Paint-4	ACT-3
Closet	11	Break/Copy	VCT-1	Rubber-1	Paint-4	ACT-3
Small Conference	12	Conference	Carpet-3	Wood-1	Paint-3	ACT-3
Sales Conference	13	Conference	Carpet-3	Wood-1	Paint-3	ACT-3
Acct Conference	14	Conference	Carpet-3	Wood-1	Paint-3	ACT-3
VP Acct Office	15	Office	Carpet-1	Rubber-2	Paint-2	ACT-2
Acct Office	16	Office	Carpet-1	Rubber-2	Paint-2	ACT-2
Acct Office	17	Office	Carpet-1	Rubber-2	Paint-2	ACT-2
Acct Office	18	Office	Carpet-1	Rubber-2	Paint-2	ACT-2
HR Office	19	Office	Carpet-1	Rubber-2	Paint-2	ACT-2
HR Office	20	Office	Carpet-1	Rubber-2	Paint-2	ACT-2

Figure 19.24

Populated room Finish Schedule

1. If you are continuing from the previous lesson, you can continue to use that file, or from the book's companion download files (available at www.sybex.com/go/introducingrevit2012), open Dataset_19_10.rvt.

2. From the Manage tab → Settings panel, click the Shared Parameters button.

    This will open the Edit Shared Parameters dialog box.

3. Click the Create button to open the Create Shared Parameter File dialog box.

4. Navigate to a folder on your local computer, and name the file **C19SP**.

5. Click the Save button to create the shared parameter file.

6. In the Edit Shared Parameters dialog box, click the New button under Groups to create a new parameter group.

7. Name the group **Wall_Direction**, and click OK.

8. Click the New button under Parameters. Using the following table as a reference, create new parameters (Figure 19.25).

NAME	DISCIPLINE	TYPE OF PARAMETER
East Wall	Common	Text
North Wall	Common	Text
South Wall	Common	Text
West Wall	Common	Text

Figure 19.25

Creating a shared parameter file for specifying the cardinal direction of walls

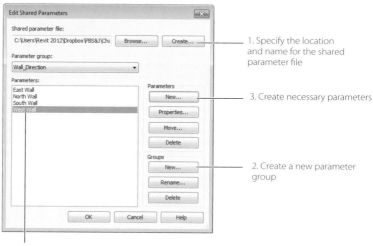

9. Click OK to close the Edit Shared Parameters dialog box.

The next thing we need to do is tie our newly created shared parameters to a project parameter.

10. From the Manage tab → Settings panel of the ribbon, click the Project Parameters button [Project Parameters].

This will open the Project Parameters dialog box.

11. Click the Add button to open the Parameter Properties dialog box.

12. Under Parameter Type, click the Shared Parameter radio button.

13. Click the Select button to open the Shared Parameters dialog box.

14. Under Parameters, select the East Wall and click OK.

15. Under Parameter Data, change the Group Parameter Under value to Identity Data.

16. Under Parameter Data, click the Instance radio button.

17. Under Categories, check the Rooms check box (Figure 19.26).

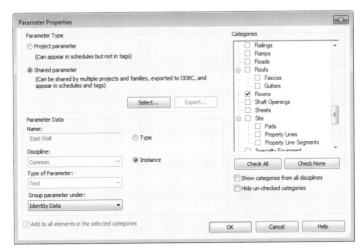

Figure 19.26

Creating a shared parameter for specifying the cardinal direction of walls

18. Click the OK button to close the Parameter Properties dialog box.

19. Repeat steps 11–18 for the

    West Wall

    North Wall

    South Wall

20. Click OK to close the Project Parameters dialog box.

    These parameters can now be added to your schedule through the Fields tab. The existing Wall Finish field will need to be removed.

    Once your schedule has been updated with your new fields, you may want to group them under the heading Walls.

21. In the Finish Schedule, select the East Wall, West Wall, North Wall, and South Wall column headings and right-click.

    This will open a context menu (Figure 19.27).

22. Click Group Headers.

    A new header is created, named Walls (Figure 19.28).

23. Save your file to the desktop.

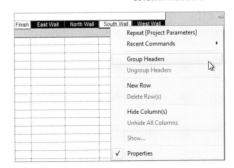

Figure 19.27

Grouping schedule column headers

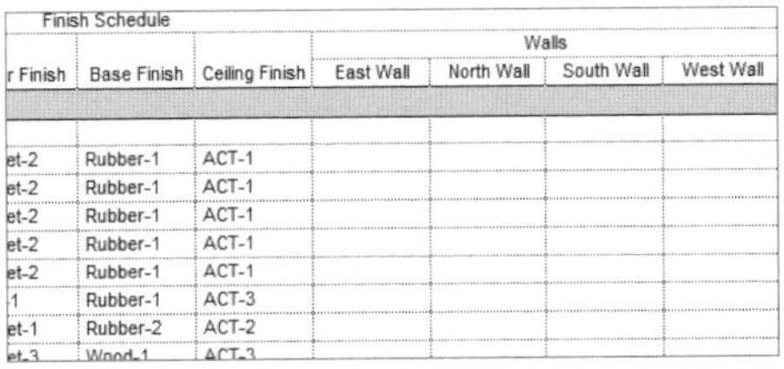

Figure 19.28

Column headers for the Walls group

Finish Elevations and Plans

When a project is more complicated than what a finish schedule can show, adding elevations and enlarged plans is necessary to clearly indicate the design. Multiple finishes can consist of various materials, such as where the carpet ends and wood flooring begins, or multiple trims and paint colors assigned to one wall, or intricate ceramic tile patterns.

Part of a successful set of plans is to convey the design clearly and accurately to the owner, contractors, vendors, and other building professionals. Basic graphic standard and construction document conventions still apply and include showing correct line weights, patterns, and notation.

Creating Interior Elevations

A straightforward way to create an interior elevation is to simply use a crop boundary. Refer to Chapter 2, Figures 2.26 and 2.27, for an explanation of crop regions.

Revit will automatically generate the elevation when you place the elevation tag. However, the program will crop to the halfway point of the outside face, cutting the line in half. The effect is less than desirable when printing. You can adjust the crop boundary to show the full thickness of these lines, but it can be difficult to achieve consistent results. This method may be the easiest solution for simple projects with few interior elevations and consistent ceiling heights.

Another solution is to create a masking region with a window showing the part of the elevation you want, as shown in Figure 19.29. The crop region is expanded out past the elevation. You create a masking region with a cutout for the part for the elevation you want to show through. You can adjust the line weights on the masking region to create a crisp drawing.

Figure 19.29

Interior elevation

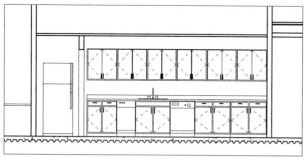

When creating a crop region, you must take care where you expand the crop—elevation tags may begin to show up on ceiling plans on the level below or the floor plan above. If your ceiling plan is set with the view range's top primary range being the level above, tags will show through. Setting this view range to offset -1′-0″ (300mm) will keep this from happening. Our next step in cleaning up the elevation in Figure 19.30 is to create a masking region.

1. From the book's companion download files (available at www.sybex.com/go/introducingrevit2012), open Dataset_19_11.rvt or continue using the file from the previous section.

2. Switch to the Break default building elevation view.

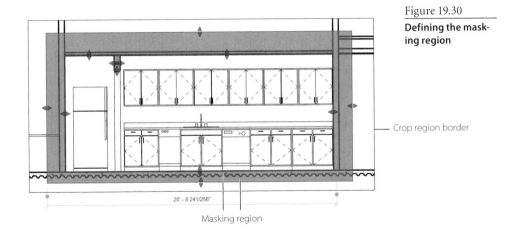

Figure 19.30

Defining the masking region

Crop region border

Masking region

This elevation view has the crop region already enabled. The next step will be to create a masking region around the elevation view to hide the geometry that we do not want to see.

3. From the Annotate tab → Detail panel of the ribbon, click the Region drop-down button and select Masking Region ⬛ Masking Region .

   This will open up the Modify | Create Masking Region Boundary tab.

4. Using the Line tool from the Draw panel—and Figure 19.30 as a reference—sketch the inner masking region boundary.

5. Using the Rectangle tool from the Draw panel—and Figure 19.30 as a reference—sketch the outer masking region boundary.

   You do not need to draw the outer masking region boundary to the edge of the crop region. We will adjust the crop region to the masking region.

6. Click the Finish Edit Mode ✔ button on the Mode panel to close out of Sketch mode.

7. Adjust the view's crop region to be inside the outer masking region line.

8. In the view's Properties palette, uncheck the Crop Region Visible check box. The results are shown in Figure 19.31.

9. Save your file to the desktop.

Figure 19.31

Cropped and masked interior elevation

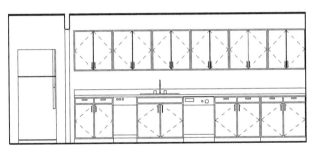

Creating Finish Plans

Depending on the complexity of your floor finishes, there are many workarounds for creating detailed finish floor plans. These include filled regions, detail lines, the Split Face tool, and the Paint tool. These methods are similar to what we would use in the CAD world. The primary drawback is that these are essentially unintelligent objects. We can use the Split Face tool and Paint tool to define a tile border, but we would not be able to extract any metadata or quantity information about the border.

A true BIM solution is to create separate floor elements for each floor finish type used in the project (Figure 19.32). So if you had a room with three different floor finishes, you would create three unique floors to represent those materials (Figure 19.33). The main drawback to this method is that it will take longer to create floors for each material type than it would to use 2D tools. The main reason to use this method is that we can extract metadata or quantity information for each floor type.

When creating separate floor elements for each floor finish, keep in mind that Architecture/Structure is responsible for the design of the slab and structural flooring. When modeling the floors, always model using real materials and thicknesses.

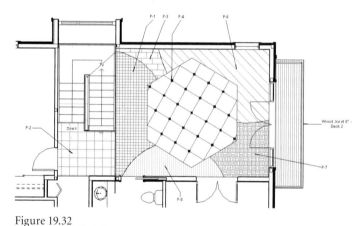

Figure 19.32

Finish floor plan

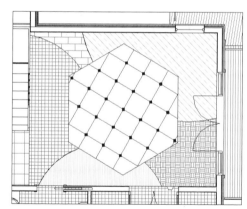

Figure 19.33

Enlarged plan view of floor finishes

CHAPTER 20

Worksharing

Worksharing in Autodesk Revit Architecture is a feature that allows multiple users to access and edit one Revit project file. It allows multiple team members to concurrently work on the same Revit project and keep changes synchronized.

While employing much of a data structure similar to a database, Revit uses a file-based approach to store projects. In a single-user scenario, one Revit user can edit a Revit file and it becomes read-only for any other Revit user trying to access the file (e.g., over a corporate network).

Worksharing is a mechanism that allows multiple users to access one Revit project file and work concurrently with a minimum of effort to control ownership of access rights for each single user. Revit will take care of access privileges in the background and synchronize all editing done concurrently by multiple users across all of them.

This chapter covers the following topics:

- Worksharing fundamentals
- Handling workshared files
- Editing workshared files
- Troubleshooting
- Best practices

Worksharing Fundamentals

When you enable Worksharing for a project file, Revit introduces a set of features to effectively assign and control ownership of all elements in the building model. First we will look at some of the terminology involved in Worksharing in order to become familiar with the basic concepts.

Overall Concept

The concept of concurrent work on a single Revit project file is oftentimes misunderstood. In practice you may hear the term *Revit database*. The word *database* sometimes suggests a client/server kind of information architecture—a scenario where remote clients feed information into a central database located on a server on the network.

This is technically not true for workshared Revit files. Revit Worksharing works on the principle of having multiple copies of the same Revit project file at the outset for every Revit user working on a particular Revit project.

Then, when users make their edits, the Revit Worksharing mechanism takes care of synchronizing all the changes done by each of the concurrently working users into a Central File and then broadcasting them back to all the so-called Local Files the users work with.

Revit also handles the necessary access control to individual elements in a workshared project. Access control is necessary because you need to avoid concurrent edits of the same element. Imagine a scenario where one user would change a particular wall from 4″ (100mm) to 5″ (125mm) while at the same time another user would try to change the same wall from 4″ (100mm) to 6″ (150mm). A conflict in the project file would occur. To avoid these sorts of conflicts, Worksharing introduces the notion of access control of individual elements in a workshared Revit project.

This allows every Revit user to work on the project file as if they were working on a single-user file and then synchronize their edits with all other concurrent users of that project. *Synchronize* here means to save one's changes and broadcast them to all other users while having one's own copy of the Revit project file updated with all the changes made by other users.

Since Revit handles synchronization of multiple users working concurrently on the same Revit project, you need to understand a few basic terms before starting to workshare a project.

Basic Terminology

Whenever you start working on a team that utilizes a workshared Revit file, you will soon hear some fundamental terms that are the *lingua franca* of Revit Worksharing, such as *save to central, worksets, relinquish permissions,* and others. To familiarize you with these most important terms, we will discuss them briefly:

Central File The Central File is the master project repository that contains all building model data. It also contains all information about the logical subdivision created in the Worksharing process as well as the ownership of the individual elements within the workshared project. It will be saved in a shared location on the network so that more than one person can access and work on the project. It is important to understand that the Central File by itself is nothing more than a container to store the information provided by all members of the team and also to send out all changes to every member.

Remember that Worksharing is based on the concept of identical copies of a Revit project file that are kept synchronized by Revit. The Central File is just another copy that aggregates all changes done by all team members and allows Revit to send those changes back to all members of the team working on that project. This means that when member A submits his edits of the project to the Central File and then member B submits her edits, member B will also see member A's changes in her copy of the Central File, which is called her Local File.

Local File The Local File is an identical copy of the Central File that resides on a team member's local workstation. It needs to maintain connectivity to the Central File in order to allow the system to manage the ownership of individual elements in the project as well as enable synchronization of changes across the team. Whenever a Local File gets synchronized with a Central File, it sends its changes to the Central File and, at the same time, picks up all the changes all other team members have made to their Local Files.

When team members collaboratively work on a project, Revit controls access of individual elements in the model to ensure that changes done by one member of the team cannot accidentally be overridden by another member of the team concurrently editing the model. There are two different approaches for handling access rights in Revit Worksharing:

Workset One possible way is to utilize worksets that can be predetermined and assigned to individual members of the team. A *workset* is a collection of elements in the building model that are assigned to and can be edited by only one member of the project team.

You can allocate elements in the building model to a workset. This workset can then be leased by a team member to edit those parts of the model contained in that workset. Common terminology is that "Laura owns workset 'partitions' now." Worksets encapsulate the idea of structuring a project into individual segments, which can be very helpful in a scenario where a project team has individuals who focus on different parts of a project, such as interior versus exterior or building shell versus construction.

Element Borrowing The second approach is called *element borrowing*. This technique allows a team member to immediately edit an element without explicitly obtaining access rights to the workset the element belongs to beforehand. Element borrowing happens automatically when a team member selects an element for modification. It requires that this element not be in use (borrowed) by another team member. Element borrowing won't allow a user to access objects assigned to or used by other members of the team. The concept of element borrowing basically allows all team members to access all parts of the model without previously structuring their workflow in detail (which would be required for a workset approach).

WORKSETS VS. ELEMENT BORROWING

While worksets and element borrowing seem like antagonistic features, they allow a well-structured team to have a fluid workflow on a project. Worksets reflect the typically planned-out-beforehand part of a collaborative project, whereas element borrowing allows the team to quickly tweak permissions on the fly. Worksets are rigid structures that reflect assigned tasks, and element borrowing reflects the need for a quick change that happens in every project, especially in a scenario of time constraints. The fact that Revit allows both approaches has proven helpful in real-world large-project scenarios since they allow proper planning and task assignments while still enabling users to quickly do a necessary change without too much overhead from access management.

Editing Requests As soon as an element is accessed by one member of the team via element borrowing or is assigned in a workset, that person will retain ownership of the element unless explicitly relinquished. Editing requests allow team members to place requests to access a specific element. The owner of the element can then explicitly grant access to it by relinquishing their ownership.

Ownership As mentioned, concurrent work on a project requires a mechanism that makes sure that a team member does not undo the changes another team member made. While in a traditional 2D or paper-based workflow this was not possible (a 2D CAD file can be accessed by only one person at a time), concurrent work on a 3D model must restrict who can do what so that conflicts don't occur. Ownership of elements means that Revit will temporarily assign particular element of a building model to one user, either by using worksets or element borrowing. As long as that particular team member keeps this ownership, no other team member will be able to access (edit) those elements unless the principal owner relinquishes them.

Element Relinquishing This term means that a user gives up ownership of elements they previously owned for editing. Those elements will now become editable again by all other team members—either by taking ownership of the worksets these elements are assigned to or by element borrowing. You can either electively relinquish your permissions when saving to central or explicitly use a feature in the Revit user interface.

Prerequisites

Some preliminary steps are necessary before setting up Worksharing in a Revit project file. The following discussion covers the most important aspects, such as how to structure a project team and which technical infrastructure is required.

One of the most critical aspects of Revit Worksharing does not necessarily depend on that particular feature; it depends more on how members share the work on a project as a team. Revit Worksharing is able to adapt to quite different scenarios.

If a team is structured to work on one project, for example, on a floor-to-floor basis, this setup can be reflected by worksharing the elements on different floors accordingly and assigning ownership of all elements on a particular level to a particular collaborator.

On the other hand, if a team is structured to share the workload thematically— meaning that one user focuses on the structural parts of the building while another user does all interior work—then you can structure worksets accordingly to fit that particular scenario.

The bottom line is that Revit will not impose a structure on how you share the workload on a collaborative project for you but is flexible enough to accommodate any practical workflow of collaboration you set up in your team beforehand.

Structuring the Project

In order to allow multiple members of the team to work on a single project file, you should consider in advance how the workload will be divided. This is by no means different from a 2D drafting environment, regardless whether it is CAD or paper based. There is no single formula on how to subdivide a project into worksets. Since virtually every element in the building model can be assigned to a workset, Worksharing can reflect most ways of team interaction on a project.

The way a project should be structured also depends on the size and kind of project as well as on the individual roles of the members in the team. Workset assignments are not mandatory since element borrowing allows multiuser access to the project without explicitly assigning elements to worksets. However, practical considerations require at least a minimum of predefinition of ownership of the building model elements.

One common approach to structure a collaborative project is to subdivide it into different topics. Your team may have individuals who focus on the structural aspects of the building while others do all interiors. Revit Worksharing allows you to keeps this approach since you can assign elements to their respective worksets.

On the other hand, if your team is composed of equally strong team members and your previous workflow was to look at a building on a by-story basis, you can also subdivide elements in the Revit model and assign ownership via worksets.

Workset assignments can be changed over the course of the project to reflect changing team configurations during the course of the project's life cycle.

Creating an Infrastructure

Worksharing requires the Central File to be accessible to all users at the same network location. This means that all members of your team need to be able to access the Central File in the same place on your network. You can check this by navigating to the file on each of your team members' workstations and checking the path in Windows Explorer. As long as it is identical, your setup will work.

You need to be aware, though, that Revit governs the Central File location via the Uniform Naming Convention (UNC) path syntax. That means that while you may see the Central File in Windows Explorer at, for example, `X:\OfficeServer\ Projects\CentralFile.rvt`, Revit will store the path as `\\OfficeServer\Volume\File\...\ CentralFile.rvt`. It is mandatory that this UNC path to the Central File be identical for all team members accessing the file; otherwise, file synchronization will fail.

Another critical requirement for Revit Worksharing is a robust and modern network infrastructure. Modern office networks in most cases will be able to handle the additional load of data created by synchronizing large Revit files between different multiple collaborators. However, legacy corporate networks that route network traffic through dedicated servers located in geographically different locations will pose a problem for efficient work with Revit Worksharing.

Finally, one aspect of infrastructure required for a Revit Worksharing environment has little to do with technology—it is the requirement of having a Revit model manager present. The classic role of project manager will—in a Revit worksharing environment—now also encompass skills to structure a Revit project using the features of Revit Worksharing. The decision as to which particular task has to be done in a project at a particular time of the design process needs to be communicated to the team and at the same time facilitated by assigning those elements to the particular team member.

These requirements mandate that the Central File reside on an office LAN in one geographic location. However, oftentimes team members wish to access the Central File through the Internet while at a different branch office or working on site. Technology to do so is being introduced with Revit Server in the Revit 2012 release cycle. Other technologies, such as hardware network caching as well as wide area file services (WAFS) techniques exist; however, the technical intricacies involved in those scenarios are beyond the scope of this introduction. Therefore, the following paragraphs focus on scenarios where Revit Worksharing needs to be set up in an office in one location.

Handling Workshared Files

Handling worhshared files is different from handling a single-user Revit file. As mentioned, Revit Worksharing conceptually depends on synchronizing identical copies of one Revit project residing on each collaborator's workstation with one Central File located on a network server. The following section describes how to technically handle this scenario.

Understanding the Principal Workflow

The basic process of worksharing a project in Revit is as follows:

1. A single user creates a project file. At that point, initial geometry and information are created.

2. A practical environment for the project should be created at this point, such as initial mass model, site information, and project information.

3. When additional team members join the project, Worksharing gets enabled in the Revit project file.

   At this point Revit allows the assignment of all existing and newly created elements to worksets, by enabling the team to logically structure the project.

4. The file is saved as a Central File at a location on the network that is accessible to all team members.

5. Team members then save the Central File as a Local File on their local hard drive (or on the network).

   Revit from now on will maintain communication between the Local File and the Central File to control ownership of individual building model elements.

Additional worksets can be created in the Local File to organize the building model into logical groups. Team members can then make changes to existing elements or add new elements either by taking control over a dedicated workset or by element borrowing.

All members of the team must save their changes to their Local File regularly. They must also save to Central to consolidate their changes with the Central File, update their Local File with changes the other team members have made, and by doing so synchronize their version of the model with the central shared model.

Team members can relinquish their ownership of entire worksets or borrowed elements at any time. Additional worksets can be acquired throughout the entire collaborative process.

Setting Up Worksharing

The following section introduces you to the basic steps to enable Worksharing in a Revit file. Before you start with the following example, you should designate two locations to save files to. One should reside on your workstation, and the other one should be located on your office network. You will use the location on your workstation to save your Local File, and the location on your office network will be designated to store the Central File. You will synchronize the changes you make to your Local File with the Central File.

1. From the book's web page (available at www.sybex.com/go/introducingrevit2012), open Dataset_20_01.rvt (Dataset_20_01_Metric.rvt).

2. On the Collaborate tab of the ribbon, click the Worksets button (Figure 20.1) found in the Worksets panel.

   Figure 20.1

   Worksets button

   The Worksharing dialog box will open with a warning message and allow you to determine initial names for the default worksets that Revit will create.

   The process of enabling Worksharing is not reversible. Once Worksharing is enabled, all Local and Central project files will retain their behavior—you cannot roll back workshared files to single-user files.

3. Click OK to dismiss the Worksharing warning dialog box.

   The Worksets dialog box will open (Figure 20.2).

Figure 20.2

Worksets dialog box

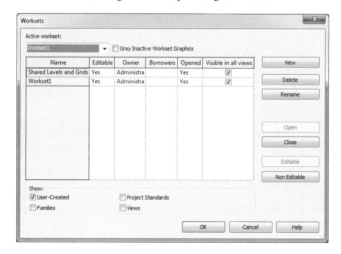

4. Select Workset1 and click Rename.

   The Rename dialog box will open.

5. Rename Workset 1 to **Exterior Elements**, and click OK.

6. In the Worksets dialog box, click New.

   The New Workset dialog box will open.

7. Enter **Interior Elements** as name for the new workset. Click OK.

You will notice Interior Elements being added to the list of worksets.

8. Click OK to close the Worksets dialog box.

The Specify Active Workset dialog box will open and ask if you want to make Interior Elements the active workset.

9. Click Yes.

You have now enabled Worksharing for the project file. The only further steps required are to create the Central File as well as the Local File.

Saving a Workshared Project File

When you save a file for the first time after Worksharing has been enabled, Revit will create a Central File. Clicking Save will create a Central File in the same location as the original (not workshared) single-user file. Clicking Save As will allow you to specify a network path where the Central File will be saved (Figure 20.3).

Figure 20.3

File Save Options dialog box accessed by clicking Save As

Continuing with the example we started in the section "Setting Up Worksharing," we will now create the Central File:

1. With `Dataset_20_01.rvt` (`Dataset_20_01_Metric.rvt`) still open, choose Application menu → Save As → Project.

2. In the Save As dialog box, click Options.

Notice that Make This A Central File After Save is checked but grayed out: That means that Revit will now automatically create a Central File when saving this project.

3. Click OK to save the project, preferably to a network location.

Next we will create the Local File:

1. Choose Application menu → Save As → Project.

2. Specify a location on your local computer to save the file.

3. Click Save.

Revit has now created the Local File. Notice that the Synchronize With Central button will become available (Figure 20.4), which means that from now on you will be able to synchronize your Local File with the Central File.

Another option for creating a Local File is to directly attempt to open the Central File. When you directly access a Central File on your network and then subsequently save it locally using Save As, a new Local File will be created and the virtual link between the Central File and the Local File will be established.

Figure 20.4

Synchronize With Central button

In a scenario where the virtual link between the Central File and the Local File already exists, Revit will allow you to automatically create a new Local File when you try to open the Central File. This option will be available on the Open dialog box when you directly try to open a Central File that already has an established virtual connection to your local workstation (Figure 20.5).

Figure 20.5

Open dialog box

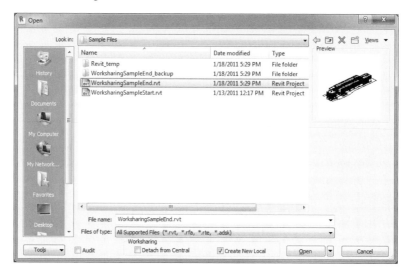

Elements and Worksets

Once Worksharing has been enabled in a Revit project, all elements will get an additional parameter that controls which workset they belong to. You will find the Workset parameter in the Properties palette, grouped under Identity Data (Figure 20.6). As long as the element is accessible to you—in other words, as long as no other user has acquired the specific workset the element belongs to or has borrowed the element—you can change the assignment of worksets for this specific element.

The Worksets Dialog Box

The Worksets dialog box (Figure 20.7) allows you to specify access permissions for individual worksets. It allows you open worksets, make worksets editable to you, create new worksets, rename worksets, and delete worksets, as well as specify the currently active workset.

Figure 20.6

Properties palette

You can access the Worksets dialog box by clicking the Worksets button in the Worksets panel on the Collaborate tab of the ribbon. Opening the Worksets dialog box will present you with a list that shows all worksets in the workshared model. The columns in this dialog box are as follows:

Name Lists the name of workset.

Editable Shows whether the particular workset is editable to you or not.

Owner Shows the current owner of this workset. Be aware that the name displayed here corresponds to the Username field found on the General tab of the Revit Options dialog box.

Borrowers Gives the name of any team member borrowing elements residing on that workset.

Opened Displays Yes if this workset is open in your current Revit worksharing session. Otherwise it displays No.

Visible In All Views This check box controls weather this workset will be visible in all existing or to-be-created views by default. By default, the check box is checked. Be aware that when you uncheck this box, all elements on that particular workset will not be visible in any new view you create unless you explicitly turn their visibility on the in Visibility/Graphic Overrides dialog box of that particular view.

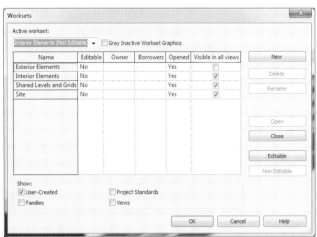

Figure 20.7

Worksets dialog box

Active Workset

This drop-down allows you to specify the currently active workset. All new building elements will now be created on the workset you choose unless you explicitly override this preset in the individual element's Instance properties.

Gray Inactive Workset Graphics

This check box is a handy feature you can use to visually emphasize which worksets are currently editable. All elements that are not residing on worksets currently editable to you will be displayed in half tone.

New

Clicking New will create a new workset. You can choose the name of the new workset in the dialog box that pops open after you click the New button.

Delete

When you delete a workset, the dialog box that appears will allow you to specify a workset where all elements that resided on the to-be-deleted workset will be moved to. Deleting a workset will not delete the elements it contained; you must specify another workset to subsequently contain those building model elements.

Rename

Clicking Rename allows you to rename an existing workset. In the Rename dialog box that appears, you can supply a new name for the workset.

Open

Clicking Open will open a workset and load all elements on this workset into your current Revit session. The Open button will be grayed out when all worksets are already open and will therefore be available only when you selectively opened a subset of worksets while opening your Local File or when you closed individual worksets before you saved your Local File prior to loading it into the current session.

Close

Closing a workset will effectively unload all elements residing on that particular workset from your current Revit session. This feature is powerful in a large project scenario where you need to control model performance. You can reopen a closed workset at any time if required.

Editable

Selecting a workset from the list and clicking Editable will make all elements of this particular workset editable for you. That means that only you can access and change those elements. No other members on your team will be able to change those elements, nor will they be able to make the same workset editable to them unless you relinquish your permissions either explicitly by clicking the Relinquish All Mine button on the Collaborate tab or marking the workset as Non Editable in the Worksets dialog box.

Non Editable

Clicking this button relinquishes your permissions on that particular workset and makes this workset available to all other team members. Elements on worksets that you made Non Editable to yourself can now be acquired either by another team member making this particular workset Editable to himself or by all other team members via element borrowing.

Show

In the Worksets dialog box all worksets in the Revit project file can be viewed all at once or filtered using the check boxes in the Show group: User-Created, Families, Project Standards, and Views.

In a common scenario you will rarely need to access worksets other than those in the User-Created group. The different classes are briefly described here:

DEFAULT WORKSET

- *Views*: For each view, a dedicated view workset is created automatically containing the view's defining information and any view-specific elements such as annotations.
- *Families*: A family workset is created for each family defined in the project.
- *Project Standards*: Each project setting is placed on its own workset. These standards include Materials, Line Styles, and the like.

USER-CREATED WORKSET

- *Shared Levels and Grids*: At the onset of enabling Worksharing, this workset is automatically created for existing grid and level objects.
- *Workset 1*: Everything that is left over is placed into this Workset.

Synchronizing Changes

You should give some consideration to establishing a plan as to when to synchronize your Local File with the Central File. Depending on your project size, number of team members, as well as technical infrastructure such as network speed, synchronizing your local changes with the Central File can take significantly more time than a normal local save would consume.

Synchronizing your Local File with the Central File can be accomplished in two ways:

- Access the Collaborate tab on the ribbon and click the Synchronize With Central button on the Synchronize panel (Figure 20.8).

- Click a similar button located on the Revit Quick Access Toolbar, right next to the familiar Save button (Figure 20.9).

Figure 20.8

Synchronize panel on Collaborate tab

Both buttons will open a drop-down menu, labeled Synchronize with Central. On that dropdown, you can choose either Synchronize And Modify Settings or Synchronize Now.

Figure 20.9

Synchronize With Central button on the Quick Access Toolbar

Synchronize And Modify Settings

Clicking Synchronize And Modify Settings will bring up the Synchronize With Central dialog box (Figure 20.10).

Here you can specify the Central File location using the Browse button. You can also instruct Revit to compact the Central File during synchronization. Be aware, though, that this will, depending on your model size, add significant time to the synchronization process.

Further settings govern the ownership of elements—you can elect to relinquish ownership of all elements you previously acquired either by dedicatedly assigning worksets to

Figure 20.10

Synchronize With Central dialog box

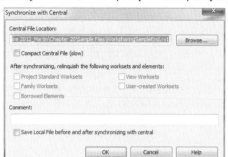

yourself or by element borrowing, or you can choose not to do so, depending on the particular requirements of your workflow at the time of saving to the Central File.

In the Synchronize With Central dialog box you can also add a comment that may be useful in scenarios where you want to track changes made to the Central File over the course of the project.

Finally, you can also specify whether or not your Local File should be saved before and after the synchronization takes place. This is especially helpful in scenarios where for any reason you want to be able to save the state of your Local File before synchronization using the backup features Revit offers for workshared files. Unchecking the check box will speed up the synchronization process, but you may lose the ability to restore your Local File to a state it was in before you attempted the synchronization.

Synchronize Now

Synchronize Now will perform a straightforward synchronization that will both push your changes to the Central File as well as pull all other team member changes that have been synchronized thus far from the Central File and update your local model file accordingly.

Synchronize Now is especially handy when you and your team have already established a working routine utilizing the Worksharing capabilities in Revit. It will perform an unconditional synchronization of your Local File and the Central File.

Reload Latest

Reload Latest allows you to synchronize your local copy of the model with all the changes other team members have made so far without submitting your changes to the Central File. All other team members will not see the changes you have made since the last time you synchronized, but you will be able to update your model to the current state of changes all other team members submitted to the Central File using the Synchronize With Central or Synchronize Now feature in Revit.

Relinquish All Mine

Clicking the Relinquish All Mine button relinquishes all ownership you previously gained in the worksharedfile either by making worksets explicitly editable to you or by element borrowing. All those elements can now be acquired by other team members by either methodology.

Show History

Clicking Show History brings up the History dialog box, where you can query any work-shared file to display its synchronization history (Figure 20.11). Comments you made using the Synchronize With Central dialog box are displayed in this dialog box.

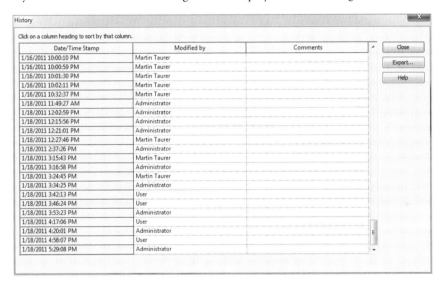

Figure 20.11

History dialog box

This particular feature allows you to either review the changes that have been made to the worksharedfile on screen or export them to a comma-delimited text file that subsequently can be imported into applications such as Microsoft Excel for reporting purposes.

Restore Backup

Using the Restore Backup feature opens a dialog box that will allow you to select a backup file. Backups of workshared files are handled differently from single-user files. This process is oftentimes referred to as a *rollback*. Backup files are created each time a user synchronizes with central or saves a local copy of the central model. Cumulative backups share as much element information as possible; that means they are incremental rather than equal in size to the entire project.

In the Browse For Folder dialog box that opens when you click Restore Backup, you can elect to use either a Local File Backup or a Central File backup folder. You will need to coordinate with your team which version of the project you want to restore before attempting to go ahead.

Once you have successfully restored a prior version of your project, you can utilize the Save As options to save it as a new Central File and then distribute it as fresh Local Files, as described previously.

> The process of restoring an earlier version of a workshared file is a time-consuming process that will require all team members' consent. It is definitely not designed for a scenario where you want to simply review a file's state from a prior date; it is used to roll back time in a project's history, but it will make any changes that happened after the chosen restore date inaccessible.

Editing Requests

Clicking the Editing Requests button brings up a dialog box that shows all pending editing requests made by other team members who tried to access elements in the model that you currently own (because you made a particular workset editable for you or because you borrowed a specific element in the model). A detailed description of the procedures required to make and grant editing requests can be found in the section "Editing Workshared Files."

Opening a Workshared File

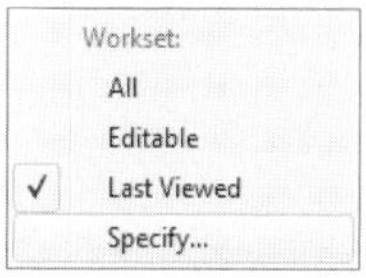

Figure 20.12

Open workshared files options

When you open a workshared file, regardless of whether it is your Local File or the Central File, a drop-down menu is available next to the Open button on the Open dialog box (Figure 20.12).

You can access the following options when you click the arrow next to the Open button:

All Clicking All opens all worksets in the file; you will see the entire model.

Editable Choosing Editable opens all elements that are editable to you, which means all elements no other team member has explicitly acquired ownership of, either by assigning them to themselves or borrowing them.

Last Viewed Selecting Last Viewed brings your Local File into the state you left it in, showing those worksets you chose to view the last time you synchronized your file.

Specify Choosing Specify displays the Open Worksets dialog box. This will put you into a position where you can select which worksets you want to open. This option is especially helpful in a large project scenario. When you use this feature, Revit will read only the worksets you explicitly choose into your local computer's memory.

In a scenario where the Central File is already very large, the Specify feature will help you cut down file load times significantly and increase the application's responsiveness while editing elements. In other words, this feature lets you open just that part of the entire model that is important to your particular needs at that time.

Detaching a Workshared File

On the bottom of the Open dialog box you will find a check box labeled Detach From Central. Clicking this check box will terminate the connection of the file you created by opening the workshared file from the Central File. Detaching a file is especially helpful in scenarios where you want to edit the file without running the risk of interfering with the other team members working in the Worksharing environment.

> Be aware that once a project file is detached from the Central File, you will not be able to reconnect the file to the Central File.

Editing Workshared Files

In the daily routine of editing workshared files, some features are frequently required to control ownership of elements and make sure that elements are assigned to the correct worksets. The following sections discuss these features.

Ownership

The concept of Worksharing in Revit is based on the application handling which team member is allowed to change an element at a specific time to avoid conflicting edits between different team members. The mechanism of element ownership is based on acquiring and relinquishing permissions to edit elements in the building model. The following section describes this concept and lists the features required to control element ownership.

Acquiring and Relinquishing Permissions

Acquiring permissions in a workshared file can be done in two ways, either by explicitly assigning an entire workset to yourself using the workset feature or by element borrowing.

Assigning a Workset to Yourself If you choose to assign an entire workset to yourself, you will need to navigate to the Collaborate tab on the ribbon and click the Worksets button. The Worksets dialog box will open. There you can select any workset that has no owner assigned yet and make it editable by clicking the Editable button.

This will make the workset editable to you, and no other team member will be able to edit elements that are assigned to this particular workset.

Element Borrowing Element borrowing means that you gain ownership of elements in the project file automatically by simply editing them. This will work only if the elements in question are not assigned to a workset that is currently editable to another team member or that is or has been edited by another team member.

Relinquishing Permissions To give up your ownership of elements in a workshared Revit file, you need to relinquish your permissions. You can do so in two different ways. First, you can synchronize your changes with the Central File by clicking Synchronize And Modify Settings found in the Synchronize With Central drop-down in the Synchronize panel on the Collaborate tab of the ribbon. In the Synchronize With Central dialog box, you can select to relinquish Project Standards Worksets, Family Worksets, Borrowed Elements, View Worksets, and User-created Worksets by clicking the appropriate check boxes.

The other way to relinquish your permissions is to click Relinquish All Mine, also located in the Synchronize With Central drop-down in the Synchronize panel on the Collaborate tab of the ribbon.

Selecting Elements

Figure 20.13
Editable Only check box

You can control the way Revit allows you to select elements in a workshared file by clicking the Editable Only check box on the bottom right of the application's window frame (Figure 20.13).

☐ Editable Only

When this option is activated, Revit allows you to select only elements that are currently editable to you or can be made editable by element borrowing. Elements that are in use by other team members or are assigned to a workset that has been made editable by another team member cannot be selected when this check box is selected.

Visual Ownership Control

Revit offers multiple ways to control the state of each element in terms of Worksharing. This section discusses the most important features.

Gray Inactive Worksets In the Worksets panel on the Collaborate tab of the ribbon you will find the Gray Inactive Worksets button. Clicking this button will gray out all elements that are currently assigned to worksets that are not in use by any team member. Be aware, though, that this feature will not reflect element borrowing, which means that even if an element is currently in use by either you or any other team member, it will still appear grayed out as long as the workset it belongs to is not made editable by any member of the team.

Icons on Elements Whenever you select an element in a workshared file, a small icon will indicate that the element is not currently editable. Clicking that icon will make the element editable for you; that means you can use element borrowing to edit this particular element (Figure 20.14).

Figure 20.14
Icon on elements

Placing Editing Requests

In a scenario where you want to access an element that is either assigned to a workset that is currently editable to another member in your team or is borrowed by another team member, Revit will bring up an error message allowing you to place an editing request (Figure 20.15). Clicking the Place Request button will send the request to the team member in question.

Figure 20.15

Placing an editing request

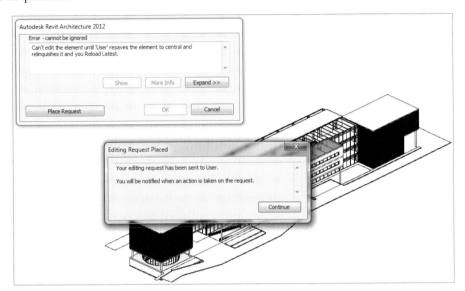

When you place an editing request, Revit will offer you a choice to either wait for the request to be granted or lose the changes you made that triggered the request and redo them once the request is granted (Figure 20.16).

Reviewing Editing Requests

There are two ways to handle editing requests that other users place. In the first scenario, as soon as a user submits an editing request to you, a pop-up window will appear, allowing you to choose Grant, Deny, or Show in response to the request (Figure 20.17). Clicking Show will open a view that displays the element in question.

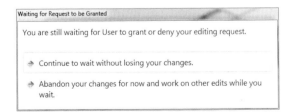

Figure 20.16

Waiting for Request to Be Granted

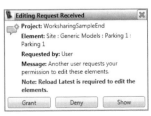

Figure 20.17

Editing Request Received

Figure 20.18

Editing Requests dialog box

Another way to review all pending editing requests is to click the Editing Requests button in the Synchronize panel on the Collaborate tab of the ribbon. This will bring up the Editing Requests window. Here you can review all pending editing requests, both your own as well as those of any other team members (Figure 20.18).

Here you can choose Grant, Deny (or Retract in case the request in question is your own), or Show in response to an editing request pertaining to those elements.

A notification will inform you of any editing requests being granted or denied (Figure 20.19).

Activating Worksets

You can control which workset will be currently set active and subsequently control which workset all new elements that you create will be assigned to. You can activate worksets by either clicking the Activate Worksets fly-out on the bottom of the application's window frame (Figure 20.20) or by opening the Worksets dialog box and setting the active workset there.

Worksharing Display

Revit 2012 introduces a new feature called Worksharing Display. This feature allows you to display the current status of ownership of elements per view. The feature is located on the window frame of each view (Figure 20.21).

Worksharing Display allows you to temporarily override the display style of any element in the particular view by the following categories:

Display Ownership Status The elements will be differently colored depending on whether they are owned by you or by any other member of the team. The example in Figure 20.22 shows a situation where two roofs (green) are currently edited by one team member while another two roofs (red) are edited by a different team member or members. The rest of the model is colored blue, indicating that those elements are not currently owned by any member of the team.

Figure 20.19

Editing Request Granted

Figure 20.20

Activate Worksets fly-out

Figure 20.21

Worksharing Display

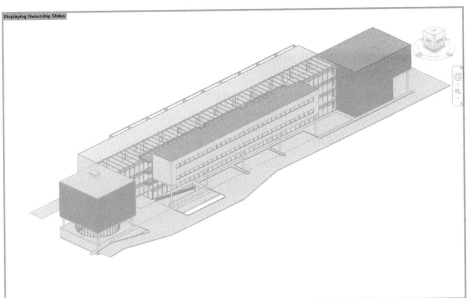

Figure 20.22

Displaying Owner-ship Status

Display Individual Owners Display Individual Owners shows a similar result as in Display Ownership Status, with the difference being that now each owner currently participating in the model is assigned one color.

Display Model Updates This display style shows any updated elements that other members of the team have so far synchronized back to the Central File.

Display Workset Assignment With this display style Revit uses one color per workset and indicates which elements of the workset assignment are using that color.

Clicking Settings will display the Worksharing Display Settings dialog box, which allows you to set up a coloring scheme for the four Worksharing Display categories. It allows you to select a line color for each line item in each category as well as control whether the color should be applied or not using the check box in the Apply Colors column (Figure 20.23).

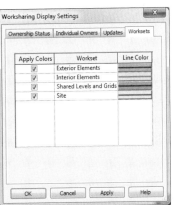

Figure 20.23

Worksharing Display Settings dialog box

Workset View Visibility

Worksharing a Revit file will also add another mechanism to control visibility of elements in a Revit project file. To control visibility of elements by utilizing the Visibility/Graphic Overrides dialog box in any particular view such as Model Categories, Annotation

Categories, Analytical Model Categories, Imported Categories, and Filters, you now will find a new tab in this dialog box labeled Worksets (Figure 20.24). This adds a powerful new mechanism for controlling visibility of elements in your project.

Figure 20.24

Worksets tab of the Visibility/Graphic Overrides dialog box

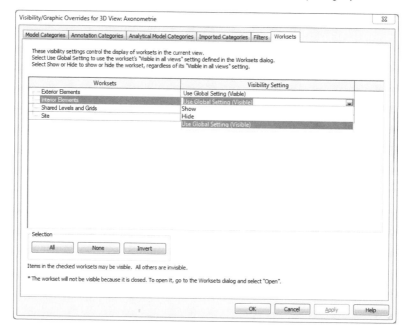

Utilizing View Visibility Controls in a Worksharing Environment

Selecting one workset in the list and clicking Visibility Setting will allow you to set the display of the particular workset either to Show, Hide, or Use Global Setting:

- Show and Hide force Revit to either display or not display the workset in question in that view.

- Use Global Setting refers to the choice made in the Workset dialog box's Visible In All views column (Figure 20.25).

Figure 20.25

Visible In All Views column of the Worksets dialog box

Name	Editable	Owner	Borrowers	Opened	Visible in all views
Exterior Elements	No			Yes	☐
Interior Elements	No			Yes	☑
Shared Levels and Grids	No			Yes	☑
Site	Yes	Administra		Yes	☑

If the Visible In All Views check box is activated, the Global Setting will be visible. When it is not activated, that workset won't be displayed in all views unless explicitly set to Show in the Visibility/Graphic Overrides dialog box.

Troubleshooting

You may find yourself in a situation where you are confronted with error messages indicating that your Local File lost connection to the Central File or that you cannot synchronize your changes to the Central File anymore. In most cases these errors occur because of network disconnections or temporary network problems that occurred when a team member tried to synchronize their changes with the Central File.

Another scenario would be that you want to revert to an earlier state of the project because of unexpected changes from outside and you elect to restart the editing of your project from a particular date.

Both scenarios are well accommodated with Revit Worksharing features.

In a situation where you are confronted with error messages during an attempt to synchronize your Local File with the Central File, we recommend that you find the best Local File or roll back the file to an earlier state, as described in the following sections.

Find the Best Local File

The first action you should take is to save your Local File. Remember, the concept of Worksharing is based on multiple team members sharing identical copies of the same file and applying their specific changes and synchronizing those with all other team members. That means that you can always use a Local File to re-create the Central File in order to avoid data loss.

Ask your team members who did what before the last successful Save to Central. Compare your files and choose which file is most advanced.

Remember, you can always elect the best file (most advanced local copy) to become the new Central File by clicking the Options button in the Save As dialog box and clicking the check box Make This A Central Model After Save.

Roll Back

Another practical scenario is that you need to restore a previous project state. A managerial decision might have been made in the context of your project, and you might need to abandon several days of work and start fresh from a particular date. Backup files are a Revit Worksharing feature that has been designed to allow you to do so.

The following section outlines the steps to take if you want to roll back your project to a previous state.

Using Backup Files

If you need to roll back your workshared project, you can do so by using the Restore Backup feature located in the Synchronize panel on the Collaborate tab of the ribbon (Figure 20.26).

It will prompt you to select a backup folder of either a Local File or a Central File and will bring up the Project Backup Versions dialog box (Figure 20.27).

Figure 20.26

Restore Backup

Here you can select any dates in the history recorded by saving the Local File or synchronizing changes to the Central File.

Clicking Browse will allow you to select a backup folder, either on your local computer or in the Central File location on your network, allowing you to use either a Local File or a Central File as the starting point of the restore process.

Figure 20.27

Project Backup Versions dialog box

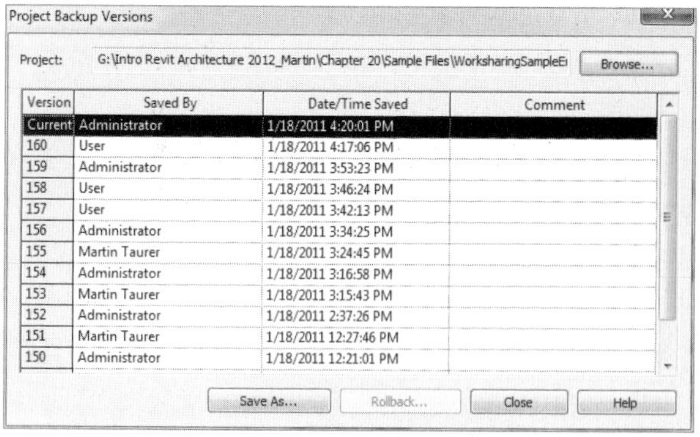

You will have two distinct options for restoring the file. One is to use Save As to create a new workshared Revit file while leaving your current file intact.

Rollback will actually roll your current file back to the point in time selected in the dialog box. Use this option with caution because once you have rolled back the current file, you will not be able to undo the rollback and cannot restore any changes made after the rollback date selected.

Best Practices

The following paragraphs summarize some of the best practice considerations commonly recommended when working with workshared Revit models:

Creating a New Local File Create new Local Files regularly. A good practice for when to create a new Local File is to do so whenever you have not been working on the model for some time while other team members were making changes. Opening the Central File and saving it locally as a new Local File will decrease the network load that would be created by trying to synchronize your outdated version of the Local File, giving you a fresh start at the current state of the project. The exact amount of time recommended between creating new Local Files varies with the number of changes that have occurred since you last synchronized your file. In a typical scenario, though, you should consider getting a new Local File every two to three days.

Auditing the Central File Open the Central File and check the Audit option; then resave and compact the file. If you do this on a regular basis, you reduce the file size and increase the overall performance when loading a large Central File. The elected team leader of your workshared Revit project should do this task. A good recommendation would be to do so at least on a monthly basis.

To perform an audit, when you open the Central File select the Audit check box at the bottom of the Open dialog box. This will display a warning that indicates that auditing a file may take a while and that you should use this process on large files to aid in performance and prior to upgrading the file to a new release of Revit.

Relinquishing Permissions When you work on a workshared Revit file, it is good practice to relinquish permissions regularly to make elements under your ownership available to the rest of the team. In a typical editing scenario where you have organized your work on a task basis, you should relinquish permissions whenever you have finished one particular task in your workflow and before starting the next. As an example, if your first task of the day is to place parking lots in the underground levels of a project and your second task will be to take care of the curtain walls above ground, then you should relinquish permissions required for the parking lots as soon as you have completed that task.

Partially Opening Workshared Files To use selective open, use the Open tool to open your local project file. In the Open dialog box, click the drop-down arrow beside the Open button. Choose All, Editable, Last Viewed, or Specify to display specific worksets when the file is opened. Click the Open button to open the file. If you select the Specify option, in the Opening Worksets dialog box, set the worksets to be Opened or Closed, and use the Open or Close buttons to display or not display the selected worksets.

The benefit of partially opening a workshared file lies in the fact that Revit will load only the elements on those worksets you selected in memory. That means you can control selectively which parts of a workshared model you want to open, which has a direct impact on your workstation's performance. Partially opening workshared projects is a powerful tool to control workstation performance, especially in large project scenarios.

The Frequency of Saving to the Central File There is no universal rule as to how often to save to the Central File since it depends on your team size, your network infrastructure, and your project size. Too infrequent synchronization puts you at risk that errors will occur during the synchronization process; too frequent synchronizations will be time consuming and disruptive for your team. A good rule is to synchronize more than once a day and whenever a modeling operation results in a significant model change.

Decoding Autodesk Revit Architecture Warnings

This appendix provides some tips and tricks for decoding Autodesk Revit Architecture warnings. Warning messages occur when Revit detects a problem while you are working in your model (Figure A.1). Warnings are issued for various reasons, including the existence of multiple rooms located in the same enclosed region or an overlap of walls and room separation lines. Warning messages (sometimes confused with error messages) inform you of a potential problem that could impact the integrity of the model, the design intent, and the reliability of your documentation.

When a warning is presented, Revit allows you to ignore the issue and continue working (Figure A.2). *Error messages*, on the other hand, require that you take immediate action to correct the problem in order to continue. Revit tracks and maintains a list of active warnings (Figure A.3) that have previously been presented to the user but that were either ignored or dismissed by the user. As long as the condition that triggered the warning is still present, Revit will track it in the Review Warnings dialog box.

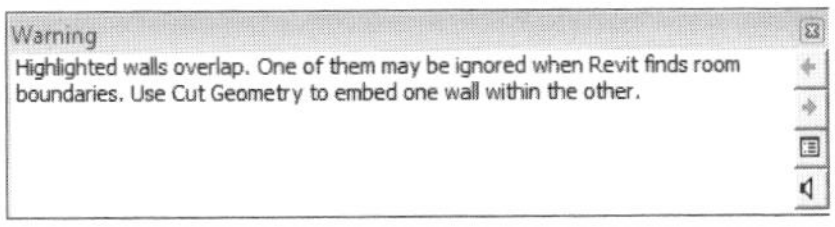

Figure A.1

Review Warnings dialog box

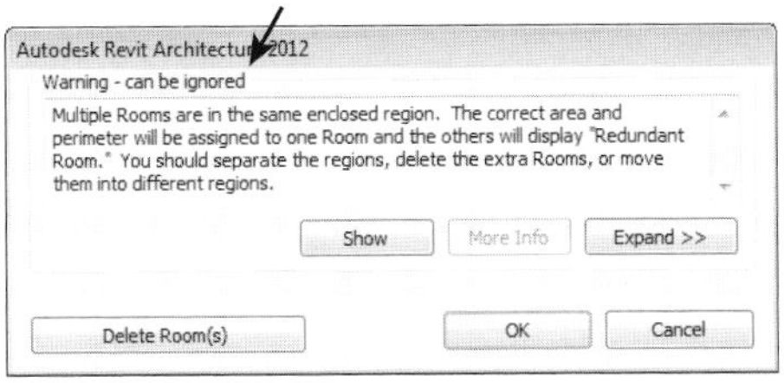

Figure A.2

Example of warning that can be ignored

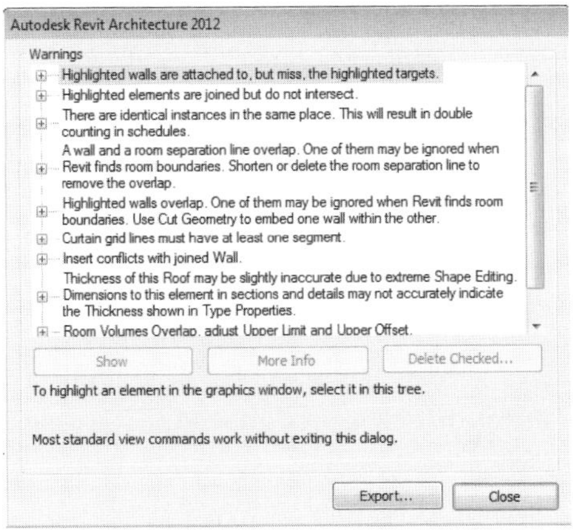

Figure A.3

List of all active warnings in the project

Warning System

As you work on projects, you will find that the creation of warnings is inevitable. It is more or less the nature of the beast. To review the current list of warnings in a project file, you access the Review Warnings dialog box. This dialog box allows you to view the list of warnings and locate particular issues for review and correction. Some warnings are unavoidable and have a negligible impact on the performance of the project and can thus be ignored. Other types of warnings have a significant impact on the performance and model/documentation integrity and should be addressed immediately.

It may not always be possible to remove all the warnings in a project. Project, size, and complexity will vary for each project. However, failure to stay on top of warnings and resolve them as they are generated will generally have a negative impact on project performance and integrity. It is also far more difficult to correct an issue that has generated a warning at a later date than at the time of the occurrence.

When a warning occurs, Revit will present a warning dialog box (Figure A.4). The dialog box will provide a brief description of the warning, and in some cases briefly describe in general terms how to correct the warning. The dialog box has six main components:

1. Issue type

2. Brief description of the issue and, in some cases, a general recommendation on how to correct the problem

3. Show button, which you can click to open a view and hightlight the conditions causing the issue

4. When applicable, the More Info button, which when clicked provides more information about the issue

5. Expand button, which you can click to show all the active warnings in the project

6. Delete button, which you can use to delete one the items that are part of the condition causing the issue

Figure A.4

Warning dialog box

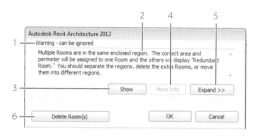

When the warning displays, the element(s) that caused it are highlighted in a user-defined color. You can select a warning heading, such as Warning 1, and all elements associated with that error will be highlighted in the drawing area. Additionally, you can select an element name and only that element will be highlighted in the drawing area. After you select the element name, you can click Show, and Revit searches views for that element only. In the warning dialog box, you can click Show to open a view and zoom in on the extents of the highlighted elements involved in the error. When you click the Show button, Revit attempts to display the elements associated with the warning(s) in one of the following ways:

- A plan view that shows all the elements.
- An elevation view that shows all the elements.
- A drawing sheet that shows all the elements.
- A 3D view.
- Any view where many of the elements are visible.
- The only view an element is visible in, if it is only visible in one view. Annotation elements generally fall into this category.

If for some reason Revit does not find a suitable view to display the elements, it opens a dialog box providing this information. While the Revit Review Warnings dialog box is open, you can perform most navigation functions, such as zoom, pan, or orbit, to get a better view of the element(s) at issue. Here are a few tips to help you locate elements related to resolving warnings:

- Create several maintenance or auditing 3D views that are used solely for the purpose of model quality control and set the Visibility\Graphic Override settings to show all pertinent categories and worksets.
- Open any maintenance or audit views before clicking the Revit Show button, because Revit will search through the current view and then open views before opening and searching all other project views.

Rooms

In this section, we'll review some common warnings related to rooms.

Multiple Room Areas

The following warning occurs when multiple room areas occupy the enclosed region:

```
Multiple Rooms are in the same enclosed region. The correct area and
perimeter will be assigned to one Room and the others will display
"Redundant Room." You should separate the regions, delete the extra Rooms,
or move them into different regions.
```

One of the simplest methods for locating the redundant rooms is to create a room schedule. This warning can be temporarily ignored but should be corrected prior to your next printing, model transmittal, or data export. Revit displays "Redundant Room" (Figure A.5) in the schedule for area and volume so that there is no duplication in the schedule totals.

To correct multiple-room areas, you can do one of the following:

- Delete the duplicate room from either the schedule or the model view.
- Create separate room regions and move the redundant room to the newly defined space.
- Move the redundant room to a new location.

Figure A.5

Room schedule displaying redundant rooms

Room Schedule 2			
Number	Name	Area	Volume
001	Family Room	381 SF	3050 CF
002	Bathroom	43 SF	343 CF
003	Mech. Room	114 SF	915 CF
005	GARAGE	412 SF	3293 CF
100	Entry Hall	55 SF	526 CF
101	WC	23 SF	183 CF
102	Living Room	425 SF	4040 CF
103	Kitchen	201 SF	1909 CF
104	Dining Room	168 SF	1589 CF
105	Lobby	54 SF	512 CF
106	Laundry	58 SF	555 CF
108	Study	173 SF	1639 CF
201	READING ROO	353 SF	3033 CF
202	BEDROOM	302 SF	2587 CF
203	BATHROOM	107 SF	852 CF
204	BATHROOM	45 SF	362 CF
206	BEDROOM	188 SF	1643 CF
211	BEDROOM	Redundant Room	Redundant Room
212	MASTER BATH	Redundant Room	Redundant Room
231	BATHROOM	Redundant Room	Redundant Room
301	ATELIER	283 SF	2467 CF

Room Tag

The following warning occurs when a tag has moved outside of the room element:

```
Room Tag is outside of its Room. Enable Leader or move Room Tag within
its Room.
```

This warning can also be temporarily ignored but should be corrected prior to your next printing, model transmittal, or data export. Figure A.6 shows the warning and room tag when it is moved outside of the room element boundary area.

To correct this situation, follow these steps:

1. Determine what room the tag belongs to. You can do so by selecting the room tag and looking for a room with a red boundary.

2. If the room tag can fit in the room, then move the tag into the room.

   If the tag will not fit into the room, then select the tag and enable the Leader option (Figure A.7) from the Options bar.

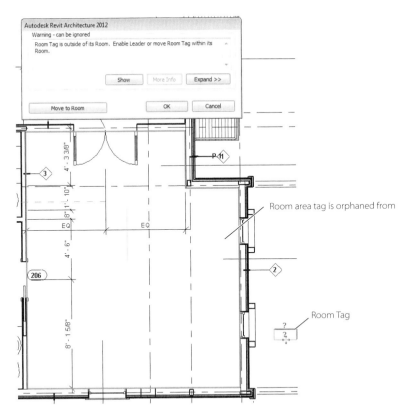

Room area tag is orphaned from

Room Tag

Checkbox for enabling room tag leader lines

Enclosed Region

You'll see this warning when a room element exists where walls or room separation lines are not enclosing it:

```
Room is not in a properly enclosed region.
```

This issue often occurs at the intersections of walls and columns or curtain walls and walls.

To correct this issue, locate the room element in a plan view and look for open boundaries or gaps in the bounding walls or room separation lines.

Room Volumes

This warning occurs when a room on a lower level has its Upper Limit or Upper Offset value set too high so that the volume from the lower room intersects with a room on a higher level:

```
Room Volumes Overlap, adjust Upper Limit and Limit Offset
```

To correct this warning:

1. Create a temporary section view of the room to help visualize the problem.
2. Select the lower-level room and then adjust the Upper Limit or the Upper Offset parameter until the rooms no longer overlap (Figure A.8).

Figure A.8

Adjusting Upper Limit and Limit Offset values for the room element

Adjust one or both of these values

Stairs, Railings, and Ramps

In this section, we'll cover common warnings related to stairs, railings, and ramps.

Number of Risers

You can add risers to the stair or remove them in Sketch mode, or change the Desired Number Of Risers setting in the Stair Properties dialog box. This Revit warning refers to the stairs not meeting its calculations:

```
The riser number is either greater or less than the number required to reach
from floor to floor.
```

This issue does not affect the documents but can signal that the stairs were not laid out properly.

This error typically results from the stairs being generated and then the floor levels shifting in height or not completing the run of stairs to meet the next level. Remember that if a stair needs to adjust to a non-floor-level height, set an offset in its instance parameters.

Riser Thickness and Tread Thickness

This warning occurs when the Riser Thickness and Tread Thickness are set to 0¢-0² (0mm) and Riser Type is set to Slanted or Straight, or the End With Riser/Begin With Riser parameter is checked:

```
Can't end Stairs with Riser because Riser Thickness is too small.
```

To correct this issue, set the riser's Type parameter to None.

Monolithic Stairs

This warning occurs for a number of reasons and is one of Revit's less helpful warning messages:

```
Can't make monolithic Stairs.
```

To fix this issue, revisit the sketch and the stair properties to confirm the parameters. The culprit may be sketch or parameter dimensioning, or the stair may not be meeting the requirements set in the type.

Check the stair sketch boundary and tread lines for integrity, especially at landings. The stair may finish the sketch, but the underside of the monolithic stair may not show as smooth.

Balusters

This warning occurs when the rail sketch in a stair is overlapping:

```
Top reference is below Bottom reference for one or more Balusters. These
Balusters are not created.
```

This issue can occur when you attempt to create a three-run stair in one stair element. You must break the stair into two runs.

Ramp

This warning occurs when the ramp was not sketched properly, or the levels changed after the ramp was created and they need to be updated:

```
The ramp is not long enough to reach the top constraint plus top offset.
Change the slope or increase the length of the ramp.
```

Remember that if you have to adjust a ramp to a non-floor-level height, set an offset in its instance parameters.

Modeling

In this section, we'll cover some common warnings related to modeling.

Column

This warning tells you that an architectural column element is completely encased in a wall:

```
Column is completely inside Wall.
```

Architectural columns are used to model column wraps around structural columns and for decorative applications. Since the architectural column is not exposed, it can be deleted. Use the Delete Checked function in the Review Warnings dialog box.

Curtain Grid Lines

This warning typically appears when a curtain wall has been modified and a grid line segment is no longer valid:

```
Curtain grid lines must have at least one segment.
```

You can usually delete the warning.

Reference Design Option

This warning typically appears when an element in a design option is trying to attach to an element or reference in the main model:

```
Design Option ' Main Model ' cannot reference Design Option 'XXXX : XXXX'
```

For example, a wall may be trying to attach to the floor in the main model. Use Show to find the element and then make the design option editable. Detach or redraw the element in the design option.

Joining Elements

This warning typically occurs when Revit is joining model objects caused by shifts in the model's geometry:

```
Unexpected join failure
```

Cutting one of these elements and then using Paste Align to paste it will clear up this issue. This warning may also indicate that a room join problem exists. Such a problem should be fixed.

Joined Elements

You'll typically see this warning when elements have been joined using Join Geometry but are not physically touching:

```
Highlighted elements are joined but do not intersect.
```

To resolve the issue, find the elements and use the Unjoin Geometry tool to remove the join. This warning can occur when a joined element is moved away from the element it is joined to. In some cases, having the elements not intersect is intentional—for example, two walls can be closely parallel but not touch and still be joined together so that a door or window opening will cut through both.

Curtain System Slightly Malformed

This warning is fairly self-explanatory:

```
Some panels in this curtain system are slightly malformed. The problem is
most likely ignorable. This problem usually occurs when a panel or parts of
a panel have been divided so that they are very narrow. To better see the
malformed panels, temporarily hide the mullion category and set display of
lines to "thin lines" (using the command on the view menu).
```

You can most likely ignore this warning. This problem usually occurs when a panel or parts of a panel have been divided so that they are very narrow. To better see the malformed panels, temporarily hide the Mullion category and set Display Of Lines to Thin Lines (using the command on the View menu).

Column Attachment

This warning appears when the floor or roof element that the column was attached to has been edited or moved and no longer covers the top of the column:

```
The highlighted column can't maintain attachment to the target. It will be
treated as unattached until it can intersect.
```

Select the column and click Detach, then Detach All from the Options bar.

Identical Instances

This warning indicates that an element was copied and placed in the same position as an existing element:

```
There are identical instances in the same place. This will result in double
counting in schedules.
```

In the Review Warnings dialog box, select and check the secondary entries and click the Delete Selected option. The only exception is if the first entry is not in the right workset or design option. Always defer to those settings first and then the order of execution.

Detach Elements

This warning indicates that a wall or walls attached to a floor, roof, or so forth are not physically attached or touching the roof or floor:

```
Highlighted walls are attached to, but miss, the highlighted targets.
```

The elements in question need to be reviewed—this condition can be intentional. The warning can also occur when the element to which the wall is attached has been moved from above or below it. This issue can be corrected by selecting the wall and clicking Detach, then Detach All on the Options bar. Be aware that the wall will return to its unconnected height and may need adjusting.

Overlapping Walls

This warning appears when two or more walls are overlapping.

```
Highlighted walls overlap. Color fills, room tags and room areas may not
behave correctly. Use Cut Geometry to embed one wall within the other or
tab-select one of the grouped overlapping walls and exclude it from the
group instance.
```

The best method for addressing this issue is to isolate both walls in a 3D view using the Hide/Isolate tool and adjust the overlap by doing one of the following:

- Deleting a wall
- Moving either or both positions (horizontally or vertically)
- Joining geometry (which could have performance implications)
- Attaching one to the other (this also could have performance implications)
- Editing the profile of either or both walls

Inserting Families into a Wall

This warning occurs when an opening (door, window, or opening family) is placed in a wall at the same location of an intersecting joined wall:

```
Insert conflicts with joined Wall.
```

This condition in some cases is intentional and can be ignored. Disallow Join can be used on the intersecting wall to remove the warning. Right-click on the Wall grip and choose Disallow Join from the context menu and the warning will disappear. Drag the wall into the insert once the join has been disallowed.

Element Detached from Its Associated Plane

This warning occurs because a wall or walls is attached to a roof or floor but does not physically touch that roof or wall. This issue can occur because the element that the wall is attached to has moved. This warning is not necessary a reflection of a constructability issue.

```
Element will be detached from its associated plane.
```

Use the Cut Geometry tool to cut one wall from the other to clean the condition.

Highlighted Walls Overlap

This warning is self-explanatory:

```
Highlighted walls overlap. One of them may be ignored when Revit finds room
boundaries. Use Cut Geometry to embed one wall within the other.
```

Adjust the wall handles so that the walls are not overlapping:

- Use the Cut Geometry tool to cut one wall from the other to clean the condition.
- Use the Join Geometry tool to address the issue if the two walls need to be in the overlapping condition.

Area

This warning occurs because an Area is not properly defined.

```
Area is not in a properly enclosed region.
```

Area separation lines are not closing on an Area Analysis plan. Find the Area element on the Area plan and look for gaps in the area separation lines.

Overlapping Lines

This warning is self-explanatory:

```
Highlighted lines overlap. Lines may not form closed loops.
```

This warning can occur when Area Separation lines overlap or do not close a space. Use Show to find the elements and delete the overlap or trim to close. The warning can also occur when you're trying to create a three-run stair where the stair and railing sketch lines that overlap on top of each other. Railings created by the stair behave oddly and generate warnings as well. Three-run stairs should be created with two stair runs.

```
Wall and room separation line overlap. Color fills, room tags and room areas
may not behave correctly. Highlighted room separation lines overlap. Color
fills, room tags and room areas may not behave correctly.
```

These conditions can affect performance as well as the documentation of the project. Use the Show button to locate the overlap in a plan view. It is helpful to temporarily change the color and thickness of the separation line in Visibility/Graphic Overrides to make it easier to see the overlap. Not all of these conditions in this section have to be corrected. There are some situations where such conditions are unavoidable.

Off-Axis Alignment

These warnings typically appear when you create elements by tracing over AutoCAD drawings where lines are drawn at a fractional degree such as 89.01°:

```
Area separation line is slightly off axis and may cause inaccuracies. Line
in Sketch is slightly off axis and may cause inaccuracies. Line is slightly
off axis and may cause inaccuracies. Ref Plane is slightly off axis and may
cause inaccuracies. Wall is slightly off axis and may cause inaccuracies.
```

This problem can also be caused by sketching or rotating elements when angle snaps are turned off, or it can result from preexisting elements when you do any of the following:

- Create an element by picking a slightly off-axis face or line.
- Align an element to a slightly off-axis reference.
- Explode an AutoCAD import that contains slightly off-axis lines.
- Create floor area faces on a mass that has slightly off-axis geometry.
- Snap defining line ends to references that are slightly off-axis (such as imported drawings or two columns that are not properly aligned).

- Snap defining line ends to references that are positioned correctly in their respective contexts but the line between them is slightly off-axis (such as snapping to two different ceiling grids).

- Draw in nonorthogonal views.

Off-axis problems should be resolved, because Revit can't create dimensions between lines that are not exactly parallel, and it can't join or cut geometry if faces are slightly off-parallel or have small gaps due to off-axis elements.

Depending on the cause of the problem, do one of the following to correct it:

- Drag the end of the off-axis element a short distance and let it snap to the axis.

- Repeat the rotation operation with Angle Snaps turned on.

- If the inaccuracy is derived from preexisting elements, correct them and repeat the operation.

- If the problem is caused by imported data, consider correcting it in the original software and reimporting it into Revit.

Autodesk Revit Architecture Tips and Tricks

This appendix provides some tips and tricks for using Autodesk Revit Architecture. You will find tips and trick on the following:

- Drafting and groups
- Working with CAD files
- Modeling
- Reducing file size
- Annotations
- Interface

Drafting and Groups

In this section we cover some tips and tricks that will aid you with working with drafting tools or annotations.

Groups

Groups can be beneficial when you have many repeating units in your project. They can also be problematic. Here are some general tips related to working with groups:

- When possible, make sure you group families and not model or detail lines.
- Avoid mirroring or rotating groups because this can cause problems.
- Avoid nesting groups, that is, having a group within a group.
- If you are having difficulty editing a group for various reasons, try creating another instance of that group and editing that. If that solves the problem, then after editing, delete the temporary group instance.
- Do not copy and paste groups; always place them. If you copy and paste into views with different orientations (i.e., east and north elevations), the result may not be what you expected.

Copy

When you select an element and then hold the Ctrl key and drag the mouse at the same time, you can create a copy. This is not a precise copy tool, but it works well for text, tags, and other elements that do not need to be copied precisely.

Working with CAD Files

While it is ideal to use only Revit geometry in your Revit projects, that may not always be possible for a whole host of reasons. In this section, we cover some tips for working with CAD files.

DWG File Cleanup

Before importing or linking CAD files into your project, it is a good idea to spend a few minutes cleaning up the AutoCAD files to improve Revit project performance. This tip provides some guidelines for working with CAD files:

- Delete anything from the drawing that is not necessary to reduce the file.
- If there are layers that are either turned off or frozen, consider deleting the geometry and the layers to reduce the file.
- Purge any unused layers, blocks, dim styles, and the like from the DWG file to lighten the file.

- Review blocks in the file. Blocks can sometimes cause issues in Revit.
- Remove any Xrefs from the file.
- Audit the DWG file to make sure there are no errors.
- If the DWG file uses hatch patterns, be aware that they may not come across into Revit correctly.
- Locate the geometry as close to 0,0,0 as possible.

Revit CAD Import Distance Restrictions

For the Revit 2010 and earlier platforms, if you imported/linked a CAD file that was more than two miles apart in the X, Y, and Z directions, Revit would throw up an error and cancel the import. In Revit 2011 and later, the distance grew to 20 miles. This step will help you clean your file to get around these issues.

If you have an AutoCAD DWG that is importing or linking and you're getting the import distance restriction error, there are several things you can do in AutoCAD. The first thing you should look at is deleting any geometry on the X and Y planes that may be outside the import distance restriction. First, verify whether there are issues with the file:

1. Turn on all layers and thaw the layers in the AutoCAD file; then do a zoom extents to see if there are any stray objects.

2. Open an elevation of a 3D view to check the Z plane for any stray objects.

3. If the CAD file contains AEC objects, in AutoCAD set PROXYGRAPHICS to 1.

To delete any stray objects, follow these steps in AutoCAD:

1. With the file open, type the command **erase** and at the prompt type **all**.

2. Type **r** to remove objects.

3. Create a window selection around the AutoCAD geometry that you want to retain.

    This step allows you to create a selection set of just those objects that are not within the geometry you want to keep.

4. Press Enter to erase the CAD geometry that you need to remove.

Now, any geometry that was outside of your windowed area will be deleted. Try importing the CAD file again.

After performing these steps, if you still get the import distance restriction error, then there might be geometry in the Z plane that is causing the issue. There are several methods to work around this problem. The following method seems to work well:

1. Configure a DXB plotter using the Add A Plotter Wizard.

2. Open the drawing.

3. Set the viewpoint of the 3D model as you want it.

4. Start the **PLOT** command.

5. Select the DXB plotter from the Name drop-down list in the Printer/Plotter area of the Plot dialog box.

6. Click OK to create the DXB format plot file.

7. Start a new drawing.

8. Start the **DXBIN** command on the command line.

9. When prompted, browse to the file you just created, and then click Open.

10. When the drawing is open, save the drawing as a DWG format file.

This creates a 2D version of the original file. If you are using AutoCAD 2007 or higher, you can also try using the **FLATSHOT** command to convert 3D solids to flattened 2D views.

Importing/Linking CAD Files

To import or link CAD files into drafting views, in the Import/Link CAD Formats dialog box, check the Current View Only option so that the CAD file is imported or linked into only the current view.

If you import or link a site plan or topographic plan, do *not* select the Current View Only option.

Modeling

In this section we provide some tips and tricks related to modeling.

Dynamic Roof Changes

To dynamically change a roof ridgeline, switch to a 3D view and select the roof to reveal the grip points. Click the grip and drag upwards or downwards to dynamically change the ridgeline.

Metal Seam Roof

To create a metal seam roof, follow these steps:

1. Create a basic roof with the desired slope.

2. Change the family type to Sloped Glazing.

3. Add curtain grid lines that correspond with the centerline-to-centerline spacing of the roof seams.

4. Add mullions for the seam at the grid line.

5. Change the panel material from glazing to solid.

Demolish Part of an Existing Roof

Use this process to demolish part of an existing roof:

1. In your project, set the Phase of the New Construction Phase (or whatever your equivalent new construction phase is called) to Active.

2. Create an in-place family using the Roof category, and name it something meaningful like **Demo Roof Void**.

3. Create a void extrusion to set the height to a larger value than what is needed so that it is easy to see.

4. Sketch the void profile.

5. Click the Finish Edit Mode button.

6. Use the Cut Geometry tool and select Demo Roof Void and the roof.

7. Click the Finish Model button.

Your roof is now cut. If you need to modify the void, then change the phase of the element being cut (the roof) to New Construction (or whatever your equivalent new construction phase is called). You can now select and edit the void. Just remember to change the phase of the element being cut back to Existing.

Placing a Picture on a Wall

Do you ever need to hang a picture, poster, or TV set on a wall? If so, use the Place Decal tool found on the Insert tab → Link panel.

Plan Regions

If you would like to show or display multiple levels within one floor plan view, then you would use the Plan Region tool. You can use plan regions for showing split-level plans or showing the roof of a portion of a building that is several stories below the level of the current plan view.

The Plan Region tool (found on the View tab → Create panel of the ribbon) lets you sketch a closed region that has its own View Range controls separate from those of the rest of the plan view. Follow these steps:

1. Open a plan view.

2. On the View tab's Create panel, click Plan Region.

3. Sketch a closed loop using lines, rectangles, or polygons.

4. In the Properties palette, under Extents, click the Edit button to the right of View Range.

5. In the View Range dialog box, specify the primary range and view depth for the plan region. Then click OK to close the dialog box.

6. In the Mode panel, click Finish Edit Mode; then, in the In-Place Editor panel, click Finish Model.

The area within the plan region will display based on the view range assigned to that region.

Reducing File Size

File size is one area that people often directly associate with the performance of a project model. There are various schools of thought on this, and a large file will take more resources to open than a small file. But project performance is based on more than just the size of the project file.

In this section you will find tips and tricks on how to reduce the file size. If file size does not have an impact on project performance, then why are we covering this? The reason is that it is still necessary to transmit files. And the larger the file, the more resources the computer has to use. So if you can reduce the file size, why not?

Purge

Periodically during the project and at the end of your project consider using the Purge Unused tool from the Manage tab → Settings panel. This tool provides options for selecting unused families and types from your file for deleting. Only those types that are not being used in the project can be deleted.

Keep in mind that not every project team member should use the Purge command. Purging a project file can result in the loss of information and should be performed only by CAD/BIM support staff or the project BIM team leader.

Faster File Opening

Before saving and closing your project, switch to your most basic view (such as the project drafting view). Then choose the View tab → Windows panel, click Close Hidden Windows, and save the file.

This works because Revit caches views that are open so that you can quickly switch from one view to another. If you save and close a file in a 3D view, when you reopen that project, Revit needs to cache the contents of that 3D view prior to displaying anything. Closing on a basic view means that there is less to cache, and the file will open much quicker.

DWG Files

Minimize the number of linked or imported DWG files.

Avoid importing unnecessary data like hatching or AutoCAD-specific linework such as construction lines. Deleting unnecessary geometry or layers will create a smaller, cleaner DWG file.

Link only essential DWG files into necessary views. If you have DWG files and you no longer require them, delete them from the model.

Avoid exploding geometry imported from DWG files. Exploding an imported DWG file will change a single managed element into hundreds or thousands of additional objects depending on the number of entities in the imported DWG.

Switch off visibility of 2D AutoCAD DWGs in perpendicular views. A 2D AutoCAD file linked into a plan view will show as collinear lines in elevation, causing performance degradation.

Linking Revit Files

Large, complex projects generally should be broken up into several different models. Ideally, during project setup, the project's creator will take into account the size and complexity of the project and will create multiple project files.

If you are working on an existing project, then splitting a project can be more complicated and may result in the loss of some data that will have to be re-created. This type of split can be accomplished by either saving the building(s) as individual Revit projects and then linking them together into a master file, or by breaking up the model using worksets. In either case, use caution.

ABOUT LINKING

When you link one Revit model into another project, Revit will open the linked model and keep it in memory. So, the more links that you have in a project, the longer it will take to open, and the more memory that will be used. This is a gray area in what is a best practice. The BIM team leader will need to weigh longer opening times and saves against a reduction in file size.

Worksets

Worksets have a negligible impact on file size. However, worksets will improve overall performance when the user displays only the parts of a project that they need to work on.

Families

Families are the primary culprit when evaluating project performance. Users tend to get carried away and not work to the proper level of detail.

Model to the correct level of detail.

Do not over parameterize. This means that you should create the basic geometry and limit the number of controls or formulas. For example, if you create a bookshelf with five shelves, consider whether it is really necessary to create parameters and controls to change the number of shelves from two to seven. The same goes with materials.

Use parameters only when appropriate. If you are creating a family that will have only one type or a one-off, then forget the parameters. Placing constraints to controls length, width, depth, and so on will just result in a larger family (RFA) file size. Granted, the size increase will be minimal, but small increases add up in the size of your projects.

Use types rather than creating separate families. For example, a project that uses one window family with two types is smaller than the same project that has two different window families, one for each window type.

Nesting isn't always a good thing. Nested families (a family loaded into another family) can provide a great deal of flexibility. For example, you can have a bookcase family and then nest a shelving system that is actually another family. There is debate over whether nested families are larger than a similar family created without nesting. What is not debated is that it takes more system resources to make changes to the model with a large number of nested families, because Revit has to recalculate everything in order to update the model.

Think about what you are modeling, where it will be placed, and the scale in which it will be placed on a sheet.

Annotations

In this section, we cover tips related to annotations and schedules.

Phases with Schedules

If you need to create a schedule that shows what phase and element are demolished, new, or existing, create a separate schedule for each phase.

Controlling Color Fills

When using color fills on your project, you can turn off the legend:

1. Open the Visibility/Graphics Overrides dialog box.

2. On the Annotation Categories tab, uncheck Color Fill Legends.

   To turn off the color in your area plan views:

1. Open the Visibility/Graphic Overrides dialog box.

2. On the Model Categories tab, expand the Areas category and uncheck Color Fill.

To turn off the actual color fill in your floor plan views:

1. Open the Visibility/Graphic Overrides dialog box.

2. On the Model Categories tab, expand the Rooms category and uncheck Color Fill.

Tag Doors by Type

There are occasions when you need to tag your doors by type rather than mark. This tip walks you through that process.

1. Open an existing door tag that you want to change to display the Door Type value in the Family Editor.

2. Select the Door Tag label.

3. On the Modify | Label tab → Label panel, click the Edit Label button.

4. In the Edit Label dialog box, select the Type Mark parameter from the Category Parameters list and add it to the Label Parameters list.

5. Remove the Mark parameter from the Label Parameters.

6. Click OK to close the Edit Label dialog box.

7. Save the tag with a new name.

8. Load the tag into your project to use.

Displaying Absolute and Relative Elevations

This tip will walk you through the process of displaying either the absolute or relative coordinates in Revit. The first step in the process is to set the true project elevation.

1. Open your project to an elevation view.

2. On the Manage tab → Project Location panel, click the Coordinates drop-down list and select Specify Coordinates At Point.

3. Click a point in your project to specify the elevation. A level is a good element to pick.

4. In the Specify Shared Coordinates dialog box, enter the known elevation for that point, and click OK to close the Specify Shared Coordinates dialog box.

5. Select the Level label, and in the Properties palette, click Edit Type.

6. In the Type Properties dialog box, under Constraints, change the Elevation Base value from Project to Shared. Changing to the Shared Elevation Base will display the coordinates that you entered in step 4.

7. Click OK to close the Type Properties dialog box.

   The elevation labels will now change to show the true (absolute) elevations.

Interface

Use your arrow keys to move objects around. This should not be used when you need to precisely move an element, but it can be great for text and other elements where placement does not need to be precise.

In Revit, when you click an element(s), if any item appears in blue, that means you have the ability to perform some kind of action.

Index

Note to Reader: **Bolded** page numbers refer to main discussions of a topic and definitions. *Italicized* page numbers refer to illustrations.

S

U

X

Z